Samuel Mānaiakalani Kamakau (1815–1876). Crayon portrait by unknown artist.

Courtesy of Bishop Museum

SAMUEL M. KAMAKAU

Ruling Chiefs
of Hawaii
(Revised Edition)

KAMEHAMEHA SCHOOLS PRESS • HONOLULU

KAMEHAMEHASCHOOLS®

Copyright © 1961
Revised Edition Copyright © 1992
by Kamehameha Schools

Inquiries should be addressed to:
Kamehameha Publishing
567 South King Street, Suite 118
Honolulu, Hawai'i 96813

The paper used in this publication
meets the minimum requirements of
the American National Standard for Library Sciences—
Permanence of Paper for Printed Materials,
ANSI Z39.48-1992 (R1997)

Printed in the United States of America

ISBN 978-0-87336-014-2, Paperbound Edition

ISBN 978-0-87336-015-9, Clothbound Edition

Library of Congress
Cataloging-in-Publication Data

Kamakau, Samuel Manaiakalani, 1815-1876.
  [Moolelo o Kamehameha I. English]
  Ruling Chiefs of Hawaii/Samuel M. Kamakau.—Rev. ed. p. cm.
  Translation of: Ka moolelo o Kamehameha I and Ka moolelo o na Kamehameha
  Includes biographical references and index.
  ISBN 978-87336-015-9 (cloth : acid-free paper).—ISBN 978-87336-014-2
  (paper : acid-free paper).
  1. Hawaiians—Kings and rulers. 2. Hawaiians—History. 3. Hawaii—History—
  To 1893. I. Kamakau, Samuel Manaiakalani, 1815-1876. Moolelo o na Kamehameha.
  English. 1992. II. Title. DU624.65.K3413 1992
  996.9'02—dc20   91-43386
                                                               CIP

24 23 22 21 20 (rev.) 6 7 8 9 10

Introduction

Samuel Manaiakalani Kamakau was the greatest Hawaiian historian ever born. Although many Hawaiians have written about Hawaiian history, none have written so voluminously or with such perception. He has remained an undiminished inspiration to generations of Hawaiians since the first publication of his work in Hawaiian language newspapers of 1842. His writing spanned a period of 34 years and he wrote nearly 300 articles, not confined merely to Hawaiian history, but explaining many varied aspects of Hawaiian life, from the complexity of chiefly society to the politics of religion.

This book, *Ruling Chiefs of Hawaii*, is only one of four edited volumes of Kamakau's extensive writings translated into English. The excerpts presented in *Ruling Chiefs* focus on the political history of our people. From the time of 'Umi, who was eight generations before Kamehameha the Great, until the time of Kamehameha III in the 1840s, Kamakau reveals the role of *Ali'i Nui* and *kaukau ali'i* in shaping our *Lāhui*, or nation. He also tells us of the coming of foreigners to our islands and of the strange diseases and other problems for which we had no ancestral answers. He tells us of that time of turmoil through which one great chief, Kamehameha, guided us in dignity and strength. He presents the life of Kamehameha so that all Hawaiians who follow him in time might share in the wisdom of that great man.

In this volume we can read of the *Ali'i Nui* who set aside the ancient *kapu* after the death of Kamehameha. We come to know these *Ali'i* intimately and watch them struggle with the terrors of massive depopulation and aggressive foreigners. We learn why certain chiefs chose to convert to Christianity and why others did not. Kamakau records his eyewitness accounts of the framing of the constitution and the adoption of Western laws. He reveals the role of American missionaries, including those who became the foreign advisors of the *Ali'i Nui*, in advocating for these changes. And, with a historian's hindsight, he speaks bitterly about such advice after the *Ali'i Nui* convert to private ownership of land and allow foreigners to own Hawaiian land.

Apart from his recording of these events so crucial to the history of our country, Kamakau is also unafraid of giving his own opinions about the changes he observed in his society. Some of them he approves of, including the adaptation of new technology from the West to suit Hawaiian needs. Other changes, such as the loss of power by the *Ali'i Nui* to foreigners that do not, and will not, love the *maka'āinana*, he denounces vehemently.

Samuel Manaiakalani Kamakau was born on October 29, 1815 at Manua'ula, Kamananui in Waialua, O'ahu. Since the law requiring Hawaiians to take two names, a Christian name and a surname, was not passed until 1840, we can assume he was probably given just one name at birth. Samuel must have been his Christian name, taken later in life, perhaps at school, after Christianity became firmly adopted in 1825.

The other two names, Manaiakalani and Kamakau, are interesting because Kamakau literally means "the hook" while Manaiakalani is the name of Māui's magical fishhook that he used to pull up land from the bottom of the sea.

At age 17 Kamakau sought Western learning and went to study at the missionary high school at Lāhaināluna. Shortly thereafter he became a teacher's helper. At age 26, he began to write articles about Hawaiian culture and history, interviewing *kūpuna* who were knowledgeable and willing to share their wisdom with him. As is still common today, *kūpuna* of Kamakau's time did not reveal their knowledge to just anyone, especially the *mo'olelo* of the *Ali'i Nui*. The *kūpuna* obviously trusted Kamakau to entrust him with their secrets, probably because he was of some *ali'i* lineage.

In 1841, Kamakau helped form the first Hawaiian Historical Association:

> . . . to obtain and preserve all historical data possible which bore on the origin of the race, and to obliterate the common belief among some foreigners who claim this is a wandering race which was lost in a storm and driven by winds to these shores . . . A great many things being circulated by these foreigners are not so. Because of the fact that these foreigners are partaking of the same food with us, what they would say now would be given much credence by our descendants, and if we do not gather these data now, after many generations our children would be like the American Indians—a race without a history.

What is incredible about Kamakau's life is that history was merely his passion; it was not his vocation. The collection and writing of history was what he did in his spare time. In order to make a living he served in various public capacities. In 1845, he was principal of a school in Kipahulu, Māui and in the following year became a school agent and tax assessor for that island. In 1848, he was appointed to the kingdom's Land Commission and in 1851 was elected from Hāna, Māui to the House of Representatives. From this time until his death in 1876, he was often elected to the legislature from various districts on Māui and O'ahu. In 1852, he became a member of the Royal Agricultural Society and in 1853 served as a district judge in Wailuku.

In the 1860s Kamakau made some drastic changes in his life. He left the Protestant religion and became a Catholic. He also moved back to O'ahu, living in Mokulē'ia and in Honolulu. It was at this time that he began to write a regular column on Hawaiian history for the Hawaiian newspaper, *Kū'ōko'a*.

From that time until his passing at age 61, he wrote for a variety of newspapers, on any and every subject in an attempt to enlighten his *Lāhui*. He was buried in Ma'ema'e Cemetery in Nu'uanu* where I like to think his spirit still lingers as an inspiration to every Hawaiian who walks in the glorious footsteps of our ancestors.

L.K. Kame'eleihiwa
December 15, 1991

*For more information on the life and work of Kamakau see also:
Chun, Malcom Naea. 1988. *I Ka Wā O Kamehameha*. Honolulu: Folk Press.
Thrum, Thomas G. 1918. "Brief Sketch of the Life and Labors of S.M. Kamakau, Hawaiian Historian." *Hawaiian Historical Society*. Honolulu.

Editor's note: *'Okina* (') and *kahako* (‾), diacritical marks which indicate correct pronunciation of Hawaiian words, are used here only in the new material in this edition of *Ruling Chiefs of Hawaii*. They were not part of the original text translation done before the book's first publication in 1961 and were not included in the index's initial publication in 1974. We have chosen to maintain the original versions and therefore have not added diacriticals to the existing text and index.

Acknowledgments

In 1961 the first edition of the English translation of Samuel Kamakau's *Ruling Chiefs of Hawaii* was published by Kamehameha Schools Press. Many contributed to make its publication possible. A group of Hawaiian scholars was first selected by the trustees of Bishop Museum to translate Kamakau's florid literary style into readable English. The group included Mary Kawena Pukui, Thomas G. Thrum, Lahilahi Webb, Emma Davidson Taylor, and John Wise. Mary Kawena Pukui then reviewed the entire translation, together with Martha Warren Beckwith, who added the footnotes. Dorothy Barrère and Caroline Curtis proofread the manuscript.

The resulting book was an immediate success, and soon became a classic of Hawaiian history. Now, thirty years later, the book has long been out of print. Kamehameha Schools is happy to publish a new edition, with significant advantages over the former edition. While the original text has remained unchanged, the new edition combines the very limited original index with the extensive index and appendices prepared by Elspeth P. Sterling and originally published as a separate booklet by Bishop Museum Press. New photographs have been chosen, and more comprehensive captions are provided. It is hoped that these additions and modifications, together with the new introduction by Dr. Lilikalā Kameʻeleihiwa will provide teachers and scholars of Hawaiian history with significant new tools with which to approach Kamakau's text.

The editors would like to thank the trustees of Kamehameha Schools/Bishop Estate for their support of this project and Dr. Lilikalā Kameʻeleihiwa, the Honolulu Academy of Arts, the Hawaiian Historical Society, and the staff of Bishop Museum for their assistance in preparing this new edition.

Kamehameha Schools Press
Honolulu, 1992

Contents

RULING CHIEFS OF HAWAII

CHAPTER I

The Story of 'Umi*

Many famous chiefs, mentioned in Hawaiian history, were descended from Hana-la'a-nui. The ruling chiefs (*noho ali'i*) of Hawaii were of that particular lineage (*mo'oku'auhau*), and with additions from those of the other islands, the genealogy of Hawaii's chiefs and their ancestors was made complete.

'Umi-a-Liloa [that is, 'Umi-son-of-Liloa] was a famous chief, and the reason for his fame was that it was he who united all of the districts of Hawaii through wars. The kingdom became his because of his humbleness and because of the prowess of his adopted (*ho'okama*) sons and his care of the god Ku-ka'ili-moku. 'Umi was of lowly birth (*lepo popolo*) [on his maternal side], but he rose until the kingdom was his through his victories in battle.

Liloa was a ruling chief, a sacred high chief (*ali'i nui kapu*). His father, Kiha-nui-lulu-moku, and ancestors were also ruling chiefs. His mother, Wai-o-lea, belonged to an Oahu family of chiefs and so did his grandmother, Ne'ula, and great-grandmother, La'a-kapu. That chiefly family belonged to 'Ewa. Liloa's wife was named Pinea. She was from 'Ewa and Ko'olaupoko [Oahu], and was his mother's younger sister. They had one son, Hakau, who was heir of the kingdom. Liloa stayed with Haua, a chiefess from Maui, and to them was born a daughter named Kapu-kini. Liloa had two children of chiefly descent. Liloa was a tabu chief who was noted for his good deeds. The other chiefs all around Hawaii remained under his rule and placed their sons under Liloa. It was customary in the olden days for some chiefs to serve others, and they became war lords (*kuhina kaua*), keepers of the treasures of the chiefs (*ali'i pu'uku*), and war leaders (*mamaka kaua*). Thus did the chiefs and sons of chiefs serve Liloa.

When Liloa began the task of erecting the heiau, or temple, of Paka'alana [at Waipi'o, Hawaii], and made the bathing pool, Mokapu, and the banks [of the wet patch] (*kuauna*) of Kahiki-mai-aea, the

*For the story of 'Umi see 2; 13, 2, pp. 74-78, 96-106; 14, Vol 4, pp. 178-234, 244-254; 18, pp. 257-266; 25, pp. 81-86; 16, pp. 265-315; 38, pp. 98-103; 26, pp. 18-29; 28, pp. 78-85; 4, pp. 62-70. For digest of the stories, see 6. All references cited by number are to be found in the Bibliography.

1

chiefs and commoners went to the mountains for *'ohi'a* logs and posts. The chief, Liloa, remained below in Waipi'o. That was the land on which the ruling chiefs lived in ancient times. He remained with one of his chiefs, named Laea-nui-kau-manamana, the son of 'Ehu-nui-kai-malino, ruling chief of Kona, Hawaii. The two chiefs made a pavement of stones leading from the bank (*kuauna*) of the place called Kahiki-mai-aea to the narrow side door (*puka pakaka*)* of the chief's residence. The long stone which Liloa himself carried on his shoulder was placed there, and inside of that the stone carried by Laea-nui-kau-manamana. Liloa called the stone he carried "the sacred slab of Liloa" (*Ka paepae kapu o Liloa*). The stone was famous down to the time of Kameha-meha I. This is why it was so well known, because of its sacredness. No chief was permitted to step upon the stone that Liloa bore on his shoulder. Only two persons were allowed on this sacred slab, Liloa, the ruler, and Laea-nui-kau-manamana, the chief who was in charge of his spittoon and the feathered-staff (*kahili*). The banks [of the wet patch] Kahiki-mai-aea and the *nioi*-wood embankment erected by Ka-hou-kapu, both very sacred symbols of chieftainship, were permitted only to them to walk upon. Their descendants were given the right to go on these places, but only those of the three highest classes, the *ni'au-pi'o*, *pi'o*, and *naha* chiefs; to them only and not to the other descendants (*pua*) of Liloa.

This was something much practiced in the time of Liloa, the worship of the god and also the building of the places of worship (*luakini, waihau, unu, ko'a*) and the erecting of stones of Kane. The ruler who did all this was Liloa, a religious chief. He kept the peace in his kingdom and his people contented and prosperous.

At one time Liloa desired to build several heiaus in Hamakua from Kukuihaele to Kowana'e and the vicinity about Kealakaha. When a house for the god was completed, Liloa, the kahunas, the favorite god, Ku-ka'ili-moku, the chiefs, and servants went up from Waipi'o to the pork-eating feast for the dedication of the chief's heiau. The procession was made a tabu one, from Kukuihaele to Wai-ko'eko'e and on to Kapulena, Kawela, and Pa'auhau. Games for the strengthening of the body were played, such as disk rolling (*maika*), dart gliding (*pahe'e*), boxing (*mokomoko*), and spear hurling (*pahuakala*). At Koholalele, the tabu for [the heiau of] Maninini was observed. Then they went on the lower side of Kowaluna and Koapapa'a. They encamped at Koapapa'a and at Ka'awikiwiki.†

---

* The *puka pakaka*, or narrow side door, would be the private entrance to the house.

† Original text in *Ke Au 'Oko'a*, Nov. 3, 1870.

Disk rolling, dart throwing, and boxing were sports enjoyed by the chiefs. At one time, when the chiefs were absorbed in playing, Liloa and one of his lesser chiefs, who served him as a guardian (*kahu*), went secretly away to visit places from Pe'ape'amakawalu to Ka'awali'i in Humu'ula and on to Ka'ula. Then they turned back from their journey. They ascended the cliff of Kealakaha and saw a beautiful young woman bathing in a stream. Women, in the olden days, were under a fixed law that forbade their living and sleeping with their husbands in the same house when "Lehua shed her tears (*e waimaka o Lehua*)" [the menstrual period]. A woman was then defiled, for the god despised (*ho'o pailua*) all bloody things. If there were two, three or more women who were "overflowed with water" they gathered at the same place which served them as a place of refuge. There a house for menstrual women (*hale pe'a*) was erected. It was tabu for any man to go by or to draw near the defiled spot lest he be destroyed for breaking the law of the god. So it was with the woman who concealed her blood and kept living with her husband, she was also put to death with him. After three to five days and when the blood ceased to flow, the woman then cleansed herself by bathing in water. The defilement was removed, and she could rejoin her husband in the sleeping house.

That is how Liloa, the ruling chief, met this woman. She was young and well shaped in body and was beautiful from her head to the soles of her feet (*kapuai*). The chief lusted after seeing this daughter of a commoner and thought of concealing his chiefly tabu and making himself free. He could not restrain his lust and desire for the woman and so he did as he wished. When he met her she was startled at seeing a man dressed in the attire of a chief and thought that she was about to be put to death. The chief asked that they do what he was desirous of doing, and the woman consented. After they had fulfilled that desire they knew that a child was conceived. The chief said, "This is my command: when our child is born if it be a girl, name her for your side of the family; but if it be a boy, name him for mine. He shall be named 'Umi. I am Liloa, and these are the tokens for the child when he grows up and seeks me in Waipi'o: the feather cape, ivory pendant, helmet and *kauila* spear" (*laau palau*). The woman heeded the words and remembered all of the chief's commands.

The woman's name was Akahi, and it was through her that 'Umi was called a low-born chief (*lepolepo*) by those of Hawaii and a free-born person (*noanoa*) by those of other places. These terms applied to 'Umi might have been right or perhaps they were not, but he was victorious and ruled the kingdom.

An account will be given here of Akahi-a-Kuleana's family for she was the daughter of Kuleana. Explanations help much to clarify. Ka-hekili was a sacred chief of Maui, one with fiery and burning tabus by which men [who broke them] were burned. Ka-hekili was regarded as being equal to a god. He was a well-known chief. His son, Ka-lani-ku-pule, was a ruling chief and while living at 'Ualapu'e on Molokai had a son, Kau-peka-moku. Kau-peka was a grandson of the sacred chief, Ka-hekili. When Kau-peka had some children by very low persons, what were those children and grandchildren called? Kamehameha-nui, son of Ke-kau-like and Ke-ku'i-apo-iwa-nui was a high chief with the fiery (*ahi*), hot (*wela*), very high intense (*i'ui'u anoano i'i*), and terrible (*weliweli*) tabus. He was an older brother of Ka-hekili, and his rule did not last a long time. He has some living descendants, some of whom are going down into the dust. What name can be applied to them? So are the descendants of Keoua, father of Kamehameha I. Some are of a different kind, half whites, and have gone away down into the dust. By what names should they be called? And so it was with the descendants (*pua*) of divine chiefs (*ali'i akua*) who beheld the children of commoners and went down to them [that is, mated with them]. There is no country person who did not have a chiefly ancestor. The *kauwa* [slaves] too had a few born of them who concealed their relationship on the side of the slave.

This is the genealogy of Akahi-a-Kuleana on the chiefly side. Kani-pahu was believed to have been the chiefly (*ali'i*) ancestor, but he was not a ruling chief. After Kani-pahu lived on Molokai and it was discovered that he was a chief, he was taken [as husband] by the ruling chiefess of Molokai. The children he had while living in the upland of Na'iwa and Kala'e became commoners. The *ali'i* wife with whom Kani-pahu lived on Molokai was Hua-lani, and these were their children: Kanaloa the eldest, then Kumu-o-ka-lani, La'a-iki, and Ka-la-hu-moku. The older children lived on Oahu, and Ka-la-hu-moku became ruling chief of Hana, Maui. Akahi's descent from Ka-la-hu-moku went thus: Ka-la-hu-moku lived with La'amea and Iki-a-La'amea was born. Iki-a-La'amea lived with Kalamea and Ka-manawa-a-Kalamea and Haua-a-Kalamea were born. Kalamea lived with Kai-ua and Ua-a-Kai-ua was born. Ua-a-Kai-ua lived with Kua-makani and Ka-nahae-a-Kua-makani was born. Ka-nahae-a-Kua-makani lived with Ka-piko and Kuleana-a-Ka-piko was born. Kuleana-a-Ka-piko lived with Ke-aniani-a-Ho'oleilei and Akahi-a-Kuleana was born. Akahi-a-Kuleana lived with Liloa, and 'Umi-a-Liloa was born. This genealogy shows that they had fallen very low and these people became dwellers [of places] from 'O'okala to Makahi'upa Point.

When Liloa went back to rejoin his chiefs, lesser chiefs (*kaukauali'i*), chiefly war leaders, intimate friends and favorites, they saw their ruling chief, Liloa, and Laea [his guardian] girded with loin cloths of ti leaves and wearing capes of banana leaves. They thought that the two had become mentally deranged or crazy. They shouted, "The chief is mad! The chief is mad!" But the two chiefs did not reveal their secret. When the sports, the dedication of the heiaus, and the enjoyment of the hospitality of the commoners were all over, Liloa and his chiefs returned to his residence, Paka'alana, and the sacred heiaus of his gods, in Waipi'o.

When it was seen that Akahi-a-Kuleana was pregnant, her husband was pleased at the thought of a first-born child, and when it was born a boy, he wanted him named for his side of the family. The mother refused and chose to name him herself. She named him 'Umi. In raising him no particular rules were observed, and he grew up into a handsome but mischievous boy. He did not mind his father, but minded his mother. When the father went fishing and returned hungry and tired, he found no food when he turned to look into the calabashes. "Akahi, Akahi, who ate up all the food?" [he asked]. The wife answered, "I do not know, for you both eat in the men's eating house, but the boy was there with some children." Her husband said, "I was very hungry and found the food all given away to children. The bananas for the god are all eaten." When the father went farming he found on his return that all the fish had been given away to children. This went on all the time. 'Umi was very fond of children and gave them all the food, fish, tapa, and loin cloths. He adopted a son (ho'okama), 'Oma'o-kamau, a boy who bore the ancestral name of 'Oma'o. This behavior of the boy's filled his father with anger, and he often gave him a beating. The mother always took the boy's part and dreaded seeing him beaten because she knew that he was the son of the ruling chief. And to be beaten by an insignificant, low commoner at that! One day as the father was giving the boy another beating, she said to her husband, "That is not your son that you are cruelly beating, but you and I have a share in rearing him. Why talk about your food and fish that are consumed by him? This is why I live with you, to feed his mouth and to give him his needs." "Whose is this child of yours?" [he asked]. His wife answered, "My child is not yours; my child is a chief and he is Liloa's." "Where are the tokens that I may recognize your son as the child of Liloa, the chief?" Akahi-a-Kuleana fetched the feather cape, the helmet, ivory pendant, and loin cloth from their hiding place. When Akahi-a-Kuleana's husband saw them, he said, "I could be killed for this. Why didn't you do the right thing by telling me that the boy is not mine and that he belongs to the chief, Liloa? Then we might have been blessed. I have beaten the boy, thinking that he was my own son. So you met with fire when he came here to Ka'awikiwiki! You have been very unkind to me, but our [young] lord will some day become a ruler." 'Umi's foster father repented of his misdeeds. Shortly after that 'Umi asked Akahi-a-Kuleana, "Let me go to see my father."

His mother consented and said, "Yes, go and see him." Then she instructed him how to go to the chief's residence, not to be afraid or to hesitate, but to go fearlessly on as there was nothing there to hurt him. "After leaving this place, you will have far to go until you reach a wide stream. Remember then that the land lying before you is Waipi'o, a land of plenty. It is a beautiful land to behold from the top of the precipice. You will see the numerous fish ponds and taro patches. The long river there is Wailoa, and on both sides of it, at the opening in the valley, and along the sides [of the cliffs] going inland are the clusters of houses." When she had finished instructing him, she dressed him in the chiefly garments left in her care for him by the chief, Liloa. After all was ready for the journey, he bade his mother farewell and said, "I will go to the place you described as my father's dwelling place. If all is well, I will take care of you all." He was a little over ten years of age at that time.

'Umi went with the son he adopted when he was a mere child. The family name was 'Oma'o, and the one he adopted was the youngest of them all, 'Oma'o-kamau. He was a fast runner and was a little taller than 'Umi. He carried a spear as they walked along to Ke'ahakea. In the evening the children played at disk rolling, sliding, and running. There was a certain boy there who was a swift runner and strong in mock fighting. His parents lived at that place. When the boy saw 'Umi in the garments of a chief, wearing an ivory neck ornament (*palaoa*), and with a helmet on his head, he wondered, for such things were not worn by boys of the back country. *Palaoa* were not common and the only one belonged to the chief Liloa. "Where are you going?" [he asked]. 'Umi replied, "We are going to Waipi'o, to the place where the chief Liloa lives." Pi'i-mai-wa'a asked, "How would it be if I went along with you two?" "Yes, you may go with us and be my adopted son." Pi'i-mai-wa'a answered, "A splendid idea, I shall become your adopted son, a son that has grown up for you in a single day. Let us go to our home, for there is food there. When my parents give me their permission, then we shall go on tomorrow." 'Umi was welcomed with honors by the parents and [they] permitted their son to go with him. They saw that 'Umi was a chief and gave him Pi'i-mai-wa'a, to live or to die in his service. The next day Pi'i-mai-wa'a was permitted to accompany 'Umi.

They went along as far as Waiko'eko'e and there they met a boy playing *ko'i* on the road. The boy's name was Ko'i. His parents received and entertained the boys at their home and consented to let Ko'i become 'Umi's adopted son. They walked together as far as the cliff of Koa'ekea, and there 'Umi gazed down on the cluster of houses nestling on a broad stretch of land surrounded by cliffs with an opening on the seaward side. They descended, walked to Lalakea pond, swam across the Wailoa Stream, and faced Ka-hau-no-ka-ma'ahala, the residence of the chief, Liloa. It was surrounded by a wooden fence. Tabu sticks were placed outside of the enclosure to mark the boundary beyond which commoners were not allowed to go. They remained outside in the sun.

When 'Umi and his adopted sons reached the outermost boundary, he asked them to wait for him there, saying, "You remain here while I go on to the chief's residence. If you hear the beating of drums, I am saved, and you will be sent for, but if after waiting you hear no sound of drums, then know that I am dead; my father has failed to recognize me." 'Umi went up to lean against the tabu sticks (*pahu pulo'ulo'u*) at the crossed sticks of the outer entrance. The outermost enclosure had crossed sticks at the entrance. When these fell,* he went on to a fence held together by cords. The gate was tied on, and the cord that would allow it to open led into the house. The cord that held the gate was released only when the password was given. 'Umi climbed over the fence, and when the executioners (*ilamuku*) of the chief saw him [they exclaimed], "The boy has broken the tabu of the chief." He went through the low side door, the tabu door of the chief's residence, and stood looking about him. Liloa sat on an elevated place with his feathered-staff bearers waving their staffs to and fro. 'Umi leaped toward him and sat on his lap. The boy had broken another tabu. The chief looked at the boy sitting on his lap and asked, "Whose child are you?" The boy answered, "Yours! I am 'Umi-a-Liloa." Liloa noticed the tokens he had left for his son and kissed and wept over him. He ordered the kahunas to fetch the *pahu* and *ka'eke* drums at once and to take the boy to be circumcized and dedicated, as was the custom for children of chiefs. The chiefly drum, Halalu', and the smaller *ka'eke* drums were sounded in Paka'alana. The chief said, "It was for this child of mine that I girded my loins with ti leaves and covered my shoulders with banana leaves. And [I also left behind] my *palaoa*."†

* 'Umi leaned against the tabu sticks to see if they would fall. He was not recognized by a guard, but by the guardian spirits of the ancestors (*aumakua*). These caused the sticks to fall and let the young chief enter.
† *Ke Au 'Oko'a*, Nov. 10, 1870.

After the ruler had blessed his son he asked, "Did you have any travelling companions?" "I did, and they are my adopted sons." [The chief said] "Go and fetch them at once." The chief said to himself, "This is a kind-hearted boy. Although he is still a child, he has made himself like a father and mother to his people. His descendants cannot fail to become rulers." The chief asked, "Where is your mother?" The boy answered, "At home. It was she who told me of you, that you are my father and a tabu chief." The chief said to 'Umi, "I gave no gift to your mother. I now say let her have the *ahupua'a* at Kealahaka for the good care given you by her and your foster father. Let that be my gift to your parents. Send one of your adopted sons to tell them and let them know that they are the chiefs over those lands."

News went abroad of the new son of Chief Liloa. This was well known at the court, and was made known to the countrysides. The people in the country places did not know very much about this chief or that. The reason for this ignorance and fear was the tabus of the chiefs and of the gods. They were tabus that caused death to the people. When the chiefs heard of the new son of Liloa, some were interested, and some despised him. They said he was indeed a chief, but not equal in rank with some. There was much discussion among themselves. Pinea taught her son, who was heir to the kingdom, not to acknowledge his relationship to 'Umi because he was born to a lowly commoner. It was well enough for Pinea to tell her son about 'Umi's humble birth, but she should have taught him to care for the gods and to take care of the big man and the little man. Then all of her words would have been of some value. They would have been like the words of Mahu-lua to her son, Ku-ali'i, "Take care of the god, and take care of the big man, the little man, and the fatherless."

When Hakau, the heir of the kingdom, heard of Liloa's new son his anger was kindled. These were the reasons for his anger: 1. The mixing of the blood of chiefs with that of commoners. 2. The relationship of the children of low-born slaves to chiefs. 3. The fear that the tabu of chiefs would be trodden by commoners. Hakau himself went before his father and said, "So you have a slave for a son, and he is to call me his brother." His father answered, "He is not to call you brother for you are a chief, a lord. My [other] son is to be a servant to you, a carrier of your spittoon, tapas and loincloth, a servant who is related by blood (*iwikuamo'o*) to you, the chief." After Hakau heard this his anger and jealousy were cooled. 'Umi dwelt there with his adopted sons, Pi'i-mai-wa'a, 'Oma'o-kamau, and Ko'i, and went to swim and dive, when they were all beaten by Hakau.

At one time Liloa made a canoe for his son 'Umi to play with,

and when 'Umi and Hakau sailed their canoes, 'Umi's went far ahead
and won. The canoe was taken away, and 'Umi was beaten by Hakau.
'Umi went home to Liloa crying, and Liloa said, "Hold back your tears."
Liloa made great favorites of 'Umi and his adopted sons.

'Umi and his companions became large men when they grew up.
When 'Umi and his adopted sons had grown up, they were skilled in
working, in spear fighting, in sham battles, in racing, and in other
arts practiced at the court of the chief. There was none in the court
of Liloa to equal 'Umi and his sons. 'Umi humbled himself before his
father, serving faithfully before him. Liloa chose some instructors
in spear fighting to train 'Umi and his adopted sons, to give them skill
in warfare. 'Umi and his companions were adept in sham battles and in
slinging stones, but the best of them all was Pi'i-mai-wa'a. He was
also a swift runner. 'Umi excelled in surfing with a canoe or a
surfboard. When Hakau's boys took part in sham battles with
'Umi's adopted sons, the latter always won the lehua [the first victim in
war—i.e. were victorious] and caused the others to flee. For this reason
Liloa made great favorites of 'Umi and his adopted sons and said, "So!
Here is the boy that will make my bones live, this child of an owl. The
chiefly child and heir to the kingdom seeks pleasure only, is fond of
women, and is cruel to the common people." Liloa was inclined toward
'Umi who heeded all instructions, served his father humbly, and was
obedient to his teachers and those in his father's court. They loved him.

When Hakau saw that Liloa loved 'Umi better than himself he
hated 'Umi and reviled, mocked, and humiliated him beyond human
endurance. Their father sought to appease Hakau from time to time
for the sake of his son 'Umi. Sometimes Liloa advised 'Umi, "After
I am dead and you are left with your lord and brother, go elsewhere
and live under others if he should mistreat and abuse you. This is
the one thing you must do, take care of the god. Whatever you have,
remember him. Though you may live in poverty, the god will have
compassion on you and reward you." When Liloa became feeble
and was about to die, he commanded that the kingdom be in charge of
the heir, Hakau, the son of his royal wife Pinea. All of the ruling chiefs
and lesser chiefs on Hawaii were to serve Hakau. He commanded
that his son 'Umi-a-Liloa be given the government-snatching god,
Ku-ka'ili-moku, and said to 'Umi, "Live humbly."

After Liloa's death, Hakau took over the government, and the
chief ['Umi] lived under him. In the first years of his reign Hakau
observed the teachings of his father, the kahunas, and counselors, and
lived a just life. He sought those who were skilled in wicker work
(haku 'ie) and had his father's corpse cleansed and woven in a wicker

covering. He also kept the houses of the god clean. But in the later
years of his rule he was lost in pleasure, mistreated the chiefs, beat
those who were not guilty of any wrongdoing, and abused the priests
of the heiaus of his god and the chiefs of his own government. 'Umi
was also abused by Hakau and was called the child of a low-born slave.
He was not allowed to eat a meal, to share a feast with Hakau, to remain
with him in the chief's residence, to use the same tapa, to gird on the
same loin cloth, or to use the same surfboard. Hakau was jealous because
'Umi-a-Liloa was handsome and good.

So 'Umi-a-Liloa and his adopted sons departed in secret. 'Umi
was afraid of being killed by Hakau. Therefore they fled by way of
the forest back of Hamakua lest they meet someone on the road. They
went by way of Pu'ua'ahuku and through a forest. Pi'i-mai-wa'a was a
good bird-catcher, and so they had something to eat in the forest until
they reached the place above Laumai'a Kemilia [called] Laumai'a
Kenahae, and there they dwelt. 'Umi sent Pi'i-mai-wa'a to tell
Akahi-a-Kuleana that they were living in the upland of Humu'ula and
that they were unable to go and dwell with 'Umi's parents. Akahi-a-
Kuleana said that it was not wise for them to live with the parents for
Hakau's overseers had been there to seek them. It was not safe to live
within the boundary of Hamakua and it was better to go to the district
of Hilo as it was a different district. It was under Kulukulu'a', and
Hakau had no jurisdiction there.

'Umi hearkened to the advice that Pi'i-mai-wa'a brought from his
mother and went to live in the district of Hilo near the boundary of
Hamakua. The name of the *ahupua'a* was Waipunalei. There were many
people there, many women of prominence, many favorite daughters,
and all were good-looking and young. 'Umi-a-Liloa was the handsomest
youth of all, and so he received four wives, twice as many as his
adopted sons. While living there his adopted sons said, "You stay
without working and let us do the farming. Our wives and parents-in-law
will do the cooking." The adopted sons observed the royal tabus of
their "father" as they lived in the homes of their wives. They said to
his wives, "Do not be careless with your husband's clothing," and they
did as they were told. 'Umi's parents-in-law were no exception to other
parents-in-law, in speaking unkindly of their son-in-law.

When the season came for bonito (*aku*) fishing down at Laupahoehoe,
the harbor from which those of that land went fishing, his adopted sons
went too. They obtained bonito whenever they went out because they
helped to man the canoes.

'Umi and his wives went sea bathing, surfing (*he'e nalu*), riding
on the surf (*kaha nalu*), and a certain chief of Laupahoehoe noticed

'Umi's skill in surf-riding. His name was Pai'ea, and he knew all the surfs and the best one to ride. It was the one directly in front of Laupahoehoe, facing Hilo. It was a huge one which none dared to ride except Pai'ea, who was noted for his skill. Gambling on surfing was practiced in that locality. All of the inhabitants from Waipunalei to Ka'ula placed their wager on 'Umi, and those of Laupahoehoe on Pai'ea. The two rode the surf, and while surfing Pai'ea noticed that 'Umi was winning. As they drew near a rock, Pai'ea crowded him against it, skinning his side. 'Umi was strong and pressed his foot against Pai'ea's chest and then landed ashore. 'Umi won against Pai'ea, and because he crowded 'Umi against the rock with the intention of killing him, Pai'ea was roasted in an imu [in later years.]

When it was seen how strong 'Umi was, he was wanted to man the bait-carrying canoe (malau), and it was discovered that he was a strong canoe paddler. Sometimes when there were many fish they were given out [to the workers] in a proper manner, but sometimes when the fish were few they were tossed one by one between the legs. Fish tossed between the legs became defiled and were not acceptable as offerings to the god. Such fish were despised by the god. Therefore 'Umi traded with another person for fish that were handed out and not tossed between the legs. If there was only one fish, 'Umi did not eat any of it, but left it for his god, Ku-ka'ili-moku. It was hidden in a cave by the trail leading down to Hokuli. Because of 'Umi's strength in manning canoes, he was called Pu'ipu'i-a-ka-lawai'a (stalwart-son-of-a-fisherman).

The disappearance of 'Umi-a-Liloa, son of Liloa, was noised abroad, but no one knew where he had gone. A certain man of chiefly blood, named Ka-lei-o-ku, noticed the low-hanging and arching rainbows over the bait-carrying canoe for bonito fishing with which 'Umi always went, and also over the cliff of Hokuli. The strangers who lived at the homes of their wives at Waipunalei were known roundabout, and so Ka-lei-o-ku guessed that the rainbows were for no one else than 'Umi, son of Liloa.

Ka-lei-o-ku took a pig and ran to offer it with prayers before 'Umi. "This is a pig with which to seek the chief [he said to himself], and if it runs and lies at his feet, this man is 'Umi." The pig ran and laid itself down at 'Umi's feet. "Are you 'Umi-a-Liloa?" [he asked]. "Yes, I am he." "Then let us go to my home." Food and all other things were ready for the chiefly guest, and Ka-lei-o-ku became his attendant (kahu hanai). The chief was grown up, and the trouble of rearing him was finished. When it was learned that he was a high chief, a son of Liloa named 'Umi-a-Liloa, fear descended upon his fellow fishermen and his parents-in-law, but he readily reassured them.

Ka-lei-o-ku became his trusted attendant and built many long houses (*halau*), ten times ten of them, for the purpose of feeding men. When people came from Hilo to Hamakua for salt they were given pork to eat [a mark of great hospitality]. Travellers from Hamakua, Kohala, and Kona who went to Hilo and Puna for birds' feathers were received in 'Umi's eating places. Before a year had gone, many people had been received, and 'Umi's hospitality gained fame. Most of the men busied themselves with farming and in the evenings were trained in warfare. News reached Waipi'o that 'Umi was living with Ka-lei-o-ku and that he was a kindly chief who cared for the big men, the little men, the old men, the old women, children, the poor, and the sick. One thing he did was to give food to people. Hakau's aged kahuna said, "He is wise in caring for a chief as he is doing. His bones shall live."

At one time the old men, Nunu and Ka-kohe, were indisposed through taking a purge. They sent a man to ask Hakau to send them food, fish, and 'awa. Hakau answered with insulting words, reviling them in such a way as to humiliate them. The old men began to plot to give the kingdom to someone else. When they heard of the goodness of Ka-lei-o-ku's beloved chief, Nunu and Ka-kohe decided to see for themselves. Ka-lei-o-ku was a younger brother of theirs, born of the same parents, conceived in the same womb, and descended from the priestly line of Lono. Ka-lei-o-ku was told of their coming and knew which day they would arrive. Everything was made ready for the day on which they were expected, and when it came Ka-lei-o-ku and all of the men went farming.*

'Umi was the only man left at home with some women. Upon arrival the old men inquired, "Where is Ka-lei-o-ku and his chief?" 'Umi replied, "Ka-lei-o-ku, his chief, and all of the men have gone farming. I am the only man left to serve you when you arrive." They asked, "When will he return?" "They will all come back in the evening. Let me prepare you some food." 'Umi grasped a large piece of wood, and with one stroke of a stone broke it into little pieces. One old man nodded to the other, "What a powerful man this is! With one stroke he breaks up a piece of hard wood and converts it into kindling." As to the fire, no sooner did the smoke curl and the pig squeal than it was ready for the roasting. The 'awa needed only the [straining] fibers, for the rootlets were already mashed. As soon as the fibers were placed in the 'awa container (*kanoa*), the pig was cooked. One of the old men said, "How strange! the mucus of my nose (*ka hupe*

* *Ke Au 'Oko'a*, Nov. 17, 1870.

o ko'u ihu) is not even cleaned and lo, the pig is cooked." It was cooked to a crisp and brought into the eating house. The 'awa was poured into coconut cups (*'apu*) and handed to the old men. In a very short time all was ready: bananas, sugar cane with outer skin removed, dog meat cooked in ti leaves, ti-leaf bundles containing chicken or *kumu* fish and all other kinds of food. The old men took them, thanked the god, Ku-ka'ili-moku, asked that 'Umi's life be preserved, and then uttered the *'amama*.

After they had eaten, they were drunk with 'awa and fell asleep in the men's eating house. 'Umi shook them, but they did not waken in the least.

When the intoxication of the old men had passed, it was evening and the people were returning from their farming. There was a great company of men, women, and children. The old men asked, "Where is Ka-lei-o-ku and the chief he serves?" "They are still in the rear," answered the men. There were so many people that they seemed an endless company. The old men scanned each one hoping to see Ka-lei-o-ku's chief, 'Umi-a-Liloa. They did not have a chance to see them all until late in the evening when Ka-lei-o-ku returned with his family. They greeted each other with affection, and after they had finished weeping the old men asked Ka-lei-o-ku, "Where is your beloved chief? We looked at the people, but there were so many that we were unable to see them all." Ka-lei-o-ku replied, "Did you not see the lone man that was here to welcome you? That is he." The old men said to Ka-lei-o-ku, "What you did to us was next to murder. So he was none other than the chief himself! If he had chosen to kill us, we would have died. We have no gift for your beloved chief except the kingdom. Let your chief have the kingdom and let our chief [Hakau] be put to death." (It was said that these old men gave the kingdom to 'Umi without any fault on Hakau's part. His death was cunningly sought by them, with bribery. So did Hakau perish. But Hawaii was always a land that killed its chiefs).

Ka-lei-o-ku asked, "How shall Hakau be put to death so that the kingdom will belong to my chief, 'Umi?" The old men replied, "Our chief shall die. His life or death depends on us. We owe much to your chief for he has made a servant of his royal self for us, for the kingdom. Thus shall Hakau die: When the tabu period of Ku arrives, it will last three nights and two days. Early in the morning the chiefs, lesser chiefs, and all of the commoners will go to the upland. Hakau and a few of his chiefs will remain to observe the tabus with us, the kahunas of the *haku'ohi'a* ceremony. That is the time for you to come with gifts of food and offerings for the heiaus. All war weapons must be wrapped in ti leaves, and stones [must be] wrapped in banana-leaf bundles. All wooden weapons such as the *pololu* spears made of *koa'ie, mamane, o'a,* and other woods should be carried on the shoulder to stick out before and behind. Then shall Hakau and his people die, and none shall save them." When Ka-lei-o-ku, the adopted sons of 'Umi, and his warriors heard this they made ready. The old men ate the fat foods for which they betrayed the kingdom of their lord.

After remaining there a few days the old men went home pretending friendship for their lord and nursing hatred and grudge in their hearts. Nunu and Ka-kohe were high priests of the priestly class of Lono. When the tabu period of Ku arrived, the kahunas made all preparations at the rising of the morning star for the chiefs and commoners to go to the upland for *'ohi'a* logs to be made into images. A large company of people departed, and when the sun appeared a procession of people was seen descending with bundles all wrapped in leaves, from the front [of the line] to the back. Some [of the bundles] looked like pigs wrapped in banana leaves. The people descended on the road from Koa'ekea, and the cliffside was thick with them. One of Hakau's attendants, named Hoe, said to him, "That is not a procession of strangers. It is 'Umi's company. It is not a procession to seek or to pay respects to their lord, because the loin cloth is girded tight around the waist (*pu'ali*), the body covering (*'a'ahu*) rolled up (*owili*) and ti leaves tied together (*pe'a*) on the head. Woe betide you, we are going to perish!" Hakau and all the others were slaughtered—chiefs, personal attendants, and stewards. Their war weapons were all taken by the warriors of 'Umi-a-Liloa. When the chiefs, lesser chiefs, and members of the court who had gone for *'ohi'a* logs heard that Hakau, the chief, was slain, that the people of Waipi'o were slaughtered, and that 'Umi had rebelled against the kingdom, the sons of the chiefs of Kona, Ka-'u, Puna, and Hilo fled in secret to their parents. They rebelled against the kingdom and gained independence for Kona, Ka-'u, Puna, Hilo, and Kohala.

After the cruel destruction of the ruler, Hakau, his chiefs, and members of the court by the rebels, all the corpses of those slain in battle were offered up in the heiau of Honua'ula in Waipi'o. It is frequently told in the tales of the skilled narrators of old that when 'Umi-a-Liloa laid the victims on the altar in the heiau—the bodies of the fallen warriors and the chief, Hakau—the tongue of the god came down from heaven, without the body being seen. The tongue quivered downward to the altar, accompanied by thunder and lightning, and took away all the sacrifices.

'Umi-a-Liloa ruled in place of Hakau, a position which he cleverly sought with the cunning of his foster father (*kahu hanai*) who showed him the way to become ruler. The rule became his in spite of the many enemies (*enemi*) who tried to prevent his getting it because they despised him for being only partly a chief (*no ke koko hapa o kona koko ali'i*). 'Umi had some children when he was living in poverty and on the charity of others. They were named Noho-na-hele (Living-in-the wilderness), Ka-punana-hua-nui (Nest-of-a-big-egg), a boy and a girl. These were born to him by a country woman while he was living in Waipunalei on the windward side of Hilo. After 'Umi became ruler, Ka-lei-o-ku was made country chief for Hamakua. 'Umi's adopted sons became chiefs, his body guards, and war lords. Akahi-a-Kuleana was sent for to live in the chief's residence. She had borne several children to her husband after 'Umi was born. 'Umi-a-Liloa cared for the daughter of Hakau, the chief. Her name was Pinea, whom Hakau named for his mother. 'Umi did this in order to preserve the rank in which there was no mixed blood. He took the daughter of his father, Liloa, named Kapu-kini, for wife. She was his half-sister. The children born to him by Kapu-kini were Ke-li'i-o-kaloa, Kapu-lani, and Keawe-a-'Umi.

At one time 'Umi-a-Liloa travelled incognito to Hilo and did not mingle with the chiefs there. They did not know what he looked like, though they had heard that he had taken the kingdom of Hakau. 'Umi went to visit Hilo accompanied by his adopted sons, and there they remained. Kulukulu'a' was chief there. They visited the chiefly residence, and 'Umi's handsome appearance and fine physique were noticed. Therefore he married the daughter of Kulukulu'a', chief of Hilo.

'Umi dwelt with the daughter of Kulukulu'a'. She owned a necklace made of finely-braided dark hair with a pendant of *wiliwili* wood (*lei palaoa wiliwili*) fastened on securely. He saw it on the night when all of the Hilo chiefs had a celebration at Kanukuokamanu, Waiakea. There was hula dancing, games of hiding stones (*papuhene*), tossing a half-coconut at a mark (*kilu*), and *loku* [?]. 'Umi saw the daughter of Kulukulu'a' adorned with birds' feathers on head and body, and about her neck was the necklace with the *wiliwili* pendant. After the celebration, 'Umi's wife, daughter of Kulukulu'a', went home. He asked her for the necklace and when she gave it to him, he said, "Is this your necklace of chieftainship?" The woman answered, "Yes, it is. Commoners are not allowed to wear one." ['Umi replied] "This is commonly worn by children and from them up to old women. The pendants (*palaoa*) of our chiefs are made of ivory, the teeth of whales. They are fastened to strands of braided hair." 'Umi then broke her *wiliwili* pendant.

'Umi-a-Liloa broke the tongue-shaped pendant of *wiliwili* wood, and when the daughter of Kulukulu'a' saw this she ran quickly to her father and said, "My husband broke my necklace in pieces. He asked, "Why did he break it?" His daughter answered, "The man said that he was ashamed of it, and that *wiliwili* pendants are worn by their commoners, from children to old women. The necklaces worn by their chiefs are made of the teeth of whales (*niho kohola a me ka niho palaoa*). Kulukulu'a' said to his daughter, "Have those men bound with ropes, and if the ivory *palaoa* of chieftainship is not produced, then they shall be slaughtered and offered as sacrifices in the heiau of Kanoa."

Kulukulu'a' commanded his warriors to bind three of the men with ropes, 'Umi-a-Liloa, 'Oma'o-kamau, and Ko'i. Pi'i-mai-wa'a was sent to Waipi'o for the *palaoa*, because it was ordered that only one day be given them to secure it, or else they should die. Pi'i-mai-wa'a ran and in a short time arrived at Waipi'o, and told the chiefs that 'Umi and his companions were in trouble in Hilo. It did not take long for Pi'i-mai-wa'a, on that selfsame day, to return and give the ivory into the hands of Kulukulu'a''s daughter. She was beside herself with joy at the sight of this new object, an ivory pendant made of a whale's tooth and attached to a necklace. She leaped and laughed with glee over her luck, but 'Umi-a-Liloa was sad at the thought of parting with the heirloom of his father Liloa. He uttered a prayer to his god, Kuka'ili-moku to let the chiefs of Hilo take care of the *palaoa* of chieftainship, Nani-koki, until the day when they should become his captives.

When the ivory was received, 'Umi and his companions were freed from being held prisoners in the house of his parents-in-law. As soon as they were released in Hilo, 'Umi and his companions returned to Hamakua and went down to Waipi'o. There he conferred with his chiefs and his father's old war leaders. It was decided to make war on the chiefs of Hilo and to go without delay by way of Mauna Kea. From back of Ka'umana they were to descend to Hilo. It was shorter to go by way of the mountain to the trail of Poli'ahu and Poli'ahu's spring at the top of Mauna Kea, and then down toward Hilo. It was an ancient trail used by those of Hamakua, Kohala, and Waimea to go to Hilo. They made ready to go with their fighting parties to Mauna Kea, descended back of Hilo, and encamped just above the stream of Waianuenue without the knowledge of Hilo's people that war was coming from the upland. Hilo's chiefs were unprepared.

A certain fisherman of Pu'ueo was at sea, catching *nehu* fish, and he noticed that the water in the ocean was dirty. He was surprised and guessed that there was war in the mountain, and it was that which caused the water to be so dirty. Some [of his companions] denied this and declared that it was a cloudburst instead of war, and that was the cause of the dirt and the reddening of the water flowing into the sea. He would not believe them and insisted that this dirt was stirred up by the feet of men. He hauled up his drawnets at once and went ashore. He did not stop to dry his nets, but cooked taro and some *nehu* fish, picked up his war spear, draped his cape of ti leaves over his back, and departed for the upland. The name of this man was Nau.

When Nau arrived away up in the upland of Ka'umana, he remained at a narrow pass, and the other side of it was the camp [of 'Umi]. He sat on a flat stone beside the stream and after opening his bundle of *nehu* fish, ate some with the cooked taro (*kuala*). 'Umi-a-Liloa's warriors noticed Nau, the noted fisherman of Pu'ueo, eating taro and *nehu* fish. It was difficult for 'Umi-a-Liloa's men to pass through to the trail. They came in single file to go through the pass, and at the narrowest part a leg had to reach out first. The spot in which he sat was comfortable and was in a depression. When someone on the other side reached out to go through, he was stabbed with a spear and fell over the cliff, dead.* This was continued until many were destroyed by this lone man who guarded the narrow pass of Ka'uamoa. Forty were killed. Pi'i-mai-wa'a climbed over the cliff and saw but one man against its side. He said to himself, "I shall kill you," and leaped over. [A cry went up] "Pi'i-mai-wa'a is dead! He has fallen over the cliff." It was Nau who died, and so there was no one to warn the chief of Hilo. When night came, the war party reached Hilo. They were supplied with torches and saw the chief's residences and the house of Kulukulu'a"s daughter. 'Umi-a-Liloa's warriors surrounded them, and the chiefs of Hilo were destroyed. Kulukulu'a"s daughter was spared, and Nani-koki, the famous *palaoa*, was restored. Regret for the loss of the *palaoa* was the cause of the war. After the battle, the districts of Hilo and Hamakua were united under the rule of 'Umi-a-Liloa.

Hua-'a was the chief of Puna, but Puna was seized by 'Umi and his warrior adopted sons, Pi'i-mai-wa'a, 'Oma'o-kamau, and Ko'i. These were noted war leaders and counsellors during 'Umi's reign over the

* *Ke Au 'Oko'a*, Nov. 24, 1870.

kingdom of Hawaii. Hua-'a was killed by Pi'i-mai-wa'a on the battlefield of Kuolo in Kea'au, and Puna became 'Umi-a-Liloa's.

I-mai-ka-lani was the chief of Ka-'u. He was blind, but noted for
his strength and skill in battle. Many chiefs who had fought against
him were destroyed. He was skilled in striking left or striking right,
and when he thrust his spear (*pololu*) to the right or to the left it
roared like thunder, flashed like lightning, and rumbled like an
earthquake. When he struck behind him, a cloud of dust rose skyward
as though in a whirlwind. 'Umi-a-Liloa feared I-mai-ka-lani. Although
he was blind and unable to see, his hearing was keen. He had pet
ducks that told him in which direction a person approached, whether
from in front, at the back, or on either side. All depended on the
cries of the birds. In former days I-mai-ka-lani was not blind, and
'Umi was never able to take Ka-'u. The war lasted a long time. 'Umi
went by way of the mountains to stir up a fight with I-mai-ka-lani and
the chiefs of Kona. He became famous as a chief who travelled through
the mountains of Hawaii, and [its trails] became the routes by which
he went to war. After I-mai-ka-lani became blind the fight between
him and 'Umi continued.

I-mai-ka-lani was never taken captive by 'Umi, but Pi'i-mai-wa'a
was crafty and studied the reason for his great strength and skill with
the spear. Not a single thrust failed its mark, and with one blow
[the victim] was torn from head to buttocks. Pi'i-mai-wa'a discovered
the reason for the skill and fearlessness of this blind man. Ducks
flew overhead and cried, and when he heard them, before, behind, or
on either side, he declared, "A man approaches from the rear." The
man who guided him about answered, "Yes, there is a man." "Where
is his club (*la'au*)?" "In front of him." He recognized it as a club
(*la'au hahau*). "Is he near?" "Yes." The blind man smote with his
club (*la'au palau*), and the other was torn from head (*puniu*) to
buttocks (*olemu*). Whenever a bird cried, there was a man. "Where
is his club?" I-mai-ka-lani asked. "On the right side." "A left stroke
will get him." When the other smote he missed, but when the blind
man smote, [his opponent] was struck from head to abdomen. As
Pi'i-mai-wa'a studied and knew every angle of I-mai-ka-lani's strength
and marvelous skill, he said to himself, "I shall kill you yet." He went
to kill the bird guards, the two men who led I-mai-ka-lani on
each side, and the forty men who carried his weapons, long and short
spears. I-mai-ka-lani thrust ten spears at a time, five with the right
[hand] and five with the left. The spears flashed forth like lightning,
and no man was able to dodge the spears when he faced I-mai-ka-lani.

All these men were destroyed by Pi'i-mai-wa'a, and the blind man was at a loss for the lack of helpers. Well could Pi'i-mai-wa'a say in a boast, "Death to him from Pi'i-mai-wa'a." After I-mai-ka-lani's death Ka-'u became 'Umi-a-Liloa's.

'Ehu-nui-kai-malino was chief of Kona. He was the father of Laea-nui-kau-manamana and was a strong man, but because of his old age, Kona and Kohala were easily taken by 'Umi-a-Liloa. When Hawaii was united under 'Umi-a-Liloa, his fame spread from Hawaii to Kauai. There was no kingdom like his. He took care of the old men, the old women, the fatherless, and the common people. Murder and thievery were prohibited. He was a religious chief, just in his rule, and so the rulers of other kingdoms brought their favorite daughters to him for wives. 'Umi had many wives of chiefly blood and he became an ancestor for the people. There is not a commoner on Hawaii who can say, "'Umi-a-Liloa was not our ancestor," and if he does, it is because he is ignorant of his ancestry. 'Umi's chiefly wife, Kapu-kini-a-Liloa, bore him the following children: Keli'i-o-kaloa a son, Kapu-lani a daughter, and Ke-awe-nui-a-'Umi a son.

Pi'ikea was [another] chiefly wife. She was the daughter of Pi'i-lani, ruling chief of Maui, by La'ie-lohelohe-i-ka-wai. She bore two children to 'Umi-a-Liloa, Kumalae-nui-a-'Umi and 'Ai-hako'ko'.

Moku-a-Hua-lei-akea was another wife of rank. She was a descendant of 'Ehu-nui-kai-malino of Kona and she bore 'Umi-a-Liloa a daughter, Akahi-'ili-kapu. 'Umi-a-Liloa lived with Ohenahena-lani, and to them was born Kamola-nui-a-'Umi. As to his children by the country women, he had many of them.

'Umi resided in Waipi'o, Hamakua, and when the island of Hawaii was united by him, he desired to dwell in Kona where the climate was warm. The chiefs lived in Kailua.

During 'Umi-a-Liloa's reign he selected workers and set them in various positions in the kingdom. He separated those of the chiefly class (*papa ali'i*), of the priestly class, of the readers of omens (*papa kilo*), those skilled in the affairs of the land (*po'e akamai o ka 'aina*), farmers, fishermen, canoe builders, warriors, and other skilled artisans (*po'e pale 'ike*) in the work they were best suited for; and each one applied himself to his own task. So it was with the governors and the head men who watched over the '*okana, ahupua'a*, and '*ili'aina* land sections.

'Umi-a-Liloa did two things with his own hands, farming and fishing. He built some large wet taro patches in Waipi'o, and farming was done on all the lands. Much of this was done in Kona. He was noted for his skill in fishing and was called *Pu'ipu'i a ka lawai'a* (a stalwart fisherman). *Aku* fishing was his favorite occupation, and it often took him to the beaches from Kalahuipua'a to Makaula. He also fished for *'ahi* and for *kala*. He was accompanied by famed fishermen such as Pae, Kahuna, and all of the chiefs of his kingdom. He set apart fishing, farming, and other practices.

Another thing that brought fame to 'Umi-a-Liloa was his battle with gods, and this was the reason: Hapu'u and Ka-la'i-hauola were godly ancestresses of his chiefly wife, Pi'i-kea. Hapu'u wanted to take one of their grandchildren to Oahu to rear because Pi'i-kea's mother, La'ie-lohelohe-i-ka-wai, belonged there. La'ie-lohelohe-i-ka-wai sent her godly ancestresses to Hawaii to bring her one of Pi'i-kea's children. When they went to get him, 'Umi-a-Liloa refused to permit any of his children to go to Oahu to be reared by Pi'i-kea's mother. He refused to let someone else bring up any child of his. So the gods killed men at night, and when day came it was seen that they were dead. So it went on night after night, that the guiltless ones were destroyed. 'Umi-a-Liloa was puzzled [and asked], "Why are these men killed by invisible killers?"

Pi'i-kea answered, "There is no other cause for their deaths except that they were destroyed by my ancestresses, Hapu'u and Ka-la'i-hauola. My mother sent them for one of our children, but you refused to give him up; and that is why the people are being killed." "How will this destruction cease?" inquired 'Umi. She replied, "Only when they have the child." He was skeptical about the death being caused by gods, but the destruction kept right on. He daringly brought war against their hands with sticks and stones, and the gods fought without using their hands. The gods won in the battle against the men. The place bears the name of Kaua-ke-'kua (Battle-of-the-gods) and Kai-a-ke-akua (Sea-of-the-gods) to this day. Hapu'u and Ka-la'i-hauola remained at home with Pi'i-kea who was pregnant at the time. One of the old women slapped her on the knees, and the child was born in the presence of the other old woman. Upon examination it was seen that the child was a girl, and she was borne away to Oahu by the gods. She was reared by La'ie-lohelohe and named Kaha'i-ao-nui-a-Pi'i-kea and Kaha'i-ao-nui-a-'Umi. When 'Umi-a-Liloa returned from the battle with the gods, lo, the child was taken away by Hapu'u and Ka-la'i-hauola.

It was said that one of the causes of the trouble was 'Umi-a-Liloa's false promises. He was asked for his children, from the eldest down, and he had promised to grant the request, but after a child was born he refused to give it up, saying that they must wait for the next one. And so it went from time to time, until the ancestresses of Pi'i-kea became angry. As a result, gods fought against men. From the beginning of 'Umi's reign until he became old, there was continued peace with his father-in-law Pi'i-lani, ruler of Maui, and with his chiefs. No battle was fought between the two kingdoms. After the death of Pi'i-lani, father of Pi'i-kea, trouble began with the heir of the kingdom.*

* *Ke Au 'Oko'a*, Dec. 1, 1870.

CHAPTER II

The Story of Kiha-a-Pi'i-lani*

Pi'i-lani died at Lahaina, Maui, and the kingdom of Maui became Lono-a-Pi'i-lani's. He was Pi'i-lani's oldest son by La'ie-lohelohe-i-ka-wai. Next to him came Pi'i-kea, then Ka-la-'ai-heana and Kiha-a-Pi'i-lani. It was said that there were two heirs to the kingdom, Lono-a-Pi'ilani and Kiha-a-Pi'i-lani, but the latter was not present at their father's death because Oahu was his birthplace, and there he was reared. Therefore the government went to Lono-a-Pi'i-lani. Pi'i-lani had commanded that the kingdom be his, and that Kiha-a-Pi'i-lani dwell under him in peace. In the first years of Lono-a-Pi'i-lani's reign all was well, and the people were content.

Lono-a-Pi'i-lani took care of Kiha-a-Pi'i-lani, and the latter cared for the people by giving them food. Lono-a-Pi'i-lani became angry, for he felt Kiha-a-Pi'i-lani was doing it to seize the kingdom for himself. Lono-a-Pi'i-lani and Kiha-a-Pi'i-lani started farming in the *ahupua'a* of Waihe'e. The ruling chief's taro patch was smaller, for the latter saw to it that his patch exceeded in size. Therefore Lono-a-Pi'i-lani grew very angry with him and abused him. He humiliated him over food and fish, and so they fought. The briny water which held *ohua* fish [and squid] was thrown into Kiha-a-Pi'i-lani's face; the tips of the squid's tentacle clung to his eyes.

Lono-a-Pi'i-lani sought to kill Kiha, so he fled in secret to Molokai. The fortress of Paku'i, above Hananui and 'Ualapuni, was surrounded [by warriors]. Kiha escaped with his life by leaping from the fortress into a *kukui* tree and went to Lanai. He was believed to have gone to Oahu, but he was on Lanai instead. He patiently bore his troubles knowing that he would not die, and that the kingdom of Maui would yet be his. He would become a famous ruler according to the predictions of those who reared him. "He would have many troubles, live in poverty, and become a famous ruler." Kiha-a-Pi'i-lani bore his troubles, his poverty, and his homeless state patiently. His life was saved by leaping from the fortress of Paku'i and fleeing to Lanai. From Lanai he sailed and landed at Kapoli in Ma'alaea and from thence

*For Kiha-a-Pi'i-lani see 13, 2, pp. 97-99; 14 Col. 4, pp. 236 254; Col. 5, pp. 176-180; 38, pp. 77-86.

22

to the upland of Honua'ula. He was seen, and the matter was reported to Lono-a-Pi'i-lani, the enemy who greatly desired his death. When it was heard that he was in Lahaina, swift runners were sent to seek and kill him, but the mana of his prayers and the help of the god saved him.

He and his wife descended by the rocky gulch of Kuanu'u and went around to the back. They lived on the charity of others at the boundary of Honua'ula and Kula, at a place named Ke'eke'e. They lived with farmers in the remote country, and because of their poverty-stricken state, neither he nor his wife had any clothing. They had nothing and had no means of making coverings for their bare bodies, and so an idea came to Kiha-a-Pi'i-lani to seek ways of getting them some tapa cloth.* Kiha-a-Pi'i-lani went to steal an anvil, a tapa beater, and beater for finishing, to help in making tapa. They had nothing at all. After Kiha-a-Pi'i-lani had stolen the anvil and other implements for tapa-making, his wife made some skirts and coarse red malos for him, but they were poorly made. He and his wife were young, handsome, with perfect physique, but they were favorite chiefly children, unaccustomed to such work. They were undergoing a bitter experience in order to appreciate the blessings they were to receive in the future. They lived in poverty, but knew of the blessings to come. Thus it was that the ancestors of chiefs and commoners knew what it was to be without. His tapa-beating anvil was called *"puka helelei"* or "hole through which things fell out." The owners of the stolen anvil accused him, and feeling ashamed he and his campanion went away in secret and lived close to the boundary of Kula and Makawao.

Kiha-a-Pi'i-lani was befriended by a woman of the place, named La'ie, and they were made welcome by her. There they lived. Many people came there to play games and to go swimming in a pool, Waimalino. Kula and a part of Makawao were waterless lands, and so this pool became a place where all enjoyed themselves and danced hulas. Although La'ie extended her hospitality to Kiha-a-Pi'i-lani, he kept his identity a secret, lest he be killed. Kiha-a-Pi'i-lani slept so much in the house that his hosts began to complain, and his wife told him about it.

There was a famine in Kula and Makawao, and the people subsisted on *laulele, pualele, popolo,* and other weeds. One night Kiha-a-Pi'i-lani went to clear a patch of ferns to plant sweet potatoes, and on that same night he made a large one that would naturally require the labor of eighty men to clear. When morning

* *Ke Au 'Oko'a,* Dec. 1, 1870.

came, the huge patch was noticed, an immense one indeed. The people said skeptically of this great undertaking, "Where will he find enough sweet-potato slips to cover the patch?" Next day Kiha-a-Pi'i-lani went to Hamakuapoko and Hali'imaile to ask for potato slips. The natives gave him whole patches of them wherever he went. "Take a big load of the slips and the potatoes too if you want them" [they said]. He went to clean a number of morning-glory vines and returned. The owners who gave him the contents of their patches had gone home. He pulled up the vines and whatever potatoes adhered to them, and allowed them to wilt in the sun. After they had wilted he laid out the morning-glory vines to bind them, laid the sweet-potato vines on them, and tied them. He went on doing this until he had enough loads for ten men to carry. Then he made a carrier ('awe'awe) of morning-glory vines, placed the bundles of slips in it, and lifted it with great strength onto his back. The sunshine beat down on his back, the 'uki'ukiu breeze blew in front of him, the 'Ulalena rain added its share, and intense heat reflected from the 'ulei vines.

One old man remarked to another, "There must be a chief near by for this is the first time that a rainbow is spread before the trees." As they were speaking a man came from below with a huge load on his back, and they called to him to come into the house. He shifted his load, saw the old men, Kau-lani and his companion, let down his burden, and entered. Each of them gave him a bundle of popolo greens and sweet potato which he ate until he was satisfied. They asked, "Where are you going?" He answered, "I am returning to the boundary of Kula and Makawao." "Are you a native of the place?" they inquired. "Yes," he replied. They said, "There is not a native from Kula to Hamakua with whom we are not acquainted. You are a stranger." "Yes, I am a stranger." They said, "The god has revealed your identity. You are a chief, Kiha-a-Pi'i-lani." He answered, "I am he. Conceal your knowledge of me and tell no one." They said, "The secrets of the god we cannot tell to others, because you have been mistreated. The man that can help you lives below Hamakuapoko, at Pa'ia. His name is 'A-puni." When they had finished talking, Kiha-a-Pi'i-lani returned to his dwelling place with his huge bundle of sweet-potato slips. One bundle of slips was sufficient to cover every mound of the whole field. No sooner were they planted than a shower fell, and the chief who made efforts at farming was pleased.

His effort was vain when he was refused help by 'A-puni. 'A-puni directed him to Kukui-ho'oleilei in Papa'a'ea who in turn directed him to Ka-luko in the upland of Ke'anae. He was again directed to Lanahu in Wakiu, and he was directed by Weua-Lanahu to go down to Kawaipapa to consult Ka-hu'akole at Waipuna'alae. Kiha-a-Pi'i-lani became a ward of Ka-hu'akole, a person of prominence. It was said that he was an able person in directing the affairs of the land, and [it was] believed that Kiha-a-Pi'i-lani would be avenged on his brother, Lono-a-Pi'i-lani. He [Kiha] did not succeed in his plot, but he was very clever in seeking a way. He dwelt at Kawaipapa, at a place called Kinahole. His wife's name was Kumaka, and she was his companion in his trials and tribulations, even in those that might mean death. He made a sister of his wife. Hana was a fertile land where taro, sweet potatoes, bananas, sugar cane, and wild fruits grew in abundance, and there was always much food to be had. Kawaipapa was rich in fish from the ponds and from the sea.

Hana had a chief to govern it, Ho'olae-makua. It belonged to the ruling chiefs from ancient days, and the ruler was a descendant of the chiefs of Hana. He belonged to a family that was noted for strong people, and Ho'olae-makua was numbered among them. He was small in size, but his hands had a very strong grip. Ka-hu'akole felt that if Ho'olae-makua sided with Kiha-a-Pi'i-lani then war could be fought against Lono-a-Pi'ilani to take the kingdom from him. Ka'uiki was the strongest fortress there was. Ho'olae had a daughter, Kolea-moku, and Ka-hu'akole believed that when she became Kiha-a-Pi'i-lani's wife, her father would aid him. Kiha-a-Pi'i-lani had a perfect physique and was good-looking from head to feet, without mark or blemish. Because he lived in comfort and ate properly, his body filled out. His constant bathing in the sea reddened his cheeks to the color of a cooked crab, and [made] his eyes as bright as those of a *moho'ea* bird. The surf on which Ho'olae's daughter surfed was called Ke-anini. It was inside of the bay of Kapueokahi, a surf that broke easily. Ho'olae's daughter was accustomed to surf-riding. Kiha-a-Pi'i-lani was used to surfing at Waikiki, and he often boasted of those with a long sweep, the surf of Ka-lehua-wehe and the surf of Mai-hiwa.

Two to four days Kiha-a-Pi'i-lani and Kolea-moku spent in surf-riding. Noticing his handsome appearance, Kolea-moku made love to him. The girl was determined to have him for a husband, but her father was set against it because she was betrothed to the ruling chief, Lono-a-Pi'i-lani. The flowers wilted in the sunlight when she saw this other man [her desire for her betrothed died away]. As they made love to each other, she asked, "Whose son are you? Where is your homeland?" He answered, "My father is Ka-hu'a-kole. Kawaipapa in Waipuna'a'ala [another name for Waipuna'alae?] is our native land, and our home is there."

For several days after that he did not go surfing. After waiting two days, Ho'olae's daughter wondered where the lover she thought so much of had gone. She remembered some houses that were once pointed out to her, and so she went by way of the upland of Waika-'ahiki to Waikaloa and on to Kawaipapa, accompanied by some women. Upon arriving on the lowland of Kawaipapa, they came to Kiha-a-Pi'i-lani's house where they were happily greeted. She was eager to be married to him. They were married, and Kolea-moku became the wife of Kiha-a-Pi'i-lani. When the news of the marriage of Kolea-moku to the son of Ka-hu'a-moku* reached Ho'olae-makua he was filled with anger. He said to himself, "I have placed a tabu on you, my daughter, which should be freed by my lord, Lono-a-Pi'i-lani. After that you could seek a husband according to your own desire. You can no longer regard me as your father, for I have sworn that you are no child of mine."

Kiha-a-Pi'i-lani and Kolea-moku had become man and wife, and before long she became pregnant. The child was born a boy and was named Ka-uhi-o-ka-lani. He became the ancestor of some chiefs and some commoners. He was carefully nurtured, and when he was able to walk it was seen that he was a very handsome boy. Kiha-a-Pi'i-lani asked his wife, "Were you a favorite of your father?" She answered, "I was a favorite daughter to both my parents and I was made much of. All of their precious possessions were mine. The fatted dogs, the tamed pigs were mine, but my parents placed a tabu on my person and not until Lono-a-Pi'i-lani, the ruler, freed it could I take a husband." Kiha-a-Pi'i-lani said, "Your parents' anger has ceased, for we have borne a child. Take our child with you and perhaps, when they see him, there will be a yearning as there was for you when they were raising you." Kolea-moku replied, "A parent's love for his child is endless." He said, "If you are a favorite child, ask your parents for some farm lands for us. If your father should offer you all of Hana, do not accept. These are the lands for us: Honoma'ele, Ka'eleku, Kawaipapa, and the two Wananalua." Kolea-moku heard her husband's request, made the child ready, and went to the parents' residence accompanied by their personal servants. When the parents saw their daughter and grandson they greeted them with the deepest affection and much rejoicing. Dogs that bit people, dogs that were fattened, and domesticated hogs were prepared for a feast to express happiness and love.

After the feast, Ho'olae-makua asked, "After living in the house of a commoner, what quest brought you here?" She answered, "My husband sent me to ask you to give us some farm lands." Ho'olae said, "Here is

*Same person as Ka-hu'a-kole (above). Ka-hu'a-kole is Son-of-a-ruling-chief; Ka-hu'a-moku is Poverty-stricken-chief.

the district of Hana, extending from Pu'ualu'u to 'Ula'ino. You two may have it." The daughter replied, "Let us have only a small portion, and you keep the rest." "Which lands would you have?" he questioned. "The lands my husband told me to ask for are Honoma'ele, Ka'eleku, Kawaipapa, the two Wananalua and Koali." When Ho'olae-makua heard his daughter's words he bowed his head in silence. Then raising it, he said, "Your husband is no commoner. He is a chief, Kiha-a-Pi'i-lani. Your child is a chief. I shall not take Kiha's part. I shall remain loyal to his older brother till these bones perish. Your husband does not want farm lands for the two of you, but is seeking means to rebel against the kingdom. The lands of Honoma'ele and Ka'eleku supply the *ohi'a* wood and *ie'ie* vines of Kealakona to build ladders to the fortress. Kawaipapa supplies the stones of Kanawao that are used in battle, and then the fortress will be well supplied. The Wananalua lands hold the Kau'iki fortress and the places below it. Koali is the fortress of Kue. I shall not take your husband's side." When Kolea-moku heard her father's words she tried all the harder to help her husband and to get her father to have compassion on him. He refused utterly and said that he would lend him assistance only when he was willing to abide under Lono-a-Pi'i-lani's rule. Ho'olae-makua took his grandson to rear.

When Kiha-a-Pi'i-lani heard his wife's report and saw that his identity had been discovered, he became very angry with his father-in-law. His anger was so great that he bided the day of vengeance when he would destroy his enemies and take the whole of Maui. He could not have what he wanted, nor were his enemies destroyed, and so he decided to go to Hawaii, to consult his brother-in-law, 'Umi-a-Liloa. 'Umi-a-Liloa had married his sister Pi'i-kea-a-Pi'i-lani. Kumaka was a chiefess of Hana and Kipahulu. When the canoe was ready, Kiha-a-Pi'i-lani, his wife Kumaka, and the canoe paddlers set sail for Hawaii and landed at Kohala. From Kohala they sailed to Maka'eo in Kailua, and when evening fell Kiha ordered the canoemen and the chiefess Kumaka to remain where they were. He said, "Stay here and if some-one should come for you, then you'll know that I am alive. But if no one comes, then trouble has befallen me. Put the ocean's space be-tween us, for yonder lies Maui, and you may go home." Kiha-a-Pi'i-lani went up to see his sister Pi'i-kea. Night had fallen, and the can-dles in the chief's house and the many houses of the chiefesses were lighted. According to the number of chiefly wives 'Umi-a-Liloa had, so was the number of their houses. Pi'i-kea and Kapu-kini had the largest houses, and they were near the enclosure of 'Umi's house.*

On the way up Kiha-a-Pi'i-lani met a man at Kamakahonu coming

* *Ke Au 'Oko'a*, Dec. 8, 1870.

home from the chief's residence and asked him about the rows of lights. The man guessed that he was from the back country or perhaps a stranger and pointed out first the home of one chiefess and then the home of another. When Kiha knew which one was Pi'i-kea's, he went on and entered. "Where is the chiefess?" he asked. "Who are you?" inquired her bodyguards. "A stranger from Maui," he replied. "Then you must be the brother of the chiefess. We heard of one that has been abused." "Yes, I am he." As soon as Pi'i-kea heard this, she wailed aloud mentioning their parents and her grief over Lono-a-Pi'i-lani's misdeeds. 'Umi-a-Liloa heard her cry and the mentioning of her parents, and guessed that she was wailing over none other than Kiha-a-Pi'i-lani, for those in Hawaii had heard of his being ill-treated by Lono-a-Pi'i-lani.

'Umi-a-Liloa gave orders at once to cook some food for the guest and to make haste. He inquired for those who had come with him, and Kumaka and the men who paddled them to Hawaii were sent for. Kumaka was brought to her sister-in-law, Pi'i-kea, who greeted her with great affection. After a joyful feast with the beloved chiefly guests, 'Umi-a-Liloa asked Kiha-a-Pi'i-lani, "What great purpose brought you to Hawaii?" He answered, "I have but one purpose in coming, to seek vengeance against my brother. Perhaps you have heard how he cruelly treated me and mocked me, and I barely escaped with my life. Our father, Pi'i-lani, commanded that we share the kingdom of Maui, but my brother took it all for himself. He sought to kill me, and so I determined to come to you two in Hawaii to help me avenge myself on my brother. What do you say?" Pi'i-kea said, "The kingdom shall be yours for our brother has wronged you. Our father had commanded that you two share the kingdom, and if one was wrong, the other would rule. It is very clear that our brother is wrong, so the kingdom is yours." 'Umi-a-Liloa asked, "What do you think, Kiha? If you wish, you may remain here in Hawaii with us." Kiha-a-Pi'i-lani replied, "That is not my wish for then I will not be avenged on those who treated me with cruelty." 'Umi-a-Liloa answered, "It is well. This shall be a year of preparation. Canoes shall be made until there are great numbers of them, then next year we shall go to make war against Maui."

Lono-a-Pi'i-lani heard that Kiha-a-Pi'i-lani was on Hawaii, and that war canoes were being built there in great numbers. The *kauila* wood of Napu'u and Kahuku, the *o'a* and *koai'e* were being made into clubs to be used against Maui. When the news of impending war reached him and his warrior chiefs, they trembled with fear.

A whole year of the making of canoes and war implements went by, and all of the warriors were well supplied. There was no war prior to that time to compare with this one, in which there were so many canoes. The first ones reached Hana, Maui while the last ones were still on Hawaii.

When the fleet of canoes arrived at Hana, Ho'olae-makua was at the fortress on Ka'uiki hill, building a tower and ladders to reach the top. The men urged him to let them stop working, for the war parties from Hawaii were drawing near. Ho'olae answered, "Continue fastening down the beams and put on the thatch of the tower." "This is no time for thatching when battle is near. The last canoes are still on Hawaii, the very first ones [have reached] Kaihalulu and are coming toward Ka-pueokahi" [they said]. "Keep fastening the beams" [he repeated].

Ho'olae was a strong man, and when those of Hawaii fought against him he proved to be a greater warrior than they. [Some of] the Hawaii canoes hardly reached the spring of Punahoa when Ho'olae killed the men [who manned them]. The canoes were forced to land at Waika-'ahiki, and Ho'olae fought them until they were compelled to flee. Some of the canoes landed below Kihahale at Ka-hu'a-kole's place. The men walked above there to battle with Ho'olae-makua. They met him on the sands of Waikoloa, in front of Kawaipapa where they fought with slings. Stones were slung at the canoes. Ho'olae kept close to a rock that is now called the Ho'olae Rock. It was so named because he kept close to it in battle and was victorious over the warriors of Hawaii. The canoes fled to the open sea, and because of the darkness of the night, they lay stretched out from Olau to Kaia'akauli.

The next morning the Hawaii war canoes pressed shoreward from Nalualele to Kaihalulu to Lehua'ula. Ho'olae-makua fought with those who slung the solid 'ala' stones of Kawaipapa, the skilled throwers of smooth pebbles of Waika-'ahiki, the expert stone-tossers of Waikiu and Honokalani, and the quick stone-slinging lads of Ka'eleku. These men used their skill with stones, and the Hawaii warriors were sent helter-skelter. Some of the canoes were broken and some were seized by Ho'olae-makua.

When 'Umi-a-Liloa arrived with the later company he heard how his canoemen were unable to go ashore and how they were held at bay by the mighty Maui warrior, Ho'olae-makua. He asked Kiha-a-Pi'i-lani, "Is there no other way of getting the war canoes ashore? We can fight them better on shore, for our present position is an unstable one." Kiha-a-Pi'i-lani answered, "There is a small harbor at Ko'olau called Wailua-iki, and if all the canoes cannot land there, there is another landing at Wailua-nui." The blocked canoes turned about and sailed for Wailua-iki at Ko'olau.

When the canoes reached Wailua-iki, they were dismantled and set upright, and in that way the innumerable war canoes from Hawaii could be beached. After all the canoes were beached the men began to go overland to the site of battle. Upon reaching 'Ula'ino, the fighting commenced at Makaolehua, and in 'Akiala at La'ahana, at Kawaikau, at Nenewepue, at Kameha'ikana's *kukui* tree, and all the way along to Honokalani and Wakiu, into the pandanus grove of Kahalaoweke, down to Pihehe, to the flats of Kalani and the spring of Punahoa. When the battle was fought with that brave warrior of the fortress on Ka'uiki hill, the small, strong-handed fellow proved his fearlessness. He drove into his foes with no thought of fear and scattered them at Kalaniawawa. The little man gave blow for blow and won the battle. Up the ladder he went into the fortress above, where none could reach him.

Next morning there was another attack, but no victory was gained. A night attack was made without success. One reason for the failure in the night attack was the cunning of Ho'olae-makua who set up a large wooden image called Ka-wala-ki'i. Every night it was brought out, dressed in war apparel with a wooden club in front of it, and set up at the top of the ladder just below the tower. This image helped the warriors in the fortress to feel at ease and to enjoy their sleep. They believed in spending the night in sleep and the day in hard fighting. Hawaii's warriors kept trying, and every night they mistook the image for a watchman and kept their distance. Early each morning the image was carried inside. Sometimes Pi'i-mai-wa'a wondered where the large man was who was seen on guard every night, but did not come out to fight in the daytime. He guessed that there was a deception.

One night the Hawaii warriors sought a way of ascending, for it was only at night that they could draw near the fortress. It was impossible to come near the hill by day, for then the expert sling-shooters [who] did not miss a blade of grass or a hair, sent the stones flying as fast as lightning. That was why the Hawaii warriors lurked in ambush and sought means of getting at their enemies at night. Pi'i-mai-wa'a gathered his weapons together one night and went up to the bottom of the ladder and up to where the wooden image stood. Pi'i-mai-wa'a twirled his war club and struck the image on the left; twirled it again and struck it on the right. He sent a spear directly toward it, and it moved not at all, but kept standing in one place. Pi'i-mai-wa'a smote with his club, called Ka-hu'e-lepo, and the two wooden objects [image and club] made a thudding sound. He said to himself, "The fortress shall be destroyed." Pi'i-mai-wa'a sent word for all of the warriors of Hawaii to assemble and to divide into two groups, one to tie rope ladders to the tower, and the other to destroy those in the fortress. In a short time the tower was reduced to nothing, but Ho'olae-makua and the warriors with him escaped. The rest were routed and leaped into the sea. His daughter and her child were saved by the command of Kiha-a-Pi'ilani. Because it was dark some people escaped, while others of their company were being destroyed.

Next day there was a search among the dead, but Ho'olae-makua was not found. Kiha-a-Pi'i-lani denied that he was dead. Kiha-a-Pi'i-lani commanded Pi'i-mai-wa'a that if Ho'olae-makua should be killed [he was] to bring his strong hands. Then Pi'i-mai-wa'a would be made chief of the fortress of Ka'uiki and the district of Hana. Pi'i-mai-wa'a sought Ho'olae above Paiolopawa, back of Kealakona, up at Hina'i, Kea'a, and 'Opiko'ula. Hands were brought back, but Kiha-a-Pi'i-lani declared that those were not the hands of Ho'olae-makua. Ho'olae-makua was found directly back of Nahiku at a place called Kapipiwai. He was killed in spite of the valor he displayed in the battle he fought. His hands were brought, and Kiha-a-Pi'i-lani and Ka-hu'a-kole confirmed that Ho'olae-makua was dead. [At first] Ka-hu'a-kole denied that he was dead. 'Umi-a-Liloa claimed that no great warrior had ever been able to escape from Pi'i-mai-wa'a. Ho'olae-makua was killed because Kiha-a-Pi'i-lani bore a grudge against him, his father-in-law, for not helping on his side. He felt no affection for him, though they were related through a common relative [Kiha-a-Pi'i-lani's son]. (Revengeful indeed was the haughty Oahuan!)

When the ruler, Lono-a-Pi'i-lani, heard that 'Umi-a-Liloa, Kiha-a-Pi'i-lani, the chiefs, warriors, and the fleet of war canoes from Hawaii were on their way, that the fortress of Ka'uiki was taken, and Ho'olae-makua was killed up at Kapipiwai, he was filled with dread and fear of death. Lono was afraid that he would be tortured like Ho'olae-makua, his great war leader. If Ho'olae who committed less was tortured by Kiha-a-Pi'i-lani, how much more would he be who had committed more! Lono-a-Pi'i-lani trembled with fear of death, and died. The war party had not reached Wailuku when Kiha-a-Pi'i-lani heard of Lono's death, and so he hastened to Wailuku. When Kiha-a-Pi'i-lani and 'Umi-a-Liloa arrived in a war canoe, Lono's corpse was gone. Kiha-a-Pi'i-lani sought the corpse to mutilate it, but it was not found. A prophet on Kauai was sent for to tell on which land it was buried. The prophet said that it was in Wailuku in a land called Pa'uniu. It was taken away again to be hidden, and so the bones of Lono-a-Pi'i-lani vanished completely. The men of Hawaii hunted, searched, delved, and sought, digging about in the lands of Wailuku and Pa'uniu, but the bones were not found.

After this cruelty Kiha-a-Pi'i-lani sought to commit was ended, he divided the lands of his kingdom. 'Umi-a-Liloa left 'Ai-hako'ko', one of his sons by Pi'i-kea, to remain with Kiha-a-Pi'i-lani. After the lands were apportioned and chiefs set over each district, land section, and *ahupua'a,* and all was at peace, 'Umi-a-Liloa returned home.

When 'Umi-a-Liloa became old, the people of Hawaii built a stone tomb for him, to hold his corpse. He commanded his sons, daughters, chiefs, and commoners all over Hawaii to hew long, four-sided stone slabs, an *anana* [about six feet] and an *iwilei* [about three feet] in length, and half of an *iwilei* in width. The stone used was the close-grained *'ala'.* These slabs were placed in the cave of 'Umi-a-Liloa at Keopu in Kailua. Because of this burdensome task imposed from Hawaii, Kiha-a-Pi'ilani killed 'Ai-hako'ko''s personal attendant in the sea. That was why 'Ai-hako'ko' lamented grievously at sea. He landed at Kapa'ahi in Kama'ole, Kula, and that place was given the name of Ka-lua-o-Ai-hako'ko' (Ai-hako'ko''s pit). The stone tomb of 'Umi-a-Liloa was not completed when he died on Hawaii.

When 'Umi-a-Liloa died, one of his adopted sons, Ko'i, heard of it and asked that he be allowed to conceal his bones completely. After the kingdom was at peace under 'Umi-a-Liloa, the land had been apportioned, and Ko'i was given the lands from Waimanu and Pololu'. He left them to his sisters and members of his household, and traveled about from Hawaii to Kauai. He returned from Kauai and dwelt in Keone'o'io in Honua'ula where he took a wife, had some children, and lived until he was well acquainted with the place.

When news of the death of 'Umi-a-Liloa reached him, he asked for his wife's brothers to accompany him to Hawaii. His wife said, "You shall not take my brothers lest they be put to death by you." He answered, "No." They sailed from Kipahulu and landed at Kohala, and there he heard more of 'Umi-a-Liloa's death. From there they continued to Kekaha, and there darkness fell. There was a man there who strongly resembled 'Umi-a-Liloa, and Ko'i went to kill him and laid him in the canoe. Ko'i and his companions set sail from Kekaha and beached their canoe at the lava bed below Maka'eo. It was then late at night. He went up and found the guards of the cave asleep except Pi'i-mai-wa'a who guarded the inside. Ko'i entered with the substitute. Pi'i-mai-wa'a knew that the body had long been promised to Ko'i. Ko'i laid the man down and took 'Umi-a-Liloa's body by way of the lava bed to the sea of Maka'eo and boarded the canoe.

The following night he reached the cliff-enclosed valley of Waimanu and entered his sister's house. When she saw him, she leaped upon him with a wail [of welcome].* As his sister leaped forward, he closed her mouth [put his hand over her mouth] and said, "Hush, do not cry. Where is your husband?" "He is in the men's house," [she replied]. "Let me go for him," and Ko'i went in search of him. When he awoke and saw his brother-in-law whom he had not seen for a long time, he leaped up to cry. His mouth was held with the warning that the children might awaken. The two men came out and met with Ko'i's sister. Ko'i said, "Hearken, you two, I came to see you before taking our lord to conceal him. With the two of you along with me our lord's bones will be out of sight. The secret is here [with the brother-in-law], and there shall he be hidden." Ko'i took his brother-in-law to his own secret cave, for he was a native son of those sheer precipices, and they took with them a rope, fire-making sticks, and kindling. When all was in readiness, they carried 'Umi-a-Liloa's corpse till they reached the sheer cliff ascended only by the tropic birds. Much has been said about this, but the accounts are not clear. It was said that the brother-in-law of Ko'i died, that he perished after being pushed off the cliff lest he reveal the secret. When Ko'i returned alone, his sister said, "Have you done away with the father of our children?" "It is our duty to conceal the bones of our lord, and to live on the product of the land" [Ko'i answered].

It is also said that Ko'i took the bones of 'Umi-a-Liloa to Maui. It is said that his bones were sought for, but could not be found. Ko'i took all the [chief's] possessions to the sheer cliff that same night and, without the knowledge of those of his household, he departed for Maui.†

* *Ke Au 'Oko'a*, Dec. 15, 1870.
† *Ke Au 'Oko'a*, Dec. 22, 1870.

CHAPTER III

The Story of Keawe-nui-a-ʻUmi

At the time of ʻUmi-a-Liloa's death the kingdom of Hawaii was at peace. He had commanded that the kingdom be divided among his two sons and Kapu-kini, the daughter of Liloa, ruling chief of Hawaii. The two sons [were] Ke-liʻi-o-kaloa-a-ʻUmi and his younger brother Keawe-nui-a-ʻUmi; they were the two heirs of the kingdom of Hawaii. At [the beginning of] their reign, the island of Hawaii was divided into two kingdoms. Ke-liʻi-o-kaloa, one of the heirs, ruled in Kona; and Keawe-nui, the other, in Hilo. The rest of the sons and daughters of ʻUmi-a-Liloa were requested to dwell as chiefs under the heirs of the kingdom.

Keawe-nui had the second kingdom with Hilo for his chiefly residence. He was a kind ruler who looked after the welfare of chiefs and commoners, and increased the number of chiefly children. He sought out all the experts of the land, the *kuhikuhi puʻuone*, the readers of earthly omens and of heavenly omens, the skilled leaders of the kingdom, strong canoemen, navigators, canoe builders, those who could right upset canoes, expert war leaders, and all other skilled workers that were able to help in the affairs of the country. He was foremost in running the affairs of the government.

Here is another thing: he sought stewards who were experts in preparing food and drink, in caring for the chief's wearing apparel, and women who were experts in tapa making, printing, dipping in perfume, and in making the chief's wearing apparel dipped in various perfumes. It was these perfumes that made the garments of the chiefs fragrant. He took many women for wives from among the daughters of ʻUmi-a-Liloa and the descendants of other chiefs. Many sons and daughters were born to him, and these became the ancestors of chiefs and commoners.

Concerning Ke-liʻi-o-kaloa: Ke-liʻi-o-kaloa was ʻUmi-a-Liloa's eldest son by Kapu-kini. He was the heir of Kona, and Kailua became his residence. He married Makuwahine-a-Palaka, the daughter of Palaka-a-Ka-ʻahu-koheo. Her mother was Ka-heana-liʻi-a-ʻEpa. To them was born Ku-kaʻi-lani. Ke-liʻi-o-kaloa had many sons and daughters, and they were the ancestors of chiefs and commoners. While he reigned, he took good care of his kingdom, his god, the priests and prophets of the god, and the common people. He lived a righteous life and heeded the teachings of the priests and prophets, but did not mind his father's advice to take care of the chiefs, the old men and old women, the orphans and the poor. When he deserted the advice of the wise, he paid attention to that of fools, thus forsaking the teachings of his father and the learned men of his kingdom. He deserted the god and oppressed the people.

These were his oppressive deeds: He seized the property of the chiefs and that of the *konohiki* of the chiefs, the food of the commoners, their pigs, dogs, chickens, and other property. The coconut trees that were planted were hewn down, so were the people's *kou* trees. Their canoes and fish were seized; and people were compelled to do burdensome tasks such as diving for *'ina* sea urchins, *wana* sea urchins, and sea weeds at night. Many were the oppressive deeds committed by this chief Ke-li'i-o-kaloa. Therefore some of the chiefs and commoners went to Hilo, to Keawe-nui-a-'Umi, and offered him the kingdom of Kona. Keawe-nui-a-'Umi and the chiefs of Hilo heard of Ke-li'i-o-kaloa's evil deeds and his disregard of the instructions of their father, 'Umi-a-Liloa.

When Keawe-nui-a-'Umi learned of the unjust rule of Ke-li'i-o-kaloa and the burdening of the common people, he was filled with compassion for the chiefs and commoners of Kona. Therefore he made himself ready with his chiefs, war lords, war leaders, and warriors from Hilo, Puna, and Ka-'u to make war on Kona. The war parties [met?] at the volcano (pit of Pele) before going on to battle along the southern side of Mauna Kea and the northern side of Mauna Loa. The mountain road lay stretched on the level. At the north flank of Hualalai, before the highway, was a very wide, rough bed of lava—barren, waterless, and a desert of rocks. It was a mountain place familiar to 'Umi-a-Liloa when he battled against the chiefs of Hilo, Ka-'u, and Kona. There on that extensive stretch of lava stood the mound (*ahu*), the road, the house, and heiau of 'Umi.* It was through there that Keawe-nui-a-'Umi's army went to do battle against his older brother, Ke-li'i-o-kaloa.

When the chiefs of Kona heard that those of Hilo were coming by way of the mountain to do battle, Ke-li'i-o-kaloa sent his armies, but they

* See 4 for an excellent account of this site. It is reached "by a fourteen mile journey from Holualoa up the old Judd trail, or by an eighteen or twenty mile trip from Kealakekua, via Pu'ulehua and Kanahaha . . . It is on the slope of Hualalai, at between 4,500 and 5000 feet elevation, with Mauna Kea and Mauna Loa towering snow-clad, much farther away." 4, vol. 17, pp. 62-70.

were defeated by the armies from Hilo. The armies of Kona were put to flight. When the armies of Hilo reached the shore of Kona the war canoes arrived from Ka-'u and from Hilo. The battle was [both] from the upland and from the sea. Ke-li'i-o-kaloa fled and was killed on a lava bed. The spot where he was killed was called Pu'u-o-Kaloa (Kaloa's hill), situated between Kailua and Honokohau.

After the death of Ke-li'i-o-kaloa, his children did not inherit the land, for the kingdom was taken by Keawe-nui-a-'Umi. The kingdom passed on to his children and grandchildren. Keawe-nui-a-'Umi became ruler of the whole of Hawaii after the death of Ke-li'i-o-kaloa. All of the children of 'Umi and their cousins served him.

Keawe-nui-a-'Umi was a famous ruler, and he governed and cared for the chiefs and commoners. He had many sons and daughters because he had many wives. These were some of his sons and daughters: Kanaloa-kua'ana, 'Ili-'iliki-kuahine, 'Umi-o-ka-lani, Lono-i-ka-makahiki, Ka-po-hele-mai, Puapua-kea, and others. They became ancestors of chiefs and ancestors of commoners. He was noted in the legend which told of his search for his favorite servant Paka'a. Paka'a was his personal attendant, an attendant from a chiefly family, one closely related, having the right to cross behind the chief and to hold his feathered staff. He was a flesh and blood (literally—bone and blood) relative, and that was how Paka'a became Keawe-nui-a-'Umi's personal attendant (*kahu*).

Paka'a was a learned man who was trained in several arts until he became an expert in them.* These were the arts in which he was trained:

1. The natural history of the land (*papa huli honua 'aina*). In this way [he] learned all about the lands from Hawaii to Kauai. He knew all there was before and behind the land everywhere. He was familiar with all the winds from Hawaii to Kauai, the direction they blew, and the way they affected the ocean. He knew each *ahupua'a* and things pertaining to land.

2. Paka'a was trained to read signs (*kilokilo*), and knew how to manage a canoe in the ocean, out of sight of land. He knew how to tell when the sea would be calm, when there would be a tempest in the ocean, and when there would be great billows. He observed the stars, the rainbow colors at the edges of the stars, the way they twinkled, their red glowing, the dimming of the stars in a storm, the reddish rim on the clouds, the way in which they move, the lowering of the sky, the heavy cloudiness, the gales, the blowing of the *ho'olua* wind, the *a'e* wind from below, the whirlwind, and the towering billows of the ocean.

* For Paka'a and Kuapaka'a see 13 2, p. 112; 14, vol. 5, pp. 72-135; 30, pp. 69-89; 38, pp. 53-67.

3. Paka'a was taught how to right a canoe upset at sea, a canoe that had turned bottom up. He was taught to read signs, to observe the clouds, to navigate over the ocean, to right upset canoes, and to know exactly how to do it, whether with the aid of a canoe roller, or [by tying a rope] where the outrigger was attached to the canoe, at the middle or at the edge of the canoe opening, the ropes to cross and run to the ends, then out to the sticks bound fast to the longitudinal sticks in front and behind. The hand held the ropes that went about the two ends, turned the keel of the canoe where the billows rose high, and forced the outrigger downward, at the same time pulling the rope taut. With one lift of the billow the water was discharged. Paka'a learned many things about righting canoes until he became an expert in all these matters while travelling on the ocean.

4. Paka'a also learned to paddle canoes. He was a strong paddler. Because of his skill in navigation he became director of Keawe-nui-a-'Umi's sea travels. He was the captain who was in charge of his voyages, having charge of the canoes that went out to the ocean and other canoes of the chief.

Paka'a was a great favorite with Keawe-nui-a-'Umi and took care of all the property in his chiefly residence. He was capable of serving his lord in any capacity: to take charge of his possessions, to oversee the preparation of his food, and to care for his clothing and ornaments. Keawe-nui-a-'Umi did not rely on others as much as he did on Paka'a.

Some time later two skilled navigators were found, and the chief noticed their ability and strength in paddling. He made them his navigators and released his captain, Paka'a. He chose Ho'okele-i-Hilo and Ho'okele-i-Puna to be captains over navigation, but no one else was given the other duties held by Paka'a.

Paka'a was dissatisfied because the duties at sea were assigned to others by Keawe-nui-a-'Umi, so he deserted his lord and secretly stole away to another land. When he ran away, he did not go to Maui or to Lanai, but resided at Kaluako'i on Molokai. Paka'a was a learned counselor and very clever in thinking. He was a deep thinker and did not choose Kaluako'i for a residence without careful calculation as to how he would fulfil his desire to regain his former position, the one that was taken from him. He thought of a way to defeat his enemies. Therefore he dwelt upon a desolate land, a land of famine. The harbor to the land [the passage through the reef] was one that twisted about here and there, called Hikauhi and Kaumanamana. Paka'a chose himself a wife from that place and married her. They had a son who was called Kua-paka'a.

When Keawe-nui-a-'Umi learned that Paka'a had run away, that he
had left him and was gone, he was filled with longing for him. The chief
ordered strong paddlers to go from Hawaii to Kauai to seek him. They
sought him on the leeward and windward sides as far as Niihau, and returned to the presence of the chief to report that Paka'a could not be
found. They had not gone to the remaining island, Ka'ula. "It might be
that a certain man at Kaluako'i, Molokai, was he [they said]. He was
accompanied by a young boy on a canoe. The boy asked us questions, but
the man did not raise his head. We inquired for Paka'a, but the boy replied that no stranger was seen there." They [the chief's paddlers] returned, leaving the two catching *uhu* fish at Kala'au Point.

Keawe-nui-a-'Umi said, "I dreamt that Paka'a's spirit told me that
he is on Ka'ula and will not come back until I, myself, go to fetch him.
He will not return with the messengers of the chief. Great is my longing
for my personal attendant. Let all of Hawaii make double canoes and
large single canoes, and let us go to fetch Paka'a."

Keawe-nui-a-'Umi sent a proclamation to every high chief and every
lesser chief for double canoes, for canoes that were joined together, and
for single canoes, to be used for the purpose of seeking the personal
attendant of the chief, Keawe-nui-a-'Umi. The chiefs were all supplied
with canoes, but there was one thing lacking. There was no double canoe
for the ruling chief. The cause of the delay in the making of that canoe
was two birds. When the tree selected for the chief was about to be
felled, these birds called from the very top of it, "Say, the log is rotten."
After the tree was felled, it was found that the trunk was rotten. The
chief hired many canoe-making experts, but no canoe was finished for
him. The chief hired bird-catchers, those who gummed birds, but none
came near enough. The naughty birds which called about the decayed
log flew away and vanished into the sky. They returned only when a *koa*
tree was about to fall.* The tree fell just after their cry of "The log is
rotten" (*puha ka waha*). The chief was weary of them!

There was a man on Oahu, named Ma'i-lele, who was an expert with
bow and arrow (*akamai i ka pana pua*). Keawe-nui-a-'Umi sent a request to Ka-kuhihewa, ruler of Oahu, to send the noted shooter.† Ka-
kuhihewa consented. When the man arrived in Hawaii he was welcomed
with honors by Keawe-nui-a-'Umi, and he was told that if he destroyed
the birds that caused the logs to decay, the daughter of Keawe-nui-a-
'Umi would be given to him for wife.

There was a certain clever boy from Kauai who was greater than
Ma'i-lele. The Kauai boy had arrived on Hawaii before Ma'i-lele and

* *Ke Au 'Oko'a*, Dec. 22, 1870.
† For the Pikoi incident see 14, vol. 4, pp. 450-463; 40, pp. 157-172.

went into the wilderness of Hawaii from Hamakua to the forest of Hilo. When he arrived at La'a he saw Keawe-nui-a-'Umi's canoe-making site, where the canoe-makers dwelt, but the chiefs had all gone to the shore to await the skillful shooter of arrows. Pikoi-a-ka-'alala', Kauai's noted arrow shooter, was already there. A native had led him to the canoe-making site. He and his companion were laden with bird feathers. When they arrived at the side where the canoes were made, the [canoe-making] experts were still there. The boy from Kauai was well supplied with a bow (kakaka kiko'o) and a bag of arrows ('eke pana pua). He asked where the birds always lighted, and [the spot] was pointed out to him by the natives, up at the very top of the tree. The head had to be bent away back to see them, and the eyes strained because they were so far up. The Kauai boy said to the canoe-making experts, "Those birds will never be hit by the arrow-shooting champion of Oahu. I know him and the way he sends forth his arrow. His arrow will only go as far as that circle of branches and come down again. A ladder will be raised to that spot, and then the ladder will be raised [again] from there up. By that time the birds will be frightened, they'll shy and fly away. They will not be hit. Now the boy from Kauai will be the one to do it." The people stupidly argued with him. Some remembered what he had said, but Pikoi-a-ka-'alala' vanished into the forest.

The Oahu champion arrived at the canoe-making site accompanied by the chief, Keawe-nui-a-'Umi, the lesser chiefs, people, and the wives and daughters of the ruling chief who had heard of his fame and the fame of the birds that caused the canoe logs to decay. Mats were spread about for all to be seated to watch the killing of the birds. When the man shot his arrow it flew as far as the spot indicated by the Kauai boy, and was unable to go any higher, so it fell. Then a ladder was made to reach to the place already mentioned. Ma'i-lele began to shoot a long arrow, which flew to the second spot mentioned and came down. A ladder was raised again until it came close to where the birds perched, but they had flown away. The cutters made much noise as though chopping down a koa tree, but the birds did not return. They were gone.

The experts who had heard the words of the boy from Kauai remembered that all he had told them was true. His words were fulfilled. They came to the presence of Keawe-nui-a-'Umi and said, "We have committed a sin to the heavenly one, to you, O chief. A certain handsome youth came here to the canoe-making site. He carried a bow in his hand and had a bag of arrows. He said, 'Your chief's enemies will not be destroyed, because the arrow will fly only as far as that place and come down again. You will make a ladder and so on. Your chief's enemies will not be destroyed. Only one person can succeed and that is the boy from

Kauai.' The boy was loaded with the feathers of the *'o'o* and the *mamo*, and so was his companion." The chief asked, "Which way did they go to shoot birds?" "No one knows where they went, maybe to the upland of La'a or Mokaulele, or Pana'ewa, or perhaps the upland of Kahupueo."

The chief said at once, "Call the bird catchers, the bird snarers, those who know where the lehua grow best and the haunts of birds, and bring them to my presence. Should my foes be destroyed, my daughter shall be the wife of the one accomplishing it, and I will give him great honors." It did not take long for those who knew the lehua thickets and forests to find the arrow-shooting boy of Kauai. He was brought before Keawe-nui-a-'Umi, ruling chief of Hawaii. The chief said, "Can you succeed in destroying my enemies?" The Kauai boy answered, "It is but a mere game for the children of my homeland." The chief asked, "Where did you come from and what is your homeland?" The boy replied, "My homeland is Kauai. Wai'ale'ale is its mountain and Kahalekuakane the place where birds are caught." "Can you kill my foes?" "They shall die."

The Kauai boy ordered the canoe-making experts to take their adzes in their hands and chop into a large *koa* tree which they thought would make a canoe for the chief. The strokes of the adzes were heard in unison, and the chopping sounded like the crackling of thunder. The birds heard the crackling just as the *koa* tree was about to fall and came to perch on the very top. The Kauai boy sat on an elevated place with a shallow calabash filled with water. The birds were reflected in the water where the Kauai boy watched them closely, watching until the necks crossed one over the other. He kept his eyes down, while men made rude remarks and used insulting gestures. They remarked on his keeping his eyes down instead of gazing upward where the birds were perched and shooting straight at them. "Then shall the birds be hit! Alas for Huahua-nana!" [Alas for the staring fool] declared the chiefs and commoners, among other things they said. Suddenly some exclaimed, "The birds are shot through the necks!" Everyone in the crowd turned to look. The arrow had gone through the neck of one bird into the neck of the bird above it. The forest was filled with the shouting of happy voices. The birds flew up into the sky, but they were followed. These were super-natural birds called Kani-ka-wi' and Kani-ka-wa'.

In the version of some, the birds did not die, for if they had their bodies would have remained in this world as proof, like many other things pertaining to Keawe-nui-a-'Umi that still remain today. Kani-ka-wi' and Kani-ka-wa', the enemies of Keawe-nui-a-'Umi, flew to the sky after they were hit by the arrow belonging to Pikoi-a-ka-'alala'.

He was the son of 'Alala' and his wife Ko'uko'u, natives of Lihu'e, Kauai. Keawe-nui-a-'Umi kept his promise, granted him his daughter, and honored him. All the lands on Hawaii where bows and arrows were used were given to him.

After the enemies of Keawe-nui-a-'Umi had flown away to the sky, a man was found who was an expert in putting on canoe parts and in hollowing the log. His name was Lulana, and he came from Kipahulu, Maui. This man's skill was noticed when he went to the upland and saw two very large trees, one on either side of the trail. These were hollow trees used as dwellings by some of the canoe-makers. When the stranger went to the upland he noticed them and said to Keawe-nui-a-'Umi's canoe-making experts, "These will make good canoes for the chief, as the centers are hollowed already." The chief's men replied, "Who would convert these hollow trees into canoes? They are used as shelters for canoe-makers, bird-catchers, and experts in canoe-making." Lulana said, "These are easy to use, for the opening is already there. They will be fine canoes, and there are no defects. If these were made into canoes for the chief, they would be excellent." The hewing began at the spot pointed out by Lulana, until both fell. The large side branches and tops were cut off, the bark stripped until none remained on the outside, the prow and stern shaped, the sides smoothed off, and the prow and stern polished smooth. The canoe was then turned up, the edges leveled, and as the canoe was already hollow, leaving only the two sides at the opening, the opening was then shaped. The opening was already there, so there was little work needed on it. The work was soon finished, and it was seen that there were no canoes to equal the canoes of Lulana in the days of 'Umi or of the ancient chiefs before him.

Word was carried to Keawe-nui-a-'Umi of the fine canoes made by Lulana, that they were beautiful and free from defects. No canoes as beautiful had ever been seen in olden times. They were twenty *anana* long [20 fathoms] and one *anana* and one *iwilei* [1½ fathoms] in depth. When Keawe-nui-a-'Umi heard of the doings of this expert who was unequalled in his skill, he was filled with happiness and joy. In no time the canoes were finished inside and ready to be hauled to the shore. Keawe-nui-a-'Umi, the chiefs, lesser chiefs, and commoners hauled the canoes to the shore of Hilo. Lulana became a favorite and was made qhief over all canoe experts (*po'e kahuna kala'i*) on Hawaii by Keawe-nui-a-'Umi.

Lulana and all the experts put together the canoes of Keawe-nui. When the pieces (*la'au*) and all the things which belong to a canoe were fitted together, the canoe which was to take the place of the outrigger float (that is, the *'ekea* canoe) was set alongside. Then the booms (*'iako*) of the canoe were put on. When the four large inner booms had been fixed, then were added the two booms for holding together the forward and rear ends of the double-canoe (*na ʻiako elua i na ʻumi o na umiʻi o mua a me hope*). Now the wash strakes (*palepale*) were set over the booms, on the inside and outside. In front were placed the bow pieces (*kua poʻi*). After the clamping down (*uma*) of the rear pieces of the canoe and the fastening with running sennit-cord (*holo ʻaha*), the platform midway between the canoes was lashed on.

Just over the arch of the main booms was set up the house for the chief, so that the chiefs could sleep on the platform. It was lashed securely (*helea*) with sennit just as for the lashing (*luʻukia ana*) of the booms. There at the big boom over the large lugs (*pepeiao*) the sail (*peʻa*) was set up (*kukia*). When the little imperfections of the canoe had been remedied, then all that was left was to sail it on the ocean.*

When Keawe-nui-a-ʻUmi went to search for his servant, Pakaʻa, all those who manned his canoe were chiefs, and all were strong paddlers who were noted for their skill in navigation. The steersmen were Hoʻokele-i-Hilo and Hoʻokele-i-Puna, the men that Pakaʻa so disliked that he ran away and wandered to a place where he would avenge himself, thus troubling his lord.

At the time Keawe-nui-a-ʻUmi sought Pakaʻa, Kiha-a-Piʻi-lani was ruler of Maui and Ka-kuhi-hewa of Oahu. The tale of the making of Keawe-nui-a-ʻUmi's fleet of canoes and his search for his favorite servant, Pakaʻa, was heard abroad.

Pakaʻa heard that he was being sought, so he made great effort to farm, and hired men from Kalaʻe, Kalaupapa, and Keʻanae to catch fish. They fished constantly until the stench of fish arose. Pakaʻa rented two inland patches of sweet potatoes and two sugar-cane fields which lay in a straight line from the upland of Punahou to the summit on the west side of the disk-(*maika*)playing site of Maunaloa. The sweet-potato and sugar-cane patches were about a mile long and about half a mile wide. Pakaʻa did his farming in the winter months when there was an abundance of rain. The plains were made fertile when the rain fell. The soil at the top of Maunaloa was composed of light gravel and ash, and sweet potatoes and sugar cane flourished. His production was great.

Keawe-nui-a-ʻUmi sailed from Hilo to Kapuʻekahi in Hana and from Hana to Kahului of Wailuku. There the chief of Hawaii met Kiha-a-Piʻi-lani, ruler of Maui. Kiha-a-Piʻi-lani was building the walls of the pond of Mauʻoni. A wide expanse of water lay between Kaipuʻula and Kanaha, and the sea swept into Mauʻoni. The two ruling chiefs met and greeted each other with affection.

Keawe-nui-a-ʻUmi left Kiha-a-Piʻi-lani and landed at Kaunakakai on

* The canoe-making passage is translated by Kenneth Emory from terms identified by Mr. Kupihea.

Molokai, with the intention of continuing to Oahu the next day. The single canoes went first, then the double canoes of the district chiefs, and then the canoe of the ruling chief, Keawe-nui-a-'Umi. The last was bedecked with red cording. So were the canoes of high chiefs marked. The bottom of the mast (*kia*) and sail (*pe'a*) and the arched parts of the sail were decorated with red cording. In the olden days the appearance of the canoes of chiefs excited admiration and awe.

The country-born son of Paka'a mistook other [the first] fleets of canoes for that of the chief of Hawaii. Kua-paka'a was often about to speak when restrained by his father's saying, "Those are not the canoes of your lord; those belong to Kulukulu'a', chief of Hilo." And so it went. The boy was wise and was quick in the use of words. He was skilled in navigation and could recite from memory every wind that blew on sea or land. He was skilled in astronomy, knew the clouds and stars; the waters that rose and fell, and those that drew toward land or away from it. He knew when the navigation star rose; when to sail at various times of the night from evening to morning; the months and the stormy days in each one all through the year. The knowledge of the son, Kua-paka'a, equalled that of his father. (How about the knowledge of those who are now considered learned? Are their skills equal to those of Kua-paka'a? And what portion of the government funds of Molokai did Paka'a spend to educate his son?)

In the narratives and calls and chants of the navigators of the chief, Keawe-nui-a-'Umi, some of the winds were not mentioned. Those all around Hawaii were.* The winds of Molokai were known to the chief's navigators, but the son of Paka'a learned all there was to know of the winds from Hawaii to Ka'ula. The boy recited to the chief the source of each wind from Hawaii to Ka'ula, asking the chief, his navigators, and paddlers to go ashore for some food and some fish. There was enough for the chief and all those of his fleet. But the boy's words were not heeded. Though the boy's wisdom was greater, Keawe-nui-a-'Umi chose to heed his skilled navigators rather than a boy.

When they had sailed as far as the point of Kala'au they met with a stormy gale, and the canoes were upset. Most of the canoes were destroyed, food and luggage swept away by the sea, and only the chief's canoe did not overturn. The navigators told Keawe-nui-a-'Umi, "This day the chief's canoes will reach Waikiki. There is no wind at Oahu, and this is but a coastal breeze. It is just some steam from the boy's mouth." The chief answered, "We must not leave the canoes that have overturned, lest it be said that I am a chief who deserts his

* *Ke Au 'Oko'a*, Dec. 29, 1870.

followers." This was a good saying and helped the boy to get his wish to destroy his father's enemies, Ho'okele-i-Hilo and Ho'okele-i-Puna. Because the chief doubted his present navigators he changed his mind about sailing to Oahu. His canoe remained until the overturned canoes were righted. When evening came they were becalmed outside the point of Kala'au. The canoes were righted, and they decided to go back to the harbor from which they last sailed.

Paka'a and his son, Kua-paka'a, were waiting the return of their lord. When he came, he was welcomed and told that the harbor [the passage through the reef] was so narrow that the canoes must enter in single file. They [Paka'a and his son] would go first and show how to avoid dangers, but they were doing this in order to conceal their plot. When Paka'a and his son went ashore, the long sheds, dwelling houses, and sleeping houses were ready for their chief. Water for his bath, fine clothing, and perfumed loin cloths were made ready. These garments were the personal property of the chief [Keawe-nui-a-'Umi] that had been cared for by Paka'a. He did just as he used to do while with the chief. The chief suspected that these were the same things that were in Paka'a's care, but he was puzzled because of the boy, Kua-paka'a. The chief's bed clothing and mats had also been taken and cared for by Paka'a.

The favorite fish of the chief were kept alive in a sea pool and taken when the chief drank his 'awa. The 'awa was kept for years as it did not spoil at all. When the 'awa was prepared in the *kanoa* container, the boy ran to the sea pool with a scoop-net and dipped up some *hinalea, kumu,* and other fish found in the deep sea. These were kept in there to be taken when wanted. That was the way of the ancients, to secure whatever the chiefs expressed a desire for. The deeds of the boy reminded Keawe-nui-a-'Umi of Paka'a because he always obtained the food that the chief was fond of.

That night the chief told the boy of his plan to sail to Oahu. The boy said that it would not do, for it was a month for storms at sea, and they would never reach Ka'ula. When it was clear, then it would do to go to Ka'ula. The chief agreed to do as the boy said.

The chief and those of his fleet remained there until their food supply was gone. Then the chief said to Paka'a's son, "The provisions of the canoes are gone. How can I obtain food to feed this hungry multitude?" The boy answered, "There is a little food, as I said to you before. There are two sweet-potato mounds and two clumps of sugar cane. Let each chief send an overseer to go with me." When the six overseers of the six districts of Hawaii went with him to the patches, they found huge patches of sweet potatoes and sugar cane.

One could run along the fields until his limbs wearied, that was how large each overseer found his patch. They went home rejoicing and told the chief, Keawe-nui-a-'Umi, of the quantity of food and sugar cane. The chief's dwelling place extended from Hikaulei to Haleolono, and there he remained for three months. After that the boy found enough food for a long voyage.

He gained the end he sought, to destroy his father's enemies. They were killed at sea. After the death of the navigators the chiefs returned to Hawaii. Paka'a revealed himself after that time.

Keawe-nui-a-'Umi was noted for the justness of his rule over the kingdom of Hawaii. There was great peace during his reign. He made favorites of his chiefs and made some governors of districts, or large tracts of land ('okana) and of ahupua'a. The common people lived in peace. He liked those who were skilled in every art and those who were strong. He was fond of women. He took his nieces and the daughters of his cousins to be his wives, and from his many wives were born sons and daughters. They became the ancestors of chiefs and commoners.

Upon the death of Keawe-nui-a-'Umi, the kingdom was divided into three parts. Kona and Kohala had two rulers, Kanaloa-kua'ana and 'Umi-o-ka-lani; Ka-'u and Puna were ruled by Lono-i-ka-makahiki; Hilo and Hamakua by Kumalae-nui-a-'Umi and his son, Makua, of Hilo.

Kumalae-nui-a-'Umi was the son of 'Umi-a-Liloa by Pi'i-kea-a-Pi'i-lani. Kumalae mated with Ku-nu'u-nui-pu'awa-lau and to them was born Makua. They were Hilo chiefs. Makua mated with Ka-po-hele-mai, daughter of Keawe-nui-a-'Umi, and to them was born I. Wars were not often mentioned during the days of these Hilo chiefs, but after the days of I came the famous battles spoken of, from the reign of Kua'ana-a-I to that of Ku-'aha'i-a-kua'ana, also in the time of Ka-lani-ku-kaula-a'a-kuahu'ia. It was in the time of Moku when the chiefs of Hilo fought a famous battle against the chiefs of Kona.*

The ruler of Kona was Kanaloa-kua'ana, son of Keawe-nui-a-'Umi. His mother was Ko'i-halawai, daughter of Akahi-'ili-kapu-a-'Umi and Ka-haku-maka-liua, a sacred chief of Kauai. The mother of 'Umi-o-ka-lani, son of Keawe-nui-a-'Umi, was Ho'opili-a-hae, of the chiefly and priestly lineage of Pae. Kanaloa-kua'ana and 'Umi-o-ka-lani were the rulers of Kona and Kohala, but it was said that the kingdom was given by command to 'Umi-o-ka-lani, and gifts were given to him. The lighted torches of other chiefs followed his, and his old

* *Ke Au 'Oko'a*, Jan. 5, 1871.

men drank 'awa constantly. It was understood that theirs was a wealthy lord.

Kanaloa-kua'ana's old priests and aged counselors passed urine like water, a sign of a chief without wealth. Therefore the old men went to urinate in his presence, and Kanaloa-kua'ana noticed how clear it was and asked, "What do you mean by coming to my presence to urinate?" The old men replied, "What was our urine like? What was its appearance, O chief?" The chief said, "I do not know what your urine is like." They answered, "Your priests, counselors, and people have clear urines because they drink copiously of water. That is because you are a poor chief. The urine of the chiefs, priests, and counselors of a wealthy chief is yellow through drinking 'awa and eating rich foods. Their lights never go out at nights." [Their nights are spent in enjoyment.] The chief said, "What must I do?" "Make war on 'Umi-o-ka-lani and take the whole kingdom to yourself." This advice of the old men started a war between Kanaloa-kua'ana and 'Umi-o-ka-lani, the sons of Keawe-nui-a-'Umi. The battle lasted a long time, and Kanaloa-kua'ana won the victory in the big battle at Pu'uwa'awa. Kanaloa-kua'ana had the whole of Kona and Kohala, districts of the island of Hawaii.*

* *Ke Au 'Oko'a*, Jan. 12, 1871.

CHAPTER IV

The Story of Lono-i-ka-makahiki*

Lono-i-ka-makahiki was a son of Keawe-nui-a-'Umi, and was chief of Ka-'u and Puna. He was sole ruler over those two districts on Hawaii. He was married to a chiefess, named Ka-iki-lani-kohe-pani'o, who was descended from Laea-nui-kau-manamana. To them were born sons, Keawe-hanau-i-ka-walu and Ka-'ihi-kapu-mahana. They became ancestors of chiefs and commoners. Lono was a chief who did not heed the advice of his priests and counselors, and so his wisest counselors deserted him and sought a better lord. Thus did Lanahu-'imi-haku and others leave him to seek a lord who listened and heeded advice. They sought another lord and dwelt with Ka-'ihi-kapu-a-Ku'ihewa on Oahu, with the hope that he was a righteous chief who listened to all that the priests and counselors taught him.

While Lono lived with his wife, Ka-iki-lani, he proved to be a bad-tempered chief, who was jealous of his wife because of her beauty, and frequently gave her a beating. They left Ka-'u and lived at Kealakekua, Kona, with other chiefs from Ka-'u. One day Lono was playing checkers (*konane*) on a large flat stone in a big coconut-leaf shed with the chiefs and chiefesses, including Ka-iki-lani. Each tried his skill with pebbles on the board of Pa'oa. There were some people there who wished to tease because they disliked the chiefess and were jealous of the beauty of her face and form. They thought of finding a cause for her to be killed by being beaten. If they should be questioned they were [some distance away] on the cliff of Manuahi. They listened in the wilderness and called out, "O chiefess Ka-iki-lani of Puna, the youth of the dark cliff of Hea sends you his regards." Ka-iki-lani heard them and began to talk loudly, "That goes forward, this flees. The white is removed, the black wins." But the mischief-makers still called loudly, making mention of her lover, in this manner, "O Ka-iki-lani, beautiful chiefess of Puna, your lowly lover Hea-a-ke-koa sends his regards." Lono and the chiefs heard, and so did all the people who were gathered there, inside and outside of the shed. Lono grasped a block of wood and

* For Lono-i-ka-makahiki see 13, 2. pp. 114-127; 14, Col. 4, pp. 256-362; Col. 5, pp. 436-450; 16, pp. 317-333.

cruelly beat his wife, unmercifully smiting her to death. When he saw that she was dead, an unhappy feeling possessed him, and he became crazy with the grief for his wife. He travelled about Hawaii, Maui, Oahu, and finally Kauai.

Upon reaching Kauai, he lost his mind completely and wandered to the wilderness. His own followers, favorites and personal attendants, went after him, but the cold and the rains drove them back. They all deserted him except one man, Kapa-'ihi-a-hilina, who followed him in spite of cold, chill, hunger, poverty, and lack of clothing. Their loin clothes were torn off by the staghorn ferns and shrubbery. They used ti leaves for loin cloths and body coverings. Their food was bananas, the hala fruit blackened and mildewed by the rain, and the wild sugar cane of the mountains. Thus they wandered in the wilderness in poverty and hunger for many months. Lono was crazed with grief for his wife. Kapa-'ihi-a-hilina took good care of him as though he were a personal attendant, one related by blood; but he was a native of Kauai who was entirely unrelated to him. This man cared for him patiently and these were among the things he did: When he cut down a bunch of ripe bananas, he saved the inside of the banana for Lono and ate the skin; the inside of the sugar cane was Lono's, and the outer skin his. Thus they ate of the food they found in the mountains. Any left-overs of the food that Lono ate, were saved by Kapa-'ihi-a-hilina. When sanity returned to Lono, they ceased to wander in the wilderness and returned to the shore.

After Lono returned to Hawaii, he attended to the affairs of his kingdom. He tended it well, and cared for strong paddlers and other men who were skilled in various arts, the soothsayers and warriors. He became a chief who earned the gratitude of his subjects.*

Lono made a favorite of Kapa-'ihi-a-hilina, a person of importance before the chiefs and other members of the court. Kapa-'ihi was made steward over all the property of the chief, but tattlers who were jealous of his being a favorite went to the chief to find fault.

When Kapa-'ihi was no longer a favorite to the chief he reminded him of their life of poverty in the wilderness of Kauai, where they wandered about hungry. Therefore great affection welled up in the chief, and Kapa-'ihi-a-hilina became a greater favorite than he was before. Kapa-'ihi-a-hilina composed a chant of affection for the chief, recounting their wanderings in the wilderness of Kauai, and this is the chant:†

* *Ke Au 'Oko'a*, Jan. 12, 1871.
† The song is translated by Pukui independently of John Wise's version in Fornander.

O Lono-i-ka-makahiki ka pua o Kalani,

Lono-i-ka-makahiki, offspring of a chief,

O Kalani kapu a Keawe i hanau.

A tapu heavenly one born to Keawe.

Hanau Kalani ke'lii ku halau,

The heavenly one was born a chief with great power,

He halau nehe Lono mai Kapa'ahu,

With the tapu of silence from Kapa'ahu,

Ka 'ahu'ula kapu o Ku-malana-hewa,

The tapu feather cape of Ku-malana-hewa.

Ua hewa, ua hewa e—

A fault has been committed—

Ua hewa ia na la he ho'omauhala,

The fault is the bearing of a grudge.

'A'ole 'ano hala i ho'omau ai e Kalani,

It is not a fault to be cherished, O heavenly one!

Ki'i malu a ka pua a kalana,

That you should want to be rid of the offspring of the district,

He kalana ka i ka hele ana,

The district through which we have journeyed,

Hele ana i 'Opikana-nui i 'Opikana-lani,

Journeying to 'Opikana-nui, to 'Opikana-lani,

I kahua a kanu'u i ka papa kalena,

To the broad tableland,

He au ka 'aina,

The foundation land,

Ka 'aina o Wakea i noho ai eo Wakea,

The land of Wakea, where Wakea dwelt,

O Wakea ka lani.

Wakea, the heavenly one.

Ka pua o Keawe i hanau,

The chief begotten of Keawe,

Hanau mamua ka hoa,

The companion was born first

Ukali aku mamuli ka hele,

Who followed him [Lono] in his wanderings,

Oi hele mai ka wa kini,

Who followed him out of days of plenty,

A hune, a mehameha, a kanaka 'ole.

Into poverty, loneliness, desolate places.

Hele ko'olua i ka nahele,

They two wandered in the forest,

I ka la'au koa kumu 'ole o Ka-hihi-kolo.

To the rootless koa tree at Ka-hihi-kolo.

Hilihili aku i ka mola palai pau,

Fern leaves were woven into loin cloths,

Hahaki i ka lauki pe'a ma ke kua,

Ti leaves were broken off and worn on the back,

Ia loa'a ke kepa 'a'ahu o kaua,

Thus were we clothed,

O hele, o hele a—

Wandering, wandering on,

O hele aʻai i ka hua pala a ka hala.

Wandering and living on the ripe fruit of the pandanus.

Hala ia la pololi o kaua e ka hoa e,

Thus passed our days of hunger, O my companion,

Ka ua kaʻeʻe, ua makani,

Through the pouring rain, the wind-blown rain,

Ka ua hoʻokinakina a nui,
A nui a kau a malie ia ua.

The ceaselessly pouring rain,
Through much heavy rain, through light rain, until the rain ceased.

Inu aku i ka awa o Koʻukoʻu,
I ka ʻawa lau hinalo ʻaʻala,
ʻAwa ʻona o Mamalahoa, he hoa e,

We drank the ʻawa of Koʻukoʻu,
The fragant-leafed ʻawa,
The potent ʻawa of Mamalahoa, O my companion.

He kaʻupu e Lono e,
He kanaka au no ka ua iki,
Ina hoʻi ha he hoa au no ka ua iki la paʻia,
He hoa i ka nahele lauhala loloa,

A friend [was I] O Lono,
A server was I in the light rain,
I was your companion in the light rain of the forest,
A companion in the long-leafed pandanus groves,

Mai Kilauea a Kahili la,

[That extend] from Kilauea to Kalihi,

O ka hala i ʻaiʻna kepa ʻia e ka manu
O Poʻoku i Hanalei la.

The pandanus [whose fruit] is pecked by the birds,
[The pandanus] of Poʻoku in Hanalei.

Hala ia mao a ka ua e ka hoa e,

There we were till the rain ceased falling, O my companion,

He hoa i ka makani lauwili Poʻaihele,
Mauka o Hanalei iki a Hanalei nui,

My companion in the hurrying whirlwind,
In the uplands of lesser Hanalei, of greater Hanalei,

Mauka mai hoʻi kekahi ua,

[In] the rain that came from the uplands,

Makai mai hoʻi kekahi ua,
Ma naʻe mai hoʻi kekahi ua,
Malalo mai hoʻi kekahi ua,
Maluna iho hoʻi kekahi ua,
Malalo aʻe hoʻi kekahi ua,
Ma ka lae hala o Puʻupaoa,

Rain that came from the lowlands,
Rain that came from the east,
Rain that came from the south,
Rain that came from above,
Rain that came from below,
Along the cape of Puʻupaoa, overgrown with pandanus,

Ilaila ka ua kike hala,

There was the rain that pelted the pandanus fruit,

Ho'owalea ike one 'ai a ke kina'u,

Drenching the sand where the sand eels fed,

He kia'u 'ai hala o Mahamoku,

The eels that ate the pandanus of Mahamoku,

Ka ua ho'opala 'ohi'a o Wai'oli.

The rain that ripened the mountain apples of Wai'oli.

He 'oli'oli au e pono o 'oe ka haku a,

I was glad that you were my lord,

O ka haku maka o Kalamanu'u,

Lord beloved by the mo'o goddess Kalamanu'u,

O ka Makalei-o-Ku kalai aku Ho'one'enu'u

By Makalei-o-Ku from which was carved Ho'one'enu'u,

Ke ana a Kalaukanikani.

[At] the cave of Kalaukanikani.

Kaniku hele ka ua i kaupaku o ka hale o moe a,

The rain patters on the roofs of the sleeping houses,

Ilaila ka ua ha'a hula i ka nahele.

Then it dances away to the forest.

Ha'aha'a ka ua i ka nahele,

Quietly fell the rain in the forest,

Lauwili ka ua i ka nahele,

Whirling came the rain in the forest,

'Ope'a ka ua i ka nahele,

The rain in the forest twisted this way and that,

Kiilihuna ka ua i ka nahele,

Drop by drop fell the rain in the forest,

Pohina ka ua i ka nahele,

Mist-like fell the rain in the forest,

Anuanu ka ua i ka nahele,

Chilly was the rain in the forest,

Ko'eko'e ka ua i ka nahele,

The rain in the forest was cold,

'Opili ka ua i ka nahele,

The rain in the forest chilled through to the bone,

Ha'ukeke ka ua i ka nahele,

The rain in the forest made one shiver,

Ho'opala 'ohi'a ka ua i ka nahele,

The rain in the forest ripened the mountain apples,

I ka nahele o La'auha'ele'ele e hele a.

In the forest of La'auha'ele'ele where we wandered.

Walea kanaka i ka helea ho'i mai,

The server went forth in peace, and upon returning,

He lalo 'ino, he lalo 'aki'aki ka ko muli nei,

He found trouble, a back-biting among inferiors,

Eia mamuli ka ukali ka'ele'ele,

About the dark-skinned man who had followed you,

Kepai ka ho'okuke a.

The favorite, who is being banished.

He nani nei hele, ua ho'okuke 'oe,	It is well that I should go, for you have sent me away,
Eia la ka hewa o ka noho hale.	The owner of the house has found fault with me.
O ka noho a ku a'e ha'alele,	Had I stayed and then gone away without cause,
Lo'aa la ko'u kina ilaila,	That would have been wrong of me,
Ko ka ohua ukali 'ino a.	Your companion, who followed you in stormy weather.
Aloha a ha'alele ia 'oe ke hele nei.	Farewell, I leave you and go.
Ia hele kikaha a'e la kaua a Hopukoa	The rain of Hopukoa passes by
A Waialoha, eia la e—	At Waialoha, and so
Aloha wale ana ka wau ia 'oe iloko o ka uahoa.	I bid farewell to you, who remain in anger.

When Lono heard this chant of Kapa-'ihi-a-hilina, relating all the places they had wandered in destitution, in hunger, poverty, cold, chill, and of their being robbed by others, affection welled up in him so that he wept and could not hold back his tears. Therefore Kapa-'ihi-a-hilina became ten times the favorite he was before.

During Lono's reign, when he tended to the affairs of his kingdom, the chiefs and commoners lived in peace. He desired to go to see Kauai, to see the places he had wandered while insane, to see Ka'ula and to plunge into the water of Namolokama. Kama-lala-walu was the chief of Maui, Kane-kapu-a-Ku'ihewa and Ka-'ihi-kapu-a-Ku'ihewa were the chiefs of Oahu on the Kona and Ko'olau sides, and Ke-alohi-iki-kaupe'a, Ka-uhi-a-hiwa, and Kawelo-'ahu were the chiefs of Kauai. Lono-i-ka-makahiki sought the good will of these chiefs when he came to meet and associate with them in a friendly manner. There were to be no wars between one chief and another.

The chiefly emblem of Hawaii was a large feathered staff (*kahili*). Hawaii-loa was the name of Lono-i-ka-makahiki's *kahili*, and these feathered staffs were not common among chiefs of the other islands. Only in Hawaii were the *'o'o* birds found in great numbers. When Lono travelled, the large *kahili* was wrapped up. When it was set up the men in Lono's canoe prostrated themselves. In this way was the Makahiki god also honored. When Lono sailed from Hawaii, his emblem was erected, and on the tops of the masts hung *ka'upu* bird [skins] like banners, the wing-spreads of which were a fathom and more in length. They were hung at the very top of the masts. His voyage to meet the chiefs of Maui was an awesome sight.

Kama-lala-walu, ruler of Maui, met him and welcomed him royally. The chiefly host and guest spent much time in surfing, a sport that was enjoyed by all. It showed which man or which woman was skilled; not only that, but which man or woman was the best looking. It was a pleasing sight, and that was why chiefs and commoners enjoyed surfing. Lono and Kama surfed until evening.

Kama's stewards and food-preparers made their chief's food ready. Lono did not say what he wished for the evening. After they had surfed, bathed in fresh water, and dressed in dry tapa, dusk came. The chiefs suggested eating. Kama's food and 'awa had been prepared beforehand, but the food that Lono wished was not ready. Lono asked for his broiled chicken, and his head steward answered, "It is not ready." The chief felt ashamed because his food was not ready. Maui's chief made Hawaii's feel humiliated by showing the readiness of his servants. Lono gave his steward, named Puapua-kea, a blow that drew blood from his nose. The meal was to be served in the chief's eating house, but nothing was ready there.

Puapua-kea, still bleeding, took a gourd container, removed from it a fine mat made from the pandanus blossoms of Puna, spread it, took out a stone fire container, some charcoal, kindling, and the fire sticks. He made a fire with fire sticks in hand, kindled it until it lighted quickly, and lighted the charcoal. He tore pieces of 'awa, put them in his mouth, grasped the chicken, tore off a wing, rubbed salt on it, and placed it on the fire; tore off a leg and laid it on the fire. He had one ball of 'awa and then a second which was enough. The steward said, "The chief did not say anything to the servant. If he had, the servant would have deserved the beating." The chicken cooked very quickly, and the 'awa was ready in a cup before the 'awa of the chief of Maui had time to take effect. Puapua-kea won the banner! [By his speed and skill he had proved himself the better servant.] The chiefs and commoners praised Puapua-kea greatly because the chief of Maui had planned to humiliate the chief of Hawaii. When the feast was ready, Maui's chief said to Hawaii's, "Let us have broiled chicken and dog cooked over hot charcoal, to remove the bitterness of our 'awa." The Hawaii chief had nothing there, and the other was well supplied. His personal servant, Puapua-kea, was ready. The ears of the dog and the wings of a chicken took but a short time to cook. Kama, ruler of Maui, said to Lono, ruler of Hawaii, "A desire has come into me for your servant. It is better that I have our servant."

["Let your servant be our servant."] Lono replied, "This is not my servant, but an important person in my court. He is my younger brother, a protector of my land. I am the chief, and he comes next to me as chief of the island of Hawaii and its people."*

When the effect of the 'awa began to wear off, the ruler of Maui asked the ruler of Hawaii, "After you have ruled until you are old, need the help of a cane, and become as bleary-eyed as a rat, who will be your successor?" Lono pointed to the person at his side, "This person here." Kama's heir replied, "Short of stature, stout and short, a shelf easily reached by a dog." Puapua-kea, Lono's heir said, "I may be a small person, but I am the small *maika* stone that can roll all over the field and win. I am the small sugar cane stalk of Kohala [whose fuzz] can irritate the nose."

The Hawaii chief then asked Kama, "After you have ruled until you need the support of a cane, become as bleary-eyed as a rat, and sprawl helplessly on a mat, who will be your successor?" Kama pointed to his younger brother, Maka-ku-i-ka-lani, and said, "This person." Lono's heir answered, "Tall, thin, spindly, and too slender. Falls easily with a gust of wind." Maka-ku-i-ka-lani retorted, "I am the tall banana tree of the wild mountain patch whose fruit does not ripen in a week. I am the long anchoring-root of the mountain. Though the wind blow, I do not fall."

After Lono departed from Maui, he made a circuit of Molokai. The chiefs of Molokai spent some time at Kalaupapa to surf. Halawa was the second-best place where the Molokai chiefs liked to surf. They welcomed the chief of Hawaii. The chiefs there enjoyed another sport, checkers (*konane*). It was there that Lono broke the *konane* board after an argument with Ka-iki-lani, a woman. Because she was fond of her board, he saved one pebble. The board could not break until his personal attendant, Hauna, arrived. There was no one more able to break the board of Ka-iki-lani than he.

Lono sailed away and landed at Lapawai, Kailua, Oahu. Ka-'ihi-kapu-a-Kuhi-hewa was the chief of the hilly Ko'olau side of the island, and Lono was graciously welcomed by him. They displayed their chiefly emblems, and the one thing that created much admiration from the chiefs of Oahu was the large *kahili* of Hawaii. Ka-'ihi-kapu-a-Kuhi-hewa tried to buy his feathered staff, but the price was high.

One of Lono's sons was named for Ka-'ihi-kapu-a-Kuhi-hewa, that is Ka-'ihi-kapu-mahana. That son of Lono was taken to Pa'ala'a, Waialua, and he became the ancestor of the people there. It was in this way that he became an ancestor there: Ka-'ihi-kapu-mahana mated

* *Ke Au 'Oko'a*, Jan. 19, 1871.

with Aila, and Ka-welo-a-Aila and Kaina-Aila were born. Ka-welo-a-Aila (also called Ka-welo-iki-a-Aila) mated with Ka-ua-kahi-hele-i-ka-wi' and Kulu-ahi, Ka-halana-moe-'ino, and Ho'olau were born.

Lono went with Ka-'ihi-kapu to surf at Kalapawai. The chief's home was named Pamoa, and the thing that was much done there was to recite the chant of Kuhi-hewa II, called Ke-alialia. Kuhi-hewa appropriated the chant for himself, for it had belonged to a woman of Kauai. Lono had learned the chant from this woman, whose name was 'Ohai-kawili-'ula. When Lono wandered insane on Kauai he adopted her as a relative (ho'owahine), and thus learned the chant. After surfing, the chiefs returned to the house. The sacred cord was set up [at the entrance], and the guards would not admit anyone with a wet loin cloth. The native chief could receive a dry loin cloth and step over his own tabu sign, but the stranger could not receive a dry loin cloth until he was able to chant one chant. Lono, chief of Hawaii, was made to feel humiliation by being refused a loin cloth unless he chanted the chant of the Oahu chief. Lono said, "My attendants composed that chant, Ke-alialia, for me and not for any other chief." The Oahu chiefs asked Lanahu-'imi-haku and others, "Is it true that the chant, Ke-alialia, was composed for Lono?" They replied, "We do not know, for we have not heard that it belonged to him. He claims that his attendants composed it when he was a child, but we deny that he had a chant like that." When Lono made comparison with his version of Ke-alialia, those who appropriated it and gave it to Ka-kuhi-hewa II failed to complete it. Lono won Ke-alialia. (This is a lengthy chant.) Fishing was another sport enjoyed by Ka-kuhi-hewa and Lono. Ka-kuhi-hewa lost in that contest of skill. In canoe-racing and other sports Ka-kuhi-hewa lost to the chief of Hawaii.

Lono sailed away to Kauai, to Niihau, to Ka'ula, and returned after being welcomed by the chiefs. One of his grandsons, Kaina-Aila, remained on Kauai and mixed with the chiefs there, thus: Kaina-Aila mated with Ka-pu-lauki' and had Kulu-i-ua. Kulu-i-ua mated with Ka-ua-kahi-lau and had Lono-i-kai-hopu-kaua-o-ka-lani. Lono-i-kai-hopu-kaua-o-ka-lani mated with Kamu and had Kau-me-he-'iwa. These were the ancestors of chiefs and commoners on Kauai. When Lono returned to Hawaii he found the chiefs still at peace. There he remained in peace with the chiefs of Kona, Hilo, and Ka-'u.

Kama [chief of Maui] grew weary of continued peace with the chiefs of Hawaii, and desired to make war against the chiefs of Kohala, Kona, and Ka-'u. He did not want to fight against the chiefs of Hilo because they were cousins of the Maui chiefs. He sent some men to spy in Hawaii. They were his half brother, Ka-uhi-o-ka-lani, a son of Kiha-a-Pi'i-lani, and [with him] a man chosen from among the fastest runners. They were to see how large the population was, and if it was large to report it truthfully. If it was not, then war could be declared against Hawaii.

The spies sent by Kama-lala-walu went to Hawaii and landed at Kawaihae in the evening. Ka-uhi-o-ka-lani ran about that same evening and returned before the canoes were dismantled and placed in the house. The keepers of the gods at Mailekini were servants of Kama, and so they concealed the canoes of the spies. When Ka-uhi-o-ka-lani returned his fellow spies and hosts asked, "Where did you go?" "I went visiting from here to the lava bed and the pond that lies along the length of the land." "Kaniku is the lava bed and Kiholo, the pond. Then did you turn back?" "No, I went on to the long stretch of sand, to the small bay with a point on that side and one on this side. There are large inland ponds." "The sandy stretch is 'Ohiki, and the walled-in ponds are Kaloko and Honokohau. Then you came back?" "No, I went on to the large rocky cape below, where there was a small bay with big groves of coconut trees. The land from there on is good, and a small village is located there." "The point that juts out is Hi'iaka-noho-lae and the sandy beach inside of that is Kaiakeakua. Next is Kailua. The coconut groves are Holualoa and Kahalu'u. Then you came back?" "No, I went to the hill below with a bay inside [the hill below which a bay reaches far into the land]. A cliff stands back of the bay, and there is a sharp ridge like the comb of a cock. There is a hole [cave mouth] underneath that leads where the smooth, water-worn stones are. I laid a section of my sugar cane right over the entrance" [of that cave]. The natives replied, "The hill is Pu'uohau; the bay is Ka'awaloa; the hole that leads in is Lepeamoa. Your swiftness is like that of a god. The day has waned into evening, and the baggage on the canoes has not been completely removed by us. This is indeed marvelous."

Next morning the spies began a circuit of Hawaii. At Kalepeamoa, Anapuka [the cave] in Ka'awaloa, they found the section of sugar cane on the cliff. (What a fast runner he was! If he tried to make a circuit of Hawaii he would have made it in a single day.) This fast runner was Ka-uhi-o-ka-lani, brother of the ruler, Kama-lala-walu. He was the son of Kiha-a-Pi'i-lani by Kolea-moku, a native of Hana. These spies of Kama-lala-walu went around Hawaii to see how many people there were. After they had been around, they returned to report to their chief, saying, "We went all around Hawaii. There were many houses, but few men. We went to Kohala and found the men only on the shores." These spies were mistaken when they denied that there were many men on Hawaii [as the saying was], "Bare of inhabitants is Kohala, for the men are at the coast." The spies had seen the land of Kohala [but had failed to see the people for] on all of the fields where sports were held from inner Kohala to outer Kohala, from Kohala of the coastal cliffs to Kohala of the inland, a crowd of people gathered every day from morning to night to play. Kohala was known as a thickly-populated land. The spies thought that if Kohala was conquered, Kona, Ka-'u and Puna would be easily taken, and they felt that Hilo and Hamakua would lend no assistance. This was true, for the chiefs of these districts were cousins of the chiefs of Maui.

When Kama-lala-walu, ruler of Maui, heard the report of his spies, he was eager to stir his chiefs, his sons, and warriors to make war on Hawaii. The prophets, seers, readers of omens, and all of the learned men of the land heard of it and came to him with their prophecies concerning the war against Hawaii. Most of the prophets and seers supported the chief's desire and gave dogs as their omen of victory [said that clouds taking the form of dogs foretold victory]. The dogs were a sign of fierceness, and so would the chief fiercely attack the enemy and gain the victory with great slaughter of the foe. Part of the prophets and seers came to the chief with prophecies denying his victory, and urging him not to go to fight against Hawaii. If the chief would stubbornly insist on war, he himself would be killed, and his chiefs and warriors slaughtered. It would be fortunate indeed if one of them would be spared if taken captive. When the chief heard them say that if he went to fight against Hawaii, then he would die, and his chiefs and warriors would be slaughtered, he made them a promise, "If I return in victory after the war, then I will burn you alive in the fire." The prophets who told him not to go said that they were not afraid of his threats. They came before him with their prophecies. Thus did Lani-kaula, Kiu, and Kaohi, and this was one of the prophecies uttered:

> The Kiu is the wind,
> A gusty, moisture-laden wind,
> That roars down to Maulukai
> And rushes up to Pauwela.
> There it flies, O Lono,
> Where Wahinekapu watches over the water Kapo'ulu.
> The sweet-potato vines of Makaili'i
> Are scorched by the sun, O Lono.

Kama-lala-walu went with his chiefs, his royal sons, the heir to the government of Maui, the warriors, and learned counselors. Upon landing in Kohala, battle began at once by the destruction of the Kohala people. The natives were put to rout. At that time a high chief of Hawaii, Kanaloa-kua'ana, the son of Keawe-nui-a-'Umi, was taken and cruelly treated. His whole skin was tattooed, his eyelids turned inside out and tattooed. Kanaloa-kua'ana was renamed Ka-maka-hiwa (Blackened-eyes) and Ka-maka-paweo (Shamed-eyes).

From Kohala, Kama-lala-walu set forth for Kawaihae, and found no one there. The people had gone up to Waimea, for all observed the services at the heiau of Mailekini. Only those of lower Kawaihae and Puako remained. The battlefield was at Waimea. Kama-lala-walu's counselors said, "Waimea is not a good battle site for strangers because the plain is long, and there is no water. Should defeat be met with by the warring strangers, they will all be slaughtered. It is better to go to Kona to fight, as there will be a resting place for the canoes. There will be no trouble in fighting."

Kama-lala-walu, the heedless chief, paid no attention, but followed the advice of two old men of Kawaihae who counseled falsely. One of them was named Puhau-kole. They said, "Pu'oa'oaka is a good battlefield and will be a great help to the chief. All the canoes should be taken apart because the warriors may desire to run back to the canoes and depart in secret for Maui. The best thing to do is to cut up the canoes and outriggers, for there are canoes enough in Hawaii. When it is conquered, there will be many canoes from Kona and Ka-'u. There will be much property and wealth for the Maui chiefs." The chief, Kama-lala-walu, listened to the advice of Puhau-kole and his companion. Their suggestions were carried out, and the canoes were broken up. Then Kama-lala-walu's fighting men went up to the grass-covered plain of Waimea.

After Kama-lala-walu's warriors reached the grassy plain, they looked seaward on the left and beheld the men of Kona advancing toward them. The lava bed of Kaniku and all the land up to Hu'ehu'e was covered with the men of Kona. Those of Ka-'u and Puna were coming down from Mauna Kea, and those of Waimea and Kohala were on the level plain of Waimea. The men covered the whole of the grassy plain of Waimea like locusts. Kama-lala-walu with his warriors dared to fight. The battlefield of Pu'oa'oaka was outside of the grassy plain of Waimea, but the men of Hawaii were afraid of being taken captive by Kama, so they led to the waterless plain lest Maui's warriors find water and hard, waterworn pebbles. The men of Hawaii feared that the Maui warriors would find water to drink and become stronger for the slinging of stones that would fall like raindrops from the sky. The stones would fall about with a force like lightning, breaking the bones into pieces and causing sudden death as if by bullets.

Maui almost won in the first battle because of Hawaii's lack of a strong champion. Maka-ku-i-ka-lani was first on the field and defied any man on Hawaii to match strength with him. Maka-ku-i-ka-lani tore Hawaii's champion apart. When Puapua-kea arrived later by way of Mauna Kea, those of Hawaii rejoiced at having their champion. Maka-ku-i-ka-lani and Puapua-kea matched their strength in club fighting on the battle site before the two sides plunged into the fight.* The first stroke belonged to Maka-ku-i-ka-lani, and his club-fighting instructor had taught him that the strokes to use on Puapua-kea were the ones that his grandfather, Ho'olae-makua, used. The upper stroke was called Ka-wala-ki'i, the lower one, Laumaki. He used the Ka-wala stroke above and the 'io below. Puapua-kea was thrown upward, the base of his ear struck, and the ear torn off. There was a thud against his skull, and blood poured from it. Puapua-kea became dizzy and fell. Maka-ku-i-ka-lani's instructor said, "The mighty warrior is not dead. You did not use the favorite stroke of your grandfather, Ho'olae-makua." Maka said, "He is dead: A handsome man needs to use but one stroke." Puapua-kea, being struck dizzy with Maka-ku-i-ka-lani's club, lay still. Maka-ku-i-ka-lani was told to strike again to see if he was dead:

After lying still, Puapua-kea arose and stood on the battle field. His teacher in club fighting, Ka-welo, suggested Wahie-'eke'eke for the upper stroke, and Hu'alepo for the lower one. He also said, "O Kanaloa-kua'ana, the strokes will be too low," because he noticed how tall Maka-ku-i-ka-lani was. Puapua-kea retorted, "The teacher's instruction ceases after leaving home. The club from tip to base could strike from head to spine." The instructor said, "Kill the mighty warrior." Puapua-kea looked at the palm of his hand and said, "He shall die, for it is marked here." They ran out on the grassy plain, and there Maka-ku-i-ka-lani was killed.

[Then] the two sides began to fight. Short and long spears were flung, and death took its toll on both sides. The Maui men who were used to slinging shiny, water-worn stones grabbed up the stones of Pu'oa'oaka. A cloud of dust rose to the sky and twisted about like smoke, but the lava rocks were light, and few of the Hawaii men were killed by them. This was one of the things that helped to destroy the warriors of Kama-lala-walu: They went away out on the plain where

* *Ke Au Okoa*, Jan. 26, 1871.

the strong fighters were unable to find water. If they did find some, it was from the little pools of Lani-maomao [rain water caught in hollows].

The warriors of Maui were put to flight, and the retreat to Kawaihae was long. [Yet] there were many who did reach Kawaihae, but because of a lack of canoes, only a few escaped with their lives. Most of the chiefs and warriors from Maui were destroyed. Those who escaped on bait-carrying canoes [*malau*] were sunk and destroyed by the Hawaii warriors. Some escaped by way of Kohala, found canoes, and returned to Maui. Ka-uhi-a-Kama, the oldest son of Kama-lala-walu by Kapu-kini, was the heir of the government of Maui. He escaped to Kekaha, on Hawaii, secured a canoe, and thus found his way back to Maui.

The person who saved him was Hinau, foster son of Lono-i-ka-makahiki. Ka-uhi-a-Kama made Hinau's name a famous one. It was said that Ka-uhi-a-Kama was annoyed with Hinau because he was a favorite of Lono-i-ka-makahiki, and sought means of destroying him. It was said that his [Hinau's] eyes were scooped out. Some say that Ka-uhi-a-Kama was not killed on Hawaii because his mother, Kapu-kini-akua, belonged there. This is shown in the genealogy of the Hawaii chiefs. Maka-kau-ali'i mated with Ka-'ao'ao-wao, and Kapu-kini-akua (female), and Keawe-nui-ho'okapu-ka-lani and 'Umi-nui-ka-'ai-lani were born. They were among the chiefs of Hawaii who took part in this war. So was Iwi-kau-i-ka-ua, another son of Maka-kau-ali'i. He was an uncle of Ka-uhi-a-Kama. These were all high chiefs of Kona in Hawaii, and there was no reason for his death in the war there. [Because of these chiefly relatives Ka-uhi-a-Kama was not killed.] Kama-lala-walu, ruler of Maui, was killed on the grassy plain of Puako, and some of his chiefs were also destroyed. Kama-lala-walu was noted for his fearlessness, and he died bravely before the chiefs and warriors of Hawaii. He showed no fear or cowardice, but went forward to meet his death. He was famed for his fearlessness, and it was made known in a chant of praise thus:

O ka huli koa nui a Kama-lala-walu,	A mighty warrior was Kama-lala-walu,
O ke aluka koa a Kama i Waimea,	A multitude of warriors had he at Waimea.
O ka huli o ka 'anapu a kaikoa,	A brave warrior he, like a flash of lightning!
O ka huli koa a Papa ia Owa',	A brave warrior of the lineage of Owa'!

O ka huli koa nui a Kama-lala-walu,	A mighty warrior was Kama-lala-walu
O ke aluka koa a Kama i Waimea,	A multitude of warriors had he at Waimea!
O Kama a Poʻokoa,	Kama, kinsmen of Poʻokoa,
A Ka-ʻaoʻao a Maka-ku-i-ka-lani,	Of Ka-ʻaoʻao and of Maka-ku-i-ka-lani,
O ke koa aliʻi o ʻUmi-ka-la-kaua.	And the chiefly warrior, ʻUmi-ka-la-kaua.

In this battle of Kama-lala-walu at Puʻu-ʻoaʻoaka in Waimea, Hawaii, his name became renowned and attached to his islands as "Maui, land of Kama." Ka-uhi-a-Kama succeeded as ruler of Maui, and his children and grandchildren became chiefs there.

When Lono-i-ka-makahiki, ruler of Hawaii, died, his children and his descendants did not become rulers of the government. His name was made famous through the Makahiki god, Lono-i-ka-ʻou-aliʻi, and [he] was thus thought of as a god of the Makahiki celebration. The name Lono was combined with the word Makahiki, thus making it Lono-i-ka-makahiki.

Lono had sons by Ka-iki-lani-kohe-paniʻo, named Keawe-hanau-i-ka-walu and Ka-ʻihi-kapu-mahana. They did not become their father's heirs. The rule went to Kanaloa-kuaʻana's descendants, but not the whole of Hawaii, only Kohala, Kona, and Ka-ʻu. Hawaii was divided into small divisions. The children of Kanaloa-kuaʻana, by Maka-kau-aliʻi's sister Ka-iki-lani, and their descendants became rulers. Kanaloa-kua-ʻana mated with Ka-iki-lani, who was older than Maka-kau-aliʻi, and Ke-liʻi-o-ka-lani, Keakea-lani-kane, and Ka-lani-o-ʻumi were born. Ke-liʻi-o-ka-lani mated with Keakea-lani-kane, and to them was born Ke-aka-mahana. Ke-aka-mahana was made ruler of Hawaii, but not the whole of it for there were other chiefs over Hilo and Hamakua. Those [districts] were held by the descendants of Keawe-nui-a-ʻUmi by Kamola-nui-a-ʻUmi, Kumalae-nui-a-ʻUmi by Ku-nuʻu-nui-a-ʻUmi, and Kumalae-nui-a-ʻUmi by Ku-nuʻu-nui-puʻawa-lau. Their children and grandchildren were the rulers of Hilo and Hamakua.

Chiefs of Kona recognized one as head over all and they all called called her their lord. They left the government to her and exalted her. Their ruler was Ke-aka-mahana, a woman. This sacred woman, Ke-aka-mahana, was married to Iwi-kau-i-ka-ua, a chief of Hawaii. Their rank was not equal as his was lower than hers for hers was of *piʻo* rank, and her family included the tabu chiefs of Kauai. Her grandfather [ancestor], named Maka-liua, was from Kauai. She was one of the *piʻo* rank because her parents were brother and sister, Ke-li'i-o-ka-lani and Keakea-lani-kane. When Ke-aka-mahana was born she was taken to Kauai to be reared, and when the chiefs of Hawaii desired a sacred ruler over their government they went to Kauai to bring her back.

This sacred woman ruled and found a husband, Iwi-kau-i-ka-ua. She despised the oldest daughter of Iwi-kau-i-ka-ua by his sister Kapu-kini-akua, and [despised] his mother. She had his mother and daughter killed and their bones mistreated. When Iwi-kau-i-ka-ua discovered that his mother and daughter had been secretly murdered, his mind became possessed with a desire to desert his wife and betray her government to the chiefs of Hilo. Iwi-kau-i-ka-ua made a circuit of Hawaii and kept torches burning night and day. This burning of torches became famous and was spoken of as the "*Kukui* torches of Iwi-kau-i-ka-ua." [Lighted torches came to be associated with him and his descendants.] His determination led him to go and live on Oahu where he married an Oahu chiefess, named Ka-ua-kahi-a-kua'ana-au-a-kane, and they had one son, Kane-i-ka-ua-iwi-lani. When he (Kane-i-ka-ua-iwi-lani) had grown up, he went to Hawaii to marry his half sister Keakea-lani, the daughter of Iwi-kau-i-ka-ua by Ke-aka-mahana. To this union was born a daughter, Ka-lani-kau-lele-ia-iwi.

After Iwi-kau-i-ka-ua left Hawaii, a war began among the chiefs of Hawaii. There was much fighting between the chiefs of Kona and Hilo, but neither was defeated. The chiefs of Kona desired Hilo, Hamakua, and La'a because of the *mamo* and *'o'o* feathers, the war canoes, and fine tapas such as the *'o'uholowai, 'eleuli, pala'a',* and *kalukalu* of Waipi'o. The chiefs of Hilo in turn desired warm food and drinking water, and tough and tender fish. Those were the wealth of Kona. The war lasted through several centuries.

It was said that the cause which started the war between the chiefs of Hilo and Kona was the cruel treatment of Kua'ana, chief of Hilo, by the chiefs of Kona. He was the son of 'I by Ho'o-lei-ali'i, a chiefess of Hana. Kua'ana was taken captive by the chiefs of Kona, pushed up and down in the sea at Kawaihae, and barely escaped with his life. He was seen by Palena, a Kohala chief, who said to the chiefs of Kohala and Kona that were forcing Kua'ana under water, "Be careful with the offspring of 'I, lest later the tough root of 'I crawl hither." Palena let Kua'ana escape by canoe, all by himself, and the wind blew the canoe until it landed on Maui. Kua'ana sought his mother, Ho'olei-ali'i, after his life was saved and found her at Hamoa in Hana.

The news of the cruel treatment of Kua'ana, a chief of Hilo, by the chiefs of Kona was heard by those of Hilo, and they prepared for war. Kuahu'ia, son of Kua'ana, was the chief war leader there. Kua'ana noticed the bonfire indicating war in Hamakua and knew that the chiefs of Hilo were going to make war against those of Kona. Kua'ana suggested to his mother that she give him some men and warriors to help his son, Kuahu'ia. When Kua'ana met his son they were very happy to see each other.

Sometimes the victory went to the chiefs of Kona, but more often to the chiefs of Hilo. Kona's chiefs fled to their fortresses, and Keakea-lani and others were taken captive when the Hilo chiefs won. Keakea-lani and her company were sent as prisoners to Maui and to Molokai. Keakea-lani was restored to Kohala where she ruled, in name only, over the districts of Kohala, Kona, and Ka-'u. The chiefs of Kona combined in fighting those of Hilo, but the victory was always Hilo's during the reigns of Kua'ana, Kuahu'ia, Ka-lani-ku-kau-la'ala'a, and Moku.

After Moku's time the Hilo chiefs ceased to reign. The rulers of Kona who succeeded Ke-aka-mahana were her daughter, Keakea-lani, and her [Keakea-lani's] son, Keawe. While the war was raging between the chiefs of Hilo and those of Kona, Keakea-lani was the ruler over the people of Kona and Kohala. The Mahi clan were the war leaders, that is, they were in charge. They were Mahi-kukuku, Mahi-'ololi', Mahi-o-Palena, Palena, Luahine, Paua, and many others in the chiefly families of Kona and Kohala. But the chiefs of Hilo were always victorious over those of Kona. In the large battle at the sheer cliffs, the chiefs of Hilo won. In the important battle at Kahina'i, Pae and Ka-lani-ku-kau-la'ala'a were Hilo's principal war leaders. After they won the battle of Hu'ehu'e the secret places and burial caves in Kona were broken open. In the battle of Mahiki, Ka-lani-ku-kau-la'ala'a and Moku were the chief war leaders of Hilo. Some war canoes were brought from Kauai by Kona-kai-ale'e and others, to aid the Hilo chiefs. They were victorious and the Kona chiefs were slaughtered. One of the high chiefs of Kona, named Ka-uaua-nui-a-Mahi, was also slain.*

* *Ke Au Okoa*, Feb. 2, 1871.

CHAPTER V

Keawe's Reign

Keawe was the son of Keakea-lani. His father was Kanaloa-kapu-lehu and his [half] sister, Ka-lani-kau-lele-ia-iwi. Ka-lani-kau-lele-ia-iwi's father was also her cousin, named Kane-i-ka-ua-iwi-lani. These were the noted rulers of Hawaii. Her husband was Ka-uaua-nui-a-Mahi, and to them was born Alapa'i-nui-a-Ka-uaua. Keawe was a famous ruler of Hawaii and was the ancestor of chiefs and commoners on that island. Keawe had many children by chiefesses and commoners. These are the children of Keawe who gained renown: Ka-lani-nui-'i-a-mamao (whose mother was Lono-ma'a-i-kanaka, a chiefess of Ka-'u and a descendant of 'I), Ke'e-au-moku and his sister Ke-kela-o-ka-lani (whose mother was Ka-lani-kau-lele-ia-iwi), Ha'o, 'Awili, Ka-lilau-moku, and Kumuhea (whose mother was Kane-'alai, a ruling chiefess of Molokai and a daughter of Luahiwa of the reigning family of Kauai). These were not the only children of Keawe, for he had many by chiefesses [of high rank], those of lesser rank, those without [rank], and by commoners. The descendants of Keawe spread from Hawaii among chiefs and commoners.

During Keawe's reign the whole of Hawaii was not united under him, for his rule was only over Kohala, Kona, and Ka-'u. He ruled over the many chiefs that were under him, and they took charge of Keawe's affairs. They were the ones who fought against the chiefs of Hilo. During Keawe's reign, Ka-'u was set aside for his son, Ka-lani-nui'i-a-mamao, and chiefly tabus were given to him. The chiefly tabu then belonged to the chiefs of Ka-'u, and the *wohi* tabu to the chiefs of Kona. So also did the chiefly tabus of the chiefs of Kona pass on to the son of Keawe. Keawe was a chief who was fond of traveling and he traveled about Maui, Molokai, Oahu, and Kauai. (Hence the saying, "Red-eyed was Keawe on Kauai, bald-headed was Keawe on Hawaii.") One noted thing that was said of Keawe was that he built a house to contain the remains of the chiefs at Honaunau, Hawaii, called Hale-o-Keawe.

When Keawe died, his bones were enclosed in a wicker container. Those which were so enclosed were said to be in the *ka'ai* (*ku i ke ka'ai*). So the saying was, "Keawe returned and remained in the *ka'ai*"

(*Ho'i o Keawe a ku i ke ka'ai*). Before he died he commanded that the government belong to his sons, Ka-lani-nui-'i-a-mamao and Ke'e-au-moku; Ka-lani-nui'i-a-mamao to be ruling chief of Ka-'u and Ke'e-au-moku of Kona and Kohala.

While Alapa'i-nui-a-Ka-uaua was living on Maui with Ke-kau-like, ruler of Maui, he heard that Keawe, chief of Hawaii, was dead. Ke-kau-like was his half-sister's (Ke-ku'i-apo-iwa-nui) husband, and his broth-er-in-law. Ke-ku'i-apo-iwa-nui-a-Ka-lani-nui-kau-lele-ia-iwi, his half sister, was the wife of Ke-kau-like and she was the first-born child of Ka-lani-kau-lele-ia-iwi by Ka-'ula-hea-nui-o-ka-moku. There was an-other reason why Alapa'i-nui-a-Ka-uaua lived with his half sister on Maui—the death of his father, Ka-uaua-nui-a-Mahi, at Mahiki by the hands of the Hilo chiefs. After Keawe's death, Alapa'i-nui-a-Ka-uaua thought of going to Hawaii to make war against the chiefs. When he made war against the chiefs of Kohala and Kona, he took them captive and became ruler of Kohala and Kona. Ke-kau-like heard of his vic-tory over all of the chiefs of Kohala and Kona, therefore he desired to make war against Alapa'i and return the government to the chiefs whose land it was. Alapa'i won this victory but the warriors of Ke-kau-like went around Hawaii and interfered with Alapa'i's wish to conquer the whole of it. Because Ke-kau-like fought against Alapa'i frequently, Alapa'i was unable to take captive the chiefs of Hilo and Ka'u.*

* *Ke Au 'Oko'a*, Feb. 2, 1871.

CHAPTER VI

Hawaii Under Alapaʻi-nui

It was during the time of the warfare among the chiefs of [the island of] Hawaii which followed the death of Keawe, chief over the whole island (Ke-awe-i-kekahi-aliʻi-o-ka-moku) that Kamehameha I was born.* Moku was the ruling chief of Hilo, Hamakua, and a part of Puna; Keʻe-au-moku of Kona and Kohala. Alapaʻi-nui, son of Ka-uaua, was living at the time on Maui with the ruling chief Ka-lani-kuʻi-hono-i-ka-moku, [half] brother of the chiefess Ke-kuʻi-apo-iwa-nui. When Alapaʻi heard that the chiefs were stirring up trouble, he went to war on Hawaii against these chiefs, was victorious in battle against them, slew them, and united the island under his own rule. Ka-lani-ʻopuʻu and Keoua (the sons of the two sons of Keawe), who were then children, he brought up to be commanders of his host.

Ke-kau-like, also called Ka-lani-kuʻi-hono-i-ka-moku, the ruling chief (mo-i) of Maui mentioned above, was then living at Kaupo engaged in building luakini heiaus for his gods. He built Kane-malo-hemo at Popo-iwi, and the war heiaus (mamala koa), Loaloa and Puʻu-makaʻa at Ku-munui and Pohoʻula. This Ke-kau-like so delighted in war that he sailed to attack Hawaii. The fighting began with Alapaʻi at Kona. Both sides threw all their forces into the fight. Ke-kau-like cut down the trees throughout the land of Kona. Obliged to flee by canoe before Alapaʻi, he abused the country people of Kekaha. At Kawaihae he cut down all the coconut trees. He slaughtered the country people of Kohala, seized their possessions, and returned to Maui.

When Alapaʻi heard how cruelly the chief of Maui had treated the people of Hawaii he felt indignation on their account and determined to carry the war into Maui. He therefore consulted his leading chiefs,

---

* Kamakau's date for the birth of Kamehameha has been challenged as over twenty years too early on the basis, first, of Kamakau's general inaccuracy in matters of dating; second, contemporary estimates of voyagers who visited the islands during Kamehameha's lifetime; third, the events of his life, which would, in case the early date is accepted, put his career as a warrior well into middle life; fourth, the contemporary record by Don Francisco Paula de Marin, who, according to Wyllie's copy of Marin's journal (in Archives of Hawaii) puts his age at death (1819) at 60 years 6 months. The whole argument has been set forth in detail by the Hawaiian Historical Society (29). J. F. G. Stokes treats of the subject also (33). On the basis of further evidence, Kuykendall favors 1753 or several years earlier as the probable birth date (17 p. 430).

under-chiefs, warriors, and fighting men. Hawaii had six districts with six leading chiefs over the districts, six bands of fighting men, six fleets of canoes. Alapa'i lived with his chiefs in Kailua in Kona. He was himself a warrior chief and might have secured the rule over the group from Hawaii to Oahu had he so desired, but he had respect for the families of the chiefs, and for his relatives, for he was connected with the ruling families of both Maui and Oahu.

You have perhaps heard of Alapa'i's war upon Maui and at Kawela. A disastrous war it was for Hawaii, this carrying of the war to Maui. When all was in readiness, Alapa'i set out for Maui with the chiefs, warriors, and fighting men in double and single canoes. The war fleet encamped at Kohala, from Koai'e to Pu'uwepa. The leader landed with the chiefs at the harbor of Kapakai at Kokoiki close to Upolu, near the *luakini* heiau of Pa'ao called Mo'okini, in the northern part of Kohala.

On the second night Ke-ku'i-apo-iwa was taken with the pains of childbirth. (This was Ke-ku'i-apo-iwa of Hawaii, the daughter of Kekela and Ha'ae. The other Ke-ku'i-apo-iwa, called Ke-ku'i-apo-iwa-nui, was the mother of Ka-hekili and others.) The night was very rainy. It was hard to find a fit place for the birth, and it was hence on one of the *lanai* adjoining the guest-house that the mother suffered the first pains of childbirth. A numerous guard had been set to await the time of birth. The chiefs kept awake with the guards [for a time], but due to the rain and the cold, the chiefs fell asleep, and near daybreak Ke-ku'i-apo-iwa went into the house and, turning her face to the side of the house at the gable end, braced her feet against the wall. A certain stranger was outside the house listening, and when he heard the sound of the last bearing-down pain (*kuakoko*), he lifted the thatch at the side of the house, and made a hole above. As soon as the child was born, had slipped down upon the tapa spread out to receive it, and Ke-ku'i-apo-iwa had stood up and let the afterbirth (*ewe*) come away, he covered the child in the tapa and carried it away. When the chiefs awoke they were puzzled at the disappearance of the child. Kohala was searched that day and houses burned. The man who took away the child was Nae-'ole, the chief of Kohala, who wished by thus getting possession of the chief's child to be appointed his *kahu* to care for the child. The child thus taken and hidden away was Kamehameha I.

Kamehameha was born at Kokoiki in Kohala in 1736.* His mother

* Kokoiki near the heiau of Mo'okini, North Kohala, is one of six or seven places in that region pointed out to Donald Walker as the birthplace of Kamehameha. Kokoiki (Little-blood) is one of the star names listed in the Kumulipo chant. In the newspaper, *Ku'oko'a Home Rula*, Honolulu, April 9, 1909, in an article on Hawaiian astronomy (after Kamoho'ula in the English column) is a note to the effect that a bright and beautiful star, which the

was Ke-ku'i-apo-iwa, daughter of Kekela and Ha'ae, both of whom belonged to families of chiefs. His father was Keoua, younger brother of Ka-lani-'opu'u, Ka-maka'i-moku being the mother of both. It was the custom from ancient times among the chiefs of Hawaii for the chief of one island to give a child to the chief of another island. This is the reason why Ka-hekili has often been called the father of Kamehameha, for chiefs of Hawaii and Maui were closely related, and this is why the twins Ka-me'e-ia-moku and Ka-manawa, who were the children of Ke-kau-like, ruling chief of Maui, were made tabu to live on Hawaii as associates for the child of Ka-hekili. In the chant of Ke-aka, wife of Alapa'i, ruling chief of Hawaii, it is said that Kamehameha was born in the month of Ikuwa:

He ua lokuloku no Ikuwa ke 'li'i.   Like the heavy rain of Ikuwa is the chief.

Another chant places the time of birth in Makali'i:

Ke kukuni aku la i ka lani nui   Intense is the heat in the vast heavens.

O Makali'i ka haoa la wela   To Makali'i belong the intensely warm days,

Hanau mai ka lani la, he aoa.   In which was born the chief, a fighter.

It is said that there was rain, thunder, and lightning on the night when Kamehameha was born. Clearly this was in Ikuwa, the month of rain, thunder, and lightning, corresponding to our February or the first part of March.

Because of her weakened condition after the birth of her first-born child, Ke-ku'i-apo-iwa did not accompany Alapa'i's expedition to Maui. After it was learned that Nae-'ole was the person who had taken the child, he was made the child's guardian, and his younger sister, Ke-ku-

---

writer takes for a planet, appeared at Kokoiki on the night before Kamehameha was born and is hence called Kokoiki. Dr. Maud Makemson, plotting the position of Halley's comet as it appeared December 1, 1758, finds that it corresponds in position and movement with the description given by the Hawaiian observer of the star called Kokoiki. If the tradition is genuine it would argue for 1758 as Kamehameha's birth year and not 1736, which is the date accepted by Hawaiian historians. The time of the year, "a stormy night in November," is corroborated by the Kokoiki tradition. The celebration of Kamehameha Day on June 11 came about in the following way. On December 11, 1871, the birthday of Kamehameha V who was at that time ruling king, a public celebration was held with horse-riding and other sports. It was agreed to make this celebration an annual event, but because of the uncertain weather in December to change the date to June. Kamehameha V died soon after, and the holiday remained as a "Day in Commemoration of Kamehameha I." (*La Ho'o-mana'o o Kamehameha I*).

nui-a-lei-moku, was appointed his [the child's] foster mother. Until Kamehameha was five years old he was brought up at Halawa, an inland region of Kohala, and then Nae'ole returned the child to Alapa'i, ruling chief of Hawaii. Alapa'i placed him in charge of Ke-aka, and from that time she became his guardian.

Upon Ke-kau-like's return to Maui from his raid upon Kohala he made his home at Kaupo, intending to return to Hawaii and ravage Waipi'o and the Hamakua district. But God ordered it otherwise, for he was seized with a violent illness, or epilepsy, called "Eyes drawn heavenward" (ka-maka-huki-lani), which defied the skill of doctors. Hence the succession to the land was settled at Mokulau in Kaupo, and Kamehameha-nui, the older brother of Ka-hekili, was made ruler over the land of Maui.

Ke-kau-like had many children by his wives (wahine) and female retainers (haia wahine). Ka-uhi-'aimoku-a-Kama by Kaha-walu was the first born; Manu-ha'a-ipo, Ke-kau-hiwa-moku and Ka-'eo-[kulani] were the children of Holau; Kamehameha-nui, Ka-lola, Ka-hekili, and Ku-ho'oheihei-pahu, of Ke-ku'i-apo-iwa-nui; Na-mahana and Kekua-manoha', of Ha'alo'u. But it was to Kamehameha-nui that the land descended, according to the command of Ke-kau-like. His mother's children were of higher rank than those of the other wives of Ke-kaulike. By the command of Ka-lani-'opu'u given at Waio'ahukini, the rule over his lands in both Hawaii and Maui descended to his son Kiwala'o'. It was from the families of these two rulers that Kamehameha II and Kamehameha III were descended.

When Ke-kau-like heard that the ruling chief of Hawaii was at Kohala on his way to war against Maui, he was afraid and fled to Wailuku in his double war canoe named Ke-aka-milo.* He sailed with his wives and children . . . his officers, war leaders, chiefs, and fighting men, including warriors, spearmen, and counselors. Some went by canoe and some overland, and the fleet landed at Kapa'ahu at the pit of 'Aihako'ko' in Kula. Here on the shore the chiefs prepared a litter for Kekau-like and bore him upland to Haleki'i in Kukahua. There Ke-kaulike died, and the sound of lamentation for the dead arose. Then, fearing the arrival of Alapa'i bent on war, the chiefs cut the flesh from the bones of Ke-kau-like in order to lighten the load in carrying the body to 'Iao [for burial]. Placing the remains on a canoe, they sailed and landed at Kapoli in Ma'alaea and thence went on to Pu'uhele, to Kaluamanu, to Waikapu', to Wahanemaile, to Kaumu'ilio, to 'Aoakamanu, to Pu'u-'elinapao, to Kaumulanahu, to Kapohako'i, to Kalua, to Kekio, to Kama-'auwai, to Kahua, to Ka'ilipoe, to Kalihi, to Kalua'oiki, to Kihahale,

---

* Ka Nupepa Ku'oko'a, Oct. 20, 1866.

stopped at Ahuwahine, laid him down at Lo'iloa, and put him away at Kapela. It was in the month of March, 1736 that Ke-kau-like died.

Alapa'i sailed from Kohala on Hawaii with a great company of the chiefs of Hawaii, his war leaders, warriors, and the district chiefs of the island, to the great consternation of the chiefs of Maui. But when he landed at Mokulau in Kaupo [Maui] and heard that Ke-kau-like was dying, he gave up all thought of war and wished only to meet Ke-kau-like and his [half] sister Ke-ku'i-apo-iwa-nui. He had heard that Ka-mehameha-nui had been chosen ruler over Maui and he had no desire to make war upon his sister's child. He landed at Kiheipukoa with all his chiefs and fighting men, commanded by the two leaders, Ka-lani-'opu'u and Keoua, who acted as spies over the district for Alapa'i. There the great chief, Alapa'i, son of Ka-uaua son of Mahi, had a friendly meeting with Ke-ku'i-apo-iwa-nui and her son Kamehameha-nui, to whom the land had descended, and with Ka-lola, Ka-hekili, and Ku-ho'oheihei-pahu, the other children of Ke-kau-like by Ke-ku'i-apo-iwa-nui.

While he was at Kihei, Alapa'i heard that the ruling chief of Oahu was making war upon Molokai. Most of the chiefs of Molokai who were being thus ravaged by the ruling chief of Oahu were of Hawaii, children and grandchildren of Keawe. They had fled to the hills, and the ruling chief of Oahu had broken down the sea walls and destroyed their fishponds. Alapa'i's sympathy was aroused, for these were his own brothers and children [relatives], and he made ready to go to their help on Molokai. He sailed from Maui and landed at Puko'o. From Waialua to Kalua'aha the fleet of Hawaii extended. The fighting was in progress at Kamalo'o with Ka-pu-lei as the battlefield. There the forces of Hawaii, joined with those of Molokai, made a formidable array. The chief of Oahu, Ka-pi'i-oho-o-ka-lani, was encamped at Kalama'ula, and the country from Kaunakakai to Na'iwa was occupied by the chiefs and fighting men of Oahu. For four days the fighting went on with equal success on both sides, for Ka-pi'i-oho-o-ka-lani had drawn up his chiefs and fighting men side by side in the shape of a square like the threshold of a door. [With this formation he] drove into the opposing forces, while a right and left wing, formed of lines of men one behind the other in the shape of a flying fish, made attacking and protecting wedges at the two sides. His leaders on the left wing were Kaua-kahi-ali'i-kapu, Ku'ihewa-ka'oko'a, Ka-'ihi-kapu-a-mahana, Kawelo-iki-a-kulu, and Lono-nui-akea; on the right wing, Ka-ho'owaha-kananuha, Ka-ho'oa'-lani, Hua, and Moko-ka-la'i. On the fifth day at Kawela the decisive battle was fought. Every able-bodied man came out of his house to fight. The Molokai forces attacked from the hills, those of Hawaii from the sea, while a great number landed from the fleet and

fought on land. The battle began in the morning and lasted until afternoon. The ruling chief of Oahu found himself surrounded by sea and
by land and hemmed into a small space. Ka-piʻi-oho-o-ka-lani died at
Kawela below Kamiloloa, and many chiefs and fighting men were
slaughtered, but some escaped and sailed for Oahu.

At the close of the war on Molokai, the chiefs were gratified by the
return to them of their lands. Then Alapaʻi determined to sail to Oahu
and take possession of that island; for he had heard that it was without
a ruling chief, Pele-io-holani being at that time ruling chief of Kauai.
Alapaʻi therefore sailed to Oahu with his chiefs and fighting men, accompanied by the chiefs of Molokai. Inquiring about the harbors on
Oahu, he was told by those skilled in such things that, "Waikiki has a
harbor, Waiʻalae has a harbor; these are both good harbors; at Waikiki
and Honolulu live most of the chiefs." Alapaʻi attempted to land at Waikiki, but encountered so much difficulty that he decided to go on to Wai-
ʻalae. Here he was driven back by the warriors of Ka-naha-o-ka-lani, the
six-year-old son of Ka-piʻi-oho-o-ka-lani who had succeeded his father.
Alapaʻi fled and put in at Koko, but was again driven back, and the
same thing happened at Hanauma. Further information about landing
places, perhaps from the experts of Molokai, revealed the fact that the
coast of Oneawa in Koʻolau was an isolated place suitable for the landing of the expedition, and he sailed thither and beached between Kane-
ʻohe and Kailua in Koʻolaupoko, at a good place for camping his numerous forces. There he made preparations for attacking Ka-naha-o-ka-lani,
and appointed Ka-lani-ʻopuʻu and his brother Keoua captains of the
army. A wonderful thing related of the child Ka-naha-o-ka-lani is
that, in every engagement, he directed his forces by the voice alone,
from the shoulders of his attendant.

Upon the arrival of Alapaʻi to war against Oahu, the [Oahu] chiefs
sent for Pele-io-holani, chief of Kauai, to come to their aid. He accordingly arrived with his chiefs and fighting men and joined with those
of Oahu to chastise the chief of Hawaii. Now there was a certain wise
counselor named Na-ʻili, brother to Ka-makaʻi-moku the mother of Ka-
lani-ʻopuʻu and Keoua, who was the chief in charge of Waiʻanae. Ka-
makaʻi-moku was at this time living at Waikele. Said Na-ʻili to Pele-io-
holani, "It would be best for you to put an end to this war and you two
become acquainted with Alapaʻi," and he continued, "You can stop this
war if you will, for the chiefs of Maui and Hawaii are related to you
and that not distantly, for they are your own cousins." "Is Alapaʻi related
to me?" asked Pele-io-holani. "You are a god, and on one side you are
related," answered Na-ʻili. So Pele-io-holani consented to a meeting with
Alapaʻi.

At this time the fighting was going on at Kaulekola in Kane'ohe, and Na-'ili went down to stop the fighting. Approaching Ka-lani-'opu'u and Keoua he kissed their hands and asked, "Where is your uncle?" Ka-lani-'opu'u said, "Alapa'i? He is at the seacoast, at Waihaukalua." "Then stop the fighting and let us go down to the seacoast." The two consented and went down with Na-'ili to the coast with the chiefs and fighting men of Hawaii, and those of Oahu and Kauai also retired. There Na-'ili met Alapa'i, and the two wailed over each other affectionately. "What brings you here?" said Alapa'i. "I have come to stay the battle while you go to meet Pele-io-holani." "Does he consent?" "Yes," answered Na-'ili. So Alapa'i agreed to stay the battle and go to meet Pele-io-holani. Then Na-'ili laid down the terms of the conference. They were to meet at Naoneala'a. The Hawaiian forces were to remain in their canoes; not one was to land on pain of death except Alapa'i himself, and he was to land without a weapon in his hand; likewise in the forces of Kauai and Oahu, if even a single chief bore arms, he was to die.*

It was the custom, when blood relatives went to war with each other and both sides suffered reverses, for some expert in genealogies to suggest a conference to end the war; then a meeting of both sides would take place. So it was that Pele-io-holani and Alapa'i met at Naoneala'a in Kane'ohe, Ko'olaupoko, on Ka'elo 13, 1737, corresponding to our January. The two hosts met, splendidly dressed in cloaks of bird feathers and in helmet-shaped head coverings beautifully decorated with feathers of birds. Red feather cloaks were to be seen on all sides. Both chiefs were attired in a way to inspire admiration and awe, and the day was one of rejoicing for the end of a dreadful conflict. The canoes were lined up from Ki'i at Mokapu to Naoneala'a, and there on the shore line they remained, Alapa'i going ashore alone. The chiefs of Oahu and Kauai, the fighting men, and the country people remained inland, the chief Pele-io-holani advancing alone. Between the two chiefs stood the counselor Na-'ili, who first addressed Pele-io-holani saying, "When you and Alapa'i meet, if he embraces and kisses you let Alapa'i put his arms below yours, lest he gain the victory over you." This is to this day the practice of the bone-breaking wrestlers at Kapua and at Naoneala'a. Alapa'i declared an end of war, with all things as they were before, the chiefs of Maui and Molokai to be at peace with those of Oahu and Kauai, so also those of Hawaii. Thus ended the meeting of Pele-io-holani with Alapa'i.

Alapa'i returned to Molokai to straighten out matters between the chiefs and the country people and enable them to live at peace with the chiefs of Maui and Lanai. Upon arriving at Maui, he found that Ka-

*Ka Nupepa Ku'oko'a, Oct. 27, 1866.

uhi-'aimoku-a-Kama, the oldest son of Ke-kau-like by his wife Kaha-walu, had rebelled against Kamehameha-nui, heir to the island. The occasion for this revolt came when stones were being carried for the building of the heiau of Wailehua. The counselor who incited him to rebellion was a kahuna named Pi-na'au. He said to Ka-uhi, "Let the weak carry stones; the work for the strong is to establish themselves upon the land." Said Ka-uhi, "What shall I do?" Pi-na'au answered, "Go to war, stand at the head of the government." They therefore seized all the food at 'Alamihi and kept it under the control of the fighting men of Ka-uhi, enough to support their needs until they reached the fortress at Kahili. Thus began the war against Kamehameha-nui.

Ka-uhi was a son of Ke-kau-like and a good soldier. He had led the attack in the wars carried on by Ke-kau-like, and was the commander-in-chief in the battles of his father's time. These were the battles of Ki'i-mumuku and Kipuka-'ohelo at Kama'ole, and of Ka-eulu and Ka-hale-mamala-koa at Kaupo, by which he established peace for his father as ruling chief of Maui. Another name for Ka-uhi is Ka-uhi-covered-by-the-shadow-of-the-cresent-moon (Ka-uhi-pu-mai-ka-hoaka).

Kua was the name of Ka-uhi's *kahu*. He went to Alapa'i and said, "I have come to you to demand the kingdom for my chief. Take your chief and make him chief of Hawaii." Alapa'i said, "I consent, but first fetch your chief to confer with me; then, if all is well, I will take my chief to Hawaii as a child of the chiefs." Then Kua ascended the fortified hill of Kahili at midday. He was a man with sore eyes, red and bleary, and was recognized as he ascended the fortified hill. Ka-uhi met him and said, "What is your errand?" Kua answered, "Your uncle, Alapa'i, has sent for you to come and confer with him. Then the kingdom will be yours; he will take Kamehameha-nui to Hawaii. That is my errand to you. So let us go down." Ka-uhi consulted his chiefs, kahunas, and soothsayers in regard to Kua's message. They answered, "To dream of canoes or of *'ulei* berries brings no good luck. So it is with the omens of the day, if you meet the hunchback, the bleary-eyed, or the rainbow in front of your path. This man who has come to you is a double rainbow of ill-luck. That we can all see." Kua said, "O chief, let us go down. Do not heed this nonsense. True counsel is to be had at the sea. Come and speak with Alapa'i." Ka-uhi answered, "I will not go down." Said Kua, "You will become a destitute chief; you despise my words when I come to secure the government for ourselves."

Ka-uhi with his war leader Ku-ka-'e'a and other warriors opened the attack against Kamehameha-nui. It was a great battle from which the forces of Kamehameha-nui fled before those of Ka-uhi. Near the house of David Malo is a breadfruit tree on which the first victim of the battle was laid. There the fighting men of Kamehameha-nui were slaughtered. Kamehameha-nui fled to Alapaʻi's canoe. Alapaʻi said, "I thought that this was a family quarrel, but it seems to be a real war of rebellion!" Alapaʻi returned to Hawaii, taking Kamehameha-nui with him, and made ready to come back and overrun the place and take Ka-uhi prisoner. When Ka-uhi heard that Alapaʻi was returning to war with Maui, he sent a present to Pele-io-holani with the request that he come to help him hold Maui, and Pele-io-holani, ruling chief of Oahu, consented.

A whole year Alapaʻi spent in preparation for the war with Maui. It was in 1738 that he set out for the war in which he swept the country. What was this war like? It employed the unusual method in warfare of drying up the streams of Kauaʻula, Kanaha, and Mahoma (which is the stream near Lahainaluna). The wet taro patches and the brooks were dried up so that there was no food for the forces of Ka-uhi or for the country people. Alapaʻi's men kept close watch over the brooks of Olowalu, Ukumehame, Wailuku, and Honokawai. When Pele-io-holani heard that Alapaʻi was at Lahaina he gathered all his forces at Honokahua and at Honolua. At Honokawai an engagement took place between the two armies, and the forces of Alapaʻi were slaughtered and fled to Keawawa. There Alapaʻi heard that Pele-io-holani had landed at Honokahua and had an army stationed at Keawawa, and he disposed his forces, some on sea and some on land. Although Pele-io-holani had but 640 men against Alapaʻi's 8,440 from the six districts of Hawaii, there were among them some famous warriors, such as Hana, a warrior intimate of Pele-io-holani, Malama-kuhi-ʻena, Moko-ka-laʻi, Kulepe, ʻOpu-hali, Kuakea, Lono-nui-akea, Pa-i-kahawai, Kawelo-iki-a-kulu, and Ka-mahu-a-koaiʻe. Pele-io-holani intended to unite his forces with those of Ka-uhi, but Alapaʻi's men held Lahaina from Ukumehame to Mala on the north, and in attempting to aid Ka-uhi, Pele-io-holani became involved in difficulty.* The hardest fighting, even compared with that at Napili and at Honokahua in Kaʻanapali, took place on the day of the attack at Puʻunene. Pele-io-holani was surrounded on all sides, *mauka* and *makai,* by the forces of Alapaʻi, led by Ka-lani-ʻopuʻu and Keoua. The two ruling chiefs met there again, face to face, to end the war and became friends again, so great had been the slaughter on both sides . . .

Perhaps the reason for this friendliness on the part of the two chiefs was the close relationship that existed between them. Alapaʻi's mother belonged to Oahu. She was Ka-lani-kau-lele-ia-iwi-nui, a daughter of Kane-i-ka-ua-iwi-lani, who was the child of Ka-ua-kahi-a-kuaʻana-au-a-kane, the daughter of Ka-ʻihi-kapu-a-Kuʻihewa. Moreover Ka-lani-

*Ka Nupepa Kuʻokoʻa, Nov. 3, 1866.

'opu'u and Keoua were own sons of Pele-io-holani through their mother Ka-maka'i-moku. While Kuali'i was still ruling Oahu, she had come to visit her mother 'Umi-'ula-i-ka-'ahu-manu, who was living at Waikele with her younger brothers, and it was at the water of Alele just above Waipahu in Waikele, 'Ewa, that Ka-lani-'opu'u was begotten by Pele-io-holani. The ruling chiefs of Oahu wore as a neck ornament an ivory whale's tooth shaped like a bud (*'opu'u*) ; the royal neck ornament of Hawaii was a tongue-shaped hook, like a tortoise-shell fishhook. Pele-io-holani named the child Ka-lei-'opu'u after the bud-shaped neck ornament of his father Kuali'i. Thus he begot Ka-lei-'opu'u.* Keoua he probably begot after he became ruling chief.

At the end of the war Kamehameha-nui became ruling chief of Maui. Pele-io-holani retired to Ko'olau on Molokai with his adviser Na-'ili and his chiefs and fighting men. The counselors of both Hawaii and Maui boasted, "Pele-io-holani, the son of Ku, belongs to Hana!" [has done his work well] W. P. Kina'u the younger, who died recently, was a descendant of the rebel chief. Kamehameha-nui ruled Maui in peace, and Alapa'i held the rule over Hawaii, to which he returned after affairs had quieted down on Maui. He had no occasion to renew the war on Maui as in the time of Ke-kau-like, the father of Kamehameha-nui, who was an ambitious chief, a lover of war and greedy for rule over Hawaii.

Alapa'i was a good ruler, one who loved the common people. His lands he had inherited from his grandfather Mahi-'ololi', the chief who led the battle of Ke-one-'ula at Pohakuomane'o when the chiefess Keakea-lani was ruler. He did not take lands from the chiefs or the commoners. He honored his wives, made feasts for them, and gave them ornaments. The chiefess Ke-aka was his favorite among them. He used to travel about the island and make his home for a time in one place and then in another.

Alapa'i lived for some years in Hilo, and it was while there that Keoua, called Ka-lani-kupu-a-pa-i-ka-lani-nui, fell ill of a lingering sickness at Pi'opi'o adjoining Wailoa in Waiakea and died there in 1752. He was mourned by the chiefs with loud wailing and with swaying of the body (*ma ka ha'a ana*) in token of grief.† His older brother Ka-lani-'opu'u was with his *kahu* Puna above Kalepolepo at the time. Puna was a chief and a famous soldier of Alapa'i's time. He it was whom Ka-lani-'opu'u urged to abduct Kamehameha I for it was rumored, perhaps justly and perhaps not, that Alapa'i was responsible for the death of Keoua.

---

* While this chief's name was Ka-lei-'opu'u, the name which people generally were permitted to use was Ka-lani-'opu'u.

† The swaying motion of an object back and forth is called ha'a. The mourner usually kneels with hands clasped behind the neck or thrown into the air or beating the breast while the body sways back and forth.

After this, began the strife between Ka-lani-'opu'u and Alapa'i. The war began on the night when Ka-lani-'opu'u went to secure Kamehameha. The chiefs were all on the alert, watching the corpse of Keoua, among them Keawe-'opala, the son of Alapa'i, Ka-me'e-ia-moku, Ka-manawa, Ke'e-au-moku, and Keawe-heulu, all chiefs who were "children" of Alapa'i, and brave fighters through whom Alapa'i's rule had been established. Puna, the *kahu* of Ka-lani-'opu'u, had a war canoe ready at a place between Pi'opi'o and Kalepolepo. Ka-lani-'opu'u took a small company with him, and a fight ensued in which he would have been killed save for the proximity of Puna and his war canoe, but Kamehameha was not secured. This was Ka-lani-'opu'u's first battle in his struggle to secure the rule over Hawaii, which finally became his through the efforts of his friends and the younger brothers of Keawe-ma'u-hili.

Ka-lani-'opu'u and Keoua were the hereditary heirs to the land of Hawaii, for it had belonged to their father, Ka-lani-nui-'i-a-mamao, and [his brother] Ka-lani-ke'e-au-moku; but Alapa'i had seized it through force of arms and had slain the inheritors. Alapa'i was a chief of high rank. Ka-lani-kau-lele-ia-iwi was his mother as well as the mother of Ka-lani-ke'e-au-moku. His father was Ka-uaua-a-Mahi, whose father, Mahi-'ololi', was executive officer (*Kuhina kaua nui*) for the chiefess Keakea-lani while she held the government of Hawaii.

After the fight at Kalepolepo there was another battle between Alapa'i and Ka-lani-'opu'u with their chiefs and soldiers at Pa'ie'ie adjoining Pua'aloa. Thereafter a great battle was fought at Kualoa and Mokaulele all the way to Mahinaakaka, at which Ka-lani-'opu'u almost lost his life. Hemmed in on all sides, he slipped on the *pahoehoe* [smooth lava rock] and two men seized him, one on either side; but he put forth all his strength, killing four of the soldiers. When two more came up and seized him he held them off, one with one hand and one with the other, and chanted these words:

He moku Ka'ula i hoa me Ni'ihau,	An island is Ka'ula connected with Niihau,
I kaulua ia Kawaihoa a Kane,	On both are the waters brought forth by Kane,
O kaulana a ka la i Halali'i la,	The sun shines over Halali'i there,
Hala ka la nalo ma Lehua,	The sun passes on and vanishes at Lehua,
Hiki ka molehulehu o ke ahiahi,	The dusk of evening comes,

Moe e no Kauai iluna ka la,   Kauai sleeps ere the sun goes
                                       down,

E ao ana no Lehua i ke kai.   Lehua lies bright in the sea.*

[Paraphrased, the lines mean: These two men I am holding both have
life from Kane. They are men in full strength. They are soon to die.
Early death comes to them. Glorious in battle am I.] Ka-lani-'opu'u's
men were victorious that day, and the chief realized how powerful his
following was in chiefs and fighting men and how strong he himself
was to break men's bones with his hands.†

After this battle at Mahinaakaka, Ka-lani-'opu'u ruled over Ka-'u
and Puna, for he was a native of Ka-'u. There were the birth sands of
his ancestors. Alapa'i dwelt in Hilo for a year and then went to live
in Waipi'o. Shortly after, he and the chiefs moved to Waimea and
others went by canoe to Kawaihae. From Waimea he went to Lani-
maomao, where he fell ill. Later he moved to Kikiako'i in Kawaihae.
There his illness became serious, and at Kikiako'i in the heiau of
Mailekini, Kawaihae, he appointed his son Keawe-'opala to be ruler
over the island.‡

---

* The rock islet of Ka'ula lies farthest west of any land in the group, and the
mention of this island and of the rock islet of Lehua west of Niihau suggests the
sunset which to the Hawaiian, as to so many other peoples symbolizes death. *Ka
wai hoa a Kane,* (The newly discovered waters of Kane) are the springs of fresh
water which Kane, incited by Kanaloa, caused to flow out of the rock at various
places in their travels over the islands. Pukui has collected such stories from Oahu,
Beckwith from Maui. Reference is made to the waters of Kane in 5, pp. 131-133;
40, pp. 32-37; 19, p. 152. *Ke ko 'eli lima o Halali'i* refers to a famous place on
Niihau where the sand used to drift so that only the leaves of the sugar cane
planted there showed above it, and the stalk had to be dug out from under the sand
by hand.

† The art of bone-breaking, called *lua* "was much practiced in ancient times
and is understood now by some old people," writes Andrews, in "A Dictionary of
the Hawaiian Language," Honolulu, 1865, but no description of its technique was
ever recorded. Andrews also mentions, "noosing men in order to murder them, as
practiced in Kauai," under the head of *lua.*

‡ *Ka Nupepa Ku'oko'a,* Nov. 10, 1866.

CHAPTER VII

Hawaii Under Ka-lani-'opu'u

It was in 1754 that Keawe-'opala succeeded to the chieftainship over the island, with the chiefs and all his relatives placed under him. A number of the chiefs, however, who were deprived of their lands murmured against him and put up a fight against him, among them some of his own relatives such as Ke'e-au-moku, Keawe-poepoe, and Ku-mai-ku; but because of the number of his supporters the battle went against them. This fight was called Kai-omo and Moku-kohekohe because the coast was so well defended that there was no place to land, and the battle had to be carried on at sea.

A canoe arrived from Kekaha and brought word to Ke'e-au-moku that Ka-lani-'opu'u was at Kapalilua [in south Kona] and was coming to make war against Keawe-'opala. Ke'e-au-moku therefore made up his mind to join forces with Ka-lani-'opu'u, and at Honomalino in Kapalilua Ke'e-au-moku came to offer his support to Ka-lani-'opu'u. When Keawe-'opala heard that Ke'e-au-moku had thus given his support to Ka-lani-'opu'u, he made ready his forces with Ka-moho-'ula as their leader, a famous fighter and skillful in maneuvering a battle. He sent his forces into South Kona by the east side of Hualalai, on the slope of Pae, and from thence to Kuapehu. Between Ke'ei and Honaunau lay the battlefield. It was bad land, with rough lava underfoot, stony and full of holes, and demanded skillful fighters. Keawe-'opala held the larger part of Kona. Those were days of constant fighting. Sometimes one side was victorious, sometimes the other, and this prolonged the war. At last Ka-lani-'opu'u's kahuna, Holo-'ae, told him that in order to defeat Keawe-'opala he must first kill Keawe's kahuna, Ka-'akau, since he was the one who held the rule in Keawe-'opala's favor. Both Ka-'akau and Holo-'ae had been kahunas of Alapa'i. Holo-'ae now served Ka-lani-'opu'u as Ka-'akau served Keawe-'opala, and Ka-'akau was seized and cruelly put to death and baked by Ka-lani-'opu'u.*

In the year 1754 Ka-lani-'opu'u became ruler over the island of Hawaii. He was the son of Ka-lani-nui-'i-a-mamao, the ruling chief of Ka-'u and first-born of the ruling chief over all Hawaii, Keawe-i-

---

* *Ka Nupepa Ku'oko'a*, Nov. 10, 1866.

kekahi ali'i-o-ka-moku, by Lono-ma'a-i-kanaka, the daughter of Ahu-a-I. The mother of Ka-lani-'opu'u was Ka-maka'i-moku, the daughter of Ku-a-nu'uanu and 'Umi-'ula-i-ka-'ahu-manu. Ka-lani-'opu'u administered his lands by placing some chiefs as landlords over the divisions of the island, called *moku*, some over the *'okana*, and some over the *ahupua'a*, and appointing landlords (*konohiki*) over small divisions of land such as *ahupua'a-li'ili'i* and *ili-'ai'aina* within the larger *ahupua'a*. Thus he divided the land among his chiefs and fighting men. He had many kahunas skilled in canoe cutting, many fishermen, and men who were strong paddlers. He selected wise counselors (*po'e kaka'olelo*), soothsayers (*po'e kilo*), and men skilled in laying out buildings (*po'e kuhikuhi pu'uone*). Ka-ua-kahi-a-kaha-ola of Kauai, a man skilled in giving counsel, became famous as a counselor in the time of Ka-lani-'opu'u and was his intimate friend. Kiko'o was a man skilled as a counselor, so also were Kai, Ka'a-loa, Ka-palaoa, and Pu'uone. Among the chiefs in the time of Ka-lani-'opu'u were many who were overseers of the army, many warrior chiefs, many leaders of maneuvers, and many instructors in knowledge. The business of war was the principal occupation of Ka-lani-'opu'u's age, which produced Keoua Kuahu-'ula, killed at Kawaihae, Keoua Pe'e-'ale, and Pauli Ka-'o-lei-o-Ku, the first-born son of Ku-nui-akea Kamehameha (Kamehameha I).

A clever chief was Ka-lani-'opu'u and an able one, famous as an athlete in all games of strength such as *honuhonu, uma, mokomoko, wala*.* But he had one great fault; he loved war and display and had no regard for another's right over land, as we shall see in his wars on Maui. Kamehameha-nui was the ruling chief of Maui, the first-born child of Ke-ku'i-apo-iwa-nui by Ka-lani-ku'i-hono-i-ka-moku (Ke-kau-like), and brother of Ka-lola, wife of Ka-lani-'opu'u, ruling chief of Hawaii. But little did Ka-lani-'opu'u care for this relationship. When he had completed the regulation of his lands on Hawaii and had lived at peace for a number of years, he went to war in 1759 with East Maui and made Hana and Kipahulu a part of Hawaii without regard for his wife, Ka-lola, and the chiefs of Maui.

Many chiefs from Hawaii at this time settled on Maui, some of them grandchildren of Keawe. As governor of the new territory and commander of the fortified hill of Ka'uiki Ka-lani-'opu'u appointed one Puna, a chief of the family of Moana who had been his *kahu*

---

* *Wala* (to be thrown backward) is a term for a certain play in a wrestling match; *uma* is a hand-pushing contest. In *honuhonu* the players sat facing with the left foot bent under and right foot extended, the right hand resting on the opponent's shoulder, the left against his side, and each tried to push the other over. This contest was popular because there was no danger of injury involved.

at the time Hawaii became his. Kiko'o, an expert in war maneuvers and a skilled orator, was his adviser, and Puna himself was a famous warrior. After Ka-lani-'opu'u's return to Hawaii, leaving Puna in charge, Kamehameha-nui came to make war upon Puna. This was a famous struggle on both sides. The chiefs of Molokai, including Ka-'ohele, Ka-'olohaka-a-Keawe, 'Awili, Kumu-ko'a, and Ka-po'e-loku, allied themselves with the ruler of Maui; the chiefs of Lanai also including Na-makeha', Kalai-manuia, Ke-ali'i-'a'a; and those of Maui who belonged to Kamehameha-nui's family, children of Ke-kau-like, as well as the veteran chiefs and their fighting men. Ka-pali-pilo is the name of this war because of the multitude of those engaged in it; from Heleikeoho to Nahiku the men were massed. The field of battle extended from Makaolehua in Akiala to Kawaihau in Honoma'ele. The hill of Ka'uiki was the fortified ground for the Hawaiian forces, a fortress celebrated in ancient days for its strength as a refuge in time of danger. It was ascended by a ladder, the body of which was made of 'ohi'a wood from Kealakomo, fastened with withes of 'ie vine from Paiolopawa. The summit was covered with kanawao plants from Kawaipaka [to serve as bedding]. The contents of the fishponds of Kihahale were heaped like an ocean on Ka'uiki. Big 'awa roots of Kualakila delighted the nostrils of the precious first-born chiefs with their aroma. Wananalua was the battlefield and the fortified walls of Ka'uiki. From Mokuhana came the whistle warning where to strike the leaping whales [their opponents]. Hana was a land beloved by chiefs because of the fortress of Ka'uiki and the ease of living there.

Long the war lasted between Kamehameha-nui and the chiefs of Hawaii. In one of the most desperate struggles they were joined by Ka'ohele, a chief from Molokai celebrated for his skill and strength. He would toss an antagonist in mid-air and tear at him, so that he was helplessly mangled when he reached the earth. Ka-makau-ki'i, a famous fighter from Hawaii, was a swift runner, so strong and sure with the spear thrust or other death-dealing weapon that he never missed a hair or even a louse on a man's head, and so quick was his grasp that he could catch a bird before it took wing. It was at Makaolehua that Ka-'ohele fought with Ka-makau-ki'i. That famous warrior got ready his sharp weapons in order to kill Ka-'ohele. Said Ka-'ohele to Ka-makau-ki'i, "O Ka-makau-ki'i, break off the point of the spear!" Ka-makau-ki'i answered, "I will not break off the point of my spear for you." It was love for Ka-makau-ki'i that made Ka-'ohele speak thus, because they had been reared together on Molokai. But since his going to live in Hawaii

Ka-makau-ki'i cared only for the glory of war. He exhausted his deadly weapons in the first attack on Ka-'ohele. The long and the short spears came rattling down thick as the leaves of the 'ohi'a and hala and beat down like raindrops upon Ka-'ohele. But Ka-'ohele stood with the spears forming a heap of defense on both sides of him. When Ka-makau-ki'i had exhausted his supply Ka-'ohele said, "To-morrow my god shall devour you."

The second day of the fight the battlefield lay between Akiala and Kewaikau where waved the coconut leaves of La'ahana and rustled the hala leaves of Pi'iholo. Ka-makau-ki'i did not appear among the fighters that day; he was among the reserves. But Ka-'ohele kept close watch of him, and because of his wish to meet him Ka-'ohele sprang into the midst of the conflict. The spears rained down upon him, and he bathed himself in them, seizing them with his right hand and with his left so that they fell harmless as grass before the wind, and the soldiers of Hawaii were tossed here and there like rubbish in a whirlwind in the rush of his onset. Ka-makau-ki'i, per-ceiving Ka-'ohele leaning toward him, turned to flee as fast as he could go. Ka-'ohele was hampered by the obstacles in his path; there was half a mile between them before he could get a fair start. The districts through which he pursued Ka-makau-ki'i were the ahupua'a of Honoma'ele, Kawela, two Ku'uku'ukamanu, two Kahalili, two Ka'eleku, Honokalani, Wakiu, and half of Kawaipapa. He overtook him at Waialanahu near Pihehe and thrust him through the scrotum with a spear. Ka-'ohele then returned to the slaughter of the soldiers of Hawaii. Ka-'ohele was a brave soldier and swift runner, a man of pleasing countenance and fine physique. But in spite of the chiefs and fighting men whom he thus slew on the side of Hawaii the fort did not surrender, and Kamehameha-nui retired leaving Hana in the hands of Hawaii.

While Hana was under the governorship of Puna there came one Mahi-hele-lima from Hawaii, older brother of Kane-kapolei, and he spoke craftily to Puna, saying, "Your child, Ka-lani-'opu'u, has sent me to get you to come to him for a secret conference, and I will meanwhile guard the fort for you." Puna consented, and Mahi-hele-lima rejoiced that his lying words had been believed. By sending Puna to Hawaii he gained the governorship of the forces on Maui and of the fortress of Ka'uiki. Puna went to Hawaii and found Ka-lani-'opu'u, who denied that he had sent for him. Then Puna knew that Mahi-hele-lima had lied to him and he said, "Ka! the cock's roost has been taken by the hen!" But he was unable to dispossess him, for Mahi-hele-lima occupied the cock's roost. He was an independent chief of Hana, Kipahulu, and

Kaupo districts, and his ancestors, both parents and grandparents, had been governing chiefs of that district.

After the war of Kapalipilo, Kamehameha-nui remained ruling chief of Maui, and he ruled for twenty-nine years. He had many wives and children, among the latter of whom were Pe'ape'a, Ka-lani-ulu-moku, and Ka-lani-hele-mai-i-luna; but none of his own children succeeded to the rule over Maui. He was taken ill at Kawaipapa on a journey about the island, and at Nenewepua in Kahalahili in Hana he ceded the lands and the ruling power to Ka-hekili, who became ruler of Maui. Reaching Hamakualoa, Kamehameha-nui died and was laid at Pihana and afterward removed to Moanui on Molokai. He was a benevolent ruler and his government was peaceful; he did not war upon chiefs of other lands or make raids upon Hawaii, Molokai, and Oahu.*

In the year 1766 Ka-hekili-nui-'ahu-manu became ruling chief of the island of Maui. He was a chief who delighted in the sport of *lelekawa*, that is cliff-leaping into a pool of water, and he is known to have leaped from a height of 360, possibly 400 feet. His favorite leaping places about Maui are well known. It was his whim to have one side of his body tattooed from head to foot. He had a weak voice, but was strong in war, an intelligent chief and a thoughtful one who kept watch at night for those who murmured or spoke evil or plotted rebellion against him. He did not sleep with women, but withdrew to a hill and built his house there. Before he became ruling chief he had a number of children by his wives. By Kau-wahine he had Ka-lani-ku-pule, Koa-lau-kani, Ka-lola, and Ka-lili-kauoha; by Luahiwa, daughter of Kane-'alai of Molokai, he had Manono Ka-ua-kapeku-lani. From his name Ka-hekili-nui-'ahu-manu comes the name of Ka-'ahu-manu [the favorite wife of Kamehameha]. Ka-hekili ruled Maui for twenty-seven years and Oahu for nine years, from the year 1782 when the battle of Honolulu took place.

For some years after Kamehameha-nui's death in 1766 and the accession of Ka-hekili, the chiefs of Maui lived in peace under his rule. But Ke'e-au-moku, son of Keawe-poepoe, had rebelled against Ka-lani-'opu'u and had come with his mother Ku-ma'ai-ku to live on Maui, to whose chiefs they were related. On Hawaii Ke'e-au-moku had set up a fort on a hill between Pololu and Honokane. Ka-lani-'opu'u had climbed the mountain and attacked him, but he got to the sea by being let down by rope over the cliff, and escaped by boat. This battle was called "Itching rock" (Pohaku-o-mane'o) and "Tearing crab" (Papa'i-haehae). Ke'e-au-moku was cordially received by the chiefs of Maui until, after the death of the ruling chief, he took as wife Na-mahana, the tabu wife of

* *Ka Nupepa Ku'oko'a*, Dec. 1, 1866.

Kamehameha-nui to whom she had borne Pele-io-holani and Kua-kini. This displeased Ka-hekili, who regarded it as an act of rebellion against his own authority. Na-mahana had inherited the district of Waihe'e where her mother, Ha'alo'u, lived with her husband Ke-kau-hiwa-moku and with Ka-lani-ku-i-ka-po'oloku and other chiefs of Molokai and Kumu-ko'a and other chiefs of Maui, for Molokai had surrendered to Pele-io-holani of Oahu.

In the year 1765 a quarrel arose among the descendants of the chief Ke-kau-like Ka-lani-ku'i-hono-i-ka-moku. Ka-hekili was living at Pihana, at Pukukalo, and at Wailuku with the chiefs, his companions and favorites, and his warriors, Ka-niu-'ula and Ke-po'o-uahi. The chiefs of Wailuku passed their time in the surf of Kehu and Ka'akau, those of Waiehu and Napoko in the surfs of Niukukahi and 'A'awa, while those of Waihe'e were accustomed to amuse themselves in the surfs of Pala'ie and Kahahawai. The quarrel arose through a certain soldier of the guard named Ka-hahana who belonged to Ke'e-au-moku and lived at Ka'apoko within the district of Waihe'e. This man went every day to his plantation and when he returned at night his wife cooked the taro tops. The chiefs distributed fish to the people and left out this man and his wife. Now Waihe'e had good fishing in ancient times; there were *maomao, a'ua'u, he'e,* and *'ohua,* besides fish that came at special seasons, like *nehu* and *piha',* but the chiefs were constantly depriving the people of their fishing rights. Ka-hahana said, "The chiefs with their women have pleasant eating of food and pig and fish. There is no one yet to interfere. The breakers roll into the harbor, the waves roll high, no one sees who the surfers are." [That is, anger rises in the heart and he will be avenged.]* Then he put on his feather cloak and helmet and went to Niukukahi and slew a man, and he seized and slew two others. Thus the battle began and lasted all that day and the next with loss on both sides, neither side having the advantage. Ka-lae-'ili'ili was the name of this battle. Ke'e-au-moku and the chiefs of Molokai fled, some by canoe and some by the mountains of Lanilili and Eke, to Ka'anapali whence Ke'e-au-moku, Na-mahana, Ha'alo'u, Ke-kua-manoha', Ka-uhi-wawae-ono, and all the families of the chiefs landed on Molokai. After a time Ka-hekili sailed to Molokai,

---

* The Hawaiian text reads, "I le'ale'a ka 'ai ana a na 'lii i ka 'ai, a me na laulau, me na ho'olua, a me ka i'a, 'ono kana 'ai ana me na wahine; i ke ka 'ole ia i ka pohuehue, kaiko'o ke awa, popo'i ka nalu, 'a'ole i ikeia ka poe nana e he'e ka nalu." [The chiefs enjoy eating *poi* and *laulau* and meat cooked in ti leaves and fish. Food eaten with the wives is delicious because the *pohuehue* vine had not been smitten to cause rough sea in the harbor where the billows roll so that the riders of the surf could not be seen.] This hidden threat refers to the practice of beating the waves with a length of *pohuehue* (*convolvulus*) vine such as grows by the seashore in order to secure good waves for surfing.

and a battle was fought there against Ke'e-au-moku called Ka-lau-o-na-kukui, and Ke'e-au-moku and his company fled by sea and landed at Hana, the eastern stronghold of Maui where Mahi-hele-lima was commander, and lived on the fortified hill of Ka'uiki. At this time was born Ka-'ahu-manu, the famous chiefess of the time of the Kamehamehas.

From the years 1775 to 1779 there was continual fighting between Ka-lani-'opu'u of Hawaii and Ka-hekili. Ka-lani-'opu'u and his forces raided Kaupo, abused the country people, and beat them over the head with clubs. This battle was called "The forehead beaten with clubs" (Ka-lae-hohoa). When Ka-hekili heard of Ka-lani-'opu'u's raid upon the Kaupo people and the seizure of their property, he sent soldiers from Niu'ula and Kepo'ouwahi, led by Kane-'olaelae; they fought at Pu'umaneone and Ka-puka-'auhuhu, and Ka-lani-'opu'u was routed. Kane-'olaelae concentrated the battle among the potato hills facing Ki'ei. The attack was led from below by Kane-'olaelae through the furrows between the hills of potatoes in direct line from Ka-lae-o-ka-'ilio, the right wing facing Pahonu and the left wing on the east of the cliff of Waipu. Kane-'olaelae was victor in the encounter and slaughtered the soldiers of Hawaii as they ascended the long hill toward Kiha-puhala. At Pa'auhau they made a stand and prolonged the struggle, then found refuge in their fleet and rested under the lee of "The point of the dog" (Ka-lae-o-ka-'ilio). In this battle the most noted warrior on the side of Hawaii was Ke-ku-hau-pi'o. He stayed the flight of the army among the furrows of the potato patch until he got entangled in the vines, and was saved only by the prompt action of Kamehameha, who brought men to his rescue. Had it not been for Kamehameha, Ke-ku-hau-pi'o would have been killed that day. Ka-lani-'opu'u and his party fled by canoe, Kane-'olaelae and his men pursuing and killing until they reached Ka-lae-o-ka-'ilio. Here Kane-'olaelae whirled his battle club in sign of victory over Ka-lani-'opu'u, the chief of Hawaii, and from this act the battle takes its name. This was the first battle in which Kamehameha became noted as a soldier, through the saving of the man who had been his master in the arts of warfare and in the profession of the kahuna. The chiefs and fighting men of Maui gave the name of Pai'ea (Hard-shelled crab) to this favorite warrior of Ka-lani-'opu'u.

Ka-lani-'opu'u returned to Hawaii embittered against Ka-hekili by the realization of his defeat, and spent a year in preparing an army made up of a body of men from each of the six districts of the island, each division led by a warrior chief. He gave to each division a name; there were I, Ahu, Mahi, Palena, Luahine, and Pa'ia. The war chief was called a Keawe. His own attendants, selected from the chiefs who excelled as soldiers, Ka-lani-'opu'u called the Alapa and the Pi'ipi'i. He built houses for his war god Ka'ili, 'Ohi'a-mukumuku at Kahalu'u, and Keiki-pu'ipu'i at Kailua as heiaus against sedition and for vengeance upon the chief of Maui. Holo-'ae was his leading kahuna, whose grandchildren were Pu'ou and Hewahewa, and he belonged to the order of Pa'ao. When Ka-hekili heard that Ka-lani-'opu'u was building heiaus for his defeat, he sent for Ka-leo-pu'upu'u, a kahuna of the order of Kaka'e, Maliu, and Malela, who had been Pele-io-holani's kahuna before his death. Under the direction of this kahuna he built the heiau of Kaluli at Pu'uohala on the north side of Wailuku; and when it was completed, the image erected, and the service successfully ended, (*i ke kaka'i ana o ka 'aha, a maika'i*), Ka-leo-pu'upu'u said to Ka-hekili, "This is the house of your god; open the sluice gate that the fish may enter."

In the year 1776 Ka-lani-'opu'u and the chiefs returned to war on Maui, and in the battle with Ka-hekili's forces at Wailuku were completely overthrown. The army landed at Keone'o'io, their double canoes extending to Makena at Honua'ula. There they ravaged the countryside, and many of the people of Honua'ula fled to the bush. When Ka-hekili heard of the fighting at Honua'ula he got his forces together—chiefs, fighting men, and left-handed warriors whose sling-shots missed not a hair of the head or a blade of grass.[*] Ka-lani-'opu'u landed his forces before noon, a great multitude filling the land from Kiheipuko'a at Kealia to Kapa'ahu, all eager with the thought that the Alapa were to drink of the waters of Wailuku. The Alapa were led by Inaina, Kua'ana, Kane-ha'i-lua, and Keawe-hano. There were 800 of them, all expert spear-point breakers, every one of whose spears went straight to the mark, like arrows shot from a bow, to drink the blood of a victim. Across the plains of Pu'u'ainako (Cane-trash-hill) and Kama'oma'o shone the feather cloaks of the soldiers, woven in the ancient pattern and colored like the hues of the rainbow in red, yellow, and green, with helmets on their heads whose arcs shone like a night in summer when the crescent lies within the moon. Ka-hekili was at Kalanihale just below Kihahale and above the plateau of Ka'ilipoe at Pohakuokahi. Said Ka-leo-pu'upu'u to Ka-hekili, "The fish have entered the sluice; draw in the net." Like a dark cloud hovering over the Alapa, rose the destroying host of Ka-hekili seaward of the sandhills of Kahulu'u, the "smoke head" (*po'ouahi*) and the "red coconut" (*niu'ula*) divisions. They slew the Alapa on the sandhills at the southeast of Kalua. There the deal lay

[*] *Ka Nupepa Ku'oko'a*, Dec. 8, 1866.

in heaps strewn like *kukui* branches; the corpses lay heaped in death; they were slain like fish enclosed in a net. This great slaughter was called *Ahulau ka Pi'ipi'i i Kakanilua* (Slaughter-of-the-Pi'ipi'i-at-Kaka-nilua). Keawe-hano, the governing chief of Hilo, was discovered by Ka-po-lua almost dead among the heap of corpses, and he alone was taken alive before Ka-hekili, because of an agreement between Ka-po-lua and Keawe-hano [that each should spare the other in battle]; but it was too late to save him for he was fatally injured.

Only two men escaped, perhaps over the top of the net when it was drawn, slipping past Manu Hopu who was at Wailua on the Ko'olau side and running along by deserted places. At Kiheipuko'a Ka-lani-'opu'u was just boastfully exclaiming to the chiefess Ka-lola and to Ka-lani-kau-i-ke-aouli Kiwala'o, "My Alapa have perhaps drunk of the waters of Wailuku!" believing that his forces would slaughter those of Ka-hekili and the chiefs of Maui, when one of the refugees stood before him and said, "O heavenly one! our men are lost; we two remain to tell of our escape. The chiefs Inaina, Kane-ha'i-lua, Kua'ana, Keawe-hano and the whole host of the Alapa are dead." When Ka-lani-'opu'u heard of the death of his men upon whose strength and skill he had depended, the dart of whose spear was like lightning, the tongue of whose sharp-pointed spear was like the upper jaw of the shark, like the tiger shark that circles the islands, he leaned his head against his hands, pressing them against his forehead, grasped his nose with one hand and pulled at it with a mournful wailing for the dead. A chill struck him, overwhelming him with the thought of the swiftness of this utter annihilation of his wild dogs, his ferocious guards, his spotted pigs that bared their teeth, all wiped out by the fearless soldiers of Ka-hekili.

Ka-lani-'opu'u turned to his defenders, the chiefs of Hawaii—to Keawe-ma'u-hili, the Keawe whose tabu was doubly twisted, twisted into knots, woven in and out, broken from the topmost branch of the expanding I family with the Mahi and the Ahu under his feet; to Ka-lani-mano-o-ka-ho'owaha-a-heulu, the highest on both sides of the Palea, that is of the Leapa; to I-maka-koloa, the dark 'awa among the hala blos-soms of Puna; to Nu'u-anu-pa'ahu, tearer-up of the cutworms of Na'alehu, the hillside that withstands the winds of Ka-'u; to Nae-'ole, growler of Kohala at Wahilani; to Kane-koa also, like the big cold raindrops of Waimea; to Nanue Ka-lei-opu, the sandpiper of Hamakua; to Ka-me'e-ia-moku and Kamanawa, the twins of the burning tabu of Ke-kau-like; to Ke-ku-hau-pi'o, the grandchild of Holo-'ae, the teacher who trained Kamehameha I in warfare; and to the royal sons and cousins of Ka-lani-ʻopuʻu, his friends and favorites, the warrior chiefs of Hawaii and the fighting men, and asked, "What about fighting Ka-hekili?" Everyone answered, "Tomorrow we will drink the waters of Wailuku and rest in the shade of Hekuawa." Thus encouraged, Ka-lani-ʻopuʻu prepared for an attack on the day following.

Ka-hekili was the younger brother of Kamehameha-nui, both being sons of Ke-kau-like whose family were ruling chiefs on Maui at that time. He prepared for the battle and Ka-hahana, the ruling chief of Oahu and Molokai, came to his aid. The great battle took place between Waikapu and Wailuku. Ka-lani-ʻopuʻu expected to enter Wailuku at Kakanilua, but Ka-hekili's men rose at dawn and occupied the sandhills of Kamaʻomaʻo, and a portion of them took their stand on the side toward Waikapu turn, so that the forces of Ka-lani-ʻopuʻu, who had supposed that the battle would be at Kakanilua, found a divided front from which spears, javelins, and other missiles poured like water. Death-dealing weapons poured down like a swift rainstorm beating the sides of the fisherman's canoe and agitating the surface of the sea like a cloudburst over the deep ocean. The terrified soldiers were surrounded and took to flight; they were driven by Ka-hekili's men like leaves before a whirlwind. The plains of Kamaʻomaʻo became like a fishpond through whose sluice gate the sea flooded, Ka-lani-ʻopuʻu's men [became] like the mullet driven by the sound of beating into the sluice gate of ʻUkoʻa; and the sea rose up to the walls. Like the fiery petals of the lehua blossoms of Piʻiholo were the soldiers of Ka-hekili, red among the leaves of the *koa* trees of Lilikoʻi or as one glimpses them through the *kukui* trees of Haʻiku. Like the creeping branches of the *ʻulei*, so moved the cloaked warriors, young and middle-aged, over the *ʻilima*-covered plain of Paholei. A chill seized Ka-lani-ʻopuʻu as he crouched in the canoe, mourning the dead who lay like fish stupefied by the poison spread by the great fisherman, Ka-hekili. Like grasshoppers on the plain, easily to be caught by women, so they lay in the heat of the sun snuggled close to the blossoms of the grasses.

Ke-ku-hau-piʻo was the most famous of the warriors of Hawaii that day. He had fought his way through and was supposed to be safe with the fleet when he was but facing the onset. A certain famous soldier of Ka-hekili named Ouli was so skilled with the sling that he could send a shot like a ball from a gun with the swiftness of lightning and a roar like thunder. Ke-ku-hau-piʻo taunted him, saying, "Where the *ʻala* stone of Ouli strikes below the soles of Ke-ku-hau-piʻo's feet, there it bursts into flame to warm them."

Of Ouli's second shot he made an offering to Ku-ka'ili-moku. At the third shot he jeered, "Say, Ouli, let me have that stone!" Ouli sent his shots like lightning, reverberating like the sound of thunder in Kona or the roar of an earthquake, shriveling the 'ilima. A distance of two miles the shots traveled.

When Ka-lani-'opu'u saw that the forces of Hawaii were surrounded by Ka-hekili's men he said to Ka-lola his chiefess, "O Hono-ka-wai-lani! we shall all be killed. Do go up to your brother Ka-hekili to sue for peace." Ka-lola answered, "It will not do any good for me to go, for we came to deal death. If we had come offering love we should have been received with affection. I can do nothing. Our only hope lies in Ka-lani-kau-i-ke-aouli Kiwala'o." "Perhaps Ka-hekili will kill my child," said Ka-lani-'opu'u. "Ka-hekili will not kill him. We will send Ka-hekili's half brothers with him, Ka-me'e-ia-moku and Ka-manawa." So Kiwala'o was dressed in the garments of a chief and attended by Ka-me'e-ia-moku bearing the spittoon and Ka-manawa carrying the kahili. As Kiwala'o advanced, splendidly arrayed, endowed with the tabu of a god and covered with the colors of the rainbow, down fell the fighting men of both sides prostrate to the ground because of his divine rank as a ni'aupi'o and the severe tabu which demanded prostration to avoid facing the sacred back of a chief. The soldiers of Maui wished to ignore the tabu, regretting the cessation of the fighting, but Kiwala'o continued on to Wailuku.

Ka-hekili had not come to the battle in person but was at the chief's house in Wailuku where he had gathered together the old men and women, the children, and a great host. When the twins and Kiwala'o saw the multitude they said, "We imagined that he was in the midst of a school of fish, but it is only red sea moss." When, at the arrival of Kiwala'o, Ka-hekili heard the words, "Here is your child," he turned his face upward [as a sign of a favorable reception]. Kiwala'o entered and sat on his chest; and they kissed each other and wailed. Afterward the twins crawled forward and kissed the hands of Ka-hekili. Kiwala'o, being tabu, could not be addressed directly. Ka-hekili accordingly asked them, "Why do you two bring the chief here? If you are in trouble you should have come up here yourselves, lest without my knowledge your chief be killed." The twins answered, "We do not believe that the chief will be killed. It is we who would have been killed had we left the chief at the shore. The chief has been sent to ask for life. Grant us our lives. If the chief dies, we two will die with him (moe-pu'u). So our royal brother commanded." Ka-hekili replied, "There is no death to be dealt out here. Let live!

Let the battle cease!" and he asked, "Where is your sister [referring to Ka-lola]?" "At the shore, at Kiheipuko'a, and it was she who sent us to the chief," answered Ka-manawa. Then Ka-hekili said to his followers, "Take the fish of Kanaha and Mau'oni and the vegetable food of Nawaieha down to Kiheipuko'a." So the two chiefs became reconciled, but Ka-lani-'opu'u's was a feigned friendship.*

Not many years later, Ka-lani-'opu'u, perhaps nursing his hatred because of his former failure, prepared to ravage the land of Maui and, sailing to Kaupo, clubbed the commoners to death on all sides. Ka-hekili, hearing of this, prepared his men for war. Ka-lani-'opu'u set sail, touched at Kaho'olawe, and from there went on to Lahaina. The people fled to Ka'anapali, and the chiefs and soldiers occupied the fortified hill of Kahili, situated just above Pa'upa'u between Kaua'ula and Kanaha. Thither Ka-lani-'opu'u sent his soldiers, and on the broad plain of Haleili at the turn above Pa'upa'u the fighting began with much slaughter on both sides. Among the valiant soldiers of Hawaii were two, Ke-ku-hau-pi'o and Kamehameha, who fought close to the fortress of Kahili. A certain two-handed soldier in the fortress, named Pua, let drive a spear with his right hand, which Ke-ku-hau-pi'o saw and dodged. Then with his left hand Pua drove another spear, which struck Ke-ku-hau-pi'o below the abdomen and stuck there. Ke-ku-hau-pi'o however did not die at this time, but lived to see, as ruling chief, Kamehameha who had distinguished himself for bravery in this battle. Ka-hahana, ruling chief of Oahu and Molokai, had sent soldiers to aid Ka-hekili. When he asked the returning soldiers how the battle had gone they said, "There was one bit of a soldier of Hawaii named Kamehameha, whom they call an *aikane* of Ka-lani-'opu'u. He was a brave little fellow."

A certain counselor from Hawaii, named Ke-a-ulu-moku, who was with Ka-hahana, often heard these words repeated about Kamehameha, and he was ashamed to be living with Ka-hahana, the ruling chief of Oahu. He was grieved to hear those jeering words spoken of Kamehameha. Bowing his body he composed a mele and, lifting up his head, instantly gave utterance to it, as follows:

Ouiui a Wa'a-kia-loa ke kane	Wa'a-kia-loa, the man, turned to question
Na Ku ka manu e ui anei,	The birds of Ku,
Uia ia Ki'i, ia Uli, ia Nana ali'i,	Questioned Ki'i, and Uli, and Nana, the chief,

* *Ka Nupepa Ku'oko'a,* December 15, 1866.

Ke kumu ali'i o na'li'i—e?

From what source sprang the chiefs?

E Ku e pehea la?

O Ku! how was it?

Pehea ua lani hou, ali'i hou?

How about the new heavenly one, the new chief?

Lani hou a laua i hanau ai, eia ho'i,

The new chief who has been born, here he is!

Eia ua lani loa, ali'i loa,

Here is the heavenly one, the chief of long lineage,

Lani o ka maka o Haloa,

Heavenly one of the bud of Haloa,

Eia ua lani o Haloa e na moku,

Here is that heavenly one of Haloa, O islands!

E pili ai ka hanu me he la ua la,

Who will make one catch one's breath as on a rainy day,

I ke kapu o Ke-aka.

Because of the tabu of Ke-aka.

Eia Ke-aka, eia Ke-aka, Ke-aka-a-Kiha,

Here is Ke-aka, here is Ke-aka, Ke-aka-a-Kiha,

Kama-ka-la-kaua-a-Kama,

Kama-ka-la-kaua-a-Kama,

Ka maka o 'Umi-ka-la-kaua i hanau,

The bud, 'Umi-ka-la-kaua was born,

Ka pua aia ali'i o Kama.

Child of that chief Kama.

Ewalu ho'i ke kama o nei ali'i,

Eight were the Kama names of this chief,

E Kama, e Kama-nu-'ena, Kama-hiki,

Kama, Kama-nu-'ena, Kama-hiki,

Kama-ola, e Kama-oho-lani,

Kama-ola, Kama-oho-lani,

Kama-kulia-a-Pe-'ape'a-'ai-uila,

Kama-kulia-a-Pe'ape'a-'ai-uila, etc.

Soon after, Ke-a-ulu-moku left Ka-hahana and joined Ka-lani-'opu'u, the ruling chief of Hawaii.

Ka-lani-'opu'u carried the war into Lanai and attacked the chiefs and soldiers in their stronghold called Ho'oki'o, *mauka* of Maunalei, which was their place of refuge. The trouble with the place was that when the chiefs and soldiers fled thither, their water supply was cut off and they were all slaughtered. The whole island of Lanai was ravaged by the forces of Ka-lani-'opu'u. At Paomai, at Keaea close to the forest, and at Ka'ohai was the place called Kamokupeu scarred by war markings of old. A certain captive who was being led to Ka-lani-'opu'u with his hands tied, as he neared a cliff asked to have the cords loosened, pretending he was in pain. Since they were so close to the cliff the men felt no fear of his escaping, but no sooner were his hands released than he leaped over the precipice. His name was Kini and he was famous for his skill in leaping cliffs. He had leaped down the rough cliff of Kukaemoku at 'Iao and Olowalu, and it was this skill in leaping down cliffs that saved his life in the battle on Lanai. During Ka-lani-'opu'u's occupancy of Lanai, the food ran out, and the men had to eat the root of a wild plant called *kupala*. This had a loosening effect upon the bowels when eaten in quantity. The war is therefore called The-land-of-loose-bowels (Ka-moku-hi') and it is a war still talked of among the descendants on Lanai.*

Ka-lani-'opu'u decided to go on to Ko'olau, Maui, where food was abundant. He went to Ka'anapali and fed his soldiers upon the taro of Honokahua. As he was sailing, just off Kahakuloa, a certain man was sitting on the crest of Pu'ukoa'e, and as the war canoes came in sight the man made a gesture of contempt. The distance from the water's edge was some two hundred feet, but Ka-lani-'opu'u prayed to his god saying, "O Ku-ka'ili-moku, give me the life of that scoffer there!" and, putting stone to sling, he struck him on the back at the first shot, thus causing him to take a misstep and fall off the cliff to instant death. At Hamakualoa Ka-lani-'opu'u landed and engaged in battle, but Ka-hekili hastened to the aid of his men, and they put up such a fierce fight that Ka-lani-'opu'u fled to his canoes. Landing at Ko'olau he slew the common people and maltreated the captives by urinating into their eyes. Descendants of people so treated are alive today. From Hana, Mahi-hele-lima, commander of the fortress Ka'uiki, joined forces with Ka-lani-'opu'u, and for six months the fighting continued. During this campaign, carried on for half a year, from 1778 to 1779, with fighting at Kaupo, Lahaina, Lanai, Hamakualoa, and Ko'olau, Kamehameha, as well as his master in warfare, Ke-ku-hau-pi'o, distinguished himself for skill and bravery in war. . . .†

* *Kupala*, also called *paha*, is a native cucurbit, species *Sicyos pachycarpus*.
† *Ka Nupepa Ku'oko'a*, Dec. 22, 1866.

CHAPTER VIII

Captain Cook's Visit to Hawaii

... It was eighty-eight years ago, in January, 1778, that Captain Cook first came to Hawaii.* Ka-'eo was ruling chief of Kauai, Ka-hahana of Oahu and Molokai, and Ka-hekili of Maui, Lanai, and Kahoolawe. The ship was first sighted from Waialua and Wai'anae [on Oahu] sailing for the north. It anchored at night at Waimea, Kauai, that place being nearest at hand. A man named Moapu and his companions who were out fishing with heavy lines, saw this strange thing move by and saw the lights on board. Abandoning their fishing gear, no doubt through fright, they hurried ashore and hastened to tell Ka-'eo and the other chiefs of Kauai about this strange apparition. The next morning the ship lay outside Ka'ahe at Waimea. Chiefs and commoners saw the wonderful sight and marveled at it. Some were terrified and shrieked with fear. The valley of Waimea rang with the shouts of the excited people as they saw the boat with its masts and its sails shaped like a gigantic sting ray. One asked another, "What are those branching things?" and the other answered, "They are trees moving about on the sea." Still another thought, "A double canoe of the hairless ones of Mana!" A certain kahuna named Ku-'ohu declared, "That can be nothing else than the heiau of Lono, the tower of Ke-o-lewa, and the place of sacrifice at the altar." (*'A'ohe kela he mea'e, o ka heiau no kela o Lono, o ka'anu'unu'u no kela o Keolewa, a o na lele kela o ke kuahu.*) The excitement became more intense, and louder grew the shouting.

The chief sent some men on board to see what the wonderful thing was. Those who went were Kane-a-ka-ho'owaha, the kahuna Ku-'ohu, wearing a whaletooth ornament to show his rank, the chief Ki'ikiki', and some paddlers. When they drew near and saw how much iron there was along the side of the ship and on the rails they said excitedly to each other, "Oh, how much dagger material (*pahoa*) there is here!" for they called iron "*pahoa*" because that was what

* For the account of Cook's visits to Hawaii see 8, vol. 2, pp. 190, 255, 530-549; vol. 3, pp. 1-169. Dibble—10, pp. 20-28—has an early abridged version evidently from the same source as Ka-makau's. Stokes attacks Ka-makau's historical accuracy in his paper—33.

92

they used in old days for their fighting daggers (*pahoa*). One of them went on board and saw many men on the ship with white foreheads, sparkling eyes, wrinkled skins, and angular heads, who spoke a strange language and breathed fire from their mouths. The chief Ki'ikiki' and the kahuna Ku-'ohu, each clothed in a fine girdle of tapa cloth about the loins and a red tapa garment caught about the neck, stepped forward with the left fist clenched and, advancing before Captain Cook, stepped back a pace and bowed as they murmured a prayer; then, seizing his hands, they knelt down and the tabu was freed. Captain Cook gave Ku-'ohu a knife, and it was after this incident that Ku-'ohu named his daughter Changed-into-a-dagger (Ku-a-pahoa) and The-feather-that-went-about-the-ship (Ka-hulu-ka'a-moku). This was the first gift given by Captain Cook to any native of Hawaii.

They called Captain Cook Lono (after the god Lono who had gone away promising to return). A man hoisting a flag they called Ku-of-the-colored-flag (Ku-ka-lepa-'oni'oni'o) after the image that stood against the outer wall of the heiau. A lighted pipe in the mouth of another gave him the name of Lono-of-the-volcanic-fire (Lono-pele). When they saw a heap of coconuts they said, "These are the fruits of Traveling-coconut (Nui-ola-hiki),* they must have killed this mischief-maker of the sea." Of a bullock's hide they said, "They must also have killed Ku-long-dog,† (Ku-'ilio-loa)! Perhaps they have come here to kill all the mischief-makers of the sea." And they returned to shore and reported all they had seen, the men's acts and their speech; how they had killed the *kupua* of the sea, Niu-ola-hiki and Ku-'ilio-loa, of which the coconuts and the hides were proof; how much iron there was lying about the floating heiau (for the Hawaiians had seen iron before); and how the men had fair skins, bright eyes, sharp noses, angular heads, and deep-set eyes. Then both chiefs and commoners, hearing this report, said to each other, "This is indeed Lono, and this is his heiau come across the sea from Moa-'ula-nui-akea‡ across Mano-wai-nui-kai-o'o!" When the priest's

* Niu-ole-hiki (or Niuolahiki, Niuloahiki) occurs in Hawaiian legend as a mythical ancestor who can take the form of man, a coconut, tree or an eel at will, and whose stretching powers serve to form a bridge along which his descendant travels from Hawaii to the land of his ancestors (Kahiki). In Tuamotuan, Marquesan, and Rarotongan mythology the name also occurs as a canoe or tree by which the hero gains some ancestral land, and is there definitely connected with ritual ceremonies.

† Ku-'ilio-loa (Ku-long-dog) is the mythical man-eating dog form of Ku, sometimes spoken of as "the man-eating dog of Hina." He comes with Lonoka'eho, the warrior with eight sharp foreheads, to Hawaii from Kahiki. Kamapua'a, the hog man, encounters and overcomes him. He guards the way to the land of Kane and Kanaloa.

‡ Moa-'ula-nui-akea is the land in Raiatea of the Society Islands from which Moikeha migrated to Hawaii.

prayer had freed the tabu and his words were ended the chief asked, "Would there be any harm in going to the heiau of the god?" The kahuna reassured him, saying, "No harm at all, for I did my work well. Only do not meddle with the things belonging to the god."

The people made ready to go on board. When Ka-pupu'u, a warrior of Ka-'eo's guard, heard of the quantity of iron on the ship, he said to the chief, "I shall go on board and take the iron." The chief answered, "The kahuna warned us not to take the god's property lest there be trouble." "Let my lands be surety for any trouble." "Just as you say," replied the chief.* Ka-pupu'u went out to the ship and, seeing a quantity of iron objects lying about, he seized some hastily and threw them into his canoe. The stranger saw him taking the iron and shot him with a gun and killed him. Then all the men in the canoes paddled ashore and told the chiefs and the people how Ka-pupu'u had died, and of the death-dealing thing which the white men used and which squirted out like the gushing forth of water. Some called the weapon a "water squirter" (*wai-ki'*), because of its squirting out like water from a bamboo; others called it a "water gusher" (*wai-pahu'*).

The strangers asked where they could find water, pointing to water with their hands, and the people told them that there was abundant supply inland. The strangers therefore went ashore to draw water. The Hawaiians, observing the way they rowed, said, "They must be nursing babies the way they lean over!" and as the men swayed as they rowed they exclaimed in surprise, "They row their canoe swaying back and forth and they seem to be bending back the tips of their paddles!" For this reason they called a boat a "doubling-up canoe" (*wa'a-pelupelu*). When the boat landed at the mouth of the Waimea river, the beach of Luhi and the opposite side of La'au-akala were crowded with people. There was not a bare spot visible. Chiefs and commoners, old and young, came from Polihale, Napali, and Ki'pu', like a rushing stream.

Some chiefs cried, "Let us kill these people for killing Ka-pupu'u!" but the kahuna Ku-'ohu said, "That is not a good thought, for they were not to blame. The fault was ours for plundering, for Ka-pupu'u went to plunder. I have told you that we live under a law; if any man rob or steal, his bones shall be stripped of flesh. The proper way to do is to treat these people kindly. For listen, you chiefs and people! I do not know whether these are gods or men. Here is the test of a god: if we tempt them and they do not open their gourd

* *Ka Nupepa Ku'oko'a*, Jan. 19, 1867.

container which holds their ancestral gods (*'aumakua*) then they are themselves gods, but if they open the sacred gourds (*ipu kapu*) [that is, if they yield to the temptation of women] then they are not gods— they are foreigners (*haole*), men from the land of Ka'eka'e and Ku-kanaloa and their companions.* Many of the old people felt doubtful, for they had heard of foreigners, but the majority of the people and the young men shouted, "A god! a god! Lono is a god! Lono is a god!" Thus the name Lono spread from Kauai to Hawaii.

When night fell, the men on the ship shot off guns and skyrockets, perhaps to express their joy in having discovered this first land of the group, Kauai. The people called the rockets "the fires of Lono-makua" and they named the flash of the gun "the lightning" and its report "Kane in the thunder." The next day Captain Cook, his officers, and some of his men went ashore with their guns in readiness, and were taken before Ka-'eo, the ruling chief, the chiefess Ka-maka-helei, and the other chiefs. They greeted him well and gave him gifts of hogs, chickens, bananas, taro, potatoes, sugar cane, yams, fine mats, and bark cloth. Captain Cook accepted their gifts; it may be that he took them to show the British people what the products of Kauai were like. To the Hawaiians he gave gifts of cloth, iron, a sword, knives, necklaces, and mirrors. The cloth they called "foreign fiber" (*a'a kahiki*) because it resembled coconut fiber. Glass they called *kilo* [from the practice of the *kilo*, or soothsayer, looking into a shallow bowl of water where he was supposed to see reflected the persons or acts about whom inquiry was made], and iron they called "dagger" (*pahoa*). They ceased to believe the foreigners to be gods. At first they had taken their cocked hats to be a part of their heads and their clothing to be wrinkled skin. Ka-'eo gave to Captain Cook his wife's daughter Lele-mahoa-lani, who was a sister of Ka-umu-ali'i, and Captain Cook gave Ka'eo gifts in exchange for Lele-mahoa-lani.† When the other women noticed that the chiefess had slept with foreigners, they too slept with foreigners in order to obtain cloth, iron, and mirrors.

Captain Cook left Kauai and sailed northwest of America through Bering Strait to seek lands to the north. To these islands he bequeathed such possessions as the flea, never known on them before his day,

* Ka'eka'e is one of the "foreign priests whom Pau-makua of Oahu is said to have brought with him on his return from foreign voyages." Ku-kanaloa is a ship-wrecked foreigner who is said to have arrived in Hawaii during the rule of Ke-li'i-o-kaloa of Hawaii or, in another version, on Maui during the rule of Ka-ka-'alaneo, and to have become an ancestor for the Hawaiian people. See 13, vol. 2, pp. 25, 106-110, 152.

† This charge is not widely accepted today. For refutation see discussion by Stokes, 32.

and prostitution with its results, syphilis and other venereal diseases. These serious diseases caused the dwindling of the population after the coming of Captain Cook.

Ka-'eo, chief of Kauai, sent Kane-a-ka-ho'owaha and Kau-ka-pua'a to Ka-hahana on Oahu to relate all that had happened at the coming of Captain Cook to Kauai and to describe the appearance of the white men. They said that their speech was like the twittering and trilling of the 'o'o bird, with a prolonged cooing sound like the lali bird, and a high chirping note. They said that they [the foreigners] were clothed from head to foot, wore triangular shapes on their heads, and shoes on their feet. Said Kane-a-ka-ho'owaha, "They were not gods for they opened the sacred netted gourd; Ka-'eo caused Lele-mahoa-lani, the chiefess, to sleep on the heiau." The leading kahuna of Ka-hahana, Ka'opulupulu, said, "They are foreigners from Hi'ikua, Uliuli, Melemele, Ke'oke'o—they are men who will possess the land." Some said, "Perhaps they are the people whom Kekiopilo, the prophet (kaula) of Kupihea, prophesied would come, white men, having dogs with long ears which men would ride upon." Others said, "These are the men spoken of by Kekio Pilakalo in the time of Kuali'i:

> A messenger is Ku from the heavens
> A stranger is Ku from Kahiki.*

There was a great deal of talk about Captain Cook.

Another canoe came from Kauai bearing Kau-a-ka-piki, another chief of lesser rank. When people questioned him he told them the story. The ship was like a heiau with a tower upon it. There were three masts with three sails shaped like a sting ray, a long stick at the prow, holes for guns along the sides, and shining holes behind. As for the men, they were fair with angular heads, their clothes were fastened to their skin and had openings on the sides over each thigh and in front; they had narrow foot coverings, and fire at the mouth from which smoke issued like Pele's fires. "What was their speech like?" asked the men. Kau-a-ka-piki tied on his loin cloth, wrapped his shoulder cape around his buttocks and between his legs, wound a piece of tapa around his head, put the stem of a cane blossom in his mouth, lighted the end, and blew smoke from his mouth. Then he stuck it inside his garment and said, "They spoke thus: 'Hi-ka-pa-lale, hi-ka-pa-lale, hi-ohi-ai, o-a-laki, wala-wala-ki, wai-ki, po-ha. Aloha kahiki, aloha ha'eha'e, aloha ka wahine [the women], aloha ke keiki [the children], aloha ka makua [the men] aloha ka hale [the house].' "

* Ku-ali'i is a traditional ruling chief of Oahu said to have lived during the 17th and early 18th centuries. For his story see 14, vol. 4, no. 2, pp. 364-434.

Thus he went on to Hawaii and Maui telling his story wherever he went.

Ka-lani-'opu'u was in Ko'olau, Maui, fighting against Ka-hekili, the chief of Maui. When Moho told him and the other chiefs of Hawaii the story about Captain Cook and described his ship they exclaimed, "That was surely Lono! He has come back from Kahiki." Pai-lili, son of Holo-'ae, who had accompanied Ka-lani-'opu'u said, "Life is ours! The god of our ancestors has returned!" Others said, "Lono is a true god to us; he has come back. We descendants of his shall have life."

While Ka-lani-'opu'u was in Wailua in Ko'olau, Maui, on the evening of November 19, 1778, Captain Cook's ship was sighted northeast of Mokuho'oniki with the prow turned a little to the southeast. It was seen at Kahakuloa, and the news spread over the island, then at Hamakua, and at evening it was seen in Ko'olau. The night passed, and the next day the ship was anchored at Ha'aluea just below Wailua. When they saw that its appearance exactly fitted the description given by Moho, there was no end of excitement among the people over the strange object. "The tower of Lono! Lono the god of our fathers!" they exclaimed, redoubling their cries at the thought that this was their god Lono who had gone to Kahiki. The men went out in such numbers to visit the ship that it was impossible for all to get on board.

When the canoes returned to shore, Kala'i-mamahu' persuaded Kamehameha and one other to remain on board, and that night the ship sailed away taking Kamehameha and his companions and by morning it had disappeared. Ka-lani-'opu'u thought that Kamehameha must have gone away to Kahiki. He was displeased and ordered Ke-pa'a-lani to bring them all back. Ke-pa'a-lani took six paddlers and a large single canoe supplied with food and water. Puhie declared that within two days and two nights they would sight the ship. Maui disappeared, and Mauna Kea rose before them out of the waves. Kamehameha, looking out, saw a white object on the wave and said to Kala'i-mamahu', "Is that a canoe or only a wave?" "Where?" "Yonder." As they watched it became clearly a canoe, and Kamehameha guessed that it was Ke-pa'a-lani come to seek them. But Captain Cook had no intention of carrying them away; he only wanted them to guide him to a good harbor on Hawaii. Captain Cook may have sailed by a map made by the Spaniards, for how else could he have found the proper harbors at Waimea, Mahukona, and Kealakekua? As for Ke-pa'a-lani he was relieved, for he had already sailed two days and nights without sighting the ship. Kamehameha pointed out the canoe to Captain Cook and then pointed toward Maui. Cook would not consent; he pointed to the ship and then to Hawaii. Again Kamehameha pointed to Maui, and the ship turned about and reached Wailua in a single night.*

It was eleven days after leaving Maui before Captain Cook entered the channel between Maui and Hawaii and sailed close to Kohala. The day was December 2, and Mauna Kea and Mauna Loa were capped with snow. He landed close to Kukuipahu, and the whole population of Kohala, men, women, and children, the aged and the feeble, flocked to the cliff-side along the coast; the place was covered with them. They came from 'Awini to Kekaha along the coast from the uplands of Waimea and Kahuwa. "Look!" they exclaimed, "How tall it is! The back looks like a hammerhead shark, the front comes to a point; it is wide in the center and will hold ever so many men." When they went out to the ship, seeing some of the strangers peering out of the holes at the back one man said, "Those are the gods of the upland of Mouths-shining-with-fat (Kanukuhinuhinu), Peep (Ki'ei) and Peer (Halo)."† Seeing one of the strangers with a telescope they said, "Long-eyes (Maka-loa) and Eyes-that rove (Na-maka-oka'a) the stargazers who see the heavens and the earth." Captain Cook bought hogs with pieces of iron and iron hoops to be used for weapons, hatchets, knives, and fishhooks. A hog a fathom long was had in exchange for a piece of iron a yard long. This was for a dagger for the chief. A commoner could not keep it; it was taken from him, and if he resisted he was killed.

Captain Cook sailed past Hamakua, Hilo, Puna, and Ka-'u and put in at Kealakekua Bay, and on January 17, 1779, he put in at Ka'awaloa Bay. Ka-lani-'opu'u was fighting Ka-hekili on Maui at the time. Captain Cook arrived during the tabu time of the Makahiki when no man could paddle out to the ship without breaking the law and forfeiting all his possessions. But when Captain Cook appeared they declared that his name must be Lono, for Kealakekua was the home of that deity as a man, and it was a belief of the ancients that he had gone to Kahiki and would return. They were full of joy, all the more so that these were Lono's tabu days. Their happiness knew no bounds; they leaped for joy [shouting]: "Now shall our bones live; our 'aumakua has come back. These are his tabu days and he has returned!" This was a great mistake. He was a long-tailed god, a

---

* Ka Nupepa Ku'oko'a, Jan. 26, 1867.

† Ki'ei and Halo (Peep and Peer) are two gods of Hawaii who come to the doors of houses and look in to see what is going on.

scorpion, a slayer of men. What a pity! But they believed in him and shouted, "Lono is a god! Lono is a god!"

Hikiau was the name of Lono's heiau at Kealakekua, and it lay close to the beach. The kahunas of the heiau were among the first, together with those who fed the god, to adopt the error of the rest of the people. The men hurried to the ship to see the god with their own eyes. There they saw a fair man with bright eyes, a high-bridged nose, light hair, and handsome features. Good-looking gods they were! They spoke rapidly. Red was the mouth of the god. When they saw the strangers letting out ropes the natives called them Ku-of-the-tree-fern (Ku-pulupulu) and Coverer-of-the-island (Moku-hali'i). These were gods of the canoe builders in the forest. When they saw them painting the ship they said, "There are Ma'ikoha' [originator of the *wauke* plant]* and Ehu (Faired-haired) daubing their canoe, and Lanahu (Charcoal) daubing on the black!" When they saw the strangers smoking they said, "There are Lono-pele and his companions [of the volcano] breathing fire from their mouths!" Another sailor who put up a flag at the masthead they called Ku-of-the-colored-ensign (Ku-ka-lepa-'oni'oni'o)."

A man named Kila stood up and told the people a story about the ship and its crew, saying:

Great and strong Pakaku' is the chief of this canoe, and his astronomers are Roving-eyes (Na-maka-oka'a) and Great-eyes (Maka-loa). As they sailed along in the ocean great Pakaku' called out to Roving-eyes and Great-eyes, "O Roving-eyes and your comrade, peer and listen! Climb the mast of our ship, gaze about, seek and look for any mischievous one who could trouble our ship. Ha'eha'e-ke!" "O great and strong Pakaku'! we have gazed and gazed. Lo! here is the mischievous one. Oho! oho! here is Ku-long-dog (Ku-'ilio-loa) with wide-open mouth before us. Here is the upper jaw of the dog extending above us; his lower jaw is beneath us. One more huge wave and we shall be devoured!" Then Pakaku' called out to the people of the ship, to Lono-of-the-volcanic-fires (Lono-pele), to Lightning (Ka-huila) and his company, to Flash ('Anapu) and his company, to Kane-of-the-thunder (Kane-hekili), to Father Lono (Lono-makua) and his company, to Steam (Mahuia) and his company, to Kuku'ena and her company, to Na-kola-i-lani and his company, and to Little-flame (Lapalapa-iki) who was in charge of the fires, "O Little-flame, Little-flame! Gaze about you, gaze about! Ready! Pause! Charge! Hoi-he-ke! Hoi-he-ke!" Then the great and mighty Pakaku' called to Shooting-water and to Exploding-water, "When I shoot, leap! when I shoot, leap! when I shoot, leap! O smooth pebbles of Great Britain! hard-grained pebbles of Great Britain! Oh, exploding waters of America! when I shoot, leap forward! when I shoot, leap!" A bullet sped forth striking

* For the myth of Maikoha' and his transformation into the *wauke* plant see 14, vol. 5, no. 2, pp. 268-271

Ku-long-dog on the forehead, splitting his skull apart. This hide here was his. The coconuts lying here are the remains of Traveling-coconut. The ropes on this ship are the intestines of Great-black-turtle (Ka-honu-nui-mae-loku). The points of the anchor are the foreheads of Lono-ka-'eho, Ku-anuenue, and Lele-ia-naha. Thus all the gods of the ocean have been destroyed.

At the conclusion of Kila's story the people said, "It is true, this is Lono, our god! this is Lono, our god!" (Perhaps this man Kila had heard Cook's name from the chiefess with whom Cook slept and had corrupted 'Captain Cook' into Paka-kuka or Pa-kuka.) Then the people brought hogs, taro, potatoes, bananas, fowls, everything he wanted, thinking him to be their god Lono.

When Captain Cook went ashore at Kealakekua the kahuna, believing him to be a god, led him to the heiau, and seated him above the altar where sacrifices were offered. The kahuna stepped back, and had a soft white tapa wrapped about his loins. Captain Cook was covered with a cloak of red tapa like that about the images. Then the kahuna prayed thus:

Your heavenly bodies, O Lono, are the long clouds, the short clouds, the peeping cloud, the peering cloud, the clouds gathering in clusters in the sky, from Uliuli, from Melemele, from Kahiki, from Ulunui, from Ha'eha'e, from 'Oma'oku'ululu', from Hakau'ai, from the land that Lono split in twain, in the lower heavens, in the higher heavens, at the foundation of Laka of Lalohana, from the foundations of the earth. O Ku! O Lono! O Kane! O Kanaloa! gods from the upper regions, from the lower regions, from Kahiki in the east and Kahiki in the west, here is an offering, a gift. Grant life to the chief, life to your children until they reach the world of light, the fruitful land. It is ended, it is freed.

Now it is doubtful whether Captain Cook consented to have worship paid him by the priests. He may have thought they were worshiping as in his own land. But he was a Christian and he did wrong to consent to enter an idolator's place of worship. He did wrong to accept gifts offered before idols and to eat food dedicated to them. Therefore God smote him.

Some days later, many women went on board the ship to offer themselves to the sailors and received in return iron, mirrors, scissors, and beads. When the women looked into the mirrors and saw their own likenesses as if alive, they scraped the quicksilver off the backs of the mirrors, but when the glass could no longer reflect their images they regretted their act. The natives took hogs a fathom in length to trade for guns, for they liked the sound of the report. They said, "Trade, trade! we will trade the hogs for your shooting-water, your exploding-water;

guns, guns, guns!" The strangers said, "No!" "Trade! trade! guns!"
"No more." "The *moa* (fowl) are all gone from Molea in Hamakua."
The natives said, "Ha! the white men know where the fish are hid.
These long-tailed gods know well, for they are taking our women on
board."

On Ka-lani-'opu'u's return with his chiefs and warriors from Maui
on January 24, 1779, he landed at 'Awili in Ka'awaloa and stayed in
Hanamua at the home of Keawe-a-heulu, who had been with them on
Maui fighting with Ka-hekili and when he saw how many women went
aboard the ship to prostitute themselves to the strangers, he forbade their
going. When the strangers could get no more women on the ship, they
came ashore at Na-po'opo'o, at Kahauloa, and on this side of Ka'awaloa,
and numerous were the *'opala haole* [foreign rubbish] born to the women.
Ka-lani-'opu'u treated Captain Cook hospitably, giving him hogs, taro,
potatoes, bananas, and other provisions, as well as feather capes, helmets,
kahili, feather leis, wooden bowls beautifully shaped, tapa cloths of
every variety, finely-woven mats of Puna, and some especially fine mats
made of pandanus blossoms. In return Captain Cook gave Ka-lani-'opu'u
some trifles. It is said that the hat Cook gave to Ka-lani-'ipu'u is in
the wrappings of the head of Keawe-i-kekahi-ali'i-o-ka-moku.

On February 4, Lono sailed away in his ship and had got beyond
Kawaihae when he discovered that one of the masts was decayed and
he had to put back to Kealakekua to repair it. The natives saw him
return, and the women took up once more their association with the
sailors, but not in such numbers as before. The natives had begun to
be suspicious, and some said, "These are not gods; these are men,
white men from the land of Ku-kanaloa." Others declared them to be
gods. Still others said, "The legends of Kane, Kanaloa, Ku, and Lono
say that they came from Kahiki; they do not lie with women.
Lono-i-ka-makahiki was a deified man, not a god." One man said, "The
woman [Lele-mahoa-lani]who was on the ship says that they groan
when they are hurt. When the woman sticks her nails into them they
say, 'You scratch like an owl; your nails are too long; you claw like a
duck!' and more that she did not understand." The natives tried to
provoke Lono to wrath to see whether he would be angry. They
reasoned, "Perhaps the god will not be angry because he has received
offerings of hogs, clothing, red fish, bananas, and coconuts, and the
god Lono has been propitiated." The natives accordingly went on
board the ship and took some iron. The sailors caught them
stealing it and shot them; then a fight began. One of the sailors
grasped the canoe of a certain chief named Palea who was an intimate

friend of Ka-lani-'opu'u. Palea defied the sailor, thrusting him to one side. Another sailor ran toward them and struck Palea down with a club. The natives fell upon the sailor, but Palea recovered consciousness, and the fighting ceased. They were afraid lest Lono kill them, hence they stopped fighting.*

Palea no longer believed in the divinity of Lono and he plotted to steal a boat. He and his men secretly took a boat from Lono's ship and, conveying it to Onouli, they broke it up in order to get the iron in it, also perhaps because they were angry with the white men for striking Palea with a club. It was this theft of a boat by Palea that led to the fight in which Captain Cook was killed. When Captain Cook and the sailors awoke in the morning and found their boat gone they were troubled; so Captain Cook went ashore at Ka'awaloa to inquire about the boat of Ka-lani-'opu'u, the ruling chief. Ka-lani-'opu'u denied any knowledge of the affair, saying, "I know nothing about it; perhaps the natives stole it and carried it away." Possibly Captain Cook did not quite understand what Ka-lani-'opu'u said. He returned to the ship, and the officers discussed the affair and resolved to take the high chief Ka-lani-'opu'u on board and hold him there until the boat was found and restored, when he was to be given his liberty. It was resolved that an officer be chosen to fetch the chief; and an officer and some marines were selected and armed with swords and guns for the purpose of bringing the chief on board the next day. However, because on that day, Thursday, Febuary 14, the officer appointed for the duty was ill, Captain Cook took his place.

Cook landed with his company at Ka'awaloa between Ka-lani-'opu'u's place at 'Awili and Keawe-a-heulu's at Hanamua. As a result of the conference held in the men's eating house before Ka-lani-'opu'u, his older chiefs, and his sons, Ka-lani-'opu'u consented to go on board the ship. Ke-ku-hau-pi'o, meanwhile, seeing Cook on his way to Ka'awaloa, hastily set out from Ke'ei with another chief named Ka-limu. The strangers, seeing a man sitting at the outrigger of the canoe wearing a feather cape, shot at him. The shot struck Ka-limu and killed him. Ke-ku-hau-pi'o then hurriedly turned back and landed at Ka'awaloa. Just then Ka-lani-'opu'u and some of the chiefs dressed in chiefly array and carrying their war-clubs, appeared on the shore, ready to go on board the ship. Ke-ku-hau-pi'o cried, "O heavenly one! stop! it is not safe on the sea; Ka-limu is dead. Go back to the house." When Ka-lola heard that Ka-limu was dead, shot by the strangers, she ran out of the sleeping house, threw her arms about the shoulders of Ka-lani-'opu'u

* *Ka Nupepa Ku'oko'a*, Feb. 2, 1867.

and said, "O heavenly one! let us go back!" Ka-lani-'opu'u turned to go back. Captain Cook tried to grasp him by the hand, but Ka-lani-mano-o-ka-ho'owaha stuck his club in the way, and Ka-lani-'opu'u was borne away by his chiefs and warriors to Maunaloia, and the fight began. Captain Cook struck Ka-lani-mano-o-ka-ho'owaha with his sword, slashing one side of his face from temple to cheek. The chief with a powerful blow of his club knocked Captain Cook down against a heap of lava rock. Captain Cook groaned with pain. Then the chief knew that he was a man and not a god, and, that mistake ended, he struck him dead together with four other white men. The rest of the party fled to their boats and shot the gun, and many of the Hawaiians were killed. Some of those who were skillful with the sling, shot stones after the boat. Of one of these named Moa the strangers said, "Mahi-moa is a bad one. He twists his sling and the stone flies forth. He who flees, dies; he who stands still, lives."

When the strangers on the ship knew that their chief was dead, they shot their guns from the ship while the natives tried to ward off the shots with sleeping mats. The bodies of Captain Cook and the four men who died with him were carried to Ka-lani-'opu'u at Maunaloia, and the chief sorrowed over the death of the captain. He dedicated the body of Captain Cook, that is, he offered it as sacrifice to the god with a prayer to grant life to the chief (himself) and to his dominion. Then they stripped the flesh from the bones of Lono. The palms of the hands and the intestines were kept; the remains (*pela*) were consumed with fire. The bones Ka-lani-'opu'u was kind enough to give to the strangers on board the ship, but some were saved by the kahunas and worshiped.

Eight days after the death of Captain Cook, friendly relations were resumed with those on board the ship. On Monday, February 23, the ship sailed and it anchored at Kauai on the 29th of that month to get water and food supplies, then sailed to Niihau and got a supply of yams, potatoes, and hogs. On March 15, the ship sailed into the blue and disappeared. This was the end of Captain Cook's voyages of exploration among these islands . . .*

Captain Cook was a [man of] Britain famous for his explorations in the Indian, Atlantic, and the Pacific oceans. He discovered lands in the ocean which were [previously] unknown. He had been but a short time in Hawaii when God punished him for his sin. It was not the fault of the Hawaiian people that they held him sacred and paid him honor as a god worshiped by the Hawaiian people. But because he killed the people he

* *Ka Nupepa Ku'oko'a,* Feb. 9, 1867. A concise account of these events drawn from reliable sources, is presented by Kuykendall, 17, pp. 17-19.

was killed by them without mercy, and his entrails were used to rope off the arena, and the palms of his hands used for fly swatters at a cock fight. Such is the end of a transgressor. The seeds that he planted here have sprouted, grown, and become the parents of others that have caused the decrease of the native population of these islands. Such are gonorrhea, and other social disease; prostitution; the illusion of his being a god [which led to] worship of him; fleas and mosquitoes; epidemics. All of these things have led to changes in the air which we breathe; the coming of things which weaken the body; changes in plant life; changes in religion; changes in the art of healing; and changes in the laws by which the land is governed.*

* Extract from *Ka Nupepa Ku'oko'a*, Feb. 16, 1867.

CHAPTER IX

Events of Ka-lani-'opu'u's Time

After the death of Captain Cook and the departure of his ship, Ka-lani-'opu'u moved to Kainaliu near Honua'ino and, after some months, to Keauhou where he could surf in the waves of Kahalu'u and Holualoa, and then to Kailua. He delighted in the hula dance. Everyone, young and old, even to the babies just able to walk, was summoned to dance before him. The most popular dances were the *kala'au* [danced to the beating of sticks one against the other], the *ala'apapa* [similar to the modern *olapa* but with a different rhythm], and the dance of the marionettes (*hula ki'i*). Both chiefs and commoners participated in the dances, Ka-lani-'opu'u, over eighty years old as he was at the time, taking part.* As he was dancing to the chant

Nu'uanu popo'i ka huna a ka ua,	Nu'uanu is drenched by the rain.
Ku-ku' ka'ale a ka makani	Great gusts of wind blow.
Hololua, holopili, holokake,	Back and forth, against the cliff, in and out,
I ke alo o ka pali ka makani	Blows the wind at the face of the cliff

with the gathering of chiefs, lesser chiefs, warriors, notables, and commoners looking on, a chief named Ka-pi'ipi'i-lani, standing among the group of commoners remarked to one of them, "The hula is amusing enough except for that silly old man's dancing!" The man addressed answered, "Don't you know who the chief is?" "Who is he?" "That is Ka-lani-'opu'u; you are a saucy upstart indeed not to know the chief!" His neighbor whispered, "Don't you know the man you are talking to is a chief? That is Ka-pi'ipi'i-lani." "Hush! don't let's get into a brawl."

While Ka-lani-'opu'u was amusing himself with the pleasures of the dance, trouble came in the form of a famine in Kona. He ordered all the products of the cultivated areas to be seized, even those which were the people's property. The people wept bitterly over this seizure of their property, and life in Kona became so uncomfortable that the chief said to his household, "Let us make a circuit of the island, eat, waste, enjoy ourselves, dance and sleep or not as we please."

* Extract from *Ka Nupepa Ku'oko'a*, Feb. 16, 1867.

Perhaps Ka-lani-'opu'u was by this time senile with age. At Kapa'au in North Kohala he selected a place at Hinakahua for sports and games such as hula dancing, *kilu* spining, *maika* rolling, and sliding sticks. Meanwhile rebellion was brewing. It was I-maka-koloa, a chief of Puna, who rebelled, I-maka-koloa the choice young 'awa [favorite son] of Puna. He seized the valuable products of his district, which consisted of hogs, gray tapa cloth (*'eleuli*), tapas made of *mamaki* bark, fine mats made of young pandanus blossoms (*'ahu hinalo*), mats made of young pandanus leaves (*'ahuao*), and feathers of the *'o'o* and *mamo* birds of Puna.

Nu'u-anu-pa'ahu, chief of Ka-'u, was also in the plot to rebel, but he was at this time with Ka-lani-'opu'u, and Ka-lani-'opu'u feared Nu'u-anu-pa'ahu. Ka-lola in the meantime was with Kiwala'o on Maui. Ka-lani-'opu'u ordered nets from Hilo and lines for albacore fishing (*aho hi-ahi*) from Puna and from Kalae in Ka-'u; and Ka-hekili and Ka-lola sent him a double canoe filled with small-meshed nets and fishlines. Because of his fear of Nu'u-anu-pa'ahu, Ka-lani-'opu'u plotted with his false kahunas to be rid of him. The kahunas said, "Let Nu'u-anu-pa'ahu be devoured by a shark so that his kahunas may not have his remains to burn in vengeance." "Yes," assented the chief, "let him be swallowed by a shark so that his kahunas cannot avenge him. Let him be swallowed whole by the shark." The kahunas boasted, "O heavenly one, the shark is ready that is to devour him. Let all the chiefs go to Kauhola at Hala'ula to indulge in surfing, the favorite pastime of chiefs. Should the surfer from Ka'wa' in Ka-'u join in the sport he will be swallowed by the shark. He will then not be able to rebel against the rule of your son, Kiwala'o." The chief agreed to this plan, and chiefs, guards, warriors, and all the members of the chief's household went to Kauhola, erected temporary shelters, and went surfing, but Nu'u-anu-pa'ahu could not be persuaded to join them. All the other chiefs and commoners went surfing, but he did not go with them.

One day when the waves of Maliu and Ka-pae-lauhala were rolling in magnificently, the cutworm-tearing son of Na'alehu resolved to show the skill he had got through practice [in surfing] on the bent wave of Ka'wa', or diving headforemost into the waters of Unahea. He reached for his surfboard and went out to sea beyond Ka-pae-lauhala. He rode in on a wave and landed at Kinaina. Again he went out and, having set himself in the way of a good wave, rode once more to land. As the wave rolled landward, a shark came in with it. It came with open mouth that showed sharp, pointed teeth. Sea water poured between

its teeth and through its gills; its skin seemed to bristle; dreadful
indeed was the appearance of that rough-skinned one. Six fathoms
was its length. Chiefs and commoners fled terrified to the shore, but
Nu'u-anu-pa'ahu, the lad who had broken *mamane* branches at Kapapala
and torn up *koai'e* vines at 'Ohaikea, did not lose courage. When he saw
that the shark was pursuing him, he steered his board for the crest of
the wave. The shark saw him on the crest and pursued him there.
Nu'u-anu-pa'ahu fled with the speed of an arrow. The shark passed
under and turned to slash; Nu'u-anu-pa'ahu struck out with his fists
and hit it in the eye. The shark dived downward; Nu'u-anu-pa'ahu
turned toward a low surf, and as he rode it the shark passed under
him. Again it turned to bite; he sped on and the shark missed.
He struck at the shark's gills, his hand found its way in, and he
grasped the gills and jerked them out of its head. The shark, wounded,
left him. Just as he was about to land, another shark that lurked near
a stone appeared with open mouth. Nu'u-anu-pa'ahu struck out at
it with his fists, hitting it back of the jaw. The shark turned and gashed
him on one side of his buttocks. Then at last Nu'u-anu-pa'ahu reached
shore. Chiefs and commoners shouted applause for his strength and
congratulated him upon his escape from death. Sounds of wailing
echoed and reeohoed.* His kahunas meanwhile saw to the securing of
the gills (*pihapiha*) of the shark and quickly began their prayers. The
leaves of the trees went dry; there was no fish to be had. "Let these
sharks die in a day," they prayed, "land on shore, be eaten by hogs
and dogs, and their flesh stink in the sun." On that very day one shark
came ashore at Na'ohaku, the other at Hapu'u. But Nu'u-anu-pa'ahu
lay suffering great pain until he died at Pololu', and there he was buried.
The natives of that place will tell you something of this, but they
will probably repeat only half the story.

During the stay at Kohala it was arranged by the chiefs and counselors
that the young heir to the rule over the land, Ka-lani-kau-i-ke-aouli
Kiwala'o, should be sent for to Waipi'o. At his arrival it was agreed
by the chiefs and counselors and by the ruling chief, Ka-lani-'opu'u,
that at the death of Ka-lani-'opu'u the rule over the land should descend
to this heir, his should be the right to perform the ritual to
dedicate a heiau, and whatever ivory [of whale or walrus tusks] came
ashore should belong to him. To the son of his younger brother, to
Kamehameha, Ka-lani-'opu'u gave his god Ku-ka'ili-moku and commanded Kamehameha to live under Kiwala'o, who belonged to the
senior branch of the family.

* *Ka Nupepa Ku'oko'a*, Feb. 9, 1867.

The heiau of Moa'ula was erected in Waipi'o at this time, and after its dedication by Ka-lani-'opu'u the chief set out for Hilo with his chiefs, warriors, and fighting men, some by land and some by canoe, to subdue the rebellion of I-maka-koloa, the rebel chief of Puna. In Hilo Ka-lani-'opu'u built the heiau of Kanowa at Pu'ueo and after dedicating it he went to stay at 'Ohele in Waiakea while his army went to fight in Puna. The fight lasted a long time, but I-maka-koloa fled and for almost a year lay hidden by the people of Puna. Ka-lani-'opu'u meanwhile awaited his capture. Leaving Hilo, he went to Ka-'u and stayed first at Punalu'u, then at Waiohinu, then at Kama'oa in the southern part of Ka-'u, and erected a heiau called Pakini, or Halau-wailua, near Kama'oa. A certain man, a *kahu* of the chief named Puhili, said, "I-maka-koloa is being hidden by the natives of Puna, but if the chief consents I will go with my god and find him." "Go with your god," said the chief. Puhili went until he came to the boundary where Puna adjoins Ka-'u, to 'Oki'okiaho in 'Apua, and began to fire the villages. Great was the sorrow of the villagers over the loss of their property and their canoes by fire. When one district (*ahupua'a*) had been burnt out from upland to sea he moved on to the next. This was Puhili's course of action, and thus it was that he found I-maka-koloa where he was being hidden by a woman *kahu* on a little islet of the sea. A man of handsome features was this I-maka-koloa. He had a fine head of hair so long that it reached to the soles of his feet. Fearing lest he be recognized by his hair he had gone secretly to this woman *kahu*, on a rock islet standing off in the sea, to have his hair cut, and that was how he came to be found. As soon as he was found, Puhili stopped his god from eating up the houses of Puna.

I-maka-koloa was taken to Ka-lani-'opu'u in Ka-'u to be placed on the altar as an offering to the god, and Kiwala'o was the one for whom the house of the god had been made ready that he might perform the offering. Some of the chiefs muttered one to another, "Our chief [Kamehameha] is left destitute!" and, making an end of secrecy, one talked with Kamehameha saying, "Listen to our counsel if you would have wealth rather than poverty. If you will listen to us you may become a chief with wealth for yourself and your descendants, but if you neglect our counsel you will be destitute." Kamehameha said, "Tell me what you advise, and I will consider whether your counsel is good or bad." Said the chief, "This is our counsel: when your cousin is making the offering to the god and has first taken up the hog and the banana to offer, do you seize I-maka-koloa and offer him to the god. The man will be your offering, and the rule over the land will

then be yours. I will not be present at the dedication of the heiau."
Kamehameha answered, "I consent. If I die it is well, and if I live so let
it be, and may the god help me." The day came when the chief, Kiwala'o,
was to perform the tabu for the heiau of Pakini by presenting the offerings. There were present Ka-lani-'opu'u, the chiefs and *kuhina* [the
executive officers, highest officers next the ruler], the war leaders
(*pukaua*) and bearers of supplies (*mamakakaua*), the warriors, the reti-
nue of the chiefs (*anaina*), and the commoners. The ceremony began at
which the heiau was made tabu. Then Kiwala'o grasped the hog to offer
it first and afterward the man. He hooked on Manaia-ka-lani, then
made the offering. Before he had ended offering the first sacrifices,
Kamehameha grasped the body of I-maka-koloa and offered it up to the
god, and the freeing of the tabu for the heiau was completed. It was
from this incident that Ka-manawa named his son Amama'-lua, Double-
freeing.*

There was great excitement among the chiefs. "This was not done
right! Kamehameha will have the rule over the land!" it was said. Some
said, "He will not rebel; both are sons of the chief; they are an elder
and a younger brother." Others said, "He will rebel; better to kill him
first." Their talk reached the ears of Ka-lani-'opu'u, and he spoke secretly to Kamehameha saying, "My child, I have heard the secret complaints
of the chiefs and their mutterings that they will kill you, perhaps soon.
While I am alive they are afraid, but when I die they will take you and
kill you. I advise you to go back to Kohala. I have left you the god;
there is your wealth." Then Kamehameha, with his wife Ka-lola, daughter of Kumu-ko'a, and his brother Kala'i-mamahu', and Ku-ka'ili-moku
the god, went by way of Hilo to Kohala, his own land, and there lived.

Ka-lani-'opu'u left Kama'oa and went to the shores of Ka'alu'alu and
Paiaha'a to fish. Then there came a school of *ahi* fish to Kalae, and all
the chiefs went down to Kalae for the *ahi* fishing. Since the distance to
Ka'iliki'i after fresh water for bathing was so great, Ka-lani-'opu'u
asked his kahunas who were skilled in pointing out proper locations,
"Is there water to be found on Kalae?" One kahuna said, "There is water
here. It is in front of the dog [a rock so called]. That dog is Ka-'ilio-a-
Lono, The-[pet]dog-of-Lono, who went to the spring for water
to drink but was caught by Pele and turned into stone. The water
bubbles up within the sea, and one must dig deep for the waters of

---

* In Ka-'u an old Hawaiian told Pukui that when I-maka-koloa was brought
to be sacrificed an old *kahu* of his who pitied him shouted out to the chiefs,
"That is not I (makakoloa) the chief, that is I his servant; I can point out to you
I the chief!" So a young *kahu*, a relative who resembled him, was sacrificed in his
place. Their descendants in Ka-'u still bear the name of I-kauwa', (I-the-servant)
and I-pa'a-puka (I who-closed-the-door [of death]).

Mana." The kahuna who thus spoke was a dwarf called "The dwarf who points out the water of Kalae." Upon hearing of this water of Kalae, Ka-lani-'opu'u set all the chiefs and commoners of Ka-'u to digging for it. Although the kahuna was right, and the fault was the chief's in not carrying out the kahuna's instructions, or perhaps because it was hard digging in the pahoehoe without foreign implements, not even the sea was found underneath. Because no water was found, Ka-lani-'opu'u was angry and had the kahuna killed who pointed out the water of Kalae.*

After the *ahi* season (*Ka wa hi-ahi*) was over, Ka-lani-'opu'u set out to return to Kona, but was taken ill; so he went to Ka'iliki'i at Waio'ahukini in Pakini and there he died in January, 1772, in the twenty-ninth year of his rule over Hawaii. He is said to have been a son of Pele-io-holani, ruling chief of Oahu, and to have been named Ka-lei'opu'u after the fashion of cutting the ivory clasp round like a bud (*'opu'u*). This the Oahu chiefs used as an ornament instead of that shape worn by the chiefs of Hawaii. He is said to have been begotten by Pele-io-holani to Ka-maka'i-moku at the waters of Alelele above Waipahu at Waikele, for at Waikele lived her mother 'Umi-'ula-i-ka-'ahu-manu with the brothers of Ka-maka'i-moku, Heulu and Na'ili. Keoua also was named by Pele-io-holani, and that is the reason why Ka-lani-'opu'u and Keoua would not fight against the chiefs of Oahu in the battle at Na-one-a-La'a and at Pu'unene and Ka'anapali, and in other battles. That is also why Ka-lani-'opu'u would not fight against Molokai in the time of Kumu-hana and Ka-hahana. Ka-lani-nui-'i-a-mamao was the legitimate husband of Ka-maka'i-moku. She had been six months pregnant on Oahu when she returned to Hawaii. There she lived until the birth of the child, and she named the child Ka-lei-'opu'u, the name given her by Pele-io-holani for the child; but the Hawaiians called him Ka-lani-ku-mai-eiwa-ka-moku.

As to the noted events of Ka-lani-'opu'u's time, the first battles he fought were against Alapa'i-nui, son of Ka-uaua. These were fought at Kalepolepo, Pua'aloa, Pa'ie'ie, Mawae, Kuolo, Mokaulele, and Mahinaakaaka, which last was the place where Ka-lani-'opu'u slipped [and almost lost his life]. The battles fought with Keawe-'opala, the son of Alapa'i, were at Ke-omo between Honaunau and Ke'ei, on the mountain of Hualalai, the battle of Pae at Kahilina'i, and the battle

---

* The spring still bubbles up in the deep sea at Mana off Kalae, and several such fresh-water springs occur in the ocean outside of Ka'wa' on the western side of Punalu'u. The chief's failure was due not to the absence of fresh water but to his inability to get at (from the coast) the underground stream which feeds this spring.

of Pu'uki'ilili' on the plains of Kawaihae. Other events were the taking of the fort of Pohakuomane'o from Ke'e-au-moku; the annexing of the fortress of Ka'uiki, together with Hana and Kipahulu, to Hawaii; and the battles with Ka-hekili at Kaupo, Lahaina, Lanai, and Hama-kualoa in Ko'olau on Maui.*

Na-maka was one of the noted men of Ka-lani-'opu'u's time. He was a man skilled in politics, oratory, genealogies, spear-throwing (*lono ma ka ihe*), the conformation of the earth's surface (*kuhikuhi pu'u one*), bone-breaking (*lua*), cliff-leaping (*lele pali*), and the interpretation of omens (*kilo*), all accomplishments which he had learned on Kauai. Then he set out to find a *haku* (lord) to whom he might impart all his learning, and Ka-lani-'opu'u was the *haku* whom he selected. Arrived at Oahu he heard that Pakua-nui was skilled in debate and in bone-breaking. This Pakua-nui was the father of Ka-'ele-o-waipi'o, a man of learning of Kamehameha's day who lived at Kailua and composed the dirges to Jesus. Na-maka met Pakua-nui at Kahaukomo in Nu'uanu, and after they had matched their skills, Pakua-nui realized the skill of the tentacle-breaking son of Kilohana and the *koai'e* wood-breaking son of Kailila'au. The shafts of wit flew, brilliant as the rainbow arching over the *hau* trees of Kahaukomo that lends its color to the *'ulalena* rain blown by the *kiowao* breeze against the *pali*, bending the *kawelu* grasses of Lanihuli; swift as the gusts that lift the leaves of the tangled lehua of Malailua. There was no limit to his knowledge. He slipped out of the grasp of Pakua-nui like an eel or wormed his way through his fingers like a slim *'opule* fish; a hard question he dodged like a blow aimed at the nose. Unable to defeat Na-maka at Kahaukomo Pakua-nui thought to make an end of him at the Nu'uanu *pali*. As they descended the *pali*, just as they came close to the cliff of Kapili, Pakua-nui crowded Na-maka a little toward the edge of the path and with a shove of his foot sent him over the cliff. Those who saw this say that Na-maka flew like a hawk poised on the wind as he sailed above Lanihuli and whirled about like a kite as the wind turned, and as it struck the *pali* he descended upon it and lit on the top of a *kukui* tree directly below Kawaikilo.

Na-maka went on to Maui; at Kahakuloa are some cliffs which he leaped, such was his skill. When he reached Hawaii he found that Ka-lani-'opu'u was already under the training of Ka-ua-kahi-a-kaha-ola, a native of Kauai who had had the same ambition as himself. Disappointed as he was, he sought and found a pupil in Hina'i, a chief of Waimea who was closely related to Ka-lani-'opu'u, thinking that if he taught Hina'i some of his arts, Hina'i would tell Ka-lani-'opu'u

* *Ka Nupepa Ku'oko'a*, Feb. 16, 1867.

about him and the chief would take him as his *kahu* to teach him all his accomplishments. He therefore taught Hina'i some things, and the chief became very skillful. Leaping cliffs was one thing he taught him, and the cliffs which he leaped are still pointed out by young people of Waimea who have been shown them by their parents.

When Ka-ua-kahi-a-kaha-ola heard of the skill of this man who was living with Hina'i at Waimea, he was sure that this must be Na-maka and he said to Ka-lani-'opu'u, "There is a certain man who teaches rebellion in your dominion. He is teaching Hina'i to leap down cliffs and over rough places without being hurt. He can leap over ridges and brooks, down cliffs, hillsides, and fortified places without coming to any harm. The result of this will be rebellion." Ka-lani-'opu'u was much perturbed. "What is best to be done?" he asked. "Have him put to death at once," replied Ka-ua-kahi. Ka-lani-'opu'u sent men to take and kill Na-maka and, if Hina'i resisted, to attack Hina'i also. But Na-maka had prepared a way of escape by digging a tunnel under his house leading to some distance, and when the men set fire to the house they were disappointed to find that he had escaped. Having thus escaped death on Hawaii, he returned to Kauai by way of Maui and Oahu. It was a prophecy of his that, "No chief over the island of Hawaii shall place his foot upon the sacred sand of Kaha-malu-'ihi, none of its war canoes shall have power to come to Kauai, without a truce having been made between the islands."

Another noted person of Ka-lani-'opu'u's time was Ka-hau-manu, a woman of Kahuwa'. She lived at Puaiea, and Hinupau who lived at Hamakua was her friend (*aikane*). Mua, the wife of Hina'i, chief of Waimea, was her traveling companion. Her burial house (*pu'o'a*) is at Kahuwa', and there her story is told.

Ke-a-ulu-moku was another celebrated man of Ka-lani-'opu'u's day. His father was the great chief Ka-ua-kahi-akua-nui, son of Lono-maka'i-honua and Kaha-po'ohiwi, but his mother belonged to Naohaku in Kohala. He was celebrated as a composer of war chants, chants of praise, love chants, prophetic chants, and genealogical chants. When he went back to Hawaii with Ka-lani-'opu'u he was homesick for the two Hamakua districts of Maui where he had lived with Kamehameha-nui and Ka-hekili. His love for the place found expression in the following lines:

Alo—ha, alo—ha—	Affectionate longing, affectionate longing,
Aloha wale o'u maku—a la—e o'u makua,	Affection for my (foster) parents, my parents,
Aloha wale o'u makua	Affection for my parents

Mai na 'aina Hamakua,

Who belong to Hamakua,

He mau 'aina Hamakua elua,

The two districts of Hamakua,

No'u mua kaikua'ana i noho ai.

Where my elder brothers live.

He ala pali na'u he mau ali'i ia,

My hillside trails are theirs to rule,

O ka hanai ana komo ke aloha,

They nurtured me until I loved them;

Lele hewa au i he mau kaikua'ana —e

I find myself with other elder brothers

'A'ole—he mau mea 'e wale no o laua.

Who are not the same to me.

He ua i pono—e—pono ia ua.

Let the rain fall, for rain is good.

A he ua i halaka', he mahala,

It patters down, it pelts down,

Pehi hewa i ka nahele,

It crushes the forest growth,

Kua'oa kanikani i ka pua lehua.

It sprinkles musically on the lehua.

Ua ua lehua, he lehua hala,

The lehua trees blossom, the yellow lehua,

Ua i ka lehua o Kailua.

When the rain comes to the lehua of Kailua.

Lehua maka konunu i ka wai,

The lehua petals are heavy with raindrops,

Konunu konunu oha'ha'.

Heavy, heavy and full-blown.

Halana makapehu wale no kie ia,

They know not the pangs of thirst

Pehu, ua mae ka maka mua o ka hinalo ho'i.

That wilt the first-blown pandanus bloom.

Ho'i ka ua ma Haneho'i,

The rain returns by way of Haneho'i,

Ma ka lae o Pu'umaile i Hoalua,

Along the brow of Pu'umaile to Hoalua,

Ma kahakua o Pu'ukoa'e,

Over the ridge of Pu'ukoa'e,

Ma ke alo pali o Huelo.

Before the face of the cliff of Huelo.

Ua poha' Kaumealani,

There it pours down on Kaumealani,

Ua ko ia e ka pua nui

The rain that brings out the full-blown flowers

Hukia aku la lilo i kai

And draws them close down to the shore.

Lilo aku la ua i ka moana,

The rain goes out to sea,

He maka o Hawini ia ua,

It falls on Hawini like teardrops,

He ua 'alo ma ka lae,

It passes along over the capes,

Nihi pali nihi lae.

It creeps by the cliffs and capes,

Nihi i ka lae o Mokupapa.
Creeps by the cape of Mokupapa.

Hele wale ka ua a kipa wale,
The rain comes uninvited,

Ka ua pe'e hala huna kai o—
The rain that hides in the hala groves below,

O—huna huna lauki.
Whose fine drops water the ti plant.

Huna ke kupa i ka hala mua a kau.
The native-born hides away the first hala fruit of summer.*

U-u-e ua wahia e ka ua o ka ho'oilo.
And weeps over the stormy rains of winter.

E ke kuawa kahi o ke kau
Oh! for the light summer showers

Nana i ho'oko'o nei ka pua!
That brought forth the blossoms!

Aui ka pua noho 'ao'ao i ke ka,
The blossoms droop with stem half-broken,

Aui e noho e na pua polo pe'a;
The blossoms hang wilted and uncared-for;

Pala ka'ao, ka'ao ka pola,
The fruit clusters, ripened above,

Loli helele'i ahu ilalo;
Mildew and fall in heaps to the ground;

Loli ka'ao ka hala me ka hinalo.
Both fruit and flowers are mildewed.

O ka hala o ka 'ohi'a lana i ka wai
The hala fruit and the mountain apples drop into the stream

I ka' i ke kahawai o Kakipi,
And are washed down in the stream of Kakipi,

Ilina iluna o ka mau'u kuku',
Washed up on thorny weeds,

I ka pua po'o o ka mau'u pu'uko'a
Up on the flowers of coarse grasses

I kahi a maua e hele ai,
Where we two have wandered,

Me ku'u wahine i ka ua hala o Kulo—li,
My wife and I, to the rain-wet hala grove of Kuloli,

A 'oia loli ke ala iho ma ka lau,
Fragrant among the leaves,

Lauhala—e a ke 'o'i'o'ina 'oe i Ko'olahale,
The hala leaves over the resting place of Ko'olahale,

'Ike aku i ka mahina hiki'alo'alo
Where we watched for the belated moon

One ku a ki'i i ke kaha o Malama,
To rise over the cinder cone of Malama.

* The yellow drupe of the pandanus (hala) fruit is cut and made into a lei to wear about the neck. One such lei is usually kept dry and not allowed to mildew in order to be used to exorcise evil spirits.

Malamalama ke one kea ke hele ia,	The white sands are plainly to be seen if we wish to go there,
Kipa ke alanui mauka o Waiakuna,	Over the upland trail of Waiakuna
He kuna—e.	Winding like the fresh-water eel.
Me he kuna kuhe la ke oho o ke kukui,	The *kukui* leaves look dark like the gobey fish,
I ka ho'olu'u lupekolo ia e ke hau	When overshadowed by the twining *hau* trees
A lipo a 'ele'ele i ka waokoa.	Deep in the dusky koa forest.
He 'ele'ele ko ke kukui noho malu,	Dark are the leaves of the *kukui* in the shade,
He lena ho'i ka lau o kekahi kukui	The leaves are pale yellowish green
O ke kukui aku i waho i ka la,	In the full light of the sun,
I ka ua ia e ka ua 'ulalena.	Watered by the rainbow-tinted rain.

Many celebrated persons there were in the time of Ka-lani-'opu'u. He himself was known for his war excursions and his unjust treatment of his commoners and young people. He was a father without love for his people.

When Ka-hekili heard of Ka-lani-'opu'u's death and of the ceding of the rule over Hawaii to Kiwala'o, he determined to retake the eastern peninsula of Maui, the part taken by Ka-lani-'opu'u and annexed to Hawaii. In 1781, he made war upon Hana. The chiefs of Hana at the fortress of Ka'uiki were Mahi-hele-lima, Ka-loku-o-ka-maile, Nae-'ole, Malua-lani, Ka-loku, those of the grandsons of Keawe and the chiefs of Hawaii who liked to live there, and those native chiefs who, together with some commoners, took the side of Hawaii. Ka-hekili divided his forces and sent part to march by Ko'olau and the rest by Kaupo, an overwhelming army. Both sides had an innumerable army and were well prepared for battle. The fortified hill of Ka'uiki, reinforced and well provisioned, provided a place of safety for the chiefs and fighting men of Hawaii. They had abundant food from Kuakaha and the districts of Pihehe and Kaho'oka'aka'ana. For a year the war continued with the loss of half the men of both sides. Those who held the hill made sallies down to the plains to fight. Ka-hekili made every effort to take the hill, but without success.

Kua-la'a-mea said to Ka-hekili, "I have heard that there is a certain old man of Hana who says that the hill of Ka'uiki can easily be taken without a struggle." "So?" "Yes, so I have heard." "What is his name and where does he live?" "Ku-la'a-hola is his name, Oleawa his home." "Will he come here if I send for him?" "Yes, he will come at the chief's command." Ka-hekili was glad to hear that Ka'uiki could be so easily taken. From ancient times until that day such a thing had never been heard. Ka'uiki had surrendered to Pi'i-mai-wa'a in the time of 'Umi because the guards fell asleep. It surrendered to Pele-io-holani because it was in fact given away by the soldiers. There were many tales about how strong was the fortress of Ka'uiki.

Ka-hekili accordingly sent messengers to fetch Ku-la'a-hola and, when he arrived not long after, eagerly inquired whether it was true that Ka'uiki could be taken without a struggle. "Yes, it is true as reported to the chief," answered Ku-la'a-hola: "It can be taken without a scratch to the skin or weariness to the hand in carrying the spear or club, or the body being burdened with a load of sling-stones. Kahiko-pawa once took the fortress and so did Kahiko-lei-ulu, but the accounts of these old battles are forgotten by the story tellers. Today Ka'uiki seems to us a strong fortress, but from this day it will be as if leveled to earth and no longer a fortified place. Anyone can climb it." "How can the fortress of Ka'uiki become a level plain?" asked Ka-hekili in astonishment. "The fortress of Ka'uiki depends upon its water supply. Cut that off and Ka'uiki will surrender for want of water." "What is the best way to do this?" "Let the chiefs, guards, and fighting men cut off the springs of Punahoa, Waika'akihi, Waikoloa, and the ponds from Kawaipapa to Honokalani on the Ko'olau side of the hill Ka'uiki and those on the Kipahulu side from Kalaniawawa to Haneo'o. Let them cut them all off at night. When the people are dying of thirst and can get no water, then they may be slaughtered." So Ka-hekili did as Ku-la'a-hola taught him, and wailing arose for the dead, for chiefs, fighting men, women, and children. Those who were eye-witnesses say there never was a more dreadful slaughter than in this war. Canoes were lowered to the rocks of Kane (*Na niu a Kane*), and Nae-'ole was the first to escape and sail to Hawaii. Afterwards Mahihele-lima escaped and landed at Kohala, but he was killed at Makapala. All the rest were slaughtered. At the heiaus of Kuawalu and Honua'ula adjoining Kuakaha and Ka'uiki are numerous ovens where the corpses of the slain were burned and left to dry in the sun; hence this battle was called Kaumupika'o. With the capture of Ka'uiki, in 1782, and the ending of the war, Ka-heili, his chiefs, war leaders, and fighting men retired to Makali'ihanau, the wide plain *mauka* [mountainward] of Mu'olea and adjoining Koali, and took up land cultivation.*

* *Ka Nupepa Ku'oko'a*, Feb. 23, 1867.

CHAPTER X

Kamehameha Wins Half Hawaii

In the month of July, 1782, Kiwalaʻo consulted with Keawe-maʻu-hili, his chief adviser (*kuhina nui*) and a younger brother of Ka-lani-ʻopuʻu, and with his younger brothers and all the other chiefs about the removal of the body of Ka-lani-ʻopuʻu to the Hale-o-Keawe at Honaunau in South Kona where it had been the chief's wish that his bones should lie in the tomb of the chiefs with the bones of former ruling chiefs. When the chiefs of South Kona heard of this bringing of the chief's bones to Honaunau, some of them formed a conspiracy to give the rule over the lands to Kamehameha. Ke-ku-hau-piʻo was both chief and kahuna, a renowned warrior and owner of the land of Keʻei. He went to Kohala to bring Kamehameha and found him and a younger brother out swimming and amusing themselves by making love to a woman. Informed of the messenger's arrival, Kamehameha and his friends went to meet him and, when all had gathered in the men's meeting house, Ke-ku-hau-piʻo addressed him thus: "O Chief! why waste time with a woman? The soldier's wealth is the only wealth worth while. Stand at the head of the government, and when you are a ruler the women will come to you like fish drawn by the stick of Makalei.* Become a worshiper of the god; stand at the head of the island. This is what I have come for. Let us go back to Kona, to your older relatives there; if they approve my plans, all will be well, for we have heard that your older brother who is ruler is coming with the corpse of the father of you two. If your brother does well by us, then all will be well; but if he treats us meanly then the land must go to the stronger." Kamehameha answered, "You have spoken well. Let us return to Kona and pay honor to the chief and to the corpse lest the chief say we are disrespectful." So they sailed and landed at

* The stick of Makalei—the fish-drawing stick "brought from Borabora by great Haumea, from Moa-nui-ʻula-akea, the sacred island at the borders of Kahiki"—has three properties; it will cause pregnancy, assist child birth, and change the features from youth to age. The romance of Makalei, in which the magical deeds performed by this stick in the hands of Haumea or of her favorite descendant play the leading part, was contributed to the Hawaiian newspaper, *Ka Nupepa Kuʻokoʻa*, between January 6, 1922 and the close of the following year when the story was discontinued because of the death of its contributor, Samuel Kai-akea Ke-koʻo-wai.

Kekaha where Ka-me'e-ia-moku was living at Ka'upulehu, and Ka-manawa at Kiholo. Now Kiwala'o was the son of Ka-lani-'opu'u, ruling chief of Hawaii. His mother was Ka-lola Pupuka-o-Hono-ka-wai-lani, daughter of Ke-kaulike and Ke-ku'i-apo-iwa-nui, chiefs of the prostrating tabu (*kapu moe*) on Maui.

When all was ready to carry the body of Ka-lani-'opu'u to Kona, Kiwala'o set sail in his double canoe accompanied by a double canoe bearing the corpse and by other canoes for the chiefs and commoners. They landed at Honomalino, South Kona, and then sailed on. Outside Honokua there came a chief from Honokua named Ke'e-au-moku, and he wailed over the body and asked, "Where will the body be laid?" A guard named Ka-ihe-ki'oi answered rudely, "It will be laid at Kailua." The chiefs of Kona knew well enough that the dead chief had commanded that he be taken to the Hale-o-Keawe, and that Ka-ihe-ki'oi was giving them a different answer. Sailing on, the party landed at Honaunau, placed the corpse in the Hale-o-Keawe, and remained at Honaunau. Ke'e-au-moku meanwhile hastened to join Kamehameha at Kekaha and inform him and the chiefs Ka-me'e-ia-moku, Ka-manawa, Ke-ku-hau-pi'o, and the rest, of the arrival of the body at Honaunau. Ke-ku-hau-pi'o said, "The best thing will be for us to sail to Ka'awaloa, Napo'opo'o, and Ke'ei. In case of fighting, Hauiki will make a good battlefield; the gulches in Ke'ei and the rough lava at Honaunau will make good ground for fighting." To this Kamehameha and the others assented. They sailed, landed at Ka'awaloa, and sent some of their men to Napo'opo'o and some to Ke'ei. When Kiwala'o heard of their coming he went to meet Kamehameha at Ka'awaloa, and they wailed and raised loud lamentation for the dead. When the wailing was ended the chief [Kiwala'o] said to Kamehameha, "Where are you? Perhaps we two are to die, for our uncle is urging us to war. Perhaps just we two will be put to death!" Now Keawe-ma'u-hili was the uncle to whom he referred. Kamehameha answered, "Tomorrow my friends and I will go to see the body of the chief," and Kiwala'o consented. The next day Kamehameha and all his chiefs wailed over the body of Ka-lani-'opu'u at the Hale-o-Keawe at Honaunau.

Then came the ruling chief, Kiwala'o, and stood at Akahipapa on the west side of the Hale-o-Keawe and announced the decree of the dead chief, saying, "Hear, you chiefs and commoners! To two of us, my younger brother* and me, has the chief left command. To him, our

* Close relatives of the same generation were thought of as equal in relationship and therefore the same term was used; likewise those of preceeding generations were referred to as *makua* (one generation older, therefore parent); *kupuna* (two generations back, therefore grandparents).

god Ku-ka'ili-moku to be under his command, and the lands which his father gave him to be his own lands; to me the command over the land. I am to be chief over the land; I cannot take what has been given to him, he cannot take what is my portion. Such is the command of the dead." Hearing this, the Kona chiefs grumbled, saying, "Unjust! unjust! The land should have been divided, three districts to one and three to the other; that would have been about right. We are impoverished. The chiefs of Hilo and Ka-'u will get everything, for this is their chief. Better that we go to war! better go to war!" Kamehameha had not thought of going to war, but the chiefs, who feared the loss of their lands, persuaded him to battle. They were determined to rebel but kept their determination a secret. Keoua Kuahu-'ula was, however, to take the first step.

Kamehameha was about to return to Kawaihae, but Ke-ku-hau-pi'o held him back and said, "Let us stay here and tonight we will go again to your elder brother." As they entered the chief's house that night a drinking party was being made ready, and Ke-ku-haupi'o said to Kiwala'o, "Let him [Kamehameha] chew the 'awa." The chief said, "Why should he chew the 'awa?" Ke-ku-hau-pi'o answered, "It was your father's command that one of you should serve the other, who was to be ruler over the land." So Kamehameha chewed the 'awa, strained it into the drinking cup, prayed and, freeing the tabu, handed the first 'awa cup to the ruling chief. Kiwala'o reached for the first cup and gave it to his intimate companion (aikane); and as this man raised his arm to drink, Ke-ku-hau-pi'o struck the cup from his hand and said, "The chief has insulted us! Your brother did not chew the 'awa for a commoner but for you, the chief." Nudging Kamehameha with his foot, he said, "Let us go back to the canoe and sail to Ke'ei, for each side will blame the other, one saying you are to blame and the other that he is at fault."

The next day Keawe-ma'u-hili urged upon Kiwala'o and the chiefs the division of the land of Hawaii; so Kiwala'o consented, told him to divide it, and said, "In dividing it, do not forget to give my brother Kamehameha some of the land." Keawe-ma'u-hili refused, saying, "This is not according to your father's command. He has the god and his old lands as was commanded. You are chief over the island, I am under you, and the chiefs under us. So was your father's command." So in dividing the land he reserved the largest portions for himself, and the rest he divided among the chiefs, warriors, lesser chiefs, favorites, and fighting men.

Keoua Kuahu-'ula heard that the land was being divided. He was a twin son of Ka-lani-'opu'u, his twin brother being Keoua Pe'e-'ale. The beautiful chiefess Kane-kapo-lei was their mother. Keoua was a handsome man, tall and broad of body, with fine features; a distinguished-looking figure with strands of hair so long that they hung down his back. That day about nine o'clock he came to the ruling chief, Kiwala'o, and said, "Are Ola'a and Kea'au ours?" The chief answered, "They have been given away; they are not ours." "How about Waiakea and Ponahawai?" "They have been given away; they are not ours." "Waipi'o and Waimea are ours?" "They are not ours; they have been given away." "Pololu and Makapala are ours?" "They have been given away; they are not ours." "The two Napu'u and the two Honokahau are ours?" "They have been given away; they are not ours." "Kahalu'u then, and the two Keauhou?" "They have been given away; they are not ours." "Then I am to have nothing in this division?" "You and I are left without land in this division. Our uncle has taken it. Our old lands you will have." Keoua went home and rallied his fighting men, his intimate friends, and his *kahu,* and bade them get food ready, don their feather mantles and helmets, hang their *palaoa* [necklaces] about their necks, take their *pololu* spears, and go to the sea as if for high diving. When the chief saw them and asked, "Where is Keoua Kuahu-'ula going with his people?" some one answered, "To the seashore for high diving." Keoua, accompanied by his *kahu* Uhai, his adopted son Ka'ie'ie, and his favorites and fighting men, went to Keomo on the east side of Ke'ei and cut down coconut trees. Now such destruction of coconut trees was a sign of war. The coconut tree was a man, said the ancients, whose head was buried in the ground with his penis and testicles above; and a man must be of the rank of a *nia'upi'o* chief to cut down such trees. When the party reached Ke'ei, some chiefs and others were out surfing, and a quarrel arose in which Keoua's party killed some of the men belonging to Kamehameha's party. Their bodies were taken to Kiwala'o to offer up at the heiau, and Kiwala'o offered up these war victims of Keoua Kuahu-'ula.

For four days skirmishes took place here and there before the real fighting began. Some of the chiefs of Kamehameha's party deserted him for Kiwala'o. Kane-koa, a favorite of Kamehameha, was one of these, and Ke-ahia, and others. The chiefs who backed Kamehameha were Ke'e-au-moku, Keawe-a-heulu, Ka-me'e-ia-moku, Ka-manawa, Ke-ku-hau-pi'o, and the younger relatives such as Kala'i-mamahu', Ka-welo-o-ka-lani, Ka-lani-malokuloku-i-ka-po'o-o-ka-lani and other chiefs of Kona and Kohala, but the greater number upheld Kiwala'o. At about nine in the morning of the fifth day the decisive battle was fought, Kamehameha's side was defeated, some of his men were killed, their bodies taken before Kiwala'o, and offered as a sacrifice by him and his kahunas. At the close of the offering a kahuna named Kalai-ku'i-'aha said to the chief, "The flood tide is yours in the morning, but it will ebb in the afternoon. Postpone the fighting until tomorrow." Kiwala'o would not listen to this advice, believing that Kamehameha's side would be defeated.

Kiwala'o's men had a long way to go from Honaunau to Hauiki at Ke'ei. Keoua had canoes ready in case Kamehameha should win.* All the chiefs had gone to the battle except Kamehameha, who was detained at Kealakekua by Holo-'ae and the prophetess (*kaula*) Pine to perform the ceremony of divination with the sacred calabashes. Said Holo-'ae to Kamehameha, "It is a day of misfortune, with defeat for both sides. One chief in your party will be killed, but when the god turns the defeat to that side then the ruling chief will be killed; but the tide is still rising; when the sun begins to decline the other side will meet defeat." Ke'e-au-moku was fighting in the rear of the battle and fell entangled by his *pololu* spear. Kaha'i and Nuhi ran and stuck him through with their daggers (*pahoa*). Kini came to retrieve his *pololu* spear and stood at his back and shouted in his harsh voice, "My weapon has caught a yellow-backed crab!" Kini was a person with a rasping voice (*leo'a-'a*). Almost dead though he was, Ke'e-au-moku heard the voice of Kiwala'o say, "Guard the ivory whale tooth (*niho palaoa*)! guard the ivory whale tooth! do not let it become covered with blood!" and he knew that he must die since the chief had no care for his own blood relative (*hulu makua*). Ka-manawa, meanwhile, seeing his plight, rushed through the thick of the fight to reach his side. As Kiwala'o gazed eagerly at the famous ornament to see that it should not get smeared with blood, Ke-akua-wahine silently aimed (*poko*) a slingstone (*pohaku 'ala'*) which struck Kiwala'o unaware, and he fell down. The men who were stabbing Ke'e-au-moku fled, and, seeing Kiwala'o lying prostrate, Ke'e-au-moku crawled to him with his shark's-tooth weapon (*lei o mano*) in his hand and cut his throat with it so that he died.

Kamehameha meanwhile had entered the fight and had made an end of Ke-ahia. This was his first victim that day. He tossed him up, and when he fell his bones were broken to pieces. Kamehameha had an affection for Ke-ahia, but Holo-'ae had instructed him to seize a man for the god. Then the chiefs and fighting men of Kiwala'o fled. Keoua and some of the chiefs ran, jumped into the sea, boarded their

* *Ka Nupepa Ku'oko'a*, Mar. 2, 1867.

canoes, and sailed to Ka-‘u; there Keoua became ruling chief over Ka-‘u and Puna. Some of the chiefs fled to the mountains. The name of this battle is Moku-‘ohai.

Keawe-ma‘u-hili was caught alive and imprisoned in the canoe shed (*halau*) at Piele in Napo‘opo‘o and guarded there for some time with the idea in Ke‘e-au-moku's mind that he was ultimately to be put to death; but some of the chiefs, among them Ka-nuha who guarded him, were sorry for him, for he was a chief of high rank, a son of Ka-lani-nui-‘i-a-mamao, the son of Keawe. Ke-kua-like-i-ka-wekiu-o-ka-lani was his mother, the granddaughter of Keawe. He was called Keawe-ma‘u-hili, that is, Keawe of double twist (*wili lua*), because of his high rank on both sides (*wili la pu‘u i ke kapu*). He was a tabu chief during the time of Alapa‘i-nui and while Ka-lani-‘opu‘u was ruling over the country. That is why the chiefs and Ka-nuha pitied him and allowed him to escape. He crossed over the mountain of Mauna Kea to Pa‘auhau in Hamakua and thence to Hilo, where he became ruling chief over half of Hilo, half of Puna, and also [half] of Hamakua. Kamehameha took Kona and Kohala and half of Hamakua. Thus the island of Hawaii was divided into three dominions (*aupuni*) under three ruling chiefs (*mo-i*).

What chief was responsible for giving Kamehameha dominion? It was Keoua Kuahu-‘ula. But did not the ruling chief, Kiwala‘o, join hands with Keoua? Yes, and that was when he broke the solemn command of Ka-lani-‘opu‘u and his proclamation at Akahipapa. In what respect was Kiwala‘o wrong? In first offering in sacrifice Kamehameha's men who had been killed by Keoua; that was as if he had consented to make war on Kamehameha. And for this reason the god transferred his power to Kamehameha. The offerings (*mohai*) and the gifts (*alana*) of Kiwala‘o were an abomination to the god. Who was the wise philosopher who foresaw in this beginning the taking of the whole island by Kamehameha? It was Ke-a-ulu-moku. Here is what he said at this period:

I ka papa o Akahipapa	At the camp ground of Akahipapa
Haawi ‘oe o kou ea o kou make.	Thou gavest up thy life, thy death.
Lilo ka hema me ke ‘akau,	The south land and the north are gone,
A la lilo—mai welawela,	There they are now lost; grudge not to yield them,
Mai ‘ea‘ea, mai puniu,	Dispute not, hold not back,
Waihoa ko ia nei ko me ko ia nei ‘oli‘oli.	Give up to him what he has gained with his joy.

and again:

I kahi one i Hauiki	... at the sand beach at Hauiki
O Kalani kela, O Kalani keia;	That was a chief, this was a chief;
Koi moku ilaila;	The stake was the island;
Koi kaʻa kumu kela,	There the property was staked,
Koi pa i ke poho,	The game was played to utter loss,
Pa i ke kumu helu palua,	He strikes the goal, he counts double,
Helu koke no i ka puni ʻeo.	He quickly counts what he has gained.
Eia koi ʻaina, puo ka lima,	'Tis he who staked the land, he clasps his hands,
Oia koi moku o ka lani.	He is the chief who staked the island.
O Kalani Kau-i-ke-ao-uli kela,	The divine Kau-i-ke-ao-uli is that one,
O Kalani-nui-lani-mehameha keia.	The divine Kamehameha the Great is this.

You will find the lines in the prophetic prayer chant called "Haui ka lani."* Kamehameha himself knew that this [victory] was but the beginning of an empire.

Kamehameha was the son of Ka-lani-kupu-a-pa-i-ka-lani-nui Keoua, son of Ka-lani-keʻe-au-moku, the son of Ka-lani-kau-lele-ia-iwi by Keawe-kahi-aliʻi-o-ka-moku. His mother was Ke-kuʻi-apo-iwa, daughter of Kekela-o-ka-lani, the sister of Ka-lani-keʻe-au-moku. Her father was Haʻae, son of Ka-uaua-nui-a-Mahi by Ke-poʻo. Ka-mehameha's younger brother was Ka-lani-malokuloku-i-ke-poʻo-o-o-ka-lani and his sisters were Ka-lani-ka-uli-hiwa-kama and Ku-hoʻoheihei-pahu, all born to Ke-kuʻi-apo-iwa. Ka-manawa was the father of some of them. Some of Keoua's [other] children were Ka-lani-mamahuʻ and Ka-welo-o-ka-lani, and their mother was Ka-maka-e-hei-kuli. One of Keoua's daughters was Ke-kuʻi-apo-iwa [also called Liliha], mother of Ke-opu-o-lani and daughter of Ka-Iola. She was called "One who was sought for a lord" (*imi ana haku*).†

---

* The quotations are taken from the chant called "Haui ka lani," 14, vol. 6, p. 384, lines 239-243; p. 383, lines 227-232.

† Fornander accepts the genealogy which makes Haʻae the son of Ka-uaua by Ka-lani-kau-lele-ia-iwi instead of Ke-poʻo-mahana the great-granddaughter of a son of Kama-lala-walu of Maui. See 13, vol. 2, p. 131, note 3. In this case he and Alapaʻi would be full brothers. Fornander makes Ku-hoʻoheihei-pahu the child of Ke-kau-like and Ke-kuʻi-apo-iwa-nui p. 213.

The news that Kiwala'o was dead and Kamehameha had become ruling chief on Hawaii reached Ka-hekili, ruling chief of Maui, while he was living in Makali'ihanau at a place called Hanalu'ukia above Mu'olea, and he sent Alapa'i-malo-iki (also called Alapa'i-kupalu-mano') and Ka-ulu-nae, younger brothers of Ke'e-au-moku and sons of Ku-ma'ai-ku, by canoe to Kamehameha to ask for canoes, for Ka-hekili wished to sail to Oahu to make war on Ka-hahana, ruling chief of Oahu. Kamehameha answered, "The chief cannot be provided with canoes; if Hilo and Ka-'u were mine, then canoes could be provided. But you two stay here with us in Hawaii and do not go back to Maui." And perhaps because of their older brother's [Ke'e-au-moku's] urging, or perhaps because they were made regent chiefs in Hawaii, they remained. But when Keawe-ma'u-hili heard of the two messengers being sent to Kamehameha for canoes and failing to get them, he sent some double canoes together with feather capes and 'o'o feathers as a gift of affection to Ka-hekili. When Ka-hekili saw these gifts of friendship his heart warmed toward Keawe-ma'u-hili, and he sent fighting men to Hilo, warriors from Kaniu'ula, led by his intimate friend Ka-haha-wai from Ka-haha-wai at Waihe'e, a brave man, father of Ke-aloha-waia and Haia'.

After the battle of Moku-'ohai, which was Kamehameha's first battle to gain rule over the island, Kane-koa, a chief under Keawe-ma'u-hili, rebelled against him, did battle against him, was defeated, fled to Ka-'u, and lived with Keoua Kuahu-'ula. Again he rebelled against Keoua, but in the battle he fled and was killed by Keoua *mauka* of Ola'a. He was a grandson of Keawe. His younger brother Kaha'i, overcome with grief for his beloved elder brother and thinking how he could avenge him, remembered the child whom they had nursed and packed about on their backs, as the one to whom to appeal for vengeance. So, laying aside his loin cloth, he went to Kona to challenge Kamehameha as a warrior. When Kamehameha, who had already heard of Kane-koa's death, saw Kaha'i coming to him in this way, love welled up within him for Kane-koa, his uncle, who used to carry him perched on his hip along the plains of Kawaihae and up the paths to Lanimaomao in the chilly winds of Waimea, while the perspiration poured down the back of Kane-koa at the ascent of Uli. So his feelings were stirred, and he hastened off his warriors to do battle against Hilo and Ka-'u. The advisers and orators quickly seconded their chief's plan to send an army, and preparations were made for some to go by land and some by canoe. As they came along by Kawaihae the campaign got the name of "Bad child" (*Kama'ino*), because the fleet at sea met bad weather, and the division over the mountain met rain and a chilly fog. The battle was fought beside the pit of Pele and was called "Battle of the bitter rain" (*Kau-ua-'awa*).

During this engagement at the pit of Pele, Keoua lay *mauka* of 'Ohaikea at Kapapala in Ka-'u, and Kamehameha decided to join forces with his fleet under the command of Ke'e-au-moku. As he was descending, just out of Pana'ewa at a place called Pua'aloa, he met the war party of Ka-hekili which had been sent to the aid of Keawe-ma'u-hili under Ka-haha-wai. Moa, who saw the encounter with his own eyes, says that these men of Ka-haha-wai were soldiers without equal. They surrounded the forces of Kamehameha on all sides. Ka-haha-wai was as hard to hold as a slippery eel; when hemmed in, his men always managed to break through. The *pololu* spears and the *ihe* spears rained down like bath water; blood flowed like water and soaked into the dry earth of that hill. The spears were entangled (*hihia ana*) like a rainbow arched on both sides. In the thick of the fight between the two sides, Kahu-'ena and Ka-haha-wai showed their skill in handling and warding off *pololu* and *ihe* spears from descending upon their forces. As they brushed aside the weapons descending upon them from all sides, their own weapons waved (*kolili*) in the air like the tail feathers (*hulu ko'o*) of the bosun bird (*koa'e*), waving (*pulelo*) in the wind.

Kamehameha's forces were badly used in these battles. Ka-lani-malokuloku-i-ke-po'o-o-ka-lani was almost killed at Hala'i. The army was saved only by getting to the sea and going aboard Ke'e-au-moku's fleet. A soldier named Mo'o who followed Kamehameha is reported to have said, "O heavenly one! do not run away in fright; it is only I." Since Keawe-ma'u-hili and Keoua had joined forces against Kamehameha there was no place for him in Hilo; he camped his men at Laupahoehoe in Hilo Paliku (Hilo by the cliff). Afterwards Kamehameha and Ka-haku'i paddled to Papa'i and on to Kea'au in Puna where some men and women were fishing, and a little child sat on the back of one of the men. Seeing them about to go away, Kamehameha leaped from his canoe intending to catch and kill the men, but they all escaped with the women except two men who stayed to protect the man with the child. During the struggle Kamehameha caught his foot in a crevice of the rock and was stuck fast; and the fishermen beat him over the head with a paddle. Had it not been that one of the men was hampered with the child and their ignorance that this was Kamehameha with whom they were struggling, Kamehameha would have been killed that day. This quarrel was named Ka-lele-iki, and from the striking of Kamehameha's head with a paddle came the law of Mamala-hoe (Broken paddle) for Kamehameha.*

While Kamehameha was encamped at Laupahoehoe, Aka-lele was sent by Ka-hekili to Hilo with strong paddlers to bring back Ka-haha-wai's war party to Maui in order that they might go to war with Ka-hahana on Oahu, and Keawe-ma'u-hili consented to their going, since he had an ally in Keoua. He gave them new canoes for Ka-hekili, and Keoua did the same. When the party was ready to start for Maui, Ka-haha-wai directed the canoes by way of Laupahoehoe, to meet Kamehameha. When he met the chief he said, "Is it to be face up or face down?" (*iluna ke alo, ilalo ke alo*) [meaning, is the sentence to be life or death?]. Kamehameha knew that Ka-haha-wai was a man sacred (*la'a*) to Ka-hekili and was not to be slain; Kikane again was a man sacred to Kamehameha, and he answered, "It is not death." Ka-haha-wai said, "It does not matter about the others; I came to you, O chief! to put my life or death in your hands lest you should say that I ran away." Then Ka-haha-wai returned to Maui with his party and once more joined Ka-hekili. Kamehameha and his followers remained at Laupahoehoe, but being unable to defeat the combined forces of Keawe-ma'u-hili and Keoua, he removed to Hala'ula and Hapu'u in Kohala. He appointed Ke'e-au-moku, Keawe-a-heulu, Ka-me'e-ia-moku, and Ka-manawa to be his secret advisors (*hoa kuka malu'*) and counselors (*hoa'aha'olelo*) in ruling the island. They alone were consulted about what would be for the good or the ill of the country.

At that time the noted warrior, Ke-ku-hau-pi'o, died at Napo'opo'o of a wound got in a sham (*le'ale'a*) battle in which he failed to ward off a spear-thrust. The point struck him where a fragment of a broken spear had previously lodged in his body, perhaps driving it into his intestines (*na'au*). Ke-ku-hau-pi'o died in 1784. One thing that brought him fame was the fulfilment of his prophecy about Kamehameha's conquest of the island in the chant called "Hikikauelia." About the same time there died in Hilo another man famous for his battle chants, chants of praise, love chants, and prophetic chants, Ke-a-ulu-moku, the author of "Haui ka Lani."

Kamehameha and his followers left Kohala and went once more to battle in Hilo against the two opposing chiefs of Ka-'u and Hilo, but in spite of hard fighting they remained undefeated. This battle was called Hapu'u and "The last of Laupahoehoe." Kamehameha then retired to Kauhola at Hala'ula in Kohala with his counselors, chiefs,

* *Ka Nupepa Ku'oko'a*, Mar. 9, 1867.

and warriors, where they spent their time in farming. In 1785, Ka-mehameha took Ka-'ahu-manu to be his wife. She was the first-born child of Ke'e-au-moku, son of Keawe-poepoe and his wife Ku-ma'ai-ku, by Na-mahana, daughter of Ke-kau-like and Ha'alo'u. Ka-'ahu-manu was one of a large family born to Na-mahana, among whom were Ka-heihei-malie who was renamed Hoa-pili-wahine, Ka-hekili who was renamed Ke'e-au-moku, Ka-lua-i-Konahale who was renamed Kua-kini, and Ke-kua-i-pi'ia who was renamed Na-mahana. Ke-aka-kilohi was the son of Ke'e-au-moku by Ka-lolo-wahi-lani, daughter of Ka-uhi-'aimoku-a-Kama and Lu'ukia. Kamehameha's children prior to his ruling over Hawaii were Pauli Ka-'o-lei-o-ku, by Kane-kapo-lei, wife of Ka-lani-'opu'u, Maheha Ka-pu-likoliko, and Kina'u. The mother of the last two was Pele-uli, granddaughter of Ke-ku'i-apo-iwa-nui and Ka-ua-kahi-akua, son of Lono-maka'i-honua and Kaha-po'ohiwi.*

* *Ka Nupepa Ku'oko'a*, Mar. 16, 1867.

CHAPTER XI

Ka-hahana Loses Oahu

Ka-hahana was a tabu chief of Oahu.* Ka-'io-nui-lala-ha'i was his mother, a granddaughter of Ka-lani-'o-mai-he-uila, daughter of Ka-lani-kahi-maka'i-ali'i and Kualu, older sister of Ka-'ula-hea, ruling chief of Maui. Elani was his father, belonging to the family of Ku-panihi and Ke-opu-o-lani. He was taken to Maui in his infancy as the foster son of Ka-hekili and was brought up with all the tabus of Maui. He developed into a handsome child with good features and lovely curling hair from which came his nickname "Pi'ipi'i" [curly head] (*hahai moa*). When he became a man he caused a breach in the tabu by making love to the lesser chiefesses and so lost the tabu of Fire (*Ahi*), Heat (*Wela*), and Extraordinary heat (*Hahana*) which had been his, and he was called Walia (*wale'ia*) [an elision, meaning "is degraded"]. Ka-hahana took for himself a wife named Ke-kua-po'i. It is said of this woman that she had no equal throughout the group. Her name was famous from Hawaii to Kauai. It had become a legend because of the splendid proportions of her body, without a flaw from head to foot; eyes lovely as a dove's; cheeks like a rosebud that unfolds its petals in the early morn; a face whose features seemed to change from morning to midday, evening, night. For such a peerless beauty the tabu was well worth losing.

The chiefs, priests, and commoners of Oahu were dissatisfied with the rule of Ku-mahana, son of Pele-io-holani. He slept late, was stingy, penurious, deaf to the advice of others, and used to take himself off to the plains to shoot rats. They therefore plotted to depose Ku-mahana, and, having succeeded in their plans, the chiefs and the leading kahuna, Ka-'opulupulu, agreed to bring Ka-hahana from Maui to rule over them. For this purpose they sent to him his mother [mother's cousin] Ke-kela, and she landed on Maui, met her son and the ruling chief and other chiefs of Wailuku, and conveyed to them the will of the chiefs and of the head kahuna of Oahu that Ka-hahana should return to Oahu. "To be at the head of the government?" asked Ka-hekili. "I believe this to be their purpose," answered Ke-kela. "Then I will not hold the boy back

* The story of Ka-hahana printed in 14, vol. 6, pp. 282-306 seems to be taken from Kamakau.

128

since you have come for him yourself; anyone else I would have refused. But I will retain his wife as surety for his treatment on Oahu." "Are not we, his parents, the persons to carry orders (*ilamuku*) for our son? This is our younger sister, and since our son has taken her as his wife it is proper that she go where he goes." Ka-hekili then turned to Ka-hahana and said, "I permit you to go. Only do me this favor, that when you are firmly established on Oahu you let the land of Kualoa and the ivory that drifts ashore be mine; let these be my property on the island." Then Ka-hahana and Ke-kua-po'i his wife, accompanied by chiefs and paddlers, sailed for Oahu and landed at Kahaloa in Waikiki, and the chiefs, lesser chiefs, kahunas, counselors, warriors, and commoners gathered from the mountains of the interior to the seacoast at the principal place at Waikiki to make Ka-hahana chief over Oahu. There was no opposition to the appointment since Ka-'opulupulu had sanctioned it. Ka-hahana was approved by all, for his rule was established without war or bloodshed.

Ka-hahana's rule over the land having become firm, he informed the chiefs, governors, and counselors of Ka-hekili's request for Kualoa and the ivory that drifted ashore, and asked their opinion. Some approved, saying, "If you desire to give this to your parent (*maku-kane*) as a reward for rearing you, it is all one to us." But the chief Ku-ka-lehua-'a-iku-lani said, "Call Ka-'opulupulu and let him decide whether to give it or not." So Ka-'opulupulu was sent for and the question put, and Ka-hahana told him that he was willing to grant these things to his parent in return for his up-bringing. The kahuna bowed his head, then, looking up, said, "O chief! if you give away these things your authority will be lost, and you will cease to be a ruler. To Kualoa belong the water courses of your ancestors, Ka-lumaluma'i and Ke-kai-hehe'e; the sacred drums of Ka-pahu-'ulu, and the spring of Ka-'ahu-'ula; the sacred hill of Ka-ua-kahi son of Kaho'owaha of Kualoa. Without the ivory that drifts ashore you could not offer to the gods the first victim slain in battle; it would be for Ka-hekili to offer it on Maui, and the rule would become his. You would be no longer ruler. Had the country been yours by conquest, it might be proper for you to reward your uncle, but your authority was given you by the chiefs because of your uncle Ku-mahana's mismanagement. Any other requests of Ka-hekili you might have granted, but not this. And be sure not to conceal from me any further secret message that Ka-hekili may send." Having heard these words of the kahuna, Ka-hahana and the chiefs and counselors congratulated themselves upon their escape from losing the dominion to Ka-hekili.

Ka-hahana became ruler of Oahu in 1773, and ruled eight and one half years. During the first of these years there were no wars as in the time of Pele-io-holani, son of Ku-i-ke-ala-i-ka-ua-o-ka-lani Ku-nui-akea Ku-ali'i, who delighted in war and whose passion for it was inherited by his son Ka-lani-'opu'u, the ravening lion of his time, who was during this period engaged in war with Ka-hekili on Maui. Ka-hekili asked Ka-hahana's help in this war, and since Ka-hekili had reared him Ka-hahana sent some of his warriors to Ka-hekili's aid; but Ka-lani-'opu'u was also a relative of his, and it was for this reason that Ka-lani-'opu'u did not go to war against Oahu or Molokai.

One of the warriors who served the two masters, Ka-hahana and Ka-hekili, was a certain lesser chief (*kaukauali'i*) named Ka-pohu. Ka-hekili built himself a chief's house called 'Umi-hale on the *mauka* side of Ka'ilipoe, *makai* of Kihahale. Any chief or commoner who paid the taxes levied in the shape of feather capes and bird feathers was looked upon with favor and admitted to 'Umi-hale, but a person who failed to pay the taxes was discredited and refused admission. Ka-pohu and Ka-'akakai went to Hawaii after feather capes and bird feathers in order to gain admission to 'Umi-hale. They landed in Kohala and Ka-'akakai went by way of Hamakua to Hilo and became friendly with Keawe-hano, the chief of Hilo. As for Ka-pohu, he went around by Kona, Ka-'u, Puna, and finally reached Hilo and there heard in some native villages that a man from Maui had become a friend of Keawe-hano and had obtained a feather cape from him. Keawe-hano's houses were situated on the beach at Punahoa, close to Pi'ihonua and facing the waves of Huia and Hikanui. Ka-pohu went along outside the fence of Keawe-hano's place and saw Ka-'akakai sitting with Keawe-hano at the threshold of the house, both wearing feather capes on their shoulders, feather necklaces about their necks, and helmets on their heads. Now when Ka-'akakai saw Ka-pohu standing outside the fence, he scowled, took up as much room as possible, and left no room in the doorway. Ka-pohu, observing their splendid apparel, chanted these words:

Po Ka'ula i ka hulu o ka manu,	Ka'ula is darkened by the feathers of the birds,
Ke nonoi a'e la ka hulu o ka manu	The feathered birds are appealing to
I komo iloko ua i Poli - e.	The rain to fall at Poli.

As soon as Keawe-hano heard these words chanted, he brushed Ka-'akakai aside and looked out. Then Ka-pohu went on boldly chanting:

Ku pololei ka 'opua ua malie	The hanging clouds stand erect; it is calm
A ka luna aku i Maunalahilahi,	On the upland of Maunalahilahi,
Eia la!	Lo, here it is!
O ka i'a a ke akua la	The fish of the god
Ua lahilahi wale.	Is thin.

Keawe-hano heard the words and called out to Ka-pohu, "Come into the house! There is food and fish in here." As Ka-pohu entered he chanted:

A Kahuku i Ola'a,	From Kahuku to Ola'a [I have traveled],
Ka uka i Pana'ewa,	To the uplands of Pana'ewa,
Ka uka o Haili,	To the uplands of Haili,
Kapili manu e,	To catch birds with lime,
Kawili manu e,	To catch birds with snares,
Kololio manu e,	To catch birds with lines,
Wiliwili manu e,	To twist the necks of birds,
O ka hulu o ka manu.	For their feathers.
'Ahu'ula mai no,	[Give me] a feather cape,
Mahiole mai no.	[Give me] a feather helmet,
Hulikua mai no.	[Give me] a feather necklace.*

To these words Keawe-hano responded, "Here is your feather necklace, here is your feather helmet, but the cape you two shall share!" No sooner had he uttered the word share (*mahele*) than Ka-pohu reached for a corner of the feather cape that Ka-'akakai was wearing and drew it over his own shoulders, leaving Ka-'akakai without any. In that short space of time Ka-pohu had gained the friendship of Keawe-hano. He turned to Keawe-hano and said, "I have two masters, Ka-hekili and Ka-hahana. If your lord goes to war against my two lords, should my lords be victorious over yours I will preserve your life that day" (*o 'oe ka'u ola nui ia la*). Keawe-hano made the same promise to Ka-pohu, and both agreed to abide by their vow.

At the time when Ka-lani-'opu'u went to Maui to fight against Ka-hekili, when the battles of Ka-moku-'ilima and Kakani-lua were fought, Ka-pohu was with Ka-hahana, ruling chief of Oahu, who was living on Molokai; and when Ka-hekili sent a messenger to tell Ka-hahana that Ka-lani-'opu'u had come to Honua'ula to attack him, and Ka-hahana sent warriors to help Ka-hekili, Ka-pohu remembering his vow to Keawe-hano, joined those who went on that mission. He went from

* *Ka Nupepa Ku'oko'a,* Mar 16, 1867.

Honua'ula by way of Ka'anapali on the day that the Alapa, also called Pi'ipi'i, attacked their foes in the battle of Kakani-lua. When he reached the battlefield, all the warriors had been slain; Keawe-hano alone remained to be put to death. Ka-pohu went among the warriors to plead with them not to kill Keawe-hano. He said to Keawe-hano, "This is not the kind of encounter implied in our vow that if your chief and his warriors and my chiefs and their warriors took part in a battle, if my chiefs were defeated and slain you would preserve my life, and so your life would be preserved by me if your chief were defeated and slain; so we should be seen as favorites of our chiefs. This evil treatment that you have suffered came as a murderous attack, and I was unable to save you." All this was spoken in a chant, for these two were skilled in uttering their thoughts in chant. I have not quoted the words here because they are too long, and you would not understand their meaning. The younger generation would not know what it was all about. Ka-pohu had told Ka-hekili of the vow, and the chief consented to free Keawe-hano and he took good care of him, but Keawe-hano died of his many wounds.

An intimate friend of his came to see him when he heard that he was dying. This was Ka-moe-au, a man very skillful in observing signs in the heavens and on the earth and all kinds of omens pertaining to the lives of men and women. Every chief held him sacred and none was permitted to put him to death; Ka-hekili himself was acquainted with him. His conversation with Keawe-hano was all carried on in chant, but because the chant is too long I have not included it in the story. Composing chants was one of the arts of the ancients. In old times one who lived in the country in poverty and hunger would chant to the chief his need of bark cloth or some other necessity, and his need would be relieved. Chants of that kind were clever and ingenious. Their composers were called "lovers of wisdom" (ake akamai) and "seekers of unseen things" (noi'i i na mea 'ike 'ole 'ia).

After the battle of Ka-moku-'ilima, Ka-lani-'opu'u returned to Hawaii, and Ka-hekili sailed to Molokai to meet Ka-hahana, who was living under tabu at the heiau of Kapukapu-akea of Wailau. The tabu being ended he went to live at Kanalu, where all the men of Molokai were making the big water taro patch of Paikahawai. The two chiefs met with many professions of affection, but Ka-hekili's was feigned; he coveted Oahu and Molokai for their rich lands, many walled fish-ponds, springs, and water taro patches. The island of Oahu was very fertile and Molokai scarcely less so, and Ka-hekili lay sleepless with covetous longing. He asked for Halawa, a large land on the northeastern side of Molokai adjoining Wailau on the north, and Ka-hahana gave it to him. Ka-hekili asked, "How about those properties on Oahu that I asked of you?" Ka-hahana replied, "You cannot have them. Ka-'opulupulu held them back." "That is strange! Ka-'opulupulu offered me the whole dominion over Oahu, but I refused it for your sake, lest I be thought treacherous to my sister's son in snatching away your land." These words had been taught to Ka-hekili by Ka-leo-pu'upu'u. They were treacherous words, designed to lead Ka-hahana to put Ka-'opulupulu to death. Ka-hekili had urged war against Molokai and Oahu, but Ka-leo-pu'upu'u had dissuaded him from attempting it while Ka-'opulupulu lived lest he lose Maui as well. The only thing to do was to poison Ka-hahana's mind against Ka-'opulupulu, and when he was put to death then Oahu could be easily taken. This Ka-'opulupulu was the kahuna who had uttered the famous words, "Open the sluice gate that the fish may enter!" Ka-leo-pu'upu'u was his younger brother, and he sought to sell the life of his elder brother in order to advance Ka-hekili and obtain honor for himself.

After his return from Molokai, when he had ruled six years over Oahu and Molokai, Ka-hahana abandoned the advice of Ka-'opulupulu and began to lay burdens upon the country people and to dig up bones from their burial places to make arrows for rat-shooting and hooks for fishing. The bones of chiefs were bartered for skirts for chiefesses and handles for kahili. Ka-'opulupulu came in vain to remonstrate with him, and the kahuna and all his followers, relatives, and members of his household tattooed their knees as a sign of the chief's deafness to his admonitions. [The word kuli means both "knee" and "deaf."]

Ka-hekili waited some years for the kahuna's death, then he sent his dear friend Ka-hui, the one who had charge over the life or death of captives and who offered up for him the first victim in battle throughout the time of his rule, and told him to take a gift to Ka-hahana and repeat to him the words that he taught him. And Ka-hui repeated to Kahahana the secret message, saying, "Your uncle sent me out of affection for you because Ka-'opulupulu has offered the dominion over Oahu to your uncle; but your uncle does not approve of this deed, since you are his nephew, and has sent me to let you know of it. Thus he commanded me." Ka-hahana did not reveal the message to any of the chiefs, kahunas, or soothsayers, but sought the death of Ka-'opulupulu lest the dominion become Ka-hekili's. Some time after, in February, 1782, Ka-hahana said to Ka-'opulupulu, "I wish to go around the island and restore the houses dedicated to the gods." Ka-'opulupulu answered, "It is a good wish, O chief! for the gods are the pillars of the dominion, and the chief who serves the gods as did your ancestor Kuali'i, will rule long, grow old, blear-eyed like a rat, well-nigh bloodless, withered as a dry pandanus leaf, tottering with age, and in the end reach the world of light. The gods give such life to a religious person, and none shall rebel against his rule. If the land becomes poor or suffers from famine or is scorched by the sun or lacks fish or servitors, the gods can be found in Kahikimelemele. There are two roads for the chief to take about the island, one which will support the dominion and make it fast so that it shall remain fixed and immovable, a second which will give the dominion to others." Now the kahuna may have been wrong in telling him about the right and the wrong road to take in order to keep the dominion. You, O reader! may guess what he meant by these roads, for your grandparents may have told you. Ka-hahana however put a different construction upon the words and thought, "So Ka-'opulupulu has offered the rule to Ka-hekili!"

Ka-'opulupulu* was living on his lands in Waimea and Pupukea when Ka-hahana went around Oahu with the chiefs, counselors, guards, kahunas, and attendants, and restored the most important heiaus, observed strictly the tabus on the heiaus, and ate of the fat of the land. At Wai'anae he restored the heiau of Ka-moho-ali'i and sent for Ka-'opulupulu. When the messenger came to him at Waimea the kahuna [Ka-'opulupulu] said, "Tell the chief that we two will come tomorrow." The next day he and his only son, Ka-hulu-pue, set out, and when they reached Ka'ananiau at Ka'ena Point he said to his son, "Let us pray that we may know whether this journey is for good or evil." When he had prayed he said, "The gods show me that we shall die. Here is the way leading to life, and here is the way leading to death." The son chose the road to life. The father said, "If we take the road you have chosen we shall not gain vengeance in this world, but if we die we shall be avenged. The chief shall die, his dominion shall be taken, and none of his offspring shall survive. It is better for us to take the road to death." The son consented. When they reached Wai'anae Ka-hahana at once ordered that Ka-hulu-pue be put to death. The kahuna called out to his son, "Take a deep breath and give your body to the sea; the land is the sea's!" The boy ran and dived into the sea of Malae and died there. Then the chiefs and the commoners, hearing of Ka-hulu-pue's death, were uneasy in their minds, but Ka-hahana paid no attention to his counselors' words, and when they reached Pu'uloa Ka-'opulupulu was killed. The leading counselor of the island being thus

* See 37, pp. 48 & 51 for description of his heiaus, Pu'u o Mahuka and Kupopolo.

dead the people lost courage, for the foundation of the dominion was shaken.*

Ka-hekili on Maui heard that the pillar which held up Oahu had been broken down. Said Ka-leo-pu'upu'u, "The end post (*pouhana*) of the dominion of Oahu has fallen, so let us take over the rule as you have so long desired." Ka-hekili answered, "Send for Ka-haha-wai and his warriors to go with me to make war on Oahu." Here are the names of the chiefs called to the war: Ke-kua-manoha', Ka'iana, Na-makaeha', Kalai-koa, Ka-mohomoho, Nahiolea, the war leader (*pukaua*) Hu'eu, Ka-uhi-ko'ako'a, and Ka-hui. Of the chief's sons there were Ka-lani-nui-ulu-moku, Pe'ape'a, Manono Ka-ua-kapeku-lani, Ka-lani-ku-pule, and Koa-lau-kani. There were also the chiefly leaders of the warriors, the (warrior companies) Po'o-uwahi, Ka-niu-'ula, Pahu-pu, and the experts with the sling and the bow and arrow. As for double canoes, these had been furnished by Keawe-ma'u-hili and Keoua from Hawaii. The companies met at Hale-kumu-ka-lani, the gods' house (*ka hale o ke akua*) at Puehuehu in Lahaina, and after the tabu period was ended they sailed to Molokai to secure fish from the walled fishponds for the journey, and their canoes reached from Ho'olehua to Kaluako'i. They sailed north of Lanai by the route called Ka-'opua-ki'iki'i and thence out to deep ocean until they felt the breeze that blew from Oahu, then heading shoreward, they entered the harbor of Waikiki.

Ka-hahana, who was then living at Ka-wanana-koa in Nu'uanu, back of Honolulu, was filled with consternation when he heard that Ka-hekili had come with a fleet of war canoes that reached from Ka'alawai to Kawehewehe, and he rallied his warriors about him. Eight of the warriors from 'Ewa and Waialua who heard the call did not join Ka-hahana, but went to fight single-handed against the host. These were Pupuka, Maka'i-o-ulu, Pua-kea, Pinao, Ka-lae-one, Pahua, Ka-uhi, and Ka-puko'a, eight in all. They went to 'Apuakehau and fought against the whole host, and when they found themselves surrounded by the Maui warriors they broke through the front lines, only to find their way of retreat bristling with more warriors and no way to turn in all Kawehewehe. Spears fell upon them like rain, but it was they who slew the warriors of Maui. At the border of Punalu'u, on the way down to Luahinewai and the coconut grove of Kuakuaaka, a Maui chief named Ka-uhi-ko'ako'a caught hold of Maka'i-o-ulu, who was a fat, clumsy person, not a swift runner but a good fighter. Ka-uhi-ko'ako'a was a tall man, muscular from head to foot. He was the father of Kina'u, the younger brother of Poki. Since the Maui men had been unable to touch the Oahu warriors with their spears or *pololu* thrown

* *Ka Nupepa Ku'oko'a*, Mar. 23, 1867.

from all sides, they thought to catch them first and then use their spears upon them; so Ka-uhi-ko'ako'a caught Maka'i-o-ulu and attempted to run his dagger into the back of his neck, but failed to pierce him. The captive meanwhile called out to his friend Pupuka (grandfather of Pi'i-lani, the sister of the late M. Ke-ku-anao'a), "Give my love to my wife and children when you see them!" Pupuka turned and, seeing his friend a prisoner, launched his spear. "Stab at my navel!" cried Maka'i-o-ulu, intending to die with Ka-uhi-ko'ako'a, but Pupuka deftly turned the spear to one side. It entered Ka-uhi-ko'ako'a's abdomen, and Maka'i-o-ulu seized it and forced it through to the back. Since the other Oahu warriors had escaped, the two of them could not carry off the body when the Maui men fled. Some say that this was the reason why the Oahuans were eventually defeated in the war, because they were unable to offer the first victim of battle upon the altar.

Three times both sides attacked, and three times both were defeated. In January, 1783, a decisive battle was fought with Kahe-iki as the battlefield. Ka-hekili's forces were divided into two companies, one under Hu'eu's leadership stationed at Kanela'au and Kapapakolea back of Pu'owaina, and the other under his own command stationed from above Hekili to Kahehuna and 'Auwaiolimu. In this battle the waters of the stream of Kahe-iki ran red with blood from the heaps of broken corpses that fell into the water; the stream was dammed back with the corpses of those who died in battle. On the ridge facing Pauoa and from thence down to Kapena another attack was made against the defense stationed back of the heiau of Kahe-iki. Confusion seized the ranks; the warriors of Ka-hahana were dispersed; Ka-hahana and Ke-kua-po'i his wife fled to the forest. Ka-hekili's wife Kau-wahine was also a noted fighter. Thus Oahu and Molokai were taken by Ka-hekili and Ka-'opulupulu's prophecy was fulfilled.

For two years and six months Ka-hahana and his wife and Ka-hahana's friend, Alapa'i, hid in the mountains and were fed and clothed by the commoners, who had compassion upon them. Thus were the misdeeds of Ka-hahana justly repaid. They were finally betrayed by Ke-ku-manoha', father of Ka-lani-moku and half brother of Ke-kua-po'i, Ha'alo'u being the mother of both. Their last place of hiding was near Wailele at Waikele in 'Ewa. Alapa'i said to Ka-hahana, "Let us kill our wife and then we shall be able to escape." Ka-hahana was more merciful, perhaps because he could not endure to lose Ke-kua-po'i, who was an incomparable beauty. He said, "Why kill our wife who has been so faithful a companion to us while we have dodged death in cold and wet, wandering here in the mountains, in the thickets of Wahiawa, in this ocean of Ka'ie'iea? Perhaps she can persuade her kinsmen to help us some day." Learning that Ke-ku-manoha' was at Waikele and Ka-lani-ku-pule and Koa-lau-kani at Kapapapuhi, Ke-kua-po'i made herself known to her brother, hoping that he would save them all three for her sake. "Where are Ka-hahana and his friend?" asked her brother. "Will you spare us three?" asked the woman. "Why should you die? are we not all chiefs?" he answered; but his words were false; he intended to give up his brother-in-law to Ka-hekili. Alapa'i urged, "O heavenly one! let us flee. We shall die if we stay here; only Ke-kua-po'i will be saved." "If Kekua-po'i is saved, we shall be also." "You will not be saved; you are a chief, a ruler by descent." Then Ke-ku-manoha' sent men to Ka-hekili at Waikiki to tell him that Ka-hahana was at Waikele. Ka-hekili ordered him to be killed and brought to Waikiki and he sent double canoes to Halaulani at Waipi'o in 'Ewa. Ke-ku-manoha' killed Ka-hahana and his friend Alapa'i, wrapped them in coconut leaves, placed them on the platform of the canoes, and took them to Kahekili at Waikiki. When he witnessed the murder of his chief, Ka-la-wela broke forth into lamentation for Ka-hahana:

O Pililua 'oe o hele lua i 'Ewa,
O ka hele 'oe a ka'u La—ni.

You two companions fled to 'Ewa,
You were gone, and [one was] my chief.

O kapiki kolo o lua ia luamea,
O mea wale ia iho i ke ku—la—
I ka oneanea i ka waile—le,

Both of you fled in destitution,
Fled to the plains in utter poverty,
To the waste places, to the waterfalls,

Nolaila ka o Ka-hapu'u-kolu
O Kapa'i-kaunalulu
O ka pahu iloko o Kekei'aiku,

Ah! there belong Ka-hapu'u-kolu
And Kapa'i-kaunalulu,
The drums in [the heiau] of Kekei'aiku.

O Hi'olani o ka pueo kani kaua

You are Hi'olani, the owl that sounds the alarm of battle

No Halaulani i Hanapou—li—
No ka welu hau i ke kai i Kupahu.

For Halaulani at Hanapouli
Through the torn hau at the sea at Kupahu.

Nolaila ka o Kaloha'iopua,
O Ka-puana-ka'u ka malama,
O ka malama ia Hiki-lei-akaka-le'a,
O Hi'onalele o Kamaka o Kemilia,
O Hiki-Nauele o Nauele kona lua.

There belonged Kaloha'iopua,
Ka-puana-ka'u was the month,
The month of Hiki-lei-akaka-le'a,
Hi'onalele, Kamaka, Kemilia,
Hiki-Nauele, Nauele his comion.

Elua laua i ka moa—na—e	Two of them are being taken to the ocean
Oia ka i ke awalau o Puʻuloa,	To the many harbors of Puʻuloa,
Iluna o Waʻa Kaiolohia la—ni.	On the chief's canoe, Kaiolohia.
Ei i lau hoe ia nei Kalani,	Speak, you paddlers who bear away the heavenly one,
O ʻoe ka iluna o ka pola waʻa—e, etc.	Upon the platform of the canoe, etc.

After Ka-hahana's death a plot was laid to murder the chiefs of Maui. Ka-hekili was living at Kailua with most of the chiefs; Manono, Ka-ua-kapeku-lani, Kaʻi-ana, Na-makehaʻ, Nahi-olea, Ka-lani-ulu-moku, and others were at Kaneʻohe and Heʻeia; Huʻeu alone was at Waialua. Those in the plot were the chiefs Elani, Pupuka, Makaʻi-oulu, Kona-manu, Ka-laki-oʻo-nui, and a great many others. Waipiʻo in ʻEwa as the center of the plot got the name of "Waipiʻo of secret rebellion" (Waipiʻo *kimopo*). The plotters were divided, Elani and his party to kill the chiefs in ʻEwa; Makaʻi-oulu, Pupuka, and their accomplices to attack Ka-hekili; Kona-manu and Ka-laki-oʻo-nui and their party to kill Huʻeu; and all to attack on the same night. But someone warned the ʻEwa chiefs of the plot and they fled to Waikiki, and Ka-hekili and his chiefs escaped in the same way. But Huʻeu, who was living at Kaʻowakawaka, Kawailoa, in Waialua, was killed on one of the Kaloa nights while his guards were asleep. To throw suspicion on others the plotters said, "Death comes from Kauai," and later they said, "Death comes from Waipiʻo." But the plot came out, and when Ka-hekili learned that Elani of ʻEwa was one of the plotters, the districts of Kona and ʻEwa were attacked, and men, women, and children were massacred, until the streams of Makaho and Niuhelewai in Kona and of Kahoaʻaiʻai in ʻEwa were choked with the bodies of the dead, and their waters became bitter to the taste, as eyewitnesses say, from the brains that turned the water bitter. All the Oahu chiefs were killed and the chiefesses tortured.

A certain Maui chief named Kalai-koa who lived at Moanalua built a long house and named it Kauwalua and, perhaps in order to make his name famous, had it filled with the bones of persons stripped, bound, and set up inside the house and all around the outside enclosure of the house.* The bones of Elani, Kona-manu, and Ka-laki-oʻo-nui were bundled up and placed beside the entrance. The house stood at Lapakea on the slope into Moanalua on the upper side of the old

* *Ka Nupepa Kuʻokoʻa,* Mar. 30, 1867.

road. Eyewitnesses said, "It was a terrible and gruesome sight. The bones were stripped, bundled together, and the skulls set upon each bundle so that, seen from a distance, it looked like a company of living men." Two men from Waialua, Pua-kea and Pinao by name, were passing by wearing fine mat shoulder capes and helmets on their heads and carrying heavy spears. As they came up toward Lapakea and passed the lower side of the house they called out, "Greetings to you all! Kalai-koa's victims are here, but Manono's return to Ko'olau." The guards, eighty in number, heard them and came outside with their spears. They had scarcely reached Kahauiki when the trouble began. "You are rebels! you are rebels!" shouted the guards, and spears, clubs, and darts began to fall about them. They were surrounded and had a hard time to struggle through. At the stone called Ka-papa-i-kawaluna that stood on the upper road of Kahauiki, Pinao turned and stabbed two men, Pua-kea stabbed two, and the men who obstructed the way scattered. This side of Kahauiki they encountered a host of warriors, and the dead fell about them like water in a bath. Pinao killed five men, and Puakea slew the same number. At the stone Palena they killed more men. The way ahead toward Waikoa'e from Mokauea and Hono'umi seemed filled with men, and death seemed certain; but, like an over-ripe breadfruit that falls of itself before the rain and rots away, so the foe scattered, some leaping into the stream of Waikoa'e and others retreating to the plain. The Maui chief, Ka-mohomoho, was in upper Nu'uanu and there the fighting ceased. The chief inquired carefully into the cause of the scrap and then spoke his mind as follows: "There was no harm in these men's words. They were good words, and showed affection for their people. Why should you be offended? They said moreover that they had been taken by Manono, Ka-hekili's son, but were not held as prisoners. It is a good thing that you were beaten. Make an end of this and go home and let these men go."

Maka'i-oulu was among the brave warriors who fought in the battle called Ka-po-luku. Had it not been for Pupuka he might have had trouble. At Manana in 'Ewa, at Kulana, and in the ravines beyond Napohakuhelu he was hemmed in by warriors who stabbed at him on all sides but without hurting him in the least, and so many were killed that they finally left off fighting. He himself fled exhausted and battle-weary to the uplands of Wahiawa and hid among the potato vines where he was betrayed by a certain farmer to those who sought to kill him, and so died. He was a brave warrior. Pupuka rallied the retainers of the chiefs of Kona, 'Ewa, Wai'anae, Waialua, and Ko'olau at Kawiwi, a stronghold between Wai'anae and Makaha, where many died of starvation or were flung over the precipice because of famine, and many perished. Ka-lani-ulu-moku, a son of Kamehameha-nui, the older brother of Ka-hekili, also rebelled and was aided by his relatives Ka'i-ana, Na-makeha', and Nahi-olea. He perished by leaping off the cliff of Olomana. Ka-neoneo, a chief of the prostrating tabu (*kapu moe*) and a son of Ku-mahana, died at Kalamake'e on the road leading up to Maunakapu and down to Moanalua. Many chiefesses of the prostrating tabu also were killed and mutilated, and thus were fulfilled the words spoken by Ka-'opulupulu the kahuna. The chiefess Kekela fled in secret to Kauai and is said to have carried with her sands from 'Apuakehau, Kahaloa, Waia'ula, and Kupalaha at Waikiki, and to have deposited them at Hulaia, Kulana, and Kane in Kauai.

The fulfilment of the prophecy uttered when Hawaii was in darkness is being seen today. The words, "Take a deep breath and give your body to the sea; the land is the sea's" contain an inner meaning which relates not alone to the conquests of Ka-hekili and Kamehameha as the chiefs who came by way of the sea and took the island of Oahu, but also to the events of these days in which we are now living. This is something for us to ponder over, to seek the actual cause of God's anger; to confess the sin that angered God; [to accept] the atonement of Christ which caused Him to be sacrificed for our sins; to offer sacrifices for our own sins; to pay for the sins of our forefathers and for our own sins by offering sacrifices to Christ. We ask, "Who forgave the crimes, evil deeds, and impious acts of Pele-io-holani, Ku-mahana, Ka-hahana, Ka-hekili, Kamehameha, and so on?" Let us turn to the words of Scripture: "A jealous God, visiting the iniquities of the fathers upon the children unto the second and third generation of them that hate me." God is still angry with the Jews, and because of their ancestors they are scattered among all nations of the world. There was David, for instance, king of the children of Israel. He repented of his sins, but when David sinned the whole Israelite nation was punished by an epidemic. God did not choose sinless man to offer the sacrifices for sins, but he chose the man who committed the sin to go up to Aaron and offer a sin offering. God accepted it, and the disease was stayed. Kamehameha was a chief who did not know the true God in heaven; but when Hawaii was threatened by a lava flow that went down toward Kiholo, Ka'upulehu, and Mahai'ula, and might have filled up the ponds with lava, he was afraid when the prophets and priests said, "The fire can be extinguished easily, and the fishponds of which you are so fond can be saved if you yourself take the sin offering and offer it with your own hands. The goddess will not heed a prophet, a kahuna, or any other chief but you alone." It happened just as the prophets had predicted, as Ka-ʻahu-manu, Ka-heihei-malie, Ulu-lani, and other royal personages were eye-witnesses. From old times it has been an important duty of ruling chiefs to invoke an answer [from the gods].*

* *Ka Nupepa Kuʻokoʻa*, Apr. 6, 1867.

CHAPTER XII

Kamehameha Wins All Hawaii

During this period there were disturbances among the country people, not only on Oahu but also on Maui. The trouble arose through one of the lesser chiefs (*kaukauali'i*) named Ku-keawe, a favorite (*aikane*) of Ka-hekili to whom Ka-hekili had given the privilege of letting his pigs run over the land of Kula and roasting them as he needed them. But he seized also the pigs belonging to the country people of Kula, Honua'ula, and Kahikinui, as far as Kaupo, and went with a large party to rob them of their wealth even with violence. This was the cause of the uprising of the country people called the "Battle of the pig-eating of Ku-keawe" (*'Aipua'a-a-Ku-keawe*). When the plundering party reached Kaupo they were surprised by some fighting men of Kahikinui, Honua'ula, Wailuku, and Waihe'e under 'Opu', and their retreat was blocked by Ka-wehena, Ka-ho'oluhina, and Ku-heana, each with his company. Hence they climbed the mountain of Haleakala in order to descend to Kamaole in Kula and fortified themselves strongly at Kapuoa, where they would have been safe had they not descended to the sea at Kamaole. Here they were surrounded by Ka-wehena's men, Ku-keawe was killed, and his body stuck up like an image toward the sea of Palauea.

When Ka-hekili and the chiefs who were on Oahu heard of the trouble on Maui they pitied the common people, and Ka-hekili gathered his younger brothers and his sons about him, and Ka-lani-ku-pule was chosen ruling chief to return and rule over Maui, 'with some of the chiefs to accompany him. Among the party were Ka-lola-pupuka Hono-ka-wai-lani, and her husband, Ka-'opu-iki, their granddaughter Ka-lani-kau-i-ka-'alaneo Ke-opu-o-lani, her mother Ke-ku'i-apo-iwa, her [Ke-ku'i-apo-iwa's] younger sister, Ka-lani-akua Ka-lani-kau-io-kikilo, Ka-lani-ku-pule himself, Koa-lau-kani, his younger brother, the war leader Ka-mohomoho, and Kapa-kahili, one of the commanders. Ka-lani-ku-pule was a chief praised for his freedom from pretentiousness. He loved the common people, would fraternize with the humblest, and was not haughty. He was spoken of thus:

Ku moku paupau	Standing upon the lowland
Ko Kanekope - pau e -	Your chiefly grandeur is gone,
Pa - u kahu akua o mua - hilu - e	Your divine state is set aside; although dignified
Ko noho ana i ka haumanumanu	You live humbly,
Ko - ki - e	Very humbly.

While he ruled over Maui, some of the chiefs of Hawaii came over and took up some land at Hana and Kipahulu on Maui. One of the chiefs was Kamehameha's own brother, Ka-lani-malokuloku-i-Kepo'o-o-ka-lani. He protected the rights of the common people, and while he lived in Kipahulu and Hana there was no sugar cane broken off, no potatoes dug up, no pigs roasted. The common people loved him and called him "The good chief" (*Ke-ali'i-maika'i*) in praise of his kind deeds, and that is why his life was spared when he was about to be made prisoner in war. Ka-lani-ku-pule, hearing that chiefs from Hawaii had taken Hana and Kipahulu, sent a body of chiefs and warriors under Ka-mohomoho to battle against them. The good chief and his warriors were at Kipahulu, the other chiefs from Hawaii were in Hana. The good chief commanded that no one should touch the property of the common people. On the day of the battle of "The-red-mantle" (*Ka 'ahu'ula*), the foe came down to Kipahulu on the Ka'apahu side of Lelekea; the hills reflected the red of Ka-mohomoho's mantle. Ke-ali'i-maika'i hastily made his war canoes ready, met the main body of warriors at the Kukui'ula, and encountered some of the skirmishers; then both sides attacked. Finally Ke-ali'i-maika'i retreated to Waipalua. Both sides had lost alike, but Ka-mohomoho had the stronger force. At Kapukai'olena in Ma'ulili the fighting was resumed and Ke-ali'i-maika'i was in jeopardy. His *kahu*, Muli-hele, saw his danger and ran in where the fight raged most furiously. Ka-mohomoho's warriors were scattered and Ke-ali'i-maika'i saved. He would have been killed but for his kahu's courage.* At Alae, adjoining Kakalahale on the main road *mauka* of Kanihoa'ia'i, Muli-hele saw a thick growth of *ka'e'e* vine and ti plant on the side of a gully; and he pointed this out to the chief as a place to hide. When the battle began again, he was standing on a rise of ground from which he could look back toward his foster son until he saw that the chief's red feather cloak was completely concealed among the vines. Then he faced the fight again, which

* *Ka Nupepa Ku'oko'a,* Apr. 6, 1867.

continued to Wailoa and down that side of Kaumakani in pursuit of the chief. The people of Kipahulu saw where the chief had hidden himself, but because they loved him they would not tell the soldiers of Ka-mohomoho lest he be killed by them. The chief remained hidden until dark, then he sailed to Hawaii and joined his elder brother. After they had greeted each other and wept, Ke-ali'i-maika'i told the story of the battle with Ka-mohomoho, the foster father of Ka-lani-ku-pule, son of Ka-hekili, and of his [own] escape and said, "You might never have seen me again but for the courage of this *kahu* of ours who saved my life." Kamehameha answered, "Had you been killed, I would have made a great slaughter in Kipahulu and struck off the heads of men, women, and children." Ke-ali'i-maika'i said, "It was because of their kindness that I was saved," and Kamehameha said, "Then we will carry on the war on Maui against the sons of Ka-hekili."

Now chiefs from Hawaii often made their home in Kipahulu. Ka-loku-o-ka-maile was chief of Kipahulu; and Hale-loa, of Kiko'o in Kipahulu. Ka-loku-o-ka-maile was the son of Ka-lani-kupu-a-pa-i-ka-lani-nui Keoua; Ka-lani-lehua was his mother. This is how the Kipahulu people came to know the chiefs of Hawaii and why "The good chief" lived at Kapo'ookalani.

Not five years had passed since Cook's landing on Hawaii when there arrived at Kauai a boat called *Alomakani* or *Olo* because it was the first boat to bring strings of beads (called *olo*) as ornaments for the neck. Next there landed at Hawaii the ship called *Kanikani*, which brought the first knives called *kanikani* and *hana'oi*. Then came the *Lokea*, bringing knives called *lokea* knives. Afterwards came the boat called *Kapilipakela*, and she was a fine boat. Then came the *Kane*, the boat that took Ka'i-ana 'Ahu-'ula to foreign lands, where he remained for three years in China and other lands. This boat landed at Kauai in 1787. After she left there came *Koki*, after her the *Arctic* (*Alika*),* then Brown, then *Kapilimaka*, then came Vancouver.* Most of these boats were ships of war or ships looking for new lands. Some among them were friendly, others were bent on destroying men and governments.

---

* The adventures of the ship *Arctic* are commemorated in an old hula song which has been put on phonograph records, subtitled "Aia i Alika." The first stanza runs:

Aia i Alika ka ihu o ka moku,	The prow of the ship turns toward the Arctic,
Ua hele a pa'ihi na pe'a i ke kia,	Her sails are made fast to the mast,
Ke liolio nei ke kaula polena,	The rigging is pulled taut,
Ua hele a pa'ihi na pe'a i ka makani	And each sail is trimmed to the wind.

One of these boats was the *Eleanor** from Liverpool, England, which arrived at Honua'ula on Maui in February, 1790. John Young came to Hawaii on this boat. Ka-lola Pupuka-o-Hono-ka-wai-lani, the former wife to Ka-lani-'opu'u, was living at this time at Honua'ula with a new husband by the name of Ka-'opu-iki. When the chiefs and other men of Olowalu and Ukumehame knew of the arrival of the foreign boat, Ka-'opu-iki was glad to go on board to trade for iron, muskets, and red cloth; but muskets were the objects he most desired. The people brought in exchange hogs, chickens, potatoes, bananas, and taro. Night fell before they had finished their bargaining, and the next day Ka-'opu-iki and others went out again to trade further; but the strangers were unfriendly and beat them off with ropes. When Ka-'opu-iki heard from the people of Honua'ula about the small boat which it was customary to keep tied to the back of the ship, he determined to steal the boat at night. At midnight when the guard on the skiff and the men of the ship were sound asleep, Ka-'opu-iki and his men cut the rope without being seen from the ship. As they were towing it along, the guard awoke and called out to those on board the ship, but he was too far away to be heard; he was killed and his body thrown into the sea. The boat was taken to Olowalu and broken up, and the iron taken for fishhooks, adzes, drills, daggers, and spear points.

The next morning when the men on the ship awoke and found both skiff and watchman missing and realized that the boat had been stolen and the watchman killed, they shot off the cannon upon Honua'ula and killed some men, among them a peddler from Wailuku, named Ke-aloha, who had come to Honua'ula to peddle his wares. Two men were held on board the ship, one from Honua'ula and one from Olowalu, perhaps because these men had given information about the theft or perhaps because the foreigners suspected that Ka-'opu-iki and the others, who had brought out the hogs and said they were from Olowalu, were responsible for the theft. That evening they sailed to Olowalu, and in the morning Ka-lola declared a tabu restricting canoes from going out to the ship on pain of being burned to death if they disobeyed. "Withered grass" (Mau'umae) was the name of this law. It belonged to Ka-lola alone and to her children and grandchildren; no other chief could declare such a tabu. It lasted three days. On the fourth the tabu was ended, and canoes in great numbers went out to trade with the foreigners. Many came from Lahaina

* This vessel was the *Eleanora*.

as well as from Ka'anapali, Lanai, and neighboring places. The canoes gathered under the ship's sides, the men eager to procure iron, beads, looking-glasses, scissors, muskets for the constant warring going on at that time, red cloth and other foreign material. Little did they suspect the terrible carnage that was to follow, a carnage without any effort to apprehend and punish the offenders or any pity for the innocent. So these Christians murdered the Hawaiian people without any more mercy than cannibal Nukuhivans show, or people of pagan lands. Canoes that drifted toward bow or stern were compelled by a shower of stones to keep amidships, and when all were clustered together, the captain was pretending to trade, and the people were busily eyeing the objects they desired, just as Aka-kane and another man had climbed upon the deck, the ship opened fire and shot the people down without mercy, just as if they were creatures without souls. Even those who swam away were shot down. John Young was an eyewitness on board the ship and has testified to the great number who were killed at this time. At noon that day the *Eleanor* sailed, and the people went out and brought the dead ashore, some diving down into the sea with ropes and others using hooks; and the dead were heaped on the sands at Olowalu. Because the brains of many were oozing out where they had been shot in the head, this battle with the ship *Eleanor* and her captain was called "The spilled brains" (Kalolo-pahu). It was a sickening sight, as Mahulu and others have reported it; the slaughtered dead were heaped upon the sand; wives, children, parents, and friends came to view and mourn over their dead; and the sound of loud wailing arose.

The ship *Eleanor* sailed for Hawaii, and a small sloop arrived there at the same time under the captaincy of Isaac Davis. John Young, called by the natives Olohana, went ashore from the *Eleanor* armed with a sword and musket to see the country. He was at this time a little over forty-six years of age. Kamehameha was anxious to secure foreigners to teach him to handle the muskets which it had been his first object to obtain. Wars were going on among the three ruling chiefs of Hawaii and between the chiefs of Hawaii and Maui. It was through the aid of muskets and of foreigners to instruct in their use that Kamehameha was able in so short a time to bring all the islands under his rule. While Young was out sight-seeing darkness came on, and when he attempted to return to the ship he was detained by Kamehameha and told not to go back to the ship but to remain as a friend (*aikane*) of the chief. Kamehameha may also have been afraid lest Young carry information of the capture of the sloop which had occurred that same day and the killing of the five men of the crew and the wounding of her captain, Isaac Davis. These men, Young and Davis, became favorites (*aikane punahele*) of Kamehameha and leaders in his wars, and from them are descended chiefs and commoners of Hawaii.

The capture of the sloop came about in this way. Ka-me'e-ia-moku coveted the muskets, iron, knives, and other death-dealing weapons of the foreigners, and he had besides an insult to avenge. While he was attempting to climb on board, the men had struck him with a rope. Although this was customary with the foreigners, Ka-me'e-ia-moku, being a man of quick temper and having nothing at hand with which to inflict immediate retaliation, nursed his humiliation and vowed to capture the first foreign boat that came his way. He was living at Ka'upulehu, South Kona, at the time, and seeing a sloop sailing by he and his men immediately determined upon its capture. Among the men who joined him in the raid were Nauki, Kuaiwa, Kuahiku, Mano-hili, Na-luhi, 'Ahu-'ole, Pe'e, and some relatives of the chief, Ka-lau-koa, Manu-hoa, Ka-nuha, and Ke-aka-o-ka-lani. They went on board the sloop, killed the five men of the crew and wounded Captain Davis. Men had little good will for each other in the days of our fathers.

Among the things obtained from the sloop was a cannon which the natives called "Robert" (Lopaka) and a number of muskets, swords, axes, powder, and clothing. These things were taken before Kamehameha together with the prisoner, and Kamehameha made Isaac Davis his friend as he had John Young, and great was his joy to find himself provided not only with foreign implements of war but with men to use them. He saw these men shoot and hit, one a chicken and the other a pig, at some distance, and was delighted with their skill. He therefore sent messengers to Keawe-ma'u-hili requesting canoes, men, and feather capes to equip a war expedition against Ka-lani-ku-pule, ruling chief of Maui. Keawe-ma'u-hili consented and dispatched the articles and the men asked for, accompanied by some of his own family, Ke-awe-o-kahi-kona, 'Ele'ele, Ka-lei-paia-hala, and Koa-kanu. In this he acted contrary to the policy of Keoua who had advised remaining neutral and not mixing in Kamehameha's wars, thinking it wrong to fight against the sons of Ka-hekili. It was for this reason that Keoua made war against Keawe-ma'u-hili.*

At the time of the gathering of the war parties on Maui Kamehameha, the chief, sailed with his counselors, chiefs, and younger relatives, the sons of Keawe-ma'u-hili, ruling chief of Hilo, and a great host of

* *Ka Nupepa Ku'oko'a*, Apr. 20, 1867.

fighting men; and that battle was called "The many canoes" (Ka-wa'a-nui) because of the size of the fleet which beached at Hana and extended from Hamoa to Kawaipapa. Ka-lani-ku-pule, the son of Ka-hekili, was living on Maui with his younger brother, Koa-lau-kani, his war leader and chief counselor, Ka-mohomoho, and other chiefs and fighting men. With him were the tabu chiefess of Maui Ka-lola, and her daughters, Ke-ku'i-apo-iwa the elder, and Ka-lani-kau-io-kikilo Ka-lani-akua the younger, and her granddaughter, Ka-lani-kau-i-ka-'alaneo Ke-opu-o-lani. Hearing of Kamehameha's approach Ka-lani-ku-pule sent an army to Hamakualoa under the warrior Kapa-kahili. The battle met at a small hill called "Bosun-bird Hill" (Pu'ukoa'e) situated on the *makai* side of Pu'umaile at Hanawana in Hoalua, and Kapa-kahili was defeated. In the evening Kamehameha beached at Halehaku, went ashore, and built temporary shelters just where he stepped foot. The feather god Ku-ka'ili-moku encouraged him to fight, for its feathers bristled and stood upright in the direction of Hina-wai-koli'i;* Kamehameha therefore lost his fear of a fight with slingshot. The next morning he saw through the *koa* and hala trees the red gleam of feather capes. It is said that he narrowly escaped defeat by Kapa-kahili's company. But reinforcements came up, Kamehameha put the enemy to flight, and pursued them along the main road or they would have rejoined their fellow-warriors at Kokomo. At the ascent of 'Opaepilau, Kapa-kahili was exhausted and was over-taken. "Slain by Pipili," Kamehameha boasted over him.

After his death the fighting ceased, and Kamehameha and his chiefs went on to the principal encounter at Wailuku. The bay from Kahului to Hopukoa was filled with war canoes. For two days there was constant fighting in which many of the most skilful warriors of Maui took part, but Kamehameha brought up the cannon, Lopaka, with men to haul it and the white men, John Young and Isaac Davis, to handle it; and there was great slaughter. Had they fought face-to-face and hand-to-hand, as the custom was, they would have been equally matched. But the defensive was drawn up in a narrow pass in 'Iao, and the offensive advanced from below and drew up the cannon as far as Kawelowelo'ula and shot from there into 'Iao and the hills about, and the men were routed. The victors pursued them and slew the vanquished as they scrambled up the cliffs. There was a great slaughter, but mostly among the commoners; no important chief was killed in this battle. "Clawed off the cliff" (Ka-'uwa'u-pali) and "The damming of

---

* Hina-wai-koli'i is a sacred mythical bird from which came the two feathers on the top of the head of the Ka'ili image. Another tradition found in Kamakau says that these feathers came from the foreheads of the birds Halulu and Kiwa'a.

the waters" (Ka-pani-wai) this battle was called. During the fight
Ka-lani-ku-pule, Koa-lau-kani, Ka-mohomoho, and other chiefs
escaped to Oahu. Ke-ku'i-apo-iwa, Ka-lani-akua, and Ke-opu-o-lani
were taken over the pass in 'Iao Valley to Olowalu, where they met
Ka-lola's party and sailed to Molokai.

While Kamehameha was at Wailuku with his followers he heard of
Ka-lola's being on Molokai with her daughters and granddaughter
and he sent word by Kikane for her not to proceed to Oahu as he was
coming to escort her to Hawaii. He sailed with a great company,
among them Ke'e-au-moku, Keawe-a-heulu, Ka-me'e-ia-moku, and
Ka-manawa, the brothers of Ka-lola, and landed at Kaunakakai. They
met Ka-lola at Kalama'ula and, when Kamehameha saw how ill she was
and of an incurable disease according to the kahuna's diagnosis, he
asked, "Since you are so ill and perhaps about to die, will you permit
me to take my royal daughter and my sisters to Hawaii to rule as
chiefs?" (He referred to Ke-opu-o-lani and her mother and aunt, Ke-
ku'i-apo-iwa and Ka-lani-kau-io-kikilo). Ka-lola answered, "If I die,
the girl and the sisters are yours." Then Kamehameha and all the chiefs
waited until the death of Ka-lola. They wailed and chanted dirges, and
some were put to sleep with the dead, and the chiefs tattooed themselves
and knocked out their teeth. Kamehameha was also tattooed and had his
eyeteeth knocked out, and the chiefs and commoners acted like mad-
men. At the end of the mourning, Ka-lola was laid away in her cave
house at Konahale. A certain chief, the son of Ke'e-au-moku by
Namahana, who became the governing chief of Hawaii, was called
"The pit at Konahale" (Ka-lua-i-Konahale) after Kalola's burial place.

After the death of Ka-lola, Kamehameha sent Ha'alo'u and Ki-kane
to Oahu. Ki-kane he sent to Ka-hekili, and Ki-kane went and landed
at Waikiki and met Ka-hekili. But Ha'alo'u he sent on a different
errand, first to go to Kauai and seek a wise man to instruct Kamehameha how to conquer all the islands of the group; second, to bring his
cousin Ke-kua-po'i to Hawaii, so much was she talked of in Hawaii.
But when Ha'alo'u had seen her, she knew that all the stories told
of Ke-kua-po'i were true, and that it would not be well to take her to
Hawaii, for there was none lovelier than she, and she would spare no
one, and Ha'alo'u had great affection for her grandchildren. As for the
first errand, Ha'alo'u knew that no man who understands deep things
should go unrecompensed, for knowledge is not to be scattered about
freely and "the laborer is worthy of his hire." There lived at Kamoku
in Waikiki a certain man of Kauai named Ka-pou-kahi, of the order of
Hulihonua, and he was skilful in the art of reading signs and omens.

When Ha'alo'u found that this wise man was close at hand, she ran quickly and offered the genealogy of her grandmother, Kane-i-kahei-lani, in exchange for the blessing for her lord. When the old man said, "What shall I give you in return, O chiefess?" she said, "This is your return gift, to tell me how the rule over all the islands may become my lord's." Ka-pou-kahi answered, "Build a great house for the god and mark out its boundaries." Ha'alo'u asked, "Where shall this house be?" "At Pu'u-koholá. If he makes this house for his god, he can gain the kingdom without a scratch to his own skin." So answered Ka-pou-kahi. Now Pu'u-koholá is at Kawaihae above Maile-kini, the two heiaus standing one above the other, and it is a resting place for peddlers who go to Waimea and Kahua.

Ki-kane, Kamehameha's messenger to Ka-hekili, threw down two *maika* stones, a black one and a white one. Ka-hekili said when he saw these stones, "This stone (the white) brings life through farming and fishing, rearing men, and providing them with food; this other stone (the black) brings war." Let the reader ponder the meaning of this answer. Ka-hekili asked, "Is Kamehameha coming to Oahu to fight?" "Yes," answered Ki-kane. "What harbor will he choose?" "It was Kiko'o's counsel to make Waimanalo the harbor and battle site." "It is too low there to cast sling stones to reach the heights. It is good only for food and fish. If stones are thrown from above nothing can save the battlefield. Who else gave advice?" "Ka'a-loa advised Waikiki as the harbor and battlefield." "That is much too low. Neither those on the sea nor those on the shore have the advantage. It is a place for cultivating food, not a battlefield. Who else?" "Ka-ua-kahi-a-kaha-ola counsels Koko as the harbor and battlefield." "A wise man! He has the right idea. The provision patches of Ko'olau are far distant. There is a good site above, large enough to fight on. Go back and tell Kamehameha to return to Hawaii and watch, and when the black tapa covers Ka-hekili and the black pig rests at his nose, then is the time to cast stones. Then, when light is snuffed out at Kahiki, that is the time to come and take the land."* "Here is another request I am commanded by Kamehameha to make of you." "Tell on." "Kameha-meha would have the gods, Olopue and Kalai-pahoa." Now Olopue belonged to the class of gods (*papakahui*) that led the spirit to or back from the spirit land. He was a god much dreaded by the warrior chiefs of old. He was in the keeping of Ka-'opu-huluhulu. Kalai-pahoa

---

* "*A kau ka pua'a i ka nuku*" (when the pig is placed before the mouth). It was a custom at death to kill pigs to feed the mourners. "*Aia kinai (a) na i Tahati*" (When the light is snuffed out at Kahiki) is a familiar phrase implying that death takes a man according to a decree of the gods, conceived as dwelling in Kahiki.

was a sacred tree of Maunaloa on Molokai, belonging to the pepper family, and exceedingly poisonous. Ma'i-ola alone was able to offset its effects. Ka-hekili gave a piece of the Kalai-pahoa to Kamehameha, who made of it the god "Kane who gives *mana* to Pai'ea" (Kane-mana-ia-pai'ea). Then both Ki-kane and Ha'alo'u returned to Molokai.

Keoua Kuahu-'ula heard how Kamehameha had gone to make war against Maui, and how Keawe-ma'u-hili had aided him to fight the sons of Ka-hekili, contrary to their agreement and dangerous to their independence. Fearing therefore lest the two join forces and fight against him, he made war on Keawe-ma'u-hili, routing him at the very start. At Alae in Hilopaliku Keawe-ma'u-hili was killed and with him the chief, Ka'o'o who was his brother-in-law. Keoua also slaughtered many of Keawe's fighting men. Having gained Hilo, Keoua thought to carry the war into Hamakua, Waimea, and Kohala, and to plunder the country people. He descended into Waipi'o and broke down the fish-ponds, drying up Lalakea, Muliwai, and all the other ponds. He pulled up the taro of Waipi'o, broke down the banks of the taro patches, and robbed the people from Waipi'o to Waimea. In Kohala, women and children were beaten, and the people cruelly treated. The low-born attacked the low-born, and the high-born the high-born [literally, "small gourds" and "large gourds"]. Such were the bitter fruits of war.*

Kamehameha, who was living on Molokai with his chiefs and fighting men, heard how Keoua had killed Keawe-ma'u-hili and ravaged Kohala. He loved his people and he said, "Alas! while I have been seeking new children my first-born have been abandoned!" He therefore returned to Hawaii with his counselors and warriors and landed at Kawaihae. Keoua was at Waimea, and Kamehameha proceeded at once to march thither accompanied by Young and Davis, but by the time he reached the place Keoua had retreated towards Hamakua. Kamehameha pursued and caught up with Keoua at Pa'auhau in Hamakua, where a battle immediately took place in which neither side gave ground, and which resulted in loss on both sides. On Kamehameha's side the cannon called Lopaka was their refuge; on Keoua's two men, Uhai and Ka-'ia'iaiea, performed great deeds of valor. They caught men up in their arms and when the cannon was fired, as soon as the shot had passed, Ka-'ia'iaiea seized the cannon. It was said that without the foreigners the fight would never have ended; no one could have told which side was victorious.†

It was at Koapapa in east Hamakua that the great battle was fought

* *Ka Nupepa Ku'oko'a,* Apr. 13, 1867.
† *Ka Nupepa Ku'oko'a,* Apr. 20, 1867.

between the warriors of Kamehameha and those of Keoua. Koapapa is a broad open plain with a grove at the south, well situated for a battlefield. The fighting was fierce, for although Kamehameha's side had muskets and powder, Keoua's men ran up and seized the muskets; but since they were unable to supply themselves with powder, neither side gained a victory. Keoua retired to Hilo; Kamehameha went back to Waipi'o and Kohala. At Hilo Keoua divided the land among his chiefs and warriors; the fat mullet of Waiakea and Pi'opi'o became theirs. He then set out to return to Ka-'u by way of Ola'a past the crater of the volcano and on to Kalanihale at Kapapala, when the division of his army which came up at the rear was completely annihilated by the volcano. This is how it happened: A pillar of sand and rock rose straight up in the air to a height above the summits of Mauna Loa and Mauna Kea, and a flame of fire appeared at its top. It looked as if a little hill were being pushed straight up by a larger one until it burst into masses of sand and rock. Some of these rocks are to be seen today at the edge of the crater and [others] at some distance away. Eruptions continued for some days and many were killed, the bodies of men, women, and children lying unmutilated just as they were when marching. Mona an eyewitness, said that the reason their group escaped was that one of the women was menstruating and so they carried tabu flags, one in front and one behind the marchers. If there had been several hundred in that group none of them would have been hurt. They did not think of Jehovah and give credit to him for their escape! Several cinder cones were heaped up near Kilauea at this time. One cone moved straight down toward the sea at Apua and in less than two weeks reached the sand at Punalu'u, where Keoua Kuahu-'ula was staying at the time under tabu. This cinder heap moved along the sand from Apua to the beach at Punalu'u where its progress was barred by the highlands at Punalu'u, Wailau, and Ninole, and there it remains at Punalu'u to this day. One of the seers told Keoua that Hi'iaka, his beloved, was angry at him for leaving Hilo, for she was enjoying the fat mullet of Waiakea. Foolish as they were in the old days, they are much more so in these enlightened times!

This strange and marvellous act of God occurred in November, 1790. Keoua was then chief over Ka-'u, Puna, and Hilo, and skirmishes were taking place between his followers and those of Kamehameha. The strife between the chiefs took the form of denying each other's pure descent from a line of high chiefs. Each was well-versed in genealogical lines, oratory, and minute details in the histories of chiefs, their birthplaces, rules of government, and the signs and omens that revealed their rank as chiefs. Both sides also had composers of meles who chanted the names of ancestors, the high and godlike rank of their own chief, and the mean ancestry of the other. This form of controversy between the two chiefs is well-known today and will be remembered for all time.

While Kamehameha was living in Kona on Hawaii, a ship landed at Keala-ke-kua commanded by Captain Kane [Captain Meares] and bringing the chief, Ka'i-ana, a grandson of Keawe-kekahi-ali'i-o-ka-moku, his father being Keawe's son 'Ahu'ula, and his mother Kau-peka-moku. He had sailed from Kauai where his brothers, Na-makeha' and Nahiolea, lived. He gave Kamehameha a quantity of muskets and cannon, and the chief made him a favorite and urged him to remain with him, saying, "Here is land, here are chiefs, here are commoners. Let us live on Hawaii. Do not return to Kauai and Oahu." Ka'i-ana had a number of relatives among the chiefs of Hawaii, among them the family of Ka-lani-kuaiwa and Ka'i-ana Ukupe, father of Ka-iki-o'ewa. He was pleased by Kamehameha's proposal and the prospect of living in the land of his ancestors and he asked that his brothers might also be sent for. To this the chief consented. Ka'i-ana was a learned man well trained in the arts of war, in laying out buildings, and in the other arts of the kahuna, the orator, the seer who explains hidden meanings, the expert in the science of government who could advise for the welfare of the country, and the genealogist. Men said of him, "Ka'i-ana is well-skilled. He has given all his death-dealing weapons and life itself to Kamehameha." For this reason Kamehameha's counselors conspired against him, and there was still another reason. Ka'i-ana had been trained in the use of [foreign] weapons by his friend, Captain Kane, during the three years in which he had traveled with him in foreign lands, years of strife between the nations of Europe and America, when ships were in danger of being seized at sea. Kamehameha therefore made him commander of his army to make war upon Keoua Kuahu-'ula. The forces led by Ke'e-au-moku and the chiefs and accompanied by Young and Davis had been forced to flee both in Hilo and in Ka-'u.*

As soon as Na-makeha' and Nahiolea arrived, therefore, a war expedition was started off for Ka-'u. The battlefield was laid out at Kalae, Paiaha'a, Kama'oa, and at Ua'ohulelua, where the struggle was fiercest. Once Ka'i-ana was forced to retreat to the fleet, once Keoua was forced back by the guns; had they fought face-to-face he would not have retreated. Keoua retired to Puna, and Ka'i-ana followed. A battle was fought at Punakoki in which Ka'i-ana displayed great valor as a soldier, rallying his men with such battle cries as, "Make the chills

* *Ka Nupepa Ku'oko'a*, Apr. 27, 1867.

run up and down, make them teeter like the tail of a plover, make them flutter like the long feathers of the *koaʻe* bird in the wind, sway like the *ʻuwaʻu* bird in the calm, make them scatter and hold their breath! Do you hear that, fellow?" One of the chiefs answered, "I am no fellow, I am Na-makeha', 'The-lightning-flash-in-the-sky.' I am 'The-eyes-of-the-ruling-chief-over-all-the-islands.' "

"And why, then, are you as slippery as slime to fall so easily and be so careless on the day of battle?" "I was at Hana in Kaʻuiki; I made my men scale the hill and they would have got to the top had not my eye been struck by a sling stone." "Ha! high indeed! to the black clouds and above, just below the constellation of Little-eyes!" [Na-makehá replied, using another name for Kaʻi-ana,] "Oh, Ka-lani-kuaiwa, son of 'Ahu-ʻula, were you the son of 'Ahu-ʻula or was I in the day of battle? I was at Laʻiepuʻao in Koʻolau. I shot downwards with my gun and the gun of Ka-lani-kuaiwa trembled." "Oh! that was too low. You shot downwards and reached just a bit above Milu, land of the dead." Thus the battle raged until Keoua's men, Ka-ʻieʻiea and Uhai, made a rush and captured the cannon. [Then] Kaʻi-ana and his fierce warriors were forced to withdraw to Kona where Kamehameha and his followers were staying.

Wars fought with *pololu* and *ihe* spears, with *kuʻia* daggers and *laumeki* blades, with slings and bows, with sharks'-teeth and *pahoa* daggers, muskets, and bayonets had proven ineffective. The power of the gods alone remained to defeat Keoua Kuahu-ʻula. Kamehameha abandoned war and adopted the advice of Ka-pou-kahi and his aunt Haʻaloʻu, to build a house for the god. He summoned his counselors and younger brothers, chiefs of the family and chiefs of the guard, all the chiefs, lesser chiefs, and commoners of the whole district. Not one was allowed to be absent except the women, because it was tabu to offer a woman upon the altar; a man alone could furnish such a sacrifice. The building of the heiau of Puʻu-kohola' was, as in ancient times, directed by an expert—not in oratory, politics, genealogy, or the prophetic art, but by a member of the class called *hulihonua* who knew the configuration of the earth (called *kuhikuhi puʻuone*). Their knowledge was like that of the navigator who knows the latitude and longitude of each land, where the rocks are, the deep places and the shallow, where it is cold and where warm, and can tell without mistake the degrees, east or west, north or south. Such knowledge, taught on Kauai, one could apply anywhere in the world; so Ka-pou-kahi had instructed Haʻaloʻu to the letter.

When it came to the building of Puʻu-kohola' no one, not even a tabu chief, was excused from the work of carrying stone. Kamehameha himself labored with the rest. The only exception was the high tabu chief Ke-ali'i-maika'i [Kamehameha's younger brother]. It is said that when this chief saw Kamehameha carrying stone, he too lifted a stone and started to carry it on his back to Pu'u-kohola'; but when Kamehameha saw him packing the stone on his back he ran and took it away saying, "You stop that! You must preserve our tabu. I will do the carrying!" Then he ordered Ka-pa'a-lani and some others to take that rock out into mid-ocean so far that land was no longer visible and throw it overboard. Kamehameha certainly thought a great deal of his brother. Thus Kamehameha and the chiefs labored until the heiau was completed, with its fence of images (*paehumu*) and oracle tower (*anu'unu'u*), with all its walls outside and the hole for the bones of sacrifice. He brought down the *ohi'a* tree (*'ohi'ako*) for the *haku 'ohi'a* and erected the shelter house (*hale malu*) of *'ohi'a* wood for Ku-ka'ili-moku according to the rule laid down for the kahuna class of Pa'ao. Had the class been that of the Nalu'ulu the god's house would have been made of *lama* wood.

As soon as the heiau was completed, just before it was declared free, Kamehameha's two counselors, Keawe-a-heulu and Ka-manawa, were sent to fetch Keoua, ruling chief of the eastern end of the island of Hawaii. These two men were skilled in preparing a dose of the slippery *hau* sap and the *uhi* root; they knew well how to use cunning and deceitful speech. Keoua was living in Ka-'u *mauka* in Kahuku with his chiefs and the warriors of his guard. Keawe-a-heulu and his companion landed at Ka'iliki'i and began the ascent of Kahehawahawa along the plains of Ke'eke'ekai. Close to the extreme edge of the tabu enclosure of Keoua's place the two got down and rolled in the dirt and began to weave their nets of speech. Keoua's people nodded at each other, and Ka'ie'iea said to Keoua, "It will be a good thing to kill these counselors of Kamehameha." Keoua answered, "They must not be killed for they are younger brothers of my father." Ka'ie'iea went on, "If these are killed he will have but two counselors left, and the government will become yours." "I can not kill my uncles." The two messengers rolled along in the dirt until they came to the place where Keoua was sitting, when they grasped his feet and wept. When the weeping was over Keoua asked, "What is your errand?" Keawe-a-heulu answered, "We have come to fetch you, the son of our lord's older brother, and to take you with us to Kona to meet your younger cousin, and you two to be our chiefs and we to be your uncles. So then let war cease between you." "I consent to go with you to Kona," answered Keoua.

He made ready to go with the fleet while most of his men went on foot over the mountain. Those who went by canoe sailed and landed at Honomalino and waited for those who went on foot. From Honomalino they sailed and landed at Ka'awaloa at Keawe-a-heulu's place. Chiefs and men went up to gather 'auhuhu to catch fish by poison for Keoua's party. Here Ka'ie'iea and Uhai again urged the killing of the two messengers, but Keoua would not consent to it. From Ka'awaloa the party sailed and landed at Kailua, and again Keoua's affection for his uncles prevailed against the advice of his warriors to kill the two men. They left Kailua and went as far as Luahinewai at Kekaha, where they landed the canoes. Keoua went to bathe, and after bathing he cut off the end of his penis ('omu'o), an act which believers in sorcery call "the death of Uli," and which was a certain sign that he knew he was about to die.* There for the sixth time his counselors urged the killing of the messengers and the return by the mountains to Ka-'u, since to go on to Kawaihae meant death. Keoua refused. He brought out all his weapons of war, his feather capes and feather helmets, and placed them in Keawe-a-heulu's canoes. He also ranged his chiefs about him in his own double canoe, those of high rank and those who had lived with him and upon whose love he could count and who would die with him. Such was the custom with chiefs of old to have many companions in death (moepu'u). Keoua knew that he was to die, and those who were with him. The people who were to be spared he sent in the canoe of his younger cousin, Pauli Ka-'o-lei-o-ku, because this was Kamehameha's first-born son, born while he was still a beardless youth, and Keoua knew that he would be spared by his father.

When all was ready, Keoua and his followers went aboard the canoes, twenty-seven in all. Keoua, with Uhai carrying the kahili and another chief carrying the spittoon, was on the platform (pola), and the paddlers took their places. Just outside of Puako' they came in sight of the plain of Kawaihae with Pu'u-kohola' standing majestic. The fleet of war canoes grouped in crescent formation like canoes out for flying fish. Keoua remarked to Keawe-a-heulu, "It looks stormy ashore; the storm clouds are flying!" The chief replied, "From whence can a storm come on such a pleasant day?" Again Keoua repeated, "It looks stormy ashore; the storm clouds are flying." They kept on their course until near Mailekini, when Ke'e-au-moku and some others carrying spears,

* "The death of Uli" refers to death caused by the vengeance of the sorcerer, since Uli is the goddess worshiped by sorcerers. The part cut off is used for the purpose of sorcery so that those who do a man to death may themselves be discovered and punished.

muskets, and other weapons broke through the formation of the fleet, surrounded the canoes of Keoua, separating them from those of Keawe-a-heulu and his followers and calling to Ka-manawa to paddle ahead. Keoua arose and called to Kamehameha, "Here I am!" Kamehameha called back, "Stand up and come forward that we may greet each other." Keoua rose again, intending to spring ashore, when Ke'e-au-moku thrust a spear at him which Keoua dodged, snatched, and thrust back at Ke'e-au-moku, who snatched it away. Kua-kahela, who was an eyewitness, says that if there had been weapons aboard Keoua's canoes some [of Kamehameha's warriors] would have been killed. Muskets were then fired from the shore, and a great commotion took place among the people, during which Kua-kahela, Keoua's kahuna, jumped overboard and, disappearing under the eyes of thousands, hid in the tabu house of Ke-ku'i-apo-iwa where he lay concealed in a roll of mats. Men said, "You were saved by your family god." This man and one other were the only ones saved of those who came in the canoe with Keoua. La'anui jumped overboard secretly while off Puako'. Keoua and all those who were with him on the canoe were killed. Had the two chiefs greeted each other face-to-face. Kamehameha might not have killed him, for he loved Keoua.*

The double canoe holding Pauli Ka-'o-lei-o-ku and his people was floating some distance away. Kamehameha beckoned to him to come ashore, there was no danger for him; but he refused until a law to that effect was proclaimed. Ka-lei-mamahu' informed Kamehameha of this, and Ke-ali'i-maikai said, "Since his older brother is dead he too should die, for if you were to die I would die with you (*moepu'u*)." But Kamehameha refused, saying, "Why should our child die, the son of our youth? His mother still lives with the tabu of Ka-lani-'opu'u, and since he came from his mother he shall find refuge there in the time of distress; he shall be saved this day." And to Ka-lani-mamahu' he said, "Proclaim the law (*kanawai*) to save our child." The chief therefore called out, "Let live! Let live! No one is to die! No one is to die. Let the captives live! Let them live! The law of the broken paddle is proclaimed!" Then Pauli Ka-'o-lei-o-ku's canoe landed on the shore, and all in the canoes were saved as well as all those who had run away. Kamehameha faithfully kept the law promising life.

In the history of Keoua Kuahu-'ula it is said that the prophetic words uttered by Ka-pou-kahi were fulfilled: "War shall cease on Hawaii when one shall come and shall be laid above on the altar (*lele*) of Pu'u-kohola', the house of god." They may not have known

* *Ka Nupepa Ku'oko'a*, May 4, 1867.

that it was the power of Jehovah which united these small dominions into a single kingdom. When Ka-ihe-ki'oi saw the chief Keoua being born on men's shoulders to Pu'u-kohola' he chanted these words of affectionate lament:

Ku'u haku i ka ua Ha'ao e,	My lord of the rain of Ha'ao,*
Ke lele a'e la ka ua,	The rain flies fast,
Ma uka o 'Au'aulele,	Flies over the upland of 'Au'aulele,
Lele ka ua, lele pu no me ka makani.	The rain flies driven by the wind.
E lele po'o ana ka wai o ka ha',	The rain drives down from the cliffs above,
Ku'u haku mai ka wai	The tears for my chief
Ha'ule po'o e.	Drop down on the heads of the people.

By the death of Keoua Kuahu-'ula and his placing in the heiau of *Pu'u-koholoa' the whole of Hawaii became Kamehameha's.*†

Ua Ha'ao (rain of Ha'ao) is the name of a rain that comes down at Waiohinu in Ka-'u and keeps that district green. Ha'ao is the name of the spring second in size of the five springs that water Waiohinu. The chant is still chanted by the old people of Ka-'u who retain their love of Keoua and hatred for Kamehameha.

† *Ka Nupepa Ku'oko'a,* May 11, 1867.

CHAPTER XIII

Last Days of Ka-hekili

When Ka-'eo-ku-lani, ruling chief of Kauai, heard how narrowly
Ka-lani-ku-pule and the other chiefs of Maui had escaped death in the
war on Maui, and how the waters of 'Iao had been choked with the
bodies of the slain in this war, he was so perturbed that he set sail
to war against Kamehameha. He set out with Pe'ape'a, son of Kamehameha-nui, his counselor of war, Ki'ikiki', Kai-'awa, and chiefs, warriors,
and paddlers, all well armed with muskets and weapons of all kinds,
and with his two man-eating dogs. [He also took with him] Maka-'eha
and Mr. Mare Amara, a man skillful in the use of arms who acted
as his gunner.* On Oahu he met Ka-hekili, ruling chief over Oahu,
Molokai, Lanai, and Maui, and persuaded him to join in a war against
Kamehameha. Ka-hekili selected a type of soldier new to Oahu called
"Cut in two" (*pahupu'*), strange-looking men tattooed black from
top to toe, with eyelids turned inside out and held up by props and only
their eyeballs and teeth left in their natural state. They were led by
Koi, Kuala-kia, and Manu-o-ka-iwi. Had the black negroes who came
later to Nu'uanu arrived at that time they might have been made
favorites and given the lands of "Black waters" (Wai-pouli) and
"Daubed black" (Hono-ma'ele)! Ka-hekili left his son, Ka-lani-ku-
pule, to govern Oahu during his absence and set out to accompany the
ruling chief of Kauai, with his chiefs, both high and low, his warriors,
the children of chiefs, and among them Ka-niu-'ula, Ke-po'o-uahi,
the *pahupu'*, and other soldiers newly picked from Oahu.

The war party landed at Kaunakakai on Molokai, and when the
Kauai chief saw for the first time, by the ovens they had left, the size
of the camp which Kamehameha had occupied he said, "Where a big
squid digs itself a hole, there crab shells are heaped at the opening."
Upon their reaching Maui, Ke-kua-po'i-'ula [former wife of Ka-
hahana] died, a woman famous for her beauty. The army camped
at Wailuku, and of Waiehu the Kauai chief remarked, "Here is the
land of the warrior to whom Kamehameha owes his kingdom [alluding

* Mare Amara, or "Mare the armorer" was "probably the gunner or blacksmith of some foreign vessel trading at the islands" says Fornander in 13, vol. 2,
p. 241, note 2.

to Ke'e-au-moku whose wife, Na-mahana, brought him the land of Waiehu]. O Kauai! stand up! This is the land where you shall leave your excrement!" The Kauai people were vulgar in their speech at best. Waiehu fell to Ki'iki'i' and it was, alas! the Kauai people who ate the poi of Waiehu. The mouth that eats food should never throw stones at the producer (*I pono i kau a na waha, mai noho a pehi wale iho*). Ka-hekili gave some of the land of Maui to the ruling chief of Kauai to be divided among his men, and Waiehu fell to Ki'iki'i'. This caused discontent among the chiefs of Maui, who had thus to lose some of their land, and they rose against the Kauai chief. A battle was fought at Paukukalo adjoining Waiehu while some of the people were out surfing. Koa-lau-kani was the hero of that day's battle. You know him and the size of his feet. He was surrounded by the Kauai soldiers and in a perilous situation, but he dodged long and short spears and showed his courage in the fight that day.

Ka-'eo-ku-lani made a circuit of the north end of the island, came with all his people, and climbed the fortified hill of Ka'uiki, and he twirled his war weapon (*la'au kaua*), called Ka-mo'o-lehua, and made a thrust upward believing he could reach the sky. Failing in this he remarked, "It is said of Hana that the sky there is low; but it is too high for my weapon, the war-eater Ka-mo'o-lehua, to touch.* I fear therefore that my spear may not be able to strike down Kamehameha. O you of Kauai! chiefs, soldiers, warriors, and dear little ones, be strong, be brave! Drink the water of Waipi'o and eat the taro of Kunaka!" Ka-hekili and his men set sail for Hawaii from Mokulau in Kaupo, and Ka-'eo-ku-lani from Hana. They landed at Waipi'o. There Ka-'eo-ku-lani carried out his vow. He wantonly destroyed everything in Waipi'o. He overthrew the sacred places and the tabu threshold of Liloa; he set fire to Ka-hou-kapu's sacred threshold of *nioi* wood and utterly destroyed all the places held sacred for years by the people of Hawaii. No one before him, not even Keoua who had passed through there the year before and destroyed the land and the food, had made such wanton destruction. Perhaps it was a sign of the downfall of the ancient tabus of Hawaii "by the kingdom of God."

---

* The demi-god, Maui, is supposed to have stood on Ka'uiki in order to separate Heaven and Earth and allow room for growing things to multiply. Hina-hanai-i-ka-malama, the supernatural wife of 'Ai-kanaka who lived on Ka'uiki, is said to have leaped from this place into the moon. A folktale relates that a man of Hana is seized and imprisoned on Kauai for some infringement of tabu and is about to be sacrificed. His little son comes to the place to offer him food, and he pretends to be satisfied with nothing but a bit of the moon which hangs so low over Ka'uiki that men can feed upon it. The credulous captor releases his prisoner in order to visit and behold this wonder.

Ka-hekili in the meantime went to Halawa in Kohala where some desultory fighting occurred while Kamehameha was in Kona. Eight-eyed-bat (Pe'ape'a-maka-walu Ka-maka-uahoa), a son of Kameha-meha-nui, performed great feats of valor. It was said that Kamehameha himself could not have overcome him in combat. His strength is shown by his famous deeds. At Kahahawai he uprooted a *kou* tree; at Napoko he pulled up the ti plant of Mulei'ula and Polipoli. He tore in pieces the banana-eating monster (*mu 'ai mai'a*) of La'auhaele. He rent the hairless one (*olohe*) of Pu'ukapele, and did other wonderful feats. At Kohala he seized men by fours, lifted them up and broke their backs so that they fell lifeless. It was not until the close of the war that his death occurred at Kapelenui-a-Haho, while Ka-hekili and Ka-'eo-ku-lani were staying at Hana and Pe'ape'a was living for a time on Ka'uiki with his followers. One day as he fired off a gun a spark fell into a keg of powder, and an explosion followed which blew up the house and burned Pe'ape'a. He was carried still alive to Honokalani in Ka'anapali and there he died. What a terrible disaster!

Wela kalani - e, wela kalani,	Burned is the heavenly one, burned is the heavenly one,
Wela Ka'uiki i ka hulili,	Burned is Ka'uiki, the top of Ka'uiki!
Pau ai Pe'ape'a-maka-walu	Pe'ape'a-of-the-eight-eyes has perished in the flames
Iluna o Hawaii Kua-uli.	On top of Hawaii of the green back.
Oia ka 'uhane e o nei	His spirit lives on,
O ka 'uhane heahea makani,	The spirit that calls, calls to the wind,
'Uhane noho i ka hala i ka pe'e,	The spirit that hides in the hala grove,
Ulu mahiehie pua hinalo,	Beautiful with its white blossoms,
Ma kai o Honokalani - o-e.	Seaward of Honokalani.

Ka-hekili sailed from Halawa and joined forces with Ka-'eo at Waipi'o. When Kamehameha heard of this he consulted his counselors and those men who understood wise sayings, and they coined this phrase, "The fish have entered the net; they are gone into the bag." Believing this to be true, Kamehameha set sail with his forces and blocked the entrance of Waipi'o Bay. He had several double canoes and a sloop owned by Ka-me'e-ia-moku on board of which were John

Young and Isaac Davis. Ka-hekili and Ka-'eo met the fleet off the Waimanu cliffs, and a fight took place at sea which ended indecisively with the loss of warriors on both sides. This battle, called Ke-pu-waha-'ula, took place in 1791. It was Ka-hekili's last battle. He and his men all returned to Maui and he died in 1793. Keoua was at this time still living, and Ka'i-ana and some of the men had gone to Ka'u to make war against him because they were unwilling, or perhaps ashamed, to make war on Kamehameha.*

Fourteen years after the arrival of Captain Cook in Hawaii came Captain George Vancouver seeking new lands for Great Britain. With his two ships he followed the trail first marked out by Captain Cook from the north Atlantic to the south, through the cold ocean of the south to the Indian Ocean and the Pacific, north and south, to the cold ocean of the north. The latitude and longtitude in the northern and southern hemispheres [were] all clearly marked so that the course was known by which he had come and the places where he had planted his feet. Captain George Vancouver was a man from the land of Albion, as it is called, in Great Britain. At that time the [Hawaiian] group was not united under one government. Vancouver was the friend of every chief and of every government. He came from the south following a course which led to Kealakekua on Hawaii, but did not stop there; he merely hove to, and inquired for Ka-lani-'opu'u. He was told that Ka-lani-'opu'u was dead and the government belonged to Kamehameha. Vancouver went on to Waikiki at Oahu and met Ka-lani-ku-pule, the son of Ka-hekili chief of Oahu, who gave him forty hogs and a great quantity of foodstuff in return for red cloth, and the two became friends. Vancouver next touched at Waimea, Kauai, and set off fireworks as a sign of its being the first land discovered by an Englishman [by Cook on his first discovery of the group]. "Atooi" was the name by which the English called it. Here he met Ka-umu-ali'i, the ruling chief of Kauai, who was a mere child at the time. His country [was] ruled by his *kahu*, Na-kaikua'ana and others, while Ka-'eo-ku-lani, his father, was still on Maui with Ka-hekili. Vancouver gave Ka-umu-ali'i the name of the British monarch King George and in return Ka-umu-ali'i gave hogs and yams of Niihau. To the red cloth called *kanekopa* which Vancouver brought they gave the names *ke-kupu-ohi* and *ke-akua-lapu* because of its beautiful red color.

Vancouver remarked at this time a decrease in the population of the country and in the number of chiefs since the time of the arrival

* *Ka Nupepa Ku'oko'a*, May 11, 1867.

of Cook, who reported the land covered with people and the chiefs numerous. This was due to the fact that on Cook's arrival so many men, women, and children had come to see Captain Cook; also Cook saw them at the time when many men had gathered for the war against Maui. The white man was then an object of wonder, and many had come to see the men with brightly shining eyes. This was not the case in Vancouver's day. Moreover, a period of war had followed Captain Cook's visit, and many had been slaughtered, baked in the imu, and pounded out of existence.

The second of Vancouver's ships, called the *Daedalus,* sailed to Ko'olau on Oahu and anchored at Waimea in Ko'olauloa, a good harbor close to Waialua and often visited by ships. It was here that the captain and the astronomer were killed. Koi, one of the tattooed men, was a man of great influence with Ka-hekili. He was a leader of the tattooed forces called *pahupu'* and a kahuna of the class of Ka-leo-pu'upu'u who had charge of the heiau and the house of Koi at Kapokea, Waihe'e, Maui. All the natives were eager to secure muskets, which they had seen kill men instantly at a distance, the year before at the battle of Ka-pu-waha-'ula'ula off the cliffs of Hawaii. Koi and his men accordingly determined to kill the foreigners in order to secure these weapons of war. When the sloop arrived at Waimea two ships' boats were sent ashore for water to the mouth of the Pili'a'ama Stream on the south side of Waimea. They were supplied with barrels and equipped with muskets, swords, and bayonets. Men from Ko'olau and Waialua belonging to Ka-hekili's black division called *pahuku'* were on the watch, and when they saw the arms carried by the captain and astronomer they determined to secure them. They persuaded the men to go further up the stream to escape the brackish waters and directed them farther up than necessary. While the men were filling the barrels and rolling them down the stream, they [Koi and his men] enticed the captain and astronomer to go to see some hogs, potatoes, and bananas that were being offered for sale, thus separating them from their party. They then stoned them with stones which they had carried concealed under their clothing. The two men who threw the first stones were Ka-pale-'ai-uku and Kua-niu. These hit the white men on the chin and knocked them down. Then they were killed. When the other foreigners saw what was happening they stopped rolling the barrels and ran to the boats and began firing at the people. The men on the ship, seeing what was going on, swung the ship around and fired at Waimea. This they continued all that day until night, when the ship lay to outside. At daylight the firing began again and this went on for five days, when they sailed for Niihau. The two men who were killed were dragged along from Waimea to Waialua and from there to Mokuleia, all because of hatred for the foreigners. In the hearts of [the plotters] there was no fear of God who had made all men of one blood. I met one of the men who did the killing and he told me, "The men were killed to get the guns; the chiefs had commanded the lesser chiefs and warriors who lived in the back country that if a ship came into those parts with guns [they were] to kill the strangers and get the guns." The guns and swords were taken to Ka-lani-ku-pule at Waikiki, and when the chief saw what Koi had seized he rejoiced to have the muskets, for those were times of war on this group from Kauai to Hawaii, war both within the island and with other islands. The land mourned the blood of men shed without cause, because of the pride and arrogance of the chiefs who desired to get land and riches at the sacrifice of human blood. Let the Hawaiians ponder these things.

Vancouver disappeared from Kauai and sailed to the northwest coast of America, to the harbors just visited by Captain Cook, and he called also at harbors in Mexico and California. He returned to the Hawaiian group and reached Kawaihae, February 14, 1793. There he was urged to sell muskets and powder, but he replied, "It is not right to sell things for killing people." Vancouver was a Christian and a true Englishman. He may well be called the father of the Hawaiian people. He was the first to point out "the true God in heaven." He is well-known as the friend of the chiefs from Hawaii to Kauai. He did not furnish some chiefs with weapons and deny them to others, but to all the chiefs from Hawaii to Kauai his advice was, "Stop making war; live in peace; be friends with each other." All the chiefs were anxious at this time to obtain guns and powder because of the wars that lasted until the whole group was brought under the rule of Kamehameha. On this second visit of Vancouver he met Kamehameha and his foreigners, Isaac Davis and John Young—called "Olohana." He thanked Kamehameha for the good care he had given the foreigners, and when they told him that the chief had given them lands he did not ask to take Young back to England, but recommended both men to the chief's care. In return for the chief's kindness to them and for the food with which he had been himself provided he gave Kamehameha a bull and a heifer brought from Monterey in California. The Hawaiians were grateful for these cattle, and because they stared so strangely they were given the name "Pig-beef" (pua'a-bipi). This was the beginning of the wild herds of Waimea and Mauna Kea.*

* *Ka Nupepa Ku'oko'a*, May 18, 1867.

At the close of Vancouver's stay at Kawaihae, on February 22, he took Kamehameha with him to Kealakekua. The chief gave him provisions to stock the ship. When there was trouble about getting fresh water he had his men take the ship's barrels and fill them with cool mountain water and return them to the ship, where the men received a few inches of iron each for their labor. When Vancouver saw Kamehameha's great following of lesser chiefs and soldiers and how the whole island was his and he was the sole ruling chief over the island of Hawaii, he advised Kamehameha to stop fighting the chiefs of Maui, Oahu, and Kauai; but Kamehameha did not commit himself on the subject. Vancouver gave him some fine clothes, and the chief in return gave Vancouver feather cloaks, feather leis, helmets, and *kahili* to be delivered as presents to the King of England.

On March 8 Vancouver left Kealakekua and sailed for Maui and on March 12 reached Lahaina. Here he met Ka-hekili, the ruling chief of Maui, a very old man at this time and strange in appearance because of his black tattooing. Vancouver told him to stop fighting and establish friendly relations with the chiefs of Hawaii. Ka-'ili-naoa spoke for him and said that Ka-hekili would agree to peace, but it was not right for the chiefs of Hawaii to raid Maui and rob and pillage without cause. Ka-hekili requested Vancouver, if he desired peace, to stay there all the time and guard him against further wars. Vancouver remarked that Kamehameha "had many chiefs in his following" (*nuinui ali'i* Kamehameha), [but because of his imperfect knowledge of the language he used the words, "is a great chief"]. Ka-hekili, thinking he referred to Kamehameha's rank, protested, saying, "Kamehameha has come up from nothing; I am a great chief." Vancouver answered, "Ho! you have few chiefs, he has many." "No, no! I am the great chief, he is not a chief!" All this time Ka-hekili was speaking of their respective ranks, Vancouver of the number of their followers, because he had seen Kamehameha's men and how many there were and how well equipped with arms. The chiefs of old were very jealous of each other. And because Vancouver had called him a "little chief" (*u'uku ali'i*) Ka-hekili called his grandchild, Ahukai, who was named after the sea-sprayed land of Waialua, "The little chief" (Ka-'u'uku-ali'i). She was the daughter of Manono Ka-ua-kapeku-lani and of Ka-'ili-naoa, who was the daughter of Mano-ha'aipo, the daughter of Ke-kau-like with Holau, who was the daughter of Ka-ua-kahi-hele-i-ka-iwi.

Vancouver went on to Oahu and landed at Waikiki. There he met Ka-lani-ku-pule, ruling chief of Oahu, and took up with him the matter of the murder of the foreigners at Waimea, saying, "Those who

killed the white men should be stoned to death for their crime."
Ka-lani-ku-pule consented to put to death those who had committed the
crime, but Ka-mohomoho, whose man Koi committed the murder,
refused to have Koi and his men killed for the foreigners. [Therefore]
some other men were brought and put to death on March 25, 1793, in
the presence of Vancouver, after which Vancouver sailed to Kauai and
from there to the west coast of America. Thus ended his second visit
to the coasts of Hawaii . . . His third visit occurred January 9, 1794
on his return from the American coast after the death of Ka-hekili
and while Ka-'eo was ruling over Maui.

After the battle of Ke-pu-waha-'ula'ula and the fighting along the
cliffs of Hawaii, Ka-hekili returned and ruled Maui for three years
and some months. In Ikiiki (May) he fell ill and, returning to Oahu,
died at Ulukou, Waikiki, in the month of Ka'aona at the age of
eighty-seven. His bones were carried away by Ka-me'e-ia-moku and
Ka-manawa and hidden in a secret cave, perhaps at Kaloko in North
Kohala. Ka-hekili was a famous chief, a tabu chief, one who ruled
men, and so sacred that whatever had touched his body was burned with
fire [after he was through with it, so that no one else could use it]. He
was a famous leaper from a cliff into water (lelekawa), sometimes
from a height of 500 or 600 feet or even higher, and he could climb
cliffs which no other person could ascend. He elected to have his skin
black; one half of his body from head to foot was tattooed black, and
his face was tattooed black, and this became an established law with
him: Any person taken in crime who passed on his dark side, escaped
with his life. He delighted in war and fought many battles with Ka-
lani-'opu'u, with Puna, with the chiefs of Molokai, with Ke'e-au-moku,
Mahi-hele-lima, and Ka-hahana, ruling chief of Oahu, and in strife
with Kamehameha. While he ruled over Maui, Molokai, Lanai, and
Oahu he appropriated to himself the gods of these islands. Here are
the names of the gods he worshiped as a means of keeping control of
the   government: Ku-ke-oloewa,   Kuho'one'e-nu'u,   Kalai-pahoa,
Ololupe, Kameha'ikana, Kala-mai-nu'u, and Kiha-wahine, Haumea,
and Wali-nu'u. These gods were deities whose heiaus were tabu and
in which human sacrifices were offered. Ka-hekili was a man prudent
in   warfare   and   skilled   in   statecraft   (kalai'aina)   and   oratory
(kaka'olelo). He took the greatest delight in feats of strength. Rolling
the maika stone was his favorite sport, and there were many maika
courses constructed from Maui to Oahu. He liked solitude and would
separate himself from the other chiefs and from his wives. He erected
living quarters on high points of land and admitted only those who

were special favorites. No woman entered his house, not even his wives; his house was set perhaps a quarter or half a mile from the house of his wife, and perhaps it was for this reason that he was so studious. He would go out at night to spy about, accompanied by his two favorite friends, Ka-hui and Ka-halawai. He did this in order to detect rebellion or conspiracy, to find out which men ate with their wives, whether men asked the gods for the life of the ruling chief when they drank 'awa, whether they were worshipers or not, whether they ate things sacrificed to the gods, and whether they were carousing at night and making false vows. He was cruel to his enemies. Ka-umu-pika'o at Hana was a place famous for the roasting of chiefs and lesser chiefs. On Oahu he had even roasted tabu chiefs in the imu. His cruelty to chiefs and people on Oahu is notorious. But God punished him for his cruel deeds for, although he had many sons and daughters, none of his children produced a long line of descendants (*puko loa i ke ao*). He was nevertheless a religious man and heeded well the laws of his gods, and this is why he was victorious over his enemies, and it was for this reason that he had half of his body tattooed black like Kane-of-the-thunder (Kane-hekili) and Kane-hekili-nui-'ahu-manu, and he lived to a good old age.

Many persons [of his time] were famous for their skill in oratory, administration, genealogies, prophecy, and knowledge of the configuration of the earth. Kane-wahine was a noted priestess, both prophet (*kaula*) and reader of signs (*kilo*). Manewa was her child, of the priesthood of Ka'eka', Maliu, and Malela, and of Luhau-ka-pawa. Ka-leo-pu'upu'u also is famous for the erection of the heiau Kaluli and for the prediction of the coming of the pestilence known as the Pi'ipi'i at Kakanilua, the downfall of the independent chiefs of Oahu, and the taking-over of the government of Oahu. Ka-'o-pulupulu was noted for his prophecy that white men would become rulers, the native population would live [landless] like fishes of the sea, the line of chiefs would come to an end, and a stubborn generation would succeed them who would cause the native race to dwindle. There were such historians as Kaha-walu, Kane-hahei, Ka-'ope'ape'a, and Kai-akea, who knew the genealogies of the chiefs.*

* *Ka Nupepa Ku'oko'a*, May 25, 1867.

CHAPTER XIV

Kamehameha's Conquest of Maui and Oahu

At the death of Ka-hekili in 1793 Ka-'eo-ku-lani became ruling chief of Maui, Molokai, and Lanai. Ki'ikiki' and Kai-'awa were his counselors, and they had chiefs and governors under them. He ruled a little over a year and showed kindness to the common people, but at the end of that time he grew homesick for his friends on Kauai and set out with his chiefs and warriors to return to his own people, stopping at Molokai to enjoy its fat fish and *kukui*-nut relish. Now Ka-lani-ku-pule and his younger brother Koa-lau-kani, heard that Ka-'eo-ku-lani was return-ing to Kauai. Not knowing what his plans might be they made prepara-tions for war, digging trenches and throwing up earthworks at Kukui, Kalapueo, and Waimanalo [on Oahu]. At Kukui a severe battle was fought in which one of the favorites, a war leader of Ka-lani-ku-pule, was shot by Mare Amara at the stream of Muliwaiolena as he stood with a feather cloak about his shoulders directing the battle with his hand. Two days and two nights Ka-'eo-ku-lani lay out at sea, then Ka-lani-ku-pule called off the fighting and the two had a friendly meeting at Kalapawai in Kailua, Ko'olaupoko. It was a day of mingled joy and weeping—joy for the ending of war, weeping for the dead in battle and also for the death of Ka-hekili.*

A few days later Ka-'eo-kulani set out to return to Kauai by way of Waialua and thence to Waimea, where he discovered a conspiracy among Kai-'awa and some other chiefs and captains of his fleet to throw him overboard in mid-ocean. Thinking that death on the field of battle among many companions was better than to die alone, he had the canoes dismantled and proceeded to make war on Ka-lani-ku-pule, joined as he was by the warriors of Waialua and Wai'anae. Ka-'eo's change of plan came to the ears of Ka-lani-ku-pule, and by November, 1794, both sides were ready to fight, and Ka-'eo won an easy victory over Ka-lani-ku-pule's forces. But during the early days of the war a couple of foreign ships entered the harbor of Kou at Honolulu, the first to enter that harbor. They were the *Jackal* and *Prince Lee Boo*, American [British] ships on an exploring expedition and equipped like

* *Ka Nupepa Ku'oko'a,* May 25, 1867.

168

men-of-war. Ka-lani-kupule at once engaged Captain Brown to aid him in this war in return for four hundred (a *lau*) hogs. A battle was fought on the plains of Pu'unahawele in which some foreigners were killed by Mare Amara. Natives also fell, and Ka-lani-ku-pule was forced to retreat. Some six days later another battle was fought in which Ka-'eo was again victorious. This gain he followed up by approaching further upon 'Ewa, hoping to push on to Waikiki which was at that time the center of government. On December 12, 1794, a great battle was fought on the ground of Ka-lani-manuia between Kalauao and 'Aiea in 'Ewa. The heights of Kuamo'o, Kalauao, and 'Aiea were held by the right wing of Ka-lani-ku-pule's forces commanded by a warrior named Koa-lau-kani; the shore line of Malie [was held] by the left wing under the command of Ka-mohomoho; Ka-lani-ku-pule himself with the main army held the middle ground between 'Aiea and the taro patches; Captain Brown's men were in boats guarding the shoreline. Thus surrounded, Ka-'eo found his men fighting at close quarters and, cut off by Koa-lau-kani between Kalauao and Kuamo'o, he was hemmed in on all sides and compelled to meet the onset, which moved like the ebb and flow of the tide. Shots from guns and cannon, thrusts of the sword and spear fell upon his helpers. Ka-'eo with six of his men escaped into a ravine below 'Aiea and might have disappeared there had not the red of his feather cloak been seen from the boats at sea and their shots drawn the attention of those on land. Hemmed in from above, he was killed fighting bravely. His wives were killed with him, and his chiefs and warriors. This war, called Kuki'iahu, was fought from November 16 to December 12, 1794, at Kalauao in 'Ewa. At the death of Ka-'eo-ku-lani who was the son of Ke-kau-like and his wife Holau, his son George Ka-umu-ali'i became ruling chief of Kauai; but, being too young to take charge of the government, his *kahu* administered it for him with power to make war.

On the afternoon [of the final day of victory for Ka-lani-ku-pule] the dead were gathered together, carried to Pa'aiau, and piled in a great heap. Among the bodies was that of Ka-hulu-nui-ka-'aumoku, a daughter of Ku-'ohu, the leading kahuna of Kauai, who had fallen with Ka-'eo and the rest at Kuki'iahu. Her body had been picked up for dead, carried with the others to Pa'aiau, and left in the heap of corpses. It was about one o'clock in the afternoon when she fell. At about ten o'clock that night she was aroused by an owl that flew over her and beat its wings on her head. She opened her eyes as from a deep sleep and found herself lying with the dead in a great heap. A guard was walking to and fro. The owl flew seaward and she followed, crawling, until she reached the sea. Then she swam to the opposite shore in spite of her many wounds and landed at 'Aiea, where the owl led her up Halawa valley into the mountains. There she found a cave and fell as if dead. While she lay unconscious, the owl flew to a former *kahu* of hers who knew the country well around Halawa, and this person brought her food and anointed her wounds. Two days later Ka-lani-ku-pule proclaimed an amnesty giving life to the captives, on pain of death if anyone, commoner or chief, kept up the slaughter. Ka-hulu died in 1834. I have seen with my own eyes the scars of the wounds with which her body was covered. Thus God showed mercy to this woman until she heard the word of God and the Holy Trinity.

After the battle of Kuki'iahu and the death of Ka-eo-ku-lani a quarrel arose with Captain Brown over the payment for the captain's help. Ka-lani-ku-pule offered to pay the four hundred hogs stipulated, but Captain Brown demanded further payment. The chiefs accordingly conspired to kill Captain Brown and his men. Ka-mohomoho advised Ka-lani-ku-pule to pay the whole number of hogs agreed upon, and when the white men asked how to salt down such a number to tell them that they might get all the salt they wanted from Ka-'ihi-kapu, with the hope that Captain Brown would accompany the boats sent for salt, and the Oahu men might seize the ships and kill the white men. Ka-lani-ku-pule consented and the plan was put into execution. They delivered tthe whole number of hogs at once, enough to fill the two ships, and when the captain asked for salt they directed him to Ka-'ihi-kapu. The tide was high when the boats came in; but when the boats loaded with salt attempted to return, the tide at Ke'ehi was low, and the boats had to wait. The ships meanwhile lay in the harbor filled with chiefs and their men who killed Captain Brown and some others. Some of the white men who went after salt were killed, those few who remained alive were taken prisoners, and Ka-lani-ku-pule took possession of the two ships well-stocked as they were with weapons and ammunition.

Ka-lani-ku-pule now thought he might sail to Hawaii and make war on Kamehameha. Three weeks later he set sail with his chiefs, counselors, and warriors filling the two ships and a fleet of canoes besides. Ka-mohomoho advised him, "Place most of the foreigners in the canoes, keep only enough of them to navigate the ships." "No, no!" said Ka-lani-ku-pule. Again Ka-mohomoho advised, "Then place the arms in the canoes and leave only the large guns on the ships." Again Ka-lani-ku-pule refused. The ships sailed from Honolulu harbor on January 4, 1795, crowded with chiefs and warriors. On the morning of January 5 all became so seasick that the boats were ordered back to Waikiki where they anchored. Ka-mohomoho said, "The white men are up to something. The reason we are all seasick is because of the stink pots of the white men that have such a bad odor!" and he repeated his advice to place either the foreigners or the weapons of war in the canoes. Ka-lani-ku-pule again refused, nor was this the last time that our chiefs have refused to obey sound advice. They refuse it even now, the historians say. On this occasion all the chiefs and their men went ashore, and no guards were set on the ships or over the canoes. Toward midnight the ship *Prince Lee Boo* was made ready to sail. Her men whistled to those on the *Jackal*, she too made ready, and they set sail with Ka-lani-ku-pule on board and his wife and a few attendants. At daybreak, when those on land looked to sea, the ships were gone. Strangely enough, off Lae-'ahi [Diamond Head] the chief and his people were sent ashore in a canoe. The men on board did not take vengeance on the chief for the death of their fellows and the capture of the ships, but even waited until daylight and sent him ashore alive. They certainly showed a true Christian spirit. These ships belonged to the United States of America. They sailed to Hawaii and told Kamehameha what had happened, even handing over to him the munitions of war of the Oahuans. Hawaii owes these men a debt of gratitude. Had Ka-lani-ku-pule not lost these arms, Kamehameha might not have been successful in bringing the whole group under his rule.*

When Kamehameha heard the whole story from his two foreign friends Young and Davis, and how Ka-lani-ku-pule had started out to make war upon him, he believed in the power of his god and he said, "Say, Ku-ka'ili-moku, seize that island." He did not know of the true God Jehovah, who rules heaven and earth and was uniting the many small kingdoms into one so that war and slaughter and the pitiless burning of bodies in ovens might cease. In February, 1795, Kamehameha's fleet of war canoes landed at Lahaina, covering the sands along the coast from Launiupoko to Mala. All that part of Lahaina given over to food patches and cane fields was at that time overrun by the men from Hawaii. At Molokai, again, the whole coast from Kawela to Kalama'ula was covered by canoes.

It is often said that in old times because of the wars when even the women were killed, [because] of the practice of infanticide, the slaughtering and assassination carried on at night, the throwing of men into hot ovens, the catching of men to use as shark bait, the lack of any place of safety for the weak, [because of all these things] death

* *Ka Nupepa Ku'oko'a*, June 1, 1867.

surrounded people on all sides; but nevertheless there seem to be fewer native people today than in those old days. Even after the tabus were abolished the land was well populated from Hawaii to Kauai with high chiefs, the favorites of chiefs, lesser chiefs, the children of chiefs, and commoners. The land was well filled with men, women, and children. It was a common thing to see old men and women of a hundred years and over, wrinkled and flabby-skinned, with eyelids hanging shut. One does not see such people today.

While Kamehameha remained on Molokai with his forces, awaiting a proper time to set sail for Oahu, he consulted with many of his counselors and orators and his secret advisers; but he never summoned Ka'i-ana-Ka-'ahu-'ula to such councils, and this made Ka'i-ana suspect that the counselors were plotting his death. These councils took place at Kaunakakai. Ka'i-ana stayed at Kamiloloa . . . Ka'i-ana told his younger brother, "I fear that the chiefs are conspiring to kill us." "What can we do to save ourselves?" asked Nahiolea. Ka'i-ana answered, "We face death whether we follow Kamehameha or the sons of our older brother." His brother said, "You have given all your weapons to Kamehameha; how then can you follow our nephews?" Ka'i-ana replied, "I was deceived by crafty words and had no idea he would do this." When the fleet left Molokai and was approaching the Kaiwi channel, Ka'i-ana leaped into his wife's canoe and rubbed noses with her. "Why this kiss?" she asked. "I am leaving you to follow the sons of my older brother; but if I die, see that I am secretly buried." Ke-kupu-ohi said, "I will not follow you, for I must go with my chief, but if your side wins, find a secret place for my bones." After exchanging farewells the two parted, and Ka'i-ana made his way to Ko'olau on Oahu and fought on the side of Ka-lani-ku-pule.

Kamehameha's fleet landed at Waikiki where it covered the beaches from Wai'alae to Waikiki. Ka-lani-ku-pule and his chiefs were stationed at strategic points in Nu'uanu at Kanoneakapueo, Kahapa'akai, Luakaha, Kawananakoa, Kaukahoku, Kapa'eli, Kaumu'ohena, and Pu'iwa, where the fighting began. At La'imi in Nu'uanu Ka-lani-ku-pule's side was routed, and there Ka'i-ana died. The chiefs and warriors of Ka-lani-ku-pule were slaughtered, but Koa-lau-kani escaped and fled to Kauai, and Ka-lani-ku-pule hid in the underbrush for a little over a year and then was captured *mauka* of Waipi'o in 'Ewa and killed. His body was brought to Kamehameha and offered in sacrifice to his god, Ku-ka'ili-moku.

By the battle of Nu'uanu, as this was called, Oahu, Molokai, and Lanai were taken; Kauai alone remained. Kamehameha now resolved

to carry the conquest to that island. Before setting out he declared a
tabu on the heiau of his war god Ku-ka'ili-moku at 'Ewa, the heiau
called Ha'ena, and he made offerings and sacrificed human sacrifices
for the freeing of the tabu. The fleet went on to Wai'anae, and the war
god was carried ashore that evening. Towards midnight they put out to
sea, intending to land at daylight in Puna harbor on Kauai, but in the
midst of the Ka'ie'iewaho channel the advance canoes encountered the
strong wind called Kulepe and were capsized. The canoes that went to
their assistance were swamped, and all might have been wrecked on
the coast of Kauai or carried out to sea by the current and lost had
they not been near enough Wai'anae to gain shelter. Because of this
disastrous ending of the war expedition to Kauai, the whole fleet
returned and remained on Oahu for over a year. This expedition was
called Ka'ie'iewaho.

Na-makeha' was a tabu chief of Maui. His mother was Kau-peka-
moku, his father was Ka-nalu-i-ho'ae, also called Ke-kau-like. These
people belonged to an order descended from Ka-'aka-lani who avoided
the sun. They must have been an odd lot to make the sun their tabu
and to belittle the sun placed by God over all living creatures on earth!
While he was living in Ka-'u Na-makeha' had been sent for to accompany Kamehameha's expedition, but he had not responded. It was said
this was because he felt ashamed to fight against Ka-lani-ku-pule, and
he was led also by the counsel of Ka-lani-huia, a kahuna of Kiwala'o
and Keoua. Na-makeha' now rebelled against the rule of Hawaii and
began to feed the men of Ka-'u, Puna, and Hilo, in preparation for
war against Kamehameha. When Kamehameha heard of this, he set
out to return to Hawaii and selected to accompany him some of the
lesser chiefs of Oahu and Maui, together with skillful orators and
genealogists of those islands, of whom Kalai-ku-ahulu was one.* Kamehameha consulted these orators in regard to placing a chief over
Oahu, but was advised as follows: "Do not appoint a chief over Oahu,
for during your absence in Hawaii he would rebel against you. The
best thing to do is to leave none but commoners on Oahu and take
the young chiefs with you. We were able to win the island only because
the foreigners carried off the munitions of war. Had the government
been supplied with arms by other ships we could not have conquered
it." Kamehameha therefore put his steward Ku-i-helani, in charge of
Oahu, and Ka-lani-moku appointed his man Ka-hanau-maika'i, to
collect taxes. Ke-kua-manoha', although among those who fought for
Ka-lani-ku-pule and plotted against Kamehameha, was left on Oahu

* *Ka Nupepa Ku'oko'a*, June 8, 1867.

because many of his relatives were among Kamehameha's followers. In September, 1796, Kamehameha returned to Hawaii to make war on Na-makeha' and his followers. The battle took place at Hilo. Na-makeha' was defeated, fled, and hid in the bush until he was captured. He was made a mock of by his enemies, and in January, 1797, with the consent of Kamehameha, he was offered in sacrifice to the gods in the heiau of Kaipalaoa in Pi'ihonua, Hilo. Many had said that Na-makeha' would never be taken by Kamehameha because he was of higher blood, but it was the higher powers who decided which should become the greater of the two. This was the last of the battles fought by Kamehameha to unite the islands. He now had brought Hawaii, Maui, Molokai, Lanai, and Oahu under one rule, with Kauai and Niihau under a different ruler.

In October, 1796, a ship [Arthur, under Henry Barber] went aground at Kalaeloa, Oahu. This ship had visited the island on several occasions during the rule of Ka-lani-ku-pule. This was the first time a foreign ship had grounded on these shores. Kamehameha was on Hawaii, but Young had remained on Oahu. All the men on the ship came ashore at night in their boats. At daylight when the ship was seen ashore Ku-i-helani placed a ban on the property of the ship and took care of the foreigners. Hawaiian divers recovered the valuables, and they were given over to the care of Ku-i-helani, but part were given by Captain Barber to the men who had recovered them.

Before the battle of Nu'uanu there were living on Oahu with Ka-lani-ku-pule Mr. Oliver Holmes, Shomisona, Mr. Lele, Mr. Mela [Miller], Mr. Keaka-'ele'ele [Black Jack], and some other foreigners. When Kamehameha conquered the island, they all came over to his side. [After the battle of Nu'uanu in 1796] Mr. Miller and Mr. Keaka built a red stone house for Ka-'ahu-manu at Apukaiao in Paunau, Lahaina.*

* Ka Nupepa Ku'oko'a, June 15, 1867.

CHAPTER XV

Reminiscences of Kamehameha

After the death of Na-makeha' there was peace from Hawaii to Kauai, and Kamehameha began to administer the kingdom for the good of chiefs and commoners. He made his uncles, Keawe-a-heulu, Ke'e-au-moku, Ka-me'e-ia-moku, and Ka-manawa, who had aided him to secure the rule, his governors (*kuhina*) and gave them large tracts of land from Hawaii to Oahu in payment for their services; Kamehameha himself had no power to recover these lands. Ka-lani-moku he made commander-in-chief (*pukaua*) and chief treasurer (*pu'uku nui*) with the duty of dividing the lands to the chiefs and commoners, to all those who had used their strength for the victory of Kamehameha. By this appointment Kamehameha waived the privilege of giving anything away without the consent of the treasurer. Should that officer fail to confirm a gift it would not be binding. Kamehameha could not give any of the revenues of food or fish on his own account in the absence of this officer. If he were staying, not in Kailua but in Kawaihae or Honaunau, the treasurer had to be sent for, and only upon his arrival could things be given away to chiefs, lesser chiefs, soldiers, to the chief's men, or to any others. The laws determining life or death were in the hands of this treasurer; he had charge of everything. Kamehameha's brothers, the chiefs, the favorites, the lesser chiefs, the soldiers, and all who were fed by the chief, anyone to whom Kamehameha gave a gift, could secure it to himself only by informing the chief treasurer.

Kamehameha had a deliberative council consisting of his counselors and chiefs selected for the purpose, and these persons handled the affairs of government in matters of war or of the welfare of the people. He sought out men who had knowledge of old methods of warfare and made them members of his council; such men as Ka-ua-kahi-a-kaha-ola, Kai, Ka-palaoa, and Ka'a-loa son of Ka-uhi. The kahuna and orator Kalai-ku-ahulu also became a member of the council. Kamehameha made laws to protect both chiefs and commoners, prohibiting murder, theft, wanton destruction of property, the taking of property without cause, robbing the weak, praying to death, and laws

175

to observe the tabus of the gods. He thus made it possible for "old men and women and children to sleep in safety by the wayside." He divided the warrior chiefs into companies according to certain classes and put every man into one of these classes: the Keawe, the Mahi, the I, the Ahu, the Palena, the Luahine, and the Paia. For young stranger chiefs he made three classes: the Okaka, the 'Ai-'ohi'a, and the Uouo.

He also regulated the fishermen. There were deep-sea nets for fishing ('aumaiewa), shallow-sea nets for fishing (laulele), nets for fishing by diving ('upena-lu'u), fishing by enticing into the net by means of a stick with a strong odor (lawai'a melomelo), aku trolling with mother-of-pearl hooks (lawai'a-hi-aku), ahi trolling with hook and line (hi-ahi), net fishing for flying fish (hano-malolo), trolling for kahala fish with hook and line (hi-kahala), and several other kinds. Mahi-luheluhe and I-ama he selected as head men over all the fishermen. He used himself to take part in the work, no matter what kind it was. He helped in preparing the fishing gear or in drawing the catch ashore, or he would go out himself to sea and take part in the labor. As soon as the catch was landed Ka-lani-moku would be sent for, and after the fish for the gods had been set aside, then would come the portion for the treasurer himself. After that the remainder was divided among Kamehameha and his wives and children, the chiefs, the king's housemates, the warrior chiefs, and all the rest. Ka-lani-moku was the highest official in the kingdom to the time of his death.

Kamehameha also selected workers in wood: makers of pololu, ihe, and laumeki spears, paddles, and canoe floats. He chose kahunas who were makers of double canoes (wa'a kaulua), war canoes (wa'a peleleu), single canoes (wa'a kaukahi), sailing canoes (wa'a kialoa)—either one-masted canoes (kiakahi) or two-masted (kialua); and kahunas who were makers of holua sleds and surf boards (papa he'enalu). He appointed head men over these kinds of work. He also appointed kahunas as craftsmen to make wooden bowls (ipu la'au), calabashes ('umeke), dishes (ipu kai), spittoons (ipu kuha), slop bowls (ipu hanowa), flat dishes (kalai pa), hand basins (pa waiholoi lima), face basins (holoi maka), bath basins (ipu 'au'au), vessels in which meat for shark bait was left to decompose (ipu kupalu mano), vessels for dyeing tapas (ipu ho'olu'u kapa), or skirts (ipu ho'olu'u pa-'u), containers for valuable possessions (ipuhokeo), for the shell fishhook (ipu pa-hi-aku), for a little shell fishhook (ipu makau ea), for human bones (ipu makau iwi kanaka), for medicinal clays (ipu kapuna), for offerings to the gods (ipu o Lono), cord holders (ipu *kuaʻaha*), and for salt holders (*ipu kuliʻu*). Wai-pa' he appointed at the head of all these crafts.

Kamehameha selected strong paddlers to paddle canoes, and he set masters over them to navigate the canoes from Hawaii to Oahu and to carry orders from the chief to the governor of the island or to the head of a district, down to the smaller divisions of each district (*ʻai-kalana, ʻai-ʻokana, ʻai-ahupuaʻa, ʻai-o-loko, ʻai-ʻili-kupono, ʻai-ʻili-ʻaina*). Ke-paʻa-lani was Kamehameha's navigator, Keawe-opu' and Na-hili were his sailing masters, and he had a number of men who carried messages of good will to the different islands. He appointed commoners to the different land divisions to cultivate *wauke*, bananas, sugar cane, taro, sweet potatoes, and yams, to raise hogs and chickens, and fatten dogs. He selected people skilled in dyeing tapas, skirts, and loin cloths, also makers of *olona* twine, net makers, and catchers of the *ʻoʻo* and *mamo* birds. He had experts in the binding of feathers for the making of feather capes, cloaks, *kahili*, feather helmets, and feather leis.

Kamehameha had tax collectors who went out to ear-mark the hogs that were given him and to see that one-tenth of the taro patches, dry-land taro, and sweet-potato cultivations were marked by sticking up one end of a sugar cane stalk as a sign where his property ended. He appointed tax gatherers for large and small properties and tax assessors to fix the tax on large and small land divisions all over Hawaii to Oahu in proportion to the size of the lands, the larger lands paying larger taxes and the smaller lands smaller taxes. The payment of these taxes was made in tapas, skirts, loin cloths, swine, dogs, chickens, mats, *olona* fiber, nets, fish lines, *ʻoʻo* and *mamo* feathers, and pearls from ʻEwa. These taxes were paid yearly and delivered at a place named by the king. On all the tracts of land in the different divisions certain days of the year were set aside as days of cultivation of food for the king, for his use and for that of the chiefs and people who lived with him. He placed restrictions on sea fisheries for periods of five months, and on the sixth month when the restriction was removed and fishing was allowed all over the land, the king and the commoners were usually the only ones to share the first day's catch, and the landlords and the commoners the second day's catch. After this the restrictions were removed, allowing all to fish for six months. At the end of this period restrictions were again placed over certain fish in order that they might increase. These restrictions were also extended to the deep-sea fishing grounds where the *kahala* were caught and the fish that go in schools, such as deep-sea squid, *uhu, aku,* and flying fish. Expert fishermen were appointed to catch the smaller fish such as 'a'ala'ihi, maikoiko, kole, 'upapalu, manini, 'opule, 'u'u, and other such fish as served for the morning meal.

Kamehameha appointed men to serve under the different chiefs as stewards. There were several hundred of these, all well-educated for the position, alert and strong. He often summoned the chiefs to come and live with him, and he discouraged their living far away in the back country where they might gather men about them and some day take it into their heads to conspire against his rule. When he saw any chief collecting a number of retainers about him, he would summon the chief to him at Kawaihae or some such place; when the provisions ran short the hangers-on had to go back to the country, but the chief was always well provided with food, fish, tapa, and everything he needed for his own wants. Kamehameha was known as a good provider, because he supplied the wants of the chiefs high and low, of those who lived with him, and of those who had no master. He did this in order that the people might speak of his kindness and of the pains he took to care for the chiefs and people; the orators were instructed to speak of his kind acts.

Kamehameha took the children of commoners and trained them to be warriors or to learn other arts. He called these "adopted children" (ho'okama), "friends" (aikane), "favorites" (punahele), or "companions" (hoa-'ai). He had a large train of chiefs and people constantly with him, and for this reason his rule was very popular. He took men who were fast runners with Ke-kua-pani'o at their head. These men were always ready to be ordered out. Ke-kua-pani'o could run from Kawaihae to Waiakea, get fresh fish, and bring it back alive to Kawaihae all in one day. Ke-pa'a-lani was his swiftest paddler; he could go from Kawaihae to Lahaina and back again to Kawaihae in the same day. What wonderful endurance men had in the old days!

Kamehameha selected men to act as teachers in the arts of wrestling (ku'ialua), dodging the javelin (lonomakaihe), warding off the javelin ('oniu la'au), boxing (mokomoko), hitting with the fist (ku'iku'i), fencing (kākā la'au) running chest up with a weight on the back (umauma), squatting and pushing (honuhonu), disc rolling (ulu maika), playing puhenehene, pahe'e, koi, turning somersaults (wala), turning somersaults backward (walakua), broad jump (pinao), leaping from a height (lele), reading signs and omens (kilokilo), pointing out locations (kuhikuhi pu'uone), the configurations of the earth (papa hulihonua), wound healing (lonopu'ha'), and all the arts of the kahuna.

The kahunas who taught the art of healing wounds were selected by Kamehameha from the descendants of Miliko'o, Puheke, and Palaha, who had been trained in the art of healing by Ka-maka-nui-'aha'ilono and Lono. One of these kahunas, Ku-a'ua'u, became Kamehameha's personal healer. Among other chiefs trained in the art of healing wounds were Ka-lani-moku and Boki Ka-ma'ule'ule. Others were educated in the art of healing chronic diseases. This is how these healers were trained: Pebbles were set in the shape of the human body. The different parts where diseases were located were marked off from the head to the feet, and the kind of disease and its symptoms were taught for each part. The healers learned to know which diseases were curable and which incurable. Then medicines were studied for each disease. When that had been learned the pupil felt over a real patient and studied his body.*

Kamehameha built heiaus for his gods. Ku-ka'ili-moku was a feather god whose feathers, it was said, had formerly grown on the foreheads of the great birds Halulu and Kiwa'a. Ku-ke-olo'ewa, Ka-haka-iki, or Maku'u† was a wooden god from a tree of Paliuli and wore a helmet on its head. Ku-ho'one-nu'u was another god made of the tree with beautiful flowers brought by Haumea from Ka-lewa-lani. It also bore the flowers, Kani-ka-wi' and Kani-ka-wa', and wore a feather helmet on its head formed out of the feathers of Halulu, Kiwa'a, and Hiapo. These were gods who seized governments, and it was through them that Kamehameha became ruling chief over the islands. 'Olopue, known also as Ka-papa-kahui, was a god that led spirits of other chiefs who were enemies into the heiaus where the spirits were sacrificed. Kameha-'ikana, Haumea, Pele, Ho'ohoku, Walinu'u, Kalamainu'u, Kihawahine, and Hi'iaka were female deities, and there were a great number of goddesses besides. Papa was the heiau of the female deities. Kane-i-kaulana-'ula, Kane-mana-ia-pai'ea, Ka-huila-o-ka-lani, and Kapo were called Kalai-pahoa gods because they were carved (*kalai*) by the stone dagger (*pahoa*) [used] as an axe. They were gods who had much *mana,* and Kamehameha built for them the house called Hale-'ili-mai'a; if a person entered this house he would die; if a bird flew upon the roof it would die; if a rat, cockroach, or any other creature came into the house it would die. One creature alone could enter and live, the lizard called *mo'okaula.* Ma'alo and Moe-luhi were the *kahu* who had charge of these gods. Kane-'alai and Ke-li'i-ku-ka-haoa were the kahunas who anointed and prayed to these gods, but they had no house set aside for them. Kamehameha built separate god houses for

* *Ka Nupepa Ku'oko'a,* June 15, 1867.
† Names for the one image.

the different gods and appointed the *kahu* of the gods to be with their god within the separate god houses and heiaus. Ka-puni was one god; Ka-'ohu-walu, Ka-'akau, Oulu, and Hiapo were flying gods [gods of sorcery]. Kamehameha had many such gods. One of his gods was a real man; Ka-ho'ali'i was his name, and he had tabus, tabu drums, and tabu flags. The white *ka'upu* bird and the eyeballs of men were the tabu laws of this god. His favorite food was the eye of a man. This god was allowed free eating with the chiefesses. Kamehameha established as heiaus for the sacrifice of human beings to his blood-thirsty gods Pu'ukohola' and Mailekini at Kawaihae; Keiki-pu'ipu'i and 'Ahu'ena at Kailua; Hikiau at Kealakekua; Kama-i-ke'e-ku' and 'Ohi'a-mukumuku at Kahalu'u; Hale-o-Keawe and the Pu'uhonua at Honaunau; and so on all about Hawaii. When Vancouver saw how religious Kamehameha was and how he worshiped in the god house and heiaus morning and evening he said, "You are a religious chief, Kamehameha, and you worship wooden images. These are not true gods; the true God is in heaven. If you wish, when I return to England I will ask King George to send you kahunas who will tell you of the true God who is in heaven and you will believe them." Kamehameha answered, "These are my gods, they are gods with *mana*; through them I gained control of the government and became supreme chief." It was perhaps because Vancouver saw how devoted Kamehameha was to his gods that missionaries were not sent here from Great Britain.

Kamehameha established yearly feasts as a time of rest from labor when men might regain their strength. At the close of the ninth month of each year a tabu was placed upon the eating of the flesh of animals or of coconuts, and at the close of the year a pig was placed on the altar (*lele*), coconuts were opened, and a feast was held lasting seven days during which time food was prepared for the occasion. It was at this time that the game god was carried around. This god was the god of . . . all sorts of athletic exercises. Food was supplied by the government out of that collected by the landlords of every district during the working days set aside for the ruling chief, and given over at once to the people for the festivities. As the god, Kapala-'alaea, and the goddess, Kiha-wahine, were borne along, the side toward the sea was tabu and the side toward the mountain was free. Anyone who broke the tabu by going on the tabu side paid a fine, but if he saw the deity and prostrated himself he saved himself from the penalty. The gods of the festival were Ka-puni, Oulu, Ka-'ohu-malu, Lono, Kaho'ali'i, and others. A ka'upu bird was mounted on a stick and borne along like a banner. Lono was fastened to a long pole and so were

Ka-puni and the other gods of the festival, and they were carried by bearers from one end of a land division (*ahupua'a, 'okana, moku*) to the other. Then they were set up and the people within that division gave contributions of whatever property they could. If the contributions were generous, of good quality, and such as the keepers of the gods approved, then the gods were let down, and the gifts given over to the *kahu* of the gods. The rest was given to all the people. Men said, "Our needs will be supplied if we live under this chief; here is food, fish, tapa, loin cloths, skirts, mats, *olona* fiber, nets, and feathers, all to be had in one day." If any district did not contribute properly on any occasion, the gods would complain. They were not laid down, and the end of it was that the section, whatever it was, was given over to be plundered. But the trick was to watch the gods, for if they were held slantwise, the plunderer must run for his life, for the gods had laid by their protecting *mana* over the plunderer, and the owners might recover their stolen property. The long god was carried about for fifteen days, when he met the short god. They were rolled up and taken back with the other gods to where the ruling chief was, and all were placed in the god houses and heiaus, and it again became tabu for men to see them. The gods were tabu objects to the common people; only the kahunas, the keepers of the gods, and the attendants at the god houses were allowed to see them. The chief also might look upon them whenever he wished to go with the keepers to worship in the heiau and the god houses, or the *'ili-mai'a* house, the *'auhau ma'ule* house, or the *'alaneo* house where men go to pray for healing. These places were so tabu that not even the favorites of the chief might enter, only the chief himself.

Kamehameha always listened to the advice of orators, diviners, kahunas, and men of skill. If he thought the advice was for the good of the ruling chief and the people he would carry it into execution immediately, but if he thought it was not for their good he would not heed it. That Kamehameha listened to the advice of others is the reason he became ruling chief. He was a patient chief and did not instantly avenge an injury. Here is an example of his leniency toward one who had injured him. At the time when he became ruling chief over all Hawaii, there were brought to him those men who had struck him with a paddle, together with their wives and children. All the chiefs said, "Let them be stoned to death!" Kamehameha replied, "The law of the broken paddle is declared: no chief or officer of execution is to take their lives. It is I who should by right be stoned." What a wonderful thing for a chief thus to mete out justice toward those who had injured him!

Kamehameha was watchful against conspirators and those who plotted at night against his rule. Did such plotters go undiscovered? After the battle of Nuʻuanu certain treacherous chiefs, Ke-kua-manohaʻ and Ka-uhi-wawae-ono, were suspected of plotting to kill him. They were living at Puʻuloa in ʻEwa. Kamehameha went there at night from Honolulu and overheard clearly the whole plot. Then he stuck his dagger, called Kauwa, into the ground [as a sign that none were to leave the house until he sent for them]. In the morning they saw it and knew that Kamehameha had been there and discovered their conspiracy. They were taken to Honolulu and treated with tolerance.

Kamehameha loved pious people. While he and his chiefs were living at Kawaihae, Kamehameha and Hoʻomakaukau went out one night to spy. At midnight an old man rose up to pound ʻawa. Hearing the pounding, the chief and his companion came up close to the house. After pounding away for some time on some scraps of ʻawa, the old man strained the ʻawa and poured it into the cup. Then he prayed for the preservation of all the chiefs, and after that he prayed for the preservation of all the chiefesses, then for the life of Kamehameha, saying, "Let Kamehameha, the good king, live to be old, until his eyebrows are wrinkled like a rat's, his skin parched like the dry hala leaf, until he lies helpless, so let him live, O god, and let me live also." The old man drank the ʻawa. At the end of the prayer Kamehameha asked, "Is all your ʻawa gone?" The old man answered, "The ʻawa is gone. I have only scraps left. Last evening I gave most of it to the god, and since I could not sleep I awoke and pounded a little and drank it without any food (*pupu*) to eat after it." Kamehameha said, "I have a little ʻawa; let my man bring you some." After they had gone away he said to his companion, "Bring him forty ʻawa stocks (*puʻawa*), twenty bundles of *paʻiʻai* (*holoʻai*), five tuna fish (*ahi*) forty *aku* fish, forty *mamaki* tapas, and twenty heavy loin cloths (*malo uaua*)." When the things were given to the old man he said, "It must have been Kamehameha and his man who came here last night!"*

At another time Kamehameha saw an old man with his grandson on his way home across the plain of Kawaihae. He was gasping under a heavy load of ti root. Pitying him, Kamehameha drew near to help him. When the load was taken from him the old man, supposing Kamehameha to be a robber, exclaimed "What are you doing! These plains are under the tabu of Paiʻea†" "Is Paiʻea then a good chief?" "Yes, Paiʻea is a good chief. He makes the old man and the old

*Ka Nupepa Kuʻokoʻa, July 6, 1867.
† Paiʻea, Hard-shelled-crab, was one of Kamehameha's names.

woman to sleep [without fear] by the roadside. He is a good chief; it is his favorites who are bad and rob others." "Bad indeed!" said Kamehameha, and he carried the old man's load until they came to the beach close to Kawaihae. Then he said, "If some men overtake you, do not tell them that I carried your load for you thus far." Some time later the old man was overtaken by Kamehameha's favorites who asked him, "Have you seen the chief, Kamehameha?" The old man was terrified, believing he would die for letting the chief carry his load; but Kamehameha was a kindly chief and a patient one.

While Kamehameha was living with the chiefs at Waimea [he was] engaged in restoring the old heiaus. When the fence of images (*paehumu*), the oracle tower (*anu'unu'u*), and the pavement (*Kipapa*) of the heiau of Uli had been restored, all the people had to go down to Puako after coconuts. When each had taken up his load to return there remained still 480 nuts unhusked. All had gone except Kamehameha and one other to whom the chief was unknown. Kamehameha turned to him and said, "It looks as if there would not be enough coconuts for the dedication in the morning." It is possible that the man recognized the chief for he replied, "They will all be there." The two put the nuts into nets and fastened them together into a huge load that stood taller than either of them. The road from Puako to Waimea is close to twenty miles in length. Occasionally when the man seemed tired Kamehameha took a turn at the load. At dusk as they neared their destination, and it came time for evening prayer, Kamehameha left the man, saying, "When you get to the heiau spend the night with the people of the place, but do not tell them that Kamehameha helped carry the load on his back." Because of this feat of strength and another later, when he took up two hogs each more than a fathom long and carried them without help, this Ku-i-helani, as his name was, became a great favorite with the chief and held an important office under him. He was allowed to have ten wives, an honor allowed to no other chief besides, and there was no home happier than his, no governor of a district to be compared with Ku-i-helani.

Kamehameha respected his wives and gave them wealth and honor.

He once gave a feast at Kailua in honor of Ka-'ahu-manu, the wife he loved best of all, a feast which was the talk of the time. Many beautiful ornamental objects were made for this feast, such as a huge *kahili* called Hawai'i-loa, and a feather lei of great value. Ka-'ahu-manu was borne by the chiefs upon a litter resting upon long poles and spread with feather cloaks and cushions, fragrant with fine perfumes. Chiefs and chiefesses carried the hem of her tapa and *pa-'u*, splendidly colored by the most skilled dyers. Ka-heihei-malie Ka-niu and Ka-haku-haʻakoi, the second and third in esteem of his wives, were also richly dressed and their rank shown by the *kahili* called Koaʻe-hulu-maʻemaʻe, which had formerly belonged to Ke-aka, the wife of Alapaʻi-nui, and had been passed down by her to her granddaughters as a sign of their rank and of their parents' affection. Next came the sacred child of Ka-lani-kau-i-ke-aouli [Kiwalaʻo] and Ke-kuʻi-apo-iwa, and her aunt, Pele-uli who was her personal attendant and the fifth of Kamehameha wives. When she appeared, the tabu chiefs from the whole group came carrying the *kahili* named ʻEleʻele-ua-lani-nui, rich and beautiful in color as the greenery of the forest. Beholders prostrated themselves before them because of the tabu. The daughters of the high chiefs and all the young chiefs acted as escort for the wives to do them honor. The celebration lasted several days, and much wealth was consumed to mark the era of peace begun by the rule of Kamehameha over the whole group from Hawaii to Oahu.

As governors over the islands of Hawaii, Maui, Oahu, and Molokai, Kamehameha appointed commoners lest a chief stir up rebellion. But later he made Ka-ʻahu-manu's brother, Ka-hekili Keʻe-au-moku, governor over Maui. Mokuhia was to have been appointed over Hawaii, but he was got rid of by a trick played upon Kane-i-halau by Ke-kua-wahine. [The two men plotted how to do away with Mokuhia.] Ke-kua said to Kane-i-halau, "I will engage Kamehameha in talk and you watch me. If I nod my head, he has consented to your putting Mokuhia to death and becoming yourself governor of Hawaii." The two then went into the presence of Kamehameha, and Kane-i-halau sat down at a distance where he could watch his friend, while Ke-kua pretended to be engaged in conversation with Kamehameha, who was really talking to someone else, while the mischief-maker nodded his head and pointed to the sky. Kamehameha nodded to the other man, and Ke-kua imitated his nod . . . Mokuhia was really killed by this means, but when Kamehameha heard of it he did not give the governorship of Hawaii to Kane-i-halau, but appointed John Young.

Another important event which occurred in the fourth year of Kamehameha's rule was the lava flow which started at Huʻehuʻe in North Kona and flowed to Mahaiʻula, Kaʻupulehua, and Kiholo. The people believed that this earth-consuming flame came because of Pele's desire for *awa* fish from the fish ponds of Kiholo and Kaʻupulehu and *aku* fish from Kaʻelehuluhulu; or because of her jealousy of Ka-mehameha's assuming wealth and honor for himself and giving her only those things which were worthless; or because of his refusing her the tabu breadfruit of Kameha'ikana which grew in the uplands of Hu'ehu'e where the flow started. Perhaps the people were all wrong, since the true God is in heaven and fills the heavens with wonders and the earth with all it contains. Kamehameha was in distress over the destruction of his land and the threatened wiping-out of his fish ponds. None of the kahunas, orators, or diviners were able to check the fire with all their skill. Everything they did was in vain. Kamehameha finally sent for Pele's seer (*kaula*), named Ka-maka-o-ke-akua,* and asked what he must do to appease her anger. "You must offer the proper sacrifices," said the seer. "Take and offer them." replied the chief. "Not so! Troubles and afflictions which befall the nation require that the ruling chief himself offer the propitiatory sacrifice, not a seer or a kahuna." "But I am afraid lest Pele kill me." "You will not be killed," the seer promised. Kamehameha made ready the sacrifice and set sail for Kekaha in Mahai'ula.

When Ka-'ahu-manu and Ka-heihei-malie heard that the chief was going to appease Pele they resolved to accompany him and if necessary die with him. Ulu-lani also went with them because some of the seers had said, "That consuming fire is a person; it is the child of Ulu-lani, Keawe-o-kahikona,† who has caused the flow," and she was sent for to accompany them to Kekaha.‡ Other chiefs also took the trip to see the flow extinguished. From Keahole Point the lava was to be seen flowing down like a river in a stream of fire extending from the northern edge of Hualalai westward straight toward Ka'elehuluhulu and the sweet-tasting *aku* fish of Hale'ohi'u. There was one stream whose flames shot up the highest and which was the most brilliant in the bubbling mass as it ran from place to place. "Who is that brightest flame?" asked Ulu-lani of the seer." "That is your son," he answered. Then Ulu-lani recited a love chant composed in honor of her first-born child as his form seemed to stand before her:

O ka maka o ku'u keiki ka lamaku',	The eyes of my son are like a burning torch,
Ke kukui monopu wela o hau-nonoli,	Glowing like the red-hot *kukui* nut,
Oia ka makamua o ke ahi 'ena-'ena,	It is the first flame to be seen in the burning fire,

---

* *Ka Nupepa Ku'oko'a*, July 13, 1867.
† A chief had several names. This is the name of Ulu-lani's son used by people in general, while the name in the chant which follows was used only by members of the immediate family.
‡ John Wise (personal communication) says, "The Hawaiians believe that the fires of Pele are dead persons who have worshiped the goddess and become transformed into the likeness of her body."

Oia kai loko i ke ahi makukuku, It is there in the bubbling fire,
Kino kuku o Kanaloa-mahe-walu, The body of Kanaloa-mahe-walu stands forth,
O ka moholi iki ka'u e mana'o iho, I suppress my cry of affection,
E mana'o, ke aloha mai la ka ipo It overpowers me, my love, like
e. that of a lover.

The flow had been destroying houses, toppling over coconut trees, filling fish ponds, and causing devastation everywhere. Upon the arrival of Kamehameha and the seer and their offering of sacrifices and gifts, the flow ceased; the goddess had accepted the offering.

The reasons given for the flow may be summed up as: first, Pele's wanting the *aku* of Hale'ohi'u and the *'ahi* fish of Kiholo; second, her anger at being denied the breadfruit of Kameha'ikana in upper Hu'ehu'e; third, her wrath because Kamehameha was devoting himself to Ka-heihei-malie and neglecting Ka-'ahu-manu. It was said that Pele herself was seen in the body of a woman leading a procession composed of a multitude of goddesses in human form dancing the hula and chanting:

Lilo ka makou kane i ka ha'awe Our husband has gone to carry
'olo'olo e the bigger load [Ka-heihei-malie]

Ha'alele ia ka ha'awe leilei e While the lighter load [Ka-'ahu-
leilei e. manu] is neglected.*

Ka Nupepa Ku'oko'a, July 20, 1867.

CHAPTER XVI

The Peaceful Transfer of Kauai to Kamehameha

Now that the affairs of the kingdom were well in hand and but a single light was to be seen burning at night, Kamehameha turned his attention to the subduing of Kauai. He accordingly ordered his chiefs to build *peleleu* war canoes and this for two reasons, first, because of the shipwreck he had experienced in the storm in the Ka'ie'iewaho channel when he tried to reach the island of Kauai, and second, in order to bring the whole group of islands under his dominion, and to satisfy the clamor of his chiefs and warriors who had endured so many privations to make him ruler, [to satisfy them] in their desire for more lands to conquer. The *peleleu* canoes were large single canoes lashed together a little apart like a double canoe, but with a covered platform at the stern to make them more seaworthy, and equipped with mast (*kia*), mainsail (*pe'a ihu*), and jib like a sloop (*kiakahi*). [Kamehameha's two *peleleu* canoes were said to have been called Ka-'aha and Ka-ihu.] Over eight hundred of these were constructed. One chief surpassed all the rest by lashing three canoes together and calling them "the triple canoes (*pukolu*) of Ka'enokane." One of the lesser chiefs, named Wai-pa', built a real ship, the first put together by a native builder since that built for Kamehameha at Kealakekua in 1794 and which Wai-pa' had inspected. The ribs were *koa* and *hau* wood, the flooring *wiliwili* wood, the nails of *kauila* wood from Napu'u [near Pu'uwa'awa'a]. (Later Wai-pa' built other ships for Kamehameha.) Five years the fleet was in building. Kamehameha's watchword (*ho'ohiki*) for this expedition was, "Let us go and drink the water of Wailua, bathe in the water of Namalokama, eat the mullet that swim in Kawaimakua at Ha'ena, wreathe ourselves with the moss [sea-lettuce] of Polihale, then return to Oahu and dwell there," none of which wishes were ever realized.

When all the preparations for the expedition to Kauai were completed, Kamehameha called together his counselors and the hereditary kahunas: Pu'ou and his son Hewahewa of the Pa'ao priesthood; Kuaiwa and Holo-io-lena of the Nahulu class; Ka-pou-kahi of the class of Hulihonua kahunas who point out locations and superintend the building of heiaus. And he appointed Liholiho, then in his fifth year, his heir to inherit the rule. This was proclaimed, and he was then for the first time given the tabu of the heiaus. Kamehameha made him the head of the worship of the gods, and he was carried by the *kahu* to be proclaimed in the heiaus of Maui and Oahu.

But when the expedition was about to start, there appeared a certain man, named Lono-hele-moa, a kind of prophet, and he said, "Do not go on this expedition. Live here in Hawaii. There is food in the uplands, there is fish on the seacoast; heaven above, earth beneath." Kamehameha answered, "I shall not remain as you advise. I shall go to drink the water of Wailua, ride the surfs of Kauai, and fulfill my oath. Then I shall return and live on Oahu." Lono-hele-moa said, "I have a piece of land here, stretching from the mountain to the sea on which I live, but in a strange land I shall have no uplands or seacoast to run to and live. A man-made canoe you have to sail away from Hawaii, but a god-made canoe it will be that brings you back again, and there will be a great pestilence." Kamehameha refused his advice, and the prophet made an oath before him that if his words did not come true his life should be the forfeit. But his words did come true. Counselors, chiefs, warriors, and commoners perished; and the ruling chief himself barely escaped the same fate. This man's prophecy must have come from God.

Six years had gone by since the battle with Na-makeha' at Kaipalaoa when the fleet called the Peleleu set sail, touching first at Kipahulu where Kamehameha erected the god house called Ma'ulili, then at Kaupo where Kane-malo-homo, Pau-maka, and Loaloa were set up and their tabu declared by Liholiho. The party then went on to Lahaina where they remained about a year feeding and clothing themselves with the wealth of Maui, Molokai, Lanai, and Kahoolawe, and worshiping the gods. Liholiho, heir to the kingdom, rededicated as dwellings for the gods (*ho'ola'a aku la i na heiau i mau hale no ke akua*) the heiaus of Haluluko'ako'a and Wailehua, Pihana, Ka-uli, Malumalu-akua, Ke-ahuku, and Olopio at Wailuku, Ke-alaka'i-honua at Waihe'e; and placed a tabu over them.

It was while the expedition was encamped at Lahaina that Ka-me'e-ia-moku, one of the four chief counselors of the kingdom and the father of Ulu-maheihei Hoa-pili, died at Pu'uki, Lahaina. Before he became too weak Kamehameha went to see him. He turned and kissed the chief and said, "I have something to tell you: Ka-hekili was your father, you were not Keoua's son. Here are the tokens that you are the son of Ka-hekili." The chief said, "Strange that you should live all this time and only when dying tell me that I am Ka-hekili's son! Had you told me this before, my brothers need not have died; they could have ruled Maui while I ruled Hawaii." Ka-me'e-ia-moku answered, "That is not a good thought; had they lived there would have been constant warfare between you, but with you alone as ruler the country is at peace." There died also at this time at Pu'unau, Lahaina, Ka'i-ana Kuku'e, son of Ka-'olohaka-a-Keawe and father of Pale-ka-luhi Ka-iki-o-'ewa.

At Oahu also the fleet remained for a year, the whole company, including Kamehameha's sons and daughters with their households and those of his brothers and sisters, his counselors and chiefs, over a hundred in each household, running into a thousand. It was at the end of this time that the pestilence appeared called 'Oku'u. It was a very virulent pestilence, and those who contracted it died quickly. A person on the highway would die before he could reach home. One might go for food and water and die so suddenly that those at home did not know what had happened. The body turned black at death. A few died a lingering death, but never longer than twenty-four hours; if they were able to hold out for a day they had a fair chance to live. Those who lived generally lost their hair, hence the illness was called "Head stripped bare" (Po'o-kole).* Kamehameha contracted the disease, but managed to live through it. His counselors all died, and many of the chiefs and their families. There died also at this time at Kapopo in Koko, Ke'e-au-moku, the man who was chiefly responsible for Ka-mehameha's rise to power. He was a younger brother of Ka-me'e-ia-moku and Ka-manawa on the side of his father, Keawe-poepoe, son of Ka-lani-kau-lele-ia-iwi, who was the wife of both Keawe and of Lono-i-ka-ha'upu [father of Keawe-poepoe]. When Kamehameha heard that Ke'e-au-moku was dying he went to see him and wept over him with deep affection; and all the chiefs wept with him. Kamehameha asked, "When you are gone will conspirators arise and take the kingdom from me?" Ke'e-au-moku replied, "None of the chiefs is strong enough to conspire against you. There is indeed one who might succeed in such a rebellion, your wife [Ka-'ahu-manu]; but if you are careful rebellion may be avoided." Kamehameha therefore declared a law that any man who slept with Ka-'ahu-manu should be put to death, and this not because he was jealous of her, but because he feared lest some man win her affections and rebel against his government; for a great many of the chiefs were her blood relations, and therefore it was that he heeded Ke'e-au-moku's warning, "The wife is the only one who might succeed in raising a rebellion against your rule."

At Ka'a'awa in Ko'olauloa died another of Kamehameha's great war

* *Ka Nupepa Ku'oko'a*, July 20, 1867.

leaders, Keawe-a-Heulu Ka-lua'apana, son of Heulu-nui. He belonged to the I, Mahi-kukulu, and the Mahi-'ololi' families [all important families of old]. At his death of the pestilence there passed away the last of the four war leaders who suffered and gave their lives for the uniting of the kingdom under Kamehameha, and who had loved the land and its people both high and low. They were men of strong character. They possessed most of the land and took care of the poor and the rich alike, but their lands are now coming into possession of wanderers to foreign lands. The sons of these four counselors who had died were appointed by the chief to fill their places. These were Koa-hou, son of Ka-manawa; Ulu-maheihei Hoa-pili-kane, son of Ka-me'e-ia-moku; Ka-hekili Ke'e-au-moku, son of Ke'e-au-moku; and Haiha Na-ihe, son of Keawe-a-Heulu. All the rights of their fathers, whatever their district holdings large and small, whatever special privileges they had enjoyed from Hawaii to Oahu, passed to these men as heirs, except those which it was impossible for the younger men to enjoy. The highest position in the kingdom was held by Hu'eu Ka-lani-moku as regent, chief counselor, and supreme war leader for the whole kingdom; and he had the power over the laws of life or death and over Kamehameha's daughters, sisters, cousins, and other chiefesses who were free to him as his wives.

After the pestilence had subsided the chiefs again took up farming, and Kamehameha cultivated land at Waikiki, Honolulu, and Kapalama, and fed the people. He fished, made huge hauls, and gave food to the chiefs and people. Thus he cared for both chiefs and commoners. In those days ships were coming into the harbor at Honolulu—merchant vessels, war ships and ships out to discover new lands. Of these the chiefs and people bought arms and gunpowder. Kamehameha had several storehouses well stocked with foreign arms, but nobody wanted money or clothing. On the part of the foreigners potatoes and yams were in great demand. The chief accordingly went into the cultivation of these foods, and grew potatoes on the hill of 'Ualaka'a between Manoa and Makiki, and yams at Ka'akopua, and sold them to the foreigners. Canoeloads of provisions from Hawaii and the other islands were distributed among the chiefs, counselors, lesser chiefs, warrior chiefs, soldiers, followers, cultivators, paddlers, runners, canoe makers, and craftsmen; no one was left out. And in the same way distribution was made to the households of the chiefs. The first portion was given to the gods, then to the ruling chief's household. The gods were the first to be considered by chiefs and people. The first fruits were sacred to the gods. The first-born children, animals, the first fruits of the land, the first fish caught, the first product of any labor was sacred to the gods. This was an old practice. It is said that in old days, although the land was thickly populated, there was abundance of fish, sometimes so many as to be washed ashore by the waves and to be used as fuel to cook other fish. Everywhere were to be seen hogs so old and long that their tusks curved back to their ears. Men and women grew very old with wrinkled eyebrows hanging down upon their cheeks. It was necessary to prop up their eyelids with sticks in order to see. This was the life to old age called "eyes like a rat" (*hau-maka-'iole*), "skin yellow like the pandanus leaf" (*pala-lauhala*), "carried in a net" (*kau i ka puaneane*), "the life given by the gods." We might cite Ku-nui-akea, Ku-i-ke-ala-i-ka-ua-lani Ku-ali'i, Kiko'o, Pu'u-one, Pele-au, Hako'oaiau, Ehu, and a thousand persons who lived to such an old age. There were many such in Kamehameha's time. While he lived on Oahu exercising the power of a chief, he administered with firmness the taxes and other activities of the whole group.

Complaints of the seizure of property in Kamehameha's time and long before are made by young people who do not understand the reasons for such seizures. This was the custom in regard to them: In the first place, if a man's wife was stolen by another, and the man loved his wife and had a large enough following, the husband and his relatives could seize all the property of the wife-stealer; if he were a chief everything would be taken—canoe, nets, hogs, and whatever his wealth consisted in, leaving him nothing. The woman would be his payment for the property. The king would not interfere; but if he restored the woman the property had to be returned. Death or seizure of property was also permitted for any other theft, the penalty being carried out by the one whose property had been stolen or by one appointed to carry out the order. In the second place, if a man failed to go to work for several days on the days set by the overseers for work for the government, the man's property could be seized. If the king had allowed the people to go without working on the land for two or three years then a tenth of the hogs and food produced in that time belonged to the king; he would appoint overseers to cut out the hogs and gather up the food for the king. Taxes were paid for the use of the land in proportion to the size of each man's portion. Again, murder was punishable by death. A single murder was committed in the time of Kamehameha, that of Mokuhia who was killed at sea by Kane-i-halau. Moreover, the tabus called for very strict penalties. For the pollution of offerings made to the gods and of those things belonging to the king or to the chiefs, the penalty was death. The laws laid down for the kahunas were more severe than those for the king. Thus was the power of the king sustained in the time of Kamehameha. Stealing (*'aihue*), seizing of property without cause (*hao wale*), ravishing (*pakaha*), indolence (*palaualelo*), and petty thieving (*ka'ili wale*), these were the things which Kamehameha taught his children and his people to avoid. They were never to take potatoes, sugar cane, hogs, or fish from a countryman without asking permission. "Kamehameha's was a government of asking" (*He aupuni noi ko Kamehameha*), was the saying.*

Kamehameha never imposed a tax upon a man's body, or taxed his belongings, or set up fences and seized a man's hogs, dogs, chickens, or servants. He did not order the seizure from the country people of the property that strayed into the land of another; he did not lay burdensome taxes on the houses, furniture, and canoes; he did not tax the farmers and sell the food thus collected to his own profit; he never forbade the people's going to the forest for firewood; he never restricted the fishing rights for long or laid a tax upon taking ti leaves. He never made the people gather pebbles and lay them in heaps to show the size of their families on Hawaii or Maui. He never shamed or abused his prisoners of war by cropping their hair close and whipping them along the street like a lot of animals. (Some of them are no doubt bad, but some are good, and they all have guardian angels). All that he did for the kingdom was for the people's good. He was just to the great man and the small. The commoners he called "first-born children." While he lived on Oahu the kingdom from Hawaii to Oahu had peace, for it was clear that all he did was not mere talk. The country people said of him, "He is a cultivator and a fisherman, a tapa beater for the fatherless." He took away from them the stigma of living in poverty. While he lived on Oahu he encouraged the chiefs and commoners to raise food and he went fishing and would work himself at carrying rock or timber. They all saw that he labored himself with his own hands. He worked at the fishponds at Ka-wai-nui, Ka-'ele-pulu, Uko'a, Mauna-lua, and all about Oahu. He made the great [taro] patches at Waikiki called Keokea, Kalamanamana, Kualulua, and cleared the land at Waikiki, Honolulu, Kapalama, Kapa'auki, Keone'ula, Kapa'eli, and all the other places; and when all the lands were under cultivation he cultivated *mauka* in Nu'uanu as far as Keawawapu'ahanui. When he went deep-sea fishing, he superintended the selection of men to beat the surface, to dive, to tie on the weights, and do other tasks required. If the water was too dark to work with one

*Ka Nupepa Ku'oko'a, July 27, 1867.

net, other nets were brought into service. For two days and two nights
the nets were left before drawing ashore, and one day's catch was
often so large that some of the fish spoiled before they could all be
attended to. This proved him to be a great fisherman. He never
allowed a man to shirk work; his rule was that all should work.

The first taste that Kamehameha and his people had of rum was
at Kailua in 1791 or perhaps a little earlier, brought in by Captain
Maxwell. Kamehameha went out to the ship with Young and Davis
when it was sighted off Keahole Point and there they all drank
rum. On his return it was evident to chiefs and people that he was
acting strangely, and, believing him to have gone crazy, they cried,
"Alas, what terrible thing has happened! You have lost your reason;
you behave strangely! What is the matter with you?" Those who came
back from the ship said, "It is the exhilarating water of the foreigners,
the sparkling water, the dancing water!" Then nothing would do but
Ka-lani-moku must get some of this sparkling water, and he was the
first chief to buy rum; afterwards the other chiefs did the same.
Never in the past had the people tasted rum or sold, in exchange for
something to get drunk on, such food as potatoes, bananas, melons,
sugar cane, mountain apples, new pineapples, ti root, or poha, now
well-known in these islands. Their forefathers [parents] are from the
borders of Kohala on Hawaii, from Hikapoloa (To-stagger-along-in-
the-dark) the father, and Lanihupo (Chief-become-foolish) the
mother.* 'Awa is the oldest drink native to Hawaii, but this itself is
not very old, for it was Lono who brought it to Ololo-i-mehani, and
Kane and Kanaloa brought it here and planted it at Alanapo mauka of
Ke'ei on Hawaii.

It was while Kamehameha was on Oahu that rum was first distilled
in the Hawaiian group. In 1809 rum was being distilled by the
well-known foreigner, Oliver Holmes, at Kewalo, and later he and
David Laho-loa distilled rum at Makaho. Kamehameha set up a still
at Kahapa'akai, and from this beginning rum-making spread over the
group from Oahu to Hawaii. Rum drinking became general, and both
chiefs and chiefesses indulged in it. Two kinds were distinguished, the
tabu rum to be drunk by men alone and not to be touched by the
women, and the free rum which women might drink but not in
company with men. The free eaters, who were undiscriminating and

* It was an old custom to use meaningful place names to indicate personal
characteristics. In this case the author sarcastically remarks that Hikapoloa
(To-stagger-along-in-the-dark) and Lanihupo (Chief-become-foolish), two places
on the border of Kohala, must have been father and mother of those overcome
by strong drink.

godless, and some of the chiefesses became inveterate topers. Rum became the custom at feasts, the men drinking their kind and the chiefesses theirs. The commoners drank everywhere. Ka-'ahu-manu was under the influence of liquor when she first gave way to her desire and, ignoring Kamehameha's prohibition, slept with Ka-niho-nui; and she continued this practice while Kamehameha was away worshiping in the god house until the guard of the sleeping house, Luheluhe by name, fearing lest someone else inform Kamehameha of their intercourse, and he be killed for concealing the matter, finally informed the chief; and Ka-niho-nui was put to death. Ka-niho-nui was the own son of Ka-lani-ka-uli-hiwa-kama, Kamehameha's half-sister through the same mother, Ke-ku'i-apo-iwa; and the chief and Ka-'ahu-manu had reared the boy. He was a great favorite with Kamehameha and with all the chiefs as well, for he was unusually good-looking, finely formed from head to foot, indeed quite the handsomest young man of his time. He was just nineteen, having been born at the time when Keoua Ahu-'ula applied to Kamehameha the insulting epithet "Long tooth" (Ka-niho-nui). It was wrong in Kamehameha to put the boy to death, but he was killed not only for breaking the law for taking the property of another. Kamehameha loved the commoners and feared lest, if Ka-'ahu-manu had a lover among the chiefs, it would lead to her rebelling against his rule, drawing her relatives away with her, and thus destroying the commoners. There was a rumor that rebellion was brewing, and hence he put his own [foster] son to death in order to put fear into the hearts of the chiefs.

In returning to Oahu after the pestilence a single thought occupied the mind of Kamehameha and that of all the people, that was the adding of Kauai-of-Mano to the kingdom. Kauai was noted for the religious character if its people, hence the name "Kauai of strong prayers" (Kauai-pule-o'o). Ka-lau-nui-ohua, the ambitious chief of Hawaii who had attempted to seize Kauai, was routed in battle outside Ka'ie'ie-waho and taken prisoner to Kauai by Kukona. Kamehameha had heard these old stories and about the powerful prayer called 'Ane'e-kapuahi belonging to Ka-maka-helei, mother of Ka-umu-ali'i. He had heard Ka-me'e-ia-moku say that Ka-umu-ali'i was his cousin, but relationship was not regarded in the old days when the ownership of land and the desire for glory were the real causes of war.*

Kamehameha had now given up the thought of going to war with Ka-umu-ali'i, believing that he could secure annexation by peaceful means. He therefore sent one of the lesser chiefs, named Kihei, as

* Ka Nupepa Ku'oko'a, Aug. 3, 1867.

his representative to invite Ka-umu-ali'i to come to Oahu to see Kamehameha and make a treaty of peace between the two. The messenger was received by Ka-umu-ali'i with great dignity and given lands and wives; he therefore never returned to report to Kamehameha. Ka-umu-ali'i instead sent his own messenger, named Wahine, with an agreement of peace and said, "Take a message to Kamehameha on Oahu, but go first to my uncle, Ke-kua-manoha', and to my cousin, Ka-uhi-wawae-ono, and they will take you to Kamehameha." Wahine brought the terms of the treaty to Kamehameha and was hospitably received and presented with large double *peleleu* canoes, the first ever given to Kauai, and with feather capes and other gifts of value. Kamehameha's message to Ka-umu-ali'i was, "Tell Ka-umu-ali'i to visit me here on Oahu." Ka-umu-ali'i was pleased with the gifts, but hesitated to trust himself on Oahu. He therefore sent his devoted friend Pahi-ko' to act as his messenger, with eleven double canoe loads and nine single canoe loads [of gifts for Kamehameha], all of which were swamped in the Ka'ie'iewaho channel except one which landed on Oahu and one on Niihau. Says the chant:

Holo mai nei no Pahi-ko'	Pahi-ko' did indeed sail
E ha'i i ka hua'olelo,	To deliver a message.
Ha'ule koke la i ka moana,	[The fleet] quickly overturned in the sea,
Auwe! auwe! auwe!	Alas! alas! alas!
Aloha 'ino ko makou po'e,	What a pity for our people,
O kuku'u nei o ka moana e!	Drowned in the sea!
I kuhi paha he puko'a ka 'ale e,	Perhaps you mistook the big waves for rocks
Kalele hewa i ka pu'ukai e.	And leaned too far to one side.

Long Kamehameha waited, hoping to meet Ka-umu-ali'i face to face. He sent messengers, but all remained on Kauai where they were given lands and wives. Finally he sent Keawe-opu, Nahili, and Isaac Davis, one of his favorite foreigners. Ka-umu-ali'i was doubtful about coming to Oahu, fearing to be served as Keoua had been. In spite of the chief's silence on the subject he could see that it was not peace Kamehameha wanted, but Ka-umu-ali'i's consent to rule under Kamehameha. He therefore sent his nephew Ka-mahole-lani and Namahana, his wife, with the high chiefs, Ha'upu and Ku'mu'mu', to negotiate with Kamehameha. They were received with great honor and given presents. To Ka-mahole-lani was given the young chiefess, Kekela-a-Ka-lani-wahi-ka-pa'a, for a wife, the same Kekela who died in 1865.

On their reporting their kind reception to the Kauai chief, Ka-umu-ali'i finally consented to visit Oahu in person, declaring, "Since my own nephew has returned alive I will now go myself; but Kamehameha has but one object in this meeting, my giving up the government to him!" He sent Luia as his messenger to inform the chief that he was arriving on Captain Winship's boat. Thus in the seventh year of Kamehameha's occupation of Oahu the two rulers met face-to-face.

Kamehameha went out to meet the boat at the sea of Mamala, accompanied by his chiefs and Ka-lani-moku, his leading counselor. Ka-umu-ali'i had with him his old kahunas learned in ancient wisdom and his war leaders, Kahe'e and Pu'u-iki. The fleet of canoes drew near, red with feather cloaks and radiant with the colors of the rainbow. Kamehameha himself was in a single canoe and he drew close to the boat [of the Kauai chief], thinking to be unrecognized; but Ka-umu-ali'i was ready to receive him, dressed in the costume of the chiefs of old, with Captain Winship and the foreigners of the ship in full dress. Davis, Laho-loa, and the war leaders, Kahe'e and Pu'u-iki, were standing on either side. When Kamehameha and his chiefs came aboard in their feather robes, Ka-umu-ali'i singled out the [ruling] chief and grasping his hand said, "Here I am; is it face up or face down?" Kamehameha disclaimed the inference, and the chief continued, "This is my gift at our meeting: the land of Kauai, its chiefs, its men great and small, from mountain to sea, all above and below, and myself to be yours." Kamehameha said, "I shall not accept your land, not the least portion of your domain. Return and rule over it. But if our young chief [Liholiho] makes you a visit, be pleased to receive him." Ka-umu-ali'i answered, "We have met, and I am now returning." Kamehameha said, "Let us land; we have food and fish and wealth; better come ashore." Ka-umu-ali'i and his wife Ke-kai-ha'a-kulou landed, and all the chiefs and followers bestowed gifts upon them.

But some of the chiefs wished Ka-umu-ali'i to be put to death, and a certain kahuna, named Ka-'umi'umi, came to Kamehameha and said, "The ivory-tusk ornament has come here; let the chief take the tusk." But the chief said, "This is not a time of war which would justify me in killing another chief and seizing his possessions." "Then I shall die, for the chief has refused to heed me," answered the kahuna. It was said that Davis knew of a plot to kill Ka-umu-ali'i at a feast at Waikahalulu where rum was drunk, and that he warned the chief. Ka-umu-ali'i was the friend of the foreigners and of the captains of the ships that touched at Kauai, and it was said that he could read and speak English. He returned safely to Kauai after a few days, loaded with gifts. Thus Kamehameha ensured peace to the kingdom.

In 1810, some time after this meeting with Ka-umu-ali'i, Kameha-meha sent a letter to King George III of Great Britain asking his protection from foreign aggression and informing him that the islands of Hawaii from Hawaii to Oahu were united under one rule. The letter was acknowledged by the premier, the king being then not of sound mind, and [he] agreed in behalf of the British government to give the protection requested.*

The deaths of several prominent chiefs and chiefesses occurred at this time. In 1809 died "The good chief" Ka-lani-nui-malokuloku-i-Ke-po'o-o-ka-lani Ke-li'i-maika'i, a younger brother of Kamehameha by the same mother and whose father was Ka-lani-kupu-a-pa-i-ka-lani Keoua. Later died Ka-ho'ano-ku Kina'u, son of Kamehameha by his wife, Pele-uli, and the father of the chiefess Ke-ahi-kuni Ke-kau-'onohi. There died also at this time the tabu chiefess, Ka-lani-kau-io-kikilo Ka-lani-akua. She was of *pi'o* rank with the *akua* and *ahi* tabus, as she was the daughter of Ka-lola and her brother, Kamehameha-nui, and granddaughter of Ke-kau-like and his half-sister, Ke-ku'i-apo-iwa-nui. It was said that she no longer desired to live and took the Kalai-pahoa poison. About this time died Ka-lani-hele-mai-iluna Paki', father of Ku-ho'oheihei-pahu Paki'.

Another event of note was the absconding of J. A. Kua-kini with the wife of the war chief Ka-lani-moku. The chief loved his wife and took her loss hard. She was Ku-wahine, the sister of Ka-niho-nui and daughter of Ka-lani-ka-uli-hiwa-a-kama. Kamehameha helped Ka-lani-moku to recover her by setting fire to the houses, not of commoners alone but those of the chiefs and even his own houses. He sent messengers about to have all property removed from the houses and then proceeded to set the houses on fire, beginning at Honolulu and Waikiki, one gang going by way of Waialae and along to Ko'olau, the other toward Kapalama, sparing nothing, then on to Kalihi, Kahauiki, Moanalua, and into 'Ewa. After one half of 'Ewa was destroyed Ku-wahine was restored, and the house-burning ceased. This was called the "Ku-wahine burning."

It was Kamehameha's wish to remain on Oahu and end his days there, but he was afraid of conspiracies in his old age; he observed that the chiefs were increasing their households and cultivating large tracts in Ko'olaupoko, Ko'olauloa, Waialua, and 'Ewa to feed their followers. They were also storing guns and powder bought from the foreigners. This caused him great uneasiness, and he gathered about him the sons of his old advisers who had been instructed by their parents;

* *Ka Nupepa Ku'oko'a*, Aug. 10, 1867.

but their advice did not satisfy him. At last came a man who, when the chief asked, "Did your father leave you any of his wisdom?" answered, "He left me a little." When the chief told him his anxieties the man said, "They are already relieved." "How am I to know that? You have not told me how you are to go about it." "They are relieved if you follow my advice. The first thing is to return to Hawaii, taking all the chiefs with you; if any refuse to go they are conspirators. Second, load all the guns and powder aboard the *Keoua,* none of it to go with the chiefs on any other canoe or ship. Allow only two followers to each chief. Third, let a great hole be made in the bow of the *Keoua* below the main deck, and when the boat has put back to Oahu do not allow the chiefs to carry their guns ashore, and [you] close up the hole." Kamehameha followed this advice with great success, and the man who gave it became a man of wealth and position with land on Molokai and Lanai and houses at those places on Maui whose names began with *wai,* that is, at Waiheʻe and Wailuku.

So in the ninth year of his stay on Oahu Kamehameha set out with all all his household . Some of his chiefs were on the ship *Keoua* on which all the weapons had been stored, but the majority were on other craft, some owned by the foreign merchants of Honolulu, two owned by Captain Winship and David ʻOpeʻa-loa, and a fleet of canoes besides. Off Kaluakoʻi Point as the *Keoua* headed for Lanai, some of the planks at the bow were broken in and the sea rushed in. There was great excitement, and all worked lest they drown. One clever man named Wai-paʻ thought he could close the hole. Like a flying bird he leaped into the high waves, right into the foaming sea, supported by a rope and carrying a piece of tarpaulin which he was able to nail over the hole and so save the ship . . . Kamehameha made use of this man later for ship building, and he became famous. The expedition returned meanwhile to Honolulu, and all the passengers went ashore, but the munitions of war were held on the ship. This first attempt of the ship to sail went by the name of "The first *Keoua*" (*Keoua mua*). After repairing and painting the ship, "The second *Keoua*" set out for Hawaii. Kamehameha and some of the chiefs sailed on Winship's boat, others on that of Captain ʻOpeʻa-loa, They touched first at Lahaina, then at Kawaihae where some of the guns were landed and put in charge of Young, then at Kealakekua where all the rest of the guns were landed and put in charge of Ka-makau at Kaʻawaloa. The ruling chief then returned to Molokai to view the *maika* course of Ka-ʻakeʻkeʻ at ʻUala-puʻe and to eat of the fat of the land of Molokai. He then went on to Lahaina and all remained there feasting and gathering wealth. Ka-hekili Ke'e-au-moku imposed a tax upon Maui, Molokai, Lanai, and Kahoolawe, and food piled up so that chiefs and people ate until they could eat no more. Still there were quantities left over; so they gave the chief the name of "Great heap" (Pu'u-nui). The return of the party after some days to Kealakekua was known by the name of Ka-ni'au-kani after a musical instrument somewhat similar to an *'uke'ke'* which was introduced and became popular at this time. It was a thin strip of bamboo with strings strung along its length and two little pieces of stick placed near the end under the strings to keep them away from the bamboo. It went also by the name of Uwinihepe, the Hawaiian for Winship.*

* *Ka Nupepa Ku'oko'a*, Aug. 17, 1867.

CHAPTER XVII

Death of Kamehameha

On Kamehameha's return to Kealakekua his first object was to pray to the gods and for this purpose he made tabu the heiau of Hikiau and then that of 'Ohi'a- mukumuku at Kahalu'u. This was the first annual tabu of the Makahiki since his return to Hawaii. There were many forms of worship in the old days. The principal purpose of the worship was to insure long life, "eyelids like a rat's, skin yellow as a dry pandanus leaf, to be carried in a net." No one prayed for the life of the soul (*'uhane*). Some believed that the soul lived forever, and that after the body died the soul would meet its guardian spirits (*'aumakua*). If these were Kane-hekili, Kane-wahi-lani, Ka-uila-nui-makeha-i-ka-lani, then if he were actually their offspring the soul would be taken to the heavens. If Pele and Hi'iaka were his *'aumakua*, then the pit of Pele would be the soul's dwelling place, and so with souls that had other *'aumakua*. People who had no inherited dwelling place for the soul would worship a dead child, a parent, some close relative, or anyone else they wished in whatever form they desired, whether a shark, or bird; and these became what were known as *'unihipili*. It was never the object itself that was worshiped. The special form of worship was evident from the kind of house built for the god. If a house of *'ohi'a* wood was erected on the grounds of the heiau it was a *haku 'ohi'a*, a *malu 'ohi'a,* an *'ohi'a-ko'*. Such a god house was one in which to pray to end rebellion, conspiracy, and war. The chiefs were fed upon pork offered at the *'ohi'a* houses and *lama* houses, called "dedicated pork" (*pua'a hea*). The ground on which the house was built also indicated its purpose. Some houses were built of *loulu* palms, or they might be mere shelters. Such a god house was for [the purpose of prayer for] the fertility of soil that had become infertile; at the death of chiefs and commoners, or at a time of trouble of any kind, such as pestilence, barrenness in women or animals, famine; hence such a god house was set up in the place where the trouble occurred. A House-of-Lono was a god house, an *'opua melemele,* for the purpose of praying for rain or crops. It was erected on the site of the altar in an old heiau. It was against famine in the hot season and drought through scarcity of water.

A Ku-'ula house was another form of god house, called a *ko'a*. Such houses and altars were erected close to seacoasts where schools of fish came, as altars for prayer to the fish gods, Ku-'ula, Hina-puku-i'a, and Kane-makua, to make the fish abundant. Many altars were set up for the prosperity of the land.

Such houses and altars could be set up by the king, the district chief, or the head fisherman alone; not all men could make such places of worship. But the Stone-of-Kane (Pohaku-o-Kane) consisting of a stone set upright in the shape of a pillar, every family and every countryman could erect as an altar where offerings were made to the god as penance for sins committed by any member of the family. Here he unburdened himself to the god by repentance for sins of the flesh and by prayer offered by the family. This Stone-of-Kane was a place of rest and refuge and the height from which a man conversed with the god in the heavens.*

The gods were worshiped and prayed to most often in heiaus of the Waihau, Unu, Hale-o-papa, Ku-'ula, Ko'a, and Loulu types. There were *'ili-mai'a, alaneo, 'auhau-ma'ule, 'ale'o, oeoe, 'anu'u kuapala,* and *lau* houses. The gods whose names were mentioned in the prayers offered were Kane, Ku, Lono, and Kanaloa. These were not gods of wood and stone, they were not gods represented by objects that could be seen with the eyes and worshiped. At the time for prayer the whole congregation assembled, then they raised their hands as a sign that the true god was in the heavens as if pointing out with the hands that the true god was in the heavens. So they uttered the prayer in unison until its conclusion, then they lowered their arms. At family prayers the men and their sons, however many in number, entered the men's eating house carrying the Gourd-of-Lono, the gourd altar. This was a calabash covered with wicker-work and provided with string handles; within were food, fish, and 'awa. A little piece of 'awa root was tied to the handle outside. This gourd was taken and laid down at the door, and the person faced outward while he made his request to the god to save the chiefs, the commoners, and his own family; then, the prayer ended, he ate the food and the fish. So it was done [morning and] evening.

The Hawaiian people had the reputation of being a pious people who worshiped the god; hospitable, kindly, giving a welcome to strangers, affectionate, generous givers, who always invited strangers to sleep at the house and gave them food and fish without pay, and clothing for those who had little; a people ashamed to trade. This was

* *Ka Nupepa Ku'oko'a*, Aug. 17, 1867.

their character before the coming of the foreigners and of Christianity to Hawaii. Now they are being taught to be close, stingy, hard-hearted, niggardly, to take pay for what is given and to be selfish. Some are following this teaching, but the larger part are still clinging to the old custom of hospitality. Those who are stingy and avaricious like Kukulu-'i, Pahia, and Ku-lei-o-iki have their names handed down to shame. How did the old Hawaiians acquire this character? They were a people who worshiped the god, who knew the story of the god, his power, wisdom, patience, good works, and long life; a people who knew of other lands and could distinguish good from evil; a people who knew the history of the ancient rulers and which had done right and which wrong. These rulers are mentioned in their prayers, legends, creation stories, genealogies; and other races besides are there named.

They did not worship idols before the coming of the Christians. No image was ever brought and put up before the congregation and knelt to in reverence. Ku-ka'ili-moku, Ku-ke-olo'ewa, Ku-ho'one'e-nu'u and the rest were never knelt to with knees to the ground. These were gods exceedingly tabu, not seen by the congregation. They were never left continuously in one heiau. Only when the tabu was proclaimed at night were they brought out, and this was the only time when these gods were borne along [except in time of war]. It was at this time that the feather gods were invoked, but only by the chief and the kahunas; the congregation waited outside the altar. These were merely signs of the gods who were not seen. The images placed along the *paehumu* were for decoration merely outside the heiau. They were not for worship, and no Hawaiian ever knelt to them.

The congregation on any great day of worship was always outside the altar at the time when prayer was offered, and the ruling chief was at the entrance of the heiau below the altar (*lele*) with his face turned to the congregation and the leading kahuna at his side. The chiefs and people remained facing the chief and the kahuna, in a kneeling position with the legs bent back straight from the knee and the body resting against them. When the kahuna reached that part in the prayer where a response by the people was called for, they raised the right hand and pointed to the heavens as a sign to the god that they were his people and asked his help, and they kept it raised for a long time. They repeated in concert that part of the prayer which belonged to the congregation, and when it came to the tabu portion, the short portion (*kumalolohia*) to trespass against which meant death, the worshipers bowed their heads without raising the body from its seated posture: then the last word was always spoken by the chief. But there was never any image set up before the congregation. This was the manner of worship in Hawaii up to the time of Kamehameha.

Kamehameha spent much time at Kailua rebuilding heiaus. With great labor he made tall images (*keiki-pu'ipu'i*) carved out of *'ohi'a* wood with grinning mouth, elongated head wearing a helmet, rounded thighs and legs, and below the feet a block of wood to plant in the ground. [These were made] as decoration outside the *paehumu*. There were forty such images on a single heiau and four hundred on some of the larger heiaus. They were erected outside the *paehumu* all around the heiau, and rows were set up on the path leading to the tabu drum. The image that stood at the sacred drum was Ku-ka-lepe-'oni'oni'o. These carved images were not objects of worship; the people did not kneel to them, nor did the kahunas worship them. They were hewn out of *'ohi'a* wood of the *hamau, pane, uhiuhi,* and *lama* species. They were made for decoration to make the god house handsome and attractive to the god when he came from heaven. For instance, in the story of 'Umi and Liloa when 'Umi offered sacrifices in the heiau of Moa'ula at Waipi'o, the god Ku came down from the heavens in a black cloud and in a rainbow (*'onohi*) and licked up the offering with a tongue of fire. These images erected outside the heiau were not regarded as sacred, for at times they were used by the people who kept the houses of the gods to fire the cook ovens. Take the story of Ka-welo when he sailed for Kauai to make war. He set a tabu over the heiau of Puehu at Wai'anae, and at the end of the sacrifice ordered that the wood of the *paehumu*, both the fence and the images themselves, be used for firewood for the expedition to Kauai. Kamehameha at this time rebuilt the heiau of 'Ahu'ena and made images for it and for Hikiau, the Hale-o-Keawe, and for other old heiaus.

Fishing was the occupation of Kamehameha's old age at Kailua. He would often go out with his fishermen to Kekaha off Ka'elehuluhulu and when there had been a great catch of *aku* or *'ahi* fish he would give it away to the chiefs and people, the cultivators and canoe makers. If word was brought that *'ahi* were plentiful at Kalae, off went the chief to the *'ahi* fishing, and he fished also at Kaulana, Ka'iliki'i, Pohue, Na-pu'u-o-Pele, Kapalilua, and at other places along the coast. During the season for flying fish he would sail to Kohala where the big schools ran and dispose of his catch to the cultivators of Kohala, Waimanu, and Waipi'o. Kamehameha made a crafty bargain with the cultivators to give a single fish for a single bundle of pounded taro (*pa'i'ai*) or a calabash of poi, and so on. The cultivators lost on this, so they sought a way to get even with him, and wrapped up a single taro in a bundle and gave it to him for a single fish. Kamehameha said, "If the fisherman drives a crafty bargain, why should not the planter retort upon him? One cannot long play a one-sided game."

During the sixth and seventh years of Kamehameha's stay on Oahu several of the captains of the boats plying to and from Manila, Macao in China, and other places, informed the king and his chiefs that the fragrant sandalwood was a valuable article of trade with the people of China.* The king accordingly, when he return to Hawaii, sent his people to the mountains after this wood, which some of the foreigners had pointed out to him as to be found on these islands. The captains McCook, Ogden, Kawelipota [David Porter?], Winship, (Winihepa), Bartow, and David 'Ope'a-loa were among those who traded this wood in Macao and Canton for woolen, silk, and cotton cloth and other commodities. On the chief's return to Kailua, that return known as the Ka-ni'au-kani after the musical instrument that became popular at the time, he ordered men into the mountains of Kona and Ka-'u to cut sandalwood, paying them in cloth and in tapa material, food, and fish. Other men carried the wood to the landings of Kona and Ka-'u as well as of Kohala and Hamakua. The chiefs also were ordered to send out their men to cut sandalwood. This rush of labor to the mountains brought about a scarcity of cultivated food throughout the whole group. The people were forced to eat herbs and tree ferns, hence the famine called Hi-laulele, Haha-pilau, Laulele, Pualele, 'Ama'u, or Hapu'u, from the wild plants resorted to. The chief immediately declared all sandalwood to be the property of the government and ordered the people to devote only part of their time to its cutting and to return to the cultivation of the land.

He himself and those who ate with him ('ai-alo) toiled with their own hands to set out a large tract in the uplands of Kailua, known as Kuahewa. When the land had been cleared and taro tops planted the whole field was covered with fern leaves as mulch. As the taro grew large enough to pull the little ones were left to grow, and it was said that the field was productive for years without wild growth. The chief did not allow his men to help themselves to taro and tops for planting, as was the custom for those in power in time of scarcity. He believed in the rights of the common people, even their right of refusal to sell.

* See 39 and 36. The sandalwood of Hawaii was discovered by Captain Kendrick of the American sloop *Lady Washington* between 1791 and 1794. Between 1810 and 1825 the trade was at its height. Kotzbue writes in 1825 that he has been told that Americans have purchased sandalwood to the amount of 300,000 Spanish dollars. On Molokai a hollow is shown shaped like the hold of a ship and said to have been used in old days as a measuring place for a shipload of sandalwood.

"You can get some over there, says Pahia," became a saying [as a taunt against such refusal]. Petty thieving, (*'aihue*), taking things without leave (*lalau wale*), robbery (*hao wale*), oppression (*pakaha wale*), taking without return (*lawe wale*), stealing (*mokio*), taking without the knowledge of the owner (*lawe malu*), were regarded as wrong in old Hawaii. It is told of Kamehameha that when he went out to find tops for planting his field he went to the place of a chief who owned a large planting of taro in upper Kuapehu. He knew that the chief was not at home but had left a favorite in charge.* Landing at Ka'awaloa he walked up to the chief's place, which was not far off, and found the man in charge returned from the god house drunk with 'awa and fast asleep. Kamehameha sat down therefore and began to rub his head. The man started up and asked, "Who is there?" "It is I, Kamehameha, come to ask Naihe for taro tops from Kuapehu." A wonderful ruling chief indeed, who could have taken anything he liked, but was thus kind and humble of heart! He was a true Christian ruler.

The attempt to sink a well at Kalae came about for two reasons. In the first place, South Point lacked water and it was an excellent place for *'ahi* fishing. It was here that Ka-lani-'opu'u had tried to find water. In the second place, Kamehameha suspected one of the Ka-'u chiefs of conspiring against him, a man named Kupake'e.† Kamehameha had tested the loyalty of the chiefs by summoning them to his presence, feeding them with food and fish, and supplying all their wants, but this man remained in the back country and fed a large following. Kamehameha desired to leave to Liholiho a united and peaceful government and he was sure that this man was endangering that peace. He therefore set sail with his chiefs, favorites, and his commoners from Kona and Ka-'u. [He took also] his expert in locations (*kuhikuhi pu'uone*) named Wai-'anae, who was to tell him how and where to sink the well. The place selected was at the spot called Ka-'ilio-a-Lono (Dog of-Lono), and the digging was begun with energy, but the rock was too hard to work without foreign tools, and they obtained no water though they did make the holes which ships putting in at this place can tie up to and which are called "The water dug by Kamehameha" (*Ka wai ku'i a Kamehameha*).

* *Ka Nupepa Ku'oko'a*, Aug. 24, 1867.
† The Ka-'u clan (*'hana*) to which Kupake'e belonged were called Ka-'u Makaha. They were a group who protected their own chief as long as he was kind to them and treated them well, but unhesitatingly slew him if he caused them unnecessary suffering. To alien chiefs they paid no attention whatever. Of their own ruling chief they said, "He alone has the right to bake our heads" (*kalua i ke po'o*). Kupake'e was in this case not rebelling against Kamehameha but merely ignoring him as was the custom of his clan.

What with digging and fishing Kamehameha prolonged his stay and made many attempts to meet the chief Kupake'e, but all his attempts to trap the chief into a meeting failed. He therefore gave up the attempt and returned with his chiefs to Kona, leaving Ke-ku'i-apo-iwa in Ka-'u with her husband Pueo, who lived in Waiohinu. They had been there but a year when it was reported that Ke-ku'i-apo-iwa had fallen ill because her husband Pueo had defiled the things offered to the gods and she had eaten them in ignorance. Her nose and mouth had become covered with running sores, and she was not expected to live. The chiefs and chiefesses agreed to make Pueo his wife's death companion (*moepu'u*), but when Kamehameha heard of this conspiracy he sent for Boki Ka-ma'ule'ule and ordered him to accompany the chiefs to Ka-'u and prevent Pueo's death by telling any chief who attempted to have Pueo killed that all men were tabu to the chief Liholiho, and that chief who attempted Pueo's death would be the death companion for Ke-ku'i-apo-iwa. The chiefess died in 1815 at Kapa'akea close to Ka'alu'alu at Kiolaka'a, Ka-'u. She was the mother of Ke-opu-o-lani and the daughter of Ka-lola-pupuka-o-Hono-ka-wai-lani, a tabu chiefess of Maui and Hawaii.

In November of this same year of the return of the chiefs from Ka-'u, a Russian warship came to Oahu and made trouble there by trying to take over the island. Kamehameha sent his war commander, Ka-lani-moku, the chief counselors, Ka-hekili Ke'e-au-moku, Ulu-maheihei Hoa-pili, Haiha Na-ihe, Pale-ka-luhi Ka-iki-o-'ewa, and Pauli Ka-'o-lei-o-ku, together with chiefs and fighting men who had joined the king (*okaka*), and others besides, with orders if the Russians were peaceably inclined to supply them with vegetables and pork. When Ka-lani-moku found that everything was peaceful, he determined to erect a fort for the protection of the city and harbor of Honolulu, and a proclamation was issued calling people from all over the island to come to Honolulu and build the fort. The district chief of Waialua, Ka-hekili Ke'e-au-moku, was so busy collecting sandalwood that his district alone failed to respond to the call.

A few days after the building began, January 16, 1816, Pauli Ka-'o-lei-o-ku died in a mysterious way. Every day he had been to the fort working in company with the men who lived with him or on his lands. On this day he had worked late and came back to his home at Kaumakapili without being aware that his kahuna, Ka-maka-uila, had declared a tabu that evening and had a pig cooked for the god. The kahuna saw him [Pauli Ka-'o-lei-o-ku] passing at dusk and called him in to keep the tabu of the god and then return home. Pauli Ka-'o-lei-o-ku observed the tabu to its close, drank a cup of 'awa, ate some pork, and went home. At the house he had Kia-loa prepare him a smoke and then went to sleep with Manono, his wife. Manono awoke late and found the chief groaning. She aroused the two tobacco keepers, Kia-loa and Ka-lohi, and they found him almost dead and foaming at the mouth. The chiefs and commoners were called and the wailing began. This Ka-'o-lei-o-ku was Kamehameha's first-born son. Kane-kapo-lei was his mother, the tabu wife of Ka-lani-'opu'u while he was ruling over Hawaii. The *kahili,* emblem of the ruling chiefess, however, was given to Po'o-uliuli. Should the reader fail to guess the reason for this man's sudden death, I can give you an explanation.

At the completion of the fort, Ka-lani-moku and all the chiefs went to work cutting sandalwood at Wahiawa, Halemano, Pu'ukapu, Kanewai, and the two Ko'olaus. The largest trees were at Wahiawa, and it was hard work dragging them to the beach. All the people were drawn into service, and the chiefs bought quantities of cloth, and some began to buy ships. The ruling chief of Kauai also secured cloth, muskets, and powder, and became the owner of several ships, two large vessels called *Kamohelani* and *Mikapako* and several smaller ones.

[In 1818] Kamehameha bought a large ship [*Santa Rosa,* under Captain Turner] which was named Kalaholile after a kind of shiny blue cloth with white figures which was brought in on this ship. The ship had however been stolen by those who sold it, and a Spanish man-of-war took it away to return to its owners. Some of those who had stolen it were caught, made prisoners, and returned to Spain, and some were hidden at Kailua and became settlers (*kama'aina*) on the land. A black man of this island, named Manuel and called Nopa, is one of their descendants. From a ship wrecked on Kahoolawe about 1809 while Kamehameha was still living on Oahu came Mikapala and W. Harper, called Lu'au-eater ('*Ailu'au*), who became ancestors of some of our people.

The search for a superior and the finding of a chief [to become one's lord ('*imi haku*)] was a custom considered high and honorable in old days and one which might carry the seeker from one end of the group to the other. On the other hand chiefs of rank sought trustworthy followers, generally among those of their own kin, to hold their *kahili* and cut their hair. War ceased when chiefs met each other and respected each other's tabus. This reverence extended from chiefs to commoners. It was thought a great and worthy object in life to go in search of a chief or for a chief to seek a trustworthy follower, and it was through the faithful care of such servants that chiefs grew strong and multiplied. The chiefs were anxious also to preserve the pure blood of their class by arranging marriages between chiefs and chiefesses. No one, not even Kamehameha himself, minded if the chief selected for his daughter was homely, old, weak-eyed, so long as he could satisfy the demand for a pure-blooded lineage. The mating to a sister or near relative, which was not permitted to lesser chiefs or the relatives of chiefs, was considered desirable between very high chiefs in order to produce children of divine rank who carried the sacred fire (*ahi*) tabu. Such a mating was for the purpose of bearing children, but the two need not become man and wife. Thus the chiefs multiplied, thrived, grew, and spread out over the land; but today we are taught that such practices are wrong.*

Kamehameha had many children of his own, but since a number died young their list is not complete. By his wife Kane-kapo-lei he had Pauli Ka-'o-lei-o-ku as his first-born. By Pele-uli Kekela he had Maheha Ka-pu-likoliko, Ka-ho'ano-ku-Kinau, Kaiko'o-ka-lani, and Kiliwehi. By Ka-heihei-malie Ka-niu he had Kamehameha Iwi, Kameha-malu, and Ka-ho'ano-ku Kina'u. Ka-lani-kau-i-ka-'alaneo Ke-opu-o-lani was the mother of Ka-lani Kua-Liholiho, Ka-lani Kau-i-ke-aouli, and Harriet Nahi-'ena'ena. Kamehameha did not ordinarily take Ke-opu-o-lani as his sleeping companion. She was his niece and of so high a tabu that he had to take off his *malo* before he came into her presence, but he desired above everything to have children of the highest rank. His wife Ka-lani-kau-i-ka-'alaneo he took, not as an ordinary sleeping companion, for she was a tabu chiefess and he had to observe the tabu in her presence, but in order to beget children of high rank by blood. When he was an old man well on in years, white-haired but with the erect body of a soldier, without the flabbiness of age, and with the features of a young man, he took two young chiefesses to warm his old age. Ke-ka-ulu-ohi was the first-born child of her mother Ka-heihei-malie and her father was Ka-lei-mamahu'; Manono's mother was Kalola-a-Kumu-ko'a and her father was Ke-kua-manoha'. One of the two bore him his last child, a girl named Ka-papa-uai. Those of his children whom Kamehameha considered in the line of succession he always treated as though they were his gods. He always called them "grandchildren." Whenever he saw Liholiho approaching he would lie with his face upward, and the child would run and sit upon his chest. When the chiefesses saw Liholiho coming they had to drop their *kapa* covering. Kamehameha's granddaughter, Ke-ahi-kuni Ke-kau-'onohi, daughter of Ka-ho'ano-ku Kina'u his son by Pele-uli, was also a tabu chiefess in whose presence the other chiefesses had to prostrate and

* *Ka Nupepa Ku'oko'a*, Aug. 31, 1867.

uncover themselves, and Kamehameha would lie face upward while she sat on his chest. Such tabu chiefs were of old a mere legend; it was only in later times that anyone was allowed to see them. While still in possession of all his faculties Kamehameha proclaimed Ka-lani Kua-Liholiho heir to the kingdom after his death, and he was taken and given the tabu of the gods in the heiau. His god, Ku-ka'ili-moku, Kamehameha gave to Ka-'owa' Ke-kua-o-ka-lani. These two, the kingdom and the god, were considered of equal importance in ancient days. So Liloa had passed the two down to his two sons, the kingdom to Hakau, the god to 'Umi, who however came into possession of the kingdom because the one to whom it was given failed to rule aright. Kamehameha now taught the two boys the history of the government and of the god.

Ka-'owa' Ke-kua-o-ka-lani was the son of Ki'i-lawe-au whose mother was Manono the daughter of Alapa'i-nui, and her father was Ka-lani-kupu-a-pa-i-ka-lani Keoua. Ka-'owa''s father was Ka-lani-malokuloku Ke-po'o-o-ka-lani Ke-li'i-maika'i, Kamehameha's own younger brother. He was a favorite child, was this Ke-kua-o-ka-lani, and Kamehameha kept him constantly with him. He was entitled to seize whatever he wished from a chief or anyone else. He would cry "Kaikaowa!" and his men would seize whatever they could. When the chiefs complained Kamehameha would reply, "It is well if he robs the chiefs and not the common people; that would be a real fault. He is a fatherless child and can do these things only while I am alive. When I am gone you will not pay any attention to him!" and these words of the chief came true.*

That he was solicitous for the future welfare of his son Liholiho and his other children is clear from the acts of his later years. He attempted to make a treaty with Great Britain. He received British war ships, officers, and men, and offered help to other British ships. He wrote to the king of Great Britain asking protection. He requested a British flag of the king to be used by the king and the officials of the Hawaiian government, and this request was granted by the premier in behalf of the ailing King George III. This same courteous treatment he gave to the Americans, provisioning their boats and, in 1810, celebrating the Fourth of July (for the first time in Hawaii) at a place called Ka-pa-uhi. Before this he had extended through Captains Ogden and Maxwell a welcome to the American officer Captain Kanaloa-ahua-kana. He did everything he could to preserve friendly relations with all countries. Troubles that arose were not of his making, and those that had to do with disputes about religion came after his time. He ordered the sandalwood cutters to spare the young trees and

* *Ka Nupepa Ku'oko'a*, Sept. 7, 1867.

not to let the felled trees fall on the saplings. "Who are to have the young trees now that you are getting old?" he was asked and he answered, "When I die my chief and my children will inherit them." He gave similiar orders to bird catchers, canoe makers, weavers of feather capes, wood carvers, and fishermen. These are the acts of a wise and Christian king who has regard for the future of his children, but the old rulers of Hawaii did the same.

Kamehameha was born at Kapaʻakai, Kokoiki, Kohala, in 1736, just after the battle of Ka-hale-mamala-koa and before that of Kawela. He died May 8, 1819, at the age of eighty-three years. Fourteen years he fought to unite the islands and he ruled twenty-three years. It was in the seventh year of his rule over the group that the return to Hawaii called Ka-niʻau-kani took place. His death occured at night at Kamaka-honu, Kailua, Hawaii. He had been noted in his youth for his strength in the three forms of wrestling and in other sports. His strength lay in his shoulders, which were broad and muscular, and in his back. His powerful jaws showed energy and determination of character; in anger his eyes became bloodshot. But his outward appearance belied his true nature, for at heart he was a father to the orphan, a savior to the old and weak, a helper to the destitute, a farmer, fisherman, and cloth maker for the needy. When he died his body was still strong, his eyes were not dimmed, his head unbowed, nor did he lean upon a cane; it was only by his gray hair that one could tell his age.

He was a long time ill, and Ka-lani-moku and Keʻe-au-moku and the other chiefs who were away cutting sandalwood on Oahu were summoned back to Hawaii leaving Boki Ka-maʻuleʻule as governor of Oahu and a few chiefs with him. At the beginning of his illness he was treated by such men as Ku-aʻuaʻu, Ka-lani-moku, Kua-ka-mauna, and others who had attended the chief before and were experts in the medicinal art. They agreed that his illness would not yield to treatment, and Kua-ka-mauna told him, "The doctors have done all they can; you must place yourself in the hands of the god who alone has power over life and death." This was done in the following manner. At the direction of the leading kahuna an ʻohiʻa house was erected for Ku-kaʻili-moku, and a man demanded of the chief as a human sacrifice to the god. The people, hearing this request, all ran away and hid in the bush until the tabu should be lifted; only a few remained with the chiefs in attendance on the ruling chief. Kamehameha, however, refused to have a human sacrifice given, saying, "Men are sacred to the chief," meaning to his son Liholiho. The gods Ku-kaʻili-moku, Ku-ka-lani-hoʻoneʻe-nuʻu, and Ku-ke-oloʻewa were like rosaries worn about the neck in time of war or danger. During such a tabu ceremony, if the kahuna was allowed to continue his prayer to the end without interruption it was a sign that his request for life was granted. Ku-ka'ili-moku was in the old days a representative who acted as messenger of the god to whom the petition was offered. A sign to be noticed during the tabu was the movement of the feathers on the head of Ku-ka'ili-moku, which would stand out like hair charged with electricity and wave like a flag as a sign of consent to the request prayed for; or the god might fly from its stand to the head or shoulder or some part of the person it fancied, and this was a sign that the request had been favorably received. If none of the signs occurred the audience broke up with heavy hearts for this meant that the prayer was not granted. On this occasion Ku-ka'ili-moku gave no sign.

At the close of the *kauila* service the weakness of the chief increased, and at the next service he sent Liholiho in his place. The chiefs and the sons and daughters of Kamehameha had heard of a kahuna who had cured many people through his *mana* obtained from the gods, Pua and Kapo. Pua was another name for Kalai-pahoa, and the mudhen (*'alae*) was a form of Kapo. It was said that if these gods were brought into a house the sick would be healed. Once before the chief had been cured by this kahuna, who had not come himself but sent the gods to the chief's house. They therefore built two houses, one for the male (Pua) and the other for the female (Kapo) god. Kamehameha grew no better but steadily worse, and after three days they took him from these houses to his own sleeping house. At the close of the day he was carried to the eating house, where he took a mouthful of food and a swallow of water, but when he was asked to speak made no reply. About ten o'clock he was again carried to the eating house and again took a mouthful of food and a swallow of water. Ka-iki-o-'ewa then asked him for a last word, saying, "We are all here, your younger brothers, your chiefs, your foreigner (Young). Give us a word." "For what purpose?" asked the chief. "As a saying for us" (*I hua na makou*). "Endless is the good that I have given you to enjoy" (*E oni wale no 'oukou i ku'u pono 'a'ole e pau*). Then John Young put his arms about his neck and kissed him; Ulu-maheihei bent down and whispered that he be given charge of his bones. Kamehameha was then taken to the sleeping house. At midnight he was again moved to the eating house, but he began to gasp for breath when his head alone was inside the eating house while his body was still in the sleeping house. He was taken back to the sleeping house, and at two o'clock that morning his soul departed and he ceased to live. This constant carrying back and forth was to prevent his dying in the eating house and to avoid the defilement of eating in a house where he had slept with women; such defilement must be avoided lest the whole race perish in consequence.*

Kamehameha died on the night of Hoku, May (Ka'elo) 14 according to the Oahu calendar, and a child of one of his daughters was named Fled-in-the-time-of-Hoku (Lele-io-hoku). A great dispute arose among the chiefs in the eating house (*hale mua*), and Ka-lani-moku reentered that house and ordered the crowd away lest those in the sleeping house (*hale moe*) hear the clamor; but there were two old men [who were particularly affected] and one remained and spoke with deep affection of the care the chief had given them. Ka-lani-moku returned to the sleeping house and the chiefs held a council as to the disposition of the body, one and another offering to take it. One chief said, "It will be impossible to hide it; let us eat him (*'ai-maka*) in order to hide him away." Ka-'ahu-manu said faintly, "This body is not ours; ours was the breath, the body belongs to one of the chiefs." Ulu-maheihei Hoa-pili said, "You have no right to the body; it belongs to my chief [Liholiho] and to me. We two alone have a right to the body; so Kamehameha willed." At the close of the council the body was carried to the prayer house to be in charge of the kahuna, and the pig for the mourning (*'u-ko'*) was cooked. This pig for the mourning was a sacrifice to the god to make the soul live again and to preserve it to live with its *'aumakua*. The kahuna offered the sacrifice and the ruling chief freed the prayer. The kahuna then said, "If his death companion (*moepu'u*) dies now we shall need but one; if we have to look for one outside we shall need four; but if we wait until he is borne to the burial place (*hale lua*) we must have ten; but if we enter the burial place and there get the death companion we must have fifteen. Therefore let one man die." With these words this kahuna's official acts ended.

The leading kahuna stood up, in his hand the pig which was to make an atonement for sin (*ho'okala hala*) for the heir to the kingdom who had been defiled by coming into contact with (*ehu ke kila*) the corpse of the dead. This offering was to purify (*huikala*) and cleanse him (*ma'ema'e*) then he must separate himself (*ka'awale*) from this place of defilement (*haumia*). This was the common custom of these people in ancient days, both chiefs and commoners. Thus runs the prayer of purification from the defilement by a corpse:

* *Ka Nupepa Ku'oko'a*, Sept. 14, 1867.

E ma ka 'ai ku, e ma ka 'ai alo,	Here is the food offered, here is the food offered in your favor,
E ma ka 'aia', e ma ka hele huna,	Here is the food for the sin offering; let him be hidden,
E ma ka hele pa'ani;	Let him go and play,
E ma ka uwe makena;	Here let there be mourning,
O kukakau a ka ho'oilina,	For the dead and for his heir,
Papae'e - A kaluako'i,	Let him be accepted where he is laid to rest,
I hemu' 'oia i heu,	Let him go in peace,
I hemu' 'oia - i hemu'.	Let him go in silence.

At the close of the purification the kahuna Hewahewa said, "Where shall the ruling chief stay?" The chiefs responded in unison, "Where indeed? Are not you the one to choose the place?" "Since Kona is unclean, there are but two places for him to stay, Ka-'u and Kohala." So the chiefs chose Kohala because the people there were more loyal to the chief. At dawn of day the body was carried to the house of the dead (*hale lua*), and then for the first time the people were aware that their chief was dead, and they bewailed him with bitter weeping and gestures of despair and recalled with deep emotion his farming, fishing, and cloth making and all his fatherly acts toward them. A man named Ke-amo-hulihia was so wrought up with emotion when he saw the body borne along that he sprang upon the bier and attempted to anger the chiefs into making him into a death companion (*moepu'u*) for Kamehameha, but since they had heard Kamehameha's command putting a tabu upon men for the chief Liholiho, they drove Ke-amo-hulihia away, and each time that he returned they refused. Ka-lani-moku also wished to be his death companion, but Ho'okio prevented him. Formerly it was customary for chiefs to show their affection in this way without caring for their own lives; it was their way of repaying their chief's kindness. In the meantime when a land was defiled by the corpse of its ruling chief, it was considered in old days the proper thing for his heir to depart to another district for some days until the bones had been cleaned (*ho'oma'ema'e ia*), covered with basketwork (*ka'ai ia*), and placed within the tower (*'anu'u*) of the heiau, as the corpses of chiefs were prepared in old days for burial. In the early morning therefore Liholiho sailed and touched at Kawaihae. When the people of Kona and of neighboring places heard of the death of the chief the voice of weeping and wailing arose and the sound of lamentation and general mourning, recalling their regret and reciting their love for their chief. It would be impossible to describe all their ways of expressing love and sorrow, even to wishing to die with him. No nation on earth could have shown more grief and affection, and these manifestations of regret lasted many days.

There were in old days few kahunas of the devil-worshiping (*'oihana diabolo*) class who prayed men to death (*kahuna 'ana'ana'*). These were a tabu class to whom did not properly belong the slant-eyed, the bold, those who went from house to house, the covetous of other men's wealth, extortioners, askers of favors. The true kahuna of this class was a person who lived quietly, was lowly, unassuming, humble of heart, not a gad-about, not a seeker of companions, not a pleasure seeker, a proud talker, or covetous, but one who suppressed his lusts. This was the kind of man who represented the true sorcerer. The one who began first to harm another by sorcery was generally the one who died first. These persons secured from the devil himself their knowledge of sorcery by burning fires (*kuni*) and by sending spirits on errands of evil (*'o*). They were eaters of filth and of things defiled. When all the land was filled with mourning Kamehameha's sorcerers prepared their little fireplaces. Some believed that Kamehameha had died naturally of disease and old age, but others contended that he had not reached an age to die but had been prayed to death, and therefore it was that the fires were started for Kamehameha. The sorcerers knew by signs that there had been an attempt to get something belonging to the chief in order to put him to death. They set up tabu flags near fireplaces and set to work. When Ka-hekili Ke'e-au-moku got drunk and broke up the kahunas' doings, the people ascribed the chief's death to Ka-'ahu-manu's family and spoke hard words against them without considering that Ke'e-au-moku was drunk at the time.*

At the end of the ten days needed to clean the bones, a small heiau was built and a tower (*'amu'u*) set up in which the receptacle (*ka'ai*) was woven which was to contain the bones. It was then the kahuna's office to pray to the god to save the soul of the dead and bring it into the company of the god in the bosom of Wakea and not leave it to dwell with Milu in darkness. These prayers for the soul of the dead were called *lupa* or *lupalupa*, or if the deceased had no (inherited) part with the god then the prayer was called a "sacrifice" (*kaku'ai*). The "lamentation" (*'ulonoku'*) and "intercession" (*kahoahoa*) were other forms of prayer offered. There were many such forms which served as a pathway to go before the god. People differed in their beliefs about the soul and the hereafter. Some thought that by worship-

ing it they could get the soul of the dead to come and act as a
guardian spirit (*'aumakua*) of the living; these are the souls that dwell
in a good place.

After the kahuna had performed his office, Ulu-maheihei prepared
to carry out the command of Kamehameha given before his death, at
the time that he gave to Ulu-maheihei the name of Hoa-pili, to secrete
his bones in a place where they could not be found. The chief's bones
belonged by right to the family of Keawe-a-heulu and to the hidden
burial places of its members from Kiolaka'a and Waiohinu in Ka-'u,
but Kamehameha doubted whether this family could keep the place
secret, for the place where the bones of their father, Keoua, were hidden
was pointed out on the cliffs of Ka'awaloa. Kamehameha had therefore
entrusted his bones to Ulu-maheihei Hoa-pili with instructions to put
them in a place which would never be pointed out to anyone. At
midnight, therefore, when black darkness had fallen and no one was
likely to be on the road and the rough lava plains of Pu'uokaloa lay
hushed, Hoa-pili sent his man, Ho'olulu, to bring the container of
wicker work in which the bones of Kamehameha were kept to Kaloko
in Kekaha. Ho'olulu, carrying the receptacle on his back and a gun in
his hand, had reached the road over the lava of Pu'uokaloa when he
mistook a rock for a man and shot at it. Some people at Kailua and
Honokohau heard the report of the gun and surmised that the bones of
Kamehameha were being carried away. The next morning Hoa-pili
and Ke-opu-o-lani took canoe to Kaloko where Hoa-pili met the man
who had charge of the secret cave and together they placed the bones
there. "The morning star alone knows where Kamehameha's bones are
guarded." It is said that the bones of Hono-ka-wai-lani's daughter,
Kalola Pupuka, and those of Ka-hekili-nui 'Ahu-manu were secreted in
this same cavern by Ka-me'e-ia-moku and Ka-manawa.

It was an old custom to hide the bones of chiefs who were beloved,
as 'Umi's bones were hidden by Koi, in order that they might not be
made into arrows to shoot rats with, into fishhooks, needles for sewing
tapa, or *kahili* handles, as is still done today. There is a story told
about the bones of Pae which illustrates this custom. Pae was a kahuna
and high chief in the time of 'Umi son of Liloa and a descendant of
Lilinoe, the woman of the mountains. His daughter Kuku-ka-lani was
the wife of 'Umi's older brother Hakau, and his son Hoe is the ancestor of the Pae family today, the living and the dead. 'Umi had been
told by his prophets and diviners that the bones of Pae would make
lucky fishhooks because of Pae's descent from Ku-hai-moana and Ku-
ka-hau-'ula, guardian gods (*'aumakua*) of fishermen. Therefore, in

order to get these bones, 'Umi was anxious to be on hand at the time of Pae's death, and although Pae was now a very old man 'Umi was accustomed to take him out on his fishing expeditions. At that time the beach of 'Ohiki as far as Ka'elehuluhulu was clear [of lava]. 'Umi was out one day fishing with his chiefs at Makaula. Pae and his sons were in another canoe when Pae was stricken with sudden illness on the sea by Hale'ohi'u and died there. 'Umi said, "Take your father ashore and when I am through fishing we will all go up to mourn him."

When they were out of earshot of 'Umi a man named Lulana, a *kahu* of Pae, said, "You sons of my lord (*haku*), let us go and hide the bones of your father, and when 'Umi returns I will tell him that we lost the body, for I have heard that 'Umi wants to get hold of his bones." They accordingly landed, hid the body, and later took the bones to the cliffs of Pali-hula'ana. 'Umi came to land at the usual place and heard the people on shore wailing, but could not see the body of Pae. "Where is the body of your father?" he asked, and the sons answered falsely, "While we were bringing him in to shore the canoe overturned and a shark took him." "Alas! how I loved Pae!" cried 'Umi, and because he was so eager to have the bones of Pae he sent out orders to the sorcerers (*kahuna 'ana'ana'*) to pray to death the shark that had taken the body of Pae. Many of the diviners and seers sought the shark and the bones of Pae, and the search extended all over Hawaii.

Finally 'Umi summoned Niho-nui-o-Kua-ka-wai-ea, a seer (*kaula*) from Kauai, with the promise of a rich reward if he found the bones of Pae.* Midway out in the channel of 'Alenuihaha Niho-nui looked and saw the spirit (*'uhane*) of Pae drinking at the spring of Kawaikapu on the cliffs of Waimanu. He therefore went and got the bones and brought them to Kailua where 'Umi was then living. 'Umi welcomed the seer with the words, "I have sent for you to find the bones of Pae which his sons tell me a shark has eaten. If this is so I will get Pi'i-mai-wa'a and Ka-lae-puni to capture and kill the shark." Niho-nui replied, "Here are the bones of Pae. Send for his sons to come here, and fashion their father's bones into hooks. Take the two with you as fishing companions and when you are out at sea boast about the bone hooks." So 'Umi took the sons of Pae fishing and the two baited the hooks. No sooner had they let them down than the *'ahi* and *kahala* fish bit at them. 'Umi then called out, "Say, Pae, hold on to our fish!" to which boasting words the sons replied with the boast, "The stars alone know where are Pae's bones. Not until you find the nest of the plover [which migrates to Alaska for nesting] will you find Pae's bones." But

* *Ka Nupepa Ku'oko'a*, Sept. 28, 1867.

at the next catch 'Umi again called out, "Say, Pae, hold fast to our catch!" The sons began to wonder and to suspect the truth and Hoe, Pae's son, began to be worried lest 'Umi's boast be true. So he went to see for himself and found that the bones had disappeared, and this was the beginning of a feud between 'Umi's family and the descendants of Pae. The story is told in the story of 'Umi and in that of Kalani-kukuma.

You have perhaps heard of the desecration of the bones of Kapu-kamola, the mother of Iwi-kau-i-ka-ua, and of those of Ka-make-hau o-ku, daughter of Iwi-kau-i-ka-ua by Kapu-kini-akua. Ke-aka-mahana, the wife of Iwi-kau-i-ka-ua, was the one who desecrated the bones of these chiefs, and this was the principal reason why Iwi-kau-i-ka-ua left Hawaii and went to live on Oahu, because of the desecration of his mother's and daughter's bones. So were desecrated the bones and skull of Ka-uhi-a-Kama, ruling chief of Maui. Many of the ruling chiefs of old, even those who were not killed in battle, had their bones thus desecrated. One crafty old chief, Kaha-kauila, father of Ka-pela, the mother of Kau-mea-lani who composed the line "Bitterly cold is Wai'ale'ale" (*Kaulilua i ke anu Wai'ale'ale - ea -*), heard that Pele-io-holani, ruling chief of Oahu, wanted to get hold of his bones at his death. Pele-io-holani had been told that Kaha's bones would make lucky fishhooks. Kaha-kauila got together his kahunas, children, followers, his servants and the chiefs who were related to him and said, "When I die do not wail for me until you have hidden my bones. Then go to the middle of Kawainui and dive about in the mud, raise a lamentation for me, and tell the people that Kaha-kauila fell into the stream and was carried down in the current." When Pele-io-holani heard of the old man's death by drowning he was much disappointed and had chiefs and people dive for the body, but it was never found. The bones were taken back to Pu'uhaoa in Hana and concealed there. The bones of Lono-a-Pi'i were sought out by Kiha-Pi'i-lani in order to desecrate them, and the people of Hawaii dug around Niu close to Pihana in Wailuku in an attempt to find them, but they were never discovered. It was for this reason that the bones of chiefs were hidden, in order to avoid such desecration.

Other ways of using the bones and so heaping reproach on the descendants of those thus treated was by making them into arrowheads to shoot rats with. The person who held the arrow for the chief would wait for a relative of the one whose bones had been used for [arrow] points. When he saw a son or relative come within hearing, he would call out, "Say, Hakau, hold on to the whiskers of this rat! Say, Hakau, hold on to the tail of our rat!" And there were other such ways of taunting a man's relatives. The family of a dead chief were often much worried to know whether his bones had been discovered, but when rat-shooting time came on and they heard meles chanted mentioning his name, then they knew that their secret burial place had been discovered. This practice was not confined to the bones of the male chiefs alone. Sometimes a mele chanted while a tapa or loin cloth was being beaten would name a chiefess, and upon examination her bones would be found to have disappeared. Taunts were uttered while out fishing. A skull was sometimes used as a filth pot or a spittoon. It was for this reason that Kamehameha had his bones so secretly hidden by Ulu-maheihei. "If I die, perhaps you will not be able to hide my bones," he said to him, and Ulu-maheihei Hoa-pili replied, "I am the only one who can do so." Ka-me'e-ia-moku had his bones hidden in a similar way. It was the custom to give such orders before death, and the general belief was that the bones of a bad chief could never be hidden so that they could not be found. Perhaps the word irreligious ('aia') is a better one to use than bad (hewa). It was those who had not prayed to or worshiped the gods whose bones could not be hidden.*

* *Ka Nupepa Ku'oko'a*, Oct. 5, 1867.

CHAPTER XVIII

Abolition of the Tabus Under Liholiho

The ten days necessary for the cleaning of Kamehameha's bones had passed, and they had been brought to the tower (*'anu'u*) within the heiau built for them where the receptacle (*ka'ai*) was woven in which they were to be deposited. [After this had been done] Liholiho, the heir to the kingdom, returned from Kawaihae to Kailua with his company of chiefs, and the days of mourning were ended. On May (Kaelo) 21, 1819, in the twenty-first year of his age, Liholiho began to rule over the people, and he ruled four years and a few months. On the day when the title of Kamehameha II was given him there were gathered to the council the chiefs in full regalia, the governors all in their feather robes, the war leaders, lesser chiefs, and the soldiers under arms. Ka-'ahu-manu was regent and chief counselor, and Ka-lani-moku was chief of the war leaders. There had been a council held beforehand in regard to the division of lands. Some held that all the lands should revert to the ruling chief and there should be a new division, but others held back, declaring that their lands had been given them by Kamehameha. The lands and the crops belonging to Kamehameha's own men and those belonging to Kamehameha became the inheritance of the new ruler. In old days it was the custom for the ruling chief to rule merely, and for the chiefs to bring his cooked food (*mo'a*) to him. The large part of the land belonged to the chiefs and the country people. Some few have today obtained titles to the land which they inherited from ancient times. For example, the land of Kiolaka'a in Ka-'u belonged to Mahi-'ololi' since Keakea-lani's time and that of the battle of Keone'ula'ula at Pohakuomane'o. Such lands were held for generations and were so held up to the time called the Mahele or Land Division. The same was true on Maui and Oahu, but there the lands had been cut up and redistributed among Kamehameha's chiefs and soldiers when he overthrew the rule on these islands.

At the council it was agreed that Ka-'ahu-manu, the royal guardian, should have the honor of announcing the last commands of Kamehameha to the heir, Liholiho, who was to become Kamehameha II. After the prayer by the chief kahuna asking blessings upon him, Liholiho came out dressed in great splendor wearing a suit presented him from England with a red coat trimmed with gold lace and a gold order on his breast, a feather helmet on his head and a feather cloak worn over his shoulders. He was accompanied by two chiefs as escort, one on either side, all in so dignified and orderly a manner as to occasion favorable comment in spite of the wild actions of some of the people, because the tabu was still on. He was there met by Ka-'ahu-manu, who spoke as follows: "O heavenly one! I speak to you the commands of your grandfather. Here are the chiefs, here are the people of your ancestors; here are your guns; here are your lands. But we two shall share the rule over the land." Liholiho consented and became ruling chief over the government. Some of the people did not like Ka-'ahu-manu's use of the word "grandfather" (*kupunakane*) instead of "father" (*makuakane*) when she spoke the chief's commands before the assembly at Kamakahonu, but it was true that Kamehameha never allowed Liholiho to be called his "child" (*keiki*) in his presence, and always called the boy "my *haku*," "my chief," "my grandson," "my treasure," or "my god."* A chief was indeed made tabu by the chief whose child he was.

Liholiho was born in November (Hanaia'ele'ele), 1797, in Hilo, Hawaii. His mother was Ka-lani-kau-i-ka-'alaneo Ke-opu-o-lani, and she gave birth to him at the age of seventeen and a half years. He was her firstborn and he was given the name Ka-lani-Kua-Liholiho. Many signs appeared at his birth. He was taken to the heiau of Kaipalaoa, and the sacred rite of the cutting of his navel cord was performed by the kahuna. Ka-'ahu-manu became his royal foster mother (*kahu*); Papa 'I'i, Kalai-heana, Ho'omakaukau, Manuia, and other relatives of Papa 'I'i, as well as certain chiefs, became his personal *kahu*. The name 'I'i was coined by Liholiho when he was a child and given to Papa, who thus became known as Papa 'I'i.† One day when Liholiho was six years old he was being carried on the back of a *kahu* to a tabu ceremony at Kupalaha south of Waikiki. As they came to the beach of Waia'ula some children who were at play, seeing the people prostrate themselves before the child, lay down on the beach. The little chief picked out a stout *'ehu*-haired boy and ran and got on his back. The attendants would have taken the boy to the temple to sacrifice as one

* Ke-opu-o-lani, the mother of Liholiho, was the daughter of Kiwala'o. Kiwala'o was the son of Ka-lani-'opu'u by Ka-lola, sister of Ka-hekili who was the natural father of Kamehameha. These two adopted Kamehameha and he grew up with Kiwala'o as if they were brothers. Ke-opu-o-lani was always called niece to Kamehameha. His children by her were therefore his grandchildren in respect to their lineage as chiefs.

† *Ka Nupepa Ku'oko'a*, Sept. 21, 1867.

thus made sacred by the chief, but the child held on to the red-headed boy crying, " 'I'i! 'I'i! 'I'i!" and in this way showed his desire for the boy as a playmate. The boy's life was saved. He became playfellow to the chief, and later had the name of Daniel 'I'i.

Liholiho was not brought up away from the presence of the ruling chief as was customary, but was constantly in the presence of Kamehameha and Kamehameha's two tabu sisters, Ke-ku'i-apo-iwa and Ka-lani-akua. If the chief made a trip to Hilo, Liholiho was taken along; on his return to Kawaihae, or Kailua, or Ka'awaloa the child came back with him. In his fifth year Liholiho was declared Kamehameha's successor and was taught to observe the tabu of the heiau and the *waihau,* instructed in erecting the *unu, ku'ula,* and *ko'a* shrines, in observing the tabu of the *loulu* ceremony in the heiau, the offering of the ivory tooth, and the different types of prayers and offerings. These were the tasks set for Liholiho in his childhood. He was a peaceable child, obedient to his guardians, and very fond of playing games adapted to his age; but he found it hard to get other children who were willing to play with him for fear of a playmate who might cause the burning down of their house or their death [because of some infringement of tabu].

Many of the old chiefs were still alive in Liholiho's day. On Oahu were descendants of Pele-io-holani, Kama-hano, Ka-neoneo, and Kapueo; on Maui were those of Ke-kau-like. There were chiefs and lesser chiefs of Hawaii descended from Kamehameha. From Ke'e-au-moku there remained Ka-'ahu-manu, Ka-heihei-malie Ka-niu, Ka-hekili Ke'e-au-moku, Ka-lua-i-Konahale, and Ke-kua-i-pi'ia and their children; Kua-kini was the only one of them who died during the pestilence. Of the children of Ka-me'e-ia-moku there were Ulu-maheihei, Kiki-pa'a, and others. Of Ka-manawa's there were Pele-uli, Koa-hou, Amama-lua, and some grandchildren. Of Keawe-a-Heulu's there were, among others, Haiha Na-ihe, Ke-oho-hiwa, and some grandchildren. Of Ke-kua-manoha' there were Ka-lani-moku, Ka-haku-ha'akoi, and Boki Ka-ma'ule'ule, besides other children and grandchildren. Of Ka-uhi-wawae-ono there were among others Ka-nahoahoa, Ke-kua-iaea, and Keoua-wahine. Of Ka'iana Kuku'e there were Ka-iki-o-'ewa, Koa-kanu, and Ka-hou-o-ka-lani, besides other children and grandchildren. There were the children and grandchildren of the family of Keawe-ma'uhili and of that of Ka-lani-'opu'u and his brothers. Of Ka-ua-kahi-akua there were Kane-kapo-lei and Mahi-hele-lima, besides other children and grand-children. There were chiefs and families of chiefs of Oahu, Molokai, Kauai, Maui. The sands of Kaiakeakua were worn down like a dromedary's back by the many feet of chiefs and chiefesses tramping over them, and at Kamakahonu could be seen at night the sparkle of lights reflected in the sea like diamonds, from the homes of the chiefs from Kahelo to Lanihau. The number of chiefs and lesser chiefs reached into the thousands.*

An extraordinary event marked the period of Liholiho's rule in the breaking down of the ancient tabus, the doing away with the power of the kahunas to declare tabus and to offer sacrifices, and the abolition of the tabu which forbade eating with women. God alone knows what brought about this abolition of the old and the introduction of the new form of worship. The death of Kamehameha was the first step in the ending of the tabus; the second was the modifying of the mourning ceremonies; the third, the ending of the tabu of the chief; the fourth, the ending of carrying the tabu chiefs in the arms and feeding them; the fifth, the ruling chief's decision to introduce free eating ('ainoa) after the death of Kamehameha; the sixth, the cooperation of his aunts, Ka-'ahu-manu and Ka-heihei-malie; the seventh, the joint action of the chiefs in eating together at the suggestion of the ruling chief, so that free eating became an established fact and the credit of establishing the custom went to the ruling chief. This custom was not so much of an innovation as might be supposed. In old days the period of mourning at the death of a ruling chief who had been greatly beloved was a time of license. The women were allowed to enter the heiau, to eat bananas, coconuts, and pork, and to climb over the sacred places. You will find record of this in the history of Ka-'ula-hea-nui-o-ka-moku, in that of Ku-ali'i, and in most of the histories of ancient rulers. Free eating followed the death of the ruling chief; after the period of mourning was over the new ruler placed the land under a new tabu following old lines. In this case Kamehameha II merely continued the practice of free eating.

The custom of the tabu upon free eating was kept up because in old days it was believed that the ruler who did not proclaim the tabu had not long to rule. If he attempted to continue the practice of free eating he was quickly disinherited. It was regarded as an impious act practiced by those alone who did not believe in a god. Such people were looked upon as lower than slaves. The chief who kept up the ancient tabus was known as a worshiper of the god, one who would live a long life protected by Ku and Lono. He would be like a ward of Kane and Kanaloa, sheltered within the tabu. The tabu eating was a fixed law for chiefs and commoners, not because they would die by eating tabu things, but in order to

* *Ka Nupepa Ku'oko'a*, Sept. 28, 1867.

keep a distinction between things permissible to all people and those dedicated to the gods. The tabu of the chief and the eating tabu were different in character. The eating tabu belonged to the tabus of the gods; it was forbidden by the god and held sacred by all. It was this tabu[sic] that gave the chiefs their high station. The tabu of the chief had to do with his birth as a *ni'aupi'o, pi'o, wohi,* or some other rank and included many tabus within the tabu of the chief. It was believed that by faithfully preserving these tabus a child born into one of these ranks would become like a god (*like me ke akua*). Because he observed the tabus of the chiefs Kamehameha became a conqueror and went from one victory to another until he had united the group under him, although he had not so high a tabu as his son Liholiho. The commoners prayed in unison, either in large audiences or in family groups, either each for himself or for his family, his chief, and the prosperity of the land. This is illustrated in the story of Ka-ua-i-mai-ka-lani and Na-maka-o-ka-pao'o, as also in the story of Lua-ho'omoe, the kahuna, and in that of Kupe.* Ka-pihe the seer prophesied in the presence of Kamehameha and said, "There shall be a long *malo* reaching from Kuamo'o to Holualoa. The islands shall come together, the tabus shall fall. The high shall be brought low, and the low shall rise to heaven." The prophecy was fulfilled when the battle was fought at Kuamo'o for the downfall of the ancient tabus. Holualoa was the long *malo* uniting the kingdom from Kahiki to Hawaii. The kingdom of the gods fell, and the believers rose to the heavens. Part of the prophecy is still being fulfilled. It was like the sayings of Ke-kio, Pila-kalo, Ke-kio-pilo, Ka-'opulupulu, and Kila prophesying the coming of the foreigners. Strangest of all was the saying about the downfall of the tabus, for there was no suggestion of this in the earlier history of our ancestors. True it is said in the history of the chiefs that Maili-ku-kahi and Ka-ua-kahi-'ili-lani relinqushed their position as ruling chiefs and gave it to the commoners; and took the firstborn children of the commoners to rear and care for. These two were known as kind chiefs, but it is not said that they abandoned the tabus. The old chiefs may not have been under so strict tabu, since the strict tabus are said to date back not more than three hundred years, but they must have preserved such tabus as were observed by tabu chiefs inside the house. The practice of burning men for [failure to observe] the tabu of chiefs is said to have been introduced in time of Ka-welo-makua and Ka-'awihi-o-kalani [as well as the prostrating tabu itself]. It was practiced by Kauai chiefs alone and descended to their heirs [on that island] until the time of Ka-ua-kahi-a-Kaho'owaha, ruling chief of Oahu, who sent Kualono-'ehu to get the tabu of Kauai for his grandaunt Kaha-malu-'ihi. This tabu was passed

* *Ka Nupepa Ku'oko'a,* Oct. 5, 1867.

on to Kualono-'ehu with the law for burning men (*kapu puhi kanaka*) and drowning them (*lumaluma'i*) for the tabu chief, and was again passed on to Kuali'i when Punchbowl (Pu'owaina) became the place for celebrating such burnings. In the time of Ka-lani-ku'i-hono-i-ka-moku the practice of burning men (*puhi ahi*) was extended to Maui.

When Ke-opu-o-lani, the only remaining high tabu chiefess, gave up the tabu with the consent of all the chiefs, the tabu system fell. In the afternoon of the day following the night of Kamehameha's death, Ke-opu-o-lani ate coconuts which were tabu to women and took food with the men, saying, "He who guarded the god is dead, and it is right that we should eat together freely." This free eating was observed as a part of the mourning ceremonies (*kumakena*). It took place only among the chiefs and did not extend to the country districts. When Liholiho was sent for to return from Kawaihae after the purification ceremonies Ke-kua-o-ka-lani objected to their return, saying, "Your grandfather left commands to two of us, the care of the government to you, of the god to me, and each of us to look to the other. Tell the messengers we two will not return for we have heard that there is free eating at Kailua." When this answer was reported to Ka-'ahu-manu she sent a high chief as messenger and told him, "Go, 'E'eke, and get your lord and return." Ke-kua-o-ka-lani again attempted to dissuade Liholiho, saying, "Let us remain. There is food in the uplands and fish in the sea, and if a messenger is again sent by your *kahu* face to face, let him fear death in the bush." Liholiho said, "I am not going to stay, I am returning." Ke-kua-o-ka-lani agreed to his going but urged him, "If the chiefs want you to indulge in free eating, do not consent." Liholiho returned by canoe to Kailua, and the next day Ka-'ahu-manu proclaimed him king. Ke-opu-o-lani then looked at the young chief and put her hand to her mouth as a sign for free eating. This was a strange thing for a tabu chiefess to do, one for whom these tabus were made and who had the benefit of them. How could those to whom the tabu rank did not belong object after that? In the afternoon she ate with Kau-i-ke-aouli, and it was through her influence alone that the eating tabu was freed. No one else dared eat with her by day because of her tabu, which was so strict that even Kamehameha had been obliged to uncover and remove his loin cloth in her presence; only at night was it less severe. Liholiho however, remembered his *kahu's* instructions and did not eat with his mother and brother. The next day he and his chiefs joined Ke-kua-o-ka-lani at Kawaihae and found him at prayer, and so finding him they too worshiped, and again a tabu was put upon free eating by chiefs and commoners and they took to games and rum drinking.*

* *Ka Nupepa Ku'oko'a*, Oct. 12, 1867.

At this time there arrived at Kawaihae a ship from France on board of which was a Roman Catholic priest. When Ka-lani-moku learned from John Young that this man held office from his government as a priest of the true God in heaven he had himself baptized by the priest as pope over the islands.

On their return from Kawaihae to Honokohau, Liholiho remained under tabu at the heiau of the god until the tabu was freed. A man came from Kailua sent by Ka-'ahu-manu. "What do you bring?" asked the chief. "Your *kahu* has sent me to say that the *ti* leaf tabu is to be declared to your god upon your arrival at Kailua.* The chief bent his head in reflection and then looked up and assented. The *ti* leaf tabu meant that Kailua was to be released from further tabus and any new tabus would not have power. It was clear to him what was going on at Kailua. He accordingly sent his messengers to fetch rum from Kailua, and for two days he and his chiefs sailed about the Kona waters in his two-masted canoe, sending every little while for more rum and cooked dog and pork. During this time at Kailua the women prepared all the tabu foods without the chief's knowledge. When the wind died down and the canoe could no longer move the *kahu* sent a double canoe and paddlers and towed the boat [of Liholiho] to Kailua, and Ka-heihei-malie hastened to open the oven of dog meat. Then Liholiho on this first night of his arrival ate some of the tabu dog meat free only to the chiefesses; he entered the *lauhala* house free only to them; whatever he desired he reached out for; everything was supplied, even those things generally to be found only in a tabu house. The people saw the men drinking rum with the women *kahu* and smoking tobacco, and thought it was to mark the ending of the tabu of the chief. The chiefs saw with satisfaction the ending of the chief's tabu and the freeing of the eating tabu. The *kahu* said to the chief, "Make eating free over the whole kingdom from Hawaii to Oahu and let it be extended to Kauai!" and Liholiho consented. Then pork to be eaten free was taken to the country districts and given to commoners, both men and women, and free eating was introduced all over the group. Messengers were sent to Maui, Molokai, Oahu, and all the way to Kauai. Ka-umu-ali'i consented to the free eating and it was accepted on Kauai. Boki was over the land of Oahu at the time, and Oahu accepted free eating. The prophecy of Ka-pihe was fulfilled.

When Ke-ao-ua Ke-kua-o-ka-lani, the son of Kamehameha's younger brother and the second heir named in Kamehameha's parting commands, heard that the ruling chief Liholiho had been made to practice free eating, he was angry with Ka-'ahu-manu and with the whole family of chiefs for forcing this upon the young chief and ending the tabu of chiefs. To

* The "ti leaf tabu" is a request to the gods to take the tabu back to themselves and leave men free. Its sign is a ti leaf.

show his own stand for tabu eating he left Kailua and sailed to Ka'awa-loa and lived there shunning free eating. There he was joined by Kuaiwa and Holoi-a-lena, soldiers of the kahuna lines of Ka-uahi and Na-hulu, who stood for tabu eating. These said, "The ungodly chiefs of old who lost their lands never sinned like this!" and urged Ke-kua-o-ka-lani to take over the rule, for it was an ancient saying in Hawaii, "The chief who prays to the god, he is the chief who will hold the rule." Ke-kua-o-ka-lani, thus encouraged by the kahunas and orators, stood out for tabu eating. Many of the commoners and chiefs, even those who had partici-pated in free eating, and the brothers of Ka-'ahu-manu themselves, wanted tabu eating. Few of the chiefs were in favor of free eating. Ke-kua-i-pi'ia, the sister of Ka-'ahu-manu and foster mother of Ke-kua-o-ka-lani's father, was sent to get him to come to Kailua and take part in free eating or at least live there in Kailua and preserve his tabu, but he refused. Disorders arose; in Hamakua one man took up arms against the government. A lesser chief named Lono-akahi was sent by Liholiho to see what was going on, and in a scrimmage he and two of his men were killed by the countrymen of Mahiki. The king and his chiefs held a council of war to determine how they could send assistance to their men in Hamakua. Ka-lani-moku said, "There is no use sending men to Hamakua. The cause of the uprising is in Ka'awaloa in the person of Ke-kua-o-ka-lani. Hew down the trunk and the limb will wither." It was agreed to send Haiha Na-ihe and Ulu-maheihei, his uncles, to go in a friendly way and bring Ke-kua-o-ka-lani to Kailua. If he agreed to come, there would be no need of making war upon him.

Just as the canoe was ready to sail, Ke-opu-o-lani came on board with-out having previously expressed any intention of so doing. Her action was the cause of the battle at Kuamo'o. "This was from God in order to end the food tabu in the kingdom." The canoe landed in the evening at Ka-'awaloa, and Na-ihe and Ulu-maheihei met Ke-kua-o-ka-lani with affec-tionate weeping. Ulu-maheihei said, "We have been sent by the chiefs and your child to come here and bring you back to Kailua. You are my sister's son, and they are blaming you for the uprising. This is only be-cause you keep aloof. Since the country is left to you both, come to Kailua and talk the matter over, [you and Liholiho] and practice free eating or not as you please." Ke-kua-o-ka-lani consented and said, "I must go first and speak with Manono, my wife, then I will go back with you; but I will never practice free eating." Na-ihe and Ulu-maheihei re-turned to Na-ihe's house where Ke-opu-o-lani was staying. "What was Ke-kua-o-ka-lani's answer?" she asked. "He has consented to go with us tomorrow." "He is an *uku* fish, a fish of Kaho'olawe; he should be drawn in as soon as he is hooked." (*He uku maoli ia he 'i'a no Kaho'olawe.*) "He has consented to go Kailua, but he has refused to practice free eating, and he is going to talk with Manono and go with us tomorrow." "I am not so sure of it. Perhaps yes, and perhaps no." It is possible that Ke-opu-o-lani had a better knowledge of the man than the others and detected something that made her doubtful, for she was a good student of human nature.

All that night a man high in the counsels of Ke-kua-o-ka-lani made the rounds calling the people to make ready to return to Kailua to take part in the practice of free eating. Hoa-pili's party felt that their mission had been successful. In reality it was but a ruse; the plan was to dispose of Hoa-pili and Ke-opu-o-lani that night. Those active in the plot were the kahunas Kuaiwa and Holoi-a-lena of the priesthood of Ka-uahi and Na-hulu, the two kahunas who had joined Ke-kua-o-ka-lani in his effort to protect free eating, but to the credit of Ke-kua-o-ka-lani be it said that he refused his men's urging to the deed. Na-ihe was said to have been sympathetic with Ke-kua-o-ka-lani's side, for he left his guns behind. The next morning when Ke-kua-o-ka-lani and his followers went to meet Ke-opu-o-lani and lined up, armed, with torches lighted and sandals on their feet, it was evident that they were prepared for war. "Are we then to start?" asked Hoa-pili. "Yes." "We take the canoe, then?" [Ke-kua-o-ka-lani answered] "I go by land with my men; they are without food and can supply themselves by land." "You think too much of your men; it is you whom we came to fetch. Let the men go by land and you come with us" [replied Hoa-pili]. "I will not go by canoe; I go by land with the rest" [Ke-kua-o-ka-lani declared]. "So you cut the navel cord, my brother, by this act," said Ke-opu-o-lani. This ended the talk. Ke-kua-o-ka-lani accompanied his men by land. "There is nothing left but war," said Hoa-pili to himself as they made ready to return to Kailua.*

The plan was for Ke-opu-o-lani to go in a double canoe and Hoa-pili in a single one. Naihe ordered Hoa-pili to land at Keauhou and wait the coming of Ke-kua-o-ka-lani, but Ke-opu-o-lani heard the order and took canoe with Hoa-pili and came to Kailua. Upon landing she was met by the chief and there was much wailing. Ke-opu-o-lani said, "I was to have been killed." "Where is Ke-kua-o-ka-lani?" asked Ka-lani-moku. "He is coming by land." "How did he receive you?" "Friendly means have failed; it is for you to act now," and Ke-opu-o-lani then ordered Ka-lani-moku to prepare for war on Ke-kua-o-ka-lani. Arms and ammunition were given out that evening to everyone who was trained in warfare, and feather capes and helmets distributed.

The next morning Ka-lani-moku encouraged his followers to go forward, saying, "Go quietly, be strong, be soldiers, and drink the bitter waters, O my little brothers! There are lands ahead, honor, wealth. Do

* *Ka Nupepa Ku'oko'a,* Nov. 2, 1867.

not turn back, whether death or life lies ahead." He then placed the carriers of food and water and marched his men to Keauhou, where they camped. Ka-lani-moku then sent Ka-heana, called also Moe-hau, [to Ke-kua-o-ka-lani's men] with the word, "Let your chief come and confer with your chief Liholiho at Kailua, and if he will consent there need be no war." Moe-hau met Kua-o-ka-lani at Kuamo'o and gave the message. "Where is Ka-lani-moku?" "Encamped at Keahou." "I command you to return to Ka-lani-moku and if he attacks to seize him and await my coming." The two were talking outside the stone wall at Lekeleke. Some of the advance scouts of Ka-lani-moku's following fired a shot. The *kahu* kissed Kekua-o-ka-lani, jumped into the sea, and swam to meet Ka-lani-moku at Kawanui. Ke-kua-o-ka-lani's scouts fired and killed some of the men and wounded two chiefs on the side of free eating, but not seriously. They were Ka-iki-o-'ewa, wounded in the calf of the leg, and Holua-loa, the friend of Ka-uhi-wawae-ono and husband of Kaka'e. These were the first casualties, and had they been fatal the battle would have gone to the tabu eaters. Ka-lani-moku's men retreated, but others, seeing how few in number the shooters were, pressed forward, the two sides met, and at Kuamo'o the battle began in earnest.

Ke-kua-o-ka-lani showed conspicuous courage during the entire battle. He kept on advancing and even when shot in the leg he fought on bravely until afternoon, when he was surrounded and shot in the chest and died facing his enemies. His wife Manono fought at his side. When he was shot she cried out to Ka-lani-moku to spare her, for he and she had the same father. "How is the chief?" he called. "He is dead." "Then it would disgrace me in men's minds for you to live." How pitiful to hear a woman plead for her life! She fell at her husband's side under a volley of shots. Kuaiwa, the kahuna who had urged the revolt, was seized at Kailua and another plotter, named Wahahe'e, who shot Puakau, and they were killed and their bodies dragged along the highway. Ku-a-ka-mauna the son of Lono-hiwa, Pe'ape'a, and Na-heana fled to the bush. Manono, the son of Ka-nau-kapu and Keawe-haku, went into hiding among the cliffs of Waipi'o; many hid in the bush and some escaped to Maui. All were finally pardoned by Liholiho and their lives spared. When the battle was over Liholiho sent Hoa-pili as war leader to disperse the commoners of Hamakua who had risen up against free eating. Hoa-pili landed at Kawaihae with his forces, marched up to Waimea, met the opposing force and killed many, but some escaped into the woods at Mahiki. This ended the armed opposition against free eating. Hoa-pili returned to Kailua which was now the center of government where the chiefs held council for welfare of the country.*

* *Ka Nupepa Ku'oko'a*, Nov. 9, 1867.

CHAPTER XIX

Hawaii Before Foreign Innovations

Before the arrival of the Puritan missionaries the lands were owned altogether by the chiefs. It is not clear to what chief the lands were first given or how the chiefs came to have absolute control of the lands (*ke kumu o ka lilo loa ana o ka mana o na aliʻi maluna o ka ʻaina*) and the commoners to be under the chiefs and do the heavy labor. It is said that the commoners themselves gave the land to the chiefs and those who won victories in war, and that the lands of those who were defeated were taken by the victors. The commoners who had held their land under the defeated chiefs were thus deprived of their holdings. It is, however, clear from the early histories of these islands that from ancient times until this time the commoners followed the fortunes of their chiefs and lived under them, depending upon them for everything, and thus obtained wealth and lands. Some of the chiefs drew about themselves a great following of commoners, went to war, won victories over a district, and divided up the land to their men and their soldiers; and it became theirs.*

If some wealthy chief's light burned late at night he was suspected, war made upon him, and his land taken. If a chief became angry with a commoner he would dispossess him and leave him landless, but the commoners submitted to the chiefs and consented afterwards to endure hard labor and work like slaves under the chiefs. It was not for a commoner to do as he liked as if what he had was his own. If a chief saw that a man was becoming affluent, was a man of importance in the back country, had built him a good house, and had several men under him, the chief would take everything away from him and seize the land, leaving the man with only the clothes on his back. Men feared in old days being driven away and having to take to the highway, or even to have suspicion fasten upon them and be killed, as often happened in old days. This seizing of the land and being driven out upon the highway was what ʻAuwae warned his family against when he advised them in his last days, "You have a long life ahead. The only thing I fear for you is having your land taken away and your being cast out upon the highway. So I advise you to go to the chief Ka-lani-kau-i-ke-aouli and buy the land of ʻOwaʻ so that it may not be taken away from you; then if Wailuku is taken, ʻOwaʻ will

---

* *Ka Nupepa Kuʻokoʻa*, Nov. 9, 1867.

be left, and you can live there securely." It was this advice of Noa 'Auwae that made H. Kawai-lepolepo go to Oahu and buy the land of 'Owa'.The king consented and gave him a deed in fee to confirm the sale. 'Auwae was a promiment man in the time of Kamehameha I up to that of Kamehameha III and worked hard to promote the interests of his lord. To this end he made the commoners labor day and night; but he had little reward for his labors, only a taste of *poi*. So it was with those in charge of districts large or small; they placed heavy burdens upon the poor under them and abused the humble, yet they themselves received little reward, nor did their children inherit wealth. These were some of the hardships endured by the poorer class in the old days.

Wars were frequent in old days and entailed robbery and murder of the common people. Hence the people desired to live under chiefs who were successful and dwelt in peace, and they would serve as soldiers under their chiefs and try to give them the rule. If a chief was victorious in war and showed seemingly superhuman power, then his men feared him and worshiped him as if he were a god. And because of their dependence upon the chief he would have many *kahu*, companions (*punahele*), favorites (*aikane*), *stewards* (*'a'ipu'upu'u*), servants (*kauwa kuapa'a*), wives (*wahine*), and women (*haia wahine*), foster children (*keiki ho'okama*), men at arms (*pu'ali koa*), and keepers of gods (*kahu akua*). Seeing themselves thus surrounded, the chiefs would lay heavy burdens upon the commoners and kill them at the slightest provocation. Hence men feared them, would lay their heads down under the feet of the chiefs, and obey their slightest word, good or bad. The story of 'Umi, the son of Liloa, illustrates this; for although the rule belonged to Hakau and not to him, and Hakau's daughter Pinea II, and her grandchild Hakau-ka-lala-pua-kea, were the heirs, and 'Umi came from a humble family, yet when he became ruling chief the people bowed to him. He had numberless wives and women and children, and the commoners knelt to him and worshiped him. But Kiha-Pi'i-lani despised 'Ai-hako'ko' and Ku-malae, the children of his sister Pi'i-kea-a-Pi'i-lani, because they were born to 'Umi. 'Ai-hako'ko' was brought to Maui, but Kiha treated him with contempt and killed his favorite *kahu*; and 'Ai-hako'ko' died of grief for him and was buried at Kapa'ahu where is the burial cave of 'Ai-hako'ko'. The young people are mistaken in giving the name Ka-lua-'Ai-hako'ko' to the coconut grove at Koa-kanu on the seacoast of Kama-'ole in Kula. . . .

The chiefs did not rule alike on all the islands. It is said that on Oahu and Kauai the chiefs did not oppress the common people. They did not tax them heavily and they gave the people land where they could live at peace and in a settled fashion. When Oahu came under the rule of Kama-pua'a, he gave the land containing the word *wai* to the kahuna

Lono-a-wohi; but later the land was redistributed by Kahiki-ʻula and the older brothers of Kama-puaʻa because the kahunas had a monopoly of the well-watered lands, and the kahuna class were given the lands of Waimea, Pupukea, Waiahole, and Hakipuʻu in perpetuity, and these were held by them until the days of Ka-hahana. Ka-hekili and Ka-lani-ku-pule confirmed this gift to the kahunas, and so did Kamehameha. Waimea was given to the Paʻao kahuna class in perpetuity and was held by them up to the time of Kamehameha III when titles had to be obtained. But there was one land title held by the kahuna class of Paʻao for many years and that was Puʻuepa in Kohala. In the same way the land of Kekaha was held by the kahuna class of Ka-uahi and Nahulu.

At the taking over of the rule by Kamehameha troubles arose. The country as a whole benefited by the uniting of the government under one head, but most of the chiefs and landlords under Kamehameha oppressed the commoners and took away their lands, thus forcing the people who had owned the land to become slaves. "They put their ears to the fuzz of the treefern," was the saying. Taxes were laid upon all holdings whether large or small and were constantly being added to, for there were many landlords and under landlords who demanded tribute. In order to avoid such oppression Kamehameha made this law: "The number of landlords haku'aina) over the keeper of the land (hoa'aina) shall be [but] one. The people (maka'ainana) shall not be made to come long distances to work for the keeper (konohiki); the chiefs and keepers shall not strip the people of their property leaving them destitute; no man shall give many feasts and absorb the property of the poor; no landlord shall oppress a person while seeking his own means of livelihood; no landlord shall compel a man to work for him who does not want to, or burden him in any way; he should be impartial and judge his people aright." It has been said that the leaders seize, grasp, take, rob, burden, oppress, and are greedy, and it is these things that make a country poor. These were the hardships endured under the old chiefs down to the time of the reign of Kamehameha III. The lesser chiefs and landlords were likely to oppress the common people and the humble farmers and the squatters on the land; therefore it was that our kind king made this law to remove the slavery imposed upon the common people by the chiefs and landlords.*

The uniting of the land had brought about excessive taxation. There was an innumerable succession of landlords, and each used the commoner to further his own purposes. The chiefesses demanded such delicacies as the dried intestines of fish, sea slugs, sea cucumbers of various kinds and sea urchins. Because of these oppressions, some men migrated

* *Ka Nupepa Kuʻookʻa*, Nov. 16, 1867.

to Tahiti or fled to Kauai to live under Ka-umu-aliʻi. Many chants were composed in those days telling of Hawaii as a land of robbers. Here is one:—

A Lahaina ʻike i ka lau o naʻulu,	In Lahaina I saw the leaves of the breadfruit,
ʻIke i ka mea maikaʻi a Hawaii,	I saw the good things of Hawaii.
E humuhumu ka waha,	But I must sew up the mouth,
E noho malie ka waha,	Keep quiet,
Ka waha o ka olala e!	Keep the mouth humble!

"Even the smallest patches are taxed" (*He ʻauhau koʻele na ka Hawaii*), was a familiar saying. Kamehameha issued the law, "Let the old men and women and children go in peace and sleep [in safety] by the wayside," but there was no law for the general welfare.

Some of the chiefs under Kamehameha, such as Alapaʻi-malo-iki and Ka-uhi-wawae-ono, were murdering chiefs who did not keep the law against killing men, but went out with their men to catch people for shark bait. If they found a man or even a woman out at night they would kill him and keep the body until it decayed and use it for shark bait. So died a very pretty woman of North Kona named ʻEleʻele on the rocks at Honokohau, and many other persons these two chiefs killed at the various places where they stayed. At Keala and Kalahiki in South Kona, at Hamakuapoko on Maui, and at Puʻuloa on Oahu, people were killed by them for shark bait. Again, it was considered a great sin to wear the loin cloth of a chief. It was because one of them had worn Ka-lani-moku's loin cloth that Ke-kua-nui and his younger brother were killed at Hikiau in Kealakekua. Ka-hinu, mother of Keawe-lua-ʻole, who lived at Lahaina was falsely accused of smoking Ke-kua-o-ka-lani's pipe and burned to death in Hamakua, Hawaii.

Revenge was another great cause of strife in old days; a feud was carried on by the descendants of those involved even up to the time of the coming of the missionaries. Pele-io-holani cherished a feeling of enmity against the chiefs of Molokai for the death of his daughter Keʻe-lani-honua-ia-kama, and at the battle of Kapuʻunoni he slaughtered the chiefs and roasted them in an oven at Hakawai in Kaluaʻaha, and he attacked the commoners inhumanly, all for revenge. Ka-hekili sought to avenge upon the chiefs of Oahu their slaying of the chiefs and commoners of Maui. They had taken Ka-uhi-a-Kama prisoner to Oahu and roasted him in an oven, and they had used his skull as a filth pot. Such acts of vengeance added to the distresses of the people. The chiefs of Hawaii and Molokai retaliated upon Pele-io-holani, as at the oven of Kuna at Waikiki and that of the chiefs at Hekili above Kanelaʻau in

Honolulu. Ka-hekili punished the chiefs of Oahu for the evil done by their ancestors and avenged the blood these had shed upon the heads of their children. So perished Ka-pueo, Ka-neoneo, Elani, and other Oahu chiefs. This inhuman slaughter was one of the causes for the depopulation of these islands. It is even said that Ka-lani-moku left the body of Ke-kua-o-ka-lani on the lava rocks after the battle of Kuamo'o instead of having it buried according to his rank as chief, [and that he did this] as an act of vengeance because Ke-kua-o-ka-lani's ancestor, Alapa'i-nui-a-Ka-uaua, had drowned Ka-lani-moku's ancestor, Ka-uhi-'aimoku-a-Kama, at Nu'u in Kaupo. He was tied and thrown into the sea at Puhele and left to the mercy of the sharks. This left bad blood in the family which broke out at the death of Ke-kua-o-ka-lani. This is no doubt the reason why Boki Ka-ma'ule'ule turned over in his mind the idea of hiding his bones in a foreign land, as was rumored after his departure. If the sins committed by the ancestors are thus cherished, they become like a smoldering flame which will burst forth upon the descendants, causing the destruction of chiefs and people. Any feeling of revenge in the hearts of our people should be rooted out, and the population be allowed to increase.

The constant wars of old days were another cause of depopulation. Among the noncombatants even women were cut down, and little children killed. In Puna, Hawaii, at Opihikao, a battle was fought in which even pregnant women and children were slain. In another famous battle at Kohala, called Kepaia, children and pregnant women were leaped upon and children trampled down. Those were indeed bloody days. Even four years after the coming of the word of God this thing happened on Kauai while George Humehume, one of the sons of Ka-umu-ali'i who had come with the missionaries to Kauai, was living with Mr. Bingham at Mr. Whitney's on Kauai. A fight took place in the back country during which few of the fighting men were killed, but many, even women and children, were shot or thrust through with bayonets indiscriminately. This fight was called the "Pig eating" (*'Aipua'a*) because the dead were left lying for the wild hogs to devour. God will no doubt require their blood of those people who so heedlessly spilled it.*

Let us see what treatment prisoners had in the time of Kamehameha. Kane-maka-kini was a warrior in Kamehameha's army, but had gone to live under Ka-umu-ali'i on Kauai. When Ka-lani-moku came to Kauai, Kane-maka-kini came to meet him bringing presents, for Ka-lani-moku was well known as an influential person on Hawaii and holder of the lands of Mahukona in Kohala under Kamehameha. On the night of the insurrection at the fort at Hipo, Ka-lani-moku ordered Ka-maka-kini to

* *Ka Nupepa Ku'oko'a*, Nov. 23, 1867.

return to Oahu on the ship *Pa'a-lua,* and although Mr. Bingham and Ke-ka-ulu-ohi were on board, Noa Ka-maunu, the captain of the ship, threw Kane-maka-kini overboard with a bag of sand tied to his feet. This was done for revenge alone. Another prisoner who had been taken by his master as a slave started with his master at Waialua to climb Kilohana. The master said, "Take the load to the rise and then come back and carry me up." The prisoner carried the heavy load to the top of the rise and then returned and began to climb again with his master on his back. He staggered along more and more slowly until finally, almost at the rise, he let his master down. For this the master shot him without pity and rolled his body down the cliff. That was the way men were treated in old days. The master however, had a hard time of it, for when he asked for other men's slaves to carry his load the answer was, "You have killed your own servant so now you can carry your own load." One of my own uncles was a foolish man always on the watch to kill prisoners. His name was Kiha Ka-lu'au 'Ehu and he was of the Okaka class of warriors. Many were the men he shot without cause and shed the blood of the innocent. Once when he was living at Kapa'a in Puna a refugee came along with his grandchild on his back, and my grandfather aimed his gun at him intending to shoot him. The man called out quickly, "Say, Nae-'ole, let me live!" If he had not used the name of one of his friends he and the child would have been killed. What a pity! I was quite a small child then, and when my uncle used to boast of his deeds I would say, "You ought to have been governor of Kauai, not Ka-iki-o-'ewa. He was just eating breadfruit *poi* in Lahaina and there he is chief of Kauai!" Is it brave to kill where there is no war? Our ancestors, Ka-pueo, Ka-neoneo, Ka-hahana, Ka-'akau, were all cut to pieces in cold blood, and their children have met the same fate. This is one of the reasons why this land became depopulated.

Infanticide was another evil practiced in pagan days and still made use of today. Women dispose of their children in secret places with the help of their husbands, parents, and of the *kahuna 'o'o,* and others besides. Women in old days killed the child within the womb by drinking medicine to poison the child, by using a sharp-pointed instrument, by beating on the abdomen, or they would throw a newborn infant into the water or bury it in the earth. Their reasons for killing the child were age, poverty, pleasure-seeking, illicit relations, jealousy, slavery, dislike of children, and shame.

Homosexuality was an evil practice with which certain people in old days defiled themselves. It was not practiced by commoners but among the chiefs and lesser chiefs, even to the extent of putting away their wives. The taking of many women as wives was a cause of trouble in old days. Women too took many husbands. This broke up the family and brought about quarreling and jealousy. Some women went off with whatever husband they pleased. Parents and friends assisted in this kind of thing so long as they could get a man or woman to take a wealthy person as mate. But one excellent thing there was in old days which is not so today, that was the guarding of the chastity and purity of the young women. Some of the boys also were guarded in old days. If they were dedicated to the kahuna class they were kept tabu; the boy's body must be kept pure. He must not cut his hair, his clothing was tabu, his loin cloth, his sleeping mats, his house, everything he had to eat and drink must not be touched by others. This was also true for the boys who were to take up some branch of learning; they were guarded from defilement. Today, licentiousness is more common than formerly.

In ancient times the land was covered with people. All the lands from Hawaii to Ka'ula were peopled except the low coral reefs. From the summits of the mountains to the shore are to be found the remains of their cultivated fields and the sites of their houses. Today in some places the ground is white with their bones, and land goes uncultivated because there are none who need it. People were famous in those days for long life with "eyes like a rat's, skin yellow as a pandanus leaf, carried on a mat." Pa'ao must have lived 447 years or more, since he came during the rule of La'au-ali'i and died in that of Ka-maka-'ohua, father of Kau-a-Ka-maka-'ohua, the wife of Hoa-lani. From them came Ipu-wai-a-Hoa-lani, the wife of Ka-'ihi-kapu-a-Ku'ihewa. From the time of La'au-ali'i to Ka-maka-'ohua there fifteen generations of chiefs. Ka-maka-'ohua was the chief who built the heiau of Mulei'ula in Kahei, Kohala, and the chief at the time that Kahu-a-ka-nini, the son of Pa'ao, had his hand cut by the Kalau-maumalei fish and died of hunger at the cliff of Pololu. That was during the time of the great drought. In Kamehameha's day many lived to be old men. Keawe-kuli-loa was one of these; he was an irreligious man, but he lived to be over a hundred years old, saw seven generations, and lived under ten different rulers.

But the race was on the decrease even before the coming of the missionaries . . . This was due in part to the merciless battles that had been fought in which the earth was literally covered with the innocent who were slaughtered . . . Many died in the mountains, fell over cliffs, or were drowned in the sea. They were killed even when they fled to another land, those on Maui killing refugees from wars on Hawaii, or those on Hawaii killing people who fled from Maui. Even castaways were slain. Infanticide was another cause of this decrease . . . but because of the laws this became more common in late days. Many were put to death in those days by sorcery, either by praying to death ('ana'ana), sending spirits on messages of death (*unauna*) or by the *hiu* or *ho'opi'o-ti'o* methods of sorcery. It was a common practice to have poison gods and images and to feed them, and people feared these things for in this way people were murdered without pity. The lower class dwindled, and the upper grew more and more wicked. Robbery and theft also were frequent crimes committed in out-of-the-way places.* Certain people, called Ku'ielua, took up robbery as a profession, were known as "wild men" (*hihiu*), and waylaid travelers at such remote places on the highway as 'O'opuola, 'Akiala, Kuanu'uanu, Hana'ie'ie, 'A'alaloloa, the cliffs of Molokai, Kahakuloa [on Maui], and so also on Hawaii, Oahu and Kauai. Add to this the practice of the chiefs of killing people for bait for shark-fishing (*hahaulua*) without any excuse, and their methods of disposing of anyone whom they thought too bold by accusing him of using some article of wearing apparel or other personal article.

Then too the foreign ships which arrived at Oahu during Kamehameha's occupation of that island brought in many diseases, especially the severe pestilence of 1804 when so many chiefs and commoners perished. In Liholiho's time when the missionaries arrived in Hawaii a large number of the old chiefs were still living, and a great number of young chiefs and chiefesses. The country districts were thickly populated by lesser chiefs and men of importance. Warriors were still living from the armies of Pele-io-holani, Ku-mahana, Ka-hahana, Ka-hekili, Ka-lani-ku-pule, Keawe-ma'uhili, and Keoua Kuahu-'ula. There were Koa-kanu, Kua-kahele, Ka-'ele-o-waipi'o and their families, and numberless others. Ke-ka-ulu-ohi, one of Ka-lani-'opu'u's wives who had seven husbands during her time, was taught to read and write during the first days of teaching the alphabet. In fact many old-timers were living at that time. As for the commoners, the land was filled with them from Hawaii to Kauai. In 1831 the school teachers began to take the census. Although it was not complete, they reported a little under 200,000. It is therefore evident that the population declined after the arrival of the missionaries even though all wars ceased, and robbery and murder were wiped out. Why this decrease? Insect pests were one cause, another was the introduction of venereal diseases, and a third the epidemics brought by foreign ships. Many such occurred during the rule of Kamehameha III. In 1826 thousands died, especially in the country districts, of an epidemic of "cough, congested lungs, and sore throat." Luanu'u Kahalai'a, George Humehume, and other chiefs died of this disease. In February, 1839, a ship arrived from Valparaiso whose Captain, Henry Peck, had died at sea. This ship brought a pestilence from which many died, Kina'u among others. In September, 1848, an American warship brought the

* *Ka Nupepa Ku'oko'a*, Nov. 30, 1867.

disease known as measles to Hilo, Hawaii. It spread and carried away about a third of the population. Among the chiefs who died were Moses Ke-kuaiwa, W. P. Lele-io-hoku, and Ka-'imi-na'auao. I know personally of two families in Kipahulu, those of 'Ili-mai-hea-lani and Kukui-'ula, in which only three persons were left out of fourteen. In Ka-pule's home at Papauluna nine died out of thirteen. At this rate more must have died than survived. In 1844 there came a severe epidemic of colds, severe headache, and dizziness. Again in March and April of 1853 smallpox was discovered by Dr. Potter at Kahaka'aulana, and it broke out in Honolulu the following May. It was first seen in the house of Ka'aione in Kaka'ako. Its first victim was a woman with a tattooed face (maka-pa'ele), and the disease raged on Oahu but did not extend to the other islands. In 1857 many died of an epidemic of colds, dull headache, sore throat, and deafness, John Young and Konia among other chiefs. Leprosy is another disease brought to this country and still prevalent. From all these diseases the native population of these islands has suffered decrease. There is also a large mortality among children and a decline in the birthrate, not because women do not desire offspring. Some Hawaiian women have as many as ten to twenty children, but few grow to maturity. In Kipahulu, Maui, a woman gave birth to ten children, but lost them all in childhood. These country women do not try to do away with their children nor do they frequent houses of prostitution, yet the death rate is large.

The Hawaiians were in old days a strong and hard-working people skilled in crafts and possessed of much learning. In hospitality and kindness they excelled other peoples of the Pacific. Cultivation of the land was their main industry. With their hands alone, assisted by tools made of hard wood from the mountains and by stone adzes, they tilled large fields and raised taro, sweet potatoes, yams, bananas, sugar cane, and 'awa; and bartered (ku'ai 'ia) their product or used it at home. Always the first food of the harvest was offered to the gods. Parents before they died instructed their children, the sons to plant and fish, the daughters to make and dye tapa and weave mats.* The land was fertile, and the principal crop on Kauai, Oahu, and Molokai was wet-land taro cultivated in ponds, artificially constructed patches, along the banks of water courses, or anywhere where the ground was soft and moist. On Maui and Hawaii where there was less wet land, dry-land taro was cultivated. On Lanai and Niihau sweet potatoes were the principal crop. On Kauai, Oahu, and Molokai also are to be seen most of the fishponds built to preserve the fish supply; very few occur on the other islands.

The Hawaiians built houses of various kinds, such as the movable

* *Ka Nupepa Ku'oko'a*, Dec. 7, 1867.

house (*naue*); the house in which secret societies met (*nauwa*); the kind in which two posts were set up to hold the ridgepole (*poulua*); the house for the gods ('*auhau ma'ule*); the house for those who were ill ('*ala-neo*); the house where certain instruction was given (*o'ahualua*); the house for the women during menstruation periods (*pe'a*); the eating house (*mua*); the sleeping house (*moe*); and the houses of worship (heiau and *loulu*). The house of a chief was made lofty with a high-peaked roof, and carefully thatched, first with some coarse material laid flat underneath and then with a covering of fine *pili* grass neatly tied and fastened to give a smooth appearance inside the house. Houses thatched with pandanus, *ti*, or banana leaves were finished with equal care. Heaps of mats completed the furnishing within. The houses of the commoners were of *pili* thatch, sometimes with cane leaves or '*uki* grass underneath, or of pandanus or cane leaves folded over, and were often built only just a little higher than the head. Many varieties of grasses were used to put a handsome finish to the house. A heiau included houses, a *lele* and *kuahu*, or raised platforms or altars for sacrifice, and *pae*, or platforms where images were set up. Chiefs' houses had two, three, and four doors, those of commoners but one or two. The furnishings for the inside of the house were made by the women. There were pillows and sleeping mats of various kinds [according to the material used and the fineness of the plaiting] . . .* For a headman, a firstborn, or a favorite child the sleeping mats were piled high. The women also made the tapa coverings for the sleepers, usually of five layers, the outside sheet called the *kilohana* beautiful in color and design.† They made tapa also for the clothing of men and women, for cloaks and skirts and also for the loin-cloths of the men, which had to be made out of tough material in order to last. Men who were disinclined to follow manly pursuits were taught to be experts in making loincloths and women's skirts and were called "dyers and printers of Ehu." Some women became experts in the making of skirts and in the use of dyes to color them, something like the calicoes of our day. The dyes used might be perfumed to give the garment a pleasant fragrance . . . In old days the daughters were made much of by the parents and grandparents and by the people in general. "Beautiful above are the cliffs of Wailau" (*Hanohano iluna ka pali o Wailau*)was the saying.

All the work outside the house was performed by the men, such as

---

* Mats listed by Kamakau are: *ahuao, ahupawehe, 'aka'akai, alokahi ane'ene'e, 'auli'i, hali'i, Kakahi, Kamaka'o, kika'a, lauli'li'i, makaloa, mu'o, pakea, pu'ao, u-e, wco.*

† Names of tapas used for bed coverings listed by Kamakau are: *aeokahaloa, 'ahapi'i, aho, alauli, holei, ihuanu, kaha, maku'e, moclola, 'o'uholowai, pa'i'ula Pala-'a, puakoali, pulo'u.* Names of tapa used for clothing listed: *'akoa ihuanuanu, ku'au'olena, niholi'ila'i, pa'i'ula, pakahi, pa'upa'u, pi.*

tilling the ground, fishing, cooking in the *imu,* and furnishing whatever the women needed in the house. This was the common rule on Kauai, Oahu, and Molokai, but on Maui and Hawaii the women worked outside as hard as the men, often cooking, tilling the ground, and performing the duties in the house as well. At the time when Kamehameha took over the rule from Hawaii to Oahu it was not uncommon to see the women of Hawaii packing food on their backs, cooking it in the *imu,* and cultivating the land or even going fishing with the men. On Maui the men showed their wives where their patches were and while they went to do other work the women brought the food and firewood from the uplands and cared for the *imu.* This was why the chiefs of Hawaii imposed taxes on men and women alike and got the name of being oppressive to the people, while the chiefs of Oahu and Kauai demanded taxes of the men alone.

Fishing was one of the chief occupations in old days. The fishhooks were made of turtle shell, dog, fish or human bones, prongs of hard wood, and other materials. Fish were caught in deep-sea fishing grounds of a depth of from thirty to forty fathoms, or sometimes of four hundred fathoms . . . Fishermen went in search of such fishing grounds and learned to locate a particular spot and to return to it again and again. They kept its location a secret from others; it was like a food dish to them. Today the knowledge of most of these places is lost. A good fisherman never let down his hook without testing the depth of the water lest the hook be caught in coral and lost. For hook-and-line fishing in shallow waters smaller hooks were used than in deep sea fishing . . . Special hooks were used with *palu,* or soft bait, to catch fish with small mouths. Line fishing was also practiced, that is, floats were used to hold hooks and lines left out over night. Sometimes very large fish were caught in this way. In rod fishing from a bank, bamboo and long slim sticks were used. *Aku* fishing was the only kind in which no bait was used. Net fishing requiring a number of men, canoes, and nets was confined to chiefs and men of high station. It required experts who knew where the schools of fish generally ran. So many fish were caught in this way that even pigs and dogs were fed. The smaller fish were caught by basket fishing . . . Torch fishing was practiced at night. The expert fishermen are most of them dead, and their art is becoming lost to this generation.*

The Hawaiians, both men and women, were expert in the art of preparing *olona* fiber from the bark of *maoli, ma'alua, hopue, mamaki,* and *papakukui.* It required intelligence to do this work properly. The fiber was soaked in water, then laid on a long slim board about four inches

* *Ka Nupepa Ku'oko'a,* Dec. 14, 1867.

wide and eight to nine feet long, and scraped with pieces of turtle shell sharpened for the purpose. This fiber made excellent twine for fishnets and carrying nets. Canoe-making was also an expert art. A canoe ka-huna must first own adzes, and these were not of iron but of stone. The best stone for the purpose was the *hokele* rock, the blue lava (*'ala' makahinu*), and the *pahoa,* and the adzes were fashioned at the crater of Pele where the *hokele* rock was to be found; at Kaluako'i on Molokai; and at other places. The finishing was done with an adze called *pupu'ole,* holes were drilled with a shell called *makoloa,* and smaller holes for sewing the panks together with a *makilihoahoa* shell; another instrument for boring holes was fashioned from a dog's bone. To see the tools these people used you would wonder how, with such crude implements, they could fashion a canoe. I have been told by Ka-uhi and Kahi-poleau who sailed on the war canoe of Pele-io-holani that his double war canoe, named Kaneaiai, and said to have been made of planks sewed together, could hold 160 men. Canoes of various kinds were used to travel from island to island for war expeditions, double (*kaulua*) and single (*kau-kahi*) canoes, the *peleleu,* and the *hoapipi.* We today could not make some of these things. Wooden food containers, finger bowls and spit-toons, made out of *kou, kamani,* and *milo* woods so highly polished that one could see one's image reflected in them and supplemented by gourd and coconut-shell dishes, adorned the feasts of a chief and were an indi-cation of his wealth . . .

The composing of meles was a skilled art in old days in which some people became famous. They composed chants about the sky, space, the ocean, the earth, sun, moon, stars, and all things. Many had secret mean-ings woven into them. They were composed of symbolic phrases (*loina*) and hidden meanings (*kaona*). There were many kinds of chant [ac-cording to their subject and purpose and the occasion for which they were composed]. There were chants in honor of ancestors (*mele ku-puna*), in praise of a land (*mele 'aina*), in praise of chiefs (*mele ali'i*), in praise of favorite children (*mele hi'ilani*), chants of gratitude (*mele mahalo*), chants of affection (*mele aloha*), chants of reviling (*kuamu-amu*), prayer chants (*mele pule*), dirges (*kanikau*), chants to put a person to sleep (*mele hiamoe*), or to awaken one (*mele ho'ala*), chants asking a favor (*mele noi*), chants refusing the request (*mele 'au'a*), chants calling to be admitted (*mele kahea*), chants given as a gift (*mele haawi*), chants of boasting (*mele ho'oki'eki'e*), prophetic chants (*mele wanana*), chants foretelling future events (*mele kilokilo*), chants of criticism (*mele nemanema*).* Some of these chants are of great value,

---

* Other forms of mele are the mele *ho'oipoipo* or love song, the mele *inoa* or name song, the mele *ma'i,* or song in honor of thhe generative organs.

some are worthless. Chants uttered in monotone (*olioli*) are prayer chants, but they are not all uttered alike. The tone is softened (*aheahe*) in places and forced from the throat (*'i'i ikaika*). Some are uttered with a sonorous (*nonolo*) sound, a gurgling (*'ola'ola'*), the chanter breathing all the while gently with a gentle rise and fall of the chest. Each word must be well uttered by the tongue with the mouth open and the teeth separate, and the mouth opened and closed without tightening the neck muscles. The ancients were excellent chanters.

In the recitation of a genealogy (*ko'ihonua*) the voice took a tone almost on one note (*kamakua*), and each word was enunciated distinctly. There was a vibration (*kuolo*) in the chanting together with a guttural sound (*kaohi*) in the throat and a gurgling (*alala*) in the voice box. The voice was to be brought out with strength (*haanou*) and so held in control (*kohi*) that every word was clear. The genealogical chant recited the ancestry of chiefs, their rank and lineage, from a period long before the peopling of Hawaii. The Ku-ali'i genealogical chant contains the Kumuuli and the Kumulipo; in that of Pele-io-holani the history of Ololo begins with ancestry of Haloa; with the time of Ka-mahana begins the Pali-ku and the line of chiefs from Puna-i-mua. It is because of the skill of these ancient people in weaving the story into their chants that their names have became a permanent possession to this day. In the chant of Ku-ali'i foreigners are mentioned and the land of Kahiki, with a description of their speech and appearance.

The composers of genealogical chants such as the *ko'ihonua, ha'iku-puna,* and *kamakua,* were men learned in the art who knew the family lines and were skilled in oratory and state-craft. Such chants were composed under tabu. Chants of prophecy and prayer were composed under the inspiration of a spirit. Chants in praise of a name, a favorite child, chants of gratitude, dirges, and many others might be composed by any person and completed in a short time. Each word had to be studied for its meaning, whether lucky or unlucky, and for its effect [in this particular connection], whether it suggested good or bad luck, a stingy or a kind person, a grumbler or a brave one. If a group worked together to compose a chant the leader would ask each composer to give a line; if there were eighty composers the chant would contain eighty lines, and these would be combined into a single composition. Two, three, or more composers could work on a single chant. The chants were skillfully composed and very pleasing and well fitted to the characteristics of the person for whom each was composed. Generally such chants were composed for chiefs, or by parents for their own children, or for favorite children. Most of them were good but some were licentious in character. The chant might be delightful on the surface, but might have a hidden meaning suggesting stinginess, a refusal to give, or anything else. Most [hearers] would not catch this meaning and would see only the pleasing picture.*

Another ancient art was that of the diviners who revealed hidden things about the land, called "Pointers-out-of-sandhills" (*Kuhikuhi pu'uone*) and "Class of changes on the earth" (*Papahulihonua*). They were able to find things hidden away from the eyes of men; they could locate water in places where water had not been found. They knew the land boundaries from Hawaii to Kauai, the running of the affairs of government, how to handle people, the location and building of houses, and whether one would live or die; they resembled the seers (*kaula*), but there were few such persons in old days and there are none today. Statesmen and orators too have passed away. The genealogists (*po'e ku'auhau*) were important people in old days. They kept the genealogical histories not only of chiefs but of kahunas, seers, land experts, diviners, and the ancestry of commoners and slaves. If a man lacked a professional genealogist then anyone who was acquainted with the art recited his ancestry until a kahuna was found to fill the position. An expert genealogist was a favorite with a chief. He was like a premier in a foreign country who watched for trouble that might come to his ruler from without, and guarded him against those who spoke disparagingly of his rank and called him slave (*kauwa*). So 'Umi was called *keiki lepo popolo* by Hakau and Pinea, Liloa's other children. That is why genealogies became tabu to commoners and the children of commoners, and why there were few who understood the art; but some skilled genealogists survived to the time of Kamehameha and even down to the arrival of the missionaries. Today there are no more such.

The Hawaiians had exercises to build up the body. Disc-rolling (*'ulu maika*) was considered one of the best of such exercises, and grounds for the sports were laid out from Hawaii to Kauai.† The player sweated freely, he had to run fast, and limbs became strengthened. He must start on a run and follow the rolling stone; sometimes he was required to pick it up on the run. In this way speed was developed, and from these disc-rolling contests professional runners were picked. Sledding (*he'e holua*) was another favorite sport, carried on sometimes over a cliffside, sometimes on the slope of a hill over a course either laid out on the ground or artificially built up, like that at Kaneaka at Keauhou in North Kona, Hawaii. This was a vigorous sport in which beginners suffered, but those who were accustomed to it guided the board with legs and arms and could keep their balance and breathe lightly as they sped faster than a racehorse or a railroad train. The runners were made of hard wood like

* *Ka Nupepa Ku'oko'a*, Dec. 21, 1867.
† See 20 for a comparative study of the game *maika* throughout the Pacific area.

the *koai'e, uhiuhi,* or *mamane,* about two and a half fathoms long and a half inch thick, tapering upward, and some four inches high. They were set in pairs six inches apart and fastened together neatly and firmly with cord of coconut fiber. In front they turned straight up and then pointed outward like the beak of a duck. The top where the person lay was woven over with fine matwork leaving a space between it and the runners. The runners were made slippery with *kukui*-nut oil or some other vegetable oil. The course was covered with stalks of *pili* grass stripped of the blade and laid evenly. Midday was the favorite time for the sport when the heat of the sun made the grass slippery and the sled could then attain terrific speed.

Other sports of strength were common. For skill in warfare, throwing the javelin (*lono-makaihe*), sham battles (*pahukala*), stone throwing (*ma'a*), and archery (*panapua*) were practiced by those who wished to become warriors. Such exercises strengthened the body and made men able in battle. The art of attack was taught (*ho'oukakaua*) in all its forms, trench digging (*kaua eli lua*), the ambuscade (*kaua po'ipo*), lying in ambush (*moemoe*), sudden attack (*powa*), defiance (*ho'ohaehae*), spying (*ho'ohalua*) and all such practices of warfare. Warriors also became proficient in missile-throwing such as *ku'ailua,* the *Ka'ala'au,* the *'ikoi.* They knew the different parts of the body, which were the vital parts and which were easiest to disable. But there was one bad thing about such training; it not only developed strength, but taught men to become highwaymen and live on the weak. Some took the training in order to become warriors, others to defend themselves against attack, but still others in order to make a living by preying upon the weak.

Nauwa houses were those in which ancestry was taught, both on the father's and on the mother's side, the land where one was born, and the signs by which one could tell the birthplace of one's ancestors. Such houses were first set up on Oahu and called "proclamation in chorus" (*nauwa*) and "a telling of ancestors" (*he ha'i kupuna*); and the study was taken up by chiefs and persons of good standing. Those who sought admission to the house had to answer questions as to their ancestors, where these ancestors came from, and their own place of birth. The chiefs feared these houses because of the blood of the commoners mixed with their own, as in the case of 'Umi, Keawe, Mahi, and I all of whom had children by commoners. Ke-ku'i-apo-iwa, the mother of Ke-opu-o-lani, objected to them saying that Hawaii had no chiefs of pure blood and "Keawe was a calabash cover." On Oahu these houses flourished, but by the time Oahu was taken over by Hawaii most of those who knew the genealogies had died. The genealogy of Mano-ka-lani-po' and Kapo-lei-a-ka-uila was united by the genealogists of Hawaii to one relating to Ka-haku-maka-liua because he had lived with Akahi-'ili-kapu, daughter of 'Umi, and from him came Ke-aka-mahana and Keakea-lani, tabu chiefs of Hawaii; but they left out Ka-haku-mai'a, the tabu wife of Ka-haku-maka-liua, to whom was born Kama-kupua from whom sprang Ka-welo-mahamaha-i'a, Ka-welo-makua-lua, and Ka-'awihi-o-ka-lani and from him again Keawe-'ai-kanaka. They took up the Oahu genealogy at Ka-ua-kahi-kua'ana-ua-kama-a-Ipu-wai-a-hue-lani and Ka-'ihi-kapu-o-ku-ihewa, and because she lived with Iwi-kau-i-ka-ua-a-Makau-ali'i, the genealogical history of Ka-ku'ihewa was connected with that of Kua-loa-ka-la'i-lani and with the ancestral line of Ke-opu-o-lani, and was united with Kane-hoa-lani for the benefit of the Hawaii line of chiefs, making it fit with that of Ka-lani-kaulele-ia-iwi-nui-a-Keakea-lani and Kane-i-ka-ua-iwi-lani.*

Most of the native arts known to the people of Hawaii are now lost. The people were kindhearted, affectionate, and hospitable, quick to learn and to carry out what was taught them. They learned to dress and to behave properly more quickly than other island peoples. The Borabora and Moa people came in contact with foreigners earlier than our people. For sixty years they had been taught the word of God, but when some of them who were working as sailors came ashore at Lahaina they wore no hats, not because they had none, but because they did not care to wear them but wrapped a piece of cloth around the head. The Rev. J. Kekela wrote: "We have reached Tahiti where our ship is being repaired, and are to remain here for some four weeks. We have attended church on the Sabbath. The Queen Pomare I saw going to church in her undergarment without hat or shoes and her husband with a coat, no hat but a cloth about his head, no shoes and a short skirt about the lower part of his body. When I entered church the preacher had on a coat without shirt or trousers but with a short skirt, and when I came out after service I saw that he had only a cloth about his head. Then again, the people take no interest in welcoming strangers, but the Hawaiians living here saw us at once and came to welcome us with demonstrations of affection, and have helped us in every way, giving us food of all kinds and bringing us pigs and fowl as we do to strangers in Hawaii. Foreigners often observe how kindhearted the Hawaiians are. . . ." Before the coming of the missionaries some of our people had gone to foreign lands and to Tahiti and learned to read and write and to speak English. Such women as 'Umi-o-ka-lani and Ponunu came home with a knowledge of writing. Some of our boys learned English in America. Here in Hawaii some chiefs had been taught English and could speak and read it. Ke-aka-kilohi, the son of Ka-lolo-ahi-lani and Ke'e-au-moku, was one; others were Ka-hekili

* *Ka Nupepa Ku'oko'a*, Dec. 28, 1867.

Ke'e-au-moku, Ka-lua-i-Kona-hale Kua-kini, and Ka-umu-ali'i, the ruling chief of Kauai and his son Ka-mahole-lani. Of Ke-aka-kilohi who died in 1812 it is said that he was a learned chief with a good command of language, knew several secret languages, and could speak in riddles so that few could understand him.

Many foreigners of different races, the red, the black, the white, came in early days to Hawaii. Some were educated and some ignorant. Some came as merchants and traders, others as laborers, and some escaped from ships where they were serving as sailors. Some were received hospitably by the Hawaiians, taken under the care of chiefs, became favorites, and bequeathed to Hawaii their posterity. Some became advisers to the rulers of the country and worked for its good; others tried to enrich themselves, were proud, and trod the Hawaiians under their feet. The greater number came from the United States of America. They associated with Ka-hekili, Ka-lani-ku-pule, Ka-umu-ali'i, and Kamehameha before the coming of the Puritan missionaries to Hawaii and had shown so much goodwill that Ka-umu-ali'i sent his son, George Hume-hume, to America to be educated. Henry 'Opu-kaha-'ia, William Ka-nui, Thomas Hopu, William Ka-moho-'ula, Pa'ula-li'ili'i, Honoli'i, Ka-lima-hauna, 'Ukali-moa, Palu, and Ka-la'au-lana, all were educated in America without paying for their education. For this and for the gift of Christianity to this people our country is indebted to America. It has shown itself a kindhearted country and a father to our government, before the time education was here and ever since we have become a Christian people. Moreover America has never tried to take over Hawaii to become a part of her territory, although thousands of Hawaiians have gone away to foreign lands and remained there.*

* *Ka Nupepa Ku'oko'a*, Jan. 4, 1868.

CHAPTER XX

Rule and Death of Liholiho

The coming of the Puritan missionaries was the important event during the reign of Liholiho. They had not come without an urgent call to this beloved land. A young Hawaiian named Henry 'Opu-kaha-'ia had gone to live in New England in the United States and had been wel-comed freely and educated there. He believed that Christianity would benefit his people, who were still under the influence of false gods. He traveled about to the cities in the eastern states urging the sending of preachers to preach the word of God to his people. Although the young man died before this was accomplished, the seed he sowed bore fruit, the missionary society gave its consent, and such missionaries were sent out as Hiram Bingham, Asa Thurston, Mr. Whitney and Mr. Ruggles as teachers, Mr. Daniel Chamberlain as a farmer, and Abraham [Blatch-ley],* all with their wives. The Hawaiian boys who came back with the missionaries, that is, George Humehume, Thomas Hopu, William Ka-nui, Honoli'i, and Pa'ula-li'ili'i, were able to reassure the Hawaiian people as to the friendliness of the relations between America and Ha-waii and to serve as guides to the missionaries upon their arrival.†

It was on March 30, 1820, after the battle of Kuamo'o, that the boat anchored at Kawaihae on Hawaii, and the news was conveyed to those on board that Kamehameha was dead, and that Liholiho, the new king, had abolished the tabus and was governing the country in a new way. The missionaries rejoiced, believing that God had blessed their coming, and they sang the hymn,"Wake, isles of the South! Your redemption is near . . . "

Since the king and chiefs were at Kailua, the ship sailed thither, and the captain went to announce their coming. Mr. Hunnewell was the ship's mate. Some of the chiefs looked upon the arrival with favor, others were doubtful, and the king himself was uncertain because his friend John Rives, called "Old woman" (Luahine) by the natives, told him that it was the religion of France which was the true religion. A council was held that lasted several days. John Young said, "These kahunas wor-ship the same God as those of our country of whom Vancouver said to

---

* Kamakau was in error. Dr. Blatchley came with the second party of mission-aries.

†Ka Nupepa Ku'oko'a, Jan. 4, 1868.

Kamehameha, 'When I go back to Great Britain let me ask King George to send you kahunas.' Let the chiefs try them out by permitting them to remain in Hawaii for a year; then, if you discover that they are not doing right, let the chiefs send them away." The chiefs took the advice of this favorite foreigner of Kamehameha. They were afraid of the white men who had already come into the country, not the runaway sailors who worked under the chiefs, but those who were doing things injurious to the welfare of the people. They agreed that the missionaries might remain on Hawaii for a year without interference with their worship or teaching, and if their work was good they might remain permanently.

White men and their children by native women had often been seen on Hawaii, but when the missionaries, men and women, came ashore at Kamakahonu and walked along the beach, the people came in crowds, men, women, and children, and exclaimed over the pretty faces of the white women, their deep-set eyes, their bonnets that jutted forward, and their long necks which won for them the name of "Long neck" (*'A'i-oeoe*). Crowds gathered, and one and another exclaimed, "How white the women are!" "What bright-colored eyes!" "What strange hats, not at all like the tall hats of the men!" "What long necks! but pleasing to look at!" "What pinched-in bodies! What tight clothing above and wide below!" John Rives advanced boldly and said, "The king does not want you here. You can stay a little while, but then you must go." The party went along the beach of One'o to visit Ke-opu-o-lani, mother of the king and the one who had abolished the tabu and introduced free eating. It must have been that the Holy Spirit inspired them to go thither, for it was she who was the mother of Christian Hawaii. They stood outside the fence of her yard and Thomas Hopu called out, "Is the Chiefess's place tabu?" The missionaries were received and exchanged greetings with Ke-opu-o-lani, Hopu acting as interpreter. He said, "These white people are kahunas of the most high God who have come to tell us of the One who made heaven and earth," and added, "Hereafter will come the great day (*la*) when all will be judged before God." The chiefs and people thought, "Is the sun (*la*) going to grow bigger?" [mistaking the word "day" for the "sun" shining above], and they said among themselves, "This traveler is telling tall tales!" and called him a romancer (*ma'oi*).

Mr. Thurston and his wife remained at Kailua, the others went on to [Oahu and] Kauai. From Hawaii to Kauai the chiefs and people received them as friends. No people could have treated them more kindly. No one begrudged their coming, grumbled, spoke unkindly of them, or raised any trouble, but all dwelt with them in peace. It was the other foreigners, local traders and settlers from foreign lands, who tried to

stir up trouble for them.* They advised the chiefs to send the missionaries away, and spread the rumor that the cellars which they dug under
their houses were to store powder in so that some day they might take
over the government. But the chiefs did not believe this; they were a refuge (*pu'uhonua*) to the missionaries and defended them in trouble. The
Hawaiian people received them as parents their firstborn children. Within
three to five years many of the people had turned to God. They went to
the missionaries in procession with gifts in their hands, saying, "What
must we do in order that God may save us?" "You must repent of your
sins, then Jesus Christ will save you." Then the people, men, women, and
children, went away to mountains and valleys, beside the streams, on the
hills, in caves, to reedy places, and to other quiet solitudes, and there
prayed with humility in their hearts. There was no place from Hawaii to
Kauai where the people did not turn and repent. The teachers advised
them, "Strive to enter in at the strait gate," and when the people heard
how it was only by fortitude that one might enter the kingdom of God,
many came from the outlying districts, worked at hard labor, and confessed their sins. They labored hard and faithfully for the teachers without asking pay because of their desire to enter the kingdom of God. The
teachers said, "Close to your sleeping houses erect houses in which to
pray for repentance," and the people in the country built houses to which
the women and girls went to repent of their sins, and the fathers and
sons the same. Two, three, and more years were required before a person
could be allowed to join the church . . .

Education made rapid progress. Immediately after his arrival Mr.
Bingham gathered some of the young people into a school. Kaomi Moe,
Kapi'o Moe, Ka-uhi-kua, Wahine-ali'i, Hulu-moi, Oliver 'Alapa, and
Maiao were some of the pupils. At the end of a year he held an exhibition at which great progress was shown. Mr. and Mrs. Thurston and
many of the other missionaries taught pupils; another foreigner taught
the chiefs at Kailua. Liholiho sent his wives and the young chiefs to
school. In April or May, 1821, the king and the chiefs gathered in Honolulu and selected teachers to assist Mr. Bingham. Kahuhu, John 'I'i,
Ha'alilio, Prince Kau-i-ke-aouli, were among those who learned English.
In April, 1823, there arrived assistants to the first missionaries, and a
start was at once made upon adapting Hawaiian speech sounds to the
English alphabet . . . As soon as the chiefs saw what a good thing it was
to know how to read and write, each chief took teachers into his home to
teach the chiefs of his household. Ka-'ahu-manu took Naomi Moe to her
home, and when all her household had learned to read and write, she
sent some of them to other islands to teach, and all the other chiefs sent

* *Ka Nupepa Ku'oko'a,* Jan. 11, 1868.

teachers to their lands in other districts to teach the people to read and write. Before the end of the year the old people over eighty and ninety years old were reading the Bible. Ke-kupu-ohi, Ka-'ele-o-Waipi'o, Ka-makau, and their families all learned to read and write; the household of Hoa-pili used to read the Bible on the Sabbath day. This was why education spread so rapidly. When the missionaries began to settle in the outer districts they found that the people already knew how to read.*

Reading aloud in unison was the method used. The missionaries were all eager in their work, and the pupils absorbed their spirit. The quickest pupils were advanced, and this made the pupils ambitious to be at the head. The teachers made great strides in their methods of teaching, not only in reading but also in writing. All followed the same method and drilled good behavior into the pupils. They were taught to bow to men and boys when they met and to bend the knee slightly as they bowed to women and young ladies. These things were impressed upon the minds of all. The old Hawaiian ways of salutation were touching noses, bowing the head, greeting with the mouth, weeping, rolling on the ground, or kneeling as a sign of submission. These were the forms taught by early Hawaiian parents. There were other forms required in the households of chiefs, but the country people expresssed their affection in these ways. Even when in modern times the old ways have been discountenanced the country people still keep up the ways of their ancestors.

The translation of the Bible was a great help in educating the people. It was ten years or more before even portions of the Bible were translated, but after that small portions put into Hawaiian, for instance Matthew, chapters 5 to 7, the first part of Luke, and the first part of the Psalms. The books of Matthew, Mark, and John, as well as other portions translated by the missionaries, Mr. Loomis had printed in America. Thus portions of the Bible were given to the Hawaiians. The chiefesses became more proficient in writing than others because they wrote all the Scripture verses translated by the teachers and used as texts for sermons and in other connections.

When Liholiho became king he gathered about him the young chiefs of every rank and the children also of warriors and of many of the commoners and made them members of his household as friends (*aikane*), favorites (*punahele*), and foster children (*ho'okama*), just as the old chiefs had done before him. The kingly crown in those days was represented by the circle of chiefs and commoners who surrounded the king. These united the people to their ruler by a bond that could not be severed in the days of Liholiho and his mother Ke-opu-o-lani, to whom the government had come down in legitimate succession and without those civil

* *Ka Nupepa Ku'oko'a*, Jan. 18, 1868.

wars which had been fought by other ruling chiefs to obtain control of the government.

One thing conspicuous during Liholiho's time was the extravagant use of liquor among chiefs and commoners; they almost bathed in it. The sale of *okolehao* and *'uwi'uwi* became a means of wealth, and they were peddled through the outer districts. Hula dancing, debauchery, and licentious indulgence became common. Some people refused to touch liquor because they did not like the taste, but the majority fell into the gutter of filth. Pa'ula-li'ili'i and other young men who had come back with the missionaries and had even taught the word of God took to drinking liquor when they saw the chiefs using it.

During the first year of his rule Liholiho sailed to Lahaina on Maui, then to Hilo, and back to Kona. It was decided at this time that the king should go to Oahu to live where Boki, governor of Oahu, and his wife Ka-lili-kauoha, Kahala-i'a and his wife Liliha, Ka-lola-ehu-kaikai and his family, Kaka'e and his family, were already making their homes. Boki took Liliha, his nephew's wife, to be his wife. The king sailed with all his household and stayed for some months at Wailuku on the way. Ka-lani-moku had preceded him because his wife Likelike was about to have a child, and Ka-hekili Ke'e-au-moku [had also preceded the King] because his wife Ke-kua-iaea was also near her confinement. At the birth of Likelike's child Lani-hau, in Honolulu, Boki and Ka-lani-moku set off so many guns that both mother and child died of the shock, so it was said. Ke-kua-iaea was taken to Kukaniloko to have her child, but it was finally born at Halemomi in Waialua; the mother later died on Kauai. On the king's arrival a great reception was given him at which the chief attraction was dancing of which the young king, then almost twenty-four, was very fond. A chiefess named Ke-ana had prepared a special performance of the stick hula (*hula ka-la'au*) in which several hundred took part. The hulas which Hawaiian chiefs danced were the *'olapa, pahu, kuolo, alala', pihi, ki'i, pa'iumauma,* and innumerable others. Liholiho established his household, which included his five wives Ka-mamalu, Ke-ka-ulu-ohi, Ka-lani-pauahi, Ke-kau-'onohi, and Kina'u; his mother Ke-opu-o-lani; his chief *kahu* Ka-'ahu-manu and Ka-lani-moku; the members of the privy council (*kuhina ali'i*) including Ka-hekili Ke'e-au-moku and his wife Ke-kua-iaea, and after her death Ka-ma'i-ku'i, who later became the wife of Dr. Rooke, Ulu-maheihei Hoa-pili and his wife Ke-opu-o-lani, Na-ihe and his wife Ka-pi'o-lani, Kua-kini and his wife Keoua; Ka-iki-o-'ewa and his wife Keawe-a-mahi; Koa-kanu and his wife Lo'eau, Ka-welo-o-ka-lani and his wife Pele-uli, Kamehameha Kau-'oko'a and his wife Kili-wehi, Boki and his wife Liliha, Kai-ko and his wife Ha-'aheo, Ka-lani-moku and his wife Likelike and after her death Akahi, daughter of Pau-elua, Kaheihei-malie and her husband Ka-nuha, Kekua-i-pi'ia and her husband La'a-nui; together with Ka-pu-likoliko, Ka-haku-ha'akoi, Ke-kikipa'a, Kalilikauoha, Ka-lola, Ke-kupu-ohi, and other chiefs of higher or lower rank, and warriors, all of whom added to the glory of his reign.*

A number of foreigners were living in Honolulu at the time of Liholiho's establishment there. Some were men of high standing, some were captains of ships, some were traders who owned stores. Among them were Jones Aluli, Mr. Parker (Mikapako), Lanai, Newalo, Captain Apiki, William Lihi'ula, Captain David 'Opealoa, Captain John Meek, Captain Meek,† and Captain Winship [Jonathan or Nathan]. There were also some foreigners who were included as native residents, like George Holmes [son of Mr. Oliver Holmes and a Hawaiian woman], Mr. Alika, Manini (Don Francisco Paula y Marin), Captain William Nuku'iole, and a great many other foreigners who lived in the city and in the country districts. Some of these were good men, but others led the king to drink and to get the country into debt. Several of them became his friends and boon companions. They enticed him to drink liquor, and soon all the chiefs and chiefesses had taken to drinking, and not one of them heeded the word of God as taught by the missionaries. The missionaries themselves became obnoxious to the other foreigners because they taught that drinking was bad for the liver and the cause of sin, that dissolute living was wrong, and the taking of plural wives a sin. One foreigner attempted to thrash Mr. Bingham, cursing and swearing at him and using vile language. No doubt when these men saw the missionaries teaching the people the word of God and advising them to do right and to live upright lives they felt that there would be no more good times for them; they therefore strove to lead Liholiho to drink more heavily, and when he was drunk they would run him into debt and sell him, not small lengths, but many bolts of cloth, and charge the goods to his name. The king also went into debt buying ships such as the *Ha'aheo, Ka-'ainoa-nui, Kuko-puka*, and several schooners and brigs like the *Ka-umu-ali'i, Ka-mahole-lani*, and *Mikapako* (Mister Parker). The chiefs also bought cloth, most of which was consumed by rot and worms, and the rest by fire. They purchased ships and turned their debts in to the king, and he

* *Ka Nupepa Ku'oko'a*, Jan. 25, 1868.

† For John Meek's obituary see 22. He was a native of Marblehead, Massachusetts, and first came to Hawaii as officer on a sailing ship engaged in the Northwest trade. In 1812 he was master of a ship touching at the port of Honolulu. The last fifty years of his life he was a resident of Honolulu and died January 29, 1875. He was "noted for his probity of character and genial disposition," was a friend and adviser of chiefs, and introduced improved breeds of cattle and horses to Hawaii. John Jacob Astor is said to have thought so highly of him as to build a ship especially for his command.

to the government. The king's favorites helped to increase the debt. They were outspoken in saying, "Let us run up the debt and make the chiefs and commoners work; they are no friends of ours, so let us get what we can while our lord is alive." The debts were met by the sale of sandalwood. The chiefs, old and young, went into the mountains with their retainers, accompanied by the king and his officials, to take charge of the cutting, and some of the commoners cut while others carried the wood to the ships at the various landings; none was allowed to remain behind. Many of them suffered for food; because of the green herbs they were obliged to eat they were called "Excreters-of-green-herbs" (*Hilalele*), and many died and were buried there. The land was denuded of sandalwood by this means.

The king made a trip around the island accompanied by his five wives, by Ke-opu-o-lani, Ka-'ahu-manu, and several chiefs and favorites, some sailing by canoe, and some going horseback. They went by way of Ko'olau and stayed at Waialua to enjoy the fat mullet of Uko'a and to catch *aholehole* fish. The king wanted to see Kukaniloko, but, prevented by a pest of army worms, all came back by Ka'ena point to Wai'anae for a stay, and then to Honolulu. He then proposed a trip to Kauai. The chiefs advised his protecting himself with a large following, but Ke-opu-o-lani said, "Do not be afraid and do not take men with you, for you will find men on Kauai," and he accordingly set sail with his wives and few friends only. On Kauai he was welcomed with great affection by Ka-umu-ali'i and with the firing of guns and ringing of bells at the Hipo fort, and loud acclamations from the people to show their respect for the royal descendant of Ke-kaulike. "Here comes the son of our lord; he alone has the right to gouge out our eyes!" was the phrase often heard. Ka-umu-ali'i stepped down from his place as ruler to act as steward for the king, preparing his food and attending to his wants in every way. Fire sticks were made ready awaiting the signal for starting the ovens in which to cook the pigs, dogs, fowl, fish, and all the things for the feast; from Makaweli to Waimea fires were started simultaneously with the speed of lightning.

The arrival took place July 22, 1821, and on July 24 a council was held at the king's house at Papa'ena'ena at which Liholiho declared that "in accordance with the words of Kamehameha I off Mamala, Oahu, Ka-umu-ali'i shall be the ruling chief of Kauai and occupy the place inherited from his ancestors, only the name of king to belong to Liholiho, the flesh and bones to be Ka-umu-ali'i's." Ka-umu-ali'i said, "Let the king take some of the lands and give them to his wives." "No, you shall retain your lands." "Will not your guardians be dissatisfied with this?" "Kamehameha I left no command in regard to the land, merely that I should be ruler." And so the council ended. Liholiho gave his fifth wife, Ke-ka-ulu-ohi, to his friend Ka-na'ina in order that none of his guardians and chiefs might question his action, since when a ruler gives away anything it must please his chiefs, and took Ka-umu-ali'i's wife Ke-kai-ha'a-kulou as one of his wives to be counted with the others. Ka-'ahu-manu was not pleased at this, feeling it to be showing disrespect to her nieces, but upon tracing her ancestry Ke-kai-ha'a-kulou was found to be of the lineage of the chiefs of Maui from Hawea, who was related to Ka-'ahu-manu; her father Kai-awa of the line of chiefs of Kauai was found to be connected with Kane-i-kahei-lani and with Kawelo son of Mahuna-ali'i, ancestor of Ka-'ahu-manu.

Many of the chiefs, seeing what a royal reception Ka-umu-ali'i had given Liholiho, sailed to visit Kauai. Among them Ke-opu-o-lani and Hoa-pili paid a visit to obtain timber for their ship *Ho'oikaika*, and Ka-hekili Ke'e-au-moku, his wife, and Ka-'ahu-manu with her household accompanied them. Ka-umu-ali'i received them all, feasted them royally, and gave them presents of clothing and whatever else they wanted. He erected houses for Ka-'ahu-manu at Papa'ena'ena. She wished while on Kauai to go in search of Nihoa, a land mentioned in the old chants although unknown to the people of her generation. She knew the mele composed by Kawelo-a-Mahuna-ali'i:

Ea mai ana ke ao ua o Kona,	The rain cloud of Kona rises.
Ea mai ana ma Nihoa	It rises over Nihoa
Ma ka mole mai o Lehua,	Beyond the base of Lehua.
Ua iho la pulu ke kahawai.	It pours down and floods the streams.

And from the mele of Hi'iaka:

Ea mai ana ma Nihoa	It rises over Nihoa
Ma ka mole mai o Lehua,	Beyond the base of Lehua,

and some other old chants in which foreign lands are mentioned. So she said to Ka-umu-ali'i, "My son, let us go in search of Nihoa." He consented, and, with William Sumner as captain and pilot, Nihoa* was found in 1822 and annexed to Hawaii.†

Upon the return of the chiefs to Oahu, Ka-'ahu-manu urged Ka-umu-ali'i to accompany them, and they set sail with Ka-'ahu-manu's household and all the chiefs of Kauai. They stopped at Waialua to see to the weighing of the sandalwood, where Ka-'ahu-manu left the expert mat weavers she had brought from Niihau. After a few days they came on to Honolulu. There Ka-'ahu-manu took Ka-umu-ali'i as her husband

---

* For Nihoa see 12 and 24.
† *Ka Nupepa Ku'oko'a*, Feb. 1, 1868.

with the consent of her brothers and sisters, but with some doubt on Ka-umu-ali'i's part until he saw that the king wished it, and he was not expected to return to Kauai. Ka-umu-ali'i was a handsome man, light in complexion and with a nose and general features like a white man's. He was rather slight in build, but he had a good carriage and dressed well. He was gentle in temper, spoke English well, was kind and simple in his ways. It would be well for the nation if there were more chiefs like him.

After this marriage the chief wished to see the other islands, and Ka-'ahu-manu was only too willing show off her new husband on Molokai, Maui, and Hawaii. One of the chiefs from Kauai who accompanied them was Ni'au, husband of Na-mahana, a noted chanter and dancer much admired by the chiefs of Hawaiii. They were called home in February, 1823, by the illness of Ka-'ahu-manu's brother, Ka-hekili Ke'e-au-moku. He was treated by foreign physicians but died March 23 at Pakaka in Honolulu. On the night that he died Kua-kini arrived from Hawaii, lay off shore with his ship, and secretly took away the body to Hawaii leaving Mr. Bingham to conduct the funeral services over an empty coffin. The chiefs did not at this time take the missionaries seriously and some of them said, "Let us see whether the foreign god has power to tell them that the coffin is empty." How ignorant are the ungodly who say there is no God! The chiefs met and appointed Ulu-meheihei governor of Maui as well as of Hawaii to fill the vacancy caused by the death of Ke'e-au-moku.

On April 27, 1823, arrived the first reinforcement to the American mission to Hawaii, including Rev. William Richards, Rev. Charles Stewart, Rev. A. Bishop, Mr. Levi Chamberlain, and Mr. Loomis, a printer.* Ke-opu-o-lani asked for two teachers to go with her to Maui and she took Mr. Stewart and Mr. Richards. She was one of the few chiefesses who showed true faith in God at this time. She had prayers offered before meals and in the morning and evening. She had living with her some Tahitian members of the English church in Tahiti, among them Ka-'au'a-moku, a single woman, and Tau'a'kane and Tau'a'-wahine who had come with Mr. Ellis from Tahiti. These religious Tahitians taught her the word of God and the road to heaven and became her helpers; Tau'a' preached to the chiefs of her household, and all instructed her in letters and music until she was able to read.

The king on his return from Kauai indulged in all kinds of wasteful dissipation, drinking and gambling, spending money continually, and going after women. Liquor flowed like water in the court and became common in all parts of the country. Hula dancing was taught all over the islands during Liholiho's reign. The queens followed the king's

---

* Kamakau is slightly in error here. Mr. Loomis came in 1820 with the first mission group.

example in vice. Rum drinking and loose living led to jealousy and murder; the king ordered that any chief or favorite who was caught with one of his wives should be killed, but the king's *kahu* saved them because of their relatives of the older generation. Ha'alo'u alone had his head cut off by Koli'i and Kahala-i'a, for adultery with the queens, while he was sleeping with his wife, Sarah Hiwa-uli, who later became John 'I'i's wife. Although a heavy drinker Liholiho was never seen under the influence of liquor. He was kind and gentle to the poor; he took orphans and children of the poor under his care; he treated the missionaries kindly; he saw to it that his younger brothers were educated; he could read and write; but when it came to expressing faith in God, he paid no attention to it. While living at Pu'uloa, Oahu with his wives he received a visit from Mr. Bingham who said, "I love you very much. You are but a young king, therefore I want you to stop drinking and loose living and become a good king, confess your sins to God, pray to him, and your kingdom will be blessed and your soul will be at peace with God in heaven." The king replied, "Give me five years more, and I will become a good man!" In the third year of his living as king in Honolulu Liholiho gave a great feast in honor of his five queens, with chiefs to hold up their trains and carry *kahili* to add to the luster of the occasion. Ka-lani-pauahi in her desire to surpass the rest threw her fine clothes to the flames, which never to my knowledge have refused wealth surrendered to them.*†

In September the king was summoned to Maui where the queen mother, Ke-opu-lani, lay dying. At her death, September 16, 1823, at Kaluaokiha in Lahaina, many persons from the back country came and offered themselves as her death companions (*moepu'u*), but Hoa-pili refused them all, saying, "It was the command of your lord that there should be no death companion, no wild mourning, because she had given herself to God." There was indeed mourning and wailing but no wild demonstration, although Ka-lani-moku allowed liquor to flow like water. Blessed was Ke-opu-o-lani to put her faith in God and save so many innocent persons from death, those who owed nothing to her and had not benefited by her wealth, but by old custom offered themselves to die with her.

While on Maui Liholiho addressed a gathering of chiefs and commoners at Kaluaokiha on the subject of his desire to visit England. He said, "Where are you, Chiefs! I am about to sail to a foreign land and I place my younger brother Kau-i-ke-aouli to be your chief [during my absence]. I go, and if I return I return; if not, then you are to have

---

* For an account of this episode see (7, p. 185). Pauahi was named for the escape of her mother Luahine from being burned to death.
† *Ka Nupepa Ko'oko'a*, Feb. 8, 1868.

my younger brother as your king," and to Kau-i-ke-aouli he said, "Live in peace with the chiefs; those lands which belong to me are yours, the lands given to the chiefs shall be theirs." Then he and some of the chiefs went on board an English whaler under Captain Starbuck and sailed for Oahu. In Honolulu chiefs and *kahu* urged him to carry out his father's command to "watch over the chiefs and the commoners," but he refused to listen. It has been said in explanation of this determination on the king's part that he was ashamed because no taxes had been collected for him or gifts received from the chiefs and people, and he had no lands left to give away; others said that he went to hide his bones. It is a fact that during Liholiho's time all the larger tracts of land were held by the chiefs, and he received only what the chiefs were willing to give him, and the government had received nothing. This was true up to 1828, when Boki Ka-ma'ule'ule gave the lands of Hilo to Kamehameha III, and he divided them among the people. In 1831 tax collectors were assigned, one to each island, but the right of collecting taxes did not belong to the king. The usual large gift taxes (*ho'okupu*) from the different islands were not collected during the rule of Liholiho. This was why Liholiho became wasteful, drank, and ran into debt, because the responsibility for the debts lay with the chiefs. When the king had put to sea he asked someone, "Is there no ship coming to take us back?" and when told there was none he said, "Ah! they have long despised us." Those who accompanied the king were Queen Ka-meha-malu;* Boki Ka-ma'ule'ule, son of Ke-kua-manoha' and now governor of Oahu, and his wife Liliha, daughter of Hoa-pili; Ka-uluhai-malama son of Ke-ku-hau-pi'o, a younger brother of Hoa-pili; Manuia, son of Ka-ulu-nae; Ke-ku-anao'a, son of Na-hiolea; Na-ihe-kukui, son of Hanakahi; No-ukana, son of Ka-manawa; Na-'ai-weuweu, son of Ke-kumu'ino; James Kane-hoa, son of John Young; and John Rives, a Frenchman and an intimate friend of the king; twelve in all. Many wished to accompany him, but he asked them to stay with his brother.

The party sailed November 27, 1823, on an English whaler under Captain Starbuck. As Liholiho went on board, the thousands assembled to see him sail set up a great wailing, and one chief almost had his clothes torn off his back for suggesting that they hold the king back. The queen remained on shore wailing and throwing up her hands and crying,

E ka lani e, e ka honua e,	O heaven! O earth!
E ka mauna e, e ka moana e,	O mountains and sea!
E ka hu e, e ka maka'ainana e,	O commoners and people!
Aloha 'oukou.	Farewell to you all.

* The name of this daughter of Kamehameha means "under the protection of Kamehameha." She was commonly called Kamamalu.

E ka lepo e, aloha 'oe,	O soil, farewell!
E ka mea a ku'u makuakane i 'eha ai e,	O land for which my father suffered,
Aloha 'oe,	Farewell,
E ka luhi a ku'u makuakane i 'imi ai e.	O burden that my father strived for.
Ke ha'alele nei maua i ko luhi.	We two are leaving your labors.
Ke hele nei no au mamuli o ko kauoha,	I go in obedience to your command,
'A'ole au e ha'alele i kou leo.	I will not desert your voice.
Ke hele nei no au ma ko kauoha i olelo mai ai ia'u.	I go in accordance with the words you spoke to me.*

As she ended these words the boat came alongside, she went out to the ship, it set sail, and as its masts sank on the horizon the faces of those on board disappeared as if going down into the grave.† After Liholiho's departure there was a period of debauchery. Guns were fired, drunken men wept and rioted, prostitutiton was rife. When this was over there still remained the heavy debts of the nation.

On the passage to England James Kane-hoa went ashore at Rio de Janeiro in Brazil, got drunk, and did not get back to the ship before she sailed. He carried all the papers and was the interpreter for the king. On the arrival of the party in London the king and queen were both ill, the queen of measles. It was not until Kane-hoa turned up on a coal ship with the letters of introduction that George IV knew that this was the king of the Hawaiian islands. He took great care of the king and sent his own physician to take charge of the case, but first Queen Ka-mehamalu died, July 8, 1824, and five days later Liholiho, Kamehameha II, died in London at the age of twenty-six, having ruled four years and some months.‡ Their bodies were sent home on a British warship. Of the company that set out five had died and the Frenchman had returned to France. King George met Boki and Liliha and the four other members of the company who remained. After expressing sorrow for the unfortunate termination of the king's visit he said, "You must return, and his younger brother shall be king. I shall not interfere in your internal troubles, but I shall guard you from outside invasion just as I did in the time of Kamehameha I." Kane-hoa interpreted these words to Boki and Liliha, Ke-ku-anao'a, Manuia, and Na-'ai-weuweu. On May 4, 1825, the warship dropped anchor in the waters of Mamala bearing the bodies of those who had sailed away living. The lamentations of the people

*"Father" and "you" refer to Kamehameha the Great.
† Ka-makau's account closely follows Bingham's. See 7, pp. 203-204.
‡ *Ka Nupepa Ku'oko'a*, Feb. 15, 1868.

rose to the skies. People rolled in the dust to express their love for their young ruler. They looked with admiration at the handsome caskets the like of which had never been seen before in this country, where the chiefs had been put away in basketwork woven of braided cord (*ka'ai*).

The chiefs met in council to make known the successor to the rule over Hawaii and to place at the head of the government Kau-i-ke-aouli the generous, whom Liholiho had appointed his heir. As he was only nine years old at the time, his *kahu* assumed control, with Ka-'ahu-manu at their head, and her brothers and the chiefs under her. Luanu'u Kahala-i'a became the child's personal *kahu*, since his former *kahu* Ka-iki-o'ewa had been appointed governor of Kauai. Boki made known the message sent by the king of England, and at Honuakaha Kau-i-ke-aouli was proclaimed king and gave his solemn oath before the people, being then but ten years of age. He arose and said, "Where are you, chiefs, guardians, commoners (*hu* and *maka'ainana*)! I greet you. Hear what I say! My kingdom I give to God. The righteous chief shall be my chief, the children of the commoners who do right shall be my people, my kingdom shall be one of letters." Ka-'ahu-manu and Ka-lani-moku encouraged this attitude of the king and declared to the people their trust in God.*

* *Ka Nupepa Ku'oko'a*, Feb. 22, 1868.

An Inland View in Atooi [Kaua'i], *One of the Sandwich Islands,* etching by J.G. Wooding after John Webber, artist with Captain Cook, 1778–79. In January 1778 Captain Cook first saw the Hawaiian Islands and anchored off Kaua'i.

Courtesy of Honolulu Academy of Arts, gift of George R. Carter (5,888)

Karakakoa Bay, Owhyee [Kealakekua Bay, Hawai'i], etching, aquatint, hand-colored with watercolor, by M. Dubourg after Thomas Heddington, artist with Captain Vancouver, 1792–1794. In January 1779 Captain Cook anchored here during his second voyage to the Hawaiian Islands. After he was killed by Hawaiians, his body was offered in sacrifice at Puhina o Lono *heiau* (place of worship) at the top of Palikapu o Keōua cliff.

Courtesy of Honolulu Academy of Arts, gift of Donald Angus (11,988)

Kaʻuiki Hill, Maui, viewed from the south. This fortified hill was the site of at least two major battles, one between ʻUmialiloa (a *mōʻī* of Hawaiʻi Island) and Hoʻolaemakua (*aliʻi ʻaimoku* of Hāna), and another between Kahekili (*mōʻī* of Maui) and the Hawaiʻi Island chiefs who had captured Hāna. After besieging the fortress for a year, Kahekili conquered the opposing forces by cutting off their water supply.

Courtesy of Bishop Museum

View of ʻĪao Valley looking seaward, West Maui. Site of a major battle between Kamehameha I and
Kalanikūpule (c. 1790). The waters of the stream were dammed with the fallen bodies of Maui warriors.

Courtesy of Bishop Museum

A *koʻa* at Maunalua, c. 1930. *Koʻa* were fishing heiau erected on the seacoasts as altars to Kūʻula, god of fishing, to promote abundant catches.

Courtesy of Bishop Museum

Stones of Kāne and Kanaloa, gods, respectively, of fresh water and ocean voyaging, at Kalaʻe, Molokaʻi, 1909.

Courtesy of Bishop Museum

Puʻukoholā *heiau*, Kawaihae, Hawaiʻi, c. 1890. A religious *kahuna* (priest) advised Kamehameha I to reconstruct this ancient *heiau* in order to gain the kingdom. After he offered in sacrifice the body of the rival chief Keōua Kūʻahuʻula of Kaʻū at this *heiau* Kamehameha became ruler over all of Hawaiʻi.

Courtesy of Bishop Museum

Temple du Roi dans la baie Tiritatéa, lithograph, hand-colored with watercolor, by Norblin after Louis Choris, artist with Russian explorer von Kotzebue, 1816. Ahuʻena *heiau,* Kamakahonu Bay, Kailua, Hawaiʻi. Kamehameha restored Ahuʻena and used it as a *heiau* for human sacrifice.

Îles Sandwich: Maisons de Kraïmokou, Premier Ministre du Roi; Fabrication des Étoffes [Sandwich Islands: Houses of Kalanimoku, Prime Minister of the King; Kapa Making], engraving by Villeroy after A. Pellion, artist with French captain and navigator de Freycinet, 1819.

Fish Ponds at Honoruru, Oahu, aquatint, published by John Murray, London, 1836, after Robert Dampier, artist with Lord Byron, British commander of H.M.S. *Blonde*, 1825. This view was probably drawn from Punchbowl looking toward 'Ewa. Until the early 1900s there were more than one hundred fishponds on O'ahu, some encompassing hundreds of acres.

Courtesy of Honolulu Academy of Arts, gift of George R. Carter (5,945)

Kālaipāhoa image. Kālaipāhoa was a poison god inhabiting statues carved from poisonous versions of the *nīoi* (*Eugenia* sp.), *kauila* (*Alphitonia ponderosa*), or *ʻohe* (*Reynoldsia sandwicensis*) trees. *Kālaipāhoa*, "carved with a *pāhoa*," also referred to the style of carving using a stone knife or axe. Dimensions: 14 1/2 in. (height) × 9 1/2 in. (width).

Rev. William Richards (1793–1847), detail of oil painting by unknown artist, c. 1845. Teacher and foster father to Kauikeaouli and Nāhiʻenaʻena. A government minister under Kamehameha III, Richards drafted the Constitution of 1840.

Keoni Ana (John Young II, 1810–1857), photo by an unknown photographer, c. 1855. Son of John Young, Kamehameha I's military advisor, and a close friend of Kauikeaouli, he was appointed governor of Maui and *kuhina nui* in 1845.

Kiaukiauli, King of the Sandwich Islands, engraving, 1826, by Edward Finden after painting by Robert Dampier. Kauikeaouli (1814–1854) was ten years old when he became Kamehameha III.

Courtesy of Bishop Museum

Nahienaena, Princess of the Sandwich Islands, engraving, 1826, by Edward Finden after painting by Robert Dampier. Nāhiʻenaʻena (1815–1836) was the sister of Kauikeaouli and the daughter of Kamehameha I and Keōpūolani.

Courtesy of Bishop Museum

Kekūanaoʻa (1794–1868) and his daughter Victoria Kamāmalu (1838–1866), photo by an unknown photographer, c. 1850. Kekūanaoʻa was a prominent chief who became governor of Oʻahu. His wife was Kīnaʻu, Kamehameha's daughter, with whom he fathered Alexander Liholiho (Kamehameha IV) and Lot Kapuāiwa (Kamehameha V).

Courtesy of Bishop Museum

Kauikeaouli, photo by an unknown photographer, c. 1853, reigned as
Kamehameha III from 1825 to 1854.

CHAPTER XXI

The Childhood of Kau-i-ke-aouli, Kamehameha III

The genealogies of Ka-lani-kau-i-ka'alaneo Ke-opu-o-lani and her ancestors were called Kumu-uli and Kumu-lipo and are to be found in the mele of Ku-ali'i and in that of Pele-io-holani and Ka-mahana, tabu chiefs of Oahu. The Oahu chiefs have no direct descendants in this world; their genealogies trace back through the ancestors of Ke-opu-o-lani who bore Kamehameha II and Kamehameha III. . . .*

Ke-opu-o-lani was born in 1780 at Pihana in Wailuku, Maui. She was the only child of her parents; Kiwala'o was her father, Ke-ku'i-apo-iwa II her mother. Her ancestors on her father's side were of the blood of chiefs who had ruled the island of Hawaii for as many generations back as the genealogies extend, and the same was true on her mother's side of the ruling chiefs of Maui. They were all tabu chiefs of divine rank. She herself was reared under tabu; at the time she was being nursed by her wet nurse (*kahu hanai wai-u*) neither chief nor commoner dared approach or touch her, and anyone who disobeyed this tabu was burned to death. Her guardians wished to exchange her for their own daughter named Kane-koa who had an excellent physique while the chiefess was homely and puny looking. They had just made up their minds to the exchange when a dog entered Kane-koa's sleeping place while both children were asleep, each in her own place, and bit off the fingers of one hand. The servant might have been the chiefess had not God willed it otherwise.

Kiwala'o was present at the birth of Ke-opu-o-lani, but he was ordered soon after by Ka-lani-'opu'u to Hawaii to become ruling chief over that island, and the mother and child were left on Maui. The child was brought up in Wailuku, Olowalu, and Hamakua on Maui.†
Ke-opu-o-lani was nine or ten years old when the great battle was fought at 'Iao in which Ka-lani-ku-pule and the Maui chiefs were routed by Kamehameha's forces. The fugitives fled across the sharp ridges of the mountains, the mother carrying the child on her back and the *kahu* carrying mother and child, until they were able to escape to

---

* *Ka Nupepa Ku'oko'a*, Feb. 22, 1868.
See Page 433 of this volume for full genealogy.
† *Ka Nupepa Ku'oko'a*, Feb. 29, 1868.

Molokai, where they remained on account of the illness of Ka-lola [grandmother of Ke-opu-o-lani] instead of going on to join Ke-ku'i-apo-iwa's brother on Oahu. They were at Kalama'ula when the chief's [Kamehameha's] messenger came with the request that they remain on Molokai instead of sailing to Oahu. After the death of Ka-lola Kamehameha took Ke-opu-o-lani to Hawaii together with the chiefesses, Ke-ku'i-apo-iwa, Ka-lani-kua, and Ka-haku-ha'akoi, and their households. At Keauhou in North Kona Ke-opu-o-lani was brought up under the name of Wahine-pio until she was a grown girl. With her mother she accompanied Kamehameha on his expedition to make war upon Ka-lani-ku-pule on Oahu, where in 1795 was fought the battle of Nu'uanu. Here one of the Oahu chiefs gave her the name of Ke-opu-o-lani in place of that of Ka-lani-kau-i-ka-'alaneo by which she had been previously called.

At Waikiki she was formally united (ho'ao) with Kamehameha but was not made his constant companion, for he slept with her only from time to time in order to perpetuate the high-chiefly blood of the kingdom. In Hilo, 1797, she gave birth to her first-born, Liholiho; her second child was born prematurely (mumuku) at Wailupe; her third child, born March 17, 1814, at Keauhou, North Kona, was Kau-i-ke-aouli, Kamehameha III; and her fourth child, born in 1815, was Harriet Nahi-'ena'ena. Ke-opu-o-lani loved her children and wept when they were taken from her to be brought up by other chiefs or chiefesses. Kamehameha, for example, wanted Liholiho brought up in his own household and the child placed in charge of Ka-'ahu-manu, the wife who was always with him. The mother yielded until it came to the last child and this one's rearing she would not give up to another.

Ke-ku'i-apo-iwa's younger sister, Ka-lani Kau-io-kikilo, was a tabu chiefess of pi'o rank. Her mother was Ka-lola and her father was Kalola's brother, Kamehameha-nui. She was called Ka-lani-akua and likened to a god; all the chiefs and people prostrated themselves before her and she was even allowed to climb about the tabu heiaus of the tabu gods, so high was her tabu. She did not like Kamehameha, thought him of inferior birth, and did not want her niece to sleep with him. It is said that this was why she took the Kalaipahoa poison and died at Honuakaha in 1808. Ke-ku'i-apo-iwa Liliha, the mother of Ke-opu-o-lani, was the daughter of Ka-lola and Ka-lani-kupu-a-pa-i-ka-lani-nui Keoua. She was a proud woman and despised the chiefs of Hawaii, saying of them, "They are from Keawe! they are from Keawe! they drip (aweawe) poi!" but the chiefs of Oahu and Maui from whom she came she held in respect.

THE CHILDHOOD OF KAU-I-KE-AOULI
Ke-opu-o-lani was not like her mother in this. She was known as a good mother, respectful to the chiefs, to her husband, and to all people. No one was ever put to death for breaking her tabu. It was she, supported by her aunts and uncles, who brought about free eating on the day when Liholiho was proclaimed king, by making Kau-i-ke-aouli eat tabu food and motioning to Liholiho to eat with the women. She caused the war for free eating against Ke-kua-o-kalani by going with Ulu-maheihei to Ka'awaloa and returning weeping to Liholiho. Had they not gone there would have been no battle at Kuamo'o. Liholiho was in favor of keeping the tabus. He would have sided with Ke-kua-o-ka-lani, and Ka-lani-moku's faction would have been killed. Ka-'ahu-manu also was responsible for Liholiho's course. He saw for himself that the upholding of the tabus was for his own benefit. Perhaps also Ke-kua-o-ka-lani was right when he said, "No ungodly chief can ever rule long; he will die without cause," for certainly both Liholiho and the chiefs who chose free eating are scattered and gone. Strange that Ke-opu-o-lani should have desired free eating against her own interests and those of her children! She and they were looked upon by the people as gods with powers like fire, heat, light, not through any feeling of inferiority on their part but through long-cherished custom. When she broke down the tabu she became a meek woman, and chiefs and people mingled on an equality.

It was Ke-opu-o-lani who first welcomed the missionaries and whose children were first taught letters, Kau-i-ke-aouli when he was six, Nahi-'ena'ena at the age of four. She herself first heard the word of God in 1820 from Thomas Hopu.* She became interested and was the first to adopt the teaching that a man should have but one wife and a woman but one husband, and she gave up having more than one husband and took Ulu-maheihei for her husband. The other chiefs and chiefesses were given over to drink and sensual indulgence. When Liholiho came to Maui and made a trip around that island she learned more of the missionary teaching. Later she went with her husband to Kauai after a load of sandalwood for their boat, the Ho'oikaika, and met the missionaries, Samuel Whitney and Mr. Ruggles. On Oahu she met Mr. Bingham, took her stand as a Christian, and gave up drinking. On April 11, 1822, the Rev. William Ellis, an English missionary of the London Society, arrived from Tahiti bringing several Christian Tahitians, Ka-'au-moku who was unmarried, and Tau-'a and Akole, each with his wife. These Ke-opu-o-lani took as

* *Ka Nupepa Ku'oko'a*, Mar. 14, 1868.

her teachers. They taught her to read and write, held religious services morning and evening, offered a blessing at meals, and taught the word of God to the household. On March 23, 1823, the governor of Maui died and Ulu-maheihei was appointed in his place. Ke-opu-o-lani took with her to Maui Mr. Richards and Mr. Stewart of the second installment of missionaries from the United States, made them her teachers, gave them one of the chiefs' places at Halehuku to live in, and taxed the people to build a covered shelter (*lanai*) and later a church for worship.

Lahaina was in those days a popular resort for the chiefs. There lived Pele-uli and Kawelo-o-ka-lani, Kau-kuna Ka-hekili, Ke-kikipa‘a, Ka-hou-o-kalani, Ke-oho-hiwa, Keoua, Pu‘ali-nui, Ka-lolo‘u, Ha‘eha‘e, Kalai-koa, Ka-‘ili-hakuma and their households, and between Mala and the farther end of Waianu‘ukole lived other chiefs. None of these paid any attention to the word of God but amused themselves at their gatherings with liquor drinking, dancing, gambling, sensual indulgence, and all kinds of such devilish doings. This was true not only on Maui but all over the islands. Even David Malo, who was one of the first teachers in Hawaii, knew little of religion and made drinking and dancing his principal pastimes. But with Ke-opu-o-lani's acceptance of the Christian faith and way of life, the chiefs in Lahaina immediately left off drinking and gathered about Tau-‘a and Ka-‘au-moku to hear the new teaching. Great numbers became true worshipers of the Lord and many took up reading and writing. Among the most proficient of these were David Malo, Daniel ‘I‘i, and One‘o. Ke-opu-o-lani's daughter, princess Nahi-‘ena‘ena, with her companions, and Ke-opu-olani's son, prince Kau-i-ke-aouli, with his companions, came to Maui at that time, and the young prince was at Halaka‘a in Lahaina with his guardians, Ka-iki-o-‘ewa, Ka-hou-o-ka-lani, and Ka-pololu.

Hardly four months had passed since Ke-opu-o-lani came to live at Lahaina when she fell ill and knew that she was to die. Liholiho was sent for. To Ka-lani-moku and Hoa-pili she said, "You two must accept God, obey Him, pray to Him, and become good men. I want you to become fathers to my children." It was to this that Ka-lani-moku referred when he said in May, 1825, at Honuakaha, "My sister [literally 'wife'], Ke-opu-o-lani, asked me to turn to God and obey Him." She became very weak and her preachers, Mr. Bingham and Mr. Stewart, baptized her by the name of Harriet Ke-opu-o-lani. Before the end of the day she was dead. Thus the highest tabu chiefess became the first Hawaiian convert.

Ke-opu-o-lani died September 16, 1823, at Kaluaokiha in Lahaina in her fifty-fifth year. The chiefs and people began to wail and carry on as usual, but Hoa-pili forbade the custom of death companions and boisterous expressions of grief, saying, "She forbade it and gave herself to God." Had not Ka-lani-moku himself heard her words he would have been the first to start the carousing for he was always the leader in such excesses. After the death of Ke-opu-o-lani, Ka-heihei-malie Ka-niu left her husband Ka-nuha in Hawaii and took Ulu-maheihei as her husband, and they became known as Hoapili-kane and Hoapili-wahine [after the foreign fashion of designating husband and wife by the name of the husband].

Ka-lani-kau-i-ke-aouli was the second son of Ke-opu-o-lani by Ka-mehameha, and she called him Kiwala'o after her own father. She was the daughter of Kiwala'o and Ke-ku'i-apo-iwa Liliha, both children of Ka-lola Pupuka-o-Hono-ka-wai-lani, and hence she [Ke-opu-o-lani] was a *ni'aupi'o* and a *naha* chiefess, and the *ni'aupi'o* rank descended to her children and could not be lost by them. While she was carrying the child [Kau-i-ke-aouli] several of the chiefs begged to have the bringing up of the child, but she refused until her *kahu*, Ka-lua-i-konahale, known as Kua-kini, came with the same request. She bade him be at her side when the child was born lest some one else get possession of it. He was living this side of Keauhou in North Kona, and Ke-opu-o-lani lived on the opposite side. On the night of the birth the chiefs gathered about the mother. Early in the morning the child was born but as it appeared to be stillborn Kua-kini did not want to take it. Then came Ka-iki-o-'ewa from some miles away, close to Kuamo'o, and brought with him his prophet who said, "The child will not die, he will live." This man, Ka-malo-'ihi or Ka-pihe by name, came from the Napua line of kahunas descended from Makua-kau-mana whose god was Ka-'onohi-o-ka-la (similar to the child of God). The child was well cleaned and laid upon a consecrated place and the seer (*kaula*) took a fan (*pe'ahi*), fanned the child, prayed, and sprinkled it with water, at the same time reciting a prayer addressed to the child of God, something like that used by the Roman Catholics:-

> "*He is standing up, he is taking a step, he walks*"
> (*Kulia-la, ka'ina-la, hele ia la*).

Or another,—

Huila ka lani i ke Akua,	The heavens lighten with the god,
Lapalapa ka honua i ke keiki	The earth burns with the child,
E ke keiki e, hooua i ka punohu lani,	O son, pour down the rain that brings the rainbow,

Aia i ka lani ka Haku e,	There in heaven is the Lord.
O kuʻu ʻuhane e kahe mau,	Life flows through my spirit,
I laʻa i kou kanawai.	Dedicated to your law.

The child began to move, then to make sounds, and at last it came to life. The seer gave the boy the name of "The red trail" (Ke-aweawe-ʻula) signifying the roadway by which the god descends from the heavens.

Ka-iki-o-ʻewa became the boy's guardian and took him to rear in an out-of-the-way place at ʻOʻoma, Kekaha. Here Keawe-a-mahi, the lesser chiefs, the younger brothers and sisters of Ka-iki-o-ʻewa, and their friends were permitted to carry the child about and hold him on their laps (*uha*). Ka-pololu was the chief who attended him; Koʻi-pepeleleu and Ulu-nui's mother [were] the nurses who suckled him. Later Ka-ʻai-kane gave him her breast after she had given birth to Ke-kahu-puʻu. Here at ʻOʻoma he was brought up until his fifth year, chiefly occupied with his toy boats rigged like warships and with little brass cannon loaded with real powder mounted on [their] decks. The firing off of these cannon amused him immensely. He excelled in foot races. On one occasion when the bigger boys had joined in the sport, a lascar* boy named Ka-hoa thought to play a practical joke by smearing with mud the stake set up to be grasped by the one who first reached the goal. He expected one of the larger boys to be the winner, but it was the little prince who first caught the stick and had his hands smeared. "You will be burnt alive for dirtying up the prince. We are going to tell Ka-pololu on you!" the boys threatened; but the prince objected, saying, "Anyone who tells on him shall never eat with me again or play with me and I will never give him anything again." Kau-i-ke-aouli was a splendid little fellow. He loved his playmates and never once did them any hurt, and he was kind and obedient to his teachers.

As he grew older, perhaps eight or nine years old, he used to go out with a boatload of boys, generally in the sail boats, *Ka-ʻai-loli* and *Ke-ʻaki-koʻowali*, although sometimes in other boats; and he would haul the sails and do any of the work without trying to assume command, for even up to the time when he became king he was simple in his ways. It was not until 1833 that he first showed himself capable of the dignity of a prince. Dressed in his ordinary frock and a rubber cap the country people would never have recognized him as their king. I

---

* A lascar is an East Indian. The project of introducing Hindu laborers into Hawaii was abandoned in 1877.

verily believe he had no equal on earth for gentleness of spirit. He loved the people, high and low alike. In November and December, 1820, the prince accompanied Liholiho and his train to Maui. With him came Ka-iki-o-'ewa who lived at Lahaina with the prince while the rest of the household, including Keawe-a-mahi, his sister Ka-hou-o-ka-lani, and his younger brother Koa-kanu, stayed at Kapa'ahu in Kama'ole, the coconut grove called the pit of 'Aihakoko. Here in Lahaina the prince's personal attendant Ka-pololu died, and Ka-lau-'alu became his guardian.

Kau-i-ke-aouli was but nine years old when Liholiho sailed to England leaving him successor to the rule over Hawaii. As he was then too young to assume command, affairs were administered by his guardians, Ka-'ahu-manu and Ka-lani-moku, and the other chiefs were under them; but as in Liholiho's time so it was even up to the time when Kau-i-ke-aouli took control, all the taxes came through the district chiefs over the *kalana, okana,* and *ahupua'a* land divisions. The common people were generous, but the chiefs and those who were on the king's own lands such as Wailuku on Maui, Waipi'o and Waiakea on Hawaii, "had their ears stuffed with cotton." The chiefs took the taxes from the land which they held and might or might not give anything to the king. They were all bent at this time upon securing honor for themselves and would give away land only to relatives or favorites or to some high chief, in which case it could not revert again to the government. The many lands held by some of Kamehameha's high officials are said to have been given them, not by Kamehameha himself who gave away little land, but by the lesser chiefs who gave to the higher. "Doing honors like Ka-umu-ali'i" was the phrase coined.

Ka-umu-ali'i became the husband of Ka-'ahu-manu before she had become interested in the Christian religion and lived with her at Pakaka, Honolulu, from 1822 to the time of his death in 1825. When he became ill, the chiefs urged him to appoint a successor to the lands of Kauai and Niihau, but he gave them no reply until, just at the last, as his sisters were at his feet and Ka-'ahu-manu and his daughter Kapo were present and Ka-lani-moku had come to his head and repeated two or three times the question, "My son, after your death who is to be your successor?" he answered, "Our 'son'." "How about the lands?" "Let the lands be as they are; those chiefs who have lands to hold them, those who have not to have none." According to his request that his body be not removed to Kauai but taken to Lahaina and buried at the feet of the chiefess Ke-opu-o-lani, he was interred at the entrance of Ke-opu-o-lani's tomb at Kaluaokiha. And at the council of chiefs it was determined to abide by his last words and give the governorship of Kauai and Niihau to his nephew, Luanu'u Kahala-i'a, for these islands had not at that time become a part of Kamehameha's territory ('aina panala'au). Kahala-i'a accordingly sailed to Kauai as governor together with several chiefs and their households who went to Kauai for the first time, namely, Ke-kau-'onohi, Ke-kai-ha'a-kulou, Ni'au, Na-mahana, and others. He took possession of the arms at Fort Hipo and he and his companions began to drink and enjoy the common pleasures of that time.

The people meanwhile mourned the death of Ka-umu-ali'i in their old manner. The men blackened their thighs; the people made circles on their cheeks, ate prodigiously, and took to other excesses. Fishponds were robbed, taro pulled, pigs killed, and other lawless acts performed. Suqh acts were often a prelude to war. All awaited the announcement of Ka-umu-ali'i's heir. Chiefs and commoners expected George Humehume to be appointed their ruling chief under King Kau-i-ke-aouli who had succeeded Liholiho. They hated the chiefs of Hawaii because they were overbearing and because they had plotted to kill Ka-umu-ali'i on Oahu when Kamehameha sent for him there, and only the watchfulness and discretion of the foreigners had saved his life. The chief had named his son "The-patient chief-of-Kamehameha" (Ke-li'i-aho-nui-o-Kameha-meha), a name which the people of Kauai misunderstood.* About noon on June 21 an eclipse of the sun took place which covered the land with darkness. The next day Mr. Bingham explained how the eclipse was caused by the moon getting between the earth and the sun. The people asked him what event it was a sign of, and he told them it was not a sign of anything about to happen, according to the ideas of his country, but an occurrence which happened naturally from time to time and was not everywhere visible at the same time. They told him that it was the Hawaiian belief that this was a sign from God foretelling some great event like war, the overthrow of the government, the death of a ruling chief, and that they believed war was imminent. Perhaps this was because they knew how Kahala-i'a had come to Kauai as governor and was living with his followers at Papa'ena'ena in Waimea.

Ka-lani-moku now sailed to Kauai to proclaim the will of the dead chief and settle government affairs and land disputes. But he landed first at Hanalei in order to have [men] dive for the bell and anchor which had been sunk when Liholiho's ship, Ha'aheo, went ashore off that coast, and he did not sail until evening for Waimea.

* Ka Nupepa Ku'oko'a, Mar. 21, 1868.

Kikala and others who had been prominent men under Ka-umu-ali'i, together with some of the chiefs from the Ko'olau side, when they heard of Ka-lani-moku's arrival at Hanalei went there to make a night attack, but found the ship already gone. Ka-lani-moku had become a religious man at this time, held family prayers morning and evening (*ka pule 'ohana*), and had prayers said at meals.

At Waimea Ka-lani-moku examined the property at the fort. He then called a council of all the chiefs and announced to them the will of their dead ruler, that "those of the chiefs who hold land, they are well off; the commoner who holds property is fortunate; the chief or commoner who has no portion is unfortunate. The lands shall continue as they now stand. Our son, Kahala-i'a, shall be ruler over you." A blind chief of Waipouli in Puna, named Ki'ai-makani, said, "That is not right; the land should be put together and re-divided because we have a new ruler," but Ka-lani-moku would not consent to this. On Friday most of the chiefs gathered at Nihoa, one of Ka-'ahu-manu's houses at Papa'ena'ena, and urged the redistribution of the land, but Ka-lani-moku again refused. On Saturday night they seized their digging sticks and attacked the fort, which they found manned by the men of Hawaii with guns. Kahala-i'a and his men were awakened by the ringing of the bell and the shouts of a woman warrior who cried, "Here come the Kauai warriors after the arms! here come the rebels! the men of Hawaii still hold the fort! it is not taken for Kauai!" Ni'au, who tried to push his way into the fort past Kahala-i'a, was shot in the mouth and killed. Several others were killed, some leaped down the cliff of Hipo and had their bones broken, others escaped by sea. The next day, Sunday, the dead bodies were turned over to the pigs. Ka-lani-moku sent the ship, *Pa'alua,* to Honolulu after reinforcements and Mr. Bingham and Mr. Whitney and their families took passage for fear of the war. It was on this trip that the captain threw Kane-maka-kini overboard to be drowned.

Recruits were drawn in from Honolulu. The Okaka, Ka'aiohi'a, Nouo, Kala'ilua, and other companies were sent to Kauai, and the *Pa'alua* sailed to Maui after Hoa-pili, the commander in chief. [On Maui] the king and all his company were still attending the burial of Ka-umu-ali'i. As the captain came ashore people knew from the position of the flag on the ship that something was wrong. Besides Hoa-pili and Ka-hekili, the chiefs Pikanele, Pua'a, Kalai-koa, Ka-makini, and Hoa-pili's preacher Tau-'a here joined [the warriors]. At Oahu guns and ammunition were provided. The Kauai men, who at first thought they would have but few men to encounter, were terrified when they saw more than ten ships arriving. The lands held by chiefs of Hawaii were tabu; Waimea and Makaweli were held by Ka-'ili-naoa and Ka-'u'uku-ali'i, and Kehaha by Ni'au and Na-mahana. On August 8 the battle of Wahiawa was fought close to Hanapepe. The Hawaii men were at Hanapepe, the Kauai forces at Wahiawa, where a fort had been hastily erected and a single cannon (named Humehume) mounted as a feeble attempt to hold back the enemy.* In the evening there was advance made, but the forces of Hawaii retired to Hanapepe for the night. A hard rain prevented the Kauai men from firing the grass that night and making a rush in the morning as they had intended. There had been a rainbow, and Hoa-pili predicted, "If the base were on the other side and the tip here we should be defeated tomorrow, but since we have the base and they the tip we shall be the winners. I believe not one of our men will fall." In the morning he encouraged his men and had his preacher, Tau-'a, offer prayer. Large numbers of Kauai soldiers had gathered on the battle-ground, but they were unarmed save with wooden spears, digging sticks, and javelins. Many women were there to see the fight. The men acted as if death were but a plaything. It would have been well if the gods had stepped in and stopped the battle. No one was killed on the field, but as they took to flight they were pursued and slain. So Kia'i-makani, Na-ke'u, and their followers met death. For ten days the soldiers harried the land killing men, women, and children. Humehume had ridden away to the mountains with his daughter and his wife, Pake. Many fled to the mountains until amnesty for all was declared. Kalai-heana neither killed nor injured any prisoner, neither did Hoa-pili or Ka-lani-moku. All the rest took prisoners and brought them to Oahu and even to Maui and Hawaii. A great deal of property was taken, among other things horses and cattle, which had become numerous on Kauai because the foreigners had given many such to Ka-umu-ali'i. On Oahu there were only a few which had been brought in by John Young and Kamehameha from Kauai in 1809; afterwards more were brought in by Don Marin.

After the battle the chiefs all came together and Ka-lani-moku redistributed the lands of Kauai. Was this right? What about Kamehameha's agreement with Ka-umu-ali'i? What about Liholiho's promise? What about the last will of Ka-umu-ali'i at Pakaka? Some Kauai chiefs were with the chiefs on Maui attending the burial of their dead ruler, some fought loyally against the rebels; yet their lands were seized with the others. The last will of Ka-umu-ali'i, who had the real title

* *Ka Nupepa Ku'oko'a*, Apr. 11, 1868.

to the lands, was not respected. Ka-lani-moku's ship, *Pa'alua*, was wrecked on Niihau, so he returned to Oahu from Kauai, and a council was held to decide upon the future of the two islands. It was decided that Kahala-i'a should not remain as ruler, but the islands be turned over to the young king, and Ka-iki-o-'ewa was appointed governor and Kahala-i'a recalled. He was said to have been very bitter against Ka-'ahu-manu on this account, but he was consoled by being made guardian of the young king, Kau-i-ke-aouli. The lands were again divided. Soldiers who had been given lands but had returned to Oahu had their lands taken away, chiefs who had large lands were deprived of them, and the loafers and hangers-on (*palaualelo*) of Oahu and Maui obtained the rich lands of Kauai.*

* *Ka Nupepa Ku'oko'a,* Apr. 18, 1868.

CHAPTER XXII

The Career of Boki

At the close of the war learning to read became popular. The chiefs saw the value of education and of the observance of the Sabbath. They learned to repeat the Lord's prayer, and teachers were sent all about the country districts. Every chief's household had a teacher, some of them women. There were as many as forty such schools in Honolulu and an equal number at Waikiki, and education spread widely in those few years. After the death of Ke-opu-o-lani her husband Hoa-pili was the leading representative of the Christian faith. Later Ka-'ahu-manu and Ka-lani-moku and their households followed suit. . . .* The young king was fully determined to have his people educated. Ka-'ahu-manu and Ka-lani-moku supported his wish. Harriet Nahi-'ena'ena also urged chiefs and commoners to live upright lives. The wish of the king, his sister, and his guardians acted upon the people like a lightning flash stimulating all hearts. The study of letters was taken up universally from the king's own household to the remotest country dwelling. Schools were established all over Oahu conducted like the schools of the hula in old days. After the second or third week they would hold all-night and all-day sessions, and as April 19 of each year approached, when all gathered for the yearly exhibition (*ho'ike*), from Kepukaki you could see lights burning all the way from the Nu'uanu Pali to Kaimuki. Each school vied with the others to make the best showing on the day of the exhibition, and the winner would receive acclaim from the public. Those schools that excelled became famous; those that made a poor showing were objects of derision.

The subjects taught were spelling in unison; reciting syllables of two letters†; reciting a refusal to keep wooden gods; names of lands, names of months; a recitation relating the emotion of the people over the death of a king in a foreign land; portions of the books of Matthew, Psalms, Acts of the Apostles, and Luke; questions relating to God; the Ten Commandments; questions prepared for the exhibition;

* *Ka Nupepa Ku'oko'a*, Apr. 18, 1868.
† Reading used to be taught by reciting meaningless syllables by rote, running the vowel changes on the different consonants in order, as: ha, ka, la, ma, na, pa, wa; he, ke, le, me, ne, pe, we, and so forth.

the desire of the rulers proclaimed at Honuakaha; the first hymn about 'Opu-kaha-'ia; and the arithmetical processes of adding, multiplication tables, division, and fractions. It was Mr. Chamberlain who first taught figures. Some schools taught how to get ready, to stand, to speak out, to take up a slate, how to place the pencil on the slate, thus: "Attention, get ready, wait, stand up, speak, give greeting." These were some of the many things taught in old days which gave reading such prestige. Ka-'ahu-manu, Kekua-i-pi'ia Na-mahana, Kina'u, Ka-lani-pauahi, Ke-ka-ulu-ohi, all the nieces of Ka-'ahu-manu and all the chiefs were taught to read. All the old chiefs, even those who were toothless, recited from memory certain questions and answers and the commandments of God given on Mount Sinai. King Kau-i-ke-aouli laid great stress on the progress of education among the whole people and he continued attending school. Mr. Bingham was one of his teachers as were also Mr. Kahuhu and Mr. Kuke of Borabora.* He took up singing and sang in the choir on Sunday with Ke-li'i-ahonui and others at Kawaiaha'o. Until his last days he never ceased working for the uplifting of his people.† When the High School at Lahainaluna opened, he sent some of his teachers, Ka-maunu, Ka-wai-lepolepo, Mahune, and others, to learn deeper wisdom and become leaders in the affairs of the government. Ka-'ahu-manu also sent her teachers to this school and so did Kina'u, Ke-ka-ulu-ohi, Ka-iki-o'ewa, Hoa-pili, Kua-kini, Keoua, and 'Ai-kanaka. The spread of knowledge was very rapid in Hawaii.

Why were Pohukaina and Hali'imaile made palace grounds for the king's dwelling? It was the desire of the chiefs to hear the word of God and be near where the missionaries lived. Waikiki had been the old place of residence for rulers. Honolulu was seldom used in Ka-lani-ku-pule's day. In Kamehameha's time the chief lived half his time at Waikiki and half in Honolulu. Liholiho made Honolulu his usual place of residence. He used to live at Kamanuwai. Houses were built above the stream of Kikihale down to Kapu'ukolo and to Ka'aloa House, the warehouse owned by Ku-i-helani, above which was Pula-holaho, the land owned by Ka-'ahu-manu which the British seized; on the beach called today Moku'aikaua and at Kaluaokapili and at 'Apua, Ka'oa'opa', and all the way to Honuakaha. Within these bound-

---

* Mr. Kuke of Borabora was born in Huahine, Society Islands in 1781 and was named after Cook, the British navigator. He was connected with the Pomare family and was a favorite of King Pomare. During his missionary work in Hawaii he served as chaplain to Kamehameha III until that king's death. He resided for some thirty-two years in Hawaii and died December 3, 1858. (See 23).

† *Ka Nupepa Ku'oko'a*, Apr. 25, 1868.

aries there were a few buildings, in Kauanono'ula, Honoka'upu, old Honolulu, and Sailors' Home. The *maika* grounds called Kalanikahua ran from the Kikihale stream in front of William Stevens' place, southeast along John Meek's place to Polelewa (Bethel Church) and along Ka-makea's coconut grove. A watercourse ran from Ka'akopua [Central Grammar School] to the fishponds of Kaho'ikekanaka *makai* of Honuakaha. The center was occupied by a few scattered houses where the foreigners lived. Liholiho and his chiefs lived at Pakaka [the end of Fort Street] and at places near the fort, where also lived the influential people and the soldiers who guarded the fort. Pohukaina and its vicinity were overgrown with vines and brambles. Ka-lani-moku's and Ka-'ahu-manu's acceptance of the word of God was their reason for living on the plain of Apahu'a. Ka-lani-moku built a large enclosure, of forest timber, adjoining King Street on the *makai* side and almost reaching Richards Street on the 'Ewa side, leaving the boundary of Hali'imaile on the *mauka* side and running along the road leading to Waikiki as far as to the edge of Punchbowl Street on the 'Ewa side of the stone house of the Rev. Mr. Ellis (Eleiti) down King Street to where it joined Hali'imaile. He also erected a large stone house, named Pohukaina, *mauka* of King street and on the 'Ewa side of the burial place of the kings. It was in this enclosure that Kau-i-ke-aouli's house stood and also Ka-'ahu-manu's and the house of her nieces Kina'u, Ka-lani- pauahi, Ke-ka-ulu-ohi, and of their guardian, Kahala-i'a, who was the king's *kahu*. Hali'imaile was the home of Boki and Liliha. The house of Lilia Na-mahana, or Pi'ia as she was called, was on the Waikiki side of the Pohukaina enclosure; and near to this where Punchbowl Street runs were Wala-wala-i-honua and Ka-polohau, and it was there that Ruth Ke-eli-kolani was reared.*

The Pohukaina enclosure was surrounded inside and out by the homes of the chiefs, the high and the lesser chiefs and the counselors and the old chiefs who desired to know about God. So great was the desire to join the church that men and women flocked in from the country districts neglecting their duties to those at home. A wife would leave her husband or a husband his wife in order to devote himself to the service of God. Such a seeker after membership in the church would come first to Ka-'ahu-manu, braving the fear the people had of her because of her blood-red eyes, and would be sent on to another; perhaps at midnight they would be sent on elsewhere and their faith questioned. Finally

* Pohukaina and Hali'imaile include the old palace grounds, now those of the Executive Building, and part of the land where the Library of Hawaii stands. Kamanuwai is on Beretania near Nu'uanu, running over toward River Street. Kikihale is on the Waikiki side of Nu'uanu Stream running from River Street to Kekaulike between Hotel and King Streets.

they were told that they must see one of the teachers who explained the word of God, for only so could their faith be known. It was these difficulties put in the way of their own simple manner of expressing their faith that made the chiefs and people so devoted to the word of God in the old days.

After the bodies of Liholiho and his queen had arrived from England, and the Council of chiefs had met and Kau-i-ke-aouli had been proclaimed king at Honuakaha, Boki was continued in the office of governor of the island of Oahu which he held under Kamehameha I and Liholiho. He put his younger cousin, Manuia, in command of Fort Ke-kua-nohu, of the fortified hill of Punchbowl, and the harbor of Kou, and made him Chief Marshall with power over life and death. Ke-ku-anao'a he put in command of the troops. These two, Boki's cousins, held the highest positions perhaps because they had both been to England and on state occasions were dressed in spick and span uniforms trimmed with gold. Na-wai-lau, Ke-aniani, Uwahi-nui, Hinau, and Ka-leo-hano also held high rank. Boki assured the chiefs that of all the information he had gained in England as to how affairs were operated in that famous nation, the things that impressed him most were the great importance given to the word of God as expressed in the cathedrals and churches of London, of which Saint Paul's seemed to him "to my mind the foundation on which was built her fame"; and the fact that those who were educated and learned in letters were the important people of the country, compared to whom the common people were like dust under their feet. The king of England [he said] lived in a way similar to the tabu chiefs of old, and he had extended his hand to them in friendship. These remarks of Boki delivered to Ka-'ahu-manu and Ka-lani-moku in the presence of the chiefs made an immense impression. They redoubled their efforts in the study of letters and of the word of God, and Boki and Liliha and the Maui chiefs Hoa-pili and his wife and Harriet Nahi-'ena'ena, for whom Hoa-pili had selected Mr. Richards as foster parent and teacher, showed great zeal in learning to read and write. The chiefs at Kailua, namely: Kua-kini and Keoua, Maheha Ka-pu-likoliko, Ka-hahana and Makulu, Ke-pupu-ohi, and all the rest were equally diligent, as were Na-ihe, Ka-pi'o-lani, Ka-makau and his wife, and the other chiefs at Ka'awaloa and Napo'opo'o.* The Hilo chiefs like Pi'opi'o and Ke-aho-lawai'a as well. All the chiefs from Kauai also, as well as from Hawaii, such as Ka-iki-o-'ewa and his wife Keawe-a-mahi, Ka-'u'uku-

* *Ka Nupepa Ku'oko'a,* May 2, 1868.

ali'i and 'Ole-loa, Ka-'iu and Ke-kai-ha'a-kulou, made great strides in knowledge of the word of God.

Boki, because of his familiarity with English customs, was appointed chief counselor to the young king and had control over all the affairs of the kingdom. At first he conducted these with great success and was praised for his good work, even by the foreigners. It was his association with some of them which later caused his downfall. Boki heard from Kauai that Kalai-wohi, a younger cousin of Ka-'ahu-manu, was plotting to depose Ka-iki-o-'ewa and seize Kauai for himself. Boki therefore made a visit to Kauai on the ship *Pa'alua*. Anchoring off the lower end of Po'o, he went ashore at Waimea, and met Ka-iki-o-'ewa, Ahu-kai Ka-'u'uku-ali'i, her mother Ka-'ili-naoa, Na-mahana and other chiefs of Kauai. After the wailing he informed the chiefs that his errand was to take back Kalai-wohi with him to Oahu. This chief was the elder brother of the blind Ka-'eo, sons of Ka-'ai-malolo and cousins to Ka-'ahu-manu. He had been put in charge of the fort Hipo and lived on the other side at La'auakala. He was now summoned to Papa'ena'ena and Boki said, "I want you to return with me to Oahu." "It is for him (indicating the chief) to give his consent to our going," answered Kalai-wohi. Ka-iki-o-'ewa said to Boki, "We will remain with our nephew and you return alone to Oahu." After two days Boki proposed an inspection of the fort. The place had been well stocked with cannon and muskets and Ka-umu-ali'i's men knew how to change the angles and range of the cannon, but after the capture of the fort by the men of Hawaii the arms had been removed to Oahu, Maui and even to Hawaii. In this examination Boki found that the [restock of] muskets had been taken away outside the fort and knew that Kalai-wohi was guilty, and Ka-iki-o-'ewa finally consented to Kalai-wohi's removal to Oahu.

In 1826 an epidemic of cough and bronchitis carried off several chiefs and commoners. The symptoms were a parched throat, followed by fever with pains in head and chest. Among those who died of this illness were Ka-lani-pauahi, mother of Ruth Ke-'eli-kolani, and George Humehume, son of Ka-umu-ali'i of Kauai, who died in Honolulu. Ka-haku-ha'akoi Wahine-pio also died of it at Moku'ula, Maui. She was the sister of Ka-lani-moku and Boki, daughter of Ka-maka-huki-lani and Ke-kua-manoha' and mother of Ka-halai'a and Ke-kau-'onohi.

Kahala-i'a was her son by Kalai-mamahu.' He was said to be perfectly formed from head to foot and so good to his people that in time of food scarcity he would sit down and share everything he had with them. Because of his personal attractions the tabu wives of Liholiho,

Ka-meha-malu and Ka-lani-pauahi, fell in love with him, and Liholiho had once entertained the notion of disposing of Kahala-i'a as Kameha-meha had of Ka-niho-nui, but he had too many influential relatives, the ruling counselors among them. "It is as easy for him to get women as to gather the thick-growing seaweed." (*Ua like no laua me Limu-nui*) was the chant sung on this occasion for Kahala-i'a. When Ka-lani-moku was ill Kahala-i'a came and wept over him and said, "I have refrained from taking the kingdom while you are alive, but after you are gone I shall take it." His anger was chiefly aroused against Ka-'ahu-manu. Ka-lani-moku repeated Kahala-i'a's words to her and his feelings toward her were well known. It came to be said of him, "The little crook in the Bent-over-one on the night that the nose is bitten" (*O ua ke'e nei paha iloko o Ha'alo'u-o-ka-po-nahunahu-ihu*), [meaning that his wrath was of no importance.]

After Kahala-i'a's death, Boki became the young king's chief *kahu* and also controlled the affairs of government while Ka-'ahu-manu worked constantly to educate the people, assisted by Ka-lani-moku, Ke-kua-i-pi'ia Namahana, and others. In 1825 she made her first trip around the island holding meetings, exhorting the people, and teaching the Lord's prayer and the confession of sin. The people were taught to go into secret places and there offer up supplication to God; they were taught of God in the heavens and of the Trinity and urged to confer with Mr. Bingham and Mr. Chamberlain (Kamalani) who accompanied [Ka-'ahu-manu] on this trip. On this and other trips Ka-'ahu-manu showed her humility by holding meetings with the humblest, and entering the poorest and meanest huts. She was not a member of the church until 1826 when she joined it with several other chiefs and was christened Elizabeth Ka-'ahu-manu. She made a trip around the island after this event and the wheel of her carriage fell into the stream of Makawai between Kane'ohe and Kualoa. In September of the same year she sailed for Maui and from there went to attend the dedication of the church of Moku'aikaua at Kailua* which occurred on September 22, 1826. In 1827, after the death in Kailua of Ka-lani-moku, Ka-'ahu-manu returned and made a third trip about Oahu preaching the word of God. She stayed at Waialua where the young king was living at Wao'ala, and it was at this time that the sparkle of a diamond was seen on the beach at Mokule'ia.

Boki, whose conduct of the government was for a few months so admirable, fell under the influence of certain foreigners like Consul John Jones, Mr. Stephen Reynolds (Lanai), and the British consul, who

* *Ka Nupepa Ku'oko'a,* May 9, 1868.

feared the conversion of the chiefs and commoners to the word of God
and used to remark, "If the missionaries stay we shall have to go, if they
go we will remain." The respectable foreigners did not share this feeling,
for the chiefs were becoming interested in the word of God. Manuia was
intimate with the foreigners, who esteemed him highly; and all three,
Boki, Manuia, and Ke-ku-anao'a, became attached to these foreigners
who were hostile to the mission. Ke-ku-anao'a became mixed up in
this hostility because it was through Boki's influence that he had
married Ka-'ahu-manu's niece, the tabu chiefess Kina'u who was to
have been the king's wife when he came of age, and both Manuia and
Ke-ku-anao'a depended for their positions upon Boki whose power no
high chief dared dispute. Had not Kina'u married Ke-ku-anao'a he
might have disappeared with Boki and two of our kings might never
have been born. Thus God in his wisdom brought about this marriage
between Kina'u and Ke-ku-anao'a.

Boki, then, became the friend of these foreigners and they would
ply him with liquor and when he was intoxicated give him goods on
credit. Thus he would buy whole bolts of cloth and boxes of dry goods
and present them to the chiefs and favorites among his followers, and
these flattered him and called him a generous chief. In this way he became even more heavily indebted to the foreigners for goods than the
king [himself, through his] purchases. In some things he was farsighted,
for he had several buildings put up on Kauai, Maui, and Hawaii for
the sale of sandalwood and paid the men [who cut it] in cloth; and
so the mountains where the sandalwood grew were full of people
working for cloth. Boki also established several stores in Honolulu
where cloth was sold, "Deep-in-debt" (A'ienui) they were called because of his heavy debts. At Pakaka was a large wooden building belonging to Liholiho. Boki's was a smaller building which had been
moved and was called "Little-scrotum" (Pulaholaho). The weighing
of the sandalwood was done by foreigners who went from place to
place for the purpose. The foreigners, finding Boki friendly and oblig-
ing, proposed a more profitable way of making money, and both
Boki and Manuia erected buildings for the sale of liquor, Boki's called
Polelewa and Manuia's Hau'eka. Since Liholiho's sailing to England
lawlessness had been prohibited, but with these saloons and others
opened by the foreigners doing business, the old vices appeared and
in a form worse than ever. Polelewa became a place where noisy
swine gathered. Drunkenness and licentious indulgence became common
at night, and the people gathered in these places for hulas and filthy
dances. The foreigners came to these resorts to find women, and Ka-
'ahu-manu and the missionaries were discussed there.

Boki and Liliha moved from Hali'imaile to live on Beretania (Pele-kane) and the British consul also bought a house there, but the king remained at Pohukaina where the king's house at that time stood. Ka-lani-moku felt very uneasy lest Boki attempt to seize the government and depose their niece and the king. He told Ka-'ahu-manu of his sus-picions and of his fear lest Boki try to make way with them. "You have no cause to be uneasy; it is I who should fear most," she said. He con-tinued, "I have no one whom I can trust to watch him. All the chiefs as well as the commoners, great and small, follow him. But I have a plan to put up a small house (*papa'ihale*) *mauka* of Kawananakoa, and in case he moves to his canefield up Manoa I will set up my little house *mauka* of Makiki, and as Ke-ku-anao'a goes back and forth to visit him and has compassion on my loneliness, I might drop him a word." These men of old could reason well, but those who were following the for-eigners were letting the strangers do their thinking for them. . . . It is this intimate relation with the foreigners and the controversies over re-ligion which have been the occasion for all the troubles in our country since the time of Kamehameha III until today. Had the chiefs and those who attained learning ruled wisely, no nation could have interfered with our independence. Hoahine, Raiatea, and Borabora are still ruled by their own chiefs without interference from the French, and so are the Tuamo-tus. Only at Tahiti and Taha'a do the French rule according to the treaty; the other islands are ruled by their own chiefs, Kaululai and Kapoa, and no foreigners hold official positions. Chiefs and people are reported to be on the increase and there has been no conflict with foreign powers.

Because of Ka-lani-moku's illness from the dropsy and the shame and worry which Boki's wasteful and drunken habits and his plots against the life of Ka-'ahu-manu occasioned Ka-lani-moku sought re-lief in a trip to Hawaii. He took with him his foreign doctor, John Pellham by name, and on February 8, 1827, Ka-lani-moku died at Kai-lua in the fifty-ninth year of his age. He was born on the summit of Ka'uiki in Hana, Maui, and had been Chief Counselor (*kuhina nui*) with the power over life and death under Kamehameha with whom he was a great favorite. He had acted as Kamehameha's treasurer, di-vided up the lands, and served as war leader. Some said that he even excelled Kamehameha as a warrior. He had become a God-fearing chief and was the cable which held fast the nation; at his death that stay was broken. Ka-'ahu-manu, Kua-kini and his wife Keoua, Na-ihe and Ka-pi'o-lani, Hoa-pili and his wife, Ke-kau-'onohi, and other chiefs were present and wept bitterly at his death . . . Some expressed their grief in extravagant ways to the terror of Dr. Pellham. One man named Kia'i-moku hung himself head down from the ridge of the house where Ka-lani-moku's body was laid, and wailed bitterly. Many persons were suspected of having caused his death.

Ka-lani-moku had been interested in the cultivation of cotton and had, in 1825 and 1826, planted large areas in cotton from one end of the group to the other. In 1826 the cultivation of sugar was begun in Manoa valley by an Englishman. Boki and Ke-ku-anao'a were interested in this project and it was perhaps the first cane cultivated to any extent in Hawaii. When the foreigner gave it up Boki bought the field and placed Kinepu in charge. A mill was set up in Honolulu in a lot near where Sumner (Keolaloa) was living. For this action Boki is to be commended.

During this year an unfortunate incident took place in the murder by Kama-kea, who had been one of Kahala-i'a's attendants before his death, of a Spaniard employed as a laborer by Don Paula y Marin. Kama-kea was drunk at the time. People going home from Polelewa saw him and Ka-mumuku holding the man under water and dragging him in the mud in the pond in the brickyard of Waiakemi. The men were arrested and placed in the fort. Ka-mumuku ran away and was afterwards pardoned; Kama-kea refused to escape. This incident led Ka-'ahu-manu and Ka-lani-moku to enact a law making murder punishable by death. Strangely enough there was no trial and no sentence of hanging passed. No doubt it was Manuia's idea. In the dark hours of morning a rope was strung between two coconut trees, a block and tackle fastened in the center, and Kama-kea was led out. As the soldiers made ready to hang him he asked John Big-feet (Wawaenui) to wait until he had offered prayer and sung a hymn. After singing the hymn, "Onward, my ever living soul," he put the hymnal inside his shirt, the loop was placed over his head, and the rope drawn. He died without a struggle. Although he had prayed and confessed his sins no minister of the gospel was there to make his last hours pleasant . . .

Kau-i-ke-aouli's assumption of control was marked by the selection of a group of young chiefs and children of important persons, of resident foreigners, and of commoners, to become his favorites, friends, members of his household, and soldiers and sailors to form his bodyguard. After Kahala-i'a's death all repaired to the uplands of Waialua adjoining Waimea, to upper Kolokini, Wao'ala, 'Aikanaka, Kaloka in upper Makaleha, and to upper Mokule'ia, to cut sandalwood. Kau-i-ke-aouli was but a boy in his thirteenth year while cutting at upper Wao'ala and lower Maeaea, but he attended to the work himself and when he sailed in his two-masted boat to Mokule'ia or other places after sugarcane, sweet potatoes, melons, pigs, and fowl, he handled the boat in true sailor fashion, dressed in his sailor blouse and cap. He hauled the ropes and helped heave the anchor, saying, "Kamehameha's kingdom of work has come." While they were in upper Waolani the men contracted a skin disease like the white pits found on the bark of the sandalwood tree, so the king's men called Hulumanu, who were in the habit of wasting their substance on women, and were called "foul rain" (*ua wekaweka*), got the name of "Birds with foul feathers" (*Hulumanu-weka*). Such a huge amount of sandalwood was cut that they could not load it all onto their own ships and had to put part on a Portuguese three-master to carry to Honolulu. The king's ship, *Ka-'ai-noa-nui*, was loaded down and put in charge of Manuia and a young Englishman named Roberts to convey to Macao, but the two managed to lose the ship and all it contained in the transaction and returned on the *Koli* under Captain Kolo without anything to show for the expedition. The king bought a larger vessel, a brig owned by John Meek's company, which was renamed the *Kamehameha* and had a figurehead of that chief dressed in a tight Norfolk jacket with a white hat on the head. The king took a trip to Maui and Hawaii to test her speed. Afterwards she was converted into a man-of-war and carried eighteen guns.

It was at this time that Kina'u and Ke-ku-anao'a were married. Ka-'ahu-manu was furious; she ground her teeth and spit fire. Here is a comic song for the occasion which pleased the young king.

Kau ke keha o Kona i ka malie,	Kona's head rests on the pillow in the calm.
Hiololua i ka la'i a Ehu-ka-ipo,	A double peace is the peace of Ehu-the-lover.
Huli 'ole ka wa'a ke holo i ka pohu,	No canoe overturns when it sails in the calm.
Hehi i ka palahalaha a ka malie,	The sea lies smooth and peaceful,
Like ka mala a Kona e waiho nei.	Lies as still as the food patches of Kona.
Waiho nui iho la no i ka la ilaila.	The sun shines down on all.
Mai Lanihau no a Keopu-e	From Lanihau to Keopu
Opu iho la iloko o ka hina'i komo 'ole.	Vacant is the fish basket into which no fish enter.
He maunu 'ole nana e ho'owale-wale,	There is no bait tempt them,
E komo ai ka i'a hei i ka'upena.	So that the fish may be caught in the net.

Scarcely had this excitement died down when Ka-'ahu-manu's stepson Ke-li'i-ahonui, on Maui, ran away with that mischievous girl Ke-kau-'onohi, but angry as Ka-'ahu-manu was she said nothing to this match because of the affair with Kina'u. It was not until Kina'u became pregnant with her first child that Ka-'ahu-manu became reconciled to what had taken place. At his birth she herself took charge of the infant, who was named David Kamehameha. A second grandchild whom she had charge of at this time was Ruth Ke-'eli-kolani.

After the king's return from Waialua, Boki set the whole district of 'Ewa, headed by Kane-pa-iki, hauling posts and rafters for a new king's house, afterwards called "The-fern-house" (Ka-hale-uluhe) because it was first covered from the top of the roof to the posts with *uluhe* ferns tied down neatly inside, and then thatched outside with grass.* About the time that the king went to live in this house, a Russian warship bearing a kind letter from Alexander of Russia arrived in the harbor and anchored in line with the warship Kamehameha . . . In this year Lahaina was fired upon by a British warship commanded by Captain Clark, and the breadfruit trees were withered by the shots; the people retreated into the valleys of Kaua'ula, Kanaha, and Kahoma . . . In the same year there came up to John Jones's wharf a British vessel commanded by a captain blind in one eye. He brought as a great curiosity two human heads belonging to two Maori chiefs, which had been cut off during the war being carried on at that time between the British and the New Zealanders. [These heads had been] preserved in alcohol in such a way as to show their handsome features, dark tattoo prints on the cheeks, and fine long hair.

In this same year the Rev. William Richards was brought to Honolulu to be tried on complaint of Captain Buckle, commander of a British whaler, the same man who had commanded the ship that took Liholiho and his company to England. Captain Buckle had on former occasions found the nation living in ignorance. The sailors used to pay for women with a piece of cloth, a small mirror, or a pair of shears, beads, a small piece of steel, a plug of tobacco, or a small coin; and for these things the women paid in venereal diseases which left them with red scalps. At the time when Mr. Richards came to live in Lahaina the pious chiefess Ke-opu-o-lani died, but Hoa-pili and his wife and other prominent chiefs and commoners had become converted and looked upon Mr. Richards as a father. When he taught them that it was wrong and against the will of God to thus prostitute themselves they listened to him and made laws against these practices for the protection of the island. The whaleships

* *Ka Nupepa Ku'oko'a*, May 13, 1868.

came in [at Lahaina] and found that they could no longer have women, and the captains began to abuse the missionaries. In 1826 Captain Buckle's ship arrived and when he heard of the prohibition he said, "It is a missionary law and a missionary tabu," but when he tried to test it out and allowed the men shore leave, they found that it was indeed a fact. The men therefore resolved to wait until dark and then go and tear down the house and beat up Mr. Richards, but the chiefs and people guarded him night and day. When Mr. Richards wrote Captain Buckle complaining of this abuse and requesting him to prevent it, Captain Buckle replied that if he would give women to his men there would be peace in Lahaina. To this Mr. Richards would not consent, and Captain Buckle was compelled to purchase outright a woman named Leo-iki, whom he took with him to Oahu.

In October, 1827, Captain Buckle received a letter from a brother in England who wrote, "A story has appeared in the papers here telling of your improper action toward Mr. Richards and how you purchased a woman of Maui with gold money." Unable to cover his shame, Captain Buckle tried to ruin Mr. Richards and made charges against him to the British consul in Honolulu, Mr. Richard Charlton, accusing Richards of libel. Mr. Charlton joined him in the charges. What was the attitude of the American consul? This same Jones had many times more than four wives, yet he walked the street with his silk top hat set on the side. He was known to be against the missionaries, and some of the foreign merchants and the deputy American consul, Mr. Stephen Reynolds (Lanai), the white-haired American, were with him in this opposition. Mr. Charlton made complaint to Boki, Ka-lani-moku's successor, and Boki, who was the king's premier, and Manuia, who was in charge of the fort on Oahu, took the part of the consul. Boki had questioned John Young as to Mr. Richards' guilt and Young had shaken his head and mumbled, "England is very big to offend; a libelous letter is very wrong." Boki therefore informed Ka-'ahu-manu and the king of Young's answer and they too and the chiefs decided that Richards must be in the wrong. The chiefs therefore wrote to Maui, "You chiefs of Maui, greetings to you. If Captain Buckle, Captain Clark, and the British consul come to get your teacher let them have him. It is a foreigner against a foreigner; let them have it out between them." The chiefs of Oahu were willing to place Mr. Richards in the jaws of the shark.*

Ka-'ahu-manu was like a mother to the people of that community, and the missionaries and their teaching were like her beloved children. Her heart was grieved over the charges made against one she loved, and

* *Ka Nupepa Ku'oko'a,* May 30, 1868.

her tears fell. Nor was she pleased to have her enemies act according to
their own will. She therefore wrote to the chiefs of Maui, Hawaii, and
Kauai to come together in Honolulu, and some of the church people also
accompanied Mr. Richards. A council of chiefs was held at the king's
home at Pohukaina above the house of Ka-lani-moku to decide whether
Mr. Richards was guilty or not. They were ignorant of the English law
in the matter. They knew that when a man committed murder he forfeited his life. If Mr. Richards were now to die for this crime it was a
pity. For two days they deliberated but could find no way to save Mr.
Richards from being put to death, since both John Young and Boki had
pronounced against him. The government had at that time no constitution ensuring a legal trial with witnesses presented on both sides to decide such a question, hence their uncertainty.

At noon of the day following David Malo and Ka-na'ina [father of
King Lunalilo] met Ka-'ahu-manu, Hoa-pili, and Ka-ka-ulu-ohi in secret
in one of the rooms of the Council House, which they entered by a
private entrance. Ka-'ahu-manu addressed David Malo while her tears
flowed, saying, "Alas! I see no way to save our teacher. Young and Boki
both say he is guilty of writing to America." Malo replied, "Is that what
he is accused of?" "Yes." "How these foreigners contradict themselves!
[Malo exclaimed] They say it is wrong to worship God, but all right to
learn writing, and now they say it is all wrong for Mr. Richards to write
a letter." Again Malo asked, "Suppose you had a spoon stolen and some
one should inform you who had stolen it, who would be to blame, the
one who stole the spoon or the one who told you who was the thief?"
"The one who stole it." "You were Kamehameha's wife and Ka-niho-
nui forced you to sleep with him. Luheluhe informed Kamehameha.
Now, I ask, which of the two did Kamehameha execute? Was it Luheluhe?" "It was Ka-niho-nui." "Is there any country in the world where
the wrongdoer is commended and the informant against him pronounced
guilty?" "Nowhere!" Light was fast beginning to break in upon the
chiefess' mind. Malo continued, "Why should Mr. Richards be convicted
and Captain Buckle who committed wrong go free?" "It is plain to me
that Mr. Richards is in the right and we have been very ignorant," Ka-
'ahu-manu replied. She then went before the chiefs and presented her
views.

The next day the king, Boki, Manuia, Ke-ku-anao'a, the British consul, and Captain Buckle presented themselves all dressed in gold-trimmed
uniforms. When Manuia urged Mr. Richards' imprisonment within the
fort, and Boki and the consul also urged this upon the Council, Ka-'ahu-
manu spoke up and said, "The chiefs have consulted about the charge
against Mr. Richards, who has been brought to trial by the British consul
because of an alleged wrong committed against a British subject within

the kingdom of Hawaii. This is our decision: Mr. Richards is not guilty of the charge made; he is innocent and we release him."*

The queen by this decision made enemies for herself of the consul and the foreign merchants and of Boki and Manuia of her own people. Manuia and the consul went out shaking their heads and waving their swords in the air, and the captains retired crestfallen. The two captains who had fired on Lahaina became Ka-'ahu-manu's worst enemies. The consul beat up one of her keepers who had chased away the consul's cattle which roamed at large all the way to Pawa'a and were eating Ka-'ahu-manu's plantings at Kapuka'oma'oma'o in Manoa. This man, Kane-kuahine, was roped about the neck by the consul and dragged behind his carriage, tossed up and down all along the plains, his chin and ribs broken, and was only saved from being killed by getting his hand inside the noose. Englishmen are certainly oppressive to the weak! It was not the missionaries alone who suffered but the Hawaiians much more . . . . I have seen with my own eyes the heads of the New Zealand chiefs dropped into the sea at the wharf near Kapapoko. In Mr. John Jones' store Mr. George Wood, the husband of Ka-maunu, threw the water in which those heads had been washed at the people who came to look at the chiefs' heads. A very cruel act!

On March 30, 1828, a three-masted ship anchored in the harbor bringing a second reinforcement of missionaries together with some Hawaiians who had been educated through the kindness of the American pople. The missionaries included the Rev. E. W. Clark (Kalaka), the Rev. P. J. Gulick (Kulika), the Rev. Jonathan S. Green (Kerina), the Rev. Lorrin Andrews (Aneru), Mr. Gerrit P. Judd (Kauka), a physician, Mr. Shepherd (Kapaki), a printer, their wives, and a single woman, Miss Maria Ogden. There were others who later went as missionaries to the Rocky Mountains in Oregon. The Hawaiians were John Palu, Haia, Ka-la'au-lana, 'Ukali-moa, and Ka-lima-hana.† Some of these assisted the missionaries and others lived like any of the people. John Palu became a favorite with Boki and married the daughter of George Holmes and Mrs. Pale.

A few months later the king, accompanied by his chiefs, Boki among them, his Hulumanu, and sailors, went to Hawaii on his warship *Ka-mehameha*, attended by other vessels, for his first visit to that island since leaving it for Honolulu. At Lahaina they were well feasted and met Nahi-'ena'ena, Ke-kau-'onohi, Hoa-pili, Ka-hekili, Kau-kuna, and all the other chiefs of that place. Here they witnessed a tragic occurrence; a man out surf riding at 'Uo was killed by a shark which bit off

---

* This story is by Dibble 10, pp. 197-198, and Remy 27, pp. 217-225.
† *Ka Nupepa Ku'oko'a*, June 6, 1868.

his limbs and left his body floating. At Hilo the party met but a poor reception. Here were Pi'opi'o, his wife Ma'alo, and other chiefs, but they gave nothing but cooked food, held onto their lands, and did not offer them to the king as was the custom . . . Boki gave the district of Hilo to the king to divide among his followers and thus uphold his dignity at this place, but the other chiefs were not pleased at Boki's action. The king went with his sister Harriet Nahi-'ena'ena and others to pay his first visit to the volcano and spent the night at Wai'owe'owe' above 'Oma'olaulau some distance *mauka* of Kapu'euhi. He was preceded, by two days, by a black man (lascar) by the name of Kinikona who had made an oath to leave his hair in the keeping of Pele and who had then joined the king's party.

Soon after the king's return to Oahu one of his ships, the *Mikapaka*, arrived from Borabora bringing home the high chief Ke-'aki-lawa, his wife Ka-hope-kahu, and a chief from Tahiti named Paraita, one of the company of Tati, grandfather of Ninito, who had given Tahiti to the French. The ship brought back coconut oil in barrels and bamboo joints, and many other valuables all of which were placed in the hands of Boki. Another of the king's ships, the *Ka-mahole-lani* under Captain Paul Sumner, arrived with Carlos Marin, younger brother of Paula, who brought back another wife, a chiefess of the Wallis (Uvea) islands, a group situated near the cannibal islands of Fiji. The ship brought also the wife's parents and Lohi'au, former wife of Carlos Marin. This was the first time that any Wallis islanders had been seen in Hawaii. They appeared to be somewhat civilized as they wore dresses woven like cloth, and outside of their outer garment both men and women wore another reaching to the feet and gathered at the back. The little fingers of the hands were amputated. The ship also brought mother-of-pearl, sponges, sea shells, and many other articles of value for the king. The ship itself was condemned as unseaworthy, and a two-masted boat was constructed at Pakaka and turned over to Carlos Marin to return to the Wallis Islands, accompanied by some Hawaiians. There he was made ruler, but he made the people work too hard constructing forts and wooden houses for himself; and the chiefs and his father-in-law, William Ka-ni'au, who had come to Hawaii with him rose up and killed him and ten Hawaiians. . . .

When Ka-'ahu-manu and the higher chiefs heard how Boki had divided up his lands in the district of Hilo among the chiefs and the king's men, they suspected him of conspiracy, for they held that the lands were really under their control. They therefore agreed not to hold the government responsible for debts contracted by him or Kuini Liliha his wife, but to consider them his personal indebtedness. The old debts contracted in the time of Kamehameha I and II and those of the ruling king, yet unpaid, all of which had with interest accrued reached the sum of $150,000 to $200,000, were alone to be included in the indebtedness of the kingdom. Of this debt the greater part was owed to American merchants. There was a rumor that the kingdom was to be taken over by the United States. This might have happened had not a constitutional form of government been declared and government revenues conserved so that its debts could be paid in full. Certain of the foreign teachers who loved the Hawaiian people, the chiefs, and the whole nation, were taken into the government, and it became an easy thing to pay these debts and deal with other abuses that had been heaped upon the government. But Boki when he heard what Ka-'ahu-manu had said about his paying his own debts said, "This is strange! I thought that the king was mine, that the government of the whole group was under my control, and that whatever I thought right would be accepted by the king, the chiefs, and the whole people! . . . The woman who is so fond of God said that one should disregard things of the body and think upon things of the spirit. I thought she cared for spiritual riches and looked upon earthly wealth as trash. Here is a proof of it! She went to Hawaii to dismantle Hale-o-Keawe, had the chiefs' bones burned, the house broken down, and the hidden bones of the chiefs brought out and shown publicly. Perhaps if she knew where Kamehameha was buried she would have his bones too made public. I know that the kings of England take excellent care of the bones of their fathers, and so were the bones of our ancient chiefs cared for. They were hidden under oath by a trusted person."

The year 1828 is notable for the visit of Ka-'ahu-manu to Hawaii to fulfill a vow that she had made to attempt the recovery of the bones of Lilinoe on Mauna Kea where her body was said to have lain for more than a thousand years in a well-preserved condition, not even the hair having fallen out. Others deny this and say her body was too well-hidden ever to have been found. Her offspring count from Hua-nui-i-ka-la'ila'i; she was the ancestress of ruling chiefs, and from her line was born 'Umi-ka-lani [father of the Mahi family on Hawaii], son of Keawe-nui-a-'Umi by Ho'opili-a-Hae. It is said that Ka-'ahu-manu did not find the bones of Lilinoe, but only those of Liloa, Lono-i-ka-makahiki, Kauhola, and Lole at Waipi'o, and these she removed to Ka'awaloa. She also removed to Ka'awaloa the bones of all the chiefs up to the time of Ka-lani-opu'u and Kiwala'o which had been netted into baskets (ka'ai) and which completely filled the Hale-o-Keawe, and she destroyed the remaining bones with fire. It was this act which embittered Boki further against her.

Another cause of complaint against Ka-'ahu-manu arose when Ka-iki-o-'ewa, finding himself deep in debt to Mr. French and other foreign merchants, was arranging to pay his debts by giving over the lands of

Kewalo and Kulaokahuʻa to Mr. French. This merchant never made any complaints in business matters, but took all the sandalwood which others refused, even white wood or small wood. He was accordingly called "Grab-all" (*Hapuku*), and several of the chiefs were indebted to him. He accepted Ka-iki-o-ʻewa's offer and made ready to erect a wooden frame building at Kulaokahuʻa on the Waikiki side at a point where the *'olohe** had sunk some time before.† Ka-ʻahu-manu heard of this and sent a man to forbid Mr. French's building on the land and issued an order that none of the chiefs was to dispose of lands or give over any to the foreigners in payment of debts, for the king alone had the power of disposing of land anywhere in the group. She was then obliged to assume the indebtedness of all the chiefs, and when the chiefs discovered that the government was assuming the debts, there was a rush to turn them over to her. This added to Boki's discomfiture.

There was also a quarrel over the succession. One of Ka-ʻahu-manu's attendants, named Ka-pau, said to Boki, "Say, [Boki] Ka-maʻuleʻule, Ka-ʻahu-manu says that her foster child is a grandniece of your foster child" (the king). Boki asked, "What did that boastful woman say about our lord?" "She was talking to Ke-ka-ulu-ohi, and we sat listening, and she said, 'Perhaps when my grandchild [Ruth Ke-ʻeli-kolani] is grown she may become ruler.' 'How?' asked Ke-ka-ulu-ohi. 'Don't you understand that Ka-ʻo-lei-o-Ku was Kamehameha's first child, and that Pauahi was his daughter, and she [pointing to Ruth] is Pauahi's daughter? She is therefore the grandniece of Kau-i-ke-aouli on the Kamehameha side.'" When Boki heard this he conceived the wish to dispose of Ka-ʻahu-manu, but he said nothing openly. One day however when he was under the influence of liquor and Harriet Nahi-ʻenaʻena had arrived from Maui and was with the king at Boki's house at Ka-ʻopua-ua just above the king's house, Ka-pa-moʻo, Boki said to the king, "You two should be married and have children so that I might bring one up as your heir and successor; then the chiefs would not dare urge your grandniece as your possible successor!" and he recounted all that he had heard. Paʻalua Ka-lani-moku went in tears to Ka-ʻahu-manu where she sat with Hoa-pili, Kua-kini, and other chiefs in the large grass house at Pohukaina. "What are you crying about"? the chiefs asked. She said to Hoa-pili, "What do you think! Boki is trying to make the rulers marry each other in order to have a successor." "He and I are of the same mind," remarked Kua-kini. Hoa-pili said, "What business is it of his? It is her place [Ka-ʻahu-manu's] to make the match!" Others among the chiefs spoke sarcas-

---

* An *'olohe* was a rude dugout canoe.
† *Ka Nupepa Kuʻokoʻa*, June 13, 1868.

tically, saying, "What wonder that the one 'girdled with the intestines of Kamehameha' should fancy himself the chief to arrange the marriage of Kamehameha's grandchildren!" All these remarks Pa'alua, who was herself a high chiefess and an attendant upon Harriet Nahi-'ena'ena, repeated to Boki, and Boki was of course furious and prepared for a tussle with Ka-'ahu-manu. Now you all know the reason why Boki was angry wth Ka-'ahu-manu! I am the only one who had that knowledge, and had I kept it to myself and God had taken me from you, the next generation would have remained ignorant of it, and that would have been a pity.

The allusion to the girdle had reference to the rumor that Boki Kama'ule'ule was the son of Ka-hekili 'Ahu-manu, and that the father because of his hatred for Kamehameha had sworn over the child that he should have the intestines of Kamehameha to serve as his loin cloth. It was because of this hatred of Ka-hekili for Kamehameha that he has left no issue while Kamehameha has several descendants living, possibly preserved by God because he was a pure-minded chief. Kamehameha knew of Ka-hekili's oath and of his hatred for him because he had killed Kiwala'o and seized the rule. Sometimes when Boki came back from bathing he would say to him, "Here is your loin cloth."

Boki was a chief of very high descent on both father's and mother's side. [Of him could be said,]

O nahili ka po loloa ia Manu'a,	The tabu chiefs of divine rank met together in Manu'a,
O ka pu kaukama i Hawaii akea,	To them was born a son in great Hawaii,
O ka pulei akea a Kiha-nui-a-Pi'ilani,	A mighty descendant of Kiha-nui, son of Pi'ilani,
A Kauhi a Kalana-honua-akea,	Of Kauhi, son of Kalana-honua-akea,
A ka makalena 'iolena uahi lena,	Of the yellow-garbed one supreme in the yellow rain.
A ka ho'ohaulani moku i o	He stands supreme over the islands.
A kela kanaka ho'ali mauna,	A man under whose tread the mountains divide,
O Ka-lani-nui-ku'i-hono-i-ka-moku. . . .	Is this Ka-lani-nui-ku'i-hono-i-ka-moku. . . .

Boki therefore claimed the king as his child and his own personal ruler whom he himself had reared, and the other chiefs who were his guardians as the king's *kahu* because of their relation to Kamehameha. Ke-opu-o-lani was connected on all sides with the Ke-kau-like line. While Kamehameha was alive Ulu-maheihei had acted as guardian to the rulers, and his word was supreme; he alone could give orders that Kamehameha obeyed. This power held also in Kau-i-ke-aouli's time. If any of the chiefs, older relatives, or *kahu* wished to consult the king about some matter, and access to the king was not to be had, they would consult Ulu-maheihei instead. This was part of his duty which had remained his from the time of Kamehameha, who had given him this position because Ulu-maheihiei was the child of Ka-me'e-ia-moku and of Koa-hou the child of Ka-manawa, two of the chiefs through whose help Kamehameha had gained the rule. For the same reason Ha'ae was a great man during the time of Ka-lani-nui-a-Mamao and in the time of Ke'e-au-moku and of Alapa'i-nui, son of Ka-uaua. So was Lono-i-ka-ha'upu in the time of Keawe. Ke-ku-anao'a held a similar position under the Kamehamehas during his old age when the old days lived again in Hawaii.

Several months passed and Boki, urged on by such foreigners as Richard Charlton and some of the merchants who hated the missionaries, determined to put an end to Ka-'ahu-manu. There was scarcely a good word said of her by these foreigners; Boki they made much of and called "a good fellow."* Their anger was especially stirred by certain laws promulgated by Ka-'ahu-manu to be observed throughout the kingdom, and supported by the chiefs from all over the group except Boki. [These were the laws:]

1. You shall not commit murder; he who puts another to death shall himself die.

2. You shall not commit adultery; he who commits this crime, man or woman, shall be banished to Kahoolawe.

3. You shall not practice prostitution; anyone guilty of this shall be imprisoned and beaten across his back with a rope, and if he still fails to keep the law shall be banished to Kahoolawe.

4. Natives and foreigners are forbidden to manufacture, sell, or drink liquor.

Ka-'ahu-manu made many laws verbally which carried weight and were observed throughout the kingdom. She prohibited the planting and drinking of 'awa, and 'awa cultivation ceased throughout the group, and peace reigned. She prohibited the practice of ancient worship, and all this ceased, and peace reigned. But at this time when so many laws, innumerable laws, laws upon laws were made, there was no peace; there was bitterness everywhere. Murder was committed, theft, adultery, worshiping of gods, drunkenness, 'awa drinking, rum drinking, and deceit.

* *Ka Nupepa Ku'oko'a*, June 20, 1868.

These swept the island out as far as to the coral beds of Waialua. As the old saying is:

O ka popo 'auhuhu ku'i aku ia,	Pound a ball of fish-poison weed,
Nana e noke aku a wali,	Leave it alone to do its work.
Ko'eke iho lena kahakai e,	The beaches will turn yellow,
Lena kohola i ka pe'ape'a i	[And] the shallow pools with its juice,
Hola ia 'ole i'a kaheka.	Even to the sea pools.
E o no ka e hola i he'e ai na 'aina,	The land was poisoned and did its deadly work
He luahi kahiko, ua noa i ka ha'i i'a.	Long ago; now it is open for another's fish.
Ua laumilo'ia na'uhane,	The spirits of these have been snuffed out,
Ua lele i ka luapau,	They have leaped into the pit of death,
Aia i ka lua mihi 'ole.	The pit where there is no repentance.

And here is another:

Ua lilo ka ea me ka hanu,	Life and breath are gone,
Ua ha'alele loa ke aho,	The last breath has been drawn.
Ha'alele lakou i ka la ka mehana,	They have left the sunlight and warmth,
Lilo lakou i ka po i kahi anu,	And gone into the night where it is cold,
Ka'a ka haka po i kahi ko'eko'e,	Passed into the night where it is chilly,
Lilo ka la ka mehana i mahana	Leaving the sun alone with its warmth.

and again:

Lumia Hilo i kaulu o ka make	Hilo is twisted in the wind of death,
Lele make Hilo.	Death flies over Hilo.
Hilo ka make ana a Hilo Paliku.	Twisted about in death is Hilo of the cliffs.
Ke uwe mai nei o Hilo-one nei la make,	Hilo of the sandy beach mourns in death,
Make loa Hilo nalo i ka poli oia.	Hilo is seized by death and hidden away in its bosom.

[The place name Hilo is here because "hilo" means "twisted in agony"] or "writhing."] There were a great many such prayers used for sorcery by these people and their *kia* prayers became an evil thing for the whole race.

Some of the laws were changed, the punishment of adultery, for example, to hard labor on the roads. But Boki kept prostitutes in the town of Honolulu, brought in profit to the country thereby, and was therefore popular with the whites, and praised in the columns of American and English newspapers. Boki was the younger brother of Ka-lani-moku, premier for the first and second Kamehamehas. Mr. Charlton, the British consul, and John Jones, the American consul, and all the other foreigners had great faith in Boki. Gray-headed Mr. Reynolds (Lanai), the American vice-consul, also upheld Boki. Mr. Jones who had children by many women who were not his wives acted as chaplain for the seamen and other American citizens who died on the island, just as if there were no American ministers to preside on such an occasion. Thus encouraged in his purpose Boki sent word by Hakiki to Ke-kahi-moku, husband of Kau-mea-lani and land agent for Boki in charge of Waikiki, to make food ready for the soldiers who were coming that night for drill. Ka-hi-lauhele lived at the streams of Pi'inaio and 'Apuakehau and was Ka-'ahu-manu's retainer and fisherman. Boki went to Waikiki that evening, and the soldiers arrived that night equipped with guns and ammunition as if for war and some white men with them. The land of Kahaloa was covered with them.

People carried the news to Ka-'ahu-manu and told her that the soldiers and white people were coming to kill her. Some of the people, the chiefs, and members of the church joined her, but most of the soldiers stayed with Boki. Ka-'ahu-manu said, "I do not fear death planned by this son of ours, but he will have to [come] himself to kill me and these grandchildren of mine who will stay by me." These were Ruth Ke-'eli-kolani and David Kamehameha, [the latter] the firstborn child of Kina'u and Ke-ku-anao'a, whose birth had reconciled her to her niece's match and whom she and Ke-ka-ulu-ohi had adopted.

When Ke-ku-anao'a, and Ka-na'ina, Ka-'ahu-manu's nephews-in-law, heard the rumor of Boki's purpose they started on horseback for Waikiki, but at Kawelo near Ma'alo, a little distance from Pawa'a, Ka-na'ina became frightened and turned back to encourage their wives and Ka-'ahu-manu while Ke-ku-anao'a proceeded alone. He went through the stream of Pi'inaio, on to Kaihikapu and Kawehewehe, entered the coconut grove between there and Helumoa, and went down the mouth of 'Apuakehau Stream to the *kou* growth at Kahaloa. It was full of people as far as the grass house of Kekahimoku close to Kualalua. Boki was there close to Kapuni with some of the chiefs and soldiers. When the people saw Keku-anao'a they shouted his name and then were silent, though a few greeted him with "aloha." He noticed that they were armed. Boki was angry and would not look at him. Even when Ke-ku-anao'a reached out for his hand and kissed him he would not extend his hand. Ke-ku-anao'a led him away to a secluded place and said, "Here am I, your younger brother, whom you commanded to remain at Ka-'ahu-manu's house and to be obedient to the voices of those whose house it was. I would not have gone there except for your command because I did not wish your words to be in vain. I have found no fault in the house of the aunt-in-law. I have heard that you were coming to kill Ka-'ahu-manu and I have left her weeping over this plot of yours." Boki answered, "I will not put those of her household to death, but I am jealous of her because of our lord" [the king]. . . .* Much more was said between the two, and Boki gave up the idea of declaring war against Ka-'ahu-manu.

Boki returned and lived at his place at Beretania and devoted himself to medicine, in which he was proficient, and all those joined him who were skilled in placing pebbles [in diagnosis], such Kaao, Kuauau, Kinopu, Kahiole, Nahinu, Kekaha, Hewahewa, and their followers and other kahunas besides. Early in 1829 Boki started work on a government road running from the west gate of the Beretania place at Kahehune (the Royal School) to 'Auwaiolimu (where the Buddhist church stands on Punchbowl) and to the Pauoa stream, then on to the opposite side of Kalokohonu, down Kaheiki, rising to 'Alekoki and then running straight to Kawananakoa. The Keanini road began at the mouth of Nu'uanu [Valley] and ran down to the *hau* grove of Kahaukomo. Here the trees grew thick and overarched the way with their shade, leaving it in old days muddy like a taro patch. It is said that in old days from Kahapa-'akai clear to Hapu'u it was a beautiful highway through charming villages with *manienie* grass on either side of the road and garden patches where grew taro, potatoes, bananas, 'awa, *wauke*, sugarcane, *olona* and all the fat things of the land. Between Kahapa'akai clear to the mouth of the valley were situated many celebrated heiaus (*luakini waihau*) where people went to worship. [These had been] erected in ancient days as war heiaus or heiaus for purifying the land; for Nu'uanu had been a magnificent battleground in those old times. Here Pele-io-holani fought against Alapa'i-nui, ruling chief of Hawaii, and so fought chiefs before and after his day. But when the *hau* trees grew so thick as to cover the road, the lovely place became a swamp where thieves and robbers took refuge. Keanini was the first to clear and widen the road and let in the light of the sun. He improved the road in order to draw lumber for building the Kawaiaha'o church. The logs were cut in Ko'olauloa, brought by canoe to Kane'ohe, and hauled over the Pali.

* *Ka Nupepa Ku'oko'a*, June 27, 1868.

Boki started to work at the *makai* road leading to Ka'ala'a and when he reached the stream of Kaheiki there stood a great rock over the stream blocking the way. Boki was trying to remove it when a man came forward and said, "Hear, O chief! leave that rock alone. The god made this rock a guardian for this place and his house is yonder (pointing upward to Kaheiki). It is a guardian for the house of the god and its name is Ho'eu. The nature of this rock is that if you move it aside it will make you move to a foreign land and you will no longer live in Hawaii. Lucky for you if a year passes before you depart." Boki's pipe lighters, Hohopa and Hukiki, reproved the man, to whom he answered, "Take care lest you be thrown onto a bed of thistles!" While working on the Luakaha road Boki found a long, pointed rock in his way and was starting to remove it when a divining kahuna named Lu'au who was skilled in pointing out locations came forward and said to him, "Do not disturb this rock; it is named Ku-of-exceeding-great-mana (Ku-manamana) and Rock-of-exceeding-great-mana (Pohaku-manamana). Not even a high chief should disturb that rock, for it covers the waters of Ka-papa-i-kawa-luna which lie below it and supply the waters of Kunawai, Kahoakane, Ko'ula, and Kewalo." Boki instantly ordered the men to remove the rock, but it extended into the soil so far that when they had dug some ten fathoms down and about the same distance either way, he gave up in despair. Lu'au also showed him Kukui-puka and other *kupua* objects *mauka* of this place.

The building of Kawaiaha'o church was completed in 1829 while Boki was cultivating taro in the uplands of Nu'uanu from Kahapa'akai to Makuku and at Keawawapu'ahanui. Cutting of the logs for the building had been begun in 1825 at Paupala'ai in Wahiawa while Keanini was chief in Ko'olaupoko, and the finishing timbers were had from Ko'olaupoko and Ko'olauloa. The building was begun in the latter part of 1828, and early in 1829 it was completed. The pulpit was built, and covered with red velvet with candlesticks on either side. The ship *Vincennes*, under Captain Finch, arrived with the chaplain, Rev. Charles S. Stewart who had been one of Ke-opu-o-lani's teachers on Maui. The king and some of the chiefs sailed to Maui to bring the king's sister, Harriet Nahi-'ena'ena, and the Maui chiefs to the dedication of the church. . . . Another ship sailed to bring the chiefs from Hawaii . . . and those from Kauai were also ordered to Honolulu to witness the grand display of the king and his sister. . . . The dedication took place on Friday, July 3, 1829, and was conducted with great ceremony. The king and his sister were seated on a litter some three fathoms long and a fathom and a half wide with heavily padded seat draped with fancy *tapas* soaked in perfumed waters, and covered with the feather cloak named Halakea-o-'I'ahu (white pandanus of 'I'ahu). Harriet [was] in front, and the king wearing a gold-trimmed suit and a feather cloak [was] seated farther back. Boki and all the other chiefs of rank carried the litter on their shoulders while Ka-'ahu-manu, Kina'u, and the other high chiefesses held up the edges of the trailing tapas. *Kahili* were placed along the sides of the litter and the famous old *kahili*, 'Ele'ele-ua-lani and Hawai'i-loa, were brought out for the occasion. Ku-ho'oheihei Paki made himself famous that day by carrying alone the great *kahili* of Ke-opu-o-lani, called 'Ele-'ele-ua-lani. Ka-'ahu-manu also did honor to her grand niece Ruth Ke-'eli-kolani, who had also a high seat and her *kahili* Po'o-uliuli, as well as a number of smaller *kahili*. The procession extended for a mile. Native soldiers and sailors from the ship accompanied the march, and Captain Finch, the ship's officers, and a band of sixty pieces joined the procession. All the missionaries were assembled. After a song, the Rev. Hiram Bingham dedicated the church. Songs were sung to the solemn notes of flute and drum, the congregation was dismissed, and the royal pair were borne out of the church.* The courteous treatment of the king and chiefs by the captain and chaplain of the *Vincennes* and the kind and religious attitude of her crew made that ship famous in Hawaii. The captain allowed the warship to take the chiefs back to Maui and Hawaii, accompanied by the king and his attendants. The captain and chaplain associated with the chiefs and were often consulted in official matters.

While Boki was engaged on his cultivation up in Nu'uanu he heard that Kau-i-ke-aouli's favorites were gone to the mountains of Wahiawa, Hale'au'au, and Lihu'e to cut sandalwood and that Paki and 'Ai-kanaka had been placed in command. He and Kuini Liliha immediately returned to their Beretania place, and the chief prepared to go to Wahiawa to cut sandalwood. He announced his plan to his brothers and all the kinsmen of Ka-lani-moku and their retainers and bought axes of all descriptions and warm flannels for his men from the stores of the white people. Just as the party was about to leave for the mountains, a British ship arrived under Captain Blind-eye (Makapa'a), the same captain who had brought the skulls of the two New Zealand chiefs, and he spoke to some white men about an island in the South Seas where sandalwood grew from the mountains to the sea. Mr. Roberts and Jack Red-face (Maka-pa'ula), the two foreigners employed in Boki's store, brought this news to Boki, and Boki immediately sent for the captain to ascertain the facts of the story. The captain said, "The island is that of Nanapua (Eromango) in 'Ainawohi (New Hebrides) south of the equator. We anchored there and my men went ashore after wood and brought back a boatload of sandalwood. It grew from the beach up into the mountains. If sandal-

* *Ka Nupepa Ku'oko'a,* July 4, 1868.

wood were made a business, boats would touch there." "What kind of people are the inhabitants of that island?" asked Boki. "The people are wild. It would be wise to go well armed."

Boki now changed his plans and prepared to sail to the New Hebrides. He picked out men from the Okaka, 'Ai-'ohi'a, Uouo, Nuku-mo'o, and other divisions of the soldiery and equipped them with arms and ammunition as if it were a war expedition and not one after sandalwood. Undoubtedly Boki had the idea of ruling in this new island and of hiding his bones there as was the old custom in order to prevent an enemy from ridiculing one's bones after death. Boki's younger cousins, Hinau, who was named for the hair of Kekaulike, and Kaleohano, who was named for the voice of Ka-hekili, Boki himself, whose name Kama'ule'ule was for the fainting spells of Ka-hekili, his cousin Ka-wohi-moku, his favorite cousin Manuia, Ka-huhu, the commander of the soldiery, Ka-po-kini of the ships, and other prominent men of the land made up the company. Manuia was cutting sandalwood at Pu'ukuo in Honouliuli when Boki asked him to join them. Counting chiefs and their retainers, ten of each chief, there were five hundred or more. The people were greatly excited. "Let us sail to Nanapua to cut sandalwood," Boki proposed, and chiefs and people cried, "Very well! there is no harm in doing that. The king's debt will soon be paid, then we will cut for ourselves and trade for clothing and money. The chief has been kind to us and fed us well. How else can we repay him?" Nothing else was thought of but the expedition after sandalwood, and more offered to enlist than the ship would hold.

For two weeks the provisioning of the ship with dried taro, poi, hard tack, flour, rice, pork, meat, raw and dried fish, water, and meats of all kinds went on. Boki gave up drinking and gay living. On the afternoon of March 28 the *Kamehameha*, a large low boat carrying eighteen guns, launched out ahead with a large number of chiefs and their retainers. This was Saturday and Boki attended a meeting at the church at which the king, chiefs, and people were present. He said, "Chiefs, teachers, relatives, and all those who have offered me help, listen to my thought (*mana'o*). My sins are known to you, my stink has gone out from Hawaii to Kauai. My sins are many; I myself am responsible for them. I am going on account of the king's debt, not for idle pleasure. Pray God to guard me." When Boki's cousins Kina'u, Auhea, and the others, heard these words they wept, and all the people with them because they loved him.* The girls, Liliha, and the king surrounded him and tried to prevent his going. On Sunday night Boki escaped from them and went by canoe to the *Kamehameha*, which was waiting off Waikiki. Manuia's ship *Ke-o-ko'i*, was not yet stocked, so the *Kamehameha* waited about for five

* *Ka Nupepa Ku'oko'a*, July 11, 1868.

days, and all this time the king wept and refused food. On December 2 Ke-ku-anao'a went out to the boat under orders from the sisters and the king to bring Boki back and not to let him sail away. As soon as Ke-ku-anao'a had gone on board he ran up to Boki, caught his hands, and tried to force him to the canoe. The two struggled until exhausted and then sat down to talk it over. Ke-ku-anao'a said, "The king has taken no food since you ran away, and the girls are worried. Come back with me. Besides, your sister Ka-'ahu-manu has not seen you." Boki answered, "I will not go back; I am ashamed because Ka-'ahu-manu has ordered all the high chiefs' debts to be paid except mine." "That is not her fault. She repeatedly asked all those who had debts to make the amount known to her. All the other chiefs told their debts, you kept yours to pay yourself. Now let us go back and wait for Ka-'ahu-manu's return, you can arrange everything with her, and your debts will be paid with the others." But Boki refused, saying, "Tell our lord the king I am going to cut sandalwood to pay our debts. Let his aunts serve him. Give my regards to him and also to his aunts," and this message was brought back by Ke-ku-anao'a to the king, and there was much wailing for Boki and those who accompanied him.

On December 3, 1829, Manuia and his wife Ka-'upena went on board the ship *Ke-o-ko'i* with two hundred others. They sailed out to Mamala to join the *Kamehameha*, and a final shot was fired as their last salute to the land they were leaving. Scarcely had the ship disappeared south of Leahi when Ka-'ahu-manu arrived with her party from Kauai where she had gone to preach the word of God. On this island the chiefs were religious and made theselves thin in order to wear tight dresses. Ka-'u'uku-ali'i, Ke-kai-ha'a-kulou, Na-mahana, Keawe-mahi, Ka-'ili-naoa Ka-iki-o-'ewa among the chiefs, as also Daniel 'Ole-loa and Simeon Ka-'iu, became the religious leaders of Kauai under the influence of Ka-'ahu-manu, and the word of God flourished there. She had been unaware of what was happening at home and when she heard of the departure she put her hands over her head and said, "It was unkind of Boki to abandon our king!"

After two or three months the *Ke-o-ko'i* returned. A lunatic had previously cried through the streets, "Manuia has gone crooked; *Ke-o-ko'i* is the ship!" (*Kapakahi Manuia o Ke-o-ko'i ka moku*). The ship stood off Mamala with her flag at half mast, and when the pilot went out to her he returned with the report that this was indeed the *Ke-o-ko'i*, but that almost the whole party were dead. Manuia's body was being brought home, but the rest had been thrown out to sea. Boki and his company were lost. At this news there sounded the wailing of the people both night and day. Those who had survived were the captain, and Mika Bala,

Mr. Kelewali, Ke-aloha-'ai, Kahi-lona, and a few others. Their story was as follows: The ships had sailed within a short distance of each other until they left Rutuma, where they stopped to buy food—pork, coconuts, yams, and other provisions. The *Kamehameha* went out ahead, but the anchor of the *Ke-o-ko'i* caught in the reef, and the *Kamehameha* sent one of her divers, Kahilona, who succeeded in loosening the anchor, and they hoped to join the other ship at the New Hebrides. Upon reaching the place they saw nothing of Boki's company. While they awaited his arrival they were stricken with an epidemic which carried off almost the entire company (although eye-witnesses say the men were often alive and breathing when thrown into the sea, and that Mika Bala objected and had a quarrel with the captain in consequence). Some of the sick were left at Rutuma, and Kukui-nui and Kekeni afterwards returned from there. The captain and Ke-aloha-'ai were suffering from swollen stomachs and falling hair. Of the two hundred who had gone on board when the boat sailed, only these few survived. Of Boki and his company they had seen nothing since leaving Rutuma, and what their fate was can only be surmised. Some say that they died, others that the boat exploded and a portion of its stern was picked up by another ship.*

* *Ka Nupepa Ku'oko'a*, July 18, 1868.

CHAPTER XXIII

Kuini Liliha, 1830 to 1831

Before sailing to the New Hebrides Boki had announced to Kina'u and Ke-ka-ulu-ohi that Kuini Liliha was to be his successor in the care of the king. All Boki's functions as governor were therefore transferred to Liliha. She took charge of the young king and she ordered all the chiefesses and women of rank who had been wives of the chiefs who accompanied Boki to join her at her Beretania place with their attendants. She treated them with such kindness that she was soon so surrounded by followers that the wind could not even touch Beretania. Liquor had been prohibited prior to Boki's sailing. After a little Liliha allowed it occasionally but barred it from women. She also looked in person after Boki's taro patches in Nu'uanu.

In March, 1830, Liliha sailed with her chiefesses on the steamer *Pupuka* to 'Ewa to look after the loading of the king's sandalwood and stayed at Wahiawa at the house of Ka-pi'i-oho whose wife was Ka-'iako-ili. There was much liquor on the boat and Liliha, all her company, and officers of the boat drank so much that they would have been wrecked at Pu'uloa had not the natives of the place come to their aid. The ship went on and stopped at Kalaehopu, and Liliha and her party stayed near the banana, *'ape,* and yam plantings along the streams of Kuhia-waho and Kuhia-loko. Meanwhile Ka-'ahu-manu, Mr. Levi Chamberlain, and other church members had been traveling about Waialua preaching the gospel. On the day when they were expected at 'Ewa Ke-ka-ulu-ohi, Ka-na'ina, Ka-ni'au, Ka-ho'oki'eki'e and others went to Waikele to await their arrival. This was on Thursday, there had been a great storm at 'Ewa and the water was running in muddy, red streams to Pu'uloa. Ke-ka-ulu-ohi sailed to the point of Pa'au'au where the flood was high and found Liliha there with the wives of Kahe-huna, Puni-haole, and Ka-lua, all drunk. At the cry, "Here comes Ke-ka-ulu-ohi!" the women leaped into the stream and disappeared among the food patches leaving Liliha, who was less overcome by the liquor than the others, to greet the visitor alone. Ke-ka-ulu-ohi gave her a kiss and asked where John 'I'i was living. Liliha directed her to his place at Haulani and offered her food, but Ke-ka-ulu-ohi refused it and went on to Waipi'o, 'Ewa, where 'I'i was.

Now this story is related to explain why the young king was taken away from Liliha. The next Saturday Liliha and her friends went to Pu'uloa to await Ka-'ahu-manu's arrival. She was warmly greeted, and Ka-'ahu-manu returned to Honolulu. Soon after, John Palu came to Liliha with a note from the king asking her to return as he was ill and also because Ka-'ahu-manu was proposing to take him on a tour of the islands. When the king saw her he said, "Ka-'ahu-manu wishes to take me away from you because you drink liquor and she is afraid you will lead me into evil. Ke-ka-ulu-ohi caught you all drunk." Liliha wailed aloud and the king joined her. She said, "If Ka-'ahu-manu asks you to go with her you must go; do not refuse her." "Boki left me in your charge; I do not wish to go with Ka-'ahu-manu!" And indeed so great was the young king's love for Liliha that he ran away from Ka-'u to Ka'awaloa. It was customary for the chiefs to travel about the islands and honor the citizens by a visit; the king had been ten times about Oahu. But everybody said that the purpose of this trip was to get him away from Liliha. The chiefs 'Ai-kanaka, Na-makeha, Ka-'eo, Ka-'ai-malalo, Ulu-maheihei, Ka-hahana, Ha'alilio, were in the party, and Ka-lau-'alu, Ka-iako-ili, Ka-'ahu-manu and her grandnieces, Ke-ka-ulu-ohi and Ka-iki-o'ewa from Kauai, and many others. Just as the party was setting off Ku-ho'oheihei-pahu Paki came to Ka-'ahu-manu and said that he would be unable to accompany her. "Why not? You are one of the king's uncles, and the king is fond of you because you are strong and handsome." "I have taken land." "Where is this land?" "It is the Fort and its lands, Punchbowl and Waikiki." Who gives you this land?" "Liliha." Ka-'ahu-manu said angrily, "Where are you, my son! You are my lord's chosen child brought up in my house. Ka-'ahu-manu has been mother and sister to you. I have trusted you, and you are turning traitor."

The purpose of this famous circuit was to encourage the people to learn to read and write, to instruct the land agents to take care of the teachers and use the resources of the chiefs' lands to maintain the teachers, and not to overburden them. Anyone who did not give heed to these words or heed the teachers' instructions was threatened with dismissal as land agent (konohiki).* Ka-'ahu-manu also pronounced certain laws orally about which she wished to instruct the people:

1. Murder is prohibited, also robbery, cheating, and stealing.

2. Adultery (moekolohe) is prohibited, also prostitution (ho'okama-kama); a man must not persuade away another's wife or a woman another's husband. Each is to have but one husband or one wife, and all must [from this time] be legally married, but those who were married

* Ka Nupepa Ku'oko'a, July 25, 1868.

before the word of God became known are to be regarded as legally married.

4. Worshiping of idols such as sticks, stones, sharks, dead bones, ancient gods, and all untrue gods is prohibited. There is one God alone, Jehovah. He is the God to worship.

4. The hula is forbidden, the chant (*olioli*), the song of pleasure (*mele*), foul speech, and bathing by women in public places.

5. The planting of 'awa is prohibited. Neither chiefs nor commoners are to drink 'awa.

6. The manufacture of liquor is prohibited, such as distilling *ti* plant and fermenting potatoes, mountain apples, and other such foods.

7. Let us seek after truth and keep the words of God. I am traveling in my old age with my chief (the king) in order to turn you to the word of God, which has come to me in my old age and which I prize. Here is my command to you, to pray to God for your chief. He is our child.

On this expedition Paia-'opio son of Paia-'ai-kuala', the land agent at Halawa, made himself famous for his skill in bringing the party safe across the raging surfs of the sea of Halawa. Lahaina [was] the largest village on Maui or on the entire group and famous as the land of chiefs, "Lahaina of the breadfruit leaves," as the old saying was. At this time [it was] the center of religious and educational interest. [Here] the party met the chiefs and commoners who were members of the church and prominent in church work, men like David Malo, Daniel 'I'i, One-'o, Kalai-koa, Pikanele, Pua'a Ka-'ohana, and the Borabora teacher Tau-'a. A blind man named Bartimeus Pua'a-iki was noted as the first convert of the church at Lahaina. Harriet Nahi-'ena'ena and Maria Hoa-pili were active in church work and had many helpers. They were, as the saying is, "Like Ka-'u (district) regal in the wind," and "Majestic as the high hills of Wailau"; they snapped like dogs at the faces of wrong-doers and were like the wild beasts when they heard anything evil said of their chief, as the saying is "Only a dog who has a master will bark."

When Ka-'ahu-manu arrived she told Hoa-pili that she had taken the king away from Liliha because she was afraid of her influence over him because of her indulging in drinking and other worldly pleasures. She described the 'Ewa incident, and suggested that he go to Oahu and teach his daughter to let liquor alone and abandon drunkenness, loose living, and wastefulness. Hoa-pili demurred, saying, "What more could I do than you chiefs have done in taking the king away from her? She is but his caretaker, the chief belongs to you." But Ka-heihei-malie said, "I will go to Oahu to see my daughter Kina'u." Hoa-pili said to Ke-ahi-kuni Ke-kau-'onohi, "You must accompany her; I fear Ka-heihei-malie will be hard on my daughter." So the two sailed to Honolulu in June on the boat *Ho'oikaika*, but they found Liliha living quietly. She had given up drinking and was devoting her time to learning to read and write under Puni-haole and 'Api'i as her teachers; and all the chiefesses and attendants who lived with her were their pupils. Kina'u and Ke-ku-anano'a were following in the footsteps of Ka-'ahu-manu and had become church members, although in Boki's time they had belonged to his party; Ke-ka-ulu-ohi and Ka-na'ina had been the first to accept the faith. Ke-ka-ulu-ohi went to visit Liliha at the house called Poli-o-keawe on the Beretania place and after the customary wailing she related to Liliha the report of her doings which had reached Maui.* Liliha said, "It is true that my name stinks, and I have been called a wicked woman. I did not lead the king to drink. It was the white people who gave him the liquor; he had many of them about him. But I have indeed done wrong." And to Hoa-pili's wife and others whom she met she admitted her fault and promised to do right.

A few days later a council of chiefs was held at the stone house at Pohukaina where were gathered chiefs, commoners, and foreigners to discuss financial matters. Three chiefesses spoke for the chiefs, Ke-ahi-kuni Ke-kau-'onohi, Ka-ho'ano-ku Kina'u, Kuini Liliha. Ke-kau-'onohi opened with the words which appear so often in newspapers today and which I then heard for the first time— "Hawaii of Keawe, Maui of Kama-lala-walu, Oahu of Kakuhihewa, Kauai of Manokalanipo." She spoke of the goodness of God, of guarding what was good and forsaking what was evil, of not worshiping other gods; Jehovah alone was the one true God. Kina'u spoke in the same way. Then Liliha spoke to the people: "Chiefs and people of my chief, hear me. The stink of my name and that of my husband Boki has spread from Hawaii to Kauai. It is said that we do evil and that we have led the young king to do evil, and so he has been taken away from me. But we are not guilty; it is the white people and the naval officers who are guilty; it is they who tempted the king, and the blame has been put upon me. But I admit I have done wrong." At these words both natives and foreigners shed tears. Then Ka-heihei-malie, who had been sitting on the stairway during the council, rose and spoke about the goodness of God and urged the people to listen to the words of Ka-'ahu-manu and Kau-i-ke-aouli and of Nahi-'ena'ena. Then she added, drawing a figure from the communal method of fishing for swordfish, "In the time of Kamehameha the fishermen swam together in a row, and if one got out of line or lagged behind he was struck by the sharp nose of the fish. So those who do not follow God's word and do not obey our king, but fall out of line, they shall be struck by the sharp sword of the law, so do not lag behind lest you be

* *Ka Nupepa Ku'oko'a*, Aug. 1, 1868.

hurt." As these words fell upon the ears of the people, they applied them to Liliha and raised an uproar and talked of war against Ka-'ahu-manu and the chiefs. When the chiefesses had gone back to Maui, preparations were actually made for the war which was called the Pahikaua, and it was rumored that no one but the king was to be allowed to enter the harbor of Kou (Honolulu).

The Lord had blessed the land during those years. Fish were so plentiful, especially at Waialua and Wai'anae, that pigs and dogs feasted on those that rotted. On Hawaii and Kauai there was the same abundance. The fish caught were the *'uwi'uwi'*, *a'ua'u*, *'opelu, akule, 'alalaua', kala, wele'a, kalaliilii* (also called *pahikaua*), *he'e kukuli'i* (called *kukuma* in honor of Manuia who died at Rutuma). At Molokai, *kawakawa, aku, and 'ahi* were simply washed up on the beach, and flying fish came in huge schools. At Wailua the *kahala* fishing grounds were so rich a man could catch as many as twenty to forty fish at one haul. Perhaps this blessing upon the land was in compensation for the difficulties into which the government was falling and the extinction of the old families of chiefs and commoners which occurred at this time.

Those who stirred up the Pahikaua war were a baldheaded man named 'Au'a and a tall man named Haia', and these jeered at Hoa-pili's wife's words as follows, finding them double-edged:

O Pahulu ke 'kua hapai 'oko'a e a   Pahulu was the ghost who could carry away a man's body,

O Ka-ulu-la'au i ka moku puakala   Ka-ulu-la'au was the man who hid e a   among the thistles.*

There were other loud-voiced, sharp-tongued men; Ke-aniani, son of Ka-nopa, Kalai-mamahu, father of a line of chiefs and a war commander, Hua, and Ka-'eo, husband of Ka-nau-kapu (who died lately at Pauka'a, Hilo). They plotted to disembowel Ka-'ahu-manu and cut off her head. The chiefs in whose behalf the war was started were Kuini Liliha and Ku-ho'oheihei-pahu Paki. Many of the lesser chiefs helped on the war. They went to the house where Boki's guns were stored at Kuaiwi in Wai'anae in charge of Ka-'apu-iki and at Waialua in charge of Noho-nihi. The men at Wai'anae, 'Ewa, and the Ko'olaus gathered at Kula-uka's place at Leleo [Webb Lane, Honolulu]. At first everything was done secretly, soldiers gathering in crowds at night at the fort where guns and ammunition were distributed, but later activities were carried on openly. Even the foreigners joined in the preparations. Kina'u and her household were much troubled. She was pregnant with the future

---

* Ka-ulu-la'au the mischievous son of Ka-ka-'alaneo was banished to Lana'i where none but spirits dwelt. He tricked the spirits and made Lana'i suitable for human residence. See 14, Vol. 4, pp. 486-489; 11.

Kamehameha V. The church people and some of the missionaries, Mr. Clarke, Mr. Judd, and Mr. Chamberlain, acted as her guards; Mr. Bingham had accompanied Ka-'ahu-manu to Maui. I often met Ke-ku-anao'a during those days going on a crooked-mouthed horse to the fort. Sometimes he was admitted, at other times the gate was closed, and on one occasion there was a plan to shoot him for breaking open the gate.*

Rumors of war spread throughout the group. Ka-'ahu-manu was marooned at Lahaina; Kina'u lived in fear of death. Ka-iki-o-'ewa and some of the other chiefs proposed going to Oahu, but Na-ihe and Kuakini said, "You cannot get to Oahu; they will shoot you down as the British did. And it is not their fault. We sent you to Oahu to speak the word of God and persuade the people to turn to right living, but you condemned and insulted them and hurt their feelings." The council of chiefs finally agreed to send Ulu-maheihei to Oahu since there was some chance of his being spared. Should he be killed they would all retire to Hawaii. He was accompanied by Pikanele, Ka-'ohana, Ka-pahu-wai, Ka-hoa-haka, the teacher Tau-'a, Keawe-a-mahi, and others. It was early morning when the boat *Ho'oikaika* reached Mamala where many boats had been forced to turn back when they tried to enter the harbor because the guns from the fort were turned upon them. Some boats, like the passenger boat of Ka-iki-o-'ewa and 'Ai-kanaka, had landed passengers at Waikiki. They prayed to God therefore for protection and passed Mamala, approached and passed 'Ula-kua, approached *makai* of Ku-loloia with mouths of the guns threatening them from the fort, but passed through safely and reached Pakaka. Pikanele said, "We may be killed if we go to the fort." "There is nothing more to fear," said Ulu-maheihei. "They would have killed us already if Liliha had been of their mind. The Lord is protecting is." They entered the fort where more than a thousand rifles were stacked together. Within were Haia', 'Au'a, Ke-aniani, Ka-honu, other chiefs, and a part of the soldiers. Liliha and Paki were at once sent for. When Ke-aniani found that Ulu-maheihei was the leader of the party he went to Liliha and said, "Our father must die; if he dies we shall be rich, if he lives we shall be poor in this world." "No, he must not die," said Liliha. "People would say we were heartless to kill the only parent we have left in the world." "This is a crafty plan of the chiefs to send us Ulu-maheihei whom they know we would not harm. It is a pity that we must destitute in this world!" The chiefs held council and Hoa-pili said, "It was your son (the king) who sent me; I would not have come for the chiefs. I put myself in your hands. What is to be my fate?" "There is no death here for you; if it had been anyone else he would have died," said Liliha. Ulu-maheihei went on, "People have

* *Ka Nupepa Ku'oko'a*, Aug. 8, 1868.

been talking about you, and I have been worried. Will you and Paki consent to dismiss the soldiers, call off the war, and let me have the fort, I to be the person to live here?" Liliha and Paki consented, and Ulu-maheihei bade Paki go to Maui and bring the king back to Oahu. Soon after, Ka-'ahu-manu, the king, and the chiefs of Hawaii and Maui returned to Oahu bringing with them the old soldiers of Kamehameha, the Palena, Luahine, and the rest.

In October, 1830, the chiefs held a council at Pohukaina in regard to the late doings on Oahu known as the Pahikaua. Ulu-maheihei was appointed to be in charge of the fort and the harbor of Honolulu, to which the words of the Kauai chant refer:

Ha'i ka nalu o Ka-lehua-wehe e	The wave of Ka-lehua-wehe breaks,
Ke hili wale la no	It rolls gently in.
Ha'i ka nalu o Ka'ahe' e	The wave of Ka'ahe' breaks,
Ke hili la no	It too rolls in.
Ha'i ka nalu o Makaiwa	The wave of Makaiwa breaks
Kupono i Kewe'ai.	Just outside of Kewe'ai.

The main things decided by the council were:

1. The removal of Liliha from the governorship of Oahu.

2. All land and other property belonging to the king left by Boki in Liliha's care to be taken away from her.

3. The removal of the king from Liliha's care.

4. J. A. Kua-kini to succeed Liliha as governor in charge of the fort and harbor, with Kahi-ahine-nui as his assistant; and Ke-loa to have charge of the Waikiki fort and the yearly rentals, with Kahuna as his assistant; and Pehu to be the land agent of Honolulu under Kua-kini.

5. 'Ai-kanaka to be the chief of Punchbowl and the lands connected with it.

6. Ka-'iako-ili to succeed Ke-aniani as land agent of the Ko'olaupoko district of which Kane'ohe was the most valuable part. The Ko'olauloa and 'Ewa districts to be divided among the chiefs' favorites.

When Ulu-maheihei saw how the chiefs had stripped his daughter Liliha of all her wealth and power and left her destitute, he regretted his own part in the affair as the cause of his daughter's ruin. "I wish I had let the chiefs get out of their difficulties themselves!" he reflected with what Pikanele called "a late repentance." The king did not approve these doings either. They say that he loved Liliha better than his other mothers. Later we shall see how, in 1834, he planned to appoint Liliha his premier, and the soldiers and foreigners had been already assembled at Beretania at night when Ulu-maheihei and Kina'u came [to protest].

On December 11, 1830, after the lands had been divided by the chiefs, Ka-ho'ano-ku Kina'u gave birth at her own house to Lot Kapu-aiwa, who became Kamehameha V.* The mother suffered greatly and became unconscious. She had taken some medicine administered by Dr. Judd, and her menstruation period was long overdue. Ka-o'o 'Opu-nui, a Hawaiian medicine kahuna, was sent for, and when she recovered consciousness and was asked whether she would have the foreign or the native doctor she pointed to 'Opu-nui. Treatment was quickly administered externally and she recovered. She was then given a dose of medicine and asked for and partook of food. The child was given to Hoa-pili to be brought up at Lahaina as his grandchild and as foster child for Harriet Nahi-'ena'ena. Kane-ma'ai-kou and his wife Ma'ele were his attendants, and Ka-lau-kele was his wet nurse.

Upon J. A. Kua-kini's coming into command of the fort in 1831, he had it rebuilt. The old fort was made mostly of adobe and some stones. In 1831 it was rebuilt with coral rock, cut by the people of Ko'olauloa and assembled down at Kukulua'e'o and Kahalepua'a, and extended to thirty-six feet in length and sixteen in height. Kua-kini stationed soldiers on guard both inside and outside the fort.

Now that there was peace all over the country Ka-'ahu-manu was anxious to stamp out all other forms of worship. She ordered foreign houses of prostitution closed, but did not molest the liquor-selling establishment run by the foreigners inside the city or the two outside, one at Pawa'a owned by a black foreigner, Mr. Allen, the other at Kalia in the coconut grove belonging to Ka-hanau-maika'i owned by the Englishman James C. Lyman.

In this year the High School at Lahainaluna was founded, with pupils selected from all over the islands. The chiefs sent their own people to this school in order to train them as teachers. They were all eager for education. The educated people were like chiefs in those days because the chiefs treated them as chiefs. They did not depend entirely on the foreigners but made every effort themselves to get an education and were supported in this by the chiefs. Today those who want an education seek help from the Evangelical Association. During this year Kina'u and her household lived on Kauai, and the large church at Waimea was built. In this year also, on June 7, came the fourth reinforcement of missionaries. The Rev. D. Baldwin (Balauwina) and his wife were stationed at Waimea, Hawaii, and moved to Lahaina in 1835. The Rev. S. Dibble (Dibela) and his wife were stationed at Hilo, Hawaii, and in 1835 moved to Lahainaluna, where they remained until Mr. Dibble's

* *Ka Nupepa Ku'oko'a,* Aug. 15, 1868.

death in 1844. The Rev. Rueben Tinker (Tiueka) and his wife were stationed at Wailuku, then at Lahaina, then Honolulu, then Koloa on Kauai, and returned to America about 1838. Mr. Johnstone and his wife, teachers, lived at Kawaiaha'o until about 1832 and taught in a school for white and part-white children which went by the name of "Mililani." Afterwards he left the mission and worked independently of it until his death.

In this year, too, great excitement was caused by a man from Wai'anae coming into the city shouting, "Boki is at Wai'anae! Boki is at Wai'anae with a warship!" The man was taken before Kuakini until his words could be verified. The people were in an uproar, some frightened, some pleased. People ran from place to place in their joy. The red dust rose in clouds from the plain of Kaiwi'ula as natives and foreigners started out on horseback for Wai'anae. The church party who had declared Boki a stinking spirit became like a blunted needle. When messengers and horsemen returned reporting all false, the man was given a hundred strokes with a rope's end at the gates of the houses of the city for his lying tale.

On December 19 of this year Haiha' Na-ihe died at Hanamua, at his house at Ka'awaloa. When the four chief counselors of Kamehameha had died their sons were made counselors in their place. Ka-'ahu-manu, daughter of Ke'e-au-moku, and Ka-lani-moku were the only others who constituted this council. But Ka-lani-mamahu was permitted to enter it and Ke-li'i-maika'i. These were the leaders in counsel in the later days of Kamehameha and in the time of Liholiho. Koa-hou, the son of Kamanawa, had died in Punahou, Hilo, in 1826. Ka-lani-moku died February 8, 1827. Now it was Na-ihe's turn. The great chiefs of Hawaii were passing away.*

* *Ka Nupepa Ku'oko'a*, Aug. 22, 1868.

CHAPTER XXIV

Hawaii Under Ka-'ahu-manu

In February, 1832, Ka-'ahu-manu sailed for Maui aboard the *Mika-pala*, Captain Na-'opala. People from all over Maui had gathered at La-haina to meet her and construct a fort at this place in order to quell disturbances from the whale ships. In one month it was completed. On this tour Ka-'ahu-manu met David Malo and said, "I want you to work hard to get an education in order to become an adviser and office holder to administer the affairs of government under my king. I do not want ignorant leaders who oppress the people and give rise to discontent among the commoners. I have been told of my brother's (Kua-kini's) unjust dealings in Hana, [who reckoned] one coconut for a roll of *olona* fiber. Hoa-pili told me of this, and when I see Kua-kini on Oahu I shall tell him that you are to be made governor of Hawaii."* Ka'ahu-manu at this time requested Hoa-pili and his associates to supply food and clothing, fish from Kai-pa'akai on Molokai, and *mamaki* fiber from Hawaii for tapa to the Lahainaluna men who had been selected to become teachers. It was wonderful what an interest the chiefs took in those days in the men whom they wanted to become teachers. I know personally that Ka-'ahu-manu carried out her promises and supplied the men and their wives with *mamaki* fiber. In those days the chiefs made much of those who sought after knowledge. From Maui Ka-'ahu-manu went on to Ka'awaloa because of Na-ihe's illness, but he died before she could get there. She met Ka-pi'o-lani, Ka-makau, and all the chiefs of Ka'awaloa and Napoopoo, then sailed for Kailua where she met Ka-hahana, Maheha Ka-pu-likoliko and the other chiefs of Kailua. From here she sailed to Kawaihae, then went to Waimea, and returned to Lahaina, where she and Hoa-pili set forth the new laws to protect the government, abolish prostitution, and require legal marriage. A few days after her return to Oahu, in May, she was taken ill and after a week moved to Manoa.

During these days of illness, on May 17, the fifth band of missionaries arrived. These included the Rev. J. B. Emerson and his wife who were stationed at Wailua; the Rev. W. P. Alexander and his wife, at Hanalei;

* *Ka Nupepa Kuoko'a*, Aug. 22, 1868.

the Rev. H. Hitchcock and his wife, at Kalua'aha, Molokai; the Rev. E. Spaulding and his wife and Dr. A. Chaplin and his wife who were stationed at Lahaina; the Rev. C. Forbes and his wife, at Ka'awaloa; the Rev. L. Lyons and his wife, at Waimea; the Rev. D. B. Lyman and his wife, at Hilo; and Mr. E. H. Rogers, a printer, who was at Kawaiaha'o, later at Lahainaluna, and died in Honolulu. The Rev. R. Armstrong and his wife did not enter a field this year. These men were great preachers and were the means of spreading the gospel and extending their influence for good. They also introduced public education and taught arithmetic, writing, geography, and Sunday School lessons. Their wives also made every effort to assist in the teaching. It is impossible to forget the Emersons who taught school from O'io point to Wai'anae.

It was Ka-'ahu-manu's earnest desire upon her return from Hawaii and Maui to work for the spread of the word of God and for the promotion of education in that word among both chiefs and commoners alike. Her face beamed at sight of the men and women who attended worship with her, and she showed her pleasure when she saw people reading portions of the Bible which were being distributed at this time. She made such persons her friends, invited them to eat with her, and often gave them food and clothing. Those of her attendants who failed to observe these things she would reprove, and her face would flame up angrily; she was friendly only with those who were religious. Even those of the lower class whom in old days she would have despised, became her companions and fellow laborers in the word of God. She believed that it was through adherence to the Bible teaching that the government of her king would be lasting. She was not pleased with those who led the king into dissipated ways. It was for this reason that Liliha and other chiefs were banished, just as in 1830 the young chiefesses, Kini Lahilahi, Ulu-maheihei, Polupolu, and others who were Harriet Nahi-'ena'ena's companions; and Konia, Alapa'i and Ka-poli in 1835 at Lahaina, and some of them beaten. She was jealous for God's work and desired that right be maintained and the people not led into temptation and evil ways. She was devoted to the people. In certain years she allowed the people to fish in the tabu waters of Oahu and forbade the landlords to prevent them from taking fish usually restricted for the chiefs, such as the *uhu, opule, he'e,* and *kahala.* For a time there were no tabu fishing grounds for Oahu. She also removed the heavy burdens imposed by the chiefs on the common people. She forbade their imposing heavy taxes and making people go long distances to work for the chiefs. The most important restriction she imposed was that placed on worshiping false gods and idols, praying people to death, catching spirits, chanting, sorcery meles, and dancing of all kinds. All these were forbidden, as also the planting or drinking of 'awa. If anyone were caught planting 'awa his land would be taken away from him.

On Ka-'ahu-manu's return from Lahaina she at once unburdened her mind to her brother Kua-kini when he came to see her, and said, "Hoa-pili and his people tell me that you oppressed the Hana people, sending them a load of coconuts and making the people bring in one bunch of olona fiber for each coconut." He answered, "I do not believe I am to blame; it must have been some of my men." "Your men could hardly have done that without your orders, but if they acted without such orders you can dismiss your men." She told him of the new laws relieving the commoners from burdensome labor for the chiefs. Today if anyone speaks of the burdensome taxes put upon the people, the chiefs cleverly avoid the blame by laying it to the members of the legislature who make and pass the laws, and Ka-'ahu-manu's devotion to the people's welfare is forgotten. On this occasion Kua-kini replied, "It is all right to make these laws for your lands, but I shall make my own laws for my lands." Of his friend Ka-nuha who was to be banished to Kahoolawe for using government money belonging to Hawaii he said, "I shall use the money of Hawaii as long as I live; after my death it can be used for the government. I am the one to be banished and not my friend Ka-nuha." At these words Ka-'ahu-manu burst out weeping and covered her head in her blankets. Late that night she became ill and at daylight was removed to her rest house up Manoa Valley at Puka-'oma'oma'o on the edge of the 'ohi'a and kukui groves. A week and a half later in the early hours of Tuesday, June 5, 1832, Elizabeth Ka-'ahu-manu died in her sixty-fourth year, while her body showed no look of age and her bearing was still impressive. Early in the morning she was brought into the city on a covered litter and it shook so much that her niece, Ka-manele, occupied it with her.*

When it became known that Ka-'ahu-manu was dead and her body had been brought back to the city, the roads leading from Manoa, Ma-kiki, Kanela'au, Kaiua, and Ko'ula, all the way to Pohukaina, were filled with people bewailing her death, some with lamentation, some recounting her good deeds with shrill voices, some chanting meles in her honor, all with love and regret for the one whom they looked upon as "the cable that held the ship of state." Thus in different ways they showed their devotion to her who had so loved the common people. The king was to be seen weeping and lamenting.

Mihalana'au i kuakahiki ka newa   Floating on the dizzy way to the
    ana,   unknown land;

* Ka Nupepa Ku'oko'a, Aug. 29, 1868.

Ke kaha ana aku nei leina aku nei liuliu,	Here a moment ago, now gone,
Liua paia aku nei i Kuanalia,	Gone away to Kuanalia,
I Analio i Analipo,	To the cave on the far horizon, to the cave below the horizon,
Lilo aku la i ka paia kua a Kane,	Gone to the place behind Kane,
I ke alanui ma'awe 'ula a Kanaloa,	On the red pathway of Kanaloa,
Ke'ehi kulani aku nei ka hele ana,	Treading as a chief on her way,
E Malolo kiha kahakulei'ohua,	On the ebb tide slipping and diving,
Ke 'li'i i kulu hi'olani i aui newa aku nei,	The chiefess has fallen asleep and left us,
I lele aku nei i ke kohiana o ka pawa,	Flying away at the time of dawn,
I ke ano kohikohi ana o ka pawa,	At the breaking of the dawn
Ka lilo ana ia ia la oia e. . . .	She has been taken from us. . . .

The chiefess Ka-'ahu-manu was born at Mapuwena, called Paliuli, at Ka'uiki, Hana, Maui, in a small cave on the side of the hill, and her afterbirth was taken and buried at Kani-a-mako' in Kawaipapa above Pihehe. She was born in 1768 after the battle of Kalauonakukui, on Molokai, which followed that of Kalae'ili'ili in Waihe'e, Maui. Her mother was Na-mahana-i-ka-lele-o-na-lani who had already borne two children to her cousin Kamehameha-nui, Pele-io-holani the firstborn, and Kua-kini-o-ka-lani the second. When both her husband and her older son died Na-mahana was taken to wife by Ke'e-au-moku, son of Ku-ma'ai-ku and Keawe-poepoe; and Ka-'ahu-manu was the first child of this union. Ka-'ahu-manu's cousin Ka-lani-moku was also born on Ka'uiki. She was therefore a chiefess of high rank, and cousin to Kamehameha through their common grandfather Ha'ae. Ha'ae lived with Kekela and and Ke-ku'i-apo-iwa, the mother of Kamehameha. Ha'ae also lived with Ka-lele-mauli, from whom came Haa'lo'u and from her came Namahana, cousin to Kamehameha. On the side of her father also, she was related to Kamehameha, for Ke'e-au-moku was the father of Keoua through his wife Ka-maka'i-moku, and Keoua was the father of Kamehameha through his wife Ke-ku'i-apo-iwa II. Again, Ka-lani-kau-lele-ia-iwi was the mother, by her husband Lono-i-ka-ha'upu, of Keawe-poepoe, the father of Ke'e-au-moku, the father of Ka-'ahu-manu. And the reader will trace other relationships. Ka-'ahu-manu was descended from the royal blood of Keawe and was connected with Ku'ihewa-ka-'upena who was of the royal blood of Ke-kau-like and related to Ka-lani-kau-lele-ia-iwi of the royal lines of Keawe and of Mano-ka-lani-po; why should it not be said of her:

A i aku ka muimuia o Palehuna,	She was like the flower of Palehuna
O ka nahele wale a Ha'i'aimalama,	In the forest of Ha'i'aimalama,
O na lehua a Kanaloa-a-ho'okau.	The lehua blossoms of Kanaloa-a-ho'okau.

After the battles in which Ke'e-au-moku attempted to overthrow Ka-hekili, Ka-'ahu-manu's parents fled from Molokai to Hana by canoe and lived as refugees, protected by Mahi-hele-lima, the governor of Hana and of the fortified hill af Ka'uiki, a district at that time held by Ka-lani-'opu'u of Hawaii. Among the chiefs and chiefesses who accompanied them should be named Ke-kua-manoha', Ka-maka-huki-lani, Ha'alo'u, and the young Kauhi-wawae-ono. Women alone attended at the birth of Ka-'ahu-manu, and these were her grandmother Ha'alo'u, 'Apo, 'Ele'ele-i-oho, and Wahine-'a'a. She was brought up in the land of Kawaipapa and was a great favorite with her father Ke'e-au-moku and the beloved child of her aunts, uncles, and grandmother. As the only daughter in the family they lavished all their affection upon her. She was an obedient child to whom the voice of her parents and grandmother was law. Ha'alo'u once said of her, "You will be a ruler some day, and all your relatives will bow in your presence," and this one day came true. Her chief charm however lay in the fact that she was kind-hearted and beautiful. She never had a wish that was not granted.

During the war between Ka-lani-'opu'u and Ka-hekili, between the years 1777 and 1779, the parents of Ka-'ahu-manu went to Hawaii with their whole household and company of attendants and followed in the rear of Ka-lani-'opu'u's army, together with the twin half brothers of Ke'e-au-moku. [These were] Ka-me'e-ia-moku and Ka-manawa ,who had the same father (Keawe-poepoe) but different mothers, Ku-ma'ai-ku being the mother of Ke'e-au-moku and Ka-noena of the twins. Keawe-a-heulu also belonged to their company. His estates were the lands of Kapalilua, Ka'awaloa, and Kealakekua; those of Ka-me'e-ia-moku and his brother under Ka-lani-'opu'u were Kekaha and the lands of that section. At the time of Captain Cook's arrival Ka-'ahu-manu was a little girl of eleven. One of Ka-lani-'opu'u's wives was Ke-kupu-ohi, the greatest beauty of that time. Ka-lola Pupuka-o-Hono-ka-wai-lani was Ka-lani-'opu'u's chief wife, and Kane-kapo-lei was another of his wives. At the time of Ka-lani-'opu'u's death Ka-'ahu-manu was still too young to take a husband.*

* *Ka Nupepa Ku'oko'a,* Sept. 5, 1868.

In 1785, which was the year of the "Kauhola" period or "Laupahoe-hoe the second" following the "Hapu'u" year, Kamehameha was living with his chiefs and soldiers at Kauhola, *makai* of Hala'ula, and culti-vating the taro patches which can be seen covering the place to this day. Ka-'ahu-manu did not become his wife while he was living in these humble circumstances. Puna and Ka-'u were at this time under the rule of Keoua Kuahu-'ula, son of Ka-lani-'opu'u by his wife Kane-kapo-lei, and Hilo and Hamakua [were under the rule] of Keawe-ma'u-hili. Kalola-a-Kumu-ko'a was Kamehameha's wife during this time of ob-scurity, but he had no children by her. Pauli Ka-o-lei-o-ku was Kameha-meha's first child, and he had him by Kane-kapo-lei, of Ka-lani-'opu'u. His first daughter, Ka-pu-likoliko, and a son, Ka-hoano-ku Kina'u, he had by Pele-uli before he became ruling chief. Later Pele-uli became the wife of Kamehameha's younger brother Ka-welo-lani, but she continued to live in Kamehameha's household.

Ka-'ahu-manu was the most beautiful woman in Hawaii in those days. The next to her in beauty was Ke-kua-po'i. To either might be applied the lines,

Kupu papa ki'eki'e iluna o Kama-oha,	High rise the tablelands above Ka-maoha,
Ka ohaoha ke kilakila o na mauna.	Proud and majestics rise the mountains.
Ui'a'a Ka'ala kela i ka lani,	Ka'ala stands in bold relief against the sky,
O ke po'okeoa ia o na kuahiwi.	The greatest of mountains.

A handsome woman, six feet tall, straight and well-formed was Ka-'ahu-manu, without blemish, and comely. Her arms were like the inside of a banana stalk, her fingers tapering, her palms pliable like *kukunene* grass, graceful in repose, her cheeks long in shape and pink as the bud of a banana stem; her eyes like those of a dove or the *moho* bird; her nose narrow and straight, in admirable proportion to her cheeks; her arched eyebrows shaped to the breadth of her forehead; her hair dark, wavy, and fine, her skin very light. Of Kamehameha's two possessions, his wife and his kingdom, she was the more beautiful. Both husband and wife brought a host of relatives and friends to the alliance. It was said that Kamehameha's long control of the government was due to this wife alone; through her all the chiefs became reconciled to Kamehameha to whom she was devoted. Although Na-makeha' was her uncle, Ka-'ahu-manu's devotion forced her father and his brothers to remain true to Kamehameha, and Namakeha' and his followers were defeated. When her uncles and brothers conspired against him, she saved him. This was the reason for Ke'e-au-moku's warning [to Kamehameha] that only if his wife conspired against him would he be in danger, and the reason why Kamehameha caused his own [foster] son to be killed and did not falter like Ku-leo-iki.

[Allusion has already been made to the story how] while Kamehameha and his chiefs were quartered at Kaunakakai on Molokai, in 1795, on their way to make war upon Ka-lani-ku-pule, Ka-lani-moku one night approached Kamehameha's sleeping house and found Ka-'ahu-manu still awake and Heulu, the father of Pi'i-a-na-i'a, holding the torch outside. Ka-lani-moku took the torch and entered, covering the light. Ka-'ahu-manu called, "The light is out!" "It is not out," answered Ka-lani-moku. She recognized his voice and asked, "Is it you?" "Yes." "You are very late." "It is because I was afraid and could not sleep, so I came to see you." Ka-'ahu-manu inquired the reason, he told her of Ka'iana's visit on his return from Kalama'ula and of his fear lest the chiefs think he had betrayed the secret council when Ka'iana said before all the chiefs, "You have I suppose pity for me, for you know that your uncle [meaning himself] is to be disposed of." Then Ka-lani-moku said to Ka-'ahu-manu, "When Ke'e-au-moku came for the chief (Kamehameha) to attend the council the chief said, 'Let this young fellow (meaning me) go in my place and he will inform me. Whatever you decide will be all right with me.' So when I came to the council I was afraid of being killed, for there sat Kalai-mamahu' on one side of the entrance and Ke-li'i-maika'i on the other side; so I stepped over and sat in front of Ke-li'i-maika'i, and Ka-lani-mamahu' spoke up and said, 'The word is this, and you are to take it to Kamehameha. Your uncle is to be slain. But if this leaks out your life is to be the forfeit.' This is why I have not been able to sleep tonight." Ka-'ahu-manu then embraced her cousin and began to wail. Kamehameha awoke and was told the story. He said, "All secrets of life or death in heaven or earth are known to Ka'iana. There will be no harm come to your cousin." Twice he had to reassure her before her mind was free of fear.*

In Kamehameha's day the god Ku-ka'ili-moku and the lands sacred to this god were places of refuge; anyone who had forfeited his life might be saved if he ran and entered one of these lands sacred to the god; no blood could be shed there. Any violator of any law whatsoever who had been sentenced to die, if he could run and enter one of these lands would be saved; his troubles would be over. So the Mamalahoa law was the means of saving many lives during a time of slaughter; when this law was proclaimed, no more slaughter was allowed; all were saved. A third means of safety was Ka-'ahu-manu. The chief [Kamehameha] treated

* *Ka Nupepa Ku'oko'a*, Sept. 12, 1868.

her as if she were a goddess. Any condemned person could be saved if Ka-'ahu-manu said the word. Her lands were also turned into places of refuge. Pu'umau in Lahaina, Waipukua in Waihe'e, Kalua'aha in Molokai, and the rest, all became places where people could be saved from death. If a man killed another and he could escape from the friends of the man he had killed and run to the land set apart as a place of refuge, he would be saved from death. In the battle of Nu'uanu between Kamehameha and Ka-lani-ku-pule many of the chiefs and chiefesses were taken prisoner—Ke-po'o-loku, Kalola Ihu-ka'ika'i, Ka-'ele-o-Waipi'o and their followers, and many others—and they were told that through Ka-'ahu-manu they might be saved, that any prisoner who appealed for life to Ka-'ahu-manu was saved, hence many sought Ka-'ahu-manu. The same was the case when Kamehameha made war in Hilo against Namakeha'; many were saved through knowing this means of safety.

There was the case of Paki, the blind man. In 1811, while Kamehameha was living on Oahu before the return to Hawaii called the Kani'au-kani, some one stole fish from the pond of a land of Waihe'e close to Kiao, called Ko'ahi, owned by Alapa'i Malo-iki, who was known as Alapa'i Kupalupalu-mano'. Paki was convicted and suffered the penalty of having his eyes gouged out. The death penalty for such crimes had been abolished by Kamehameha, but theft was not common in those days for fear of losing the eyes. Paki after this loss lived with a canoe-making kahuna at Paukauila on the north side of Waihe'e. One evening he prepared 'awa for the kahuna, but took none himself. While the kahuna lay stupified by the 'awa the blind man felt his way to the place where the axe was kept, then to where the man was sleeping, felt for his neck, and cut off his head. He then crawled a distance of half a mile to a place of refuge called Kukuipuka, sacred to Ku-ka'ili-moku, Kamehameha's god. Another case was that where three men killed a fourth, and then ran to the land of Paunau in Lahaina belonging to Ka-'ahu-manu. Two of them ran faster than the third and succeeded in getting there, but the third was caught at Pahumanamana and killed by his pursuers.

Ka-'ahu-manu was the most favored of Kamehameha's wives. She was valued at half his kingdom. All her requests were granted. She was allowed to enter the meetings of the high council, and after the death of Ke'e-au-moku her father, at Kapokapo in Koko in 1804, his seat in the council fell to Ka-'ahu-manu, a privilege not given to her brothers Kahekili Ke'e-au-moku and Kua-kini, during Kamehameha's lifetime. After the death of the old counselors of Kamehameha one each of their children made up this high council, and others who entered there were Kalaimamahu', Hu'eu Ka-lani-moku, and Ka-lani-malokuloku-i-Kepo'o-kalani [a younger brother of Kamehameha I who] had the privilege of entering whenever he chose. Ka-'ahu-manu was however the only chiefess admitted to the council and she had great influence there. All the chiefs had the utmost confidence in her, and her commands were uniformly obeyed. This was because her mind ran in the same channels with those of the old counselors who had passed on before her. Whenever a member of the family obtained land, whether a district, an *ahupua'a*, or some smaller division, the whole family were informed of it, and the property divided among them all. Each member worked for the good of the others and they thus learned to love each other. The home of one was the home of all, and they were all well acquainted with each other, as was common with the chiefs of old. This accounts for their devotion to each other. When Ka-'ahu-manu became the wife of Kamehameha all the families of chiefs looked up to her uncles and brothers, and the whole family became known largely through her position. This working for the common good of the family was a fine practice which it would be well for our people today to emulate. Ka-'ahu-manu was a truly royal personage. She was proud, she loved beautiful things, and took pains to show her rank; she was a comely woman and took pride in keeping herself well dressed.*

Ka-'ahu-manu showed her dislike for rivals in beauty or goodness, but attractive women from the country or even from the king's household she would send for and try to make friends (*aikane*) with them or take them as favorites (*punahele*). She would even hire them to work for her, for she loved to show her authority, and since she could not have men about her she had to depend upon the attentions of women. She hated to hear scandal about men and, whenever she heard any such lewd talk, words of wrath would pour out from her mouth like the spouting of a whale in the waters of the sea. It was fearful to see her eyes turn red and hear her exclaim, "What! what! how strange! is that so?" and then she would begin to swear. That was her nature during Kamehameha's and Liholiho's time. People were afraid to enter her house. Women feared her most, for she treated men better than women, with whom she was always surrounded. But all this was changed during the rule of Kau-i-ke-aouli, after Ka-'ahu-manu had accepted the word of God. She was true to her people; she made favorites of toothless old women and old loose-jawed men and would pray with them. She made them her brothers and ate with them, and they shared her secret counsels and her activities in the church. Wherever tapa of the best quality was made, from Hawaii to Oahu, the finest patterns were always brought for Ka-'ahu-manu to see first. She must be the first to see the fattened hog, dog, poultry, or the pet dog. The fattest fish from the ponds, the

* *Ka Nupepa Ku'oko'a*, Sept. 19, 1868.

plumpest goby fish ('o'opu), and the most fragrant sea moss were all tabu for Ka-'ahu-manu. She was treated with the utmost respect and honor, but she was not given the ceremonial tabu which would have been hers according to her rank as a tabu chiefess.

She was thus honored as the daughter of Ke'e-au-moku, the most aggressive of the men who had made Kamehameha ruling chief. His had been the first blood shed for the king at the battle of Moku'ohai, in which he took a leading part. Her station was higher as the wife of Kamehameha than that of Pele-uli, Kiki-pa'a, and Ke-oho-hiwa, who were also daughters of those who had fought for Kamehameha. This was not due to her beauty and regal bearing alone, but to the number of chiefs who bore some relationship to her, more even than those related to Kamehameha. Several times the chiefs of her family wanted to rebel against the chief but were prevented through her loyalty and devotion. Kamehameha's younger blood brothers (kaikaina pono'i) so called, were also "brothers" of Ka-'ahu-manu. Ulu-maheihei, for example, thought more of her than his own daughter Liliha. Ka-iki-o-'ewa and other chiefs also considered her before their own children, for their power came to them through her.

Women in those days were especially devoted to their brothers, and brothers to their sisters. It was common to see younger sisters sitting in their brothers' laps. Brothers chanted verses composed in honor of their sisters, and sisters of their brothers as a sign of devotion. Ka-'ahu-manu showed great affection toward every member of her family. If any of them fell ill on another island she would hasten to go to their assistance. Thus she fulfilled the golden rule, but within her own family only. She was also a devoted wife. At one time after the period called the Kaipalaoa, about 1789, Kamehameha deserted Ka-'ahu-manu and lived entirely with Ka-heihei-malie, whom he treated as his wife. Ka-'ahu-manu suffered so much from this separation that one dark night she swam from Ke'ei in Kekaha to Honaunau, a distance of five or six miles, expecting every moment to be devoured by sharks, but rendered reckless by love and grief and not caring what became of her. From this feat came her law called the "Ocean-swimming law."* The parents of the chiefs and chiefesses taught them that love for one's husband could be forgotten, but Ka-'ahu-manu answered:

---

* Mrs. A. P. Taylor relates (Personal communication) that a young retainer named Luahine insisted upon swimming with Ka-'ahu-manu because of his love for her, even after she ordered him to return. Twice he was exhausted and would have been drowned had not Ka-'ahu-manu forgotten her own troubles and ordered him to rest his arm on her shoulder. Thereafter he was called "Old woman who rested on Ka-'ahu-manu" (Luahine ke ka'awe o Ka-'ahu-manu). Ka-'ahu-manu landed at Kekaha and hid in a cave, where she was discovered by an ancestor of Mrs. Manuel Reis by the constant barking of her little dog at the mouth of the cave.

O ke kane ka mea aloha,
The husband is the one beloved.

Pau ke aho au e ho'ohaehae,
Weary with labor have I been for his sake,

Luhi ia 'oe he hoa manu e i e,
Weary for you, O my bird-like companion.

Me he manu la Keolewa i ka la'i,
Like a bird is Keolewa in the calm.

Ka ha'ale o Wai'ale'ale i ka lani,
Wai'ale'ale rises high in the heavens,

Ka Lipolipo o Ha'upu i ke ko'olau,
Ha'upu is dark and green in the north,

Nu iho ia i ke kula o Koholalele,
There are groans on the plain of Koholalele.

Lele ka huna pua kukui i ka makani,
Torn blossoms of the *kukui* are tossed about by the wind,

I ke kipaku a ke Ko'olau-wahine
Tossed from their stems by the Wind-of-the-North,

Oka'i ka 'ohana pua i Wailua,
The flowers are flung about at Wailua,

He ilina na ka puahau Ka-lehua-wehe,
Hau flowers of Ka-lehua-wehe are flung in heaps.

E wehe wale no 'oe i ka hihia ua pa'a,
How can you untangle what has been firmly knotted?

E 'ole e hemo—he 'ai kuli ke aloha,
It cannot be unraveled, for love is deaf to reason

Aia a wahawaha lono i kau e
Until rejected, then it will listen.

But Ka-'ahu-manu was also devoted to her parents. When Ke'e-au-moku died she mourned him deeply. These are some verses from the dirge she composed when he died at Kapokapo in 1804:

Aloha wale hoi 'oe—
Love to you,

O 'oe ho'i kekahi a Ka-maka-a-ola-o-Kane,
To you who were like Ka-maka-a-ola-o-Kane,

O 'olua ia Lani
For you two were chiefs,

Elua ia Lani nui pueo 'ula,
Two great chiefs like two red owls,

E Kaha'i-lani-moku, o Kaha'i-ku,
Kaha'i-lani-moku, Kaha'i-ku,

O ke ku haili lani kapu o Kane,
The sacred tabu chiefs of Kane.

O ka pohaku lani ia i halulu aku nei,
Like a peal of thunder is your tread

I ka'a pono aku nei ma ke alo o Wakea,
Reverberating to the presence of Wakea,

E ke kama lani a Ka-lani-honua-kini,
Here is the divine child of a multitude of sacred offspring,

O ku'u makuakane lani,
My father and chief,

Hoa aloha wale ia la
My beloved companion,

He aloha ia la e
My loved one.

Aloha aku au a pau ke aho,
I am breathless with grieving for you,

Uwe aku ho'i o ka hoa mai ke anu,
I weep for my companion in the cold,

O ku'u hoa mai ka ua 'apo pu'e kahi,
My companion of the chilly rain.

'Apo mai ana ke ko'eko'e,
The chill encircles me,

E ho'opuni mai ana ke anu,
The cold surrounds me,

A poniponi i ke anu 'a'ohe wahawaha,
Purple with cold not rejected,

Elua no wahi e mehana ai,
Only two places to find warmth—

O ke ahi lalaku i ke hale,
The bed mate at home,
    (literally, the blazing fire
    within the house)

O ka lua o ke ahi, o ka lua kapa,
The tapa covering is the second warmth,

I ka lua poli o ka hoa e mehana'i e
Found in the bosom of a companion.

Eia la, aia la, eia la e—
It is there, it is there, it is there.

She joined with her sisters and brothers in mourning in like manner for her mother, and told of her grief and affection for her parents:

Ku'u makua, i ke hale uluo'a kanaka,
My mother in the house well-peopled,

Hale malumalu komo po'o o maua,
House into whose shelter we entered

E ho'omaha ai i ka wela ke hele—
To rest from the heat of the way,

Hele ku'u makuahine me ke aloha,
Love to my mother who has gone,

'Auwana wale iho ko au i Kuahea,
Leaving me wandering on the mountainside.

O 'oe o ka wahine 'ai makani,
You are the woman consumed by the wind

'Ai makani malana'i-e—
Consumed by the trade wind,

E 'ai e 'ai ana i ke aloha,
Consumed, consumed, consumed with love,

E 'ai e ana i ke aloha o na makua,
Consumed, consumed with love for parents.

Kenakena i ke aloha o na keiki,
Bitter with grief for the children,

O kou kaikaina muli poki'i,	For your beloved little sister,
O Poki'i-kauna, o ku'u kaikaina	For the four younger sisters, for
e—	my younger sister.

After the death of Kamehameha's old counselors who had assisted him to rule, Kamehameha feared for the stability of his government and therefore he made Ka-'ahu-manu the pillar and cornerstone for the state. He dealt out death, she saved from death. Any descendant or relative of Kamehameha who started a quarrel with a relative of Ka-'ahu-manu was put to death, unless saved by Ka-'ahu-manu. Kamehameha cherished her as if she were a goddess or an ivory-tooth necklace to adorn his neck. She was as carefully protected as if she were living in the sacred place of a heiau. He feared lest, if she escaped from her nest, all the fledgelings also would leave it with her, hence she was carefully guarded until the death of Kamehameha.*

Not a month had passed after his death before the people of Hawaii had abolished the eating tabus and the husband ate with his wife and family. Who were responsible for forcing free eating upon the people? Ke-opu-o-lani, Ka-lani-moku, and Ka-'ahu-manu; the people were benefited, and family ties drawn closer by this means. With the help of God, these chiefs became the means of enlightening the nation to whom at this time the true light was but faintly visible, and to cause it to shine as we see it today. The time of conflict is past, the time of budding leaves is here. Ka-'ahu-manu should never be forgotten, friend as she was of chiefs and commoners. Many a journey she made in her old age into the outer districts, humbling herself in order to help spread the word of God alike among the whole nation.

One of her famous deeds was the expedition to locate Nihoa in 1822 . . . and to annex it to the group. This name was given to some of her houses and enclosures, and children were named after this land rediscovered by Ka-'ahu-manu. Her marriage to Ka-umu-ali'i, as her second husband, was also a noted event. He was a religious chief, and it is said of him that he "died in the faith." 'Io-lani-makua and Ka-umu-ali'i often said, "Let us have faith in God, the Chief above all," and, "Trust in the good God that our souls may be saved in the world to come." . . . The missionary Mr. Samuel Ruggles was called "the child of Ka-umu-ali'i, the chief ruling over Kauai." Ke-opu-o-lani and Ka-umu-ali'i were the first of the chiefs to become followers of the true God, the first fruits of the kingdom of God in these islands. Afterwards Ka-lani-moku, Ka-'ahu-manu, and others of the royal family saw the light of Christianity . . . In the speech made by Kau-i-ke-aouli at Honuakaha when he

* *Ka Nupepa Ku'oko'a,* Sept. 26, 1868.

was eleven years old we see the result of Ka-'ahu-manu's efforts to turn his mind to God:

Chiefs and people, give ear to my remarks. My kingdom shall be a kingdom of learning.
> I rejoiced when they said to me,
> Let us go to the House of Jehovah,
> Let us come and sing to Jehovah,
> Let us sing joyfully to Jehovah with psalms,
> For Jehovah is a great God,
> He is King over all the gods.
> We are the sheep of his pasture,
> And as sheep we are led by his hand

On this day when we hear His voice let us not harden our hearts, but let us give our hearts and bodies to Him, and our lives to Him, that we may live in peace in this world. Jehovah our God shall be with us, and His power will turn our hearts to Him. Let us go in His way, obey His mandates, and adhere to all His restrictions.

Let our hearts be holy before Jehovah our God, that we may go forth in His ways and keep all His commandments, in order that our souls may live in the world to come. Let us keep our earthly laws, in order that we may live here in peace, because our nation is His.

Let us not keep gods of wood and stone. Let us cast off all evil things from our body. Let us have one God, Jehovah.

Let us not take His name in vain or break His laws or His commandments.

Let us keep holy the day of Jehovah. Let us not commit murder; let us not commit adultery; let us not commit theft; let us not speak falsely; let us not be hypocrites; let us not be gamblers; let us not commit infanticide; let not the husband forsake his wife; let not the wife forsake her husband. Do not conspire; do not break the laws, because it would be wicked. These things determine right from wrong; let us therefore forsake those sins which will contaminate our bodies.

It is right that we strive hard to learn letters and to understand His words, that we may know the nature of His message. Let us be diligent, men, children, women; let us be strong. Those of you who are teachers, be faithful in teaching your pupils. It is my great desire that the poor, the rich, the chiefs, the men, the commoners, and all the children of our nation acquire knowledge and know how to read the Word of God, because He has been kind to us, and has sent this great message to us to enlighten us and to redeem us.

Therefore, let you, the chiefs, be educated by the judges of this earth. Be obedient to Jehovah in fear and rejoice with trembling. Blessed are those who trust in Him.

Kau-i-ke-aouli*

* *Ka Nupepa Ku'oko'a*, Oct. 3, 1868.

Who can say after reading this speech that the king was ignorant and had no real love of God in his heart? Yet he was but eleven and a half years old when he spoke, in 1825, at Honuakaha. The young princess, Harriet Nahi-'ena'ena also, although but nine years old, showed a similar desire in words full of sound sense and devotion to God's word. It had always been the habit of the commoners to offer prayer for the king and the chiefs; here the surprising thing is that in the prayer of this young ruler she placed the commoners first and the chiefs second. So also did Kau-i-ke-aouli. But Kamehameha himself also called the commoners his first-born children . . . This is a thought worth considering.

The speech of Harriet Nahi-'ena'ena, dated Oahu, July, 1825, reads:

My greetings to all of you missionaries. God is indeed merciful, and His patience is great in giving us these blessings. Jesus our Lord who will save us is gracious.

I am revealing to you my thoughts. My heart yearns for God, and I feel that I am indebted to Him because He gave His Son to die to save sinners of this world, and His blessed blood was shed to cleanse my sins of body and soul.

My heart is yearning to trust in Jesus, my Lord and Savior. I pray God to turn all the commoners and chiefs to Him. This has been my constant prayer, that God bless our kingdom, and that the nation as a whole be purified so that the devil may be without power over this nation.

H. Nahi-'ena'ena

The speeches of the guardian chiefs in their effort to build up Christianity and spread education throughout the nation follow here. Ka-lani-moku's is dated December 10, 1825.

My greetings to you all, my brethren, chiefs, missionaries, native teachers, pupils, and all people of these islands. I am truly thankful because of the new kingdom of God as now given us, for it makes us servants of Jesus Christ.

My desire is that we love God who has given us the Word of Life. Let us keep His commandments and turn to do right, forsaking evil. Let us not follow sinful ways.

Let us be mindful of the good words of Jesus who gave us His blessed blood to save our souls.

Let us strive in our hearts to follow the words of Jehovah, our Heavenly Father, and let our thoughts be right.

Let us praise our God Jehovah and Him only. We have no other God. He made us and is keeping us. Let us offer Him our prayers in the evening and in the morning. Let us keep Sabbath day as the day of remembrance of Jehovah our God, and let us put away all labor on this day. This is God's only day, for we can labor six days in the week, but the seventh day we should remember as the day for the good of our souls and as a day of repentance of our sins. We must remember our God.

I wish also to say that I am always mindful of God's words and my heart yearns for His salvation. I am jealous for God's words and have forsaken my old ways and I want a new heart in me.

My beloved King Liholiho once said to me that my wife and I should learn how to read and write. Ke-opu-o-lani requested that I obey God in order that my soul might be saved so that I might meet her in that beautiful place in the future, in the Kingdom of God. At the death of Ke-opu-o-lani my love for her became much greater. I want to keep her request that I keep to the right. And when the King sailed to that foreign land I wept for him.

Ka-umu-ali'i too died in the faith and he instructed me to take good care of Kauai, for the land and all the people belonged to the king. I therefore went to Kauai and some made war upon us, but God kept us. On the way to Niihau again my thoughts were of God, and from then on I became afraid of evil and I am now afraid to do wicked things.

I have given my body, my soul, and my heart to God and I am His servant. I am now repenting of my old sins. I am praising God at this time. It is His grace that I want, for He alone knows my sins; He knows my body and my soul.

I want all the people to obey Jehovah, all of the chiefs and rulers and all the commoners as well, from Hawaii to Kauai. Let us faithfully keep the laws of God and the ten commandments given us by Jehovah. These laws are of benefit to all nations. I desire also that we trust in Jesus Christ, that our souls may be saved by Him. My greetings to you. God in His great mercy bless you.

Ka-lani-moku*

Elizabeth Ka-'ahu-manu's speech to the people is date December 20, 1825.

I wish to address you all, my brethren, chiefs, people, friends, women, teachers, pupils, and workers in behalf of the word of God; you old people of my own and of my king, from Hawaii to Kauai, greetings to you all.

I desire to inform you of my wishes and I want you to listen to me. I want you to learn what is right in order that you may acquire righteousness and that our hearts may be of one mind. I want you to grasp my thoughts and those of my king, in order that you may accept the word of God.

We are extending to you the blessed word of salvation which God has given us. You must strive hard to acquire righteousness that you may obtain salvation both in this world and in the world of God to come.

My heart yearns for you in hope that we may all be able to go to the

*Ka Nupepa Ku'oko'a, Oct. 10, 1868.

presence of God our Father. Let us all trust in Jesus that we may be saved by God. My heart has accepted the word of the God from above. My heart is now reaching out to you because I feel for you and am devoted to you.

You must obey the laws of Jehovah. Keep the Sabbath day holy and be obedient to the word of God, for by doing so we shall have salvation.

The word of God will gladden our hearts when we understand its goodness, because it is full of the love of the great Lord for us.

We must do the right thing here in order that we may live with God over there.

The axe is at the trunk of my tree, and I do not know when the Lord will take away my soul. Let us therefore be steadfast in our efforts to keep the beautiful word of our Lord before the coming of the great day of our judgment.

We, chiefs and rulers of these islands, set up in times past altars to sin, but these have been cast aside and we now have salvation from God.

My wish and belief is to give my heart to God who is my trust and my delight.

Let us therefore love God and request of Him to make us worthy, that the laws of God may be safe in the hearts of men, that the Holy Spirit may enter and abide there, that we may obtain salvation from Jesus Christ our Savior. My blessing be with you all.

Elizabeth Ka-'ahu-manu

These are the thoughts of a Christian devoted to her ruler and to her people in her desire to improve the condition of the government by taking the word of God as a foundation upon which to build a greater nation. Not she alone but all the chiefs assisted in this move for a better government with the word of God as a foundation, for to this the Hawaiian nation was committed. The Hawaiian nation was in all respects a Christian nation. Some of her good deeds to bring about this end are well known. The tabu relating to free eating was at that time the only tabu broken by Liholiho; the deifying of images was still practiced. When Ka-'ahu-manu became a Christian she had all the images burned and ordered an end put to the practice of kahunaism. When she heard that some of the chiefs and people had been deifying the bones of chiefs deposited in the Hale-o-Keawe at Honaunau, Kona, and at Waipi'o in Hamakua, she gathered up the bones and deposited them in the cliffs of Ka'awaloa and burned the debris. Her name was heaped with abuse for this deed, but she really did place the bones where they would be undisturbed.

Ka-'ahu-manu was the first convert of the Kawaiaha'o church. Some of the chiefs and chiefesses of her family on Oahu followed her example so that there were eight others baptized on the same day, December 4,

1825, but Ka-'ahu-manu was the first convert and the one who led the others into the church. With her were Ka-lani-moku, A. Ke-li'i-ahonui, Lydia Na-mahana, Ke-kua-i-pi'ia, Gideon La'a-nui, Simeon Ka-'iu, Deborah Ka-pule Ha'akulou, and R. Ka-lai-'ai-aulu. On Maui Ulu-maheihei, Ka-heihei-malie, and other chiefs followed her lead, and there were others on Kauai and Hawaii. All followed her from the highest to the lowest because of the laws she had made which brought protection to the poorest. She took the blind Bartimeus as her friend, made counselors, companions, and friends of the religious, visited the missionary families in their homes, and spent her time reading those parts of the Bible which had been translated. In her old age she learned to read and write and figure. At her death there was no one her equal to fill her place.*

*Ka Nupepa Ku'oko'a, Oct. 17, 1868.

CHAPTER XXV

Roman Catholicism in Hawaii

Much has been said about the Roman Catholic religion in Hawaii.* Some say that the Roman Catholics came here first with Ku-kanaloa in the ships known as Spanish during the time when Ka-hou-kapu ruled on Hawaii and Ka-ka'alaneo on Maui, and that this Christian form of worship resembles the image worship of Hawaii.† There are indeed a few things which show clearly that the Christian form of worship was mixed with the native at that time. In the first place, the action of the whole congregation in pointing the right hand to heaven when praying in unison, so testifying that God is in the heavens. Second, the erecting of images outside the *luakini* and other heiaus in order to give an appearance inspiring fear and awe, and the decorating of images with beautiful flowers from the wildwood, like the *'ie'ie* vine, the *palai* fern, leaves of the *pala* fern, and other wild plants. Third, the manner in which the priest goes to worship; upon approaching the altar he bends his knees, kneels, and then offers prayers after which he stands up and sprinkles the altar with the purifying water to which a bit of *'olena* root has been added, then faces the audience and sprinkles them with this water to purify them from sin and uncleanness. The Roman Catholic form of worship resembles the ancient Hawaiian and also that of the Jews. [It is therefore argued that] the Roman Catholic came with the Spanish ships and the Christian and pagan forms of worship were mixed together.

On the altars and places of sacrifice in the ancient *luakini* and other heiaus there were crosses. The place occupied by the kahuna was laid smooth with stones in the shape of a cross, and the ground was covered with stones. If this not clear to you I will show you the heiau of my forefathers called Ka-hina-ola, not even a stone of which has fallen. The separate sections built for men and women, and the terraces and walls still stand, testifying to the truth of my words. The place is left in peace; no man or woman has entered there from times past until now. The women were prohibited from approaching the most sacred altar; they

* For two partisan accounts of the establishment of the Catholic mission in Hawaii see 42; 7, pp. 311, 373, 415-423, 504-514, 536-558, 589-592.
† See 9 and 31 regarding the possible visits to the Hawaiian Islands of Spaniards prior to 1778.

were allowed only on the terrace known as the "House of Papa." Only chiefesses like Ni'aupipi'o and Ka-lani-kau-io-kikilo were allowed to hear the prayer of the kahuna, but [even they] were not allowed to touch the images of the goddess placed on the left hand side of the altar and decorated with 'ie'ie vine, palapalai fern, and maile vine. On the right side were the male gods similarly garlanded. On one of the terraces just in front of the kahuna and directly above the kuahu, or altar, the burnt offering was laid. That was the platform of the ruling chief. Images were brought from another place and set on the terrace, perhaps those of Ku-ho'one'e-nu'u or Ku-ke-olo-'ewa according to the kind of house built within the enclosure, whether an 'ohi'a, loulu, a lama, a haku'ohi'a, a malu'ohi'a, a lamaa'ehu, a lamauli, or a halaloa; and there were many such houses, according to the information given me by my grandfather, Ku-i-ke-ala-i-ka-ua-o-ka-lani who was called Kupi . . .

The Jewish religion it is believed was brought here during the time of Auanini, ruling chief of Oahu, by a ship that arrived at Mokapu under the captain Ulupau accompanied by his wife Maria (Malaea) and others who were called Olomana, Aniani, and Holo-makani, names to be found today in Ko'olaupoko and which were given to these people from the meaning of their foreign names. "A sailor has dragged his anchor in all ports" (Kauo ulupau ka holo Kahiki), was an ancient saying. The young people today use the words without knowing their connection with the people who came from Kahiki and landed first at Mokapu in Ko'olaupoko. These people are believed to have been Jews, and calculating the time that has elapsed since then by the generations [of chiefs] it must have been hundreds of thousands of years ago.* Paumakua the chief of Oahu, grandson of Auaniani, was a famous traveler among the southern islands and brought back the little people called dwarfs (kupali'i) and his story tells of the "whirlpool of the dotted seas" (mimilo kai o Manowai kai'o'o). Ka'eka'e, Maliu, and Malela were religious people, kahunas whose form of worship and whose tabus were like those of the Jews. According to the Bible the Jewish tabus resemble those of the Hawaiians.

Before the arrival of the ministers of the Congregational denomination called Puritan there arrived at Kawaihae, in the latter part of 1819, a French ship [the Uranie under Captain Freycinet] on board of which was a Roman Catholic priest. This was the time when Liholiho was still staying at Kawaihae, and the chiefs were divided over the matter of free eating. Ka-lani-moku, accompanied by John Young and others, went on board. The captain and the clergyman asked Young what Ka-lani-moku's rank was, and upon being told that he was the chief counselor (kuhina nui) and a wise, kind, and careful man, they baptized him into

* Kamakau is here probably influenced by the note upon the heiau of 'Umi in 28.

the Catholic Church without his knowing whether what he was doing was right or wrong. He knew what was happening only when he felt the water upon him and the sign of the cross (*kuhikuhi*). We know the skill of the man who knows how to hook the breadfruit, especially that of the topmost branch. It is thick with gum and sticky on a rainy day. What a wonder that the oven was not lighted, and the food carried cooked aboard the ship! Clever are these children of Kalai-haohia (Hew-and-grab) . . . Perhaps strengthened through constant prayers to God.*

It was difficult for the chiefs to act as they pleased in choosing for Hawaii when the Roman Catholic religion came to the country during the time when Ka-'ahu-manu was acting head of government. She attended to all the affairs of the kingdom and laid down the laws. The chiefs and commoners had to obey her. Kamehameha III was still too young to rule. The chiefs throughout the group, the prominent persons, and land agents were under her orders. Whatever religion she chose, that was the religion of the government. On July 9, 1827, a French ship arrived bringing three Roman Catholic priests, Father Alexis Bachelot, Father Abraham Armand, and Father Patrick Short, the first a Frenchman, the other two British; and with them came some laborers. They lived at first *makai* of Kapauhi at the house of a foreign carpenter named Moore *mauka* of the place belonging to Mr. George Wood, the husband of Ka-manu, [a place] which had been given him by Boki close to Ka-'opua-ua's place. On their arrival they found a native woman named Louisa (Rika) who had lived among the Spaniards in [the Ladrone Islands] and had already converted many of the people of Kalaepohaku and Pu'unui to the Catholic religion. These converts used to assemble together at Kikihale to worship, and they offered their prayers in Spanish. This Louisa was the woman who [later]stubbornly refused to change her religion and was taken to Maui by Ka-'ahu-manu to be abandoned at Kahoolawe. But the Rev. William Richards objected to this and she was brought back to work in the bulrush swamps at Waikiki.

When the priests arrived, the followers of Louisa together with a number of the wives and the Spanish members of the household of Don Francisco Paula y Marin (Manini),† and some other foreigners who

* *Ka Nupepa Ku'oko'a*, Oct. 24, 1868.

† For the obituary notice of Don Marin (Manini) see 21. Don Francisco de Paula y Marin came to Hawaii in 1793 or 1794. He was a native of old Spain and is said to have been a member of the Spanish expedition to the Northwest Coast at the time of Vancouver. He died October 30, 1837, at the age of 64 years. For an account of his activities in introducing valuable fruits and vegetables to Hawaii see 41. Vineyard Street in Honolulu is named from the grapes he introduced and grew upon his property between Vineyard and Kukui Streets. The prickly pear cactus is called *panini* (originally *manini*) after this foreigner. A copy, transcribed by Wyllie, of Don Marin's diary, which was kept between the years 1809 and 1826 is preserved in the Archives of Hawaii; the original has been lost.

were familiar with the Catholic [Church] in their own land joined with the priests, and these were the first fruits of the Catholic religion. A dwelling place was quickly secured consisting of several buildings, one of them a large grass hut with gables on the right and left ends, large doors on the Waikiki and 'Ewa sides, and many windows. At the west end of the house was a large window, and there stood the altar decorated with lights, with arches wrapped in red cloth, and images of Jesus and the cross on the altar. On the second Sabbath of the opening of the church news spread that a second religion was being established at Ka-pauhi, and it was that of Marin's country. And many Hawaiians came to see what it was like. They were amazed to see the lights burning on the altar, the three priests dressed in white, and everybody kneeling, but they could not understand the words of the prayers. The majority of the congregation was made up of foreigners. There were a few native worshipers, but the prominent people followed after the religion upon which the chiefs relied.

During the first two years the Roman Catholics had many followers, and I did not see that these were objected to or forbidden to worship during those years. It was said that Boki, because of his enmity toward Ka-'ahu-manu, helped the Catholic priests. Here is an incident: During the Rev. Mr. Bingham's absence at one time, Mr. Levi Chamberlain had charge of the services on the Sabbath with Mr. Kuke and Kahikona of Borabora as interpreters. One Sabbath Kuke was conducting the afternoon service, and the church was filled with chiefs; the king also was present with Kina'u, Ka-ulu-ohi, Ka-'ahu-manu, and other members of the royal family. The preacher had given out the text, "The king's heart is in the hands of the Lord; as the rivers of water he turneth it whithersoever he will," when Boki entered. When he heard the preacher explaining and comparing the meaning of the text he stood up and said, pointing with his hand, "Here! here! here! where are you, you preachers? I do not want you to give the heart of my chief to God. You are sorcerers who are offering the heart of my king to God and you will cause him to die" (*i ke auau*). This caused a commotion in the church, and Mr. Chamberlain said, "You are mistaken, Boki. These are the words of God written by holy men of God." "These are not the words of God, they are your own words, and you brought them here and changed them into Hawaiian words. I shall take my king; we are not coming to church any more. We shall seek another religion." Boki acted thus on the strength of his own rank as chief, without fear of his sister and nieces. There was much excitement in the church, but the young king read the English Bible and saw that the words were those of God and told Boki that he was mistaken. At that time the nation was without the Hawaiian Bible.

During the first years after the coming of the Roman Catholic priests, while Boki was still living here, there was little trouble and they baptized one hundred twenty-four members, but soon after Boki sailed away, in 1829, their religion was prohibited; Ka-'ahu-manu personally forbade the people to attend Catholic services, and the priests were ordered not to hold Sabbath services. Those who came together secretly to worship were put in chains inside the fort, but some still refused to abandon their worship. Kiha-wahine of Kalaepohaku was one of the first to be put in chains. On December 24, 1831, the ship *Waverly* (*Makau-wahie*) under the command of Captain Sumner was charged to take the two Catholic priests who still remained, Father Bachelot and Father Patrick Short, back to their own country. Captain Sumner was a Britisher who had lived here many years and was well acquainted with the chiefs. He had married a native wife and had a family. He was the captain of Hawaiian ships and had often sailed to Spanish ports. Hence Ka-'ahu-manu charged him with the task of taking the Spanish priests back to their own country. On the day when the ship was to sail Ka-'ahu-manu went to meet the priests at their own house. She offered them her hand, saying "I have come in person to see this done so that there may be no rumor that you were unjustly treated. You two have done very wrong. It is not good to preach two religions to the natives. It will cause disagreement among the people of my king. This is a small land. I have therefore come in person to meet you both and take you to the boat." There had been rumors that the priests had said they would not leave the country, and were not afraid even though the chiefs killed them or burned them alive. Ka-'ahu-manu had heard these rumors, and that was why she came herself to see that they were put on the ship.* The Hawaiian woman named Kiha-wahine was sent away with the priests. She claims that they were taken to California and landed at a desolate place where for three days they were almost famished. Is this true or not? (The editor, L. Ho'oponopono, says it is not true.) Ka-'ahu-manu then required the Catholic converts to join the Protestant religion, and all did so but some ten members among whom were Mehe-'ula and Uheke, and they were made to do hard labor at Makiki, building stone walls. In January, 1832, Louisa and other members of the Catholic faith were made to work in the bulrush swamps at Pawa'a and Mau'oki; some hid away in caves and holes and others pretended to conform.

Ka-'ahu-manu based her persecutions upon urgent reason such as the following: She believed that the kingdom of God was like the kingdoms of the world, that the authority of the chief over the government was to be united with the power of God, and that the people should follow the

* *Ka Nupepa Ku'oko'a*, Dec. 19, 1868.

the religion of their chiefs. She believed that the establishment of different religions would cause family quarrels, bring about dissension, and so make trouble for the government. She firmly believed in unity of belief for chiefs and commoners alike and a similar form of worship. She objected to the Catholic religion because of its similarity to the pagan in the use of images and in bowing and kneeling before them. She objected to it because it led to rebellion against the authority of the chiefs, and might lead to the killing of the chiefs, the laying of burdens upon the commoners and blinding their eyes. She declared that chief or commoner who turned to the Catholic Church was a traitor against the Hawaiian government.

Many opinions have been expressed in regard to these reasons urged by Ka-'ahu-manu against the Catholic faith. Some say that the Protestant missionaries urged this action upon Ka-'ahu-manu; some deny that they had anything to do with it.* Some of the missionaries argued that Catholics were Christian and not pagan, but Ka-'ahu-manu answered, "My king has established free eating, and the idols have been destroyed; my king and I do not wish to return to the old practice of bowing and kneeling before images." Some said therefore that the persecution of the Catholics was Ka-'ahu-manu's own idea. After her death those who had suffered persecution were all released, and for a year they lived without practicing their faith. This was probably because the whole country was in tumult. The island of Oahu was entirely given over to licentiousness. The power of the government was in abeyance, and the married people gave themselves up to all kinds of sensual indulgence. During the last part of the year 1833 Elizabeth Kina'u became chief counselor and governor of Oahu. She held opinions similar to Ka-'ahu-manu's and persecuted the Catholics severely. Among the Catholics brought to the fort to be tried were the women Ka-uila, Ka-ua-lua, Kiha-wahine, and the men Pa'ele and Ka-ihu-mua, and everyone knows how severely they were handled because they would not abandon their belief. For six or seven years such persecutions lasted.†

In September, 1836, a British Roman Catholic priest arrived, the Reverend Arsenius Robert Walsh. He was not banished, but was warned by the chiefs not to preach to the natives. He did not obey this order, but debated with Protestant ministers, preached to the natives, and baptized them secretly. On April 17, 1837, the banished priests, Father Bachelot and Father Short, returned on the ship *Clementine*, having

* For refutation of this charge see the letter of Kamehameha III to the American Consul, dated October 28, 1839, assuming full responsibilty for the action taken by the Hawaiian government against the introduction of Catholicism to Hawaii, 7, pp 553-555.

† *Ka Nupepa Ku'oko'a*, Dec. 26, 1868.

heard of a treaty between the British and Hawaiian governments. For thirty-three days they were allowed to live in peace at their former residence. On May 20, the governor Ke-ku-anao'a, accompanied by Ka-la'au-lana and others, arrested them and dragged them forcibly back to the ship. This caused a riot between the foreigners and the persons who had conducted the arrest. After the priests had been put on board, the British flag was hauled down. The men and the captain of the ship left the ship, and the flag was taken to the British consul's and burned in front of Mr. Stephen Reynolds' yard (where the Royal Hotel stands). For this the Hawaiian government was given the blame; the British consul threatened that they should suffer for it. The two priests remained alone on the ship which served as their prison. Kina'u sent word to the king at Lahaina and he returned word, "I will follow the action of my guardian in banishing them; order them to board the boat and depart." There they remained therefore until July when two warships arrived, a British and a French, under the command of commodores of those countries. The king was sent for and the troubles immediately settled. It was agreed that the priests were to be allowed to land until they could find a ship to take them away. One sailed soon to Valparaiso, Chile, but the French priest remained because of illness. The chiefs complained, and he sailed away [in the schooner *Honolulu* bought and rechristened *Notre Dame de Paix*] and died at sea, attended by Father Maigret, a French priest who had not been allowed to land on Hawaiian soil.

Kina'u was a brave woman. She had not feared the threats of the French and British captains even when their fists were shaken in her face, but remained true to what she thought right. The captains and the British consul did their best to frighten her into giving way to them, even brandishing their swords in her face, but she would not give in. She had the courage of a man. Had she been one, she would have been a second Kamehameha, to whom she bore a remarkable resemblance. But the kingdom of God is not like the kingdoms of this world. It is not right to burden a native with a fixed belief. A government has a right to control human rights, wealth, and property, but not to forbid a human being from worshiping according to his own Christian belief.

The arrival of the Roman Catholic missionaries in 1827 was due to John Rives, the Frenchman who had lived on Hawaii and associated with the king and his chiefs. John Rives came to Oahu as steward on a merchant vessel which arrived from Spanish and Norwegian ports while Kamehameha was living on Oahu. Rives spoke English fluently and was requested by Liholiho to become his friend and instruct him in the English language; and the captain of the ship granted this request. Rives became Liholiho's friend, and the prince and Ka-'ahu-manu called him "Luahine" (Old woman). He lived the life of a Hawaiian prince, had a tabu symbol made for him, was given considerable property on Oahu, Molokai, Maui, and Hawaii, and became a great favorite with the young king whom he instructed in English both during Kamehameha's life and after Liholiho became king. He also had several children born to him. When Liholiho sailed to England Rives accompanied the king as interpreter. On their arrival in England Rives proceeded to France where he represented himself as having accompanied the king of the Hawaiian islands, and as being a great favorite with the king and the chiefs. He said that the king had agreed to have him come to France and invite the Roman Catholic priests to Hawaii. All of this would have been true had Liholiho returned alive. Rives boasted of the generosity of the Hawaiians, both chiefs and commoners (the loss of this trait today is to be regretted). The Archbishop of Paris consulted Pope Leo XII in Rome, and the pope agreed to send priests of the order of the Sacred Heart to Hawaii. It was thus that Bachelot and his companions happened to come here. When the bodies of the king and queen were brought back to Hawaii, and the chiefs learned that Rives had gone to France after Roman Catholic priests, Ka-'ahu-manu took away all Rives' lands and gave them to others. Hearing that his return would not be welcome to the party in power, Rives went to Mexico and lived there until his death, and his wife and children never saw him again. But in 1827 the boat arrived bearing the priests and laborers and all their belongings [to found a Catholic mission in Hawaii].

Elizabeth Kina'u, Ka-'ahu-manu's successor died March 4, 1839, and her position as counselor-in-chief was given to Miriam Ke-ka-ulu-ohi. Many troubles came to the government during Ke-ka-ulu-ohi's time occasioned by the persecution of the followers of the Roman Catholic religion by the chiefs. On July 9, 1839, there arrived from Tahiti the French warship *Artemise*, commanded by Captain Laplace. It entered through the Mamala channel, docked in Honolulu harbor, and its captain sent word to the king and chiefs that he had been commissioned by the king of France to stop the persecution of the Roman Catholics, and to exact penalties from the government for these acts of persecution. The conditions he laid down as pleasing to the king of France were: first, the granting of permission to the Roman Catholics to share equal rights of worship with the Protestants; second, the granting of a piece of land to the French people for the erection of a church where Roman Catholic priests might officiate; third, the immediate release of the Roman Catholics who had been imprisoned; fourth, the payment of the sum of $20,000 delivered into the hands of Captain Laplace on board the *Artemise* as surety for the carrying out of the terms of the treaty, the money to be returned when the French government was assured of their fulfillment. The captain said, "When the king fully understands this treaty ('*olelo ku'ikahi*) he will act upon it as the only way to secure peace to his country, and to remain ruler over it at peace with the rest of the world. He must be quick (*e wikiwiki 'oia*) about signing it, and so follow the action of the queen of Tahiti in allowing Roman Catholics to worship in her country. Otherwise war will be made, and all the damage suffered by foreign residents will be charged upon the Hawaiian government."

The governor Ke-ku-anao'a and the chief counselor Miriam Ke-ka-ulu-ohi, together with the chiefs, commoners, and the foreign residents, were very much disturbed by these demands. A council was held, and it was decided to accept the terms at once without waiting to hear from the king; and Miriam Ke-ka-ulu-ohi and Mr. Richards delivered the money on board the French ship.* Captain Laplace was delighted to find that all his demands had been compiled with except the signing of the treaty, and came to shake hands with the king's representative, who assured him that the king, when he realized that it was the only way to save his throne, would not hesitate to sign the order to secure peace for their weak government. He did in fact sign on his return from Maui, but some say that had Kina'u been the king's counselor at the time the bullets of France and the bullets from Punchbowl would have echoed through the air. The Roman Catholic prisoners were all released, and on May 13, 1840, Bishop Rouchouze (Tepano) arrived with a party of priests on the *Clementine* under Captain Dudoit from the islands of Mangareva and Nu'uhiva. During the next seven months, between May and December, the number of 2,523 persons were baptized by the Roman Catholic bishop. After this more Roman Catholic priests came and were distributed over the islands of the group. They brought as helpers carpenters, builders, blacksmiths, and other craftsmen, and sisters also who taught in the schools.†

[In the missing numbers of the *Ke Au 'Oko'a* and in this issue the affairs of the Roman Catholic mission in Hawaii are further discussed. The correspondence between Captain Mallet and Kamehameha III and the premier Miriam Ke-ka-ulu-ohi, which may be found printed elsewhere in full, is explained. The country people had taken sides for and against the Protestant mission and that of the "Pope." These troubles were stirred up in the schools and churches established in the country districts. The public opposition on the part of the priests to the religion accepted by the chiefs led to disputes within the family, to the damage of

*Ka Nupepa Ku'oko'a, Jan 2, 1869.
† Ka Nupepa Ku'oko'a, Jan. 9, 1869.

churches and schools belonging to the Catholics, the refusal to grant licenses to marry to Catholic priests, and the petty antagonisms which the enmity between the two camps engendered. The Catholics again appealed to force and Captain Mallet endeavored to adjust the difficulty, and at the same time to secure better terms of entry for French wines. The king and the chiefs were perplexed, inclined to follow the policy fixed by the two powerful premiers who had passed away, but aware of the trouble which this policy had caused the government, so that, as the saying was, "Ka-'ula-hai-malama plays hide and seek; Ke-ku-hau-pi'o (Stands-leaning) is her father; she leans on the canoe side and rests against the back of the canoe" (*Pe'ekue Ka-'ula-hai malama, o Ke-ku-hau-pi'o he makua hilinai a'e i ka palekai, kalale moku a'e mahope*). This means that she tries to shield the true offender by dodging direct questions. They tried to reconcile the two religions by commanding; first, that the schools and churches stop disputing and live in peace; second, that freedom of religious worship be allowed without opposing anyone; third, that the school, marriage, and other laws of the land be carried out as they stood until they could be adjusted; fourth, that the school agent was to take precedence of the land agent (*konohiki*) in settling disputes about school grounds; fifth, that no churches were to be built in future upon any land without the consent of the high chief to whom the land belonged.]*

* *Ke Au 'Oko'a*, Mar. 18, 1869.

CHAPTER XXVI

Premiership of Kina'u

Ka-'ahu-manu was the famous queen who established God's kingdom on Hawaii and who converted chiefs and commoners to the worship of the one God and punished severely those who worshiped other gods, those smart people living in beautiful houses who say it was not Ka-'ahu-manu, to the contrary [not withstanding]. Many controversies raged before this was brought about. Many blame her for the persecutions of the Roman Catholics. Today the kingdom is blessed by allowing freedom in religion. It was because of the lack of wise advice that upon the shoulders of Ka-'ahu-manu, the chiefs, and the government was placed the blame for this persecution of the Roman Catholics. When she died her nieces stood firmly for the good cause for which she strove. Ke-ka-ulu-ohi joined Kawaiaha'o church on March 2, 1828 the third occasion in the history of the church on which members were received into it, and Kina'u on March 7, 1830. These chiefesses were of the same firmness of character as Ka-'ahu-manu, and their husbands took a similar stand. They too were like parents to the people, but the time in which they lived was not so peaceful as was that of Ka-'ahu-manu.

Not many months after Ka-'ahu-manu's death Kau-i-ke-aouli turned to sinful pleasures as is the way of chiefs, whose thoughts turn where flow their desires. The gossip among the chiefs and abroad in country places was that it was Kaomi who had seduced the king, but this was not true for he had shown a fondness for such tempting delights even before Kaomi became his favorite. Even when Ka-'ahu-manu was alive, at the time when they were making a tour of Maui and Hawaii, gossip about him had been raised at Kailua and was known to Ka-'ahu-manu. She tried to put a stop to it by reminding the king how they had labored to teach to the people righteousness according to the word of God, and how the king had himself laid down the law that "the chief or commoner who commits adultery shall be punished by being put to hard labor," but the king would not listen to her. "The lover has been deaf even from ancient times." The king said, "Let me work at hard labor as the law that I have made for my kingdom says." Ka-'ahu-manu gave him a young chiefess to become his wife by marriage, but he would not consent. The story was that he worked at hard labor to punish himself for his sin. Among the white traders it was reported that, "The king of Hawaii has been punished according to the law of the missionaries, and has built a fence for the cattle pen of the missionary, Hiram Bingham." This pen began at the northeast corner of Beretania (Pelekane) [the place now occupied by the English church and called "Britain"] and ran directly to Punchbowl and along the eastern side of the hill straight to Makiki, then turned down *makai* of Punahou. The space between Makiki and Punahou where stood the long stone called the Pohaku Ke-opu-o-lani belonged to the king. The king worked, and the chiefs, members of his household, and his favorites (the Hulumanu) aided him. Strange indeed in view of the saying, "The body of the king is sacred"! The white residents and consuls of the city said, "You do not rule the country. It is Ka-'ahu-manu who rules. In our countries the law does not apply to the king but only to the chiefs and common people. This is a law of the missionaries." So the king was angry, and after Ka-'ahu-manu's death all Oahu turned to evil ways.

Kaomi was the son of a native of Borabora named Moe, and a Hawaiian woman named Ka-hua-moa, so he was part Boraboran and part Hawaiian. He was a friend of Ka-'ahu-manu's brother, Ka-hekili Ke'e-au-moku, and became a favorite of the king not because he was well-educated and intelligent, but because he knew something of the art of healing, could tell the symptoms of diseases, had learned from Boki and Ka-'o'o how to diagnose a disease by feeling the body of a patient and [could prescribe] the proper medicine to cure it. Since his advice was successful the king conceived a great liking for him. He had moreover the power to tell a funny story entertainingly, and for these reasons he was admitted to intimacy with the king. When the king took up sinful ways he gave Kaomi the title of "joint king, joint ruler" (*moi ku'i, aupuni ku'i*), appointed chiefs, warriors, and guards to his service, and made his name honorable. Any chief, prominent citizen, member of the king's household, or any man at all who wanted land, clothing, money, or anything else that man might desire, applied to Kaomi. He had the power to give or lend for the government. Landless chiefs were enriched by Kaomi and landless men also received land through him. The king's love of pleasure grew, and evil ways that had been stamped out were revived. The natural impulses of the old days—prostitution, liquor drinking, the hula—came back. The liquor distilleries were again opened. Only in the district of Waialua was the distillation of liquor not allowed. All kinds of indulgence cropped up. People poured in from Hawaii, Maui, and Kauai, for on Oahu the marriage laws were not observed, but on the other islands the rulers were strict in their enforcement of Kau-i-ke-aouli's law. Such infringements of the law as knocking out the teeth,

tattooing, tobacco smoking, and other small sins were punished by working on the road. . . . No one of the chiefs dared attempt to turn the king
back to right living. Not even his foster mothers, Kina'u and Ke-ka-ulu-
ohi, could utter a word. The king's mind was set. Only once did his mind
seem to give way and that was when his sister, Harriet Nahi-'ena'ena,
came to take him to Maui to live until the confusion ceased on Oahu.
This was in June, 1833, and the king consented to please his sister; but
on the night for sailing, June 21, when his sister had called for him at
Kapamo'o and they had gone hand in hand down to the boat, the sister's
arm about her brother's neck, as they came close to Mr. French's house
he excused himself to her to enter the house and did not return. He had
vanished leaving his sister weeping and wailing for her brother.

The chiefs, Ke-ka-ulu-ohi and David Ka-mehameha, accompanied her
from Oahu to Maui. They left Papohaku on Molokai, crossed Maunaloa and came down to Pala'au on their way to visit Hoa-pili and his wife
on Maui. Hoa-pili was the one who had been placed in charge of the king
by Kamehameha and whose voice carried weight with him, according to
the command, "Hoa-pili is the father of the young princes." It was
rumored over Maui that the king was going to appoint Liliha premier
to replace Kina'u, and it was for this reason that Ke-ka-ulu-ohi wished
to consult Hoa-pili, since the many attempts made by Harriet Nahi-
'ena'ena to influence the young king failed. Not only was Kuini Liliha
to be appointed premier with the office of governor of Oahu, but Paki
was to be the assistant premier and governor. These chiefs had been
treated as of inferior rank in Ka-'ahu-manu's day, this was why Kina'u's
party were so indignant and why they sent for Hoa-pili to decide the
matter.

On a night of November, 1833, when the consuls, prominent white
residents, chiefs, officers of the government, and members of the army
were gathered for the appointment of Liliha and Paki, Hoa-pili came
with Ke-kaua'i-'ele'ele to Kina'u's house where Ke-ka-ulu-ohi and her
companions were staying. Kina'u said to Hoa-pili, "I sent for you to give
your opinion in a matter of right or wrong." "What is it about?" "This
is what it is about: Tonight Liliha is to be apponted premier of the kingdom. This will perhaps be to your advantage for she is your daughter
but we must suffer." Hoa-pili bowed his head and then lifted it again and
said to Kina'u, "My daughter is but a tenant, the house is yours. You
are the daughter of Kamehameha; we are but tenants." Kina'u said, "It
must perhaps be as the king wishes." Hoa-pili, without thought for his
own advantage, replied, "If you want the premiership of the kingdom
the place is yours." "How can that be? [she asked]. No chief is allowed
to enter the king's place. It is guarded by soldiers with guns and by

foreign guards. A chief who enters dies." "They would only fire off a gun" [Hoa-pili answered]. So it was agreed to go that night to the king's house at Hale-uluhe on the Beretania grounds.

The party consisted of Elizabeth Kina'u, Ke-ku-anao'a, and two armed men, Kani-ku and Ka-'ai-pua'a; Ke-ka-ulu-ohi and Ka-na'ina with two armed men, Halali and Kilinahe; and Ulu-maheihei Hoa-pili with Ke-kaua'i and Ka-'umi'umi. The yard was lined with soldiers armed with guns and swords, foreigners behind them, and officers mounted on horses and carrying swords. Ulu-maheihei went first, then the young women, and after them the escort. In defence of the dignity of their rank as chiefs they risked their lives, and did not wait to be announced as daughters of Kamehameha. As they drew close to the white soldiers they were recognized and someone told the king. He called out, "Come in!" and wept aloud as he kissed his foster mothers whom he saw again for the first time, and the foreign soldiers hearing the wailing withdrew. The king asked Hoa-pili, "Why did you come here?" Hoa-pili replied, "We came because we had heard rumors that you were going to appoint Liliha premier of the kingdom. You must first kill me before making my daughter premier lest I be blamed as her parent. Here is the daughter of the house of Kamehameha. Let her serve you. My daughter is but a tenant here." The king answered, "I love these two and I also love Liliha, but these two I love because they keep my laws." Hoa-pili said, "Do me this favor to place the duties of the kingdom upon her who is here ready to serve you." "I consent, but Liliha must hear of this," said the king. Liliha was called and was found drunk.

Some days later the party met the king again, namely, Hoa-pili, Kua-kini, Ka-iki-o-'ewa, Kina'u, Ke-ka-ulu-ohi, Liliha, Ke-kau-'onohi, and the rest, and the king agreed to appoint Elizabeth Kina'u his premier and the governor of the island of Oahu and of the fort, in place of Kua-kini; and Kua-kini returned to Hawaii and continued to serve as governor of that island.

Elizabeth Kina'u became premier during a period of riotous pleasure-seeking. Law was set at naught. Fighting, murdering, adultery, prostitution, plural marriage, disregard of the marriage law, drunkenness, and the distilling of liquor went on all over Oahu as far as Kalae-okala'au and Ka'ie'iewaho. Beyond these points the laws were effective. In Honolulu lips smacked over the flesh of baked dog. The chiefs who took part in this new regime were Liliha, Paki, and many chiefs of high and of low rank, government officials, and all of the household of the king. They did just as they pleased, neither standing up nor prostrating themselves in the presence of the king. Kaomi, the joint ruler, reigned supreme. In such days the piety of some of the church members was all the more conspicuous. The members of Kawaiaha'o church stood firm. They held prayer meetings which the chiefesses, Kina'u, Ke-ka-ulu-ohi, and other prominent members attended. During these troubled years the missionary teachers were active in encouraging the people in the word of God, in teaching school, and in sending pupils to Lahainaluna to be educated. It was the same in Waialua. The church members remained steadfast and kept up the schools. But in other places all over Oahu there were no religious meetings held, and the schools were dead. In 1834 the premier issued the following proclamation:

> To the teachers and people: Stand fast by the right, do not be highminded; do not worship amiss, for Jesus is the one God; He is life, power, holiness. He will help us in our labor. You teachers, do not turn the minds of your pupils to things of darkness. Look to the word of God where they will learn the right. Do all you can to stamp out liquor.
>
> Kina'u

Some people were delighted with the government of Kaomi, and some were disappointed and angry, but their wrath was in vain for the king himself indulged in sinful pleasures, disliked advice in these matters, and would not be "enticed to do right," as he himself put it. Some of the chiefs murmured against the king because his mind was so fixed on evil ways, and they made a secret plan to kill Kaomi, and a certain chief named Ka-iki-o-'ewa was to carry it out. He went with a servant named Ka-ihu-hanuna, carrying a war club in his hand, to the yard of Kaomi (near the present publishing house of the *Ku'oko'a*) and ordered the servant to tie Kaomi's hands behind his back with a rope. Kaomi did not order the guards to kill Ka-iki-o-'ewa in accordance with the law that "the chief who enters Kaomi's house shall die." He allowed himself to be bound and put to death if death it was to be. Ka-iki-o-'ewa led him into the presence of Kina'u inside the fort. When she saw Kaomi with his hands tied behind his back she cried out in alarm to her uncle, "Alas! what are you doing to the king's favorite? The king will think that I have a share in this. Let him go, or this crime will rest upon us all!" Ka-iki-o-'ewa said, "Who is ruler over the kingdom? You are the ruler. Give your consent to the death of this trouble-maker." At this moment the king hurried in, dressed in the scant clothing he was wearing when a guard had run to inform him that, "Kaomi is being killed by Ka-iki-o-'ewa." The king himself untied Kaomi's bonds. Ka-iki-o-'ewa sprang forward and grappled with the king, over and under they fought until the king held Ka-iki-o-'ewa fast. Then words poured from Ka-iki-o-'ewa's mouth declaring, "You are not the ruler over the kingdom if you keep on indulging yourself in evil ways!" but the king did not answer him. (Ka-iki-o-'ewa must have been insane.) Kaomi was released and went back with the king to Ka-hale-uluhe, and the king's place was made tabu; no one was allowed to enter it.*

During this troubled year of 1834 some of the young chiefs died, among them Ke-ola-loa, the son of Pauli Ka-'o-lei-o-ku and the brother of Konia, who was to have been the husband of Princess Harriet Nahi-'ena'ena, and Ka-'ua'a-moku-o-Ka-manele, the daughter of J. A. Kuakini, governor of Hawaii, who was affianced to Kamehameha III. Both these young chiefs were about twenty years of age.

Ulu-maheihei Hoa-pili who acted as the King's leading *kahu*, and Ka-iki-o-'ewa who was also his guardian, were induced by Elizabeth Kina'u and Miriam Ke-ka-ulu-ohi to live on Oahu and observe from the outside the doings of their ward. Even they however dared not cross his wishes lest he become morose, although when religious people came to him he always met them graciously. It was also observed that when one said, "Here comes Ulu-maheihei," he quickly bade, "Hide the rum!" That might have been because Hoa-pili was the king's *kahu*, but for John 'I'i also when those outside exclaimed, " 'I'i!" the glasses were immediately flung aside. So with the missionaries and the pious people however humble who went to visit the king. He was deferential and agreed affably to stop his pleasure-seeking and intoxication. It was believed that the only reason why he was so slow to quit drinking was because he was influenced by certain chiefs—Liliha, Paki, and others. The entire blame of his conduct however was laid upon Kaomi, the joint king. Then the rumor went about the city and spread to the other islands that "Elizabeth Kina'u is to become ruler of the kingdom." The king with Kaomi, the chiefs, and favorites, made a circuit of the island, and it was rumored that there would be a fight when the king returned to enter the city. Some said, "Perhaps it is only Ka-iki-o-'ewa's ravings." When the king's company reached Moanalua a mounted cavalcade set out from Honolulu to meet it. The end of this cavalcade was at the school at Kaiwi'ula when the king's mounted company entered the fort. There the king met his foster mother Kina'u and the chiefs, and the sound of wailing arose as they greeted each other.

The king associated himself graciously with the pious chiefesses and his guardians and allowed Kina'u and Ulu-maheihei to put a stop to dissipation outside the city, but the chiefs insisted upon distilling liquor and there were many stills in Ko'olaupoko, in Kona, in 'Ewa, and in Wai'a-nae. Ulu-maheihei was appointed marshal to put a stop to liquor drinking and distilling. At Kailua he smashed a still belonging to a chiefess, named Ka-lola, related to the king; and poured out the liquor. The still

*Ke Au 'Oko'a, Jan. 7, 1869.

belonging to Kaomi and a company of chiefs at Kekele was [also] broken up, and other stills in Ko'olau were demolished. Ulu-maheihei went around by 'Ewa as far as Wai'anae where two stills were reported which belonged to Kuini Liliha and the old chiefess Pu'u-he'ewale, a relative of Toti; and these were not spared by Hoa-pili, but broken up and the liquor poured out. Liquor distilling and drinking ceased in the country districts except when the king was present. Another important act of the chiefs was to restore wives and husbands to their legal spouses on the other islands. Among these were some lesser chiefs and prominent citizens, but they were for the most part commoners. In the midst of wailing they were arrested by the chiefs and placed on ships bound for Kauai, Maui, and Hawaii. There was great excitement but it rapidly subsided, peace was restored, and as a result the whole nation turned to do right according to the word of God.

Hoa-pili and the others remained on Oahu until the confusion was at an end, and order restored all over Oahu; then he returned with Ka-heihei-malie and the other chiefs to Maui. Later Harriet Nahi-'ena'ena returned to Maui on the ship *Ho'oikaika* accompanied by her attendants, Konia, Alapa'i, Ka-holo-lio, Ka-poli and others, and by some chiefesses who were members of the household of the royal daughter of Ke-opu-o-lani. At Lahaina Hoa-pili came on board on his way to Kailua, Hawaii, to arrange for the marriage of his princess [Harriet Nahi-'ena'ena] with her affianced husband, Lele-io-hoku. At Kailua he found the chiefs gone to the cattle pens at Waimea. He sailed on to Kawaihae, met Kua-kini at Waimea, and easily gained his consent to the marriage of their nephew, according to the ancient practice of chiefs to seek a chief (*'imi ali'i*) or a lord (*'imi haku*). Lele-io-hoku arrived with a numerous company of followers, Hua-lena among others, and the marriage was about to take place when a letter came from the king proposing that it be delayed, and the boy entered at the Lahainaluna school in order that he might be educated and his mind matured before marrying the king's sister. The chiefs and missionaries were pleased with this evidence of serious thought on the king's part, believing that his sister might outlive him and herself become ruler. Lele-io-hoku entered Lahainaluna school and after he had obtained some education the two were married in the Waine'e church on Wednesday, November 25, 1835, the Rev. William Richards performing the ceremony. In January 1836, Harriet Nahi-'ena'ena and the chiefs went to live at Wailuku *makai* of Kahulu. When she became pregnant the Oahu chiefs bade her come there to give birth, and Kina'u built her a house called Ka-hale-kauila where she awaited the arrival of the child whose birth was the cause of her last illness.

She nursed the child, but it was sickly and died, and the mother was very weak. Her brother the king took her to a place *mauka* of Ka-hale-uluhe where she died, December 30, 1836, at the age of twenty-one.

Great was the king's grief over the death of his sister. He wailed aloud reciting the story of her birth and how he alone was left (of those two) to rule the kingdom. Chiefs and commoners lamented for the chiefess whose children they had hoped to see carry on the line of ruling chiefs. The king arranged to have her laid away on Maui, the land where her mother, Harriet Ke-opu-o-lani had been laid away, "in the calm of Hauola." He brought the three-masted ship *Quixote,* equipped it as a warship, and renamed it *Kai Ke-opu-o-lani.* When all was ready for the ship to sail with the remains of Nahi-'ena'ena to Maui, the king thought of the country whose people he loved, of the laws which had been made for it, and he began seriously to consider for himself the Christian teaching. He recalled how Maui was a land noted for abiding by the laws: where both chiefs and commoners worshiped God and were obedient to Ke-opu-o-lani's command to observe the laws and pray to God; a land in which the first high school had been established to shed the light of knowledge and wisdom; and he hesitated to carry the remains of his sister back to the land where people were so loved by her, while he himself was so imperfect in his observance of the law. They would wonder at him because of the laws he had made for the protection of the race. On February 14, 1837, therefore, King Kau-i-ke-aouli, Kamehameha III, was married with great ceremony to Kalama Ka-paku-haili, the daughter of I-'ahu-'ula and Na-ihe-kukui, the marriage ceremony being performed by the Rev. Hiram Bingham at the home of the bride's adopted parents, Miriam Ke-ka-ulu-ohi and Charles Ka-na'ina. The wife received the supreme title of Queen (*ka Mo'i Wahine*).

The funeral of his sister followed, and the body was carried on board the warship and conveyed to Lahaina under the escort of a number of schooners carrying a large company of chiefs, prominent citizens, favorites, and soldiery. The body remained on the ship while a roadway was prepared by cutting down breadfruit trees and *kou* trees of Molakia and covering the way with sand, then a layer of grass, and finally mats spread all along the path. [This roadway] began at the horse gate at Pana'ewa, ran *mauka* until it reached the old highroad of the ancestors at the corner of Maluo's lot, then turned to the left side of Lahaina and went *mauka* of Kapahumanamana and *mauka* of Mr. Baldwin's, Mr. Richard's, and Kalai-koa's places, came out by the breadfruit tree on which was laid the first victim of battle, then went on to Kane-ma'i-kou's place and *mauka* of Ka-nau-o-pua'a's to 'Alio, then turned seaward of Molakia facing the north and descending to the sand of Makalaukalu, down to the sluice gate of Mokuhinia, and down to Halehuki, called also Halepiula. That was the route taken by the funeral procession.

On the day of funeral many high chiefs gathered, such as the king and queen, Kina'u, Ke-ka-ulu-ohi, Kuini Liliha, Ke-kau-'onohi, Ke-ano, and many others who were the last of their race to be entitled to the great royal *kahili* from which have branched off the *kahili* of today with their variegated feathers. This last funeral and service of prayer concluded the weeping and lamentation of the chiefs and people of Maui for their beloved princess. As for Kau-i-ke-aouli, such was his love and regret for his sister that he continued to live on Maui for eight years. He built her a mausoleum at Moku'ula and placed there also the bodies of their mother Ke-opu-o-lani and other chiefs. He made the day of his sister's death a public holiday, ordered guns to be fired from the government forts from Hawaii to Kauai, and gave big feasts every year in its celebration. That was the first Memorial Day instituted in Hawaii. The island of Molokai was turned over to the king; and his favorites, the Hulumanu, divided it among themselves with his consent, and it became theirs in fee simple at that time.

Not much of importance happened in the kingdom during these years with the single exception of the return of the Roman Catholic priests to Honolulu. . . .* The years in which the king lived on Maui were peaceful years. While the queen was being tenderly guarded at the time of the birth of Ke-aweawe-'ula, the king's cousin, Keoni Ana *'opio* [John Young, Jr.], the husband of Alapa'i, one of the king's favorites, was caught with her and condemned by the king to die. The black flag was hoisted for a week as a sign of death. The chiefs consulted how they could secure a reprieve for him, but could find no way out; the king was not to be approached, and no chief was allowed to come before him. The king and the two women, the queen and Alapa'i, were living day and night outside the enclosure of Moku'ula while the chiefs were assembled in Hale-piula in conference, not knowing what to do with the king's decree, "Let the man die!" which had been sent them by his messenger. The king himself had given to Ka-leo-o-ke-ko'i authority to act as his spokesman and report to him the words of the council. Four or five days they debated the life or death sentence, then it occured to Hoa-pili-wahine what to say, and the chief was pardoned. "This man will become the king's favorite," said some, and so it was.

When Mr. Richards returned from a visit to the United States his place as minister at Lahaina had been filled by Dr. Baldwin, and Mr. Richards had been withdrawn. Hoa-pili therefore requested that Mr.

* *Ke Au 'Oko'a*, Jan. 14, 1869.

Richards become instructor for the king and his court, since he had been a father to the chiefs of the royal family at Lahaina and to those of all Maui, and had carried them through their troubles. William Richards had been sent to Hawaii as a minister of the Puritan faith. He became Queen Ke-opu-o-lani's minister, and expounded to the chiefs and prominent persons of Lahaina the meaning of the Scriptures and of the ten commandments of God. And he explained how the law was a thing to bring good government and peace to the land for both chiefs and commoners, and how the chiefs should stop laying burdens upon the poor. The older men such as Hoa-pili, Kalai-koa, Pikanele, Pua'a Ka-'ohana, Daniel 'I'i, David Malo, One-'oa, and others gathered to learn of Mr. Richards. When Ka-'ahu-manu lived among the Maui chiefs the most prominent people became famous for their discussion of the laws by which the land should be governed, and Ka-'ahu-manu thought highly of the Maui chiefs. They were not influenced by the hope of gain or favor; they did not discriminate between the chief and the lowliest citizen; the law must punish all alike. One of the high chiefs, a son of Hoa-pili named Kau-kuna Ka-hekili who had great wealth and owned land from Hawaii to Kauai, to whom belonged the whole island of Lanai and who never lacked for money or wealth, nevertheless became entangled in the law, was made by his father Hoa-pili to work on the road, and was sent to Kahikinui to cut down trees. Many of the chiefs of Maui were made to work in that way, for the law was strictly observed. It was thus that Mr. Richards had taught the chiefs of Maui, "The power of the law must be alike over rich and poor; in order to govern peacefully the law must have power over all alike"; and these few words had given him such a reputation for fairness and effectiveness that the king now chose Mr. Richards as minister and instructor in the affairs of government. He then wished to provide a living for his teacher, and Mr. Richards accepted a reasonable sum for his living expenses. He worked hard, but asked no large payment for his labor; six hundred dollars, on which to support a wife and family was his pay in return for his heavy duties. He served as delegate for the king to the great countries of the world to confer upon the independence of the Hawaiian kingdom; he was minister of education and president of the Land Grants commission until his death. Is this not a glorious record?

Upon his appointment as instructor to the king Mr. Richards at once started a school of political economy among the chiefs and favorites of the king. He translated the writings on political economy of the ministers of the interior and the experts of France, Great Britain, and America, those of Washington, Newton, and a number of persons expert in increasing the wealth of a country, in determining in what the

wealth of each country consists, the principles of wealth, and how in-
animate things like fire, wind, water, and lightning, may become the
servants of man through the application of skill and knowledge. Mr.
Richards did not translate the whole of such books.* Whatever else he
undertook he never ceased teaching the principles of government to the
king. By means of these lessons in political economy with the chiefs he
was educating them to confer together as leaders of other governments
did, to compare the constitutional form of government with governments
which had no constitution, and to see that the constitutional form of
government belonged to those governments which were most famous and
whose king, chiefs, and people were most advanced. Such governments
excelled in knowledge and wealth and represented progress in the search
after wealth and trade. Thus the minds of the chiefs became enlightened.
"So this is it! [said they] Here is the way to gain wealth and honor."
Perhaps these chiefs were right, perhaps wrong. Should not these children of the chiefs, who had been educated in the schools and become
trained and clever, have been able to guard well the government as in
the time of Kamehameha I? Was it a mistake for the king to say, "When
the children come out of the Royal School the white leaders may be dismissed"? One thing was right according to their standard, all others
were not. Some of the "ti-leaf lickers" were under the influence of others,
their heels never trod on the sands of Hauiki [they never learned how
to make money].†

Aloha ka pali o Koloa,	Greetings to the cliffs of Koloa
Ke alo huli i Waihanau e,	That turn to face Waihanau,
Hanau, Hanau,	Hanau, Hanau,
Aloha wale ka hoahanau,	True aloha to my kinsmen
Ka hoʻi wale i ke kahaloa e	Who turn to go on the long trail
Hoʻi wale—hoʻi wale.	Empty handed! empty handed!

* The book of political economy translated for the mission is entitled *No ke
Kalaiaina*, printed at Lahainaluna, 1839, 1840, pp. 1-248. A copy is preserved in
the library of the Hawaiian Mission Children's Society.

† For "ti leaf lickers" (*palu lau-i*), an expression of ridicule, Pukui gives the
following explanation: When Kamehameha conquered Oahu he took his company
of men from Hawaii to Waimanalo where a feast was prepared. The numbers were
so large that the hosts ran out of poi. The natives knew of a sticky mud resembling
poi to be found in the pond of Kawainui and they filled the calabashes with the
substitute. Those who ate first had the food, those who came last were given the
substitute. In place of meat they licked the leaves without recognizing the deception.
The poor among the Hawaiian today call themselves "ti leaf lickers"; they are too
late for the feast. People from Hawaii say of Oahuans, "Oahuans are inhospitable"
(*Oahu maka ʻewaʻewa*) and those from Hawaii and Oahu say of Maui people: "men
of Maui have not enough brains to fill the head," literally, "have spaced brains"
(*poʻo hakahaka*). "Hauiki" is formed as a play upon the words *uhau*, "to strike"
and *iki*, "small." The idea is that they fail to get even the least wealth.

Some think that the change in the government came about so soon because the king, chiefs, and their favorites were trained in political science only and knew nothing about the land and the daily life of the people and the way the chiefs of old lived. Others think that Mr. Richards was the cause of the government getting into the hands of foreigners. This may or may not be true. Mr. Richards was chosen as their leader to teach the chiefs to understand the ways in which other races of men lived.

The power of the government was distributed between the king and the chiefs. The ruling chief alone could not pass a decree; the chiefs passed a law and then waited for his decision upon it. He could not do anything of himself or seize the property of another chief and give it to one of his favorites. When there were no written laws the chief also had a right to a share of the taxes. When all the taxes had been collected in the presence of the ruling chief a part was portioned out by the treasurer among the other chiefs. Of the portion remaining, part was given by the ruling chief to members of his household, to his own servants and favorites. All the personal property of the chief, such as food, clothing, store houses, tools, fishing implements, houses for storing cloth, and temporary houses, belonged to him and his chiefs; and the chiefs portioned them out each to his own people according to what had been given them. . . . Kamehameha did not unite the islands for his own benefit nor did he hire the chiefs with the profits from the government. He had no property before he became the head of the government. This was why the chiefs had a share in everything. When the chiefs who had helped Kamehameha to unite the islands died, they left the government and all its benefits to the descendants of Kamehameha and to their own descendants whole and entire, all this wealth for which they had spilled their blood in a hundred battles. When the constitution and the written laws were made, then the power of the chiefs was thrown down and only that of the king remained.

During this period in which Mr. Richards was teaching political economy to the chiefs, in 1838 to 1839, there came an epidemic of mumps called "swollen chin" (auwae pahaha) brought on the ship Quixote. This ship had been dispatched to America under Captain Henry Pease, and on its return stopped at Valparaiso in Chile where it contracted the disease. The captain went insane, jumped overboard, and was drowned. The ship stopped at Tahiti and spread the epidemic in that country, and on February 17, 1837, it came to port in Honolulu. (Mr. Cummins, the husband of Kau-maka-o-kane, was on that boat. It brought the first cargo of calico prints of a kind called paukeaho.) That was how the epidemic

spread, among both old and young over the entire group, although few
died of it. When however a single one of the high chiefs of the kingdom
succumbed to the disease it was like the death of half the nation. Of
this disease died the premier Elizabeth Kina'u, and Ka-iki-o-'ewa, ruling
chief of Kauai.

Ka-heihei-malie Hoa-pili was the mother of Kina'u; Kamehameha I
was her father. They had three children: Kamehameha Kapu-aiwa born
at the present Mission House at Hawaii in 1801, Kamehameha Ke-ku-
aiwa, born on Oahu in 1803, and Ka-ho'ano-ku Kina'u born on Oahu in
1805. Pele-uli and Ka-welo-o-ka-lani brought up their niece from her
birth and gave her the name of Ka-ho'ano-ku Kina'u, which was the
name of one of Kamehameha's sons by Pele-uli, father of Ke-ahi-kuni
Ke-kau-'onohi, and the name chant of these Kina'us is now played on a
wind instrument and sung to a modern tune. When Kamehameha and the
chiefs returned to Hawaii, the foster parents of Kina'u accompanied him
with their adopted daughter. At his death she was about fourteen years
old. In fulfillment of his command that his daughter and granddaughter
should have but a single husband, Kina'u became one of the wives of
Liholiho while she was very young.

When Liholiho sailed for Britain he took with him only one wife, and
this left three of his wives, Pauahi, Ke-ahi-kuni Ke-kau-'onohi, and
Kina'u without a husband.* Luanu'u Kahala-i'a took under his protection
Ka-lani-pauahi and Ka-ho'ano-ku Kina'u. Ke-ka-ulu-ohi was under the
care of another husband. This left Ke-ahi-kuni Ke-kau-'onohi without a
husband to care for her. Kahala-i'a kept the two women under his care
until the return of the ship [*Blonde,* Captain] Lord Byron from England, bearing the bodies of the king and queen. All the chiefs thought
that the boy King Kau-i-ke-aouli would be Kina'u's husband when
he came of age. On the ship returning from England were the two
chiefs, Boki and Liliha, and Boki's four younger relatives, Ke-ku-anao'a,
Manuia, Na-'ai-weuweu, and James Kane-hoa. So the relatives went to
Boki each with his request "in memory of the ice of Cape Horn."
Manuia, whose thoughts turned upon that treasure which decays, asked
for the fort and harbor of Honolulu, and Boki said, "That is yours." But
Ke-ku-anao'a, whose mind turned to that treasure which endures without end, thought well over the importance of his request and said, when
he came to Boki, "I have come to ask you for the thing which I long
for most when we reach Oahu." "What is it that you long for?" "The
daughter of Kamehameha to be my wife." Daring as was this request it
was granted. Children were born to him by this daughter [descendant]
of Ka-ku'ihewa, chiefs who were grandchildren of Kamehameha and

* *Ke Au 'Oko'a,* Jan. 21, 1869.

rose to honor. Manuia's dignity was soon ended; from Ke-ku-anao'a descended the kingship.

When the boat arrived, Pauahi and Kina'u were still with Kahala-i'a. Ke-ku-anao'a had a wife, Ka-lehua by name, who had been his from the time of Kamehameha and he had a son by her named Pa'a-lua who was perhaps his own child. Wise indeed was this choice of the traveler over seas. Within a few years Pauahi became the wife of Keku-anao'a, and Kina'u of Kahala-i'a. Pauahi was carrying Ruth Ke-'eli-kolani at the time, and that is why Ruth was said to be "double headed" (po'olua), that is, a child of two fathers, which was considered a great honor by chiefs of that period. Kina'u was also pregnant with her first child by Kahala-i'a, the child called Kamehameha. Pauahi died in giving birth to Ruth, and Kahala-i'a died of an epidemic of whooping cough which carried off a number of the chiefs at this time. This left Kina'u without a husband and Ke-ku-anao'a without a wife. At the death of Kahala-i'a who had held the office of guardian to the boy king with authority over the affairs of the government, while the boy's older relatives watched over the king's conduct, Boki was appointed to the vacancy at the same time that he served as governor of Oahu. There was much rejoicing among his followers. He appointed Ke-ku-anao'a commander-in-chief of the army, both regular and reserved forces, and it was a grand thing to march in brass buttons and cocked hat, things to which the Hawaiian people were unaccustomed and which were seen at the court only on the arrival of a war ship. Evidently the Hawaiian government was trying to imitate [foreign] fashions. Upon Ke-ku-anao'a and Manuia Boki showered favors, perhaps with the idea of luring them into the land of mirage, and on the return of the chiefs with the king from hewing sandalwood at Wao'ala in Waialua, Elizabeth Kina'u became the permanent wife of Ke-ku-anao'a according to the binding form of Hawaiian marriage (ho'ao).

From Elizabeth Kina'u were born five children of divine rank, David Kamehameha the firstborn, Moses Ke-ku-aiwa the second, Lot Kapu-aiwa the third, Alexander Liholiho the fourth, and Victoria Ka-mamalu the fifth. The eldest was taken to be reared by Ka-'ahu-manu, who was still living, for it was regarded as a great honor for the chief to be reared by his grandparents, and for the chiefs to rear their children's children. This made the chiefs beloved. It was a rule among the chiefs for a wealthy chief to take and rear the child of a poor chief. Chiefs always regretted it when a chief or perhaps a ruling line lacked descendants. Some chiefs hid their children in the backwoods, and brought them up as commoners, and some children ran away into the back country and became countrymen. In 1834 a chief's child was found who had been brought up in the country under the name of Ka-puni-'ai. His name was Kai-ehu and he was Ulu-maheihei's younger brother and the son of Ka-me'e-ia-moku born at the time of the battle of 'Iao Valley. Ka-me'e-ia-moku told Hoa-pili to search for and find his younger brother, but no one knew where he was staying. He was in fact peddling fish at Ka'ana-pali for some back countrymen who had no idea whose child he was, and it was not until this year that he was discovered. This was why the chiefs appointed a number of *kahu* to watch over a chief's child. Kinau's second child had as his guardian Ka-iki-o-'ewa of Hawaii who was appointed governor of Kauai. The third child was adopted by Harriet Nahi-'ena'ena, who was reared by Hoa-pili and his wife, chiefs of the island called "Haven of Pi'i-lani" [Maui]. The fourth child was adopted by the king. The fifth child was chosen by the chiefs of Hawaii to be their chiefess, and the mother kept this child to herself and would not give it to the chiefs to rear. . . .

Kina'u died on April 4, 1839, in the stone house of Ke-ka-ulu-ohi, in her thirty-fifth year while she was still young, beautiful, and unwrinkled. She was survived by her six children, one born to Kahala-i'a and five to Ke-ku-anao'a. In her youth she indulged in gaiety and drinking and had many faults, but once she was induced by Ka-'ahu-manu's good example to give up such pleasures and turn to the right and to the word of God she followed steadfastly in the way she had chosen. She was the first to start the regular prayer meetings, and it was she who converted her cousin Paki to faith in the God of power. Paki and Liliha were two of the chiefs who still lived for pleasure and liquor drinking after the days of Kaomi's downfall. When the prayer meetings were re-established at Waialua, Kina'u, Paki, and some others gave up liquor and turned to the word of God, and Paki became religious through the influence of Kina'u. During the years in which she acted as premier she became noted for her upright handling of the affairs of the kingdom and her dealings with the American traders who were living in the capital, and with the consuls of other governments. The American consuls were making trouble at this time for the government by cheating the chiefs into signing papers which made over Hawaii as surety for the debt. At this time Kina'u and the chiefs became friendly with a foreign trader named Brinsmade (Perinemese) and helped him when he became consul for the American government. His trading company established the first sugar plantation at Koloa, Kauai. He was called "Kina'u's consul," and he did many things to benefit the country and to help pay the debts to the American foreign traders living in Hawaii. Throughout her premiership Kina'u was efficient in carrying out the duties of her office. If she heard that the king was coming from Maui, double canoes loaded with provisions would be awaiting the king's party at Le'ahi and Kawaihoa, and everything needed for the king's entertainment would be ready on land. It was a rule among the old chiefs to respect and protect the chiefs. As Kina'u was dying, just as she was drawing her last breath and was unable to speak, Kau-i-ke-aouli arrived from Maui with some of the chiefs. Deep was his grief when he saw for the last time the aunt and co-worker in the kingdom whom he so greatly loved; he wept and the chiefs and commoners with him.*

* *Ke Au 'Oko'a*, Jan. 28, 1869.

CHAPTER XXVII

Troubles Under the Premiership of
Miriam Ke-ka-ulu-ohi, 1839-1843

This year 1839 was a year of heavy troubles. Many chiefs died in this year, and there was trouble with the French government. Scarcely was the mourning over for Kina'u when word came that Pale-ka-luhi Ka-iki-o-'ewa had died after a serious illness. The king sent Ulu-maheihei to Kauai to attend to the burial of the body and keep things in hand until he could arrange for a successor, and he placed Keawe-a-Mahi, the wife of Ka-iki-o-'ewa, as ruling chief for Kauai.

Ka-iki-o-'ewa was a chief of high rank. His mother was Ke-kiko'o-la Ka-lani-kau-lele-ia-iwi; his father Ka'iana-kuku'e Ka-'olohaka-a-Keawe. He was thus a cousin of Kamehameha on both sides, by an older brother on one side, by a younger on the other. He was born at Waimea on Kauai in 1765 and died in 1839 in his seventy-fourth year. He was reared on Kauai, and at the time of Ka-lani-'opu'u's death he was a grown man living under Kiwala'o at Hilo. Between 1782 and 1790 when Kamehameha was at war with Keawe-ma'u-hili, some of the chiefs of Hilo joined Kamehameha and some of Kamehameha's chiefs joined those of Hilo. It was about these years that Ke-aulu-moku composed the chant for Ka'iana-kuku'e which appears in the 13th part of the mele of Haui-ka-lani referring to his joining first one side and then the other. When Keawe-ma'u-hili was killed by Keoua Kuahu-'ula, then that chief's followers joined Kamehameha, Ka'iana-kuku'e among them with his sons Ka-iki-o-'ewa and Koa-kanu, his daughters, and all the chiefs of Hilo. After the battle of Koapapa'a therefore, Ka-iki-o-'ewa fought on the side of Kamehameha and was present on the day of battle when Hawaii and Oahu were united under one chief. Once he was almost killed in battle; at another time he almost died of a beating administered by a *konohiki* chief whose wife he had stolen, a woman named Na-hau-kapu. Perhaps this man was merely fulfilling Kamehameha's law that "the thief must die." He tied Ka-iki-o-'ewa's hands, feet, and neck with a rope. Kamehameha had retired to the tabu district of Mailekini below Pu'ukohola' when the news reached him, and he at once took canoe and landed at Waipi'o. 'Uhu'uhu was put to death, and Ka-iki-o-'ewa set free. While Ka-iki-o-'ewa was with the king, Kamehameha gave him his sister Ka-lani-ka-uli-hiwa-kama for a wife, and Ku-wahine was born. By Na-hau-kapu, Ka-iki-o-'ewa had another daughter, Likelike. He became guardian of one of Kamehameha's sons, no other than Kau-i-ke-aouli, Kamehameha III. After the rebellion on Kauai the chiefs met in Honolulu and gave up the island of Kauai to the boy king. Luanu'u Kahala-i'a retired as district chief, and in 1825 Kau-i-ke-aouli chose his guardian Ka-iki-o-'ewa to be district chief of Kauai.

At that time Ka-iki-o-'ewa was living at Lahaina with the young king. He had no knowledge of the word of God and took pleasure in drunkenness and sensual indulgence. The foreign traders and liquor sellers were his boon companions. He joined Boki in drinking and did not become converted to the word of God while Boki was alive, but indulged with him in the pleasures of drink. Only when Boki sailed away and was lost in the land of Nanapua did Ka-iki-o-'ewa begin to think seriously about the word of God. Even before that Ka-'ahu-manu's frequent visits to Kauai had converted many of the chiefs and commoners of that island such as S. Ka'iu, Ka-pule Ha'a-kulou, Oliver 'Alapa, Na-hinu, and later Daniel 'Ole-loa, Ahukai Ka-'u'uku-ali'i, Keawe-a-Mahi, and a great many others. When Ka-iki-o-'ewa turned to the word of God in his old age he remained steadfast for it. Under minister Samuel Whitney he tried hard as an old man to learn to read and write in order to read the Bible, and he learned by heart the lessons taught him by the preacher on the Sabbath. He loved to read the Bible. He and his wife Keawe-a-Mahi used to read God's word every Sabbath at his houses in Ulukou at the place called "Canaan" (Kana'ana) and they taught Sunday School in the church. At the opening of the Lahainaluna school he was eager for knowledge and wisdom to spread among his race and he sent his teachers to study and supported them at the school. Ka-'ana'ana', Na-imu, Malua-'ai-koa, Oliver 'Alapa, 'Opu-nui-'eke, Na-'aina-ko, and Kahi-'umi'umi were among those sent by him to Lahainaluna. His activity and kindness in thus spreading the faith on his island proves him a Christian chief.

Before the mourning was ended for Kina'u and Ka-iki-o-'ewa, another sorrow came to the chiefs in the death of Kuini Liliha. She was the daughter of Ka-lili-kauoha the daughter of Ka-hekili 'Ahu-manu, king of Maui and Oahu, and of Ulu-maheihei Hoa-pili. Her death is said to have been caused by poison mixed in her liquor by her own relative. She had already taken a drink and went back for another. After finishing what was left in the bottle she fell down moaning and foaming at the mouth and died. Few of the chiefs were so beloved by the common people as Liliha. It is said that never before had there been heard such lamentation for the death of a chief as on the night that she died at Leleo, and her body was brought back to Honolulu. The river of Kikihale was stamped dry by the feet of people of all ranks and races crossing over to the city. Common people loved the name of Liliha, little children loved Kuini Liliha, and when she died they tattooed their skins with the words "Liliha Leleo" as an everlasting memorial of their affection. Her body was sent back to Moku'ula at Lahaina on Maui and placed with that of the princess Harriet Nahi-'ena'ena, and chiefs and commoners bewailed her life with a sorrow that abides in the hearts of many.* As a chiefess she had not obeyed the word of God. She loved pleasure and drink; these were the things she desired. She was a chiefess who was beloved by all the commoners.

In the same year as died Kuini Liliha there died another chiefess, Ke-ano-meha or Ke-ano, daughter of Ka-po'o-loku the mother, and Ka-lani-hele-mai-iluna the father. She was a chiefess of high tabu rank and an older relative of the generation of Liliha and of Kau-i-ke-aouli the king.

On January 2 or perhaps 3, 1840, died Ulu-maheihei Hoa-pili in the stone house at Waine'e after struggling many days for breath. During these days of weakness he asked that there be no general wailing after his death, and that only one man go to announce his passing. He was a pious chief born during the rule of Ka-lani-'opu'u on Hawaii in 1775, and he died in 1840 in the sixty-fourth year of his age. His mother was Ke-li'i-o-ka-hekili, daughter of Kane-kapo-lei daughter of Ka-ua-kahi-akua who owned the sea cucumber (*loli*) ovens of Kaupo. His father was Ka-me'e-ia-moku, one of the tabu twins of Ke-kau-like, an uncle of Kamehameha, and one of the four war leaders who fought his battles and established his rule . . . and whose children were given positions as chief counselors and governors of districts after the death [of the four war leaders]. That is how Ulu-maheihei came to be selected for the office of counselor for the kingdom. An even greater honor was his than his father had enjoyed, for Kamehameha gave him Ke-opu-o-lani as his wife in order to guard the ruling tabu family of Hawaii. None of the other sons of the four war leaders had such an honor conferred upon him.

In his younger years Ulu-maheihei was something of an athlete, tall and robust with strong arms, light clear skin, a large high nose, eyes dark against his cheeks, his body well built, altogether a handsome man in those days, given to pleasure-seeking and licentious ways and a great liquor drinker. Once on Oahu he and Ka-pahu-wai were returning from a spree at Kewalo when, as they were crossing the plains of Kahu'a, they encountered at Ko'ula Kamehameha's great wild bull. Ka-pahu-wai was a dignified man of erect bearing, handsome and powerfully built, some

* *Ke Au 'Oko'a*, Jan. 28, 1869.

six and a half feet in height with redbrown (*'ehu*) hair and light skin. He was only partially intoxicated and when he saw the bull tearing up the ground in a rage he was afraid. When the bull attacked them he saved himself on the banks of the fishpond of Ko'ula leaving his companion, who was too drunk to save himself, to fall victim to the bull. When Ulu-maheihei saw the bull charging toward him be sobered up and challenged it with the words, "O bull, I will be your death!" When it charged with horns lowered he seized the bull by the horns and twisted its head about until the animal fell down, and then beat it to death. In Kamehameha's last days when he was old and feeble there was no chief whom he could trust except this chief. "Ulu-maheihei knows everything inside and outside" (*O Ulu-maheihei wale no, ia ia oloko, ia ia owaho*) was the saying, alluding to matters that came up at court. When Kamehameha was king, it was Ulu-maheihei who led the forces in the struggle with the rebels at Waimea on Hawaii. In the time of Kamehameha III he commanded the forces against the rebels of Hanapepe, Kauai, at the battle of Wahiawa. Some of the rebels were slain and mercilessly treated, and their bodies cast to the hogs; some were taken captive. Ulu-maheihei beqame noted as a war leader for his victory over the rebels.

The island of Maui, the "haven of Pi'i-lani," is famous as the place where the word of God was first accepted as the guide to good conduct. There first the chiefs and prominent persons sought guidance in the faith, and there the word of God was first made the basis for the law when all Hawaii was in confusion. At the haven of Pi'i-lani was the word of God first used to protect the laws and to punish wrong-doing and law-breaking. At the haven of Pi'i-lani laws were proclaimed and enforced against adultery, prostitution, liquor drinking, stealing, taking life and other misdeeds. Chiefs and commoners were subject to punishment, and it was Ulu-maheiihei, or sometimes Kalai-koa, who acted as judge to pronounce sentence. Even a chief who broke the law was made to work on the road; if he was caught breaking the marriage law he might be sentenced to stone breaking until he died. There were too many petty laws made at this time at the haven of Pi'i-lani, such as laws against smoking, tattooing, knocking out teeth; and this and that petty law demanded hard labor as penalty. Not even the king had power to pardon. The persons who helped Ulu-maheihei in making the laws were the Rev. 'William Richards, Kalai-koa, Ka-'ohana Pua'a, Kua, Kamauna, Daniel 'I'i, and at times David Malo. The reason why Ulu-maheihei made such stiff laws for Maui was because he was a man of faith who depended upon the word of God. He had given up chiefly dignity and wealth in this world for the life of the spirit and the good of

Jesus Christ the son of God. He was a man direct and just in his dealings, no double-dealer but straightforward and truthful. He was a pious man, sincerely penitent for his evil life. Both Richards and Baldwin are witnesses to his acts. He left a dying request that his body should not be honored according to the custom of chiefs in old days, but should be placed with the worshipers of God in the churchyard of Waineʻe.

Ulu-maheihei was a learned man skilled in debate and in the history of the old chiefs and the way in which they had governed. He belonged to the priesthood of Nahulu and was an expert in priestly knowledge. He had been taught astronomy and all the ancient lore. Richards would bring to him any question about the ancient customs or tabus, and he could explain them all. He was proficient in the genealogies of chiefs even where they were obscure; David Malo and others would go to him with puzzling questions, and he was able to explain them. It was at the court of Ke-opu-o-lani and Ulu-maheihei that the chiefs first took up the arts of reading and writing. Extraordinary how difficult it is for old men and women to acquire the alphabet which is taught to children in their early years! Tau-ʻa and others from Tahiti were their first teachers, and Ulu-maheihei learned to write letters in his old age and encouraged the teaching of the primer to the young; and that court became famous for the encouragement of learning and skill of every sort. He often traveled about the islands preaching the doctrine of the Trinity and encouraging the commoners to turn to the right teaching of God's word and to guard the Ten Commandments of God and the laws of the king of the land. What peaceful times those must have been when the rulers themselves taught the laws of the land, and those against murder and drunkenness were preserved! The commoners all obeyed their king. And how about the chiefs at that time? Perhaps they were just asleep awaiting the time to come when the shirts were made ready and the pockets filled.

Ulu-maheihei welcomed the missionaries to the island and gave them land for churches and enclosed yards for their houses without taking any payment. The Rev. Mr. Green at Wailuku was given a church lot and a yard lot for the pastor's house, and land for cultivating food for the pastor's family. So also was the Rev. Mr. Hitchcock at Kaluaʻaha on Molokai, Armstrong at Haʻiku in Hamakualoa, and Conde' (Coaede) at Hana. Ulu-maheihei personally marked out these lands and took no pay for them. Such generosity was common to all the chiefs and to the king as well; a tract of a hundred acres was sometimes given. There was some slight trouble at Kohala about the land given to the missionaries *mauka* of Nunulu. The missionary Isaac Bliss wished to exchange it for land *makai* of ʻIole; the *konohiki* in charge of the land objected, but when Mr. Bliss (Belika) complained to Ulu-maheihei the missionary was given the *makai* land and left that of Nunulu . . . When the Rev. Mr. Bingham was living in Honolulu the house lot of Kawaiaha'o and the land at Punahou were given outright; Mr. Richards too was given a number of houselots and the land tracts (*ahupua'a*) of Haleu and 'Opae-'ula, and Mr. Thurston the house lot and tract of Hinaloli. The missionaries were given land by the chiefs without any payment. They left these to the American Board when they moved away from the land, and those missionaries who wished to own the lands given by the chiefs bought them of the American Board . . . They were clever people!

When the high school at Lahainaluna was built the chiefs consented to the erecting of the schoolhouse and the houses for teachers and pupils, and to the pupils' cultivating potatoes on the land of the school and on the hill, but the rich lands above and below the stream were for the natives of the places. In 1835 the missionaries at the yearly council appealed to the king and chiefs for more land, for the pupils often went hungry. The king consented and left it to Ulu-maheihei to give whatever land was right in his judgment. He gave, under protest of the natives who owned the land, the taro land by the stream of Kanaha on the side toward the sea to the taro land of Kelawea cutting the water taro patches of Kaukahoku, running straight down to Kumu'ula and down to the stream and rising and cutting the land of Ho'olulu and ascending to the *pali*. This was the boundary toward the sea. The *mauka* boundary was the stone *mauka* of Rev. Lorrin Andrews' place and straight down to the brook and running straight along and rising to the *pali*. All the taro cultivations were below Makaili'i and adjoining Kukuikapu. And there were two cattle pastures: the plain of Ku'ia to Kaua'ula turning upward as far as Kahili, and the plain of Pana'ewa between Kanaha and Kahoma where is the plain of Pahalona. These were the lands given by Ulu-maheihei, and when the chiefs complained and said that these were their lands given by Kamehameha, and that all their taro land had been taken away and nothing left but a few breadfruit trees, Ulu-maheihei answered, "It is a fine thing; do not get excited about the land. Give your land to those who are seeking knowledge. This is the thing which will establish the government of your chiefs . . . Knowledge is fundamental to living as a chief." When Elizabeth Kina'u visited Lahainaluna in 1837 she gave more land extending to the creek of Wao.

Another good work for which Ulu-maheihei is celebrated was the building of the stone church at Waine'e in 1827. Churches and meeting houses were erected from Hawaii to Kauai, some of them large buildings thatched with *pili* grass, or with pandanus, ti, or sugarcane leaves. But at Lahaina was erected a noble building such as for size and height had never been seen before in Hawaii, some 120 feet long and 48 feet wide and two stories in height, with big glass windows. Such was the memorial built by Ulu-maheihei and his family in Lahaina to honor their own names and the name of their teacher, the Rev. William Richards. Another notable achievement was the erecting of the fort to guard the village against rioting from the whalers and foreign ships and from law breakers. Here were deposited the weapons of war, the great cannon, the shoulder guns, the rifles, the swords, the powder, as in the days of Kamehameha. It was at this same time that the stone church called Ka-lani-kahua of which Armstrong (Limaikaika) was the pastor was built at Ha'iku. After his return from Nu'uhiva where nothing could be accomplished, it was proposed to place missionaries in the country districts, and Ulu-maheihei went with Armstrong and others for this purpose. There was already a large church erected by Kahale'ohu, but later Ulu-maheihei urged the building of a stone church, and that called Kalani-'ohua was built by Ka-'auwai and others. He ordered Wahie, the kono-hiki who was over Hana district, to build a large church at Kuakaha on Ka'uiki. So [also] at Ka'anapoli and on Molokai. Ulu-maheihei became noted for his activity in church building and in spreading the word of God. A chief of true piety was Ulu-maheihei and he died in the faith of life through the sinless blood of Jesus Christ the beloved son of God.

When Kina'u died there was no one to take her place as premier. According to the old custom, if a ruling chief had no children of his own, the child whom he took to bring up and whom he had trained became his heir and succeeded to his position; even a child so taken by the king, if he had no child of his own, would succeed to the kingship. But Victoria Ka-mamalu whom Kina'u had retained to bring up was but five months old at the time of Kina'u's death. The king therefore looked for a premier among the blood kin of Ka-'ahu-manu who had been premier for Kamehameha I and Kamehameha II, and selected Miriam Ke-ka-ulu-ohi-o-Mano for this office, and she became premier during the time of Kamehameha III, when the first constitutional law was made for Hawaii.* She was an intelligent premier, careful in her decisions, but she was easily led by those who were flatterers and speech makers.

Here are some of the events of her time. She made Kahoolawe and Lanai penal settlements for law breakers to punish them for such crimes as rebellion, theft, divorce, breaking marriage vows, murder, and prostitution. Kahoolawe was the prison for the men and there was no protection for them; the government furnished them with food, but they suffered with hunger and some died of starvation and some few in the sea. Death by starvation was so much more common than by sea that some of the prisoners swam at night from Kahoolawe to Honua'ula, stole a

* *Ke Au 'Oko'a*, Feb. 4, 1869.

canoe from the people there, paddled to Ukemehame and 'Olowalu, stole food at night and went back again to Kahoolawe. Those who were being punished for adultery filled the canoe with food and paddled for Lanai, where, rounding the cliff of Kaholo and Kaumalopau, they landed at Ka'ena where was the large tract of land called Ka'a where the women were imprisoned who were being punished for adultery, and some of the men took their women and ran away with them to the mountains of Maui. This was a notable event of Ke-ka-ulu-ohi's time. Some petty chiefs were sentenced to Kahoolawe, namely Ka-nuha and Kini-maka. Ka-nuha was saved through the influence of Kua-kini the governor of Hawaii, but Kini-maka was sent to Kahoolawe. He was the son of Ka-hiko-loa, and his father was Kapi-iwi; he was younger brother of Ho'olulu and they were younger relatives of Ulu-maheihei. It was through Ulu-maheihei's written command that he was condemned as a rebel and sentenced to ten years on Kahoolawe, but after seven years he was pardoned. The law in those days was never very clear and left one to grope in the dark.

Another noted event of Miriam Ke-ka-ulu-ohi's time was the coming of the war ship *L'Artemise*, commanded by Laplace, sent by the government of France (at that time ruled by Louis Phillipe) because of the persecution of the Roman Catholic priests and their disciples under the Hawaiian government. Some of the charges made were not true, but many were witnesses of the cruel treatment they had received. It was reported that the women were undressed to the skin, tied to a post, and whipped with ropes, and other things were done bitter to recall. Pictures of the people being beaten with ropes and of the persons who were imprisoned were published in some of the newspapers by the foreigners living at the capital of Honolulu, and the reason for their persecution was made clear by Mr. Jones, the consul for America. These doings were reported to the French government, and a warship was sent commanded by Commodore du Petit-Thouars, a high official of the French government, and a treaty made with the king. After the commodore left the persecution still went on, as is shown not only by written reports but by the testimony of eye witnesses, and two years later the warship *L'Artemise* arrived, commanded by Captain Laplace, a man well known for stirring up trouble by hasty action and making reprisals upon weaker peoples. His charges were perhaps true, but were there not other reasons for his drastic action? Had not the matter something to do with the advantage the government of France hoped to gain from trade with Hawaii? The treatment of the Catholic priests was no new policy; it began as much as ten years before the government of France interfered for freedom for the teaching of the Catholic faith, affirming that persecuting and ill-treating the French priests of the Roman Catholic faith was like ill-treating the French government and the king of France, for the priests had been sent in the name of the French government. Captain Laplace demanded the signing by the kingdom of Hawaii of a treaty, demanding among other things the freedom of the Roman Catholic priests to make converts. . . .

Some of the more thoughtful and intelligent of the foreigners said that Ke-ka-ulu-ohi was justified in promptly binding the government to pay the thousands of dollars of surety demanded by the French captain. Her action came from a true love for her king and her people and a care for the property of the people of other races living under her king's protection. . . . Others of the foreigners and of their hangers-on among the people called her a timid and cowardly premier unlike Elizabeth Kina'u. . . . But there was no warship during Kina'u's premiership threatening bombardment; there was angry talking but no command to make ready a warship for attack, no threat that if the treaty were not granted there would be war. Ke-ka-ulu-ohi was wiser than the king's cabinet ministers and the chief justice in agreeing to the demands and not attempting to resist by force and thus waste the resources of the kingdom in powder and balls. In accounts of this incident published in books and newspapers, the action of the chiefs has been ridiculed for consenting so readily to Captain Laplace's terms. They are said to have been terrorized by the cannon balls of the warship and hence to have agreed to everything. [These accounts] do not praise Ke-ka-ulu-ohi's action, but would have had the French treaty rejected. Some of the clauses to which they object are those providing that a Frenchman who gets into trouble with the law shall not be tried by the native judges but by the French consul and a jury composed of white people; and that the bringing in of French wines and brandies is not to be prohibited. But a treaty similar to this last clause had already been made with Great Britain. Why was there no complaint made against this treaty? Is it not true that France was a rival of Great Britain? These clauses could make no trouble for the country; other nations were filling the land with liquor. The clauses which brought difficulty were those which concerned religious tolerance and the establishment of schools. The parents who were Roman Catholics quarreled with the teachers in the schools for influencing the children on the side that denied the pope, and kept their children out of school. Over the garden patches there were bitter quarrels which had to be taken to the Catholic priests and the chiefs for settlement. Some parents objected when the Catholic priests made the circuit of the country districts, and ordered them back to Honolulu saying that the treaty held good only for Honolulu. Another cause of dispute was the customs duties. Ministers of religion on both sides were released from taxes by the government; but in some ports duties were imposed upon the goods of the Catholic priests, the goods were seized, and there was trouble, those on the Catholic side saying that the treaty had been broken. Religion therefore became one of the major causes for the troubles of that period. It brought the French warship asserting that "the treaty has been broken! the treaty has been broken!"

Scarcely four years later there came to the government during Miriam Ke-ka-ulu-ohi's premiership a still greater trouble, not one that allowed for adjustment, but one which threatened to bring down the whole roof over their heads. This was the high-handed seizure of the country by the government of Great Britain without any reason save that of robbery. The root of the trouble really lay in the generosity and affection which characterizes our chiefs and this whole nation. Ka-lani-moku had been generous enough to give, without any payment, his houselot *mauka* of the then Mahoe house to Mr. Richard Charlton, the consul who had come from Bolabola to represent Great Britain in Hawaii. The deeds were made out to include also a house lot belonging to Ka-'ahu-manu extending from Pulaholaho to the hotel run by Mr. Lotta Manini. Neither Ka-'ahu-manu nor her heirs knew of the giving away of this lot. The consul built a stone house in Ka-lani-moku's lot just above the Mahoe house, as both Ka-lani-moku and Ka-'ahu-manu observed . . . The chiefs argued that it was the Ka-lani-moku lot that belonged to the consul, and that Ka-'ahu-manu's land, that is Pulaholaho, could not be taken by the consul, but must be returned to the heirs then living. They did not agree to Admiral Gimet's plan to give the place to the consul of Great Britain. This was one thing that made trouble, and there were other small matters of which the consul had complained to the British government. What these were may be seen by examining Captain George Paulet's demands.*

The following letters tell the story of how the kingdom of Hawaii was given to the queen of Great Britain. It was on February 25, 1843, that the transfer was made public. The translations into English [of the king's letters] and those into Hawaiian of Paulet's letters were made by G. P. Judd, secretary and interpreter for the kingdom.†

Her Britannic Majesty's Ship *Carysfort*, Oahu, 11th of Feb., 1843,

Sir,—Having arrived at this port in her Britannic Majesty's Ship *Carysfort*, under my command, for the purpose of affording protection to British subjects, as likewise to support the position of her Britannic Majesty's representative here, who has received repeated

* *Ke Au 'Oko'a*, Feb. 11, 1869.
† The Paulet correspondence is quoted from Bingham's translation 7, pp. 592-598).

insults from the government authorities of these islands, respecting which it is my intention to communicate only with the king in person:

I require to have immediate information by return of the officer conveying this despatch whether or not the king (in consequence of my arrival) has been notified that his presence will be required here and the earliest day on which he may be expected, as otherwise I shall be compelled to proceed to his residence in the ship under my command, for the purpose of communicating with him.

I have the honor to be, sir, your most obedient, humble servant.

George Paulet, Captain.

To Ke-ku-anao'a, Governor of Oahu, etc., etc.

Honolulu, February 11th, 1843

Salutations to you, Lord George Paulet, Captain of H. B. M. Ship *Carysfort*:—I have received your letter by the hand of the officer, and with respect, inform you that we have not sent for the king, as we were not informed of the business, but having learned from your communication that you wish him sent for, I will search for a vessel and send. He is at Wailuku on the east side of Maui. In case the wind is favorable he may be expected in six days.

Yours with respect,

M. Ke-ku-anao'a.

H. B. M. Ship *Carysfort*, Honolulu Harbor, Feb. 16th, 1843

Sir:—I have the honor to acquaint your Majesty of the arrival in this port of H. B. M. ship, under my command, and according to my instructions I am desired to demand a private interview with you, to which I shall proceed with a proper and competent interpreter.

I, therefore, request to be informed at what hour to-morrow it will be convenient for your Majesty to grant me an interview.

I have the honor to remain your Majesty's most obedient, humble servant, George Paulet, Captain.

Honolulu, February 17th, 1843.

Salutations to you, Lord George Paulet, Captain of Her Britannic Majesty's Ship *Carysfort*.

Sir:—We have received your communication of yesterday's date, and must decline having any private interview, especially under the circumstances you propose. We shall be ready to receive any written communication from you tomorrow, and will give it due consideration. In case you have business of a private nature we will appoint Dr. Judd our confidential agent to confer with you, who, being a person of integrity and fidelity to our government, and perfectly acquainted with all our affairs, will receive your communications, give all the information you require (in confidence), and report the same to us.

With respect,

Kamehameha III.

Ke-ka-ulu-ohi.

Her Britannic Majesty's Ship *Carysfort*, Oahu, 17th Feb., 1843.

Sir:—In answer to your letter of this day's date (which I have too good an opinion of your majesty to allow me to believe it ever emanated from yourself, but from your ill advisers), I have to state that I shall hold no communication whatever with Doct. G. P. Judd, who, it has been satisfactorily proved to me, has been the prime mover in the unlawful proceedings of your government against British subjects.

As you have refused me a personal interview, I enclose to you the demands which I consider it my duty to make upon your government; with which I demand a compliance at or before four o'clock P.M., tomorrow (Saturday), otherwise I shall be obliged to take immediate coercive steps to obtain these measures for my countrymen.

I have the honor to be your Majesty's most obedient humble servant,

George Paulet, Captain.

Demands made by the Right Honorable Lord George Paulet, Captain R. N., commanding her Britannic Majesty's Ship *Carysfort*, upon the king of the Sandwich Islands.

First. The immediate removal by public advertisement, written in the native and English languages and signed by the governor of this island and F. W. Thompson, of the attachment placed upon Mr. Charlton's property; the restoration of the land taken by the government for its own use and really appertaining to Mr. Charlton, and reparation for the heavy loss to which Mr. Charlton's representative has been exposed by the oppressive and unjust proceedings of the Sandwich Islands government.

Second. The immediate acknowledgment of the right of Mr. Simpson to perform the functions delegated to him by Mr. Charlton; namely, those of Her Britannic Majesty's acting consul; until Her Majesty's pleasure be known upon the reasonableness of your objections to him. The acknowledgment of that right and the reparation for the insult offered to Her Majesty through her acting representative, to be made by a public reception of his commission and the saluting the British flag with twenty-one guns—which number will be returned by her Britannic Majesty's ship under my command.

Third. A guarantee that no British subject shall be subjected to imprisonment in fetters, unless he is accused of a crime which by the laws of England would be considered a felony.

Fourth. The compliance with a written promise given by King Kamehameha to Captain Jones of the *Curacoa*, that a new and fair trial would be granted in a case brought by Henry Skinner, which promise had been evaded.

Fifth. The immediate adoption of firm steps to arrange the matters in dispute between British subjects and natives of the country or others residing here, by refering these cases to juries, one half of whom shall be British subjects approved by the consul, and all of whom shall declare on oath, their freedom from prejudgment upon, or interest in, the cases brought before them.

Sixth. A direct communication between His Majesty Kamehameha and Her Majesty's acting consul for the immediate settlement of all cases of grievances and complaints on the part of British subjects against the Sandwich Islands government.

Dated on board H. B. M. Ship *Carysfort*, at Oahu, this 17th day of February, 1843.

George Paulet, Captain

[The following letter was sent to Captain Long, commander of the U. S. S. *Boston*]

H. B. M. Ship *Carysfort*   Oahu, Feb. 17th, 1843

I beg to inform you with my compliments that the H. B. M. Ship *Carysfort* is prepared to bombard this town at the hour of four o'clock Saturday if the articles that I have requested of the King of this group of islands have not been agreed upon by that hour.

I am, with regards, your humble servannt
George Paulet, Captain

[The king's answer was as follows:]

Honolulu, Feb. 18th, 1843

Salutations to Rt. Hon. Lord George Paulet, Captain of H. B. M. Ship *Carysfort;*

We have received your letter and the demands which accompanied it, and in reply, would inform your lordship that we have commissioned Sir George Simpson and William Richards as our Ministers Plenipotentiary and Envoys Extraordinary to the Court of Great Britain, with full powers to settle the difficulties which you have presented before us, to assure Her Majesty, the queen, of our uninterrupted affection, and to confer with her ministers as to the best means of cementing the harmony between us. Some of the demands which you have laid before us are of a nature calculated seriously to embarrass our feeble government, by contravening the laws established for the benefit of all.

But we shall comply with your demands as it has never been our intention to insult Her Majesty, the queen, or injure any of her estimable subjects; but we must do so under protest, and shall embrace the earliest opportunity of representing our case more fully to Her Britannic Majesty's government through our minister, trusting in the magnanimity of the sovereign of a great nation which we have been taught to respect and love,—that we shall then be justified.

Waiting your further orders,
With sentiments of respect,
Kamehameha III
Ke-ka-ulu-ohi.

[Two letters follow arranging for an interview. Since the demands made were such as the country could not possibly accept and remain independent, the king made a provisional cession of the group to Great Britain until its case could be brought directly before the queen of that country.]

In consequence of the difficulties in which we find ourselves involved, and our opinion of the impossibility of complying with the demands in the manner in which they are made by her Britannic Majesty's representative upon us, in reference to the claims of British subjects; We do hereby cede the group of islands known as the Hawaiian (or Sandwich) Islands, unto the Right Honorable Lord George Paulet Capt. of her Britannic Majesty's ship of war *Carysfort*, representing her Majesty Victoria Queen of Great Britain and Ireland from this date and for the time being; the said cession being made with the reservation that it is subject to any arrangement that may have been entered into by the Representatives appointed by us to treat with the Government of her Britannic Majesty, and in the event that no agreement has been executed previous to the date hereof, subject to the decision of her Britannic Majesty's Government on conference with the said Representatives appointed by us; or in the event of our Representatives not being accessible, or not having been acknowledged, subject to the decision which her Britannic Majesty may pronounce on the receipt of full information from us, and from the Right Honorable Lord George Paulet.

In confirmation of the above, we hereby affix our names and seals, this twenty-fifth day of February, in the year of our Lord one thousand eight hundred and forty-three, at Honolulu, Oahu, Sandwich Islands.

Kamehameha III.

Ke-ka-ulu-ohi.

A Provisional Cession of the Hawaiian or Sandwich Islands having been made this day by Kamehameha III., King, and Ke-ka-ulu-ohi, Premier thereof, unto me, The Right Hon. Lord George Paulet, commanding Her Britannic Majesty's Ship *Carysfort* on the part of Her Britannic Majesty, Victoria, Queen of Great Britain and Ireland; subject to arrangements which may have been or shall be made in Great Britain, with the Government of H. B. Majesty.

I do hereby proclaim,

First, That the British Flag shall be hoisted on all the Islands of the Group: and the natives thereof shall enjoy the protection and privileges of British subjects.

Second, That the Government thereof shall be executed, until the receipt of communications from Great Britain, in the following manner:—namely, by the native king and chiefs and the officers employed by them, so far as regards the native population; and by a Commission, consisting of King Kamehameha III., or a deputy appointed by him, The Right Honorable Lord George Paulet, Duncan Forbes Mackay, Esquire, and Lieutenant Frere, R. N., in all that concerns relations with other powers (save and except the negotiations with the British Government), and the arrangements among Foreigners (others than natives of the Archipelago) resident on these Islands.

Third, That the laws at present existing, or which may be made at the ensuing Council of the King and Chiefs (after being communicated to the Commission), shall be in full force so far as natives are concerned; and shall form the basis of the administration of justice by the Commission, in matters between foreigners resident on these Islands.

Fourth, In all that relates to the collection of the revenue, the present officers shall be continued at the pleasure of the native King and chiefs, their salaries for the current year being also determined by them, and the archives of Government remaining in their hands; the accounts are, however, subject to inspection by the Commission herebefore named. The Government vessels shall be in like manner; subject, however, to their employment if required for Her Britannic Majesty's service.

Fifth, That no sales, leases, or transfers of land shall take place by the action of the Commission appointed as aforesaid, nor from natives to Foreigners, during the period intervening between the 24th of this month, and the receipt of notification from Great Britain of the arrangements made there; they shall not be valid, nor shall they receive the signatures of the King and Premier.

Sixth, All the existing bona fide engagements of the native King and Premier shall be executed and performed as if this Cession had never been made.

Given under my hand this twenty-fifth day of February, in the of our Lord one thousand eight hundred and forty-three, at Honolulu, Oahu, Sandwich Islands.

George Paulet,

Captain of H.B.M.S. *Carysfort.*

Signed in the presence of

G. P. Judd, Rec. and Int. to the Govt.
Alex. Simpson, H. B. M. acting Consul.

On the day when the land was taken away the king made another proclamation to the people which was not submitted to the chiefs and officers of the warship for their acceptance, but which showed that in the opinion of the king and his ministers the land had been given [under compulsion] contrary to their wish and without just cause, and they believed that it would be restored.

Where are you, chiefs, people, and commons from my ancestor, and people from foreign lands? Hear ye, I make known to you that I am in perplexity by reason of difficulties into which I have been brought without cause; therefore I have given away the life of our land, hear ye! But my rule over you, my people, and your privileges will continue, for I have hope that the life of the land will be restored when my conduct shall be justified.

On February 25, 1843, the British flag was raised on the flagstaffs of the forts in Honolulu and on Punchbowl, British officers were sent to raise the flag on Maui, Hawaii, and Kauai, and the Hawaiian kingdom became a part of the kingdom of Great Britain. The protection of foreigners and natives alike was given over to British officers in the town of Honolulu. Mr. D. C. Mackay (Keki) was made marshal; and Mr. Frere R. N. and Captain Lord George Paulet were made the officials to regulate affairs with foreign governments, except that the king had chosen Sir George Simpson and Rev. William Richards delegates for the king to adjust the difficulties between the kingdom of Hawaii and the kingdom of Britain, and to request the governing powers of the world to acknowledge the independence of the Hawaiian kingdom. The king did not leave the British agents to untangle matters with Great Britain, but sent his own messengers to straighten matters out with the ruling powers.

[The numbers of the Ke Au 'Oko'a from Feb. 25 to Mar. 11 are missing and also March 25. These numbers probably relate the restoration of the group to the Hawaiian government under Rear Admiral Thomas on July 31, 1843, and the disavowal by his superior officer in the Pacific of the hasty action taken by Lord George Paulet. The story is taken up again in the midst of the work of the commissioners William Richards and Ha'a-lilio to secure recognition from the governments of Great Britain, France, and Belgium for the independence of the kingdom of Hawaii.]*

* *Ke Au 'Oko'a*, Feb. 18, 1869.

CHAPTER XXVIII

A Constitutional Monarchy, 1839-1845

There was trouble between the British and the Americans living in the kingdom of Hawaii. The chiefs had been converted to the faith of the Puritan missionaries from America and had been influenced by these missionaries to make laws for the whole country [enforcing the strict code of conduct laid down by the Puritans of that day]. This aroused black demons of opposition among other foreigners. The British consul claimed the land given to British foreigners to use and which, according to the old laws, still belonged to the chiefs. The officers of a British warship made so much trouble for the chiefs that they decided to appeal to the powerful governments of the world for recognition of the independence of the Hawaiian kingdom. King George III had already shown respect for the nation when he sent the bodies of its king and queen back upon a battleship . . . King William IV and Queen Adelaide sent their kind aloha to Kamehameha III. So also did Victoria when she ascended the throne of Great Britain. Waves of trouble were dashing over the kingdom, and chiefs and commoners were overwhelmed in their foam while the pilots guiding at the back of the canoe were often themselves in consternation.

In 1841 a prominent Englishman named Sir George Simpson, an official in a wealthy firm from Oregon, arrived on a ship of the firm and stayed for a time with his son in Honolulu. He saw how men of his country had taken advantage of the gentle Hawaiian race and how seriously the chiefs took the bold words of the foreigners who spoke of the wrath of the French and British governments, and he offered to act as ambassador to the queen of England to obtain from her and her cabinet official recognition of King Kamehameha III as an independent ruler over an independent country. This would prevent foreigners from making further trouble in the kingdom, of whose difficulties the queen knew nothing. He proposed that he and William Richards be sent to gain this recognition. The king and chiefs therefore chose Sir George Simpson as their delegate, and Mr. Richards prepared a statement telling how the kingdom was well-equipped to care for itself, and the people were intelligent and Christian. To show their progress in intelligence he described from the beginning how they had been educated and the laws that had been promulgated, fifty-one sections or more. In the latter part of the year 1842 Mr. Richards and the Honorable T. Ha'a-lilio were sent by the king as delegates to seek recognition for Hawaii.

They sailed from Lahaina and landed in Mexico. They had escaped the perils of the sea, but the still worse hardships of the land were before them. Mexico was a land of robbers, a wilderness of thickets and forests, with deep rivers, high precipices, and deep crevasses inhabited by bears and other wild animals. Ha'a-lilio wrote to Dr. Judd from Weletabu, Mexico:

> Our bodies were wearied by the length of the road. There was heat and cold. We were wet with the rain and with snow. We crossed mountains and streams penetrating deep into the wilderness of Mexico. We have swum rivers lying at the foot of mountains. We have been cold and hot, have suffered hunger, and have ridden all day on the backs of mules.

In order that their mission should not be known to their enemies they did not travel by way of Panama but through the mountains to Mexico City, guarded by soldiers, and from thence went aboard steamer and arrived in Washington, the capital city of the United States of America. This country agreed to the independence of Hawaii on December 19, 1842, but the bill was not finally passed until the intentions of the European governments were learned, since America considered herself the mother country of the group. It was the country from which trading ships were first sent and the trading ventures of the chiefs started, and the land to which leading Hawaiians had been sent for education. She had taught them to read and converted them to the worship of the Christian God. She had first led them to make treaties with other countries. From the letters of Daniel Webster it was clear that she would not hesitate to acknowledge the independence of the country.

Mr. Richards and Ha'a-lilio next sailed to England where they were assisted by Sir George Simpson, and they told about the foundation already laid for good government, the elementary and high schools established, the Christian churches, the legislation enacted, and the fitness of the country for independent government. The ministers of Britain delayed their answer, being doubtful of what Mr. Richards said, and the papers were left with Sir George Simpson while Richards and Ha'a-lilio sailed on to France. Here Ha'a-lilio "drew his last breath in a foreign land" (*a waiho i Ka'ea na iwi o kamahele*). The French government was friendly; it did not raise objections, but agreed at once to the independence of the group. There was now only the meeting of the high officials at London for both governments to pass upon the independence of Hawaii. Mr. Richards went a second time to France. A letter from M. Guizot, the minister of France, is dated January 4, 1844. At London on November 28, 1843, the independence of the Hawaiian group was acknowledged in plain words, "*He aupuni ku'oko'a o ke aupuni Hawaii.*" The cultivators rejoiced; they had won their first point and had seen their crop bear its first fruit. They continued their efforts for the independence of Hawaii. The French government still waited for papers from Mr. Dudoit, the consul, to adjust the difficulties with Laplace. Mr. Richards went on to Belgium, and some twelve days after our officials had written to the minister of foreign affairs, Mr. Gobele, they received his answer saying that Belgium had agreed to recognize the independence of the country . . .*

On his return to Hawaii Mr. Richards placed all the papers in the hands of Robert C. Wyllie, secretary for foreign affairs. Gerrit P. Judd was, on November 4, 1843, appointed assistant secretary of foreign affairs and treasurer, and he filled other minor offices for the king, but finding his eyesight failing and his health suffering from so many duties, he gave up the assistant secretary-ship on March 26, 1845. Great Britain, France, and Belgium had now agreed to recognize the independence of the country. On July 6, 1844, the acknowledgement of the independence of the kingdom which had been tentatively given by the United States on December 19, 1842, was ratified . . . Daniel Webster wrote expressing satisfaction in the fact that Hawaii had by its kind treatment of American shipping made it possible for American ships to sail the Pacific. Should anyone make trouble for the chiefs of Hawaii it would be disadvantageous to America which sent to Hawaii the largest number of ships of any foreign country. It was therefore the right and privilege of the American government to see to it that the government of the group continued as it was, and that no other government took possession of it or established more favorable trade relations with it. He thought it not necessary to make a treaty or to send any new official representative, but made the consul the official for the [United States] government to look into all complaints made against the [Hawaiian] government by American citizens.

Friendly intercourse with Great Britain had been begun at the time of the visit of Captain Cook in 1778 and of Vancouver in 1792, 1793, and 1794 during the rules of King George of England and Kamehameha of Hawaii, and that friendship was not broken until February 25, 1843, when the chiefs were charged with wrongdoing, and the king gave up the government of the country and appealed to the British queen. She gave the country back its independence. Only one thing remained unsettled and that was the question of the land claimed by the consul. It was proposed that if the land claimed by the consul was not occupied or used

* *Ke Au 'Oko'a*, Apr. 1, 1869.

in any way by others it was to be his; the chiefs agreed to his using the land but not to its remaining permanently in his hands. The consul wrote again, and everything was adjusted amicably to all parties. [A treaty was sent through Captain Miller, as passed September 12, 1843, and Lord Aberdeen wrote asking for the same treatment for Great Britain as was given other foreign nations and agreeing that no one of them should ever take away the independence of the land. Admiral Thomas had already come and returned the kingdom to the king and his chiefs. It was clear that these governments were anxious to help the chiefs of Hawaii and not to weaken them. And although there were still faulty sections in the treaty with France, and these objections were stated to Captain Miller and to Lord Aberdeen, the king appreciated the kindness and good will of the nobles of Great Britain and did not ask them to make anew the objectionable clauses. This covers the main points of Kamakau's discussion.]*

The old laws had allowed a life or death sentence upon the wrongdoer. They were administered by the ruling chief who represented the head of the government. Breaking of the higher laws was punished by death, of the minor by seizure of property. During the tabu days of the god of the ruling chief it was tabu to eat flesh, to sleep with one's wife, to eat coconut flesh. It was tabu for a commoner to worship his own god at his own shrine; this was punishable by death. A chief who observed the worship of his god was called a religious chief and his kingdom one that would be peaceful and enduring like that of Ku-ali'i who lived 175 years. My grandmother saw Ku-ali'i with her own eyes. He died in 1730 and my grandmother in 1825, and I myself lived eleven years with my grandmother. She is a witness to the life from god granted because Ku-ali'i respected the law of his god.

Among those laws that helped to sustain life (*kalana ola*), laws for the fisherman, the tapa maker, the dyer, the house builder, the provider of those things which benefit the body and bring about the general peace and welfare of the race, may be classed those laws which provided for the pardon by the ruling chief of transgressors of the law. This word itself, "life sustaining," is an excellent word and occurs in the prayer chants and chants of praise to the god and the chiefs. Stealing and falsifying were crimes that stripped the bones of flesh. The wicked and the greedy ended upon the altar of sacrifice. These good laws were all observed throughout the time of Kamehameha. The Puritan missionaries instructed us that the law was the established word which determined the rights of kings, chiefs, and commoners. The chiefs understood the rights of the king, but their own rights and those of the commoners were

* *Ke Au 'Oko'a*, April 8, 1869.

not very clear. They were like a luxuriant tree whose leaves have been stifled by the dodder (*kauno'a*) vine which draws from the tree sustenance for itself, drying it up, draining it dry, and destroying it. The chiefs and commoners were those who made for the honor and glory of the king, but the king was like the dodder vine drawing upon the sap of the tree; if the chiefs and commoners were sapped how would the ruling chief fare? The chiefs objected to placing the new constitution over the kingdom, seeing that little by little the chiefs would lose their dignity and become no more than commoners. Kamehameha III protected his chiefs and paid from the treasury those who were members of the privy council. The laws drawing up the new constitution were made just before the death of Elizabeth Kina'u, and the reason why they were passed was because the old chiefs were dead, those who had refused absolutely to approve the new laws except in the matter of protection from crime and keeping the peace among the people. It was William Richards who drew up the constitution, and the king selected Boas Mahune to represent him and Jonah Kapena to represent Kina'u in drawing it up. Kina'u died before its completion, and it was finished under the premiership of Miriam Ke-ka-ulu-ohi; and chiefs and commoners rejoiced because they had a constitution based upon the Holy Scripture.* The king offered it June 7, 1839, . . . and on October 8, 1840, it was signed and became the law for the Hawaiian kingdom.†

Upon this first constitutional main post of the kingdom of Hawaii were erected other laws like the lengthwise beams, the rafters joining the upper ridgepole and thatched even to the ridge, and the trimming that completes the house. The kingdom of Hawaii was now a constitutional (*kumukanawai*) monarchy. Because this first constitution was promulgated at Lua'ehu, Lahaina, it was called the "Lua'ehu constitution." The king was given the first right in the kingdom, the chiefs the second, the commoners the third. But because of the affection existing between the commoners and the chiefs the people did not take advantage of the benefits conferred upon them by the constitution; the people who most benefited from it were the foreigners. In a constitutional government it is not the administrators who can be blamed for bad government, but the legislators who pass the laws. . . . The legislature is the source through which taxes are imposed. It is beneficial when it enacts beneficial laws which will be for the good of people and chiefs. The legislature is the parent; it

* *Ke Au 'Oko'a*, April 22, 1869.

† For the text of the Constitution of 1840, here omitted from Ka-makau's Hawaiian text in full, see "Constitution and Laws of the Hawaiian Islands established in the reign of Kamehameha III," Lahainaluna, 1842, translated from the Hawaiian text, "*Ke kumu Kanawai a me na Kanawai o ko Hawaii pae'aina, Ua kauia i ke kau ia Kamehameha III*," Honolulu, Oahu, 1841, together with the revision of April, 1841, at Lua'ehu, Lahaina, and the April, 1843, revision. See also 34.

considers in advance what will be for the success, comfort, and progress of the race in just dealing and in developing sources of wealth and increase of population. If the legislature fails to deal justice impartially the result is disastrous. Most of the nations of the world have obtained a constitutional form of government through war and bloodshed. In no other Christian nation in the world have the king and chiefs voluntarily given a constitution for the governing of their people. Nations without a constitution must depend upon the will of their king and chiefs for the administration of law. If the chiefs are kind and affectionate like those of Hawaii there is peace, but cruel rulers may cause their subjects distress. Under a constitutional government complaints by the people may be brought before the legislature as to a parent, where the question can be considered and settled according to its merits. This is the advantage of a constitutional government. The rights of the common people in relation to the king and the chiefs may be there judged. Before the constitution was granted the people were not treated equally; some were favored and some burdened and distressed; and heavy taxes fell oppressively upon the common people.*

Taxes were imposed upon an island according to its yearly yield. The ancient tax was imposed annually during the Makahiki upon the different land divisions; if the amount paid was unsatisfactory it was not the tenants who suffered but the landlord who was sent out upon the highway. The chiefs who went from house to house collecting the personal property of the people were disliked, and the people did not care to remain with them. But grandparents would advise their grandchildren to remain with chiefs who cared for their people, and the lands of such chiefs can be recognized today by the presence of old coconut trees which survive. The care and support of the common people by the chiefs was the main cause for the regard in which the chiefs were held in old days when there was no law; and that regard has been handed down in the hearts of the people and cannot be displaced until their offspring go to live in other lands and under other governments.

These observations are to be made in regard to the new laws: First, the appointment of chiefs, landlords, land agents, and under-overseers over the land divisions was done away. Because of the confused way in which the taxing was done in old days much of the property was hidden away from the chiefs who owned the land. Such collections [which the people hid away for their own chiefs] were called "added heaps" (*pu'u o komo*). Second, the restriction of certain seas for the chiefs to fish in worked no hardship in old days when there was so much fish that it was often used for firewood. Third, certain trees like the sandalwood in Ka-

* *Ke Au 'Oko'a*, Apr. 29, 1869.

mehameha's day were restricted for the chiefs, but in old days the wood was free; the large trees as well as the small could be cut by the people for canoes and paddles. Fourth, in old days people who lived in out-of-the-way places were heavily burdened by labor performed for chiefs, landlords, and land agents. But although the work was hard, that today is even more so when families are broken up and one must even leave his bones among strangers. In the old days, the people did not work steadily at hard labor but at several years' interval, because it was easier then to get food from the fishponds, coconut groves, and taro patches. Hogs grew so fat that the eyelids drooped, bananas dropped off at a touch, sugarcane grew so tall that it leaned over, sweet potatoes crowded each hill, dogs fattened, fish cooked with hot stones in the early morning filled the food gourd, and a man could eat until he set the dish aside. This was the generous way of living under a chief who made a good lord; the people were fed and every wish of the chief was gratified. Labor done in the patch of the chief was a rental paid for the use of the land and everyone was benefited thereby. Today the working man labors like a cart-hauling ox that gets a kick in the buttocks. He shivers in the cold and the dew-laden wind, or broils in the sun with no rest from his toil. Whether he lives or dies it is all alike. He gets a bit of money for his toil; in the house where he labors there are no blood kin, no parents, no relatives-in-law, just a little corner for himself. In these days of education and Christianity there is no regard for the old teaching of the ancestors. In those days the boys were taught to cultivate the ground and fish for a living, the girls to beat out tapa and print patterns upon it, and to work well and pray to the god, and they were taught that it was wrong to be indolent and take to robbing others. These teachings were held in esteem in old Hawaii, and the land was rich and its products varied. . . . Fifth, by the constitution parents with large families were assisted by the government. Parents with from three to ten or more children were released from taxes. Why was this good practice changed? What is the use of imposing taxes and spending large sums on insane asylums when families [of healthy children] are impoverished and many die for want of proper remedies? . . . Sixth, another famous law provided for the care of old people who had been ill a long time. It is useless to give to those abroad and leave your own people to suffer, throwing away your dimes in the dark while there remain distress and poverty. . . . Seventh, another useful provision would be for trained persons living in the country to have a certificate signed by the king or his minister so that appointments might be made from those persons as a reward for their energy. This would stimulate an interest in education in the hope of securing a better position, of becoming a chief, or a counselor for the king or for the governing ministers or chiefs. Parents would then be anxious to have their children educated, or, if they had no children, would adopt others and educate them to bring honor to the name of such parents. Foreigners were appointed to the principal offices because native Hawaiians had not the necessary knowledge, but now that there was a chance to train the children in higher learning the chiefs promoted this movement and the eight seas [the eight channels between the islands] were short to cross for parents who realized the benefits of Lahainaluna for their children's education. "My kingdom is a kingdom of learning," said Kau-i-ke-aouli.*

Nani na lehua kapili wai a ka manu,	Beautiful is the lehua where birds are snared,
Nani na lehua lu lehua a ka manu	Beautiful the lehua scattered by the birds,
Nani na pua o ka a'ea'e,	Beautiful are the blossoms of the a'ea'e,
Nani na 'ulu hua pala i ka lau,	Beautiful the ripened breadfruit among the leaves,
Nani na ki'owai o Kalawari,	Beautiful are the pools of Calvary,
Nani wai o ua nei i ka pali,	Beautiful are rain-filled pools in the hills,
Paku aku la i na pali,	Hidden from sight among the hills.
Hio na lua o na wai i ka makani,	The wind blows shaking the dew from the leaves
Noho paku i ke kuahiwi,	Of the close-grown thickets of the mountain.
E ho'i ma Hiku i ka uka,	The month of Hiku returns to the uplands
Ka lala i ka wai la ku'ua,	Where the rain forms streamlets,
Ku'ua mai manu'u kelekele	Streamlets that swell into rivers
Ho'okelea mai e ka la,	Sparkling in the sun.
O Maku'ukaokao, o Makilihoehoe,	Here is Maku'ukaokao, Makilihoehoe
Ka lala i ka na'auao la ku'ua,	Whose learning flows like a stream.
Ho'onu'u iho a ku kahauli.	Eager these to be honored men.

But how about the people who strive for an education today? They are no better off than the unlearned; luckless fishermen who make no better catch than the ignorant. After graduating from high school they turn to hard labor for a living. . . .

* *Ke Au 'Oko'a*, May 6, 1869.

[Some of] those good provisions of the law given by the king for the government of Hawaii were done away with at the next legislature composed of representatives of the people. When the king alone had power to give laws he showed his goodness and wisdom as a chief in the constitution he gave. He believed that the time had come when some of the commoners would become sufficiently educated to do intelligent skilled labor, and the people and the government would be benefited by the introduction of skilled employment. Now in the days of Kamehameha who united the group under a single ruler, the division of labor was well marked. There were farmers, fishermen, canoe hewers, board hewers, paddle makers, calabash makers, and so on; each craftsman in wood had his particular craft in which he was skilled. So the beaters of tapa and stampers of patterns were each a separate class of craftsmen and it was the same with other callings. There were hog raisers, dog raisers, chicken raisers. The canoe paddlers (po'e hoe) were separate from those who knew the art of righting an overturned canoe at sea (po'e kama-i-kahuli-pu), and the star gazers (kilo hoku). Those who had to do with the government also had each his special function. There were experts in dividing the land (po'e kalai-'aina), experts in the configuration of the land, experts in location, counselors, astronomers, praying kahunas of the class of Pa'ao and of the class of Nahulu, kahunas of Lono-puha who practiced healing, and prophets (kaula). All these had separate functions. The different arts of war were distinct; spear throwing for example, had its special masters. Genealogists were a distinct profession, and all experts were divided according to their class.

Kamehameha collected skilled workers from the country districts and developed in each profession a class of teachers whose knowledge became the working arm of the government. If he heard from one chief or another of a learned man he immediately made him one of his attendants and gave him land. Land was the principal reward he gave to such skilled persons, either a whole district or a parcel of land. His favorites were provided with food, fish, and clothing; his fishermen with canoes and nets; the canoe builders also with the implements of their work. He developed new arts. In ship building Waipa' who died in 1832 was the most famous, but many ships were built in Kamehameha's day by other native Hawaiians who had not been taught by foreigners but depended upon their own skill and knowledge. Waipa' built some ships out of *wiliwili* wood to go with the *peleleu* fleet, others for the Ka-ni'au-kani return to Hawaii, and still others in the time of Kamehameha II. He was a chief and untaught. The new art of blacksmithing was introduced in the time of Kamehameha. Waipa' wrought the iron nails for shipbuilding, pounding up old gun parts and other junk. He made steel wedges (*ko'i* kila), axes (ko'i lipi), flints (ko'i kahela), planes (ko'i holu).....Hawaiians all over the islands took up blacksmithing.

But when learning began to spread all these skilled people who had been so well known in the days of first three Kamehamehas were lost sight of. All learning was looked for in the high schools. That is why the Hawaiians have not shone as craftsmen. In the school they may have learned navigation and know all the rules by which to find latitude and longitude by the sextant, by the sun and Mercury, by the moon and stars, by heaving the lead, and all other means of directing the ship into the desired haven. But upon emerging from the school and seeking a place in which to show their skill, what do they find? Some become school teachers, some preachers, some are in government, some make a living in ways suited to the uneducated, but the larger number become idlers. Many of them would like to go into something worth-while but are prevented by poverty, and cannot take up any kind of work they would be fitted for. They may trade among the islands in tortoise shell, feathers, coconut oil, shells for bracelets, and other objects which are sold at moderate prices. The practice of trading in Japan, China, the Spanish islands, on the Columbia river, and in California, the captaining of ships to carry on this trade, are these not a just cause for renown to the Hawaiian government and people? They may return to the work of their ancestors and cultivate the land, fish, and peddle their products to preserve the life of themselves and their children. They are just lost like one hidden away in a clump of grass, and the government tax is their master. All this learning concerning the circuit of the sun, the planets, the comet, and the nature of the atmosphere of the heavens, even delving down the bowels of the earth like a spider—of what good is it? Where is it leading?

It is said that in old days the countries of Europe were peopled by indigent folk, but the government aided the thoughtful man to gain knowledge so that he might be of benefit to his country.... In these days when knowledge has increased and the nations have grown in wealth and strength some of the European nations are helping the farmer and the mercantile classes. But the Hawaiian government is afraid to sponsor a steamship line with California to preserve commerce with our people, lest the small return on the investment cause the company to fail. Before the government had a constitution it had difficulty with finances, but now we have a system of taxation which brings in money to the treasury which, like as reservoir of water, constantly flows forth in brooks and streams and in the early and latter rains pours its moisture over the forest and into the green fields leaving the dry land barren. It is the foreign rain that wets the dry plain. So the race limps along on tottering feet, stumbling along weakly, while thinking people allow their thoughts to sleep until they are laid away in their graves.

Before the constitution was established all property rights for both chiefs and commoners were unstable; the entire control over the land was vested in the king. According to the opinion of learned men the land belongs to the common people, and property rights are to be vested in the commoners. In old days the inheritance of the family burial place, the caves and secret burial places of our ancestors was handed down from these to their descendants without the intrusion of a single stranger unless by consent of the descendant, so that wherever a death occurred the body was conveyed to its inheritance. These immovable barriers belonged to burial rights for all time. The rule of kings and chiefs and their land agents might change, but the burial rights of families survived on their lands. Here is one proof of the people's right to the land.*

With this right of the common people to the land is connected an inherent love of the land of one's birth inherited from one's ancestors, so that men do not [willingly] wander from place to place but remain on the land of their ancestors. The Kona man does not wander to 'Ewa or Ko'olau, nor does the 'Ewa man change to Waialua. Whether rich or impoverished and barren, his love is unchanged; he cannot treat the land with contempt. However good the land on which he later lives he will wish to return to the land of his birth. The land so worthless in the eyes of a stranger is good to him. But today the habit of going away for an education or sailing abroad has undermined this old feeling for the land. In old days captives might be carried away in war or friends and favorites taken into the households of chiefs, but on the whole the common people remained on the land inherited from their ancestors, and a family lived continuously on the land of their birth. True the chiefs had the right to the fruits of the land and the property of the people, and when a chief was overthrown in war his followers also moved on. But it was they who were the wanderers; the people born of the soil remained according to the old saying, "It is the top stone that rolls down; the stone at the bottom stays where it is" (*O ko luna pohaku no ke ka'a ilalo, 'a'ole i hiki i ko lalo pohaku ke ka'a*). Some chiefs laid claim to certain land sections in old days, but it is not clear that the residents born on the land held no rights therein. At any rate there are families who have lived on the same land from very ancient times. In that way the land belonged to the common people. Land irregularities arose during the time of the wars of Kahekili and Kamehameha. The land belonging to the old chiefs was given to strange chiefs and that of old residents on the land to their

* *Ke Au 'Oko'a*, May 13, 1869.

companies of soldiers, leaving the old settled families destitute. During that period they left the lands of their birth and settled on other lands. But for the most part the common people remained on the lands inherited from their ancestors. Strangers move about but native sons remain.

At the time of the constitution the *kuleana* were divided into three parts, one for the king, one for the chiefs, and one for the people. There were certain days in the month to work for the king, certain days for the chiefs, and certain days for themselves. In the first years of the new law there was some grumbling. Some worked the prescribed number of days without seeing what benefit they got out of it, others complained when they were sent to work at a distance. To the foreigners the establishment of a constitutional form of government was very gratifying. Perhaps they foresaw the passing to them of the land under the constitution and its laws, and the benefits which the government and the chiefs would share with them, leaving the old natives of the land a slavish people whose voice was scarcely heard and whose petitioning was but a useless journey for all the attention they got. The people who gather the *pulu* and clear the wild land, those who cut away the staghorn fern are not those who benefit by the richness of the soil. The saying was that those who ate the products of the soil were those who merely heard that rains had fallen on Hawaii [absentee landlords]. The native sharpens his digging stick, and then comes along a clever man who knows how to enrich the government and fill its coffers to overflowing. The paddler knows by their undulations the swelling wave and the surf wave and the mounting of the sea spray, but the shaping of the paddle requires expert skill with the axe edge in the hands of the *koai'e*-wood paddle-makers on Pu'ukapele. The stranger has no more skill with the axe than the worn-out hewers of Hawaii, but not ten Hawaiians combined have the skill and wit to equal that of the stranger in the legislature.

The Hawaiian people believed in William Richards (Rikeke), the foreigner who taught the king to change the government of the Hawaiian people to a constitutional monarchy and end that of a supreme ruler, and his views were adopted. The people had entire confidence in John Ricord, the foreign lawyer who inaugurated the system of cabinet ministers for the different departments of government, one for foreign affairs, an attorney general, a minister of education. His law book is called the book of laws "establishing the cabinet minister of the Hawaiian islands." The people had entire confidence in Dr. Judd (Kauka), and he was the foreigner who regulated the foreign office and worked for the good of chiefs and commoners. He worked for the payment of the government debt inherited from the old kings, and as a result the debts have all been paid and the government is prosperous with a cash balance in the treasury and a well-established standing, a race born under Hoku.* It was these foreigners who set up the posts and laid the cornerstone of the constitution. The people of today, however learned they may be, are mere stone-carriers and lime-mixers. Among Hawaiians they are called "A people who draw the spawn of the squid for bait for the fishermen" (*He po'e 'u'u maunu palu 'ala'ala na kekahi po'e lawai'a*). The Hawaiian learning and skill becomes no more than a lazy sea washing up foam over the stones. Morning is all time for labor; when the sun is high the eyes blink drowsily and desire for effort is gone. The Hawaiian knows as much as the stranger, but he [the stranger], no matter how small his knowledge may be, sharpens it well and puts forth effort until he reaches the peak.

By the old constitution certain days of work belonged to the landlord. "Prison days" these are called today, because men were arrested for absenting themselves; "Landlord days" they were called in ancient times. In each month there were three work days for the king, and three for the district chief or the landlord. That made for each man thirty-six days a year for each [king and chief or landlord]—seventy-two work days all together. If a man had to go a long distance to labor for money then his land paid the tax. Before the written law there was no uniformity in the number of days of work for the king or chief. In some districts only twelve days a year were required, and the work done benefited all alike. If a wall was being built the days set apart for the landlords and land agents were spent in building the wall. If pigs were to be raised, the landlord furnished the food and the pigs raised were divided with those who raised them. The landlord was not discharged for missing a day's work now and then, but for not collecting the right amount of tax at the Makahiki. The land agent was like a parent over the people of his district. Not all were alike; some were oppressive and took the property of the commoners, but their lands did not prosper and their people's ears were plugged with *pulupulu* [they were disobedient].†

* Root vegetables planted under Hoku, the day of the moon directly following full moon, are supposed to be specially productive.

† *Ke Au 'Oko'a*, May 20, 1869.

CHAPTER XXIX

Passing of the Chiefs

The famous events in the kingdom of Hawaii in the time when Ke-ka-ulu-ohi was premier, were told abroad. There had never been a time when there was so much trouble in the kingdom from the outside as in the time of Ke-ka-ulu-ohi. There was also some local trouble, but it melted away and the kingdom was entirely freed of it. She beheld the faces and the dead bodies of the messengers who were sent to gain the independence of the kingdom of her ruler. It was obtained, and her eyes saw it, but she did not partake of the fruits of that great blessing ere she died on the seventh of June, 1845.

Let us turn back to scan the lives of other chiefs who died while she held the premiership of the kingdom. She held it for six years and two months. I am going to relate an account of certain famous high chiefs, that they may be remembered by the generations of the future.

Ka-pi'o-lani died in Honolulu in the early part of the year 1841. She was born in Hilo during the reign of Ka-lani-'opu'u, in 1781. Her mother Ke-kiki-pa'a was the daughter of Ka-me'e-ia-moku and the sister of Ulu-meheihei Hoa-pili. Her father was Keawe-ma'u-hili, a high-ranking chief and a sacred one in the time of Ka-lani-'opu'u. He was the only chief made tabu according to the royal tabu of Hawaii. He was the Keawe whose genealogy was doubled and multiplied [in the blood lines] of Hawaii according to those who are skilled in genealogies. He had the right to walk on the banks (*kuauna*) [of sacred patches], on the sacred platform (*paepae*) of Liloa, and to the *nioi* wood of Kahou-kapu that was streaked and darkened at Paka'alana. Because he was a great and high chief some of the chiefs of Kona were sorry when he was taken captive at Napo'opo'o at the battle of Moku'ohai. Therefore he was secretly liberated by Kanuha, a chief who guarded him. As several other chiefs were agreeable to this freeing of Keawe-ma'u-hili by Kanuha, the latter went unpunished. Keawe was led by way of the mountain to Pa'auhau in Hamakua and later became the ruler of Hilo.

When Kamehameha was at war with the chiefs of Hilo, Ka-pi'o-lani almost died when they fled to the forest. Those who were in charge of her (*kahu malama*) tossed her into a clump of ferns (*'ama'uma'u*) because her weight retarded them when danger was near. Another man, in walking through the forest, heard a child's cry and drew near to investigate. He discovered that the wailing voice belonged to his chiefess who had been cast aside. He picked her up and ran with sorrow for her in his heart. The name of the man was Ho'omii. This we know, Ka-pi'o-lani might have died. If an enemy had found her, then she would have been killed. . . . The power of God cared for her and preserved her life. When Keawe-ma'u-hili died in a battle with Keoua Kuahu-'ula, the chiefs of Hilo joined forces with Kamehameha. Ka-pi'o-lani and her brothers, the sons of Keawe-ma'u-hili, went to live with Kamehameha. Ke-kiki-pa'a was a cousin of Kamehameha, and Ka-me'e-ia-moku and Ka-manawa were her fathers (makua kane). Therefore when Keawe-ma'u-hili was killed by Keoua Kuahu-'ula at 'Alae in Hilo-pali-ku [East Hilo], Ke-kiki-pa'a and her daughter Ka-pi'o-lani followed Kamehameha. Ka-pi'o-lani was reared with tabu at Kealia in South Kona. When she grew up several heiaus were erected for the gods of Ka-pi'o-lani, and she went to impose the tabu for them according to her royal rank. The very sacred part of the heiau was tabu to chiefesses, and no woman, royal or otherwise, escaped death when she drew near to it. Only the sacred chiefesses, whose tabu equalled that of a god, went into the Hale-o-Papa and ate of the dedicated foods of the heiaus. So was Ka-pi'o-lani's tabu in ancient times when she grew up. Chiefesses had various husbands, but when she was wedded to Haiha Na-ihe she remained with him up to the time when the chiefs departed for Oahu with the peleleu fleet. Ka-pi'o-lani was among those who accompanied Kamehameha to Oahu. While the chiefs were there an epidemic called 'oku'u arrived and many died of it, both chiefs and commoners, from Hawaii to Kauai. Ka-pi'o-lani caught the disease and her hair fell out. The sparing of her life was a blessing from God.

When Kamehameha and the chiefs of Hawaii returned home on the royal journey called Ni'au-kani, she was among those returning to Hawaii, after which she made her home at Ka'awaloa. When Kamehameha died at Kamakahonu, Kailua, she was one of the chiefs who, in their ignorance, mourned (ka'a kumakena) for him with unseemly behavior. This shameless behavior was called an affectionate mourning (kumakena aloha ali'i) for the chief.

The battle of Kuamo'o, which was fought over the free eating of the sexes, was won by those in favor of a free-eating government. While the question was being debated between those who favored the freeing and those who desired to retain tabu eating, Ka-pi'o-lani and her husband were in doubt over the free-eating. When it became widespread in Kailua Ka-pi'o-lani came to partake in the free eating while her husband adhered to the old ways. After the free-eating government became established all doubt and desire to remain in the old ways of the wooden images was removed.

Only the royal tabu remained with Ka-pi'o-lani. She was a chiefess whose eyes bespoke her royal lineage, and those who were not well acquainted with her feared her. Her eyes reddened when she became angry and she did not associate with those of low rank (*noanoa*) and country people. None dared to stare at her in their desire to see her honored person or at seeing her for the first time. She liked amusements (*le'ale'a*) and intoxication, and spent much time in seeking fun as was customary with chiefs. Where her heart could find pleasure there went her mind and body, paying no heed to any advice. Advice only vexed her. Only a few of the chiefs heeded.

When Liholiho, Kamehameha II, was on Oahu Ka-pi'o-lani learned to read and she joined Kameha-malu in seeking knowledge in reading and writing. She learned to do both and often attended the missionary school at Kawaiaha'o. When the king, Liholiho, and the queen sailed to England the troubles in the kingdom had ceased. The chiefs were not drinking so much, the interest in hula, in sex-attracting games at night (*'aha 'ume o ka po*) and other defiling amusements had decreased.

When the rulers departed for England, Ka-pi'o-lani still continued in pleasure seeking. Reading and writing were highly regarded but not the worshiping of God as one of the finest experiences to be had by a person. She had often heard the teachings of the missionaries and the sermons on the Sabbath. She was a bright person and wrote down the sermons of the ministers and preachers on the Sabbaths with her own hand and offered grace at table (*pule 'aina*) and family prayers (*pule 'ohana*).

After her return to Hawaii she settled on the land belonging to herself and her husband at Ka'awaloa, and established the teaching of reading and writing to those of their household and to the commoners of their lands, Ka'awaloa and Kealakekua. There were also meetings of encouragement and she selected two men already versed in the alphabet to instruct her people.

Ka-pi'o-lani encouraged learning and converted her husband Na-ihe to righteousness, but the families [of their people] were unstable and frivolous (*uwehewehe o kalua 'apana*). The two continued to strive in righteousness, and such prominent people as Kamakau, Ke-po'o-kulou and others, and the lesser chiefs all joined with her. Her name became famous as belonging to a religious chiefess. She sailed to Kailua to meet with the ministers (*kahuna pule*) for the purpose of strengthening her faith and to repent of her sins. She became famed as a mother of righteousness, according to the word of God, and as a friend of missionaries.

Here is another thing: her faith in the word of God, her trust in Him and her belief that the deified gods of her ancestors were worthless. She believed that the earth-consuming and volcanic fires were creations of Jehovah and were nothing to be feared.

She was the first chiefess to go and see the volcano in 1823. Many were priests of Pele who came to her to warn her not to go down to the pit lest she perish. She replied, "Jehovah is the great God who made heaven and earth and it was He who made the volcano. I am going down to the pit to behold His wondrous work." Going to the crater was something that was fraught with fear and dread, and all travellers who passed on the trail near the crater did so with gifts, offerings, and prayer chants, without touching any of the foliage and fruit near it lest the cold rains ('awa) and storms ('ino) come, and they perish. It was feared and dreaded in ancient times. Ka-pi'o-lani had no doubt that the power of the gods defied by men had fallen away. The God who held the power was the One who was not created by man and that was the Holy Trinity. When she upheld the name of Jehovah God, she triumphed over the priests of Pele who falsely prophesied her death. Therefore she became famous as the first chiefess to descend to the crater of Pele. From that time her faith was established that Jehovah was God and King eternal. Therefore she strived for and upheld the righteousness of the great God and the entering into Jesus' sheepfold. She was one of the first fruits in the church of Jesus here in Hawaii. She entered the sheepfold of Jesus Christ and was baptized in the church of the Lord to be a disciple of Jesus, in the month of October, 1825. She preceeded Ka-'ahu-manu and others but followed Pua'a-iki Batimea that same year.

Ka-pi'o-lani became known as a religious chiefess who lowered her royal prestige and became as a mother to the lowly commoners and the poor. She associated with everyone, talked with all, discussed their troubles, and prayed with the humble. She visited the sick, those in trouble, and aided the poor who were in poor health. The causes that had made her feared were all gone. Old men and women and the religious had no fear of standing in her presence for she was their friend. Ka-pi'o-lani's table was ready to share a feast with them in love, but the wrong-doers were fearful of her and dared not approach her presence. On the lands belonging to herself and her husband at Ka'awaloa and Kealakekua she placed a strict law against drinking intoxicants. Anyone caught drinking was fined five pigs a fathom in length; so it was with adultery, prostitution, idolatry and other sins committed on their lands.

Ka-pi'o-lani was like the foreigners, and the duties of a foreign (haole) woman were those that she undertook. She and the girls of her household were adept in mixing bread dough, in baking bread, cake making, making rolls, soups, frying, and the preparation of all kinds of foods. Her table was laden with the food of the foreigners.

Her household was well kept. The attire of the women was neat and tidy and resembled that of the foreigners. Those who waited on the table wore dresses (*pukiki*). She constantly wore dresses as well as linen *holo-kus* of all kinds. She was comparable to a foreign woman. A sewing basket was always near her left hand and she took her work along with her wherever she went, even to the homes of the missionaries. Ka-pi'o-lani was known as a woman who wasted no time. While at home she frequently sewed or sought other pursuits of the missionary women. When she rode on horseback at Kailua or in the upland of Kuapehu where the missionaries lived, she used only the sidesaddle with her sewing basket on her left arm. Whether she rode on Maui or Oahu this was still her custom. The chiefs and commoners called her the white (*haole*) chiefess. When she travelled on the Sabbath her basket contained a Bible, a writing tablet and a lead pencil; and whatever sermon the preacher gave was jotted down as well as comments on the sermon.

When there was a lack of the Word of God, before it was translated into the Hawaiian language, it was in the sermons of the preachers on the Sabbath and on Wednesdays that one heard the verses from the Holy Scriptures. Many were the verses written down by Ka-pi'o-lani in her writing tablets, and her knowledge was great. When the Bible was printed hers became her sleeping companion. She divided the time of day into periods for work, for eating, for praying, for reading and teaching the Bible to relatives and members of her household, for a women's gathering, and to meet with the missionary teachers. The home of Ka-pi'o-lani and Na-ihe was close to that of their missionary teachers at Ka'awaloa.*†

When Mr. Samuel Ely (Eli), the missionary teacher who lived with Ka-pi'o-lani at Ka'awaloa in West Kona and was made pastor of the congregation there, saw how ill Ka-pi'o-lani was, and Mrs. Ely spoke to her of their affection for her Ka-pi'o-lani said, "I will obey God's will. If God wills it I will go to live with God and be freed from sin. Before I was afraid to die, but that is ended through Christ." This was in July, 1824. In August she went to Oahu and there met Mr. Richards and they talked together. She said, "Among the chiefs I hear nothing but talk about dress, lands, money, buying and selling, the kingdom, and things of that sort. I desire to hear about Jehovah, Christ, and the holy kingdom of heaven. . . . There I shall have joy, and my pain will be re-

---

* For an account of Ka-pi'o-lani from which Ka-makau seems to have drawn in part see 3, pp. 183-195. In 35 is a charming silhouette of the chiefess.

† *Ke Au 'Oko'a*, June 3, 1869.

lieved." Mr. Ely asked her about her joy in the house of God. She said, "I have joy in my heart when I listen to the words of Christ. When I learned of God my heart yearned toward him. When I learned of heaven my heart climbed to heaven. That is the way it is with me. It seems as if I had two hearts, one that loves Christ and the word of God, the other that does not desire to pray and go to the Sabbath service and the meetings." . . . In November, 1926, Mr. Ely wrote of her, "Perhaps there is not another woman in this group of islands who recognizes more clearly the meaning of true faith in God."

Ka-pi'o-lani's home at Kuapehu in Ka'awaloa impressed the visitor with its beauty, order, and absence of drunkenness. It was thanks to her skill, good management, wisdom, and care that the house was so beautiful and even grand with a nice yard planted with beautiful and rare flowers such as were not to be seen anywhere on these islands, not even in the king's court, save at Kuapehu alone. Nor was its mistress to be found sleeping on the mat, playing cards, or amusing herself in improper ways. Nothing improper was ever done in her presence. There might be a meeting going on, a Bible reading, or if not that she might be teaching her women companions to sew tight dresses, shirts, trousers, coats, vests, to make quilts out of tiny pieces, clean house, and to live with dignity. She used to receive strangers and the missionaries with kindness and send her horses freely for the use of strangers who were sightseeing at Kailua, since in those days only the chiefs and the richer foreigners kept horses. If visitors wished to visit the volcano she sent them by canoe to Ka-'u, and she would furnish them with provisions for the journey and order her men to take nothing for their services. She would also help the poor. Some four months before she died she made the circuit of Ka-'u, called at the homes of the poor, and saw their distress; she gave them her own clothes and mats and wept and prayed over them. At Hilo she was overjoyed to meet the missionary teachers and she did much good there, going into the high school and encouraging the pupils. One of them named Hoa-'ai has told me how she wept as she was praying, urged the pupils to become educated in order to help the government, and said that true education was the fear of God.

But Ka-pi'o-lani had a disease of the breast, and the foreigners urged her returning to Kona and putting herself under Dr. Andrew's treatment. He sent her to Honolulu, the doctors advised her to have the breast removed, and she consented. They cut away the greater part and she did not move or groan or cry out. When Dr. Judd asked her if she suffered she said, "It is painful, but I think of Christ who suffered on the cross for me and I am able to bear it." After some days she was better and met some of the chiefs and the young king. Hearing that she was one of the chiefs appointed to legislate for the land, she prepared to sail to Lahaina; but going about so much in the heat of the sun to see her friends she was overcome with a fever, and she died in Honolulu on May 5, 1841, the same day of the year as her birth.

Ka-heihei-maile Hoa-pili-wahine died of croup at Lua'ehu, Lahaina, and was taken to the mausoleum at Waine'e. She was born in 1778 at Kawaipapa, Hana, Maui, in the days when Ka-lani-'opu'u and the chiefs of Hawaii were at war with the chiefs of Maui and had taken Hana and the fortified hill of Ka'uiki. Mahi-hele-lima was the governor, and Ke'e-au-moku and his family were living at Hana under his protection. Hana was in those days a noted place famous for the fortified hill Ka'uiki, the surf at Puhele, the fresh-water bathing pool of Kumaka, the diving at Waiohinu, the flying spray of Kama, the changing color of the fronds of the *ama'u* fern, the yellow-leafed 'awa of Lanakila, the delicious poi of Kuakahi, the fat shell fish (*'opihi*) of Kawaipapa, the fat soft *uhu* fish of Haneo'o, and the juicy pork and tender dog meat dear to the memory of chiefs of that land, moistened by the *'apuakea* rain that rattles on the hala trees from Wakiu to Honokalani. At the time when Ka-lani-'opu'u returned to Hawaii to see Captain Cook, called Lono, all the chiefs returned with him to Hawaii, and Ke'e-au-moku also left Hana, went to live at Honokua in Kapalilua, and later moved westward with his wife and children to Honomalino and Miloli'i.

Ka-heihei-maile was a chiefess on both sides of the family. Her mother was Na-mahana-i-ka-lele-o-ka-lani, the daughter of Ka-lani-ku'i-hono-i-ka-moku [Ke-kau-like], descendant of Ka-lani-ke-li'i-ka-uhi-lono-honua-a-Kama and of Ka-lani-kau-hea-nui-o-ka-moku, ruling chief of Maui. Her father was Ke'e-au-moku the child of Ka-ma'i-ku and Keawe-poepoe; but she was of double paternity, the reputed child of Kane-koa, a great chief descended from Keawe, begotten at the Kawapo'ele at Pihehe, Kawaipapa. She was a large, plump, and handsome child, tall for her age at twelve, and at fifteen perfectly proportioned, with light skin and pleasant, brilliant eyes. She was given the name Ka-niu "The coconut," and she and her sister Ka-'ahu-manu were called "the hospitable daughters of Ke'e-au-moku." In the year that Kamehameha met Vancouver at Kealakekua, Ka-heihei-malie was married to Kalai-mamahu', the younger brother of Kamehameha by the same father Keoua; and he was the husband of her youth before she was fully ripened. On July 16, 1794, on the day of Ma'ule of the Kaulua tabu days she gave birth to her oldest daughter, who was named Ka-hahai-ka-'ao'ao-kapu-o-ka' (meaning "passing over to the side of the rising one" [that is, to Kamehameha]) and for the tabu day of Ku and Lono she had the name Ke-ka-ulu-ohi. Kamehameha came for the child at its birth, and she admitted that it was his niece but did not consent to give it away because she was in love with her husband and wanted the child to be his. She expressed her love for her first husband Kalai-mamahu' and for her daughter in the mele beginning,

Clear the weeds from the royal patch before the rain falls—
O wele iluna ka mala lani a ka ua—

It was five or six years after the battle of Kaipalaoa that Ka-heihei-malie was married to Kalai-mamahu'. She matured with child-bearing into a stately and beautiful woman, and Kamehameha took her away from his brother to become his wife, a very strange act on his part. She was made very tabu, and he lived with her to the great grief of Ka-'ahu-manu. She bore him two daughters and a son, one of whom died. Their names were Kamehameha Kapu-aiwa, Kameha-malu Ke-kua-iwa-o-ka-lani, and Ka-ho'ano-ku Kina'u.* Unlike his other wives she took no other man to herself while Kamehameha lived. Ka-'ahu-manu who was also under tabu, one whose infringement brought death, nevertheless was a flirt (liked the taste of food); but Ka-heihei-malie was never a woman to indulge in flirtations, and her name was never coupled with gossip. She may have had her longings, but she remained true to her husband; and her children were never rumored to have been born of a double paternity like so many of the chiefs. Double paternity was considered an honor because it gave a double or triple line of chiefly descent, thick and intermingled, and formed an honorable ancestry doubly blessed in such riches and knowledge as chiefs desire. Not so Ka-heihei-malie, who considered herself sufficiently honored with the root already established. Kamehameha was her uncle, and both he and Ke'e-au-moku were directly descended from Ha'ae. He had descended from Keawe and Ka-lani-kau-lelei-a-iwi, whose son Ke'e-au-moku was, and Ka-heihei-malie was the child of the two fathers Ke'e-au-moku and Kane-koa. Hence she and Kamehameha were of one blood, he a Mahi-'ololi and she a Mahi-'ololi; he an 'I and she an 'I, both equal; he a Ku'ihewa and she a Ku'ihewa, there too they were alike; he a Mano-ka-lani-po and she a Mano-ka-lani-po, both born under the same feather cloak and both descended from many lines of chiefs; one could not yield in rank to the other. Indeed Ka-heihei-malie was descended from families of very high rank, of tabu rank, thrice tabu and four times tabu. The sun, the moon, and the stars recognized their tabu signs from old days down to the time of the change in the government.

The death of Kamehameha made the first separation from the man she had lived with for twenty years. There was no woman of his household whom Kamehameha loved so much as Ka-heihei-malie. He loved

* Ke Au 'Oko'a, June 10, 1869.

her more than Ka-'ahu-manu and once deserted Ka-'ahu-manu for her. That was the time when Ka-'ahu-manu threw herself into the sea to drown herself and be eaten by sharks. Kamehameha is never known to have deserted Ka-heihei-malie, but it has often been said that she did not love him so much as her first husband Kalai-mamahu' from whom Kamehameha took her away. Since he was the ruling chief and of equal rank with herself, no one had any right to object or would have dared to, lest he be called a traitor; but that she loved her first husband is proved by her refusal to grant Kamehameha's request to have her daughter by Kalai-mamahu' adopted as his own child.

She mourned for Kamehameha a year and then was married to a man named Ka-nuha. In September, 1823, she heard in Hawaii of Ke-opu-o-lani's death and sailed at once for Lahaina to attend the burial ceremonies. The chiefs had all assembled at Lahaina, the body of the chiefess had been concealed, and Ulu-maheihei was in mourning. After the days of mourning were ended Ka-heihei-malie became the wife of Ulu-maheihei, they became converted, were married under Christian vows, and took the names of Hoa-pili-kane and Mary Hoa-pili-wahine [the Hawaiian form of Mr. and Mrs.]. At this time she had not thought much about religion. The chiefs took to drinking and sensual indulgence after the death of the chiefess [Ke-opu-o-lani], but Ka-heihei-malie listened to the word of God as taught by the missionaries although in her heart she still enjoyed life and fun. Hoa-pili had accepted the word of God because of Ke-opu-o-lani. Ka-heihei-malie turned to Christianity first, and Ka-'ahu-manu followed.

After her marriage with Hoa-pili she became as steadfast a Christian as she had formerly been a pagan. She started a school in Lahaina for the older women of rank and all the influential people of Lahaina. Under the teacher Ka'a-moku they learned rapidly to read and write Bible texts, for it was the Bible in which they most delighted. It was like the circle of nets at the catch of flying fish, the circle that met in the *lanai* of the stone house at Waine'e. She delighted in the women's meetings which were held among the commoners at Ka'anapali and Olowalu. The chiefs worked fervently to spread the word of God in those days. Ka-heihei-malie was, like Ka-'ahu-manu, firm and intense in speeding the work of the Lord although she did not, like Ka-'ahu-manu, tour the whole group of islands. Her name became famous; the island of Maui became a pillar of fire for the cause, although some of the old people still remembered its ancient glory. Like Ka-'ahu-manu Ka-heihei-malie was furious if anyone repeated scandal, and her eyes would turn red if she heard of any wrongdoing; the guilty one had to pay a pig or be put in irons until his sores festered and he was reduced to skin and bones.

Such was her treatment of a woman named Mika-paka whom some foreigners took away on a ship. Some were imprisoned and made to work at hard labor on the roads. Those jealous for the kingdom of God believed in severe treatment for offenders. This may or may not have been right; but if the law is made to keep the peace in a country then let love and compassion be the ruling principle. Well known are her words to Liliha when she pointed out to her the way of God. But in her last days when she was nearing death she spoke in such a way that people were doubtful about her true sympathies. On the night she died, in January, 1842, she was taken to the stone house of Kuloloia at Waine'e, and when King Kau-i-ke-aouli's second son, Ke-aweawe-'ula-o-ka-lani II, was brought to her, she took him in her arms and said, "Alas! my lord! the chiefs are all gone whose lord thou art!"

Ka-lua-i-Konahale Kua-kini lived as a ruling district chief until he was a feeble tottering man. He died at his home in the handsome wooden house of Hulihe'e at Honua'ula in Kailua, Hawaii, at nine o'clock in the morning, December 9, 1844. He was born in 1791 at Kahalu'u on Hawaii and was called Ka-lua-i-Konahale (The-burial-cave-at-Konahale) after the grave of Kalola at Kalama'ula on Molokai. When [his half brother] Kua-kini died of the cholera at the beach of Wai'alae, the name Kua-kini was given to Ka-lua-i-Konahale. This name was for the multitude [of chiefs] at the back (*kuakini o ke kua*) of Kamehameha-nui, son of Ke-kau-like. [Ka-lua-i-Konahale Kua-kini was known as John Adams by the foreigners.] These two Kua-kini were the own brothers (*kaikunane pono'i*) of Ka-'ahu-manu through the same mother, Na-mahana-i-ka-lele-o-ka-lani, but their fathers were different. Keawe Ka'i-ana, son of 'Ahu'ula, son of Keawe of Hawaii, was the father of Kua-kini, and Ke'e-au-moku was the father of Ka-lua-i-Konahale Kua-kini. He was therefore a chief of double paternity, a thing that elevated the prestige of the chiefs of old, and thus connected the chiefs of Maui with those of Oahu, and those of Hawaii with those of Kauai.

At the birth of the child [Kua-kini] there was a great hula at Kahalu'u, and the name hula (*hula inoa*) was being danced for the birth of the new son to Na-mahana and Ke'e-au-moku. Visitors came to bring gifts (*ho'okupu*), and among them was Ka-mehe-'ai-ku who had gone away and hidden in the country and slept with a man and given birth to a child. She was a cousin of Ke'e-au-moku, and when she was discovered among the spectators at the hula Ke'e-au-moku gave the child to her to suckle and gave with him the land of Keauhou; and Ka-mehe-'ai-ku took the little chief to Keauhou and there nourished him until he was grown. Kua-kini was a fine-looking man with a proud carriage and a handsome rosy face; he was a thoughtful man. As a child he occupied himself chiefly with sailing canoes. As he grew older he and his brother Ka-hekili Keʻe-au-moku entered an English-speaking school and became two of the four among the chiefs—namely, George Ka-umu-aliʻi, Ke-aka-kilohi, Ka-hekili Keʻe-au-moku, and Kua-kini—who were able to understand and read the English language. Like his elder brother he was fond of the foreigners and entertained them at meals. There were foreigners living at Hana, Waikapu, Honokawai, Waialua, and on all the lands of Ka-hekili on Maui and Oahu; and when that chief died they came under Kua-kini. Perhaps this is the reason why he is said to have handled so much money, much of which he lost under the hands of his *kahu*. . . .

At the time of Kamehameha's sailing to Oahu with the *peleleu* fleet, Kua-kini went with his parents as part of the company who attended the chief. When his parents died of the cholera he was a grown man with a fine bearing, soft eyes like a dove's, and a feminine face very attractive to women. At one time he took Kau-wahine, the wife of Ka-lani-moku, and hid her away. Ka-lani-moku grieved over the loss of his wife, and Kamehameha gave him permission to burn down the houses of chiefs and commoners; that burning was a famous one in history. So with [Ka-ʻoʻo] the beautiful wife of Kamehameha's favorite, Ku-i-helani, the governor of Oahu. She was the same Ka-ʻoʻo who was the wife of ʻAuwae of Wailuku. As the wife of Ku-i-helani who was her last husband she was tabu; no man dared take her on pain of death or confiscation of property. One evening when there was a *maika* game going on at the *maika* grounds of Kalanikahua at Kikihale, Kua-kini came with the chiefs to look on and there found Ka-ʻoʻo the wife of Ku-i-helani and desired her, and she consented to meet him that night. His wish was satisfied, but he was discovered by the guards and set upon by the husband. He fled and jumped over a stone wall, and the rocks fell on his foot and broke it so that he was thenceforth lame.* Those who had betrayed him were afraid lest they be killed, and the chiefs came and begged Kamehameha to put Ku-i-helani to death. The chief [Kamehameha] was at Waiʻanae and he sent Ka-paʻa-lani to tell Ka-lani-moku to put Ku-i-helani to death. Ka-lani-moku refused, but told the messenger to tell Kamehameha that he would give as compensation the land of Ka-paʻa-lani and the rest of Ku-i-helani's lands at Maunalua. Kua-kini almost died of his broken foot, and his uncles Ka-uhi-wawae-ono and Ke-kua-manoha' came and took him to Puʻuloa and treated him until he recovered.

Kua-kini went to Hawaii at the time of Kamehameha's return thither, and became the chief's intimate (*aikane*), but it is said by Lono-makaʻi-

* *Ke Au ʻOkoʻa*, June 17, 1869.

honua that he [Kua-kini] did not care for this association. He had been taught the ancient priesthood and had placed a tabu on the heiau and the *loulu* palms of Kona while his father was living, and had been given the name of Ki'ipalaoku. At one time he and his *kahu*, Ke-oho-ku-puni, learned a prayer of sorcery from the teacher Kalou'ulu called the "Lingering prayer" (*pule lolohi*). Kua-kini was a man who did not seek society, but was quiet, generous, and patient, and made his favorites and *kahu* his friends. When Liholiho sailed to Oahu Kua-kini had already taken his luggage to the canoe when the king came and stood by his canoe and said, "Are you one of those sailing to Oahu?" When Kua-kini assented the king said, "Here is the land of Hawaii; there is food in the upland and fish in the sea; take it and eat, and we will go to Oahu." That is when Kua-kini became district ruler of Hawaii and lived like a king, and it was said of him, "It was not so in Kamehameha's time." Of this family of chiefs he was the one who disliked Kamehameha; Ka-'ahu-manu and Kalani-moku were the members of the family who were devoted to him [Kamehameha].

Kua-kini was a liquor-drinking, pleasure-loving chief, a hula dancer and patron of thieves. He protected famous plunderers, and the seaport at Kailua was noted as a port where ships were plundered. When his older brother Ka-hekili Ke'e-au-moku died, and he came to Oahu to take the body back to Hawaii, he brought with him a famous thief called White-head (Po'o-ke'oke'o) who in February, 1823, plundered Mr. Newell's store, carrying off the loot in carts in broad daylight so that strings of beads (*pukeawe*) were scattered on the road. This was the house of Mr. Reynolds (Lanai) at the Royal Hotel.

When he became converted he gave up all these ways. His wife Keoua was also converted, and all the chiefs of Kailua followed suit, and the chiefs of Hawaii and his intimate friends and chosen companions from the time of Kamehameha on; the sands of Kaiakekua were crowded with people as of old. He built a church of God at Kailua, a great *luakini* named Mokuaikaua, the largest church in the islands. Outside it was made of wattled ti stalks. Later he built a big church at Waimea called Mahiki; Kalahikiola at Nunulu in Kohala; Ele'io at Hamakua; Haili at Hilo; and Ku'olo at Ka-'u; all [were] famous churches of his building. So he helped to spread the word of God and the word grew; and he helped to educate all the people and teach them to read. He was friendly to both religious denominations, the Calvinists who denied the pope's authority, and the Roman Catholics who came later. Kua-kini was the chief who first received the Catholics on the island of Hawaii at the time when people's minds were inflamed against them. He received them affectionately and let them live at one of Ka-'ahu-manu's old houses at Keaho until their house, on land given them by him, was ready for occupation. Here they were protected; elsewhere their houses were broken down, and the food taken from the pupils who had been converted by the Roman Catholics.

At the time when the constitution was proclaimed, Kua-kini did not have a clear idea of its regulations. He appointed judges and tax assessors, but allowed his followers to secrete the proceeds. When he was asked about the property which should accrue to the government he said, "Let me eat the moneys of Hawaii until I am dead, then the wealth may go back to the government. My lord placed me here to eat of the fat of the land. He is a fool who cannot live at ease in a land as roomy as this; the rains of Hilo produce a good crop." At the death of his wife Keoua, she had no child, but he had one daughter, named Ka-manele, by Ka-niu-'opio-ha'aheo. In 1839 he married in Hilo a very young woman named Puna-hoa, and she was his wife until he died at Kailua in 1844 in his fifty-third year. He was still a young man but stiff in his legs, and it was of this trouble that he died.

Miriam Ke-ka-ulu-ohi died at her stone house at Pohukaina, at six o'clock in the morning, June 7, 1845; in her fifty-first year. She was born at Keauhou in North Kona, Hawaii, July 27 [sic], 1794, the year before that in which Kamehameha and the chiefs sailed to make war against Ka-lani-ku-pule, son of Ka-hekili, at Nu'uanu. She was born on a tabu day of the tabu of Kane, the first-born of Ka-heihei-malie in her virgin days when she was just developing into a magnificent beauty, proud in bearing, handsome beyond compare. Since the child was the first-born of this family of chiefs, she became a favorite above all the other grandchildren of Na-mahana and the family of Ke-kua-manoha' and among the connections of the uncles and cousins of Ka-'ahu-manu, and was looked upon as the head of the family. Here is her genealogy:

Liloa   Pinea-a-i-ka-lani   Hakau
    Pinea-a-i-ka-lani was younger sister of Wao-ia-lani, both chiefesses of Oahu.

Hakau	Kuku-ka-lani-a-Pae	Pinea
Ke-ano-meha	Pinea	Hakau-ka-lala-pua-kea
Keawe-nui-a-'Umi	Hakau-ka-lala-pua-kea	'Ili'iliki-kuahine
'Ili'iliki-kuahine	Ke-li'i-o-lono-a-ka-lamakua of Oahu	Pua
	Hinau Ka-uhi-a-hape	
Pua	Maka-ku-a-lono-kini	'Iliki-'ele'ele
'Iliki-'ele'ele	'Umi-iwi-'ula	'Umi-iwi-'ula
Mahi-'ololi'	Kepo'o	Ka-uaua-a-Mahi
Ka-uaua-nui-a-Mahi	Ka-lele-mauli	Ha'ae
Ha'ae	Ha'alo'u	Ha'alo'u
Keke-malolo-ke-aka-lani [Ke-kau-like]		Na-mahana-i-ka-lele-o-ka-lani

Kane-koa)	Na-mahana-i-ka-lele-	Ka-heihei-malie
Ke'e-au-moku)	o-ka-lani	
Kalai-mamahu'	Ka-heihei-malie	Ke-ka-ulu-ohi

Liloa	Haua	Kapu-kini (w)
'Umi	Kapu-kini (w)	Ke-li'i-o-kaloa (k)
		Kapu-lani (w)
		Keawe-nui-a-'Umi
Keawe-nui-a-'Umi	Ko'i-halawai	Kanaloa-kua'ana

Ko'i-halawai was the daughter of Akahi'ili-kapu and Ka-haku-maka-liua, sacred chiefs of Kauai to whom belonged the sacred drum of Holoholoku and the sacred stone in the water of Iolani. Kanaloa-kua'ana was the chief whose face was tattooed by Kama-lala-walu, chief of Maui.

| Kanaloa-kua'ana | Ka-iki-lani | Ke-li'i-o-ka-lani (w) |
| | | Keakea-lani-kane (k) |

Ke-li'i-o-ka-lani and Keakea-lani-kane married, and two very sacred children were born, one for Kauai and one for Hawaii, but only Hawaii's survived and that was Ke-aka-mahana.

Iwi-kau-i-ka-ua-a-	Ke-aka-mahana	Keakea-lani-wahine
Maka-kau-ali'i		
Kanaloa-i-ka-iwi-lewa	Keakea-lani-wahine	Keawe
or Kanaloa-kapu-	(m. her makuakane)	
lehu		
Kane-i-ka-ua-iwi-lani	Keakea-lani-wahine	Ka-lani-kau-lele-ia-iwi
son of Iwi-kau-i-	(m. her brother)	
kane of Oahu		
Ka-'ula-hea-nui-o-ka-	Ka-lani-kau-lele-ia-iwi	Ke-ku'i-apo-iwa-nui
moku		of Ka-'ula-hea
Keawe	Ka-lani-kau-lele-ia-iwi	Ka-lani Ke'e-au-
		moku (k)
		Kekela (w)

See the first history written by Mr. Dibble and David Malo and other pupils at Lahainaluna in 1835. Ulu-maheihei and 'Auwae denied Ke-ku'i-apo-iwa's descent from Keawe.

This Ke'e-au-moku was the chief who built, at 'Apua in Kanaloa, a fleet of canoes which were burned.

Ke'e-au-moku	Ka-maka'i-moku	Keoua
Keoua	Ka-maka-hei-kuli	Kalai-mamahu'
Kalai-mamahu'	Ka-heihei-malie	Ke-ka-ulu-ohi-mano

This is not all the genealogy of this chief. It would take ten genealogies to cover all the ancestral lines with which this chief was connected. But in old times it was tabu to use the whole genealogy of any chief but the ruling chief; only for him was the whole genealogy recited.

A chief's ancestors are enumerated in his ancestral chants and also in those of favorite children even among commoners. In Ke-ka-ulu-ohi's ancestral chants published in the *Ku'oko'a* are inserted genealogical chants of the chiefs of Kauai and genealogies of chiefs of Oahu, Maui, and Hawaii. Kamehameha and his chiefs composed these chants. In the canoe chant of Ke-ka-ulu-ohi* the names of all of them are mentioned as appointed to various offices according to the occupations of their ancestors; for example, Kalai-mamahu' and Ka-lani-hele-mai-i-luna-ka-moku were the ones to prepare the adz for hewing the canoe, and they carried the adz and cut the canoe. Boki was the chief priest to cut off the branches and to hollow out the opening of the canoe; Kamehameha was the priest to finish off the inside and make the keel straight. Ka-'ahu-manu was the priestess to draw the canoe to the lowlands and into the canoe house; Ke-ali'i-maika'i was the priest to put the parts together; Ulu-maheihei, Ka-iki-o-'ewa, Koa-hou, Ka-welo-o-ka-lani Koa-kanu, Na-ihe, Kalai-moku, Ka-hekili Ke'e-au-moku, Ka-lua-i-Konahele, and all the other chiefs were to prepare and fasten the cords, and Kau-kuna Ka-hekili was to offer the prayer to bless the canoe. Kamehameha was the leading kahuna, Poke the prayer, Kane-'aha-kini the god, Ku-ka'ili-moku the sacred name of Ke-ka-ulu-ohi, and she [Ke-ka-ulu-ohi] had other names of gods. Clearly Ke-ka-ulu-ohi was a favorite chiefess.

And when she became such a favorite of her parents and grandparents and all the chiefs, there were perhaps no families of chiefs that did not prostrate themselves and serve her in this way except the family of Ka-lani Ke-li'i Ka-uhi-lono-honua descendant of Ka-'ula-hea-nui-o-ka-moku of Maui; these observed their own strict tabus, and those of Hawaii fell before them. For example, it is well known among the chiefs that Ka-'ahu-manu snubbed Ku-wahine for winding Ke-ka-ulu-ohi's skirt about herself, and Ku-wahine wailed aloud with shame. But Ku-wahine was herself the daughter of Ka-lani-ka-uli-hiwa-a-kama Pi'ipi'i, the daughter of Ke-ku'i-apo-iwa, and was the sister of Kamehameha, born from the same womb as he, and Ke-ku'i-apo-iwa was the daughter of Ke-kela-o-ka-lani, the daughter of Ka-lani-kau-lele-ia-iwi by Keawe. Ka-iki-o-'ewa was Ku-wahine's father, and he was hurt by Ka-'ahu-manu's snub and sent for a genealogist, Kau-loa-iwi from Molokai, who composed the chant of Owela-ka-lani (Heat-of-the-heavens) for Ku-wahine. But if we examine the ancestral chants of the sons and daughters and grandchildren of Na-mahana-i-ka-lele-o-ka-lani, it is perfectly obvious that they have upheld the Maui side of the line and the chiefly tabu of Ke-kau-like and ignored the side of Hawaii. There was no one family of chiefs on Hawaii set up as lord above the other chiefly families; they were all rated alike and all, from first to last, high chiefs and low chiefs alike, had *kahili* at their back. It was said that Ke-kau-like-

---

* When a favorite child has a canoe or house or any new object of value constructed a chant is composed in its honor in praise of the chief for whom it is made.

wahine and Ka-uhi-o-keka were the children of Ke-kau-like of Maui, but others say they were Keawe's children. Keawe-ma'u-hili is known to have been Ke-kau-like's son. Kalai-ku-ahulu was the composer who glorified the names of the chiefs of Hawaii in chant. After the battle of Nu'uanu he included the chiefs of Hawaii with those of Maui, Oahu, and Kauai, at which time he composed the chant called "Seeking the single-masted canoe" (*O uiui a wa'a kialoa*) as the ancestral path of Ke-a-ulu-moku. But those skilled in the genealogies of Kauai were indignant because the relationships he traced were connecting lines merely and not those of direct descent.

Ke-ka-ulu-ohi was brought up at Kahalu'u and Keauhou by Na-mahana and Ke'e-au-moku, her grandparents, who fondled her as if she were a feather lei from the precious *mamo* bird. Her father Kalai-mamahu' made his trusted *kahu*, Kahi-kaheana, and his [Kahi-ka-heana's] household her *kahu*.* This man's children and grandchildren, Ka-niuhi and Ka-'aha and their families, became Ke-ka-ulu-ohi's *kahu* through her father Kalai-mamahu'. She was a girl with a fine physique, pretty youthful features, a fair skin, and a rather husky voice. [As already related] she came to Oahu when Kamehameha sailed with the *peleleu* fleet, and there, through cholera, lost all her family except her grandmother Na-mahana, and her brothers. In 1809 Ke-ka-ulu-ohi became Kamehameha's wife at 'Apuakehau, Waikiki, and was kept under strict tabu in a guarded house where she and her mother studied the old customs and the genealogical lines of the chiefs under Kalai-ku-ahulu and Ka-holo. The tabu however was not strictly kept; it was up only to deceive Kamehameha. Her family had become rich and powerful, and if any man who pleased Ka-'ahu-manu was attracted by her adopted daughter she allowed their association in secret. At the death of Ka-mehameha, Ke-ka-ulu-ohi became one of Liholiho's five wives. While he was at Pu'uloa the king gave her, as a token of friendship, to one of his favorites (*aikane*), and Ka-na'ina thus became her husband. To him in 1834, at the age of forty, she bore her first male child, W. C. Luna-lilo, who might have been a blessing to his country had he established a line of descendants.

At the time of Liholiho's death Ke-ka-ulu-ohi had not accepted the word of God. She knew how to read and write and had learned a good deal in the schools, but she was addicted to drink and pleasure-seeking until the death of her half-brother Kahala-i'a. Then she accepted God, turned to the missionary teachers, repented of her sins, and became a believer. On March 2, 1828, she was baptized into the Kawaiaha'o church under the name of Miriam Ke-ka-ulu-ohi and became the third to enter

* *Ke Au 'Oko'a*, June 24, 1869.

the church. From that time she was noted during Ka-'ahu-manu's life-time for her firm stand for righteousness, and after Ka-'ahu-manu's death cooperated with Kina'u to use her power and influence in further-ing the work for which their aunt had striven, whether rightly or wrongly. At least the kingdom became wiser and more learned. After Kina'u's death Miriam Ke-ka-ulu-ohi was appointed premier for the government, and her interest turned to pleasure, honor, and wealth. She fell into sin and took to dancing and chanting. At the time of the birth of Ke-aweawe-'ula II, son and heir of King Kau-i-ke-aouli and his wife Ka-paku-haili, there was a great hula going on at Lahaina. In March Miriam Ke-ka-ulu-ohi was appointed guardian to rear the child (*kahu hanai*), repented of her sins before a great number in the church at Wai-ne'e in Lahaina, made a vow, and signed her name to the temperance pledge never to touch intoxicants again. From that time she was stead-fast in her adherence to the church. When her uncle Kua-kini died, she and Lele-io-hoku were his heirs. They quarreled about the property, but it was given to Lele-io-hoku and she received the lump sum of $20,000, one tenth of which she gave for the kingdom of God and the remainder she divided among the young chiefs Moses Ke-kuaiwa, Lot Kapu-aiwa, Victoria Ka-mamalu, and W. C. Luna-lilo.

A fall from a horse at Lahaina which broke her thigh bone caused her long suffering. When she was a little better and able to walk with a cane, she accompanied the king and chiefs to Oahu for the convening of legis-lature and to meet the delegates who had gone to foreign lands to seek independence for the kingdom. On April 9 she fell ill with fever and could eat nothing, only sip a little lemonade. By the 27th she took to her bed and fainted often; and by June 2 her eyes grew dizzy and her skin pained like a boil. She died on June 7, 1845, in her fifty-first year before her body showed any sign of age.*

* *Ke Au 'Oko'a*, July 1, 1869.

CHAPTER XXX

Legislative Problems, 1845-1852

In October, 1848, originated the legislature which established the laws of the king and the chiefs of the land and those appointed by the king with the approval of the chiefs who had assembled at Lua'ehu, Lahaina, in 1841. In old days it was tabu for the high and low chiefs (*ali'i* and *kaukauali'i*) to confer together. In matters of life and death or in difficult questions of policy it was for the high chiefs alone to decide; they held their councils in secret, and the ruling chief acted upon their counsel. It was by his action that their counsel became known. But that time was past and a new era had come. The principal business of legislature was to confirm or correct the constitution and to supplement it by other laws defining other powers of the king, the chiefs, ministers, land-claim officials, and other officers of the government, and to give the chief justice power to overrule the acts of tax gatherers and judges. A number of other laws were passed making adjustments between the chiefs and the people. The Rev. William Richards was the one who formulated the law and brought it before the king and chiefs for their approval. When he had read it he explained that in order to prevent the commoners from disputing over the law, it was the custom for the governments of America and Europe to give them a voice in the working of the laws, by allowing representatives chosen by ballot to enter the legislature and work with the chiefs in enacting the laws. In April, 1841, when the legislature met at Lua'ehu, not only the king and chiefs but several representatives of the people were elected to sit in the assembly. David Malo and Ka-'auwai of Maui and L. Kolona Hala'i were the first representatives [of the people] to enter the assembly with the chiefs and become the mouthpiece of the common people and explain their difficulties.

At the time there was not much trouble with legislation and with the assessment of taxes, but it was difficult to find men to represent the country districts.* There had been some confusion because of the exactions of the tax collectors and the school teachers and land agents. The land agents bribed the tax assessors and they became corrupted and oppressed the people. But on the whole, although a good many laws were passed and the commoners were not successful in getting their side rep-

* *Ke Au 'Oko'a*, May 20, 1869.

resented, the laws were light. In 1842 there were still too few representatives for the country districts. Those elected were Jacob Malo and Kapae for Hawaii, David Malo and S. M. Kamakau for Maui, Paul Kanoa and L. K. Hala'i for Oahu, and David Pa-pohaku for Kauai. Paul Kanoa was made secretary for the House of Nobles (ali'i). The two houses were separated, and the laws passed included: a law for the banishing of persons to other lands; a new law for tax assessors; a law in regard to runaways; a law adjusting the form of a trial; a notice of the return of properties by the government to the legislature; a law concerning taxation, duties, and properties of the government; a message appointing an interpreter and secretary for the government; a law of adjustment; a new law for the schools; a law abolishing certain taxes; and a law appointing an official to guard the properties of the government. The two houses were empowered to elect some judges, two chosen by the House of Nobles and two elected by the people, to become supreme judges for the government to meet with the king to hear cases appealed from the lower courts and such cases as concerned life and death, which could not be tried in the lower courts. Rich or poor, chief or commoner, could bring suit here without paying fees and without hiring lawyers. [Ka-makau does not approve of this but does not make it clear why.]

Governors were also appointed for Maui and Kauai. Both houses met to choose the nominees, but the power of voting lay with the Nobles. All were unanimous for Ke-kau-'onohi as governor of Maui, and John Young, Jr. of Kauai. William Richards tried to have them send Ke-kau-'onohi to Kauai, but they refused, saying, "Where the king lives, that is where Ke-kau-'onohi belongs." This decision was backed by all the chiefs and by Ke-ka-ulu-ohi the premier. . . . William Richards argued for John Young because he understood a little English and since there were many whale ships and other foreign boats calling at Maui he would make a better escort for the king and represent him better before the officers of the battleships and with delegates from foreign lands. The chiefs must have known that it was upon the rights of the chiefs and the ruling king that government had been established and not upon such things as these, but they gave up their will and John Young became governor of Maui. I was astonished, for I had believed that the ballot was really to determine an election according to the will of the greater number, but here the chiefs had given up their will to that of a single person.

So Ke-kau-'onohi became governor of Kauai and John Young of Maui, and he really did fine work there. He became Chief Justice for the island and made circuits to learn the duties of tax assessors and judges and land agents and officers of peace. He stopped crime in the country districts and urged the police to observe Kamehameha's command "that the old women and men and children sleep in safety by the wayside." It was so peaceable that plover were not afraid to alight. [Plover are migratory birds nesting away from the group, hence a veiled allusion to foreigners who make money in Hawaii and go away to spend it.] There was real peace on the island, no murder, no drunkenness in those years. On Oahu Ke-ku-anao'a also made circuits and saw to the efficiency of tax assessors, judges, school masters, officials, land agents, police, and commoners. Here too plover were unafraid and mice ran about squeaking openly. If an official was guilty he was quickly dismissed, if a land agent he was put to shame before his master. . . . Thus the governors presided as chief justices for their islands and made circuits to proclaim the laws of the kingdom and the commands of the king to respect the right.

Another achievement of this legislature was to appoint officials to look after the property of the kingdom, and Hon. Gerrit P. Judd was appointed Chamberlain with Timothy Ha'a-lilio and John 'I'i as treasurers (pu'uku) with power to settle the government debts. Their first step was to sell at auction the fleet of canoes of the district chief of Hawaii; Kuakini came from Hawaii for the sale. That was the beginning of piling up money to pay the government debt. Before that the government had been helpless. The king and chiefs had used government property merely for purposes of their own pleasure, but when the law came into effect the king was powerless to give away property without the consent of the legislature. Now that a paid official at a thousand a year and two officers at two hundred yearly were at work, the kingdom began to pay its debts and became prosperous and efficient.

During the period of the trouble with Lord George Paulet not much was done in the legislature. They waited for the return of their delegates from Europe. . . . After the return of William Richards with the body of Ha'a-lilio, on May 21, 1845, the legislature gathered, composed of the nobles and the elected representatives of the people and the former officials, G. P. Judd for the Department of the Interior, R. C. Wyllie for foreign affairs, John Ricord Assistant Attorney General, and Hon. William Richards as delegate to the foreign powers who had recognized the kingdom as an independent power. The reports of the various departments were heard beginning with that of Richards and Ha'a-lilio in seeking recognition for the government. Chiefs and people wept when they heard the account read by R. C. Wyllie of the hardships they had endured.*

After the death of Ke-ka-ulu-ohi in 1845, John Young, Jr. (Keoni Ana) was made governor of Maui, and the king appointed him to the

* *Ke Au 'Oko'a*, May 27, 1869.

premiership to succeed Ke-ka-ulu-ohi, not because of learning or intelligence but because he was a favorite and the choice of the king. The commoners were pleased because he was of the blood of the chiefs and a Hawaiian born, as the son of John Young, Kamehameha's favorite foreigner, and a Hawaiian woman from a family of chiefs, hence part Hawaiian and part foreign. He was pleasing in his manners toward the commoners and a good talker, and he helped the humble when they got into trouble with the chiefs or land agents. As governor he often toured Maui, Molokai, and Lanai, and kept up the old duty of the governor to keep the peace, to teach and explain the laws of the land to the commoners, and put a stop to all mischief, dissipation, or idleness. The country was peaceful with scarcely a murder during the year in which he served as governor and premier.

There was then a change made in office of premier. More *koai'e* wood paddles were cut on Pu'ukapele [the place on Kauai where this wood was found] in order to give the government more oarsmen to paddle. A learned man had arrived with knowledge of the law, and the foreigners who were holding office in the government hastened to put him forward by saying how clever and learned he was and what good laws he would make for the Hawaiian people. The truth was, they were laws to change the old laws of the natives of the land and cause them to lick ti leaves like the dogs and gnaw bones thrown at the feet of strangers, while the strangers became their lords, and the hands and voices of strangers were raised over those of the native race. The commoners knew this and one and all expressed their disapproval and asked the king not to place foreigners in the offices of government lest the native race become a footstool for the foreigners. Here is one of letters they sent.

King Kamehameha III   Lahainaluna, July 22, 1845

A point for discussion: Some time ago your servant (*kauwa*) sent for some of the old people who had lived in the time of Ka-hekili and of Kamehameha I, and we talked about how the government was administered in their day. The old men said, "In the time of Kamehameha the orators (*po'e kaka'olelo*) were the only ones who spoke before the ruling chief, those who were learned in the words spoken by the chiefs who had lived before his day. When the chief asked, 'What chief has done evil to the land, and what chief good?' then the orators alone were able to relate the deeds of the chiefs of old, those who did good deeds and those who did evil deeds, and the king would try to act as the chiefs acted who did good deeds in the past." Then I said, "Dependence upon those things which were done in the past is at an end; the good which is greatest at this time is that which is good for the foreigner. At the time when the government was taken we were in trouble, and from foreign lands life has been restored to the government." . . . The old men said, "We love devotedly the king, Kamehameha III; but perhaps the kingdom would not have been taken away if we had not lost the old good ways of our ancestors and depended upon the new good ways. That is why a struggle for supremacy has arisen and plots of evil. Perhaps it is not Great Britain alone which has these treacherous thoughts. There may be men living right among us who will devastate the land like the hordes of caterpillars the fields; they hide themselves among us until the time comes, then they will be on the side of their own land where their ancestors were born. Here is another thing: the king has chosen foreign ministers, foreign agents (*luna*). This is wrong. The Hawaiian people will be debased and the foreign exalted. The Hawaiian people will be trodden under foot by the foreigners. Perhaps not now, or perhaps it will not be long before we shall see it. The land will be diminished, the length and the breadth of it. Another thing, the dollar is become the government for the commoner and for the destitute. It will become a dish of relish and the foreign agents will suck it up. With so many foreign agents the dollar will be lost to the government through the cleverness of foreigners and their cunning, and instead of good coming to the Hawaiian people, strangers will get the benefit from the wealth of the government.

"And therefore we believe that we ought all to stand together against the foreigners holding office in Hawaii. Let chiefs be placed in the vacancies and do not let all of the government positions go to foreigners." "What chiefs are there who are able to fill the vacancies?" I asked. "There are Lele-io-hoku, Paki, and John Young." I said to them, "Perhaps these men are already at work, or perhaps they are not able to handle the work of the posts given to foreigners. They are puzzling positions for the ignorant. Perhaps the people of Lahaina and Wailuku were mistaken in thinking that the powerful nations agreed to the independence of our government; perhaps they agreed only if we governed intelligently. Who of us knows enough to translate the laws of Great Britain into the language of Hawaii and take the right of the country for the right of this?* That is what America did and France and all the independent governments of Europe, and the good laws of those governments will become beneficial to Hawaii. Therefore I disapprove of the people's protest against foreign officials since it is the desire of the rulers of Great Britain, France, and the United States of America to educate our government in their way of governing, as I have heard. I understand this to be the command of Her Majesty Queen Victoria who rules the empire of Great Britain and Ireland, and of King Louis Phillippe who rules France. These rulers believe that the Hawaiian group has a government prepared to administer laws like other governments and hence it is that they allow Hawaii to remain independent. We ought therefore not to object to foreign officials if we cannot find chiefs of Hawaii learned enough for the office."

The old people spoke again: "This is an amazing thing! Let us see it with our eyes! The laws of those governments will not do for our government. Those are good laws for them, our laws are for us and

* *Ke Au 'Oko'a*, July 1, 1869.

are good laws for us, which we have made for ourselves. We are not slaves to serve them. When they talk in their clever way, we know very well what is right and what is wrong. Kamehameha was not taught in the school, but his name was famous for good government. We do not believe that Kamehameha would put faith in the skill and cunning of strangers. He depended upon his own skill and judgment and upon that which he found within his own kingdom; he never accepted without question the advice of others or of foreigners. He had some foreigners like the foreign doctor Naea and the captains Barber, George Beckley, and Winship, and there were a great many other honored and clever foreigners living with Kamehameha, but it was never heard that he followed completely the advice of the foreigners, and he never made them members of his secret council to discuss good government. It was a British foreigner who advised Kamehameha, 'Do not shelter foreigners, for they are graspers of land.' Entertaining foreigners therefore is the beginning which will lead to the government's coming into the hands of the foreigner, and the Hawaiian people becoming their servants to work for them. And by and by you will see the truth of it. We shall see that the strangers will complain of the natives of Hawaii as stupid, ignorant, and good-for-nothing, and say all such evil things of us, and this will embitter the race and degrade it and cause the chiefs to go after the stranger and cast off their own race.

"Give our greeting to the king and the chiefs, but we say what we think and what is our opinion."

I place our words before the king and his minister. I am one of the least of his servants who is seeking wisdom.

S. M. Ka-makau

S. M. Kamakau: Nuʻuanu, Oahu, August, 1845

Kindly greetings to you with kindly greetings to the old men and women of my ancestors' time. I desire all the good things of the past to remain such as the good old law of Kamehameha that "the old women and the old men shall sleep in safety by the wayside," and to unite with them what is good under these new conditions in which we live. That is why I have appointed foreign officials, not out of contempt for the ancient wisdom of the land, but because my native helpers do not understand the laws of the great countries who are working with us. That is why I have dismissed them. I see that I must have new officials to help with the new system under which I am working for the good of the country and of the old men and women of the country. I earnestly desire to give places to the commoners and to the chiefs as they are able to do the work connected with the office. The people who have learned the new ways I have retained. Here is the name of one of them, G. L. Kapeau, Secretary of the Treasury. He understands the work very well, and I wish there were more such men. Among the chiefs Lele-io-hoku, Paki, and John Young are capable of filling such places and they already have government offices, one of them over foreign officials. And as soon as the young chiefs are sufficiently trained I hope to give them the places. But they are not now able to become speakers in foreign tongues. I have therefore refused the letters of appeal to dismiss the foreign advisers, for those who speak only the Hawaiian tongue.

My kindly greetings to you old women and old men, and let S. M. Ka-makau confer with you there. He is the one through whom to send me your greetings that all may be well with us throughout our lives.

Kamehameha

It was clear to us from this letter how deeply concerned the king was for our good and how completely he was working for the good of his own race and how he was giving his own people, chiefs and commoners, the offices which they could fill; and only those which they could not fill were being given to foreigners, and that when the young chiefs were sufficiently instructed in the English language the offices were to be given back to them; and that the new ways of civilized governments were to be added to the old ways of the Hawaiian government. . . . The king therefore appointed, October 29, 1845, Robert C. Wyllie to be Minister of Foreign Affairs, G. P. Judd Minister of the Treasury, William Richards Minister of Education, John Ricord Attorney General; and these foreigners administered the affairs of the government both foreign and internal.

Robert C. Wyllie showed himself skillful in handling affairs with foreign governments. Gerrit P. Judd demonstrated his ability in so handling the wealth of the kingdom that the treasury was full to overflowing. He was also praised for upholding the rights of the native race and advancing those who were educated, stimulating a desire to get an education among boys who wished to become famous. This giving of government positions to the native sons of the land brought joy to the commoners. John Ricord's work was to use the laws of the civilized world as a foundation and adapt them to the conditions of the people in Hawaii. He was a man whom Kamehameha III trusted. He said openly that the laws of the Bible were not adapted for use by modern governments; they belonged to the people of God, a Jewish race descended from Abraham, a race begotten for everlasting life. The laws of Rome, that government from which all other governments of Europe, Western Asia and Africa descended, could not be used for Hawaii, nor could those of England, France, or any other country. The Hawaiian people must have laws adapted to their mode of living. But it is right to study the laws of other peoples, and fitting that those who conduct law offices in Hawaii should understand these other laws and compare them to see which are adapted to our way of living and which are not. So when the offices of the advisers to the king were divided, a law book was made to regulate the duties to be performed by each, and during these years each was busy with his own duties and had no assistants appointed. . . .*

The Land Grants (*kuleana*) Board was a branch of the Department of the Interior. The king appointed [in 1845] five officials called the Board of Commissioners to Quiet Land Titles, a president and four others, to investigate each man's right to his land grant, both those who had lands from Kamehameha III and those whose grants came before his time. [At the beginning of 1848 occurred the division known as the *mahele* by which the lands were divided between the king and the chiefs, at the end of which the king owned approximately one half of all the land and the chiefs the other half. The king now divided his land into two parts one of which became the crown lands owned by the royal family as represented by the king, the other the government lands. It was further decided that as the government had an interest also in the chiefs' lands, this interest might be commuted and his land become the inalienable property of the chief only by a payment of money or by a surrender of part of the land to the government. Most of the chiefs followed the latter course, and this added, in 1850, aprroximately one third of the chiefs' lands to the government holdings. At the end of 1849 the commoners also secured rights to land. The Privy Council earlier passed a resolution giving the people the right to land actually cultivated by them without commutation to the government. All such claims were to be filed by February, 1848. The land, under ancient custom, had been held by the ruling chief alone, and parceled out by him to his followers, subject to return to the ruling chief at the death of the follower, or treason on his part toward his chief. At the death or subjugation of the ruling chief the land reverted to his heir or conqueror for redistribution. Theoretically the ruling chief had the ultimate claim to all the land. It now became individual property to be used or sold to another according the will of the individual owner.]† An old resident on the land could appeal for a paper to give him the right to the land on which he lived. So some commoners obtained much property by this means, but others lost their land through ignorance, favoritism, or interference by chiefs and land agents. The chiefs were selling their lands to foreigners and to those who had no grants, and those who were thus turned out became wanderers without any property and had to become contract laborers and serve people like slaves. The foreigners profited by the arrangement and were well taken care of by the government. It was the race who owned the government who were not defended (*hi'ipoi*).

* *Ke Au 'Ok'a*, July 8, 1869.
† For this summary of the land legislation I am indebted to 17, 1, and 15.

This can not be true of other independent governments of the world whose people dwell quietly under the shadow of the flag of their government and of their birthplace. . . . The Hawaiian race live like wanderers on the earth and dwell in all lands surrounded by the sea. Why have they wandered to strange land and other kingdoms of earth? They say because they were burdened by the law of the land. The time when all these people went away was that in which the chiefs took up learning letters, and made the new law for governing the land which is called the missionary law. The government of Hawaii became famous through the new law. The foreigners were benefited and they have stayed here because they like new lands, but the people of Hawaii waited for the benefits of the government under the law from strange lands. For fear of the law they went, and were not seen again in this Hawaii. Of our own people 651 sailed for the east on foreign ships, and many others are unaccounted for. At Papeete in Tahiti there were 400 Hawaiians, in Oregon 500, at Paita in Peru 50, and many have gone to Nantucket, New Bedford, Sag Harbor, New London, and other American ports. Many wail there and never return to this group. Some went to Nukuhiva, the Micronesian islands, New Zealand, and to the bush ranges of California, and lived like wanderers in foreign lands. What a pity!

William Richards became Minister of Education and president of the Board of Commissioners to Quiet Land Titles. He was a capable man in in his position as educator. . . . He did his work for the land grants honestly, and no scandal was ever connected with his name. He investigated carefully the land claims of the humble people. But during the year that he was president the common people were not ready to put in petitions for their title to different parcels of land. They were rather stupid about it, and those who were grasping took the land of the ignorant and entered it under their own names, while others got the land by lying and flattery. The agents worked patiently and tried to help the native sons of the land, but the greater benefits of the law went to the foreigners who thus secured the right to live on the land although they were not of the land. . . . Richards sailed to Lahaina where grants were issued for Lahaina and Wailuku, but mostly for Honolulu. The chiefs were the first to put in their petitions, then the foreigners because they knew that the door was open to them. The important positions were held by men of their own race who would give them what they wanted. The foreigners tried to gain favor with the chiefs in order to get lands that in old times were refused them by the chiefs, and we have that condition to which the proverb refers, "It is only a broken gourd that needs mending" (*He naha ipu auanei o pa'a i ka hupauhumu*). There was no powerful chief to stand back of the people and put together again the parts that were broken to pieces. It is a wonder that the land survives at all as a so-called independent kingdom when the rock that forms its anchor is shattered by the storm.

[A condensation of Kamakau's report follows]* On August 1, 1846, Mr. William Richards as Minister of Public Instruction read to the legislature his report of the schools in the kingdom. When, in 1823, the language had been reduced to an alphabet and a primer printed, the king Kamehameha II, the prince Kau-i-ke-aouli and the princess Nahi-'ena'ena, and other chiefs entered school and within a year could read in the Hawaiian language. Schools increased all over the islands as fast as there were teachers to teach them, and the number of pupils enrolled for the present year was 15,393. Between 1824 and 1846 about 80 books were published covering 65,444 pages. In 1827 a beginning was made in printing the Bible; in 1832 the New Testament was printed; in 1839 the whole Bible was in the hands of the Hawaiians.

In the Royal School in Honolulu the children of chiefs were educated. Seven years from its beginning all the children were still there; death had never entered its yard and there was little illness. The pupils were like a happy family. The first lesson taught was belief in righteousness and in God, the second was instruction in the English language. Instruction was given in surveying and electricity, chemistry and other natural sciences, mathematics, astronomy, and the history of foreign lands. The pupils were bright and delighted their teachers. They grew up to be dignified and god-fearing so that the kingdom did not lack what it greatly needed, wise and virtuous chiefs. Mr. and Mrs. Cooke were in charge of the school, assisted by Mr. Thomas Douglas. In 1831 the high school at Lahainaluna opened. In 1836 a girls' school was opened at Wailuku. In the same year the Hilo boarding school for boys was opened on Hawaii. The girls were taught, besides the ordinary subjects learned at school, how to sew, knit stockings, and spin, and how to be good housekeepers. At Wai'oli on Kauai there was a mixed school of fifty pupils which had then been running four years. An agricultural school, opened at Waialua on Oahu by Mr. and Mrs. Locke, had to be closed because of the death of its promotor. The Roman Catholics were opening a school at Ko'olua [at 'Ahuimanu] and had a high school in Honolulu with several hundred students. A school was opened in Honolulu under Mr. and Mrs. Andrew Johnstone for the children of foreign fathers and Hawaiian mothers, called the Oahu Charity School, and this Mr. Richards thought should continue to receive government support. A private

* These reports in translation were printed by royal authority by the Polynesian Press, Honolulu, and may be consulted at various Honolulu libraries in the Ministerial Reports for 1845- 1848. They are therefore omitted from this translation.

school for girls was conducted by Mrs. Gummer with especial attention to "ornamental needle work and other essential branches of female education." Mr. Robert Gordon coducted a school for children of foreign parents. Punahou Academy was opened for the children of missionaries. [End of condensation.]*

The Rev. William Richards became Minister of Education October 29, 1845, and died November 7, 1847. He was born in the United States of America August 22, 1793, and died in his fifty-fifth year. He was sent here as an ordained minister by the Board of Missions of the society of Puritans in Boston, Massachusetts, and arrived August 27, 1823. He and Rev. C. L. Stewart and their wives were sent to Maui in answer to the request of the chiefess Ke-opu-o-lani for missionary teachers for her own household. He did many good things during his residence at Lahaina and traveled throughout the whole island of Maui. He cared for the members of his parish, taught, encouraged, and preached of spiritual things and of righteousness as taught in the word of God. He used to go to the houses of the sick and care for them and treat them; he treated the chiefs and the missionaries who were ill. The humblest might go to Mr. Richards and find help in trouble. He would assist women in childbirth, both Hawaiian and missionary mothers, and never took pay for his labors even when he came at night to relieve the sufferer. All his care was for the good health of the people, for there was no foreign doctor in Lahaina in those days. . . . He would even go to Wailuku or into Hamakua to help sick people, whether pure Hawaiians or missionaries. His affections were not set upon wealth or honor, and he was paid very little by the government up to the time of his death. He was a father and foster guardian (*kahu hanai*) to the chiefess Harriet Nahi-'ena'ena, heir to the throne, and guarded her and led her aright, and she became noted for her intelligence, good works, and steadfastness in the word of God. Not for her alone, but for the chiefs high and low, for prominent people, and for the humble as well who were in trouble, he was a father and leader who could explain what was right and what was wrong. So also for the judges and land agents (*konohiki*) and the tenants (*hoa'aina*). He would attend also to any difficulty with church matters and always with such careful diligence that the people had full confidence in him in any trouble.

Another of his achievements was the translation of parts of the Bible into Hawaiian. He translated Isaiah, Joshua, and Palms 1-75, Mark, Luke, John, Acts, Corinthians I, James, and Jude, and he also wrote the history of animals and other short histories. After he became the king's special counselor he translated the book on Political Economy and the

---

* *Ke Au 'Oko'a,* July 15, 1869.

Book of Laws and the laws called those of Lua'ehu. His books became guides for the whole race. Who can doubt the good that he has accomplished?

After his death the king appointed Mr. Richard Armstrong Minister of Public Instruction and Mr. William Low presiding head of the land grants. Mr. Armstrong belonged to one of the Puritan missionary families. He was a very careful worker, and the Hawaiian people held him in affection. He advanced the cause of education, was active in the work himself and made himself acquainted with high and low alike. He traveled often from Hawaii to Kauai to learn for himself which teachers were diligent and which slothful and what each should be paid. . . .* With the appointments of Mr. Richards and Mr. Armstrong to take charge of public education there was an end to the dissensions which had arisen in the schools because of the high-handed and disputatious attitude of those who opposed the religion of the pope. After the treaties with France and Great Britain the government helped to preserve neutrality.

John Ricord as Assistant Attorney General [and the next year as Attorney General] helped to adjust the legal difficulties of the government and at the time of his resignation had laid the foundation for the future government of the kingdom. The closing words of this deeply-loved man were contained in his report read before the legislature, April 28, 1847. There was one very important law giving power of attorney to the officials who gave the land grant titles. . . . This law would have been better had the time for registering titles been extended for twenty years. Very few of the people living in the country were educated and knew how to apply for their titles. Others wanted to remain on the lands under their chiefs, and when the trading days came, and the chiefs leased their lands to the foreigners [and these people were obliged to leave them], they learned their mistake and were left to wander in tears on the highway. The fish of Piliwale are stranded; the sea has left them high and dry. Some people were just ignorant, but the foreigners who had waited a long time to take the land for themselves were all ready, and when the door was thrown open for natives and strangers alike they could well laugh; land was what they wanted. It would have been better moreover if, when the law made the sale of government lands available, these could have been sold so reasonably, to the descendants of Kamehameha alone, that his toil and blood might not have been spent in vain. His children do not get the milk; his adopted children have grasped the nipples and sucked the breasts dry.

Among all the foreign ministers there was one of their own blood whom the Hawaiians trusted, and he was John Young son of Keoni Ana

* *Ke Au 'Oko'a,* July 22, 1869.

who was said to be born of the daughter of Ke-ali'i-maika'i Ke-po'o-ka-lani. Her mother was Ka-li-o-ka-lani, hence Young belonged to the chiefs and was looked upon with special favor by the king. [His report was read before the legislature August 1, 1846.] Certainly if all his work were recounted we should see that this Hawaiian was capable of filling an important government office. The story is that the blind chief, I-mai-ka-lani, had four men to carry his weapons, two on each side, and had trained birds to give warning when an enemy was approaching, and he would ask how many enemies there were and in which hand the weapon was held and would kill the enemy with his own weapon. Thus he vanquished any number of warriors. But at the battle of Ka-pali-i-uka, Pi'i-mai-wa'a first drove the birds away and then killed the guards; the blind man lost his way without a guide and was killed by Pi'i-mai-wa'a. Some may have thought that John Young was not a trained man [since he had not an English education], but he could read and write Hawaiian even though he had not attended school. Hawaiians readily imitate and can memorize what they hear, or if they see any object can duplicate it exactly. In the old days of Kamehameha I and II and in those of Kamehameha III before laws were made, they built ships, did blacksmithing, carpentering, tailoring for the king and chiefs, and did many other things imitated from the foreigners. Hawaiians built the first sugar mill and made fine molasses. But when the constitution was made, men ceased to practice these crafts. Here is something to think over. Men were glad in those days to work hard and acquire a name for skill in order to find a chief. The name of carpenter to So-and-so, blacksmith to So-and-so, boat-builder to So-and-so, made both man and chief famous. And for pay he received land, a strip out of a great district to live upon at ease, and food, tapas, and fish nets. These were the reward he received, delightful to his heart as a soft, gentle rain. But today all the craftsman gets is a quarrel over property, a blow at the chin and at the head.

The Holy Bible is a thing to be reverenced, but the learned use it to smite at the chin and the head of their fellows [an allusion to the custom of disputing over Bible texts and doctrines]. There were no such disputes in old times. A man showed his skill and the chief who would listen was the chief to live with. If his lord would not listen he sought a new lord. So Ka-ua-kahi-a-kaha-ola came to Hawaii and found Ka-lani-'opu'u; Lanahu-'imi-haku came from Hawaii and found a lord on Oahu in Ka-ku'ihewa; Lama came from Hawaii and found a lord on Kauai in Kawelo-mahamaha-i'a-pela; Ka-pou-kahi sought a lord on Hawaii in Kamehameha. So it often happened that a kahuna would study first and become skilled and then seek a chief, if no great chief then a lesser one, and so the skilled men did in old days to make their names known. Have the clever men today any profound knowledge? Today the whole nation is being taxed, and the teachers are being paid by the government, and as to the knowledge they get I do not feel sure about it. I had no teacher to teach me the alphabet and numbers, but I acquired knowledge without going through the elementary school. No one ever taught me to add, multiply, subtract, or to divide the remainder into fractional parts and change these into decimals. I entered high school without taking up the preparatory steps. . . . We learned and sought after knowledge like Ka-ua-kahi-a-kaha-ola. The government did not pay for our teachers; the pupils themselves taught each other with great patience.

We learned geography, navigation, physical geography, geometry, mathematics, latitude and longitude, calculations of time, the firmament, the earth, astronomy, science, about thunder and lightning, comets, flying stars, maps, places mentioned in the Bible, religion, anatomy, the study of mankind, oratory, reading, laws, charts for sailing, calendars, singing by note and ordinary singing, and some were taught drawing and making plates for printing. . . . All these things were taught to us while we were still wearing the loin cloth, for we were still girded with the loin cloth when the Lahainaluna school was built in 1831 and up to 1840. . . .*

The burden of taxes for public education would be worth-while if the pupils could have the delight of handling the instruments for determining latitude and longitude, watch time by the telescope and determine the meridian of the sun, see the sun, moon and stars and their motions in the heavens, the lightning and what it does. Such things are an important part of education. . . . The king and Isaac of Pu'uloa are getting rich by running the salt water into patches and trading salt with other islands. How would it be to have a steam engine at Hilo to make salt until the land is full to overflowing? Or if a steam engine could spout clouds of steam, that would descend and irrigate the mountains of Hualalai so that Kailua might become a land of rivers. That would delight Kameha-meha as a result of changing old things for new. At Wailuku a factory was set to weaving cloth, and David Malo made some spinning wheels and spun thread and had his own cloth made. Kua-kini spun some thread in Hawaii and sent it to the factory and had cloth made out of it. That ended the old craftsmanship.

John Young as Minister of the Interior did his work well. He used his knowledge of Hawaiian learning with whatever he could learn from this new period and what he could pick up in the homes of the chiefs. It is only the glutton who fails to gather knowledge in the presence of chiefs. Little boys and lads from the country may prove that they are of

* *Ke Au 'Oko'a*, July 29, 1869.

Ulunui. Before the laws were passed people made money by building cat-boats (*wa'apa kuapo'i*) and one- or two-masted schooners and trading from one port to another and between the islands peddling Hawaiian products, and many enriched themselves in those years. Lahaina was perhaps the best-known port for shipbuilding and trading. But when the law was established some were punished for peddling foreign goods without license, and more than half the traders left the business. [The report of Judge Ricord, March 28, 1848, answers some of these com-plaints. The peddlers could sell home-grown products and home manu-factures without license, but must have licenses for foreign goods. This was to encourage home production and force foreigners who came to trade to pay for the privilege. A boat owner who traded to another must also have a license. Branding of animals was also provided for. There seem to have been misunderstandings in carrying out these laws.]

The great thing done in the years 1848 to 1850 was the giving of titles to owners of inherited land (*kuleana*). During these years commissioners were appointed to search titles and to travel from Hawaii to Kauai and try cases affecting the division of the *kuleana* of the chiefs, land owners, and commoners. The writer of this history was one of these commis-sioners and he traveled about Molokai, Maui, and Hawaii. The king Kamehameha V was one who helped in this work. Anyone who brought suit had his case tried before the commissioner. The trouble was that some neglected to take out the papers of appeal, others refused to do so and continued to live under their landlord (*konohiki*), and some just let their land go and are regretting their stupidity today. Some let it go because of the expense attached to the appeal, but most were awake and listened and carried out the law and have become landlords over their lands. No chief or land agent has power to disturb their holding. It be-longs to them within and without, above and below; it is theirs to sell or not; the government alone is king over them and has power to tax them. Few people at that time appealed to have their claim adjusted; perhaps the rest are now regretting it. After the adjustment of claims had been made then the land was surveyed and the blue prints were col-lected. After this the Board of Commissioners to Quiet Land Titles was disbanded and the Department of the Interior handled the sales of land.

An epidemic of measles accompanied by dysentery occurred in this year, 1848, of which several thousand died, some chiefs and prominent persons among them. Deaths occurred especially among old people. There died of the high chiefs Lele-io-hoku, Kua-kini's heir; Moses Ke-kua-iwi, the second son of Kina'u and heir of Ka-iki-o-'ewa ruling chief of Kauai; and Ka-'imi-na'auao, the foster son of Kamehameha III. The epidemic broke out first in September in Hilo, Hawaii, brought by an American warship, and spread during 1849 until July when it increased twofold. Some of the Hilo chiefs were stricken and Ka-nuha and Ka-iwi died. The disease spread to Maui and Kai-heʻe-kai took it; then to La-haina and on to Oahu, where men fell in masses, then to Kauai and Nii-hau. . . .

Another noted event was the arrival in July or August, 1849, at Hilo of a French warship under Admiral de Tromelin. Kamehameha was at Hilo at the time visiting the volcano and the old rocks of ʻUmi called Pokahu-o-Hanalei on Mauna Loa, and traveling the road which the old chiefs used to travel.* At their meeting the admiral made himself agree-able and the king and his adopted son and heir Alexander, Kamehameha IV, sailed with him. But in Honolulu the French consul complained to the admiral that the government had broken the treaty with France be-cause of the smashing of the china of the Roman Catholic priests at Kailua by the tax assessors of Kapeau, which according to treaty should have been entered free of duty, and because some persons went upon the premises of the priests to argue with them and used abusive language; and he demanded protection from the government against such persons. He made other complaints which roused the anger of the admiral, who demanded the dismissal of Kapeau as governor of Hawaii. When the king refused, the admiral sent his men ashore and the marines broke up the cannon and the guns and poured the powder into the sea and treated Ke-ku-anaoʻa, the governor of Oahu, shamefully. The king ordered them [his soldiers] not to do battle and they obeyed although it looked like an easy thing to crush that line of marines. . . . The foreign races are quick-tempered and hold nothing sacred in their anger, not even kings or chiefs. They are afraid of nothing and even curse God. Few are the ships on which, from captain to sailors, their language is not filthy and blas-phemous. . . . What Christian government so renowned for education and prayers to God yet lives peacefully without going to war? They never leave their kings without guards to watch over their lives. Their minds are constantly filled with fear and evil desires.

The Hawaiian nation loves its king and chiefs. If a chief expresses a wish, his people see to it that his words are not spoken in vain. The foreigners saw this and made this country their home and never thought of returning to their own land. They made Hawaii their own country to dwell in and leave their bones to whiten in. All the old foreigners who lived here in the time of Kamehameha and before have died here in Ha-waii, and their descendants are among us. Some of the foreigners who

* *Ke Au ʻOkoʻa*, Aug. 19, 1869.

came to trade and invest have also stayed; few have returned to their own governments. As for the missionaries, some returned and others have become old residents here (*kama'aina*) and their children have taken up the works of their fathers and helped to educate the people and work for the kingdom of God. Some of their children have bought land and become owners of stock farms and sugar plantations and have made slaves out of some of the people with work. And some have become steersmen and navigators for the government. The Hawaiian people welcome the stranger freely; rich and poor, high and low give what they can. The strangers call this love ignorance and think it is good for nothing. The love upon which they depend is a love based upon bargaining, good for nothing but rubbish blown upon the wind. The younger people are beginning to follow the foreign teaching. They are not a race of beggars who go begging from door to door however much they may trouble their blood relations in this way, but it is an old custom when a man is on the road to ask and receive entertainment. They were taught not to take, but to ask. The poor, blind, lame, and crippled, were seldom seen; they were cared for by relatives, orphans were unknown. If one found a waif and attempted to take him in and make him a kind of servant, his blood relations would come and snatch him away unless he were being brought up like an own child. But today the government is doing the asking; it is sending papers from one end of the group to the other and asking what each will give. . . .*

By 1850 the Hawaiian government had been established as a constitutional government with the power over life or death, wealth or poverty, sorrow or joy, love or unkindness, for the whole nation. In that year was established a House of Representatives of the people (*Hale 'aha'olelo 'oko'a ko na Lunamaka'ainana*) comprising twenty-seven members who met separately from the House of Nobles (*Hale 'aha'olelo o no na 'li'i*) under rules of procedure following the rules government the legislature of the United States of America. In looking back it seems as if this House elected from the common people did most of the work. Most of the bills for improving conditions in the country were introduced in this House, and it was this House which prevented oppressive taxation of the commoners. . . . The Hon. William L. Lee presided over the Legislature and everything ran smoothly. New laws were made and old laws dropped. Mr. Lee was spokesman for the people, John 'I'i for the chiefs, and Dr. Judd for the king. These three were empowered to make new laws for the government to be published in 1852 in the Hawaiian newspaper *Elele* (Messenger) a copy of which was to be distributed to each member of of the legislature so that all could discuss the new laws before their pro-

---

* *Ke Au 'Oko'a*, Aug. 26, 1869.

visions came to vote.* In 1852 the House of Representatives met in their house of assembly called Maunakilika, presided over by the Hon. W. L. Lee. Some awkwardness was caused by the distance apart of the two houses of legislature when some question came up which required joint action, and a lump sum was voted to build a House of Parliament. This is the house that stands outside the old fort of Ke-kua-nohu; the old court house was in the yard of Captain Neal which was sold to the Roman Catholic convent. Business houses were set far apart in those days. The legislature did a great deal of work that year. Women and girls, and boys under twenty, were made exempt from poll tax and women were made exempt from making tapa and twine for the land agent. Taxes on cats and some other minor things were abolished.

In this year 1852 the Planters' Association (*hui mahi'ai*) was formed, in whose annual meeting the members took as much pleasure as they used to take in attending the Makahiki festival of old after the *hiu-wai* bathing. . . . A thousand dollars that year and six hundred annually was the sum appropriated by the government for the association. The chairman set aside this money this money for the planters. What became of it? Perhaps it was used for the Planters' Association of Lihu'e, Kauai to which this chairman belonged. Perhaps for flower growing, for the same chairman tried to set aside lands about the fort for farming and flower growing. Perhaps flower growing is a proper vocation for the government, perhaps not. On East Maui there was a Planters' Association in which all worked together year after year for more than thirty years. This is the way it worked: The idea of the association was to plant taro and when they had thirty or forty acres planted to divide the work and do a little at a time, a house for one, a stone wall for another, an 'awa plot for a third, and so on for each partner in the association. Then they got saddle gear, good horses, fine clothes, hogs, cattle, and they got all sorts of food ready for a feast, the first feast of the association. The feast lasted for a week and was run at a loss, but it was not discontinued because their hearts were set on it. This stimulated the members to take an interest in planting. Perhaps if their representatives had asked for some thousands for the association the kingdom might have been bene-fited by seeing large areas of land put into cotton, 'awa, sugarcane, and coffee; and peoples' interest might have been aroused in the work. But it was the foreigners who received attention; if a foreign association asked for an appropriation for some small enterprise they received it.

* For the constitution of 1852 see "Constitution granted by His Majesty Ka-mehameha III by and with the advice and consent of the Nobles and Representa-tives of the people in Legislative Council assembled," June 14, 1852, Honolulu, 1852, together with the "Rules of the House of Representativs," 1853 (printed in Hawaiian and English).

The king and the chiefs started a planters' association at Kawaiaha'o called the Planters' Association of the King, and each member was taxed for it, but it soon disbanded because it was agreed that each member was to farm on his own land, and there was no incentive to arouse enthusiasm. No boy enjoys a game without a playmate nor would a boy progress in his lessons without schoolmates. No minister enjoys preaching to an empty church, and so it goes with the world. . . .

The new laws proposed in this legislature were a great gain, but they were not all passed in the upper house. One that I think would have been of advantage to the people proposed to have the judges (*lunakanawai*) elected and dismissed by the people instead of by the governors of the island. Some judges did not uphold the laws, led immoral lives, drank, and indulged in unlawful practices for which they punished others. They punished adulterers and drunkards according to the law, but some were known to have women and to be themselves drunkards, and it was the common people who suffered from this. Another law which the upper house did not pass proposed to have the tax assessor (*luna'auhau*) chosen by vote of the people since it was the people who had to pay the taxes. . . . Another proposed to have the governor (*ali'i kia'aina*) so elected because it was the people who suffered under poor government. . . . Before the time of Kamehameha the head of a district was appointed by the ruling chief and he had the power to act for the ruling chief. After the time of Kamehameha and up to the time of the constitution the power of the governor (*kia'aina*) was lessened and he served under the chief justice, the ministers, and others heads of the government. His duties were given to the marshal, the customs officer, the Minister of the Treasury, the Minister of the Interior, the Board of Education, the Chief Justice, and into other hands. . . .*

There were however some changes passed by the House which the Nobles did not vote down. One important one was that bills which had to do with internal taxes must come first before the House but in case of foreign difficulty the king and the House of Nobles had the united power to impose taxes. The people were also given the power of controlling government properties. A bill apportioning government funds must first be presented in the House of Representatives. . . . The king also agreed to pay legislators three dollars for each working day and mileage for traveling expenses. . . . The law that brought the greatest benefit was that which gave the legislature the right to audit the books of the government officials . . . in order to prevent suspicion of misuse of funds. . . . So the new law was passed in May, 1852, and the occasion was celebrated by the firing of a salute of twenty-one guns from Punchbowl, and it became the

* *Ke Au 'Oko'a*, Sept. 2, 1869.

law governing this group of islands. This was the second law given by Kamehameha III. The first was that called the constitution of Lua'ehu for which the king alone was responsible. The king saw how the chiefs and the *konohiki* oppressed the commoners, took their lands and their plantings, and robbed them of their fishnets and canoes, and he gave laws to protect them. But because the first law was defective, the king asked the two houses of the legislature to correct it, and in 1852 the new laws were confirmed.*

* *Ke Au 'Oko'a*, Sept. 9, 1869.

CHAPTER XXXI

Death of Kamehameha III

To a people living happily in a pleasant land with purple mountains, sea-girt beaches, cool breezes, life long and natural, even to extreme old age [to these people], with the coming of strangers, there came contagious diseases which destroyed the native sons of the land. No longer is the sound of the old man's cane heard on the long road, no longer do the aged crouch about the fireplace, no longer do those helpless with age stretch themselves on their beds, no longer do they remain withering in the house like the cane-blossom stalks plucked and dried for the dart-throwing game. We are praying to God that we may reach the length of life of our forbears. We build churches, labor day and night, give offerings to charity and the Sabbath dues, but the land is become empty; the old villages lie silent in a tangle of bushes and vines, haunted by ghosts and horned owls, frequented by goats and bats.

The smallpox came, and dead bodies lay stacked like kindling wood, red as singed hogs. Shame upon those who brought the disease and upon the foreign doctors who allowed their landing! The ship displayed the yellow flag, and the pilot went out and returned without going on board and told the chiefs that the ship had disease aboard and a foreigner had taken it. So the chiefs sent Dr. Porter Ford to the ship. He told the chiefs what the disease was, and the chiefs and foreign ministers allowed the man to be brought ashore at Kahaka'aulana and the foreigners on the ship to be quarantined for a few days at Kapua on the south side of Waikiki. The chiefs really wanted to send the ship away without landing, but they yielded to the foreign ministers. Three months later the disease broke out like a volcanic eruption. It started at Kikihale on the northwest side of town in Ka-'ai-one's yard, it is said, among some washwomen who lived in the house. The family hid the disease. In this same yard was an assistant doctor called Kentucky (Kinikake) Desha. Friends went in secret to see the girl until the eruption turned yellow, and then it was reported to the government and Dr. Judd, Dr. Rooke, and other doctors were called in. This was in May, 1853, and legislature was in session. A strict quarantine was declared, but it was too late; the house should be thatched before the rainy season (*ako e ka hale a pa'a, a i ke komo ana i ka ho'oilo, 'a'ole e kulu ia e ke kuaua o ka Hilinehu*). On

Thursday the case was discovered and on Friday it was isolated at the house for storing ox carts at Honuakaha on the south side of town, and this became a receiving station for smallpox patients. On Saturday the marshal (*ilamuku*), acting under orders of the government, set fire to the house from which the patient had been removed. People in town from other islands went to see it burn and then returned to Maui, Hawaii, Kauai, where they broke out themselves and spread the disease to these islands. Some went to Koʻolau, ʻEwa, Waialua, Waiʻanae, and the Waiʻalae beaches. Everywhere there was mourning and lamentation.

The disease spread through the row of houses on the northwest side of Maunakea street seaward of the infected house and then cut straight out to Kapuʻukolo. From Maunakea street it passed to the Kikihale Stream and up Nuʻuanu street to the land *mauka* of Waikahalulu and down to the beach at Kapapoko. The house at Honuakaha was crowded, and Mr. Johnstone's house on Kahuʻa plain was taken as a hospital and the other houses in the yard put to use. A hundred were stricken in a day; scarcely one out of ten lived. The writer went into the hospital and saw for himself how fatal the disease was, even under foreign doctors. If the pimple was spotted and pointed there was hope of cure; in from ten to fifteen days the patient was well. When the throat first became sore a gargle of *kukui* juice and *ʻohiʻa* bark was used, the patient bathed for seven days, and the skin covered with a paste which caused the scabs to fall off. The writer himself saved over a hundred persons [with such treatment], and some are living today whom he treated at Kipahulu where the government could not care for patients. Eruptions in the hair took longer to cure, and those who had the disease longer became pitted so that they show the marks today.

From the last week in June until September the disease raged in Honolulu. The dead fell like dried *kukui* twigs tossed down by the wind. Day by day from morning till night horse-drawn carts went about from street to street of the town, and the dead were stacked up like a load of wood, some in coffins, but most of them just piled in, wrapped in cloth with heads and legs sticking out. When the graveyard at Honuakaha was filled, Keoneʻula was taken for a burial ground and the plains of Kaiwiʻula and the rocky land of Mauʻoki and Laepohaku. From Maunalua to Moanalua in the district of Kona the dead lay buried. Death spread to ʻEwa, to Halawa, to Waimanalo, until it surrounded Oahu. Some large tracts were entirely denuded, some had but a few survivors. Not a family but bore its loss.* On Maui there was not a member of the Board of Health who did anything to care for the sick as they were cared for by the government in Honolulu and places in its vicinity. The police just

* *Ke Au ʻOkoʻa*, Sept. 9, 1869.

carried them away to some distant place and left them without medical care or proper food. The whole population was wiped out from Wakiu, the uplands of Kawaipapa, Palemo, and *mauka* of Waika'akihi in the Hana district, and so for Kipahulu and Kaupo.

The reason why so many died was, first, through ignorance; second, through incredulity; third, through not listening to advice. They had had no experience with contagious diseases nor had their grandparents before them except during the cholera epidemic of Kamehameha's day, and when the smallpox came they regarded it with curiosity rather than with fear. Only when they saw the dead strewn like *kukui* branches did terror fall upon them. The wife nursed the husband or the husband the wife, and when the children fell ill the parents nursed them. This is how the disease spread. Those who did not go near a house where there was disease did not fall ill. . . . It was among the commoners that the deaths occurred. Few of the chiefs died and among the members of the legislature not one was overtaken by the disease although they looked after the people and helped bury the dead. It was said that God preserved them because they were the law makers, and He also preserved the king and the royal family. For six months the epidemic lasted, by October its rage seemed spent. Ten thousand of the population are said to have died of this disease.

The year 1854 was celebrated for the disputes that arose in the legislature, the first over the payment for the medicines used by the doctors and for their attendance during the epidemic, one doctor in particular who had done his best to help save the lives of the people, becoming out of patience with the whole nation because the dispute lasted so long and was even carried over to the next session. The second [dispute concerned] the valuation of a piece of land governed by the queen. This land covered that part of Waikahalulu adjoining the sea and called today 'Aina-hou. The queen wished to sell it. The king (whose petition was presented by the writer of this history) put its value at $30,000, the legislature at $15,000. The question was debated from Monday until Saturday when finally it was put through at a compromise for $20,000 and the king graciously accepted the offer. But the next week the dispute began again because the Chief Justice pointed out to the committee of the House that the queen had no right to sell the land as it belonged to the government, and it was only their consideration for the queen that would make them give her $15,000, and this sum was accordingly passed as a gift to the queen. . . . But it seemed to the writer that the chief justice was arguing without knowing anything about the granting of land right. . . . If his opinion was correct that the queen had no right to the land of Waikahalulu toward the sea, known as Kuloloia, then the legislature had not the least right to give to the queen money for which the commoners had been taxed. This would be favoritism. The money which the commoners earned with the sweat of their brows, the poor people whose bodies were worn and their clothes ragged and their noses running, should not be so wasted. . . . The queen should prove her claim to the land before the courts. The Hawaiian historian was firm and the House voted not to give any money to the queen. When the Nobles heard of the vote, which corresponded with the wish of the majority, they too refused the money to the queen. A committee was sent to confer with the king, but he refused to see them as he wished to take the case for the queen before the land court. He therefore sent for the British lawyer, Montgomery, to try his suit for the property of the queen.

As soon as the town heard that the king was bringing suit for the land of his queen the British consul, Miller, came to the house of Ka-'eo where the king often stayed, with an offer to purchase the property for his government for $80,000. The king refused to sell to another government. Then came a letter from a company formed of the wealthiest citizens of the town of which Dr. G. P. Judd was chairman, offering $100,000 for the land, and again the king refused. The king said, "I do not want to sell the land of my queen to another government, as it is close to the port where ships anchor. I wish to sell it to my own government at a reasonable price and I left it to the legislature to decide this price. But first, you vote to give a sum of money, and then to give a smaller sum. [Then you] say there is no right of property, and now you vote to give nothing, and to take the land for the government. You cannot get anywhere in this way." The two houses were much upset when they heard this, and they voted to purchase at $22,000 and to have the principal left in the hands of the government not to be drawn for ten years and the queen to draw the interest. This land so bought by the government is situated on the east side of the harbor of Kou and extends from Pakaka to Kaka'ako [that is, from lower Fort street to Kewalo basin] and is called 'Aina-hou . . . Had he sold to another government the land would have yielded a much larger sum, hence the king showed in this transaction that he placed the good of his country before the personal gain of his wife. On the whole the legislative session of this year, 1854, was one of long disputes which prolonged the session and brought the expenses up to between $20,000 and $30,000, and the king's speech adjourning the session was not a friendly one.

This year, 1854, was marked by the death of Kamehameha III, the king so beloved by the whole people and by the men of other races who lived in the country. Perhaps no king born to the throne ever made a better ruler. . . . He made all men free and equal. There were no slaves with backs bent by labor, none with the corners of the eye tattooed, no pipe-lighters for others, none who were born servants, neither free eaters (*noa*), despised slaves (*kauwa*), none with a mark on the forehead. The tabus of the chiefs were all done away. . . . Many kinds of tabus run through a chief's veins; many kinds of tabus belong to the chiefs as gods; the kahuna's tabus pertain to the gods, but it is the chiefs for whom the tabus are carried out; the kahunas are the executors (*ilamuku*) who carry on the tabus of the gods, and the younger generation are those who carry on the chiefs' tabus. Although these tabus were all abolished before Kamehameha II became king, nevertheless they were all well fulfilled in Kamehameha III whose tabu was greater than any king or chief on earth. . . .*

A little schooner with two masts, well manned with captain and sailors, ready to sail out on the far ocean. Such is the Hawaiian kingdom. A little kingdom, but it has been given a room in the great exposition in Paris, the only government from the Pacific to be represented. The European governments are astonished to see the sign outside the Hawaiian room at the exposition. They cannot believe it. A race of man-eaters are the Hawaiian people, are they not? And do they really have a government? And have they a room here? Then they examine the exhibit and see a cloak made out of bird feathers, a wreath of bird feathers, and a number of other objects from ancient times. They see the products of the country—sugar, molasses, rice, coffee. At the office of the Hawaiian government they find books from the first *pi-a-pa* primer to books large and small, the Bible, and newspaper files beginning with the *Lama Hawaii* and the *Kumu Hawaii* and ending with the *Au 'Oko'a* and the *Ku'oko'a*. Books for education, books of laws from the beginning to the present time. The office has a quantity of Hawaiian manuscripts. The men interested in education look at each other and say, "This cannibal island is ahead in literacy; and the enlightened countries of Europe are behind it!" Hawaii is a country with a constitution, with laws and by-laws; its throne is established by constitutional authority. Most of the European countries are still ruled by the power of the king and nobles alone. Hawaii is ahead of them.

Soon after the adjourning of the legislature the king went to Oneawa in Kailua for vacation and seemed restored in health. . . .† He went fishing and sea bathing at Kailua and really felt better. His feelings of nausea and the convulsions caused by indulgence in drink left him as he lived a temperate life. Another month he passed at Kikiwelawela in He'eia and at Ahulimanu and was pleasantly entertained by the Roman

* *Ke Au 'Oko'a*, Sept. 16, 1869.
† *Ke Au 'Oko'a*, Sept. 23, 1869.

Catholic priests. The people believed that he would turn to Catholicism. It may or may not be so, for the minds of chiefs run with their desires like a river whose course is directed into fresh channels with the rainfall. The queen and the minister of the interior went down to visit the king, and the queen saw how much better he looked. After a few days she was ready to go back to the city. "Tomorrow I return," she said. "I will take you back," said the king. "No, we return alone. You are much better here." She feared that if he got back to the city the foreigners would get him to drinking again. The king however promised to return to Koʻolau and he escorted the queen back to the palace as was indeed the old established etiquette.

But when he reached the city a warship had arrived and he was detained for an audience. Then Piʻikoi invited the king to attend his house warming at Kewalo and the king consented and rode out that evening with the queen and the minister of the interior and some of the chiefs. The table was loaded with everything good to eat, but there were no strong drinks, only ale and beer. The royal party left after the feasting and toasts, but at the palace the queen noticed that the king's horse was left saddled. "Are you going to ride again?" she asked. "I will come back right away," he promised. He returned to the feast where the drinking had now begun and remained drinking until midnight, when he returned to the palace. The queen saw that he had been drinking and exclaimed, "So you went back to drink again!" The king answered meekly as he was wont to do when he had been drinking, and said, "Let us go outside where it is cool." The queen demurred lest he take cold, but he insisted and they prepared to sleep outside. He lay on a sofa at the side of the pile of sleeping mats with the queen watching at his head until the king fell asleep with Ka-ʻeo and the rest at some distance from them. Shortly after she heard him breathing heavily and cried out, "Wake up! wake up! you must have taken cold; let us go into the house." She lifted him and called John Young to help carry him into the house. Dr. Rooke was sent for, and by morning the king was better, but suffering from headache. He asked for brandy, but the queen hesitated until some one advised it. The headache was cured, the king was able to walk, and he took a drink secretly. Nausea and convulsions followed, and he was delirious and had to be put to bed. The attack came on at the house of John Young in Kinaʻu's yard, and he was carried to his own house at Hoʻihoʻi-ke-ea in the palace yard. A second doctor was called in, an Englishman named Smith, and this man informed the foreigners waiting outside that the king was dying. The queen was grieved. She and the chiefs saw him sleeping and believed that his illness would soon be over as at other times, and here it was being noised about town that he was dying, and the commoners were hushed and broken-hearted and the town fast becoming demoralized.

At eleven in the morning on Monday, December 16, 1854, the cannon boomed its signal and the flag at half-mast gave warning of his death. Our parent Kua-papa-nui had passed on with the procession that moves on forever. The whole nation heard the report, from 'Ewa and the Ko'olaus, from every mountainside; and the foreigners within the town, both strangers and those of the land. The sound of wailing rose and increased like the clamorous sound of the breaking waves. It beat upon the ears insistently and mournfully like the reiterative strokes of the tapa stick in the hands of the cunning craftsman who beats out a fine cloth. Like the plaintive voice of the yellow-feathered *lale* bird singing its dirge, was the tremulous voice of the queen, lost in the thousands of voices of the crowd who stood without. For a year or more she wept aloud, longer than was known of any other queen for a royal husband, even those who wear black in sign of mourning but seldom shed real tears, and after a few months turn to idle jesting and foolish romances.

When the common people of the land knew that their ruling chief was dead they raised their lamentations to heaven that Kane-breaker-of-the-heavens might hear and pour down rain to fall as tears upon the earth. Some sailed to Oahu to weep with the queen. The inter-island boats *Manuokekai* and *Kalama* and the sailing ships that touched in such numbers at the islands were crowded to overflowing. The queen invited the huge procession of mourners to enter the tabu grounds [of the palace] where orange and mango trees stood weighted down with fruitage, and the gates were thrown open and the body of the king taken into the palace until the time of the funeral, and the public allowed to enter and mourn him there as they wished. On January 10, 1855, the bier was lifted and carried away. It was a fine day after a time of rain, the roads were dry again and the highway was crowded with people of all races come to see the funeral procession of the king.

King Ka-lani-waiakua Ka-lani-kau-io-kikilo Kiwala'o-i-ke-kapu, Kamehameha III, died at Ho'iho'i-ke-ea in the palace yard, December 16, 1854. He was born at Keauhou at North Kona, Hawaii, on the day of Hune on the 11th day of Hinaiaeleele, August 17, 1813 by the English calendar, although some claim March 17 as the date. He lived only a little over forty years, but these years were rich in achievement; no one could find fault with any of his acts. Why did all lament him? Because his deeds were in the cause of truth. He worked to benefit chiefs and commoners alike.

He attained to the ruling power when he was but eleven years of age. . . . In his speech at Honuakaha he proclaimed "The government of learning" in which chiefs should teach commoners and each one teach another. Teachers were distributed about the islands, and only those who could not walk stayed away from school. Some schools had a hundred, some a thousand pupils. From children to bearded men, all were gathered into the schools. Buildings went up over night to serve as school houses; if a landlord refused to build he lost his post. A line separated those who could read from those who could not. The concert exercises by which they were taught delighted the people. The rhythmical sound of the voices in unison as they rose and fell was like that of the breakers that rise and fall at Waialua or like the beat of the stick hula in the time of Pele-io-holani and Ka-lani-'opu'u.

A ea mai ke kai o Waialua,	Let the sea of Waialua rise,
Wawa no 'olelo 'oko'a i pali,	Let the roar echo over the hills,
Nunu me he ihu o ka pua'a hae la,	Rumble like the grunt of the wild pig.
'Ako ka lau o ka nalu pi'i i ka pali,	Let the rising wave break the leaf from the cliff.
Ku pali Kaiaka i ka 'ino,	Kaiaka cliff stands above the storm,
'Ino ka lae o Kukuilau'ania,	Stormy is the cape of Kukuilau-'ania,
He Maka-nui.	Windy indeed it is!
Makani me he ao la ka leo o ke kai,	The voice of the sea rises upon the wind
Kuli pa'ia wawa ka uka a Lihu'e,	Deafening those in the uplands of Lihu'e,
O me he 'oka'a la i ke kula,	As it is borne over the plain,
Ke kula hahi a ke kai e halulu nei,	The rumbling of the sea treading upon the plain.
Halulu ma ke Ko'olau,	Rumbling over Ko'olau,
Ho'olono 'Ewa,	'Ewa hearkens,
'A'ole i 'ike i ka po ana a ka nalu,	She has not seen the rising of the waves
Kuhihewa wale no Wahiawa - e.	And mistakes it for Wahiawa.

Because they took so much pleasure in the old chants, they used the old tunes for the recitations in unison:

Mai malama hou i na akua la'au,	Do not keep any more wooden gods,
E huli kakou i ke 'li'i ola mau,	Turn to the Lord of eternal life,
Maika'i e ho'onui i ke akua maika'i,	Give praise to the good God,

Pela mai 'Io-lani ko Hawaii,

So says 'Iolani (Kamehameha II) chief of Hawaii.

Ua hiki mai nei ke kanawai mau,
Ke hau'oli nei ko kakou na'au,
Ko 'Io-lani makua Ka-'ahu-manu
  me Ka-umu-ali'i,
E mana'o i ke Akua ko luna ali'i.

Hither have come the eternal laws,
Our hearts rejoice in them,
'Iolani's foster mother, Ka-'ahu-manu, and Ka-umu-ali'i
Taught us to believe in God, the king above.*

Na laua kakou i kauoha mai,
E paulele mau i kee akua maika'i,
I ola ka 'uhane o kakou a pau,
Ka puaneane ke ao malama mau,

They two have counseled us
To have faith in the good God,
That our souls may be saved
To dwell in the land of eternal light,

A kaua mai nei ka po'e kimopo,
Ua malama mai Iesu ia kakou,
Iehova ke Akua ka kakou e hapai,
I ka pu'uhonua kakou e ola ai.

And when foes come to oppose us
Jesus will give us His care.
Jehovah is the God whom we laud,
Our refuge in whom we find life.

That is how the government of learning moved along quickly so that within half a year there were thousands of persons who knew how to read, write, and spell. The governor of Kauai had his own teacher, so had the governor of Maui, and this humble writer was one of those who taught. Many of these old-time teachers are still living. Of the pupils who entered the first, second, and third classes at Lahainaluna, half of were elementary teachers whose knowledge and capacity had been tested before the missionary teachers, and the chiefs had selected from among them those whom each wished to educate at Lahainaluna. That is how the government of learning moved ahead. . . . "I want a government of learning," said the king, and the chiefs supported him.

The king said, "I give my kingdom to God." . . . At this time the country was filled with people, two or three times four hundred on each large estate, up to five times four hundred. Schools were built in the mountains and in the crowded settlements. Waipi'o had school houses near the coast and in the uplands. At Kahalepo'ai, Hauone, Kalakoa, Wahiawa, Halemano, and Kanewai there were large villages with teachers and schoolhouses; so at Lihu'e, Kalena, Maunauna, Kake, and Pu'uku'u. There were several school houses and teachers for each district. Hono-uliuli had over ten school houses with their teachers. The lowest number of pupils to each school was 50 up to 200 or more. Oahu was then thickly populated. It is sad to see how in so short a time whole villages have

* *Ke Au 'Oko'a,* Sept. 23, 1869.

vanished leaving not a man. . . . And as the kingdom of letters moved quickly so also moved the kingdom of God. . . . The teachers performed both duties, they taught letters and promoted the kingdom of God. Singing and prayer came first, then testimony. There were church meetings on the Sabbath and on Wednesday evening, meetings for testimony on Thursday and Friday, and meetings of the women as well. . . . The whole nation took up the duty at the command of the king alone without aid from the missionaries. They read print, they went to prayers, to meeting, to testimony services, to the preaching services, and when they sang, they sang their songs as they had their old chants to the tunes of the *'ala'apapa* hula of Kukueuhi and others, and quavered like the *'alala'* hula of Kawaikuapu'u and his school. So sang Ke-lou Ka-makau, Ka-'ele-o-waipi'o, Ku'oko'a, and the rest. They sang their songs with the belief that the kingdom of God would not be displeased with their way of singing so long as it was sung with a humble heart by a penitent, one whose prayers were uttered in faith.

During these years when a teacher became the leader for the kingdom of God in Hawaii no one questioned the division between the old and the new religion. There was only one principle of division in the kingdom of God, all that did not belong to it was sin. God did not say this or that was wrong; it was the kingdom of God which was the dividing line. The kingdom of Hawaii became a kingdom that worshiped God. The chiefs upheld the hands of Ka-'ahu-manu, and the nation turned to the truth. No one during those years could be seen worshiping in the old way; no one was to be seen inspired by a spirit, possessed by spirits, practicing sorcery; there was not much 'awa drinking; no fire places for burning in the *kuni* sorcery were to be seen, nor any of those ancient practices which had passed away at the time of free eating in Liholiho's day. It was a time when all Hawaii turned to do homage to the kingdom of God. The plover flew in peace, the rat squeaked without fear in his hole, the shark showed his teeth unmolested in the wave, there had never been such peace before.

Some of missionaries thought it wrong to protect this government of God; the kingdom of God is not a kingdom ruled by a king [they said]. Perhaps this was not the king's thought in joining the kingdom which he ruled as chief with the kingdom of God. He did not mean to give up his rule as chief, but to make God the protector of the kingdom and of his rule over it. That was his real thought. God was to be the judge to set his kingdom to rights, and that was why he commanded the whole nation to learn to read and to turn to the word of God. Strange indeed were the hard thoughts of the missionary! . . . So they girded up their loins, sharpened their knives, and chose which part of the fish they would take, one the side piece, another the belly, one the eyes, another white meat, and another red meat. So they chose as they pleased. When the last man of them had come they were treated like chiefs; lands were parceled out to them; they were given the same honors as Ka-umu-aliʻi. Yet they found fault. Now you want to close the door of heaven to the Hawaiians. You want the honors of the throne for yourselves because you sit at ease as ministers upon your large land. . . .

Kamehameha III wanted his race to become god-fearing people, to become ministers of the gospel. In Ka-ʻahu-manu's day there were many such; for example, Ka-hana-nui, Na-ʻaoa, Ka-makahiki, Wahine-aliʻi, Kaʻi-ana, Puni-haole, and others. These men may have been ignorant, but they knew their Bibles, and the chiefs and people, the rich and the poor, were led to God. Then there were ministers appointed who were helped by the government through the legislature to consult with the king. The kingdom of Hawaii became famous because of these words of Kamehameha III. Rich, aye rich! It could be cut up, salted down, hung out to dry; it filled the big drying frame, the little drying frame until the smell of it was wafted from one end of the islands to the other end. This was the result of the land-giving fishermen of the chief. The hands trembled with eagerness to give with the right hand, with the left hand, until the head nodded, the chin swayed wearily. It was grabbed openly and passed on behind the back. Great lands were theirs until they were full of pride; they built little houses, big houses, fine wooden fences, grand sleeping houses; there was not a grain spared by the plover, the bird from Kahiki. All was included in the saying, "I give my kingdom to God."

It was said at Honuakaha that a man should not leave his wife or the wife her husband. The chiefs and prominent people had at this time many wives, and Kamehameha ordered that polygamy should no longer be practiced, but a man must have but one wife and he was to choose the wife he was most fond of, and the woman must choose one husband and they two were to be married before God and become one before God. Marriage was held sacred at this time when marriage took place before the minister, but when marriage could be performed by secular law marriage became a pastime for the wealthy man or the loose woman. Married today, divorced tomorrow. In Ka-ʻahu-manu's day the law was enforced and peace reigned.

The king said that the Christian Sabbath should be strictly kept. . . . The Hawaiians saw how the missionaries kept the Sabbath during the first years after they came to Hawaii; no work of any kind was done, no kindling of fires. After a time the Sabbath became a day of pleasure, and people did just as on week days, and for four or five years it was not observed, but when the king's proclamation was made the Sabbath was strictly kept all over Hawaii from 1825 to 1827, and the day became a day of rest for the race. It amazed a Hawaiian to see the day so disregarded as it was on the American coast where the day was not so strictly kept as in Hawaii. In California I saw people hammering, washing, ironing, and doing other work on the Sabbath day.*

"Do not become drunkards," Kamehameha proclaimed in his speech at Honuakaha. The chiefs upheld his words; Ka-'ahu-manu and Ka-lani-moku aided and approved, and liquor was prohibited in the back country. A month had not passed before all the stills were shut down, no liquor flowed, and drinking places and places of amusement were closed both in town and in the country.

Holokapapa a ke 'lii 'aimoku o Kalani	The word of the chief rules over all,
Ku ke hula ha'a ka papa mahimahi.	All move together to enforce the chief's wish.

Ka-'ahu-manu upheld her chief's words lest they be uttered in vain and the tabu became extremely strict; severe penalties were laid down. 'Awa was prohibited and all liquors, even those imported from other countries. Foreigners were forbidden to sell or even give liquor to Hawaiians. Boki helped enforce this prohibition. He had just returned from England with the bodies of the king and queen and at that time he was doing well. There was hope of putting an end to liquor drinking in the group, and Kau-i-ke-aouli's name became famous for this achievement. Even the foreigners' saloons were closed. So with his other prohibitions against murder, adultery, stealing, gambling, infanticide, and sedition. Ka-'ahu-manu proclaimed these laws from Hawaii to Kauai, and the terrible book of the law was given by word of mouth from her lips to uphold her chief in establishing the peace and prosperity of his kingdom. The king's laws were just and good in these early years of the kingdom. They were kept throughout the kingdom and caused education and Christianity to spread rapidly; in these days when there was no written law the nation had a higher standard of right living than some enlightened nations.

These are the works of note which the king accomplished in his youth. He had a mature mind and brought things to pass which really benefited the nation. . . . But his greatest achievement was the change in the form of government to a constitutional monarchy and to a kingdom based upon law. Without this change the kingdom of learning and the kingdom that worshiped God could not have had peace. This benefit the king gave willingly, not in answer to any appeal by the nation to him or to the

* *Ke Au 'Oko'a,* Sept. 30, 1869.

chiefs. It was God alone who charged him with this gift to the nation. The constitution established the king in the right to his possessions and his kingly honor; it provided for the possessions and wealth of the kingdom; it gave to the common people a right to the taxes and the property of the kingdom.

Is it the fact of our having a Christian and literate government that has brought us prosperity? In America there has just been fought a terrible war, a war of devils, costing hundreds of thousands of dollars, to free those who were kept in slavery. It is said that the word of God came to Britain in the time when the disciples of Christ lived and that the Bishop of Rome founded the kingdom of God there. Over six hundred years ago in the time of King John, Britain had a constitution. . . . Has the government always weighed the good of the common people against that of the nobles? Britain is like a huge glass water bottle, smooth and round and glittering outside. The nations praised her and admired her smooth shapeliness and variegated colors, but within were all sorts of stinging, prickly things—sea urchins, sand burrs, the thorny-seeded *nohu* creeper. For years the commoners sought for rights in the land from the nobles, and qould not get the land. The nobles of Britain took away the land from the Irish so that the chiefs and commoners of Ireland lived in poverty, and the Irish had to give gifts to the king and to the church. That is why that land is so rebellious against Britain. The British took the land of the Hindus in Asia; 190,000,000 people are in that land and bitterness and rebellion are in that land. Nor is that all. There are Newfoundland and New Zealand where also there is unrest. How have education, the worship of God, the constitutional forms of government bettered the provinces of Great Britain? . . .

The benefits given by the constitution are those which provide a better life for the common people. In first place, the fishing rights were made free to commoners, and tabu fish have been made free. Second, the small taxes to different land agents were abolished. Third, the taxes paid by women and the confiscation of property to pay taxes were abolished. Fourth, the tabu upon various trees such as *koa, kauila, o'a, koai'e,* sandalwood, and upon such birds as the *mamo* and *'o-'o* from which feathers were taken, has been abolished. Fifth, those who have many children or old people to care for, as well as feeble and deformed persons were freed from taxation. Sixth, Christian worship was introduced. Seventh, ownership of land as freehold was made possible for commoners.* Eighth, protection was given to a man from search and arrest within his own house. Ninth, the roads were improved, such as the Pali Road which has been made serviceable for a horse and carriage. Fifteen

* *Ke Au 'Oko'a,* Oct. 7, 1869.

generations ago Kiha son of Pi'i-lani paved with rocks and straightened the roads of Molokai and Maui and these roads are still preserved today. Ehu, son of Kuaiwa, was another road maker. He was chief of Kona and built a road from the uplands of Kona into Ka-'u which is called "the way of Ehu." Maui, son of Kalana, was one of the ancient chiefs of Maui who made roads twenty centuries ago. The roads in his day were straight and the people were accustomed to running along straight roads; so when certain persons ran after Maui to kill him he made the road go zigzag and it was called "the zigzag road of Maui" (*ke alanui kike'eke'e a Maui*). One is at Waikane and Waiahole in Ko'olaupoko on Oahu, and one at Keka'a between Lahaina and Kaanapali, and another at Kealakahakaha in Kahakuloa on Maui. In Kamehameha III's day the road was a benefit to the poor. But the greatest benefit of all derived from the constitution was the fact that all this was given out of love. The constitution was called "the coming of life," "the granting of life and peace,"—*Ka-la-hiki-ola, Kalana-ola, Kuapapa-nui.*＊

Some people say that the Kamehamehas won the kingdom through successful warfare. Kamehameha made the daughters of his war counselors, who gave him the kingdom, his wives; and their descendants thus became heirs to the kingdom for which Kamehameha had striven. Ka-ho'ano-ku Kina'u was considered for the succession to the kingdom because he was grandson of Ka-manawa, one of the war leaders who fought to place Kamehameha over the kingdom. Ke-kuaiwa Kamehameha was considered because he was a grandson of Ke'e-au-moku, another of the war counselors who faced death for Kamehameha. But at the death of Kau-i-ke-aouli he was succeeded by Kamehameha IV, and it was said that for the first time a grandchild of Kamehameha held the rule over the kingdom for which Kamehameha had himself striven. How did it happen, then, that Kamehameha II and Kamehameha III were chosen rulers over the group? The chiefs disputed about the succession while Kamehameha was living, and Kamehameha asked the opinion of men skilled in genealogies and of the orators and those who knew about government in ancient days. Some of the chiefs and governors thought that the old standards should not count in the succession. But the skilled men told Kamehameha that in order to keep the kingdom united as he left it and prevent its falling to pieces at his death, he must consolidate it under one ruler and must leave it to an heir who was in the ruling line from his ancestors. He should therefore appoint Liholiho his heir and his younger brother, Kau-i-ke-aouli, to succeed him because, although they came from the side of the defeated chiefs who were his enemies and not

＊ A high chief who is a wise ruler and lives like a father to his people, never allowing them to know fear or distress, is spoken of as Kuapapa-nui.

one of whom had aided him to gain the kingdom, they were *pi'o* chiefs belonging to the line of chiefs who owned the rule from their ancestors. Ke-opu-o-lani and her mother, Ke-ku'i-apo-iwa Liliha, and her younger sister, Ka-lani-kau-io-kikilo Ka-lani-akua, were tabu chiefesses of Maui, and they had all fled to Molokai with their mother, Ka-lani-ka-uli-hiwa-kama Ka-lola on acocunt of whose illness they had been overtaken there by Kamehameha before they could reach Oahu. Ke-opu-o-lani was the daughter of Kiwala'o, son of Ka-lani-'opu'u, and heir to the kingdom of Hawaii, who was killed in the battle of Moku'ohai by Kamehameha's warriors. Was Kiwala'o's an unbroken line of succession to the chieftainship over Hawaii? Perhaps so. Ka-lani-'opu'u ruled Hawaii; his father, Ka-lani-nui-a-mamao, ruled Ka-'u and Puna. Keawe ruled Hawaii; his mother was Keakea-lani. The ruling chiefs branched out. There were a multitude of children born to them, but the kingdom could be given to but one. That line of chiefs must become separated as the ruling family and the other relatives must become retainers, executors, and attendants upon that family. How about the mother of Kiwala'o and Ke-ku'i-apo-iwa? Kalola was their mother, descended from a ruling family of Maui with the fire tabu of that island. Ke-opu-o-lani was the child of these two,and Kamehameha II and III were her children. The inheriting of the kingdom by these two chiefs put an end to rebellious thoughts and gave peace to the country. During the long reign of Kamehameha III no civil war arose nor did sedition of any kind disturb it peace.*

* *Ke Au 'Oko'a*, Oct. 14, 1869.

APPENDICES

Appendix I

BATTLES OF/AT

Appendix II

DATES CITED IN TEXT

The following quotation from John F. G. Stokes should be kept in mind before accepting Kamakau's dates:

> Briefly summed up, most of Kamakau's dates in the traditional period related to people who were dead long before he was born; he had no opportunity of ascertaining the dates through tradition, because Hawaiians did not use year dates; he was the first to expound the dates and did so without explanation of their source or his method of obtaining them; they were not accepted by his native contemporaries who, on the other hand, assailed his historic accuracy. . . . There can be no question that the dates now applied to the traditional period of Hawaiian history should be scrutinized most rigidly before acceptance. ("New Bases for Hawaiian Chronology," *41st Annual Report of the Hawaiian Historical Society,* 1932, p. 31.)

1730	Kuali'i dies, 369
1736	Birth of Kamehameha, 210
1765	Battle of Ka-lae-'ili'ili, 83; Ka-iki-o-'ewa born, 350
1766	Ka-hekili becomes ruling chief, 82; Kamehameha-nui's death, 82
1768	Birth of Ka-'ahu-manu, 309
1772	Ka-lani-'opu'u dies (1780), 110
1773	Ka-hahana becomes ruler of Oahu, 130
1775	Birth of Hoapili, 352
1775-1779	Continual fighting between Ka-lani-'opu'u and Ka-hekili, 84
1776	Ka-lani-'opu'u returns to war on Maui, 85
1777-1779	War between Ka-hekili and Ka-lani-'opu'u; Ka-'ahu-manu moves to Hawaii, 310
1778	Cook arrives in Hawaii, 92; Cook off Ko'olau, Maui, 97; Ka-heihei-malie born, 385
1778-1779	Kalani-'opu'u fights around Maui, 91
1779	Cook arrives at Kealakekua, 98
1780	Ke-opu-o-lani born on Maui, 259
1781	Kehekili makes war on Hana, 115; birth of Ka-pi'o-lani, 379
1782	Battle of Honolulu, 82; Ka'uiki fortress captured, 116; Kiwala'o consults with advisors about removal of Ka-lani-'opu'u's body, 117; Ka-'opulupulu killed by Ka-hahana, 133
1782-1790	Kamehameha at war with Keawe-ma'u-hili, 350
1783	Decisive battle between Ka-hekili and Ka-hahana's forces, 136
1784	Ke-ku-haupi'o dies at Napo'opo'o, 126
1785	Kamehameha takes Ka-'ahu-manu for wife, 127; "Kauhola" period or "Laupahoehoe the second," 311
1787	Boat *Kane,* landed at Kauai, 144
1789	Kamehameha deserts Ka-'ahu-manu, 315
1790	*Eleanora* arrives at Maui, 145; explosive eruption at Kilauea, 152
1791	Battle of Ke-pu-waha-'ula, 162; rum introduced to Hawaiians, 193; birth of Ka-lua-i-konahale Kuakini, 388
1792-1794	Vancouver's visits to Hawaii, 368
1793	Death of Ka-hekili, 162, 168; men punished for *Daedalus* incident, 166; Richards born, 406

1831   Teachers began to take census, 236; tax collectors assigned to each island, 256;
            Kuakini has Fort rebuilt, 304; Catholic priests sent home, 328; Lahainaluna
            opens, 405
1832   Mr. Johnstone leaves Kawaiahaʻo, 305; Ka-ʻahu-manu sails for Maui, 306; fifth
            band of missionaries arrives, 306; Ka-ʻahu-manu dies, 308; death of Waipa, 374;
            New Testament printed, 405
1833   Kinaʻu becomes governor of Oahu, 329; Nahi-ʻenaʻena tries to take King to
            Maui, 336
1834   Death of two young chiefs, 339; Kai-ehu found in country, 348; Lunalilo born,
            394
1835   Rev. D. Baldwin moves to Lahaina; Rev. S. Dibble moves to Lahainaluna,
            304; marriage of Nahi-ʻenaʻena and Lele-io-hoku, 340; missionaries appeal for
            more land at Lahainaluna, 355
1836   Rev. Walsh, Catholic priest, arrives, 329; Nahi-ʻenaʻena moves to Wailuku,
            340; Nahi-ʻenaʻena dies, 341; girls' school opened in Wailuku; Hilo Boarding
            School opened, 405
1837   Fathers Short and Bachelot return, 329; Kau-i-ke-aouli marries Kalama, 341;
            Quixote arrives from Tahiti, 345; Kinaʻu visits Lahainaluna, 355
1838   Rev. Tinker returns to U.S., 305
1838-39   Epidemic of mumps, 345
1839   Ship brings pestilence, 236; death of Kinaʻu, 331, 348; arrival of French ship
            Artemise, 331; Ka-iki-o-ʻewa dies, 350; Kuakini marries Puna-hoa, 391; entire
            Bible printed, 405
1840   Arrival of Catholics under Bishop Rouchouze, 332; death of Hoapili, 352
1841   Death of Ka-piʻo-lani, 379, 385; meeting of chiefs at Luaʻehu, 396
1842   Richards and Haʻalilo leave for Europe; America agrees to Hawaiian indepen-
            dence, 367; death of Ka-heihei-malie, 388
1843   Hawaii transferred to Great Britain, 359; restoration by Admiral Thomas, 365;
            England recognizes independence of Hawaii, 368
1844   Epidemic of colds, 237; death of Rev. Dibble, 304; letter from M. Guizot, 367;
            U.S. ratifies recognition of Hawaii, 368; death of Ka-lua-i-konahale Kuakini,
            388, 391
1845   Judd gives up assistant secretaryship, 368; Ke-ka-ulu-ohi dies, 379, 391, 395;
            Richards returns with body of Haʻa-lilio, 398; Richards appointed Minister of
            Education, 406
1846   Richards reads education reports, 405
1847   Richards dies, 406
1848   Measles introduced, 236; Legislature originated, 396; epidemic of measles, 410
1848-1850   Giving of land titles, 410
1849   Arrival of French ship; incident involving Catholics and Governor of Hawaii, 411
1852   Laws published, House meets, 412
1853   Smallpox discovered, 237, 416
1854   Celebrated for disputes in Legislature, 418; death of Kamehameha III, 422
1855   Burial of Kamehameha III, 422
1857   Cold epidemic, 237
1865   Death of Kekela (chiefess), 195

Appendix III

HEIAU NAME AND/OR LOCALITY

'Ahu'ena, Kailua, Kona (Hawaii), 180, 203

Ha'ena, Ewa (Oahu), 172
Halauwailua, SEE Pakini
Hale-'ili-mai'a, 179
Hale-o-Keawe, Honaunau (Hawaii), 64, 117, 118, 180, 203, 285, 322
Haluluko'ako'a, Lahaina (Maui), 188
Hikiau Kealakekua, Kona (Hawaii), 99, 100, 180, 200, 203
Honua'ula, Hana (Maui), 116
Honua'ula, Waipi'o (Hawaii), 14

Kahe-ike, Honolulu (Oahu), 136
Ka-hina-ola (?), 324
Kaipalaoa Pi'ihonua, Hilo (Hawaii), 174, 220
Kaluli (Ka-uli) Pu'uohala, Wailuku (Maui), 85, 167, 188
Kama-i-ke'e-ku, Kahalu'u, Kona (Hawaii), 180
Ka-moho-ali'i, Wai'anae (Oahu), 134
Kanemalohemo, Kaupo (Maui), 66, 188
Kanoa, 16
Kanowa Pu'ueo, Hilo, 108
Kapokea Waihe'e (Maui), 163
Kapukapu-akea, Wailau [Waialua], Molokai, 132
Ke-ahuku, Wailuku (Maui), 188
Ke-alaka'i-honua, Waihe'e (Maui), 188
Keiki-pu'ipu'i, Kailua, Kona (Hawaii), 85, 180
Kuawalu, Honua'ula (Maui), 116

Loaloa, Kaupo (Maui), 66, 188

Mailekini, Kawaihae (Hawaii), 58, 77, 150, 180
Malumaluakua, Wailuku (Maui), 188
Maninini, Kohalalele (Hawaii), 2
Ma'ulili, Kipahulu (Maui), 188
Moa'ula, Waipi'o (Hawaii), 108, 188, 203
Molokini, Kohala (Hawaii), 67
Mulei'ula, Kahei, Kohala (Hawaii), 235

Nu'uanu at mouth of valley (Oahu), 291

'Ohi'a-mukumuku, Kahalu'u, Kona (Hawaii), 85, 180, 200
Olopio, Wailuku (Maui), 188

Paka'alana, Waipi'o (Hawaii), 1-2
Pakini Kama'oa, Ka'u (Hawaii), 108
Papa, 179
Pau-maka, Kaupo (Maui), 188
Pihana, Wailuku (Maui), 82, 188, 217
Puehu, Wai'anae (Oahu), 203
Pu'uhonua, Honaunau (Hawaii), 180
Pu'u-kohola, Kawaihae (Hawaii), 150, 154-55, 158, 180
Pu'u-maka'a, Kaupo (Maui), 66, 188

Uli, Waimea (Hawaii), 83
'Umi, Hualalai (Hawaii), 35

Wailehua, Lahaina (Maui), 73, 188

Appendix IV

Appendix V

SAYINGS

Alas for Huahuanana (alas for staring fool), 40
Anger rises in the heart, 83
Bare of inhabitants is Kohala, 57
Beautiful above are the cliffs of Wailau, 238
Be careful with the offspring of I, 62
Cock's roost has been taken by the hen, 81
Dream of canoes or *'ulei* berries, 73
Even the smallest patches are taxed, 232
Eyelids like a rat's, 200
Eyes like a rat's, skin yellow as a pandanus leaf, 235
Fish have entered the net, 161
Fish of Piliwale are stranded, 407
Flowers wilted in the sunlight, 25
Girdled with the intestines (reference to Boki), 287
Hawaii of Keawe, Maui of Kama-lala-walu, 300
He is an *uku* fish, 226
Hi-ka-palale (imitation of speech of Cook's men), 96
House should be thatched before the rainy season, 416
It is only a broken gourd that needs mending, 404
It is the top stone that rolls down, 376
Ivory tusk ornament has come here, 196
Kamehameha's was a government of asking, 192
Ka-'ula-hai-malama plays hide and seek; Ke-ku-hau-pi'o is her father, 333
Keawe returned and remained in the Ka'ai, 64
Kukui torches of Iwi-kau-i-ka-ua, 62
Lahaina of the breadfruit leaves, 299
Lehua shed her tears, 3
Let the weak carry stones, 73
Let us go and drink the water of Wailua, 187
Lights never go out, 45
Like Ka'u, regal in the wind, 299
Log is rotten, 38
Majestic as the high hills of Wailau, 299
Moa are all gone from Molea, 101
Only a dog who has a master will bark, 299
Open the sluice gate, 85
Pele-io-holani, son of Ku belongs to Hana, 75
People who draw the spawn of the squid for bait for the fisherman, 378
Red-eyed was Keawe on Kauai, 64
Sailor has dragged his anchor in all ports, 325
Their heels never trod on the sands of Hauiki, 344
There shall be a long *malo*, 223
Where a big squid digs itself a hole, 159
You can get some over there, says Pahia, 205

Appendix VI

Kamakau's genealogy of the Hawaiian chiefs is presented here, with slight revisions. Through some mishap, in Kamakau's original version the twenty generations from Maweke to Kane-kapu-a-ku'ihewa were printed in ascending-generation order, with no indication of the reversal from the usual order. Dr. Kenneth P. Emory of Bishop Museum corrected this error and added appropriate headings for the several sections.

In a footnote Dr. Emory also supplied the Hawaiian text for the sentence in which Kamakau stated the nature of the genealogy. Dr. Emory amended the translation, believing that *pali ku* does not stand for a "hard wall which obscures," as it was first translated, but for Paliku, the parent of Huli-honua, who starts the genealogy. Ololo is the father of Kumuhonua, who begins the second section of the genealogy. Hence these two names are used to designate these sections.

The genealogy of Ke-opu-olani recorded by Kamakau is here printed in full.* The reader will see that more than one genealogical line is traced.**

*Ka Nupepa Ku'oko'a, Feb. 22, 1868.
**"O ka hui ana o na kumu o keia mookuauhau o ka Paliku pakiki keia o ka mookuauhau o na kupuna kahiko." (Original translation: "The connecting of these foundation lines is like a hard wall which obscures the genealogies of the old ancestors." Emory's translation: "The joining of the sources of this genealogy is in the nailing together of the Paliku, the genealogy of the ancient ancestors.")

Paliku Genealogy: To Wakea's mother; Papa's father

Huli-honua	Ka-aka-huli-lani	Laka
Laka	Ka-papa-ia-leka	Ka-mo'o-a-lewa
Ka-mo'o-a-lewa	'Ole-pu'u-ka-honua-lani	Malua-po
Malua-po	Lawe-a-ke-ao	Kini-lau-e-mano
Kini-lau-e-mano	'Upolu	Halo
Halo	Kini-ewalu	Ka-mano-o-ka-lani
Ka-mano-o-ka-lani	Ka-lani-a-noho	Ka-maka-o-ka-lani
Ka-maka-o-ka-lani	Kahua-o-ka-lani	Ke-oho-o-ka-lani
Ke-oho-o-ka-lani	Ka-mo'o-ka'lani	Ka-lei-o-ka-lani
Ka-lei-o-ka-lani	Ka-'opua-hiki	Ka-la-li'i
Ka-la-li'i	Ke-ao-mele	Ha'ule
Ha'ule	Loa'a	Walea
Walea	Lanea	Nana-nu'u
Nana-nu'u	Lalo-o-haua	Lalo-kona
Lalo-kona	Lalo-o-hoaniani	Po-kinikini
Po-kinikini	Po-lehulehu	Po-manomano
Po-manomano	Po-hako'iko'i	Honua-po-i-luna
Honua-po-i-luna	Honua-po-i-lalo	Kupukupu-a-nu'u
Kupukupu-a-nu'a	Kupukupu-lani	Ka-mole-o-ka-honua
Ka-mole-o-ka-honua	Ke-a'a-o-ka-honua	Kapai-a'a-o-ka-lani
Kapai-a'a-o-ka-lani	Kani-ke-ka'a	Ohemo-ku
Ohemo-ku	Pina'ina'i	Makulu-ka-po
Makulu-ka-po	Hi'ona	Mili-po-mea
Mili-po-mea	Hanahanai-au	Ho'okumu-ka-po
Ho'okumu-ka-po	Ha'ao	Lu-ka-hakona
Lu-ka-hakona	Ni'au-lani	(Ku-ka-lani-ehu
		(Kupu-lana-kehau

Ololo Genealogy: To Wakea

Kumu-honua	Hala-iho	Ahu-kai
Ahu-kai	Halo-lena	Ka-pili
Ka-pili	Alana-'ina'i	Kalua-ka-pua
Kalua-ka-pua	Hele-i-luna	Kalua-kahiko
Kalua-kahiko	Ka-po-ha'a-ia	Kahiko-lupa
Kahiko-lupa	Lu-kaua	Kahiko-lei-kau
Kahiko-lei-kau	Ku-pomaka'i-ka-'eleue	Kahiko-lei-ulu
Kahiko-lei-ulu	Kane-maka'i-ka-eleue	Kahiko-lei-'ula
Kahiko-lei-'ula	Ha'akoakoa-ke-au	Hakoakoa-la-ia
Hakoakoa-la-ia	Kane-ia-koa	Kupo
Kupo	Lani-kupa	Nahae-i-luna
Nahae-i-luna	Ke-ao-a-lani	Hanai-kini
Hanai-kini	Hanai-i-luna	Ke-ake-nui
Ke-ake-nui	Lahea-manu	Ka-hi-ahi-naki'i-akea
Ka-hi-ahi-naki'i-akea	Lua-hina-ki'i-papa	Ka-lua-a-hina-ki'i-akea
Ka-lua-a-hina-ki'i-akea	Wahine-ki'i-papa	Lima-hina-ki'i-ukea
Lima-hina-ki'i-ukea	Ono-ahi-naki'i-papa	Hikua-naki'i-akea
Hikua-naki'i-akea	Walu-a-nahi-naki'i-papa	I-wahi-naki'i-aka
I-wahi-naki'i-aka	Loha-na-kupapa	Wala-ahi-lani-nui
Wala-ahi-lani-nui	Owe	Kahiko-lua-mea
Kahiko-lua-mea	Kupu-lana-kehau	Wakea

From father of Papa to Nana-'ulu and 'Ulu

Ku-ka-laniehu*	Kaha-ka-ua-koko	Papa
(Nobody knows clearly who the ancestors of this woman are.)		
Wakea	Papa-hanau-moku	Ho'ohoku-ka-lani
Wakea	Ho'ohoku-ka-lani	Ha-loa
Ha-loa	Hina-mano-ulu-ae	Waia
Waia	Hulune	Hina-ualo
Hina-ualo	Hau-nu'u	Kakai-hili
Kakai-hili	Hau-lani	Wai-loa
Wai-loa	Kihi-wao-o-pau'i-anea	Kio
Kio	Ka-mole	Ole
Ole	Hai	Pupue
Pupue	Kama-hele	Manaku
Manaku	Hiko-'ale	Kahiko
Kahiko	Kaea	Lu-ka-hakona
Lu-ka-hakona	Ko-'ula-mai-ka-lani	Luanu'u
Luanu'u	Ka-wa'a-maukele	Ki'i
Ki'i	Hina-ko-'ulu	Nana-'ulu
		'Ulu

'Ulu Line

		(Nana
		(Kapu-lani
'Ulu	Kapu-nu'u	(Nanaiea
Nanaiea	Ka-hau-mokule'ia	Nana-aia-lani
Nana-aia-lani	Hina-kina'u	Wai-ku-lani
Wai-ku-lani	Ke-kau-i-lani	Ku-hele-i-moana
Ku-hele-i-moana	Mapuna-ia-'a'ala	Konohiki
Konohiki	Hika-uku-lena	Wa-wena
Wa-wena	Hina-mahuia	Akalana
Akalana	Hina-ka-wea	(Maui-mua
		(Maui-hope
		(Maui-ki'iki'i
		(Maui-kalana
Maui-kalana	Hina-ke-aloha	Nana-maoa
Nana-maoa	Hina-kapa'i-kua	Nana-ku-lei
Nana-ku-lei	Ka-hau-ku-honua	Nana-kaoko
Nana-kaoko	Ka-hihi-o-ka-lani	Ka-pawa
Ka-pawa	Ke-kuku-luhi-o-ka-lani	Hele-i-pawa
Hele-i-pawa	Ko'oko'o-ku-mai-lani	'Ai-kanaka
'Ai-kanaka	Hina-hanai-a-ka-malama	Puna-i-mua
		Hema

*Ka Nupepa Ku'oko'a, Feb. 29, 1868.

Puna Line

Puna-i-mua	Ha'ina-lau-mai-ka-lani	Ua-mai-ka-lani
Ua-mai-ka-lani	Kahili-o-ka-lani	Au-anini
Au-anini	Weli-ha'a-kana	Lono-ho'onewa
Lono-ho'onewa	Loiloi	Pau-makua
Pau-makua	Heana-nui-o-ka-lani	Moe-ana-i-mua
Moe-ana-i-mua	Ala-hoe	Ku-makaha
Ku-makaha	Moemoe-a-'auli'i	Nana

(To Moemoe-a-'auli'i's family belonged Kamapua'a and the Pele family.)

Nana	Hoaka-lei-kani	Lua-hiwa
Lua-hiwa	Kilohana	Ahu-kai
Ahu-kai	Ke-aka-mili	La-a-mai-kahiki

(Ke-aka-mili was chiefess of the Iku-nu'u, Iku-lani, Iki-la'a and La'a ranks.)

La-a-mai-kahiki	Hoaka-nui-kapu-'ai-helu	(Lauli-a-la'a
	(Wao-lena	(Ahukini-a-La'a
	(Mano	(Kukona-a-La'a
Ahukini-a-La'a	Ha'i-ka-ma'i'o	Kama-hano
Kama-hano	Ka'auea-nui-o-ka-lani	Lua-nu'u
Lua-nu'u	Ka-lani-moe-i-ka-wai-kai	Kukona
Kukona	Lau-puapua-ma'a	Mano-ka-lani-po
Mano-ka-lani-po	Nae-kapu-lani	(Kau-maka-mano
		(Na-punua-mano
		Kaha'i-a-mano

(Nae-kapu-lani was granddaughter of Maka-li'i of the heavens inland of Kapa'a in Kapahi on Kauai.)

Kau-maka-a-Mano	Kapo-inu-kai	Ka-haku-a-kane
Ka-haku-a-kane	Mano-kai-ko'o	Kuwalu-pauku-moku
Kuwalu-pauku-moku	Hame-a-waha-'ula	Ka-haku-maka-paweo
Ka-haku-maka-paweo	Ka-haka-a-kukua'ena	Ka-lani-kukuma
Ka-lani-kukuma	Kapo-lei-a-kuila	Ka-haku-maka-liua
Ka-haku-maka-liua	Ka-haku-mai'a	Kama-kapu
Kama-kapu	Pa-wahine	Kawelo-mahamaha-i'a
Kawelo-mahamaha-i'a	Ka-pohina-o-ka-lani	Kawelo-maku-lua
Kawelo-maku-lua	Ka-'awihi-o-ka-lani	Kawelo-'ai-kanaka
(through a *pio* marriage)		
Kawelo-'ai-kanaka	Naki	Kawelo-a-naki
Kawelo-a-naki	Ka-laka-hinalo	Kawelo-'ehu
Kawelo-'ehu	Kaioe	Kaha-malu-'ihi
Kaha-malu-'ihi	Kane-kapu-a-ku'ihewa	Ka-ho'owawaha-o-ka-lani

(Kaha-malu-'ihi came from the sacred sands of Waimea. Ke-aka-kanaloa was her brother.)

Maweke Line to Kane-kapu-a-ku'ihewa

Maweke
Mi'i-i-'ele-ali'i
Mo'ikeha
Ho'okamali'i
Kaha'i
Ku-o-Lono
Maelo
Lani-hewa
Kahuoi
Pua'a-a-Kahuoi
Maili-ku-kahi
Kalona
(Piliwale)
Ku-kani-loko
Ka-lani-manuia
Ka-'ihi-kapu-a-Manuia
Ka-ku'ihewa

Naio-lau-kea
Wehe-la-nani
Hina-ululu
Ke-ahi-'ula
Kehenu
Kane-aka-lele'oi
Laulia
(Akepamaikalani)
Pelea
Nono-nui
Kane-pukea
Kike-nui-a-'ewa
Pa'a-kani-lea
Luaia
Lupe-kapu-ke-aho-makalii
Kau-nui-a-kana-hoa-lani
Kaha'i-ao-nui-a-Kaulana

Mi'i-i-'ele-ali'i
Mo'ikeha
Ho'okamali'i
Kaha'i
Ku-o-Lono
Maelo
Lani-hewa
Kahuoi
Pua'a-a-Kahuoi
Maili-ku-kahi
Kalona
(Piliwale)
Ku-kani-loko
Ka-lani-manuia
Ka-'ihi-kapu-a-Manuia
Ka-ku'ihewa
Kane-kapu-a-ku'ihewa

Maweke Line to Kiwala'o

Maweke
Ka-lehe-nui-a-Maweke
Hina-kai-mauli-'awa
Mua

Ku-a-mua
(through a *pio* marriage)
Ka-walewale-o-ku
Ka-'ula'ula-o-ka-lani
Ka-imihau-o-ku
Moku-o-loe
Kalia-o-ka-lani
Ke-opu-o-lani
Kupanihi

Lua-puloku
Ahu-kai
Ma'eu-nui-o-ka-lani
Ka-piki'o-ka-lani
Halau-lani
Lani-nui-a-Ka-ihu-pe'e

Ka'akaua-lani
Kaua-kahi-a-Ku'ihewa
Ka-ua-pena
Ku'ihewa-ka-ua-'upena
Ku'ihewa-ka-walu
Papa'i-ka-ni'au
Ka-lani-nui-ku'i-hono-o-
  ka-moku

Ka-lani-'opu'u
Kiwala'o

Naio-lau-kea
Ka-hinalo
Ka-hiwa-ka-'apu
Ka-'omea

Kapu-a-mua

Una-'ula
Kalu-'ai-olowalu
Loe
Ka-pihe-o-lalo
Kua-a-'ohe
Kaohi-a-kanaka
Kahua-o-ka-lani

Mumu-ka-lani-ohua
Ka-hilina'i-o-kahiki
Ka-ulu-hinalo
Ka-la-a-ka-hinalo
Ka-ihu-pe'e
Kauhi-'ili-'ula-a-Pi'i-lani

Ka-ku'ihewa
Ka-puna-wahine
Kawelo-a-ka-lani-kala
Ka-loa-iwi
'Umi-a-liloa
Ka-'ula-hea-nui-o-ka-moku
Ke-ku'i-apo-iwa I

Kalola
Ke-ku'i-apo-iwa II

Ka-lehe-nui-a-Maweke
Hina-kai-mauli-'awa
Mua
(Ku-a-mua
(Kapu-a-mua
Ka-walewale-o-ku

Ka-'ula'ula-o-ka-lani
Ka-imihau-o-ku
Moku-o-loe
Kalia-o-ka-lani
Ke-opu-o-lani
Kupanihi
(Lua-puloloku
(Niu-popo-ula
(Kahaoi
Ahu-kai
Ma'eu-nui-o-ka-lani
Ka-piki'o-ka-lani
Halau-lani
Lani-nui-a-Ka-ihu-pe'e
(Hoa-lani
(Ka'akaua-lani
Kaua-kahi-a-Ku'ihewa
Ka-ua-pena
Ku'ihewa-ka-ua'upena
Ku-ihewa-ka-walu
Papa'i-ka-ni'au
Ka-lani-nui-ku'i-hono-o-ka-moku
(Kamehameha-nui
(Ka-lola
(Ka-hekili
(Ku-ho'oheihei-pahu
Ka-lani-kau-i-ke-aouli-Kiwala'o
Ka-lani-kau-i-ka-'alaneo-
  Ke-opu-'o-lani

Appendix VII

Ka Nupepa Kuʻokoʻa

1866:
Oct. 20, 69; Oct. 27, 72
Nov. 3, 74; Nov. 10, 77, 78
Dec. 1, 82; Dec. 8, 85; Dec. 15, 89; Dec. 22, 91

1867:
Jan. 19, 92; Jan. 26, 98
Feb. 2, 102; Feb. 9, 103, 107; Feb. 16, 104, 111; Feb. 16 (extract), 105; Feb. 23, 116
Mar. 2, 121; Mar. 9, 126; Mar. 16, 127, 131; Mar. 23, 134; Mar. 30, 138
Apr. 6, 140, 143; Apr. 13, 151; Apr. 20, 147, 151; Apr. 27, 153
May 4, 157; May 11, 158, 162; May 25, 167, 168
June 1, 171; June 15, 174, 179
July 6, 182; July 13, 185; July 20, 186, 189; July 27, 192
Aug. 3, 194; Aug. 17, 199, 201; Aug. 24, 205; Aug. 31, 208
Sept. 7, 209; Sept. 14, 211; Sept. 21, 214, 220; Sept. 28, 216, 222
Oct. 5, 218; Oct. 12, 224
Nov. 2, 227; Nov. 9, 228, 229; Nov. 16, 231; Nov. 23, 233; Nov. 30, 236
Dec. 7, 237; Dec. 14, 239; Dec. 21, 242; Dec. 28, 244

1868:
Jan. 4, 245; 246; Jan. 11, 248; Jan. 18, 249; Jan. 25, 251
Feb. 1, 253; Feb. 8, 255; Feb. 15, 257; Feb. 22, 258, 259; Feb. 29, 259
Mar. 14, 261
Apr. 11, 268; Apr. 18, 269, 270; Apr. 25, 271
May 2, 273; May 13, 280; May 30, 281
June 6, 283; June 13, 286; June 20, 288; June 27, 291
July 11, 294; July 18, 296; July 25, 298
Aug. 1, 300; Aug. 8, 302; Aug. 22, 305, 306; Aug. 29, 308
Sept. 5, 310; Sept. 12, 312; Sept. 19, 314; Sept. 26, 318
Oct. 3, 319; Oct. 17, 323; Oct. 24, 325
Dec. 19, 328; Dec. 26, 329

1869:
Jan. 2, 332; Jan. 9, 332

Ke Au ʻOkoʻa

1869:
Jan. 7, 339; Jan. 14, 342; Jan. 21, 346; Jan. 28, 348, 352
Feb. 4, 356; Feb. 11, 359; Feb. 18, 365
Mar. 18, 333
Apr. 1, 368; Apr. 8, 369; Apr. 22, 370; Apr. 29, 371
May 6, 373; May 13, 376; May 20, 378, 396
June 3, 383; June 10, 386; June 17, 389; June 24, 394
July 1, 395, 400; July 8, 403; July 15, 406; July 22, 407; July 29, 409
Aug. 19, 411; Aug. 26, 412
Sept. 2, 414; Sept. 9, 415, 417; Sept. 16, 420; Sept. 23, 420, 424; Sept. 30, 426
Oct. 7, 428; Oct. 14, 430

1870:
Nov. 3, 2; Nov. 10, 7; Nov. 17, 12; Nov. 24, 17
Dec. 1, 21, 23; Dec. 8, 27; Dec. 15, 33; Dec. 22, 33, 38; Dec. 29, 43

1871:
Jan. 5, 45; Jan. 12, 46, 48; Jan. 19, 54; Jan. 26, 59
Feb. 2, 63, 65

Bibliography

(SOURCES REFERRED TO IN THE FOOTNOTES)

1. Alexander, W. D. *A Brief History of the Hawaiian People*. New York, 1891.
2. Alexander, W. D. "History of Umi—His Birth and His Youth," in *Hawaiian Annual for 1888*, pp. 78-85, abstracted from his article in the "Maile Wreath," June 1864.
3. Anderson, Rufus. *History of the Sandwich Islands Mission*. Boston, 1870.
4. Baker, A. S. "Ahua a Umi," *Hawaiian Annual for 1917*, pp. 62-70.
5. Bastian, Adolf. *Die Heilige Sage der Polynesier*. Leipzig, 1881.
6. Beckwith, M. W. *Hawaiian Mythology*. New Haven, 1940.
7. Bingham, Hiram. *A Residence of Twenty-one Years in the Sandwich Islands*. Hartford, 1848.
8. Cook, James, and James King. *A Voyage to the Pacific Ocean . . .*, vols. 1-3. London, 1784.
9. Dahlgren, E. W. "Were the Hawaiian Islands visited by the Spaniards before their discovery by Captain Cook in 1778?" in *Kngl. Svenska Vetenskapsakad Handl.*, vol. 57, no. 4, pp. 1-220, 1916.
10. Dibble, Sheldon. *History of the Sandwich Islands*. Honolulu, 1909.
11. Emerson, O. P. "Bad boy of Lahaina," in *Hawaiian Historical Society Annual Report for 1920*, No. 29.
12. Emory, Kenneth P. "Archeology of Nihoa and Necker Islands," in *Bernice P. Bishop Museum Bulletin* 53, 1928.
13. Fornander, Abraham. *An Account of the Polynesian Race*, vol. 2. London, 1880.
14. Fornander, Abraham. "Fornander Collection of Hawaiian Antiquities . . . I-III," in *Bernice P. Bishop Museum Memoirs*, vols. 4, 5, 6, 1916-1920.
15. Hobbs, Jean. *Hawaii, a Pageant of the Soil*. Stanford University, 1935.
16. Kalakaua, David. *Legends and Myths of Hawaii*, edited by Daggett. New York, 1888.
17. Kuykendall, R. S. *The Hawaiian Kingdom, 1778-1854*. University of Hawaii Press reprint, 1947.
18. Malo, David. *Hawaiian Antiquities*. Bernice P. Bishop Museum Special Publication 2, 2nd edition, 1951.
19. McAllister, J. Gilbert. "Archeology of Oahu," in *Bernice P. Bishop Museum Bulletin* 104, 1933.
20. Northwood, J. d'Arcy. "The game of *Maika*," manuscript in Bernice P. Bishop Museum.
21. "Obituary of Don Francisco Paulo de Marin," in *Sandwich Islands Gazette*, November 4, 1837, p. 3.
22. "Obituary of John Meek," in *The Friend*, February 1, 1875, p. 9.
23. "Obituary of a Tahitian," in *The Friend*, January 1859, p. 5.
24. Palmer, H. S. "Geology of Kaula, Nihoa, Necker," in *Bernice P. Bishop Museum Bulletin* 35, 1927.
25. Pogue, J. F. *Ka Moolelo Hawaii*. Honolulu, 1907.
26. Remy, Jules. *Contributions of a Venerable Savage to the Ancient History of the Hawaiian Islands*, trans. by W. T. Brigham. Boston, 1868.
27. Remy, Jules. *Histoire de l'Archipel Havaiien*. Paris and Leipzig, 1862.
28. Remy, Jules. "History of Umi," trans. by W. D. Alexander, in *Hawaiian Annual for 1888*, pp. 78-85.
29. "Resolutions Adopted by the Hawaiian Historical Society, July 8, 1935," in *Hawaiian Historical Society Annual Report for 1935*, no. 44, pp. 6-18.
30. Rice, W. H. "Hawaiian Legends," in *Bernice P. Bishop Museum Bulletin* 3, 1923.
31. Stokes, J. G. F. "Hawaii's Discovery by Spaniards . . . Theories Traced and Refuted," in *Hawaiian Historical Society Paper No. 20*, 1939.
32. Stokes, J. G. F. "Origin of the Condemnation of Captain Cook in Hawaii," in *Hawaiian Historical Society Annual Report for 1930*, pp. 68-101.
33. Stokes, J. G. F. "New Bases for Hawaiian Chronology," in *Hawaiian Historical Society Annual Report for 1932*, no. 41, pp. 23-65.
34. "Summary of the Laws of June 7, 1839," in *Hawaiian Spectator*, vol. 2, 1839.

35. Taylor, Mrs. Persis G. *Kapiolani: A Memorial.* Honolulu, 1897.
36. Thrum, T. G. "Early Sandalwood Trade, Hawaiian Version," in *Hawaiian Annual for 1906,* pp. 105-108.
37. Thrum, T. G. "Heiaus and Heiau Sites," in *Hawaiian Annual for 1907,* pp. 48, 51.
38. Thrum, T. G. *More Hawaiian Folk Tales.* Chicago, 1923.
39. Thrum, T. G. "The Sandalwood Trade of Early Hawaii," in *Hawaiian Annual for 1905,* pp. 43-74.
40. Westervelt, W. D. *Legends of Old Honolulu.* Honolulu, 1915.
41. Wyllie, R. C. Address, *Royal Hawaiian Agricultural Society, Transactions 1,* 1850, pp. 46-49.
42. Yzendoorn, Father Reginald. *History of the Catholic Mission in the Hawaiian Islands.* Honolulu, 1927.

This index combines the entries from the very limited index of the original edition with the extensive index originally published as:

INDEX TO RULING CHIEFS OF HAWAII BY S.M. KAMAKAU

Prepared by ELSPETH P. STERLING

Originally published by:

Department of Anthropology
Bernice P. Bishop Museum
Honolulu, Hawaii
February 1974

Index

maheihei Hoapili, 188; cousin of Ka-umu-ali'i, 194; son of Keawe-poepoe and Ka-noena, 310; son Kai-ehu reared unknown in the country, 348; father of Ke-kiki-pa'a and grandfather of Ka-pi'o-lani, 379

Kameha'ikana, deity of Ka-hekili, 166; female deity, 179; tabu breadfruit of, 185, 186

Kameha'ikana (Maui), 30

Ka-meha-malu, SEE Kamamalu

Kameha-malu, child of Kamehameha and Ka-heihei-malie, 208; full name, 386

Kameha-malu Ke-kua-iwa-o-ka-lani, SEE Kameha-malu, child of Kamehameha

Kamehameha, ship, 279, 283; on which Boki sailed for New Hebrides, 294-96

Kamehameha, son of Kahala-i'a and Kina'u, 347

Kamehameha I, 140, 221; birth at Kohala, 66-68, 210-11; placed under care of Ke-aka, 69; Keoua dies, Ka-lani-'opu'u goes to get, 76; first-born son, called Ku-nui-akea, 79; saves life of Ke-ku-hau-pi'o, given name of Pai'ea, 84; distinguishes himself at Lahaina, 89; in Maui campaign, 91; sails off with Cook from Ko'olau, Maui, 97; designated heir to Ka-lani-'opu'u's god, 107; urged to make offering of I-maka-koloa, 108; seizes prerogative from Kiwala'o, returns to Kohala, 109; returns to Kona at Ka-lani-'opu'u's death, 117; lands at Ka'awaloa for uncle's funeral, 118; chews *'awa* for Kiwala'o, 110; war breaks out with Kiwala'o, various chiefs desert and back him, 120; enters battle at Ke'ei in which Kiwala'o dies, 121; becomes ruler over one-third of Hawaii, 122; ancestry and relatives, 123; refuses canoes to Ka-hekili, launches battle against Hilo and Ka'u, 124; unable to defeat Keoua, retires to Kohala, 126; detains Young on Hawaii, 146; befriends Davis, launches attack on Maui, 147; lands at Hana, carries battle to 'Iao, 148; asks Ka-lola for her daughters and granddaughter, sends Ha'alo'u to seek a wise man from Kauai, is tattooed, 149; sends messenger to Ka-hekili and asks for gods, 150; returns to Hawaii from Molokai to check Keoua Kuahu-'ula's raids, 151; receives Ka'i-ana, makes him commander of his armies, 153; at Kona, abandons war and makes plan for Pu'u Kohala, 154; builds *heiau*, sends messengers to bring Keoua, 155; meets Keoua and party, witnesses his death, spares Pauli, 157; Hawaii becomes his, 158; size of his camp at Kaunakakai, 159; meets Vancouver, 164, 165; warned by Captain Brown's men, launches attack on Maui, Molokai, 171; defeats Ka-lani-ku-pule at battle of Nu'uanu, 172; fails in attempt to take Kauai, returns to Hawaii to subdue

uprising, 173, 174; how he administered his kingdom and treated the people, his gods, accomplishments, anecdotes, wives, the great lava flow at Hu'ehu'e, 175-86; makes preparations to subdue Kauai, appoints Liholiho his heir, 187; ignores prophecy regarding Kauai, learns he is son of Ka-hekili, 188; contracts *'oku'u* on Oahu, his counselors and chiefs die, 189; laws and regulations during time of, life under, 191-92; first tastes rum, sets up distillery, 193; puts Ka-niho-nui to death, this name given by Keoua Ahu'ula, sets about to acquire Kauai, 195-96; sends letter to King George III, "Ku-wahine burning" incident, 197, 389; advised on how to handle possible conspiracy, returns to Hawaii, visits Molokai, Maui, 198-99; tabu *heiau* on Hawaii, 200; rebuilds *heiau* on Hawaii, 203; orders sandalwood cut, plants taro against famine, 204; seeks water at Kalae and to see Kupake'e, 205; sends men to investigate Russian warship at Honolulu, 206; buys stolen Spanish ship, 207; wives and children, 208; gives kingdom to son, god to nephew, treatment of foreign governments, 209; birth date and place, date of death and place, character and death of, last words, 210-11; preparations and disposal of body, 212; manner in which he referred to Liholiho, 220; his death first step in ending tabus, 222; confirms Oahu lands belonging to *kahuna*, makes laws relating to oppression of poor, 231; treatment of prisoners in time of, 233; declares Ka-umu-ali'i ruling chief of Kauai, 252; takes Ke-opu-o-lani to Hawaii, marries her, 260; brings horses, cattle to Oahu, 268; resides at Waikiki, Honolulu, 271; Ka-'o-lei-o-ku, first child, 286; his alliance with Ka-'ahu-manu and her influence, 311, 313, 315; incident of Ka'iana on Molokai, 312; father of Kina'u, two other children with Ka-heihei-malie, 346; gives Ke-opu-o-lani as wife to Hoapili, incident with his wild bull and Hoapili, 352; gathered skilled men together, 374; comes for Ke-ka-ulu-ohi at birth, 385; takes Ka-heihei-malie for wife from brother, 386; mentioned in canoe chant, 393

Kamehameha II, SEE Liholiho

Kamehameha III, SEE Kau-i-ke-aouli

Kamehameha IV, SEE Liholiho, Alexander

Kamehameha V, SEE Kapu-aiwa, Lot

Kamehameha, David, son of Kina'u, 280; son of Ke-ku-anao'a, 290; accompanies Ke-ka-ulu-ohi to Maui, 336

Kamehameha Day, 68

Kamehameha Iwi, child of Kamehameha and Ka-heihei-malie, 208

Kamehameha Kapu-aiwa, child of Kamehameha and Ka-heihei-malie, 346, 386

Kau-a-ka-piki, lesser chief of Kauai, describes Cook to people on Oahu, 96

Kaua-ke-kua (Hawaii), 'Umi fights gods here, 20

Ka-ua-lua (w), persecuted, 329

Ka'uamoa, narrow pass of, 17

Kauanono'ula, Honolulu (Oahu), 272

Ka-uaua-nui-a-mahi, 66, 110; chief of Kona, 63; husband of Ka-lani-kau-lele-ia-iwi, 64; father of Alapa'i, 76; father of Ha'ae, 123

Kaua'ula (Maui), 89, 280, 355; stream, 74

Ka-uhi, Oahu warrior, 135; father of Ka'a-loa, 175

Ka-uhi, sailed on Pele-io-holani's canoe, 240

Ka-uhi-a-hiwa, chief of Kauai, 52

Ka-uhi-'aimoku-a-Kama, son of Ke-kau-like, 69; rebelled against Kamehameha-nui, other name, 73; sends to Oahu for help, 74; father of Ka-lolo-wahi-lani, 127

Ka-uhi-a-Kama, son of Kama-lala-walu, 60; ruler of Maui, 61; bones desecrated, 217; death avenged by Ka-hekili, 232

Ka-uhi-ko'ako'a, war chief, 135, 136

Ka-uhi-kua, early studies, 248

Ka-uhi-o-ka-lani, son of Kiha-a-Pi'ilani and Kolea-moku, 26; reared by Ho'o-lae-makua, 27; spared at Ka'uiki, 31; half-brother of Kama, sent as spy to Hawaii, 56

Ka-uhi-pu-mai-ka-hoaka, SEE Ka-uhi-'aimoku-a-Kama

Ka-uhi-wawae-ono, 221; chief, 83, 232; suspected of plotting against Kamehameha, 182; cousin of Ka-umu-ali'i, 195; friend of Holua-loa, 228; accompanied Ka-'ahu-manu's family, 310; uncle of Kuakini, takes care of him, 389

Kauhola, bones removed to Ka'awaloa, 285

Kauhola (Hawaii), 106, 126; Kamehameha living at, 311

Kauhola, period, 311

Kau-i-ke-aouli (Kamehameha III), 269; son of Kamehameha and Ke-opu-o-lani, 208, 229; studies English, 248; designated chief in Liholiho's absence, 255; receives Hilo lands from Boki, 256; made head of government at nine, 258; born at Keauhou, 260; forced to eat tabu food, learns letters, 261; at Lahaina, 262; sacred rank, his birth, 263; babyhood, his nature, 264; house in Honolulu, 272; cuts sandalwood, sails boat, 278; sails for Hawaii, 283; visits volcano, 284; sails to Maui for Nahi-'ena'ena, dedication of Kawaiaha'o Church, 292-93; tries to prevent Boki sailing for New Hebrides, 295; taken away from Liliha, makes tour, returns to Oahu after Pahikaua war, 298; regrets chiefs' treatment of Liliha, 303; speech made at eleven years old, 318; signs treaty with French in regard to Catholics, 332; turns

to sinful pleasures, builds stone wall at Makiki, 334, 335; refuses to go to Maui with Nahi-'ena'ena, wishes to appoint Liliha as premier, 336; is dissuaded by Hoapili, and chiefesses, 337; saves life of Kaomi, allows a stop to dissipation outside city, engaged to Kuakini's daughter, 338, 339; grieves over Nahi-'ena'ena's death, reforms, married Kalama, 341; builds mausoleum for Nahi-'ena'ena, incident of Keoni Ana 'Opio, 342; expected to be husband of Kina'u, 346; adopts Alexander Liholiho, 348; selects Ke-ka-ulu-ohi as premier, 356; drawing of the constitution, 370; "My kingdom is a kingdom of learning," 373; second son, Ke-aweawe-'ula-o-ka-lani II, 388; trusts Ricord, 402; Ka-'imi-na'auao, his foster son, incident involving French, Catholics and governor of Hawaii, 411; goes to country for health, 420; death of, full name, birth, 421-22; why chosen to succeed Kamehameha, 429

Ka'uiki (Maui), hill, fortress, 25, 28, 31; taken by forces of 'Umi, 30; fortification of, 80; 84; annexed by Ka-lani-'opu'u, 111; Ka-hekili attempts to take, 115; falls to Ka-hekili, its history, 116; Ka-'eo-ku-lani at, thrusts war club at sky, Ka-lani-moku born, 277

Ka-uila (w), persecuted, 329

Ka-uila, religious service, 211

Ka-uila, wood, of Napu'u and Kahuku, 28

Ka-uila-nui-makeha-i-ka-lani, 'aumakua, 200

Kauka, SEE Judd, Dr.

Kaukahoku, taro patches of Maui, 355

Kaukahoku, Nu'uanu (Oahu), 172

Kau-ka-pua'a, sent to Oahu to tell of Cook's arrival, 96

Kau-kuna Ka-hekili, 262, 267, 283; son of Hoapili, punished, 343; mentioned in canoe chant, 393

Ka'ula, island near Ni'ihau, 38, 44, 52, 76

Ka'ula (Hawaii), 3, 11

Ka-'ula-hea, ruling chief of Maui, 128; SEE ALSO Ka'ula-hea-nui-o-ka-moku

Ka'ula-hea-nui-o-ka-moku, 222; husband of Ka-lani-kau-lele-ia-iwi, 65; ancestor of Ka-lani Ke-li'i Ka-uhi-lono-honua, 393

Kaulana (Hawaii), 203

Kau-lani, offers hospitality to Kiha-a-Pi'ilani, 24

Kaulekola, Kane'ohe (Oahu), 72

Ka-uli, Maui heiau, SEE Ka-luli

Kau-loa-iwi, genealogist from Molokai, 393

Kaulua, tabu day, 385

Ka-uluhai-malama, son of Ke-ku-hau-pi'o, 256

Kaululai, Tahitian chief, 277

Ka-ulu-nae, younger brother of Ke'e-au-

Errata

Page 47   "Vol.," not "Col." in asterisked material.

Page 256   "Naukana," not "No-ukana."

Page 430   "account," not "acocunt;" "two, and," not "two,and;" "disturb its peace," not "disturb it peace."

Ruling Chiefs of Hawaii
Revised Edition

Samuel Mānaiakalani Kamakau

This is the history of Hawai'i from the great chief 'Umi, eight generations before Kamehameha the Great, through the reign of Kamehameha III. Major events include Kamehameha's birth, rise to power, and consolidation of the Hawaiian kingdom; the arrival of Captain James Cook; the coming of traders and missionaries; and politics of the Hawaiian kingdom through the death of Kamehameha III in 1854. Written from 1866 through 1871 by one of Hawai'i's greatest historians, *Ruling Chiefs of Hawaii* is an essential element in any collection of Hawaiian resources.

"Samuel M. Kamakau painstakingly recorded the oral traditions and histories of the Hawaiian people prior to the sweeping cultural changes of the later 19th century. His masterwork, *Ruling Chiefs of Hawaii,* begins with the account of 'Umi, the famous unifier of Hawai'i Island, and continues with the lives and reigns of various Big Island kings up to and following the arrival of Captain Cook. Kamakau provides a Native perspective on the critical period of change following European contact, especially following the death of Kamehameha I and through the rule of Kamehameha III. No historian, anthropologist, or other scholar of ancient and early modern Hawai'i can afford to be without this key source close at hand."

Patrick Kirch
Author and Director, Hearst Museum of Anthropology
University of California at Berkeley

"S.M. Kamakau's body of work is the cornerstone of the edifice of Hawaiian history."
Herb Kawainui Kane
Artist and author

"S.M. Kamakau was the most prolific writer of the Hawaiian Kingdom. His vast historical knowledge was highly respected by his own people and has become the foundation of most Hawaiian scholarship today. Rich in cultural insight and detail, Kamakau's writings illuminate our understanding about the lives and practices of Hawaiians of old."
M. Puakea Nogelmeier
Author and Hawaiian language specialist

Cover photo courtesy of Bishop Museum

KAMEHAMEHA SCHOOLS

www.kamehamehapublishing.org

FSC
www.fsc.org
MIX
Paper from
responsible sources
FSC® C008955

ISBN 13: 978-0-87336-014-2

9 780873 360142

90000